D1291640

Albania

and the

Sino-Soviet Rift

CENTER FOR INTERNATIONAL STUDIES
Massachusetts Institute of Technology

STUDIES IN INTERNATIONAL COMMUNISM

Albania and the Sino-Soviet Rift
William E. Griffith

WILLIAM E. GRIFFITH

Albania and the Sino-Soviet Rift

THE M.I.T. PRESS
Cambridge, Massachusetts
1963

LIBRARY OF CONGRESS CATALOG CARD NUMBER: 63-10880
PRINTED IN THE UNITED STATES OF AMERICA

Foreword

This book is the first in a series that the Center for International Studies plans to publish in connection with our recently inaugurated research project on international Communism. In general terms the studies planned and in progress will examine the interaction between domestic factors in various countries affecting the fortunes of local Communist parties and the impact of the growing divergence within the Communist movement as a result of the Sino-Soviet rift and other circumstances. Geographically, attention will be focused on three major areas: Latin America, Europe, and East and Southeast Asia. The project will be directed by Dr. William E. Griffith, the author of this first volume.

Three years ago the question "Why Albania?" would have been natural; today the importance of the Soviet-Albanian break seems clear, but its background, causes, course, and significance have remained largely unexplored. I think it fair to say that this book presents the first detailed, systematic, and documented examination of these matters. It thus contributes to an understanding of the international Communist movement as a whole as well as of Albania's specific role in recent events. Dr. Griffith, who has had extensive experience in East European affairs, is the author of a forthcoming work on the East European thaw, 1953–1956.

MAX F. MILLIKAN
Director, Center for International Studies
Massachusetts Institute of Technology

Cambridge, Massachusetts
November, 1962

Preface

The field of international Communist studies is still a young one, and the public outbreak in 1960 of the Sino-Soviet dispute has complicated and enlarged it. Of all its aspects, the Albanian break with the Soviet Union and the alliance with Communist China have been perhaps the most unexpected and least understood. It is my hope that this book will provide a preliminary reconstruction of the background, course, and significance of the events and also make available the major documents on the Albanian side.

The reader may well ask: Why so much about Albania? First, it is perhaps the European country about which the least is known in the West. Second, the documentation concerning recent Albanian developments has been almost entirely unavailable to the scholarly public. Third, an adequate analysis of their course and significance must cover Albanian and Balkan historical factors, Albanian internal developments, Tirana's relations with Moscow, Belgrade, and Peking, and their significance for the international Communist movement in general. Fourth, as contrasted with the 1948 Soviet-Yugoslav break, in this case there is available sufficient documentation to provide a detailed and important case study of a successful revolt of a small satellite against Moscow, this time within the context of the Sino-Soviet dispute. Last, the methodology used in this book, that of the intensive deciphering and analysis of esoteric Communist communications, is still under dispute; this book will hopefully provide more evidence of its effectiveness.

All the translations of the documents have been either made or revised from the original languages. Appropriate accents and diacritical marks have been used; their omission, too frequent in American scholarly works, is in my view no more justified in East European languages than it would be in French or German. Current Albanian orthography (i.e., the regime's version of the Tosk dialect) has consistently been used.

Contemporary history is always a jealous mistress; it can never hope to tell the complete story, least of all in Communist affairs. Yet the Sino-Soviet dispute and its Albanian aspect have already gone through several cycles and will presumably go through more; this preliminary analysis may serve to stimulate further study and other, less provisional, more complete appraisals.

In a book involving so many countries, languages, and problems acknowledgments are inevitably numerous. My work on it was made much easier by the help given me by my research assistants: Joan Barth, Peter Prifti (who made possible my use of Albanian sources), Daniel Tretiak, and László Urban, and by my secretary Mina Parks. Typing and retyping was faithfully done by Constance Boquist, Kathleen Kohlman, and Lila Rose, and indexing by Jean P. S. Clark, Peter Prifti, Joan Gettig, and Jane Gross. I have benefited greatly from comments by many friends: Donald L. M. Blackmer, James F. Brown, Zbigniew Brzezinski, Richard V. Burks, R. Rockingham Gill, Harry Hamm, Wolfgang Leonhard, Nicholas C. Pano, Herbert Ritvo, Robert Schwanke, and Stavro Skendi. The responsibility for the book's contents and errors, however, is mine alone. The Center's indefatigable editor, Richard W. Hatch, is primarily responsible for making it as readable as it is. Finally, I must record my deep gratitude to the Center's director, Max Millikan. The Center's unique and irreplaceable atmosphere, the challenge and opportunities it offers to its members, without which this book could not even have been written, are primarily his creation. Only we who have the privilege of participating in them can fully appreciate how much we owe him.

WILLIAM E. GRIFFITH

Cambridge, Massachusetts
November 27, 1962

Contents

Abbreviations

ADN	*Allgemeine Deutsche Nachrichtenagentur* [official East German news agency]
AFP	*Agence France Presse*
Agerpress	Official Romanian press agency
ASRPSh	*Anuari Statistikor i Republikës Popullore të Shqipërisë* (Statistical Yearbook of the Albanian People's Republic)
ATA	Albanian Telegraphic Agency
BBC/SU	British Broadcasting Corporation, *Summary of World Broadcasts,* Soviet Union
CB	"Current Background" (U.S. Consulate General, Hong Kong)
CC	Central Committee
CCP	Chinese Communist Party
CDSP	*Current Digest of the Soviet Press*
CENTO	Central Treaty Organization
CGIL	*Confederazione Generale Italiana del Lavoro* [Italian PCI-PSI Trade Union Federation]
CMEA	Council for Mutual Economic Assistance
CPR	Chinese People's Republic
CPSU	Communist Party of the Soviet Union
CRU	[British Broadcasting Corporation, Overseas Service], Central Research Unit
ČSSR	*Československá socialistická republika* (Czechoslovak Socialist Republic)
DDR	*Deutsche Demokratische Republik* (German Democratic Republic [East Germany])
DRV	Democratic Republic of Vietnam

ENI	*Ente Nazionale Idrocarburi* [Italian state oil monopoly]
ESE	*Economic Survey of Europe* (Geneva: Economic Commission for Europe)
FYP	Five-Year Plan
IUS	International Union of Students
JPRS	Joint Publications Research Service [U.S. Government translation service]
KSČ	*Komunistická strana Československa* (Communist Party of Czechoslovakia)
LCY	League of Communists of Yugoslavia
MPR	Mongolian People's Republic
NATO	North Atlantic Treaty Organization
NCNA	New China News Agency [*Hsinhua*]
NKVD	*Narodny Komissariat Vnutrennikh Del* (People's Commissariat for Internal Affairs [of the USSR])
NPC	National People's Congress [of China]
PCF	*Parti communiste français* (French Communist Party)
PCI	*Partito comunista italiano* (Italian Communist Party)
PCUS	(see CPSU)
PKI	*Partai Komunis Indonesia* (Indonesian Communist Party)
PPSh	*Partia e Punës së Shqipërisë* (Albanian Party of Labor)
PSI	*Partito socialista italiano* (Italian Socialist Party)
PZPR	*Polska Zjednoczona Partia Robotnicza* (Polish United Workers [Communist] Party)
SCMM	"Selections from China Mainland Magazines" (U.S. Consulate General, Hong Kong)
SCMP	"Survey of the China Mainland Press" (U.S. Consulate General, Hong Kong)
SEATO	Southeast Asia Treaty Organization
TANYUG	Official Yugoslav news agency
TASS	Official Soviet news agency

WDSOE	*Wissenschaftlicher Dienst Südosteuropa*
WFTU	World Federation of Trade Unions
WPC	World Peace Council
YCP	Yugoslav Communist Party
YFPR	Yugoslav Federal People's Republic

Fierce are Albania's children, yet they lack
Not virtues, were those virtues more mature.
Where is the foe that ever saw their back?
Who can so well the toil of war endure?
Their native fastnesses not more secure
Than they in doubtful time of troublous need:
Their wrath how deadly! but their friendship sure,
When gratitude or valor bids them bleed,
Unshaken rushing on where'er their chief may lead.

—Byron, *Childe Harold's Pilgrimage,* II, lxv

CHAPTER ONE

The Background

Introduction

This book attempts to describe, document, analyze, and place within an over-all context one aspect of the Sino-Soviet rift:[1] the dispute and in late 1961 the break between the Soviet Union and Albania.

Why pay so much attention to Albania? For Moscow, is not Tirana only the most convenient polemical symbol for Peking? Can it seriously be maintained that this smallest, poorest, most isolated, most Balkan, most primitive of all the East European Communist states has played any significant independent role in the continuing struggle between the two Communist giants?

In my view it can, nor is this the first time this has been true. As the British Ambassador in Constantinople wrote to the Foreign Office in 1880, when Albanians, not yet independent and harassed by their neighbors, were already casting about for a new protector to replace the tottering Ottoman Sultan,

> . . . the Albanian excitement cannot be passed over as a mere manoeuvre conducted by the Turks in order to mislead Europe and evade its will. . . .[2]

[1] Donald S. Zagoria, *The Sino-Soviet Conflict 1956–1961* (Princeton, 1962); Zbigniew Brzezinski, *The Soviet Bloc,* 2nd ed. (New York: Praeger, 1961), especially the epilogue, "The Impact of the Sino-Soviet Dispute," pp. 409–442, "Patterns and Limits of the Sino-Soviet Dispute," *Problems of Communism,* IX, 5 (Sept.–Oct. 1960), pp. 1–7, and in Kurt L. London, ed., *Unity and Contradiction* (New York: Praeger, 1962), pp. 392–408, and "Deviation Control: A Study in the Dynamics of Doctrinal Conflict," *American Political Science Review,* LVI, 1 (Mar. 1962), pp. 5–22; G. F. Hudson, Richard Lowenthal, and Roderick MacFarquhar, eds., *The Sino-Soviet Dispute* (New York: Praeger, 1961); Richard Lowenthal, "Schism Among the Faithful," *Problems of Communism,* XI, 1 (Jan.–Feb. 1962), pp. 1–14; David A. Charles, "The Dismissal of Marshal P'eng Teh-huai," *The China Quarterly,* No. 8 (Oct.–Dec. 1961), pp. 63–76; a special issue on polycentrism of *Survey,* No. 42 (June 1942), and another on the XXII CPSU Congress and East Europe, *Problems of Communism,* XI, 3 (May–June 1962).

[2] Ambassador G. T. (later Lord) Goschen to Lord Granville, Secretary of State for Foreign Affairs, July 26, 1880, in *Accounts and Papers,* 1880, Turkey, No. 15, LXXXI, quoted from J. Swire, *Albania: The Rise of a Kingdom* (New York: Richard R. Smith, 1930), p. 54.

Ours is an age of nationalism. Since Stalin's death Khrushchev has been unable permanently to prevent the encroachment of national interests upon the unity of the "camp of socialism" and the consequent erosion of Soviet control over it. The Sino-Soviet dispute has made clear that for the first time since 1929 there once again exists a genuinely international Communist movement, no longer wholly dominated by the Soviet Union, riven with disputes, and increasingly polycentric in practice.

The significance of Albania's present role may perhaps be better understood if one thinks back to an analogy in the late forties and fifties. When in 1948 the Soviet-Yugoslav break[3] occurred, few if any observers thought that in 1955–1956 Yugoslavia would play the role it did in loosening up the East European scene. Without this 1948 break, it seems fair in retrospect to conclude, the Polish and Hungarian events of 1955–1956 would at the very least have occurred in a different, and for Moscow less serious, context; indeed, particularly in Hungary, they might well not have occurred at all. Yet the Moscow-Belgrade break did not arise primarily from causes external to the Soviet Union and Yugoslavia, but rather from Tito's determination to resist Stalin's efforts to infiltrate, to subvert, and thus to control the Yugoslav Communist Party, security police, and army.

There is of course an enormous difference between Yugoslavia and Albania. Albania has always been much weaker than Yugoslavia and has always needed, and been under the influence of, some foreign protector. In 1948 Belgrade, unlike Tirana, had no powerful Communist foreign protector like Peking. Yet Tito did have two potential protectors: first, the West, and second, the increasingly powerful neutralist powers, with whom he could ally and maneuver. One of the essential preconditions of Albania's break with Moscow was assured Chinese support. The basic common factor shared by Yugoslavia and Albania is that the distance of China from Albania, like that of the United States from Yugoslavia, plus the geographical location, history, and leaderships of both these Balkan countries, guaranteed that neither, as a result of accepting American or Chinese support, would become a puppet of its protector but rather would increase its own degree of independence of maneuver in foreign and domestic affairs.

Finally, recent Albanian words and deeds have been permeated by a degree of ferocity, violence, and sheer recklessness which cannot but

[3] See *The Soviet-Yugoslav Dispute* (London and New York: Royal Institute of International Affairs, 1948); Robert Bass and Elizabeth Marbury, eds., *The Soviet-Yugoslav Controversy, 1948–1958* (New York: Prospect, 1959); Adam Ulam, *Titoism and the Cominform* (Cambridge, Mass.: Harvard, 1952); Brzezinski, *The Soviet Bloc,* 2nd ed., pp. 37–40, 63–64.

engender in Khrushchev and the Soviet leadership a high level of rage, increased still further by the frequent reprinting of the Albanian fulminations by the Communist Chinese.

Albania: Historical Background

Why has Albania so far successfully defied Moscow? There are three main reasons:

1. Support by the Chinese, with whom the Soviets remain reluctant to break.
2. Geographic isolation from the Soviet Union, which makes impossible intervention by the Red Army as in Hungary.
3. The unity of the Albanian Communist leadership, and the resultant inability of Moscow to infiltrate, factionalize, and create a pro-Soviet majority in it.

But why has the Albanian leadership been so united and decisive in its defiance? Certainly the common experience, like the Chinese, Yugoslav, and North Vietnamese Communists, of having conquered power by armed struggle rather than having been handed it by the Red Army played a significant role. True, the whole postwar history of Albanian Communism was one of factional struggle and constant bloody purges. But the very extent of the slaughter freed Hoxha and Shehu of many potential opponents and intimidated most others, while, as always in Albanian history, the remaining leadership was bound together by ties of blood shared and shed in common.

But these reasons alone do not explain the whole story. Only a knowledge of the long, complex, and profoundly Balkan history of Albania[4]

[4] For Albanian history, see Robert L. Wolff, *The Balkans in our Time* (Cambridge, Mass.: Harvard, 1956); L. S. Stavrianos, *The Balkans Since 1453* (New York: Rinehart, 1958); Stavro Skendi, "Beginnings of Albanian Nationalist Trends in Culture and Education (1878–1912)," *Journal of Central European Affairs*, XII, 4 (Jan. 1953), pp. 356–367, "Beginnings of Albanian Nationalist and Autonomous Trends: The Albanian League, 1878–1881," *American Slavic and East European Review*, XII, 2 (Apr. 1953), pp. 219–232, "Albanian Political Thought and Revolutionary Activity, 1881–1912," *Südostforschungen*, XIII (1954), pp. 159–199, "The Political Evolution of Albania, 1912–1944" (New York: Mid-European Studies Center, mimeo. series, No. 19, Mar. 8, 1954), and *Albania* (New York: Praeger, 1956), pp. 1–59; Robert Schwanke, "Bildung von Nation und Staat in Albanian," *Österreichische Ost-Hefte*, III, 6 (Nov. 1961), pp. 453–462 (with valuable bibliography); R. V. Burks, *The Dynamics of Communism in Eastern Europe* (Princeton, 1961); Amedeo Giannini, *L'Albania dall' Indipendenza all' Unione con l'Italia (1913–1939)*, 4th ed. (Milan: Istituto per gli Studi di Politica Internazionale, n.d. [1940]); J. Swire, *Albania, The Rise of a Kingdom* (New York: Richard R. Smith, 1930); Alfred Rappaport, "Albaniens Werdegang," *Die Kriegschuldfrage*, V, 9 (Sept. 1927), pp. 815–844; Ludwig von Thallóczy, ed., *Illyrisch-Albanische Forschungen*, 2 v. (Munich and Leipzig: Duncker & Humbolt,

can make clear why in 1960 Hoxha defied Khrushchev. Five permanent historical factors are especially important: the ever-present menace to Albania's independence represented by its more powerful hostile neighbors; its lack of internal, religious, and social unity; the xenophobia of its people and the internationalism of much of its élite; the large Albanian irredenta in southwestern Yugoslavia (Kossovo-Metohija — the "Kosmet"); and the relatively more violent Albanian nationalism than that of its neighbors, due to the country's underdevelopment and more recent independence, and itself a part of the generally more primitive, violent, and "Balkan" Albanian traditions, behavior patterns, and political life.

Of all the Balkan peoples the Albanians were the last to achieve effective national consciousness and unity of action. Thraco-Illyrian by stock and language and after the Turkish conquest 70 per cent Moslem (a much greater percentage than in any other Balkan country), they have neither ethnic nor overriding religious ties to their Slav, Greek, or Italian neighbors. They are divided into two groups, the northern Gegs and the southern Tosks. The largely illiterate and semibarbaric Gegs, partly Roman Catholic and fiercely hostile to the Orthodox Serbs, lived until independence in a mountain tribal society characterized by blood feuds and fierce clan loyalties. The Tosk plainsmen along the coast were more civilized from centuries of Greek and Italian influence as well as foreign travel, but their landless and in part Greek Orthodox peasantry was in the grip of the Moslem landlords (beys) and of a one-crop grain economy subject to violent economic fluctuations — a classic pattern for the growth of Communism.

Although Albanians, and particularly the Moslem majority, are traditionally xenophobic, the Albanian élite long played a role on the international scene. In the multinational Ottoman Empire Albanians made up a significant percentage of the multi-ethnic Moslem ruling élite. From 1453 to 1623 eleven out of forty-nine grand viziers were Albanian, as were the Sultan's Guard, the Constantinople garrison,[5] and Mehmet

1916), especially Theodor Ippen, "Beiträge zur inneren Geschichte Albaniens im XIX. Jahrhundert," I, pp. 342–385, Ludwig von Thallóczy, "Das Problem der Einrichtung Albaniens," II, pp. 85–218, Karl Thopia, "Das Fürstentum Albanien," II, pp. 219–289; Charles R. Salit, "Albania as an Index to European Prewar Diplomacy," (unpub. Ph.D. diss., Harvard, 1938); Vandeleur Robinson, *Albania's Road to Freedom* (London: Allen & Unwin, 1941); "La République populaire d'Albanie," 1ère partie: "L'évolution politique," *La documentation française, Notes et études documentaires,* No. 1843, Mar. 2, 1954; 3ème partie, "Évolution économique et sociale," *ibid.,* No. 1845, Mar. 6, 1954; George M. Self, "Foreign Relations of Albania" (unpub. Ph.D. diss., Chicago, 1943); Franz Borkenau, *European Communism* (London: Faber & Faber, 1953), pp. 396–408.

[5] Stavrianos, *op. cit.,* p. 501.

Ali's dynasty in Egypt. The Porte spread Albanian military colonies throughout Greece. Ottoman domination of Albania also produced a large-scale and mostly Tosk emigration, from nationalistic and economic motives, first to Italy and then to Egypt, Romania, Greece, Bulgaria, and the United States. Since the ninth century, Albania's neighbors — the Greeks, Serbs, and Bulgarians — submerged but not destroyed by the centuries-long domination of the Sublime Porte, showed far greater nationalist and expansionist tendencies. After the heroic initial resistance to the Porte of the Albanian hero Skënderbeu [Scanderbeg] in the middle of the fifteenth century, Albania became an object, not a subject, of Balkan politics. It thus inevitably fell far behind the other Balkan states in the drive for and attainment of independence. (The predominantly Moslem Albanians, unlike their neighbors, could still participate as equals in the Ottoman ruling élite.) By 1909, Greece, Serbia, and Bulgaria had wrested their liberty from the Turks and begun modernization, thus profiting in power as well as in territory from Albania's economic backwardness and political weakness. When in the late nineteenth century Albanian nationalism finally arose, it was therefore from the beginning on the defensive against its already independent neighbors.

Thereafter, the primary objective of Albanian foreign policy has remained the obtaining of territorial independence for as many Albanians as possible and preserving it against the constant threat of partition by its hostile neighbors. Serbia and Montenegro wanted northern Albania; Greece wanted southern Albania ("Northern Epirus"). All three, and Italy, maintained that an inevitably weak Albania was an invitation to conquest by a hostile power and therefore a menace to them. Weak and surrounded by enemies, the Albanians could only search constantly for a powerful foreign protector, the more powerful and above all the more distant the better.

In the nineteenth and early twentieth centuries the two nearest great powers were Austria-Hungary and Italy. Both had territorial and sphere-of-influence ambitions in Albania, if only to check hostile influence — for the Austrians the Slavs, for the Italians the Austrians. However, in order to prevent the Balkan powder-keg from exploding and because they could never agree (as neither Albania's neighbors nor the Great Powers have until this day) upon how the country should be divided, the other Great Powers, aided by varying degrees of Albanian resistance, prevented Serbia, Montenegro, and Greece from partitioning the Albanian-speaking area. In 1878 the Treaty of San Stefano incorporated a large number of Albanians into Montenegro, Serbia, and Bulgaria. This number was greatly reduced at the subsequent Congress of

Berlin by Austro-Hungarian and Italian pressure and by the activity of the first effective Albanian domestic nationalist organization, the "League of Prizren." Centering in the by then Serb-ruled Kosmet, the League demanded autonomy for Albania but, lest it be further partitioned among its hostile neighbors, under continued Turkish sovereignty.

Albanian nationalist agitation began among Albanian colonies abroad, notably in Italy, Romania, and Greece, and later in the United States. It was greatly encouraged by the realization of the Albanian élite, in Constantinople and elsewhere in Turkish service, in Albania, and in exile abroad, that the Porte, defeated by the Russians in 1877 and forced by the 1878 decision of the Congress of Berlin to cede Albanian-speaking territory to its neighbors, could no longer protect them. Initially stimulated by the Porte, the League of Prizren was later dissolved by Constantinople when from the Ottoman viewpoint it got out of hand. Thereafter the Albanians alternately rose against the Ottoman Empire and helped to defend it when it was attacked by its anti-Albanian neighbors.

At first the Albanian nationalists were greatly encouraged by the 1908 Young Turk revolt; but its centralizing, Ottomanizing, and repressive tendencies rapidly and finally alienated the Albanians from Constantinople. After the Balkan Wars, in 1912 the intervention of the anti-Serb Austro-Hungarians and (to a lesser extent) the Italians produced an independent Albania, which each preferred to domination by the other or by the Slavs. Even so, some five hundred thousand Albanians in the Kosmet region were incorporated into Serbia, while the Greek occupation of Korçë (Koritza)[6] and Gjirokastër (Argyrokastro) in the south, the Montenegrin of Shkodër (Scutari) to the north, and the Serb of the northern fringe of the newly independent state were ended only by pressure from the Great Powers. Albania's first ruler, Prince Wilhelm of Wied, remained in the country only half a year; Esad Pasha Toptani, a representative of Serb influence, then took power.

When the First World War broke out, with approval of the Entente powers the Greeks occupied the south of the country ("Northern Epirus"), the Serbs and the Montenegrins the north, and, first of all, the Italians the strategic port of Vlorë (Valona). In 1916, after the Central Powers' Balkan victories, Albania was occupied by Austria-Hungary in the north[7] and by France and Italy in the south. When Italy

[6] Except for Tirana, I have throughout given the Albanian spelling of place names, with the Italian in parentheses when the name first appears.

[7] For German and Austro-Hungarian war aims in Albania, 1914–1918, see the detailed and definitive account, based on comprehensive unpublished German and Austro-Hungarian archival material, in Fritz Fischer, *Griff nach der Weltmacht* (Düsseldorf: Droste, 1961), pp. 397, 400 (ftn. 7), 406, 411, 459, 465, 566, 651.

entered the war, its price in the secret Treaty of London (April 1915) included annexation of Vlorë and Sazan (Sasseno) and control over central Albania, the north being assigned at Russian insistence to Serbia and Montenegro, and the south, as the Greeks, French, and British wished, to Greece. In 1917 Lenin published and repudiated the Treaty of London, thus creating pro-Russian and pro-Soviet feeling among the few left-wing Albanians. One Albanian delegation at the Versailles Conference demanded, as a minimum, independence within the 1913 boundaries, if necessary under an American mandate. As a maximum, they wanted all ethnically Albanian territories incorporated into Greece, Serbia, and Montenegro since 1878, i.e., the Kosmet, the northern Greek province of Chamuria (Çamëria), and much more,[8] with allegedly one million Albanians — as many again as within the 1913 frontiers. The other delegation, led by the pro-Yugoslav Esad Pasha, also claimed to be the only Albanian representation; through him Belgrade hoped thus to control the whole country. Nevertheless, the Great Powers would almost surely have agreed to the *de facto* partition of the country had the American President Wilson not refused to accept[9] the Treaty of London. Esad Pasha was murdered in Paris by an Albanian student, his supporters in northern Albania were overcome by Albanian insurgents, Albanian resistance to partition increased, and in 1920 an independent Albania within its present boundaries was recognized by the Great Powers and admitted to the League of Nations. Even so, in 1921 Yugoslavia again occupied some Albanian territory in the north and instigated some of the northern clans to revolt; only the threat of sanctions by the Great Powers forced it to withdraw. (The final demarcation of the Albanian-Yugoslav border was not agreed upon until 1926.) In 1923 Greece occupied some southern Albanian villages; after initially resisting pressure from the Great Powers, it finally withdrew the next year.

Yugoslavia, Greece, and Italy, having thus failed to occupy and annex parts or all of Albania, then attempted to exercise influence on the country. In 1921 the first postwar Albanian government was formed by the Populist Party, officially led by the Tosk Orthodox Bishop Fan Noli[10] (the first time an Orthodox Tosk had played such a prominent role). It

[8] Giannini, *op. cit.*, p. 65; decision of the National Assembly of Lushnjë, Jan. 21–Feb. 9, 1920, in *ibid.*, p. 236; first memorial of the Albanian delegation to the Peace Conference, Feb. 12, 1919, in *ibid.*, pp. 241–247.

[9] Wilson to the British and French governments, London, Feb. 25, 1920, in Giannini, *op. cit.*, p. 264.

[10] Noli had emigrated to America at an early age. With the aid of Koço Tashko's father, a well-to-do Albanian living in Alexandria, he had graduated from Harvard (1912), having in 1908 founded in Boston the autocephalous Albanian Orthodox Church, and returned to Albania after the First World War.

was actually dominated by Eshref Frashëri, a Moslem Tosk bey from Korçë; Ahmed Zogu, a young Geg chieftain, was also prominent in it. (The oppositional Progressive Party was dominated by the landowning beys and violently opposed to agrarian reform.) There ensued a succession of unstable coalition cabinets, increasingly and dictatorially dominated by Zogu. In 1924, as a result of an Army coup, Zogu fled to Yugoslavia, and Noli formed a short-lived, left-wing government which recognized the Soviet Union and proposed a radical reform program. But as Noli later wrote, in a classic description of the liberal dilemma,

> By insisting on the agrarian reforms I aroused the wrath of the landed aristocracy; by failing to carry them out I lost the support of the peasant masses. . . .[11]

At the end of 1924, with Yugoslav military support, Zogu returned in triumph, first as president and after 1928 as king. Noli fled to western Europe and then back to Boston. Some of his young left-wing intellectual followers went to Moscow. Zogu exchanged his Yugoslav protectors in 1926 for Italian economic, and in 1927 military, aid.[12] Following an attempt by Zogu in 1932 to dilute Italian domination by increasing trade with Yugoslavia and Greece, in 1934 an Italian naval demonstration resulted in even greater Italian influence.

Italy subsidized the permanently deficitary Albanian economy and dominated its economic life until the German army arrived in 1941. The vast majority of the population was illiterate; health and living conditions were very low; and, except for some handicraft in the towns, there was practically no industrial labor force. Albania's very slow economic development in the interwar period was determined by the role assigned to her by Italy, that of a supplier of industrial and agricultural raw materials.[13] Exports, however, covered only about 40 per cent of her imports; the deficit was primarily made up by Italian loans.[14]

[11] Quoted in Swire, *op. cit.*, p. 444. For a far from totally unfavorable Communist view of the Noli regime, see Reshat Këlliçi, "Unforgettable Days in Tirana in 1924," *Nëndori*, VIII, 10 (Oct. 1961), pp. 155–183.

[12] Italo-Albanian Treaty of Friendship and Security, Nov. 27, 1926, in Giannini, *op. cit.*, pp. 301–302; Italo-Albanian Defensive Alliance, Nov. 22, 1927, *ibid.*, p. 174.

[13] Two-thirds of her exports went to Italy; one-half of her imports came from there. Albanian exports were primarily agricultural but also included some oil, chrome ore, and bitumen, the production of which the Italians began. See *Anuari Statistikor i R.P.Sh. 1959* (Statistical Yearbook of the Albanian People's Republic) (hereafter *ASRPSh*) (Tirana: Drejtoria e Statistikës, 1960), pp. 168–169.

[14] Between 1927 and 1939 the average value of imports was 24.9 million franga and that of exports 9 million franga. Albanian emigrants' remittances also helped to make up the trade deficit. See *Economic Survey of Europe* (hereafter *ESE*) 1960, Ch. VI, p. 2. Italian economic penetration of Albania began in 1925 with the signing of an agreement for the exploitation of Albanian natural resources and

In April 1939, Mussolini occupied Albania;[15] in 1940, allegedly to stop Greek mistreatment of the Albanian minority in the northern Greek province of Chamuria, he invaded Greece, but the Greeks soon pushed the Italians back and occupied the southern quarter of Albania. The initial Albanian anti-Italian and therefore pro-Greek feeling was soon reversed once the Greeks again moved to annex "Northern Epirus." In April 1941 the Germans overran Yugoslavia and Albania and officially "re-incorporated" the Kosmet[16] plus (nominally) the Greek province of Chamuria into Albania. Although this move failed to gain the Germans and Italians as much Albanian popular support as they had hoped, it did favorably influence the nationalistic Tosk beys and Geg chieftains. Later in the war the German-sponsored "autonomous" Albanian regime, composed largely of Gegs from the Kosmet, enjoyed some popular support.

The modern history of Albania has thus been one of foreign influence or domination, territorial irredentism, and permanent insecurity. Almost all politically conscious adult Albanians today, and certainly the present Albanian Communist leadership, have grown up convinced that Albanian independence is constantly threatened by foreign control or partition, that the return of the Kosmet is prevented by "Yugoslav chauvinism," and that these threats to Albania can be averted only by the intervention of one or more of the Great Powers. Only this conviction makes comprehensible the risks that Hoxha, Shehu, and their associates were willing to take in 1960 and the fury and endurance with which they have defied Khrushchev.

The Albanian Communist Party: Historical Background[17]

When in 1924 Bishop Noli fled to the West, a few of his young leftist adherents went to Moscow. There they belonged to a committee (first

---

the creation of an Albanian currency and National Bank (in Italy!) as a framework for the institutionalized Italian subsidies (*ibid.*). The Italian government and private Italian firms also granted long-term loans for public works, livestock raising, construction of the port of Durrës, etc. (Skendi, *Albania,* p. 225).

[15] See for documentation, Giannini, *op. cit.*, pp. 352–365.

[16] See "Die albanische Minderheit in Jugoslawien," *Wissenschaftlicher Dienst Südosteuropa* (hereafter *WDSOE*), VI, 1/10 (Sept.–Oct. 1957), pp. 163–169.

[17] There is no adequate history of Albanian Communism; the following account is reconstructed from conflicting Yugoslav and Albanian sources. The Yugoslav sources are primarily Vladimir Dedijer, *Jugoslovensko-Albanski Odnoši (1938–1949)* (Yugoslav-Albanian Relations 1938–1949) (Belgrade, 1949), trans. into Italian as *Il Sangue Tradito. Relazione Jugoslavo-Albanesi 1938–1949* (Varesi: Editoriale Periodici Italiana, 1949); *Livre blanc sur la politique hostile du gouvernement de la République Populaire d'Albanie envers la République Populaire Fédérative de Yougoslavie* (Belgrade: Secretariat of State for Foreign Affairs of

formed in Vienna) which later became affiliated with the Balkan Confederation of Communist parties and through it with the Comintern.[18] The committee included the poet Sejfulla Malëshova (Noli's former private secretary), the intellectual Lazar Fundo, and the self-educated Ali Kelmendi. In 1930, Kelmendi, the only Geg of the three, returned to Albania and began organizing Communist groups there. Forced to flee again by Zogu in 1936,[19] he fought in the International Brigade in Spain. He then went to France, where he became the senior member of the

---

the FPRY, 1961); Milovan Djilas, *Conversations With Stalin* (New York: Harcourt, Brace and World, 1962); and M. Milić, *Danashnja Albanija* (Contemporary Albania) (Belgrade: Sedme Sile, 1962). The Albanian sources (hitherto little utilized in Western published material) are from the PPSh Institute of Party History: Vangjel Moisiu, *Lufta për Krijimin e Partisë Komuniste të Shqipërisë (1917–1941)* (Struggle for the Creation of the Albanian Communist Party); Ndreçi Plasari, *Krijimi i Partisë Komuniste të Shqipërisë 1939–1941* (The Formation of the Albanian Communist Party) (both Tirana: Instituti i Historisë së Partisë pranë K.Q. të PPSh, 1957); Veli Dedi, Zhavit Struga, Fane Veizi, and Mediha Shuteriqi (Jasa), eds., *Dokumenta e Materiale Historike nga Lufta e Popullit Shqiptar për Liri e Demokraci 1917–1941* (Documents and Historical Materials on the Struggle of the Albanian People for Freedom and Democracy 1917–1941) (Tirana: Drejtoria e Arkivave Shtetërore të R.P.Sh. 1949) (hereafter *Dokumenta e Materiale*); *Dokumenta Kryesore të Partisë së Punës së Shqipërisë* (Principal Documents of the Albanian Party of Labor), 2 v. Tirana: Instituti Historisë së Partisë pranë K.Q. të PPSh., 1960, 1961) (hereafter *Dokumenta Kryesore*); Ndreçi Plasari, "The Strategy and Tactics of the Albanian Party of Labor During the National Liberation Struggle," *Buletin i Universitetit Shtetëror të Tiranës, Seria Shkencat Shoqërore* (Bulletin of the State University of Tirana, Social Science Series), XV, 4 (1961), pp. 187–189. See also Wolff, *op. cit.;* Burks, *op. cit.;* Julian Amery, *Sons of the Eagle* (London: Macmillan, 1948) and the penetrating review of it by F. B. [Franz Borkenau], "Rote Skipetaren," *Ost-Probleme,* II, 39 (Sept. 28, 1950), pp. 1233–1236; Brigadier "Trotsky" Davies, *Illyrian Venture* (London: Bodley Head, 1952); "History of the Albanian Communist Party," *News From Behind the Iron Curtain,* IV, 11 (Nov. 1955), 3–10, and V, 1 (Jan. 1956), pp. 22–30; V. [iktor] M. [eier], "Politische und ideologische Wurzeln des albanischen Kommunismus," *Neue Zürcher Zeitung,* April 13, 1957; Stavro Skendi, *Albania* and "Albania within the Slav Orbit: Advent to Power of the Communist Party," *Political Science Quarterly,* LXIII, 2 (June 1948), pp. 257–274; Branko Lazitch, "Le dossier du Parti communiste albanais," *Est et ouest,* XIII, 267 (N.S.) (Nov. 16–30, 1961), pp. 6–16; Dedijer, "Enver Hoxha Fights for Survival," *The Times* (London), Feb. 22, 1962, p. 11; Hamm, *Rebellen gegen Moskau;* Jani I. Dilo, "The Communist Party Leadership in Albania" (Washington, D.C.: Institute of Ethnic Studies, Georgetown University, 1961).

[18] The committee was first called *Konare* (National Revolutionary Committee). In 1928, after it was purged of "elements who had compromised with imperialist countries," it was renamed *Çlirimi Nacional* (National Liberation), and published a newspaper *Liria Kombëtare* (National Liberty). See Nov. 8, 1941, resolution in *Dokumenta e Materiale,* Document 572, pp. 492–503.

[19] Moisiu, *op. cit.,* p. 59, gives 1935 but *Dokumenta e Materiale,* p. 376 (Document 424, Sept. 10, 1936), gives 1936 as the year of his flight. For Kelmendi, see Ali Kelmendi, *Militant i Shquar i Lëvizjes Komuniste Shqiptare* (Distinguished Militant of the Albanian Communist Movement) (Tirana: Instituti i Historisë së Partisë, 1960).

small group of Albanian Communists; among them was the young student Enver Hoxha. Through publishing a newspaper and other means they tried, with little success, to encourage Communism in Albania.[20] In 1938 Kelmendi and Malëshova reportedly enticed Fundo from Paris to Moscow, where Malëshova's attempt to have him killed by the NKVD was frustrated only by the intervention of Georgi Dimitrov. (Fundo then returned to Paris, broke with Communism, and went back to Albania before the Second World War. From there he was deported to Italy and after Mussolini's fall returned to Albania, where he became a political advisor to the nationalist partisans; he was killed by Communist partisans in 1944.)[21]

Albanian interwar Communism arose out of a mixture of nationalist and ethnic hostilities, religious differences, internationalist tradition, economic discontent, and Western Communist influence. In the interwar period there were some young Tosk and fewer Geg[22] intellectuals who revolted against the traditional society. These intellectuals, who had been educated in France or Italy or in French or American schools in Albania, hated the traditionalist Geg chieftains and Tosk beys, and they could no longer hope for a career in the multi-ethnic international Ottoman bureaucracy (yet they remembered the opportunities it had offered). They felt that both Albania's economic development and their natural desire to use their Western education[23] for their own and their country's advancement were frustrated by Zogu's dictatorial rule, by the hostility of traditionalist chieftains and beys, and by the lack of opportunities in Albania's underdeveloped society and economy. But there were other internal Albanian reasons. Most of these frustrated intellectuals were Tosks. They hated the traditional Geg leadership of the country, whom they considered more primitive and less educated than themselves, and they were equally hostile to the Tosk landowners whose one-crop (grain) economy left the landless peasants at their mercy. Furthermore, in the Geg north the clan system still prevailed, and the relationship of its members to their chiefs was therefore primarily one of personal loyalty rather than of economic subordination. In

[20] Cf. the probably exaggerated account of their activities in Moisiu, *op. cit.*, p. 38.

[21] Cf. *Dokumenta e Materiale,* p. 519, ftn. 93. According to Amery he was clubbed to death.

[22] While I am unable to accept completely the theory of Burks, *op. cit.*, p. 147, and Meier, *op. cit.*, that Albanian Communism was primarily a revolt of Tosk intellectuals against Geg domination, this factor did play a significant role in its development. Cf. Hamm, *op. cit.*, pp. 100–101, and conversations with Skendi and Schwanke, April 1962.

[23] Which, ironically enough, Zogu had made possible for young Tosks, the principal pool of talent from which he could train a new, centralized bureaucracy.

the Tosk south, however, the chieftains had become large landowners (beys) and the population a landless agricultural proletariat, while its relatively greater economic progress and foreign influence had also produced a small group of intellectuals, sociologically and psychologically as well as economically alienated from the beys.[24] Elsewhere in East Europe, in Romania or Croatia for example, many similarly frustrated intellectuals turned to fascism. In Albania as in Serbia, however, fascism was the ideology of the Italian enemy, and for the Albanians that of the hated Greece of Metaxas as well. Like such young Yugoslav intellectuals as Djilas, a few young Albanian intellectuals became Communists.

Enver Hoxha, the first and to date the only head of the Albanian Communist party is a son of a Tosk Moslem landowner from Gjirokastër. After attending the French lycée at Korçë, in 1930 he received an Albanian state scholarship at the University of Montpellier, which after a year he lost for "neglect of his work." Thereupon he went to Paris and came under the influence of a small group of Albanian Communists living there in exile, including Ali Kelmendi and Lazar Fundo. In 1933 he went to Brussels, where he became private secretary to the Albanian Honorary Consul and subsequently studied law at the University of Brussels. In 1936, without having obtained a degree, he returned to Albania, where for a time he taught French, first at Tirana State Gymnasium and then at the Korçë lycée.[25]

Mehmet Shehu, the present Albanian Prime Minister, also a Tosk, was educated in the American Vocational School in Tirana, at the Naples military college (from which he was expelled after a few months for left-wing political activity), and then at the Tirana officers' school. In 1938 he went to Spain; there he became Acting Commander of the Fourth Battalion of the "Garibaldi" (Italian) Brigade in the International Brigade and joined the Spanish Communist Party. He retreated with the Brigade to France, where from 1939 to 1942 he was interned; during this period he joined the Italian Communist Party. In 1942 he was released and, under Italian escort, returned to Tirana,[26] whence he immediately fled to join the Communist partisans.

Hoxha's pattern of birth, education, and experience was more nearly typical of the post-1945 Albanian Communist leadership than one might

[24] Cf. Hugh Seton-Watson, "Intelligentsia and Revolution, an Historical Analysis," *Soviet Survey,* No. 29 (July–Sept. 1959), pp. 90–96, and "The Role of the Intelligentsia," *Survey,* No. 43 (Aug. 1962), pp. 23–30, and Viktor Meier, "Albanien im Schatten Jugoslawiens," *Aussenpolitik,* XIII, 7 (July 1962), pp. 469–478, at p. 471.

[25] Skendi, *Albania,* pp. 326–327; Burks, *op. cit.,* pp. 63–64.

[26] Skendi, *Albania,* pp. 341–342.

think. As in most Communist parties in underdeveloped countries, its leaders were largely of middle-class origin and intellectual by training and taste. About half of them were educated abroad. Well over three-quarters of the postwar leading Albanian Communist cadres were of middle-class origin, the highest percentage in any East European Communist party; likewise, its percentage of workers was the lowest.[27] Some were proletarian in origin, such as the Tosk tinsmith Koci Xoxe and the Geg carpenter Tuk Jakova; antagonism grew between them and the intellectuals.[28]

In the late 1930's the few Albanian Communists fell into factional struggles and impotence. They were almost totally ideologically disoriented, particularly by the 1937 Comintern popular-front line and by the 1939 Italian invasion of Albania.[29] By the summer of 1939 the Yugoslav Communists were already planning to set up and control an Albanian Communist party, and Miladin Popović, head of the Kosmet regional Communist group, established contact with the northernmost Albanian Communist group at Shkodër.[30]

When emissaries of the Yugoslav Communist partisans, headed by Popović and Dušan Mugoša, arrived in Albania in 1941, in accordance with Tito's orders, to organize a Communist party, they found "ideological confusion"[31] and "real chaos"[32] in the various Albanian Communist groups. Of the four most important, the oldest was *Puna* (Work) in Korçë, which included the intellectuals Enver Hoxha, Pandi Kristo, Koço Tashko, and Nako Spiru, and the proletarian Koci Xoxe. Another, the only Geg one, was in Shkodër; it included Zef Mala, Tuk Jakova, and the woman intellectual Liri Gega.[33] The relatively nationalistic *Zjarri* (Fire) in Tirana was headed by Andrea Zisi. Finally, *Të Rinjte* (Youth), which had split off from the Korçë group, included Anastas Lulo, Sadik Premte, Hysni Kapo, an intellectual from Vlorë,

[27] Burks, *op. cit.*, pp. 21, 52, 63–64.

[28] See proceedings of II Plenum of PPSh CC, Berat, Nov. 1944, quoted in Dedijer, *Il Sangue Tradito*, pp. 94–99.

[29] See the Nov. 8, 1941, and the April 1943 YCP resolutions, quoted in Dedijer, *op. cit.*, pp. 3–4.

[30] *Ibid.*, p. 4, citing a YCP CC resolution; cf. Milić, *op. cit.*, p. 21.

[31] Alqi Kristo, "Recollections," *Nëndori,* No. 11, Nov. 1961, pp. 96–100, at p. 96. According to a Yugoslav source ("Twenty Years of the Albanian Party of Labor," *Borba,* Nov. 8, 1961), Koço Tashko and "representatives of other Albanian Marxist groups" came to the Kosmet in October 1941 "to ask for help from Yugoslav comrades."

[32] Popović to the Yugoslav CC, May 21, 1942, quoted in Dedijer, *op. cit.*, p. 8.

[33] In 1961, Mugoša claimed that Mala favored the Italian occupation in the hopes of their incorporating the Kosmet and Chamuria into Albania ("Radio Belgrade Interviews Dušan Mugoša, Secretary of the Regional Communist Committee of the Kosmet," *Flaka e Vllaznimit* [Skopje], May 1, 1961).

and Bedri Spahiu, an officer from Gjirokastër. After some initial difficulties with the Korçë group, Popović and Mugoša got all the groups to merge except *Zjarri* (whose nationalism, the Yugoslav emissaries felt, initially made it hold back), organized partisan warfare operations, and on November 8, 1941, formed the Albanian Communist Party.[34]

The Albanian Communist partisans' program of social and economic revolution so antagonized the nationalistic Geg chieftains and the Tosk landowning beys that these two élite groups became inclined if necessary to come to terms with the Italians and later with the Germans to prevent the loss of their wealth and power. This was the more true because they wanted to keep the Kosmet, which the Italians had "returned" to Albania in 1941 and whose retention the Albanian Communists, owing to their post-1941 domination by the Yugoslavs, could not support. In addition, the non-Communist élite had become much more suspicious of the Communists. With British and Yugoslav help, the Albanian Communists carried on a long and finally successful partisan struggle. By 1944, under Yugoslav direction, they had manipulated most of their internal foes into collaboration with the Germans, outmaneuvered the British, and successfully filled the power vacuum in Albania left by the Nazi defeat.[35]

Until 1948 Albania remained a Yugoslav rather than a Soviet satellite. It did not, for example, participate in Cominform meetings; it was represented in them by the Yugoslavs. Like the Yugoslav Communists, and all Communists coming to power by their own efforts in underdeveloped countries, the Albanian Communist leadership followed left-extremist, "Stalinist" policies at home and abroad. The Yugoslavs, allowed by the Russians to deal with Albania pretty much as they wished, distrusted such intellectuals as Hoxha: they were too international, too Westernized, and not sufficiently amenable to Belgrade's desires; they supported those of proletarian origin, particularly Xoxe. Tito's pre-1948 Balkan Federation plans involved the incorporation of Albania (including the Kosmet), along with Bulgaria and Greece, into Yugoslavia as a constituent republic, a move which Stalin opposed.[36] They also included the use of Albania as one of the bases for supporting the Greek Communist partisans, an operation which in 1948 Stalin demanded that Tito abandon.[37]

[34] Resolution, Nov. 8, 1941, in *Dokumenta e Materiale,* Document 572, pp. 492–503 (with, of course, no mention of the two).

[35] See Hugh Seton-Watson, *The East European Revolution,* 3rd ed. (New York: Praeger, 1956), pp. 139–146.

[36] See Vladimir Dedijer, *Tito* (New York: Simon & Schuster, 1953), pp. 272–273, 302–303, 321; Djilas, *op. cit.,* pp. 133–186.

[37] Djilas, *op. cit.,* pp. 171–186.

During the Second World War, Albanian agriculture was hardly touched except for requisitions, but industry, particularly in the extractive branches (oil, bitumen, chrome, copper), was greatly expanded.[38] A cement factory and a small copper-processing operation were set up. For the first time, some quite extensive road- and bridge-building took place, thus providing one of the essential prerequisites for the postwar industrialization. At the end of the war Communist economic reorganization, under Yugoslav tutelage, was rapid and ruthless. The almost entirely German- and Italian-owned foreign properties were confiscated, as well as those of the upper classes (as "collaborators" — which in a sense most of them were); nationalization was rapid[39] and total; currency reforms[40] eliminated the possibility of inflation; the 1945 introduction of rationing[41] made the population totally economically dependent on the regime; and extensive financial aid from UNRRA[42] and especially from Yugoslavia[43] made the beginning of economic development possible. In 1945–1946 a radical agrarian reform redistributed nearly half of the arable land.[44]

Agricultural production improved during the 1946–1949 period, and animal population and grain production,[45] in large part through extensive draining of marshland,[46] reached new highs. Industry, however, except for coal and electric energy production, remained below wartime peak outputs;[47] Yugoslavia could not supply the necessary investment goods. Even so, Yugoslav credits reached great heights. In 1947 they were 58 per cent of state income;[48] in 1948 nearly half.[49] The economic integration of Albania into Yugoslavia moved forward rapidly, another indication of Tito's intent to incorporate the country into a Belgrade-dominated Balkan federation. Yugoslav-Albanian treaties provided for common price and currency systems, common customs frontiers, and joint economic planning. Joint Yugoslav-Albanian corporations were organized in transportation, mining, foreign trade, and banking. Albania was certainly intended by Yugoslavia to become a constituent

[38] Table 6.3.

[39] *ESE* 1960, Ch. VI, p. 5.

[40] Skendi, *op. cit.*, p. 215.

[41] *ESE* 1960, Ch. VI, p. 5.

[42] Skendi, *op. cit.*, p. 228.

[43] *Ibid.*, pp. 221, 230.

[44] The agrarian reform affected 173 thousand hectares out of a total of 393 thousand, or 44% (*ESE* 1960, Ch. VI, p. 5).

[45] See Tables 6.4, 6.5.

[46] Cereal acreage increased from 264 thousand hectares in 1946 to 319 thousand hectares in 1949. (Skendi, *op. cit.*, p. 166.)

[47] See Table 6.3.

[48] Skendi, *op. cit.*, p. 230.

[49] *Ibid.*, p. 221.

member of Tito's Balkan Federation plan.[50] From the economic viewpoint, therefore, the 1948 Moscow-Belgrade break meant release from economic as well as political tutelage by Belgrade.

Analysis of 1941–1948 Albanian Communist factional struggles, although far from easy, throws great light on how close Hoxha and Shehu came to being eliminated by the Yugoslavs and thus throws much light on their anti-Yugoslav motivation in 1960. Much of the available evidence about it, in Dedijer's books on Albania, was based on reports by Popović, Mugoša, and other Yugoslav "controllers" of the Albanians and reflects the official Yugoslav Communist view, strongly slanted against Hoxha and in favor of Xoxe. The Albanian material is strongly slanted against Xoxe and for Hoxha, in favor of the Korçë group and against the others; it also entirely omits any reference to the pre-1944 Yugoslav control over the Albanian party, and in the 1945–1948 period it presents only Xoxe, and not Hoxha, as under Yugoslav influence.[51] Finally, both sides greatly underplay and are often deliberately silent on the Kosmet issue.

Under Yugoslav direction, but probably with the Korçë group's enthusiastic support, the first purges of the new Albanian party occurred in early 1942, encompassing many of the leaders of the *Të Rinjtë* and *Zjarri* groups, the ones the Yugoslavs had initially suspected.[52] The first wartime difference of opinion over a major political issue of which we are aware was over the Kosmet. The Yugoslav Communist Party in 1928 and again in 1940 had endorsed the "return" of the Kosmet to Albania,[53] and the few Albanian prewar Communists presumably did also.[54] However, when in 1941 the Yugoslav Communist partisans

[50] *Ibid.*, pp. 229–231. For Yugoslav interest, as early as 1944, in including Albania in its projected Balkan federation, see Albanian messages to the YCP, *Livre blanc*, pp. 132–133 (Docs. 88, 89, from Doc. 11178, LCY Archives).

[51] E.g., *Dokumenta Kryesore*, I, p. 379.

[52] Dedijer, *Il sangue tradito*, pp. 89–94, *inter alia* citing from and quoting a letter of Sept. 22, 1942, from Tito to the Albanian CC, the full text of which (Doc. No. 4829, LCY archives) is in *Livre blanc*, Doc. 85, pp. 123–126; see also *Dokumenta Kryesore*, I, pp. 52, 59, 77; cf. Milić, *op. cit.*, p. 22, who states that at an April 1942 meeting in which this purge occurred, Dishnica, Gega, and Kapo were elected to the Central Committee. At this same time the Gjirokastër regional committee was dissolved and its political secretary, Bedri Spahiu (purged in 1955), blamed for its "serious errors" (*ibid.*, p. 475, ftn. 48). For a later CC denunçiation of Spahiu for a too conciliatory attitude toward the Balli Kombëtar, see *ibid.*, p. 479, ftn. 66. For the text of a message on Albanian developments from Tito to the Cominform, see *Livre blanc*, Doc. No. 85, p. 127 (Doc. No. 15592, LCY archives).

[53] See "Die albanische Minderheit in Jugoslawien," *WDSOE*, VI, 1/10 (Sept.–Oct. 1957), p. 164, quoting resolutions of the 4th YCP Congress at Dresden in 1928 and the 5th at Zagreb in 1940.

[54] Mugoša in 1961 accused the pre-1941 Korçë and Shkodër Albanian Communist groups of this. See an interview of him on Radio Belgrade at the end of April 1961, in *Flaka e Vllaznimit* (Skopje), May 1, 1961.

founded the Albanian Communist Party, they suppressed any such Albanian sentiments; they were not publicly revived until 1960, when Hoxha once again asserted Albanian interests in the Kosmet.[55] At the August 1943 Mukje joint conference of the Albanian National Liberation Council (including and dominated by the Communists) and the nationalist Balli Kombëtar, the Communist representative, Ymer Dishnica, agreed to a compromise formulation that the Kosmet's fate should be determined by a postwar plebiscite. This was immediately repudiated by the Albanian party leadership at the insistence of its Yugoslav overlords.[56]

This Albanian Communist attitude toward the Kosmet, which has remained constant until the present, has some although far from total resemblance to the attitudes of the East German, North Korean, and North Vietnamese Communist parties, all three ruling in divided countries and therefore inclined toward extremism at home and abroad. For many Albanians, including some Communists, the Kosmet is the smaller part of an Albania which has been partitioned since 1912 and whose reunification remains a national goal. Nevertheless, except for the 1941–1944 period, independent Albania has never included the Kosmet and there has been no immediate prospect that it will. Finally, the addition of the militantly Moslem Gegs in the Kosmet would worsen the situation of the Tosks, the Roman Catholics, and the Orthodox. For all these reasons the Kosmet is an important and often underestimated (although not a decisive) issue in Albanian politics.

According to the Yugoslav version,[57] at the November 1944 Berat Central Committee Plenum, antagonism reportedly emerged between the "intellectuals," including Hoxha, Gega, Spiru, Dishnica, and Malëshova,[58] and the "proletarians," led by Xoxe and favored by the

[55] *Zëri i Popullit,* June 3, 1960.

[56] Dedijer, *op. cit.,* pp. 79–80, 95–96 (ftn. 27), pp. 115–117 and Milić, *op. cit.,* pp. 25–26; *Dokumenta Kryesore,* I, pp. 476–478, ftns. 57, 62, and an Albanian CC circular, *ibid.,* Doc. 23, pp. 153–154. See a letter of Nov. 1943 from the Yugoslav CC to the Albanian CC, quoted in *ibid.,* pp. 116–117. Allegedly (*ibid.,* p. 116) Malëshova and other "nationalist" intellectuals were also for the incorporation of the Kosmet into Albania; probably most were (see a report from Vukmanović-Tempo to the Yugoslav CC, Aug. 8, 1943 [Doc. No. 1962, LCY archives] in *Livre blanc,* Doc. No. 87, pp. 130–131). See also Jorgji Sota re Dishnica in *Zëri i Popullit,* Oct. 16, 1960. Milić (*loc. cit.*) states that at a subsequent CC plenum Xoxe condemned the Mukje decisions, Dishnica and Hoxha were criticized, and Hoxha confessed and made self-criticism, and the plenum condemned the Mukje decisions. In 1961 Mugoša declared that all the Albanian Communist leaders favored the incorporation of the Kosmet and Chamuria, a charge which although intended by Mugoša to defame them as territorial revisionists was and is probably true. ("Radio Belgrade Interviews Dušan Mugoša," *Flaka e Vllaznimit* [Skopje], May 1, 1961.)

[57] Dedijer, *op. cit.,* pp. 94–99; Milić, *op. cit.,* p. 26.

[58] Who returned to Albania from France only in the middle of 1943.

Yugoslavs.[59] After criticizing Hoxha, Dishnica, and Malëshova for being too "intellectual" and discriminating against the "proletarians," and Hoxha for his conciliatory attitude toward the Balli Kombëtar and for his inefficiency, Xoxe succeeded in expelling Gega (with whom Hoxha allegedly intended to replace Xoxe) from the Central Committee and preventing Spiru's[60] election to it; Hoxha made abject self-criticism. (According to the Albanian version,[61] the Yugoslavs there launched an attack on Hoxha.) In May 1944, at Mugoša's insistence, Dishnica had been purged from the Central Committee,[62] but Hoxha later made him minister of health.

Immediately after the war, from the viewpoint of the Yugoslavs[63] and of Xoxe, Hoxha continued his sins. Allegedly under Malëshova's influence, he praised de Gaulle and France, resumed diplomatic relations with Italy, allowing some Albanians to study there and Italians in Albania to be repatriated, and in general took a pro-Italian attitude. (It is quite likely and entirely in accord with Albanian historical tradition that Hoxha was trying to decrease his total dependence on Belgrade; it seems very doubtful, however, that the Yugoslav accusations against him of having wanted to start agricultural collectivization slowly[64] are correct.)

At the Fifth Albanian Plenum, in February 1946, Xoxe succeeded in expelling Malëshova from the Politburo and Central Committee, allegedly for right-wing views on internal and foreign policy and on economics.[65] In the next year Xoxe expelled Dishnica from the party.

59 Although Albanian Communists have denied to the writer that any such antagonism in fact existed, it seems probable that, as elsewhere in eastern Europe, it to some extent did.

60 According to Dedijer (*op. cit.*, p. 97), Spiru had unsuccessfully tried to persuade the Yugoslavs to remove Hoxha, and for that purpose had written them a letter in Italian (photostat: Dedijer, *op. cit.*, pp. 206–207) calling Hoxha "mediocre," "sectarian," and a man with "no leadership qualities." This, if true, may have in part accounted for Hoxha's failure to support him in 1947.

61 *Dokumenta Kryesore,* I, p. 382.

62 Xoxe to the Berat plenum, quoted "from the stenographic notes" by Dedijer, *op. cit.*, p. 96.

63 Dedijer, *op. cit.*, pp. 126 ff., quoting *inter alia* (pp. 127–128, 130–131) a dispatch to Belgrade in June 1946 of the Yugoslav Minister in Tirana.

64 *Ibid.*, pp. 145–146.

65 "From the Conclusions and Decisions of the 5th Party Plenum," Feb. 21, 1946, in *Dokumenta Kryesore,* I, Document 45, pp. 270–278; *ibid.*, p. 269; "Letter of the Party Central Committee in Connection with the Opportunism of Sejfulla Malëshova and Its Denunciation by the Party Central Committee," May 10, 1947, *ibid.*, Document 50, pp. 334–340; Dedijer, *op. cit.*, pp. 131–133. The official post-1948 Albanian version is still (e.g., in *Dokumenta Kryesore, loc. cit.*, in Jorgji Sota, "The Strength of the Party Is Derived from the Steel-like Unity of Its Ranks," *Zëri i Popullit,* Oct. 16, 1960, and in the Nov. 7, 1961, Hoxha speech, *Zëri i Popullit,* Nov. 8, 1961, and Document 14) that it was Hoxha who (correctly)

In June 1946, the Albanian version runs, Hoxha attempted to launch a counterattack against the Yugoslavs but was frustrated by Xoxe, his associate Pandi Kristo, and Nako Spiru.[66]

By 1947 the factional struggle in the Albanian leadership had become more complex, violent, and involved in the deteriorating relations between the Soviet Union and Yugoslavia.[67] By late 1947, Xoxe and his associates, under Yugoslav direction, were intensifying their efforts to merge Albania into Yugoslavia. Much of the Albanian leadership, and in particular the intellectual Nako Spiru (the first husband of Liri Belishova), opposed this Yugoslav plan. Hoxha, although also opposed to it, did not as yet dare to resist it openly but, probably with secret Soviet encouragement, secretly sabotaged it.[68] Spiru, increasingly anti-Yugoslav[69] and driven frantic by Xoxe's attacks (and probably by Hoxha's lack of open support), in November 1947 committed suicide.[70]

His suicide was the occasion for a serious worsening of Soviet-Yugoslav relations. According to Djilas' 1962 version, the Soviets had already been intriguing with Hoxha and making complaints to the Yugoslavs:

> Why were the Yugoslavs forming joint-stock companies with the Albanians when they refused to form the same in their own country with the USSR? Why were they sending their instructors to the Albanian Army when they had Soviet instructors in their own? How could Yugoslavs provide experts for the development of Albania when they themselves were seeking experts from abroad? How was it that all of a sudden Yugoslavia, itself poor and underdeveloped, intended to develop Albania? . . .[71]

In January 1948, allegedly because of Spiru's suicide, Stalin summoned Djilas to Moscow to discuss Yugoslav-Albanian relations but upon his arrival once again declared (probably in an attempt to entrap or lull Belgrade): "We agree to Yugoslavia swallowing Albania"[72] and, as be-

---

purged Malëshova. Hoxha may also have been opposed to him, but Xoxe led the drive against him. Vukmanović-Tempo told Dedijer in 1949 (*op. cit.*, pp. 53–54; cf. *ibid.*, p. 78) that in 1943 when he was in Albania Hoxha, Dishnica, and some other Albanian CC members were opposed to setting up a supreme military command before further negotiations with the anti-Communist Balli Kombëtar, while he and Xoxe favored it; however, such statements made after the 1948 Yugoslav-Albanian break must necessarily be treated with caution.

[66] *Dokumenta Kryesore,* I, p. 383.

[67] As pointed out by Wolff, *op. cit.*, p. 288.

[68] Djilas, *op. cit.*, pp. 171–186. According to the Albanian version (*Zëri i Popullit,* June 22, 1958), the Albanians "rejected this proposal."

[69] *Dokumenta Kryesore,* I, p. 484, ftn. 96.

[70] *Ibid.*, p. 388.

[71] Djilas, *op. cit.*, pp. 135–136.

[72] Cf. Hamm, *Rebellen gegen Moskau,* p. 36; *Zëri i Popullit,* June 22, 1958.

fore, agreed with the Yugoslavs that the "proletarian" Xoxe was preferable to the "Westernized intellectual" Hoxha.[73]

However, Stalin was probably only trying to entice Tito into a more difficult position[74] while already secretly encouraging Hoxha against Xoxe and the Yugoslavs. In any case, Soviet-Yugoslav relations continued to worsen. Moscow discovered Dimitrov's (and Tito's) Balkan Federation plans, and in February, Kardelj and Bakarić having joined Djilas in Moscow (Tito pretending illness so as not to have to go), Stalin protested the Yugoslav plans to send army and air force units to Albania as support for the Greek Communist rebels, declared that Moscow had not been consulted on them, and insisted that Yugoslav support of the Greek Communist rising must cease lest the United States intervene to quell it. He also denounced Tito's and Dimitrov's Balkan Federation plans (which included Albania and Greece) and Dimitrov's support of a customs union between Bulgaria and Romania, declaring that there should instead first be a Yugoslav-Bulgarian federation which Albania should then join.[75]

The Soviet-Yugoslav crisis had direct and drastic repercussions in Albania. There Xoxe (with Belgrade's support) launched an intensified offensive to overthrow Hoxha and to bring the Albanian leadership totally under his (and Yugoslav) control.[76] At the Albanian Eighth Plenum in February–March 1948[77] Hoxha was forced to make self-criticism for allegedly supporting Spiru (although he did not lose his position as General Secretary), and Xoxe succeeded in expelling from the party Liri Belishova (Spiru's wife), Malëshova, and Dishnica, and removing Shehu as a candidate Central Committee member and Chief of the General Staff. In addition, according to the Albanian version,[78] the plenum endorsed Xoxe's proposal that the Soviet military advisors be withdrawn and that the Albanian and Yugoslav armies be merged. Had the break not occurred, Hoxha's and Shehu's days were numbered; Stalin probably saved them from Xoxe's firing squads.[79]

[73] For the Yugoslav version, see Djilas, *loc. cit.*, and Dedijer, *Il Sangue Tradito*, pp. 182–184; for the Albanian, resolution of the 11th Albanian CC Plenum, Sept. 13–24, 1948, *Dockumenta Kryesore*, I, Document 56, pp. 376–404, and of the First Congress, Nov. 8–22, 1948, *ibid.*, Document 58, pp. 423–465.

[74] According to the Albanian version (*Dokumenta Kryesore*, I, p. 386), Hoxha did resist it and was denounced by the Yugoslavs and Xoxe as a result.

[75] Dedijer, *op. cit.*, pp. 152, 168–169, 182–183.

[76] *Dokumenta Kryesore*, I, pp. 387–388. At the time it was announced that he had been "killed while cleaning his revolver" that same year, only in early 1948 after Xoxe gained still more power to be declared a suicide "conscious of his treason" and, after the 1948 Moscow-Belgrade break, "a victim of the dirty intrigues" of the Yugoslavs (*ibid.*, p. 402).

[77] Djilas, *op. cit.*, pp. 135–136.

[78] *Ibid.*, p. 143.

[79] Dedijer, *Tito Speaks*, pp. 273–303.

When in 1948 the Moscow-Belgrade break came, Hoxha, in the best tradition of Balkan blood feuds, demonstrated his determination and willingness to purge and if necessary kill any deviationist elements. First it was the turn of the genuinely pro-Titoist Xoxe, secretly tried and executed in 1949[80] after his initial attempt to jump on the anti-Yugoslav bandwagon[81] had been foiled by Hoxha's gaining Moscow's approval to purge him.[82] (Hoxha and Shehu, much more than Xoxe, were the genuine Albanian "national Communists.") Shehu, Belishova, Jakova, and Spahiu were rehabilitated.[83] After Xoxe's execution Shehu rose rapidly; in 1951 he replaced Jakova as Minister of the Interior and in August 1953, after Stalin's death, he became Deputy Prime Minister.[84] Hoxhu relinquished the Prime Ministership to Shehu only in 1954 while remaining First Secretary.[85] (There have been many rumors of hostility between the two, and it seems prima facie probable, but no specific evidence about it is available; since 1960, however, their common danger has probably driven them together.) By 1953 only three members of the original Albanian Central Committee, Hoxha, Jakova, and Spahiu, were still members; the latter two had already been demoted and were purged in 1955,[86] and all the others had been purged before. Hoxha alone is now still a member.[87]

The period of predominantly Soviet economic influence in Albania began in September 1948, when the first joint economic agreement was concluded; it was supplemented during Hoxha's 1949 visit to Moscow. In February 1951 it was extended to 1955.[88] After the establishment of CMEA in February 1949 the other East European satellites also began to support Albania.[89] By 1949 some 38 per cent of Albanian state revenue came from credits and grants-in-aid from Soviet bloc countries,[90] and

[80] For his demotion at the Sept. 1948 IX Plenum, see *Dokumenta Kryesore,* I, p. 402 (cf. Milić, *op. cit.,* p. 32); for his expulsion, trial, and execution, *Dokumenta Kryesore,* I, pp. 405, 484–485, ftn. 97; for the resolution of the PPSh First Party Congress, Nov. 8–22, 1948, *ibid.,* Document 58, pp. 423–465 (see Milić *loc. cit.,* for alleged opposition to Hoxha at the Congress). For a list of those purged with him, see Solajić, *Borba,* March 21, 1961.

[81] *Documenta Kryesore,* I, pp. 389–391.

[82] Seton-Watson, *The East European Revolution,* pp. 227–229, and Dragutin Solajić, "Obvious Facts," *Borba,* March 19, 20, 21, 1961.

[83] *Dokumenta Kryesore,* I, p. 404.

[84] *Zëri i Popullit,* Aug. 2, 1953.

[85] *Ibid.,* July 21, 1954.

[86] *Dokumenta Kryesore,* I, p. 485, ftns. 98, 99; II, pp. 61–68, 411–419.

[87] For details on 1949–1953 Albanian purges, see Solajić, *Borba,* March 21, 1961.

[88] The USSR bought the exports of Albania at doubled prices. Imports from the Soviet Union were to be delivered at half price. Furthermore, the USSR renewed all the credits previously given by the Yugoslavs. *WDSOE,* 1958, No. 3, p. 43.

[89] *Ibid.,* p. 44.

[90] Skendi, *op. cit.,* p. 221.

an intensified program of economic development, particularly in industry and mining, began under Soviet direction. During the 1951–1955 period industrial production value increased nearly three times; the surge forward was particularly rapid in the extraction and building material sectors.[91]

But in 1953 Stalin's death, and in 1955 Khrushchev's rapprochement with Belgrade, threatened Hoxha with Soviet-imposed destalinization and re-subjection to the hated and feared Yugoslavs. In view of how nearly he had been purged by the Yugoslavs and Xoxe in 1948 and of his bloody revenge against Xoxe in 1949, he could have had few illusions that anything less than his leadership was at stake.

The initial impact in Albania of Khrushchev's 1955 rapprochement with Tito was considerable, but the only evidence available is Hoxha's charges in June of that year (after the Belgrade Declaration) against Jakova.[92] The latter had already been demoted, on rather general grounds, in 1951; now, along with Bedri Spahiu, he was finally purged. According to Hoxha's charges, at an Albanian Central Committee Plenum in April 1955 (the month before the Belgrade Declaration), Jakova "attacked the general line of the party" from "Trotskyist" and "bourgeois nationalist" (i.e., pro-Yugoslav) positions. Specifically, he allegedly demanded that party history be rewritten so as to make clear that it had been founded not by Hoxha but by "certain foreign persons" (i.e., the Yugoslavs), that all those purged be rehabilitated (i.e., presumably primarily Koci Xoxe), and that the Tosk version of the written language not be imposed upon the Gegs. Clearly all these charges were intended to make Jakova out to be pro-Yugoslav; presumably they did not label him so directly because of the Soviet-Yugoslav rapprochement. Whether or not Jakova and Spahiu, anticipating that after the Soviet-Yugoslav rapprochement Moscow would replace Hoxha, were already trying to profit from this by getting their bid in early is unclear; but that Hoxha thought they were trying or would try seems probable. Jakova's purge was at least prophylactic, at most Hoxha's first and efficiently early countermove against the consequences of the Soviet-Yugoslav rapprochement.

After Stalin's death the approaching Soviet rapprochement with Yugoslavia and the consequent decline in Moscow's political interest in Albania also resulted in 1953–1955 in a reduction in the Soviet and East European flow of capital goods to Albania and a consequent heavy

[91] *ASRPSh,* 1959, p. 41, Tables 6.2–6.3.

[92] PPSh CC Plenum, June 15–17, 1955; *Dokumenta Kryesore,* II, pp. 411–419.

cut in Albania's machine and equipment investments.[93] Hoxha managed in part to offset this decline in Soviet-controlled aid by obtaining some Chinese economic support, first evident in a small long-term loan agreement between Peking and Tirana signed at the end of 1954.[94] During this 1951–1955 period Albanian agriculture continued to improve, especially in grain production, but at the end of 1955 an intensive collectivization drive reversed the trend.[95] (One may assume that at least one of the motives in this drive was Hoxha's desire to establish more reliable political controls over the peasantry in view of Khrushchev's rapprochement with Belgrade earlier in the year.)

As the events of 1955–1956 in East Europe[96] have shown, a successful thaw there requires the confluence of three components: mass discontent both economically and nationalistically induced; intellectual ferment within the party and among literary and cultural figures; and splits in the ruling élite both in Moscow and in the satellite concerned.[97] Mass economic discontent in Albania was as always endemic. Nationalistic discontent had not only declined after Hoxha's 1948 break with Yugoslavia, which gained for him some of the same kind of popularity that Tito obtained from breaking with Moscow, but the traditional Albanian nationalistic fear of Yugoslavia, Greece, and Italy was in his favor. Intellectual ferment in so underdeveloped a country as Albania was bound to be small. Splits in the Soviet leadership certainly existed, as well as changing Soviet policies. The latter were particularly signifi-

[93] Particularly the USSR and Czechoslovakia drastically cut their imports:

	(Millions of leks)	
	USSR	*Czechoslovakia*
1953	1,062.2	330.9
1954	535.7	212.6

SOURCE: See Table 6.1. Investments in machinery consequently declined from 2,206.8 million leks in 1952 to 1,880.2 million in 1953. In 1954 they were only 557.0 million, but in 1955 they rose again to 1,281.6 million leks (*ASRPSh* 1959, p. 142). This situation caused serious unemployment in Albania (Hoxha to the 4th Congress of the Albanian Women's Union, *Zëri i Popullit,* Oct. 18, 1955).

[94] On Dec. 7, 1954, Communist China granted a long-term loan to Albania. In the same month Peking sent 20,000 tons of wheat, 100,000 meters of silk, 2,000 tons of rice, 2,000 tons of sugar, and so forth, as a gift to the Albanian people (*WDSOE* 1958, No. 3, p. 44).

[95] See Tables 6.3, 6.4. Annual stock rose only 1 to 2 per cent during the 1950–1955 period (Table 6.5), while population increased by 14 per cent (*ASRPSh* 1958, p. 21). Owing to extensive land reclamation, mechanization, and credits, however, agricultural production increased 15 to 25 per cent (Table 6.4). After the renewed collectivization both livestock and agricultural production declined rapidly (Tables 6.4, 6.5). Cf. *Dokumenta Kryesore,* II, pp. 347–383.

[96] For detailed treatment, see Brzezinski, *The Soviet Bloc,* pp. 182–268, and the author's forthcoming *The East European Thaw 1953–1956.*

[97] Cf. Hugh Seton-Watson, "Five Years After October," *Problems of Communism,* X, 5 (Sept.–Oct. 1961), pp. 15–21.

cant for Albania, as for Hungary and Bulgaria; one of Tito's prices for the Moscow-Belgrade rapprochement toward which Khrushchev aimed was the removal of his enemies Hoxha, Rákosi, and Chervenkov. Tito played a significant role in the removal of Rákosi,[98] and probably in Chervenkov's as well.[99] It seems quite probable, as the Albanians have frequently maintained,[100] that Tito also tried to eliminate Hoxha, who had successfully revolted against him and executed his ally Xoxe.[101]

Judging by their subsequent purge, it seems likely that there was in 1956 a significant minority in the Albanian party élite which hoped to profit from the probable Yugoslav and Soviet plan to overthrow Hoxha and Shehu. It may well have included Jakova and Plaku, who were purged, and Gega and Ndreu, who were shot, after the Hungarian Revolution.[102] Gega's past record indicates that she was anti-Yugoslav and pro-Soviet, Plaku's that he was probably pro-Yugoslav and pro-Soviet,[103] Jakova's that in 1955 he was pro-Yugoslav. But basically they were probably like Schirdewan and Wollweber in East Germany,[104] opportunists speculating on a change in the Soviet line; like them, they guessed wrong. Hoxha and Shehu, like Ulbricht, were saved by the Hungarian Revolution.

Albanian party élite opposition to Hoxha reached its peak at the April 1956 Tirana city party conference.[105] The only detailed account of its course, unfortunately, is a 1961 Yugoslav one, published in the aftermath of the May 1961 Tirana show trial[106] and thus suspect both

[98] Ferenc Vali, *Rift and Revolt in Hungary* (Cambridge, Mass.: Harvard, 1961), p. 236, and Griffith, *op. cit.*

[99] Brzezinski, *The Soviet Bloc,* p. 198, and Griffith, *op. cit.*

[100] E.g., at the May 1961 Tirana trial, in the final speech of the prosecutor, *Zëri i Popullit,* May 26, 1961.

[101] *Bashkimi,* Nov. 24, 1956. For the 1956–1957 events, see reports by three Western correspondents who visited Albania: V.[iktor] M.[eier], "Albanien unter 'stalinistischen' Polizeiregime," *Neue Zürcher Zeitung,* April 28, 1957; Marc Marceau, "Mystérieuse Albanie," *Le Monde,* June 27, July 1, 4, 1956; Harrison Salisbury in *The New York Times,* Sept. 9–13, 1957. See also "Comment le P.C. albanais se déstalinise," *B.E.I.P.I.,* No. 157, April 1–15, 1956.

[102] *Bashkimi,* Nov. 24, 1956.

[103] Plaku stated in 1961 (*Borba,* May 27, 1961) that he had in 1957, before he fled to Yugoslavia, complained about Hoxha and Shehu first to the Soviet and then to the Yugoslav Central Committee.

[104] See Melvin Croan, "Dependent Totalitarianism: The Political Process in East Germany" (unpubl. Ph.D. diss., Harvard, 1960, publication forthcoming), and Griffith, *op. cit.*

[105] See subsequent Albanian attacks against this meeting, e.g. during the May 1961 Tirana "plot" trial (ftn. 106, *infra.*).

[106] Solajić, "Obvious Facts" (IV), *Borba,* Mar. 22, 1961; "The Trial in Tirana," *Borba,* May 28, 1961; cf. Milić, *op. cit.,* p. 44, and the summary (without citing the article as source) in Lazitch, *op. cit.,* p. 13. The only contemporary Albanian account, in the resolution of the May 1956 PPSh 3rd Congress, is brief and unenlightening (*Dokumenta Kryesore,* II, p. 481).

as to source and occasion. (The Yugoslavs have every interest in exaggerating the opposition to Hoxha.) Nevertheless, it is probably closer to accuracy than any Albanian account yet published.[107]

According to the Yugoslav account, the conference, held in the aftermath of the Soviet Twentieth Congress and presided over by Minister of Defense Beqir Balluku, was attended by 450 delegates plus many Central Committee and Politburo members. When the conference opened, the delegates

> . . . criticized the conditions in the party, the negative attitude toward the masses, the absence of party and socialist democracy, the economic policy of the leadership, etc. They also asked for explanations to be given about the numerous executions carried out since 1949, they called for a rehabilitation of old Communists forcibly removed from responsible posts. . . .[108]
>
> Several delegates requested that the topics of discussion should be the Twentieth Congress of the Communist Party of the Soviet Union, the cult of the personality, the case of Koci Xoxe, relations with Yugoslavia, party democracy, and the standard of living. . . .[109]

"But," one of the Yugoslav accounts (so correctly) continued,

> the number of graves was too great, and the list of victims too long, for Enver Hoxha to agree to renounce the road which he had chosen. . . .[110]

True; but that was not all the story. Just as the fear of "German revisionism" has helped to maintain Gomułka in power in Poland, so has the Yugoslav danger helped to keep Hoxha ruling in Albania. His own remarkable combination of ruse and ruthlessness has also stood him in good stead.

When, the Yugoslav account continues, Balluku was unable to keep the crowd quiet, on the third day Hoxha finally appeared. At first he was conciliatory, declaring that

> the Tirana party organization was not anti-party, but only that certain comrades were erroneously appraising the events and the general conditions. He admitted that certain mistakes had been committed. . . .

Even so, one officer, a Colonel Iljas Ahmeti, continued to defy him, declaring "While you were speaking I was listening to you, now you must listen to me!" Seeing that the conference was getting out of hand, Hoxha soon changed his tactics, attacking his accusers, pressuring the delegates, and forcing the adoption of a favorable resolution. Then, the

[107] I would be less skeptical of its accuracy than Hamm, *op. cit.*, p. 40.
[108] "The Trial in Tirana," *op. cit.*
[109] Solajić, *op. cit.;* Milić (*loc. cit.*) adds that the delegates demanded the rehabilitation of Jakova and Spahiu as well as that of Xoxe.
[110] "The Trial in Tirana," *op. cit.*

conference over, Hoxha struck: All those who had spoken up on the first day were expelled from the party and imprisoned or vanished. The party opposition had struck too soon. To the best of our knowledge — and precious little we have — there were no more public signs of it in 1956.

How much pressure Moscow brought against Hoxha between April and October 1956 is unclear. After the Twenty-Second Congress Hoxha declared that in April and May 1956 Suslov and Pospelov had tried to persuade him to rehabilitate Xoxe.[111] (When one remembers the role played in Rákosi's fall by the rehabilitation of Rajk, one can well understand why Hoxha refused to do this.) The Albanian Third Congress in May 1956 passed without incident; the purges of Xoxe, Jakova, and Spahiu were endorsed. After the Soviet suppression of the Hungarian Revolution, Hoxha rapidly liquidated the opposition in the party leadership; Khrushchev alleged at the Twenty-Second Congress that Liri Gega, one of them, was shot while pregnant.[112]

There was probably also some Albanian intellectual revisionism, arising from the Western education of many Albanian intellectuals, the influence of Yugoslav, Soviet, Polish, and Hungarian revisionism, and the few verbal gestures toward destalinization which Hoxha felt compelled to make. But the continued effective control of Hoxha and the party *apparat* over literary and cultural publications,[113] plus the numerical and cultural weakness of Albanian writers and other intellectuals, made any published indications of it few and far between. In May 1956 the Albanian literary monthly did carry an article by a leading literary critic, presumably written in March or April before Hoxha crushed the dissent at the April Tirana city party conference. This article, which contains almost all the humanist themes which were so characteristic of East European revisionism in 1956, deserves quotation at some length:

> Life is neither simple nor superficial. It is *very complex* and quite profound. . . . People are not all alike. They have different desires and aims; they love and hate different things. It is the duty of the writer to show the cause of these differences and reveal the roots of these manifestations of life and the soul of man. These roots are to be found in social classes, in the economic condition of men, in their manner of life. . . .

[111] Pospelov headed the Soviet delegation to the Albanian 3rd Congress in May 1956 (*Pravda,* May 25, 1956); see Hoxha speech of Nov. 7, 1961, *Zëri i Popullit,* Nov. 8, 1961, and Document 14.

[112] *Pravda,* Oct. 29, 1961, and Document 11.

[113] For Albanian literature in general, see Giuseppe Schirò, Jr., *Storia della Letteratura Albanese* (Milan: Nuova Accademia Editrice, n.d. [1959]), and "Die Literatur im heutigen Albanien," *WDSOE,* VI, 5/6 (May–June 1957), pp. 90–91. For PPSh literary control, see 3rd Congress resolution, *Dokumenta Kryesore,* II, pp. 474–475.

> Men are not machines. They are living beings, with feelings and desires, with personal or political ambitions, with virtues or vices, which distinguish them from the other. Therefore, the people of a social group, in addition to the things which they have in common, as a result of their economic status — which constitutes, as it were, the physiognomy of their group — have also their individual traits.

The author came back again and again to the idea that people cannot be explained merely in terms of classes: "Class characteristics make up the skeleton of the personality" but his "individual traits" give him flesh and blood. The conditioning factors in the life of man "are not determined entirely by his economic situation, although this is the basic factor; they are also determined by his environment and his individual traits."[114]

Nor did the aftermath of the Hungarian Revolution completely destroy this somewhat unorthodox spirit. At the Congress of the Albanian Writers Union in May 1957 one critic spoke in striking terms of the necessity of controversy and tolerance as opposed to keeping quiet about the negative aspects of Albanian life.[115]

The nationwide fear of renewed domination by the hated Yugoslavs, his own ruthlessness, and the anti-Yugoslav and anti-revisionist impact of the Hungarian Revolution on Soviet policy are the major factors which enabled Hoxha to remain in control. He and his associates, however, must have rightly thanked themselves rather than Khrushchev for their salvation; they must have vowed never again to allow themselves to be pushed by him so close to destruction and, if possible, to escape from his hazardous tutelage.

Having been so seriously threatened by pro-Yugoslav Soviet policies in 1955 and 1956, in late 1956 Hoxha was quite naturally the first and most violent in renewing the attack on the Yugoslavs after the Hungarian Revolution.[116] The Chinese joined him somewhat later for other reasons, within the context of their 1957 radical shift to the left. The "hundred flowers" liberalization campaign had gravely disappointed, as the Soviet sputnik had emboldened, Mao and most of his associates. More important for Hoxha, Mao, alarmed by the Hungarian Revolution, had become convinced that Tito's influence, and Khrushchev's sup-

[114] Riza Brahimi, "Some Problems in Our Literature," *Nëndori,* No. 5, May 1956, pp. 135–137. In a footnote to the article Brahimi quoted the Russian writer Konstantin Paustovski, one of the leaders of the Soviet literary thaw, thus giving one indication of where his humanism came from.

[115] Koço Bihiku, "Problems of Criticism," *Nëndori,* Special issue, 1957 (proceedings of the Congress), pp. 165–170, at pp. 166–169.

[116] E.g., Hoxha in *Pravda,* Nov. 8, 1956, and to the PPSh CC, *Zëri i Popullit,* Feb. 1, 1957. See Salisbury from Tirana in *The New York Times,* Sept. 10–13, 1957.

port for it, were dangerous to the Chinese concept of bloc cohesion.

Albanian economic developments during the 1956–1959 period also throw some light on the developing tension between Moscow and Tirana and the Peking-Tirana rapprochement. During 1956 and 1957 Chinese credits (i.e., subsidies) to Tirana rose rapidly. While in 1955 they had represented only 4.2 per cent of Albania's total passive trade balance, in 1956 they were 17 per cent, and in 1957 they were 21.6 per cent.[117] Probably at least in part to meet this Chinese challenge, Soviet aid to Albania also rose rapidly. In early 1957 Moscow canceled 422 million rubles in credit and gave Tirana a new 31-million-ruble credit to make possible the end of food rationing. Later in 1957 Moscow granted a new 160-million-ruble loan to Albania, and the East European satellites followed suit.[118] By 1958–1959 capital was pouring into Albania from all over the bloc so rapidly that it sometimes could not be absorbed.[119] The passive trade balance increased 150 per cent during these years.[120]

All this resulted in rapid Albanian economic growth. The labor force rose rapidly in size and technical know-how. [121] Crude oil production tripled;[122] by now it is being refined exclusively in Albanian refineries. Iron and nickel ore extraction, which began in 1958, grew rapidly.[123] Production in the light and food industries also improved.[124] Agricultural production, however, continued to decline. In spite of an increase of 12 per cent in arable land[125] and of more than double the number of tractors,[126] in 1959 crop production was 10 to 25 per cent lower than the pre-collectivization (pre-1955) averages.[127] Consumption standards,

[117] Computed from Table 6.1.

[118] *WDSOE* 1958, No. 3, pp. 43–44.

[119] "Transportation Machines for Chromium and Laboratory Drilling Mills Imported in 1957 Were Still at Warehouses," *Zëri i Popullit,* Dec. 8, 1959; cf. *ibid.,* Jan. 28 and Feb. 12, 1960.

[120] See Table 6.1.

[121] See Table 6.2.

[122] See Table 6.3.

[123] The following table gives some indication of rise in raw material production:

	Electricity	*Chrome Ore*	*Copper Ore*	*Coal*	*Cement*	*Bricks and Tiles*
			(1950 = 100)			
1955	398	234	172	476	280	431
1959	816	475	741	705	467	837

SOURCE: Computed from Tables 6.2 and 6.3.

[124] Light industry production was 17 times and food industry production 4 times higher in 1959 than in 1950. Even so, this was in large part due to broadening of the variety of items and to decline in home production rather than to increase in agricultural production. For statistics, see Table 6.2.

[125] *ASRPSh* 1958, p. 51; *ASRPSh* 1960, p. 121.

[126] See Table 6.5.

[127] See Table 6.4. Livestock were lower as well, although less so; see Table 6.5.

particularly of industrial materials, improved rapidly. Even more important, however, was the transformation in literacy,[128] health,[129] education,[130] and living standards,[131] and the establishment of a social security system.[132] Hoxha's popular support was probably thereby somewhat increased.

Only when the Chinese decided, secretly in 1957 and openly in 1960, to challenge Soviet domination of the bloc did they seriously look around for allies whom they were ready and willing to support.[133] Hoxha and Shehu, on the other hand, became increasingly alarmed at Khrushchev's renewed policy of "peaceful coexistence" and international détente, which, they correctly assumed, would result in a renewed Soviet rapprochement with Yugoslavia and consequent extreme danger for themselves. Finally, Hoxha and Shehu had remained extremist — indeed, Stalinist — in their internal policies and for this reason as well naturally sympathized with the new Chinese extremism. As Professor Brzezinski has pointed out,[134] Mao and Hoxha in 1960, like Tito in 1948, were "left extremist" deviationists vis-à-vis Moscow. This seems characteristic of indigenously based deviationist Communist regimes, as opposed to Gomułka's; the Polish party, not strong enough to be extremist, can successfully be moderate only with Moscow's support.

It is more difficult, however, to chart the course and speed of development of the Sino-Albanian alliance. As yet there is little specific published material available concerning it. However, a detailed comparison of the Soviet and Chinese positions on the ideological and foreign-policy issues during the early stages of the Sino-Soviet dispute with the Albanian positions on these same issues indicates, as is shown by Table 1.1, that Sino-Albanian convergence and joint opposition to Soviet positions (above all, naturally, on the Yugoslav issue) increased rapidly

[128] By 1955 illiteracy was eliminated among adults under forty (*ESE* 1960, Ch. VI, p. 9).

[129] During 1950–1959 the number of physicians increased from 129 to 378 and medical institutions from 67 to 125. Malaria, in prewar times the greatest cause of death, had practically been eliminated (*ibid.*).

[130] The University of Tirana was established in 1957, and many Albanian students went to the Soviet Union and to East European countries.

[131] A total of 66,800 square miles of housing were built in 1956; 103,832 in 1957, 184,809 in 1958, and 216,000 in 1959. From 1956 to 1959, 11,483 apartments were built by the state and 27,806 single-family houses by private citizens with state credits (*Bashkimi,* April 24, 1960).

[132] Established in 1953, with pensions for old age and disability; made mandatory in 1959 and the pension raised from 50 to 75 per cent of basic salary (*Zëri i Popullit,* Jan. 7, 1961).

[133] Cf. Daniel Tretiak, "The Founding of the Sino-Albanian Entente," *The China Quarterly,* No. 10 (April–June 1962), pp. 123–143.

[134] Zbigniew Brzezinski, "Albania Defies the Kremlin," *The New Leader,* XLIV, 13 (Mar. 27, 1961), p. 8.

TABLE 1.1

Parallels in Sino-Soviet-Albanian Ideological Positions, 1956–1959

Date	*Issue*	*Soviet Union*	*China*	*Albania*
Feb.–Apr. 1956	Destalinization	Khrushchev delivers secret attack on Stalin at 20th Congress, CPSU	Maintains official silence on attack from Feb. to Apr.	Maintains official silence on attack from Feb. to Apr.[1]
Apr. 1956	Cult of the Individual	Sharp criticism of Stalin	Reserved criticism	Reserved criticism[2]
Spring and Summer 1956	Explanation of occurrence of Cult of the Individual	Unique occurrence	Recurrence possible	Unique occurrence[3]
Fall 1956	Tito's Pula Speech re Hungarian Revolution	Reasoned attack on Tito's stand re Hungary	Relatively mild attack	Violent attack[4]
Oct. 1956	Rise of Gomułka in Poland	Views Gomułka with misgivings	Supports Gomułka	No support given to Gomułka*
Apr. 1957	Algeria Solidarity Week	(No report in Albanian press of SU support)	Pledge of strong support to "Algerian brothers" carried in Albanian press	Pledge of strong support for "sacred cause of the Algerian people"[5]
Nov. 1957	Sputnik assessment	Soviet power a deterrent to war by imperialists	Imperialists threaten new war	Imperialists threaten new war[6]
Dec. 1957	Local war	Advances views to discourage local wars	Advances views to encourage local wars	Supports continuation of local wars[7]
Fall 1957–Spring 1958	Balance of Power (East vs. West)	Socialist camp stronger than before	Socialist camp overwhelmingly superior	Balance of power in favor of socialist camp[8]

Date	*Issue*	*Soviet Union*	*China*	*Albania*
Spring 1958	7th Congress of the League of Yugoslav Communists	Selective attack on LCY program	All-out attack	All-out attack[9]
Spring 1958	CPR Theory of Permanent Revolution	Looked upon with disfavor	. . . .	No overt support for theory*
May–June 1958	Yugoslav revisionism	Intermittent attacks on Yugoslavia	Blistering, relentless attacks	Blistering, relentless attacks[10]
Summer 1958	Attitude toward West	Détente seen possible	Militant attitude advocated	Militant attitude favored[11]
Summer 1958	Middle East crises (landing of U.S. troops in Lebanon)	Calls for negotiations	Use of force suggested initially	Supports call for negotiations[12]
Fall 1958	View of world war	Both West and East would suffer	Imperialism only would be destroyed	Imperialism would be destroyed[13]
Fall 1958	CPR communes	Generally uncomplimentary view	. . . .	Consistently enthusiastic appraisal[14]
Fall 1958	Taiwan Strait crisis	Hedges on support of CPR	. . . .	Unqualified support of CPR[15]
Nov. 1958	CPR Doctrine of Egalitarianism	Implicit disapproval of doctrine	. . . .	Warm endorsement[16]

Date	*Issue*	*Soviet Union*	*China*	*Albania*
Jan.–Feb. 1959	Inevitability of war with capitalism	War not inevitable	Possibility of war exists	War can be avoided[17]
Apr. 1959	Evaluation of U.S. policy	Sees trend to moderation and rationality	No change seen; calls for strengthening defenses	No real change; urges increased vigilance[18]
Summer 1959	Arrest of Communist leader, Farajallah al-Hilu, by Lebanon	No protest issued	Protests arrest	Protests arrest[19]
Summer 1959	Revolt of Communist Party of Iraq	No support given	Supports revolt	No support given*
Aug.–Sept. 1959	Negotiations with the West	Optimistic re results	Skeptical of results	Guardedly skeptical[20]
Fall 1959	Nature of imperialism	Becoming peaceful	Unchangeable, vicious	Essentially hostile[21]
Fall 1959	Peaceful coexistence with West	Strong approval	Open disapproval	Highly skeptical[22]
Sept. 1959	Khrushchev's visit to U.S.	Great victory for peace and socialism	Condemns Khrushchev's negotiatory tactics	Endorses visit[23]
Oct. 1959	Sino-Indian border dispute	Neutral position	. . . .	Sympathetic to CPR[24]
Nov. 1959	Rome Resolution	Western Communist parties support SU doctrine of democracy	No comment	No comment
Dec. 1959	Stalin's birthday anniversary	Balanced account of Stalin's virtues and vices	Glowing account of Stalin's virtues	Glowing account of Stalin's virtues[25]

SOURCES to Table 1.1: The contrasting Soviet-Chinese positions are taken from Zagoria, *The Sino-Soviet Conflict,* pp. 39–287; the Albanian ones are indicated in the footnotes.

[1] The first indications of Khrushchev's secret speech did not appear in the Albanian press until late March, 1956.

[2] Enver Hoxhă, "Marxism-Leninism Teaches That the People Are the Creators of History," *Zëri i Popullit,* Apr. 14, 1956.

[3] "A Document of Great Significance," *Rruga e Partisë,* July 1956, pp. 13–21.

[4] See *Zëri i Popullit,* Nov. 23, 24, and 29, 1956.

[5] *Bashkimi,* Apr. 9, 1957.

[6] Hoxha's speech on the 40th Anniversary of the October Revolution, *Bashkimi,* Nov. 3, 1957.

[7] *Bashkimi,* Dec. 26, 1957.

[8] Behar Shtylla's foreign-policy speech, *Zëri i Popullit,* Mar. 20, 1958.

[9] "In Opposition to the Theory and Practice of Marxism-Leninism, *Zëri i Popullit,* May 4, 1958.

[10] *Bashkimi,* May 24, 1958; Hoxha's speech to the 7th Congress of the Bulgarian Communist Party, *Zëri i Popullit,* June 4, 1958; "Modern Revisionism Must Be Fought Without Mercy Until It Is Completely Destroyed Theoretically and Politically," *Zëri i Popullit,* June 22, 1958.

[11] Hoxha's closing speech to the 7th Congress of the Bulgarian Communist Party, *Zëri i Popullit,* June 8, 1958; Mehmet Shehu's speech welcoming Viliam Siroký of Czechoslovakia to Albania, *Zëri i Popullit,* June 25, 1958.

[12] "Remove Danger of War Before It Is Too Late," *Zëri i Popullit,* July 20, 1958.

[13] Shehu's speech at Tropoja, northern Albania, *Zëri i Popullit,* Oct. 26, 1958.

[14] Hoxha's speech on the 9th Anniversary of CPR, *Bashkimi,* Oct. 2, 1958.

[15] "Put an End to the Dangerous American Provocations in the Far East," *Zëri i Popullit,* Sept. 3, 1958; Declaration by the Albanian Government on the Taiwan Situation, *Zëri i Popullit,* Sept. 16, 1958.

[16] Communiqué on the Plenum of the Central Committee of the Albanian Party of Labor, Nov. 3–4, 1958, *Zëri i Popullit,* Nov. 5, 1958.

[17] "For the Defense of Peace and the Security of Peoples," *Zëri i Popullit,* Feb. 3, 1959.

[18] "Inspired by Leninism, the Peoples March Toward Communism," *Zëri i Popullit,* Apr. 22, 1959.

[19] *Zëri i Popullit,* Aug. 20, 1959.

[20] Enver Hoxha, *Zëri i Popullit,* Sept. 22, 1959.

[21] Haki Toska's speech on the 42nd Anniversary of the October Revolution, *Zëri i Popullit,* Nov. 7, 1959; Ramiz Alia, "Report by the Foreign Affairs Committee," *Zëri i Popullit,* Dec. 26, 1959.

[22] Hoxha, "Sixteen Years Under the People's Power," *Zëri i Popullit,* Nov. 29, 1959; Hoxha, "Knowledge and Culture in the New, Socialist Albania Have Become the Property of the Masses," *Zëri i Popullit,* Dec. 18, 1959.

[23] "Mission of Peace and Goodwill," *Zëri i Popullit,* Sept. 15, 1959.

[24] "Rational Path for Resolving Misunderstandings," *Zëri i Popullit,* Nov. 14, 1959.

[25] "J. V. Stalin — Distinguished Marxist-Leninist and Loyal Defender of Leninism," *Zëri i Popullit,* Dec. 22, 1959.

* *Note:* On such issues as the rise of Gomułka, the Chinese theory of the permanent revolution, and the revolt of the Communist Party in Iraq, Albania does not seem to have taken a definite stand.

after the Hungarian Revolution in spite of initial and unsuccessful attempts by Khrushchev to keep the Albanians in line,[135] and became almost total in 1959. (In retrospect, Khrushchev's visit to Albania that year must be viewed as a final unsuccessful attempt to avert Hoxha's alliance with Mao against him.)[136]

Nevertheless, a word of caution is in order. It is doubtful, and certainly not demonstrable, that Hoxha wanted to take sides totally with Peking and against Moscow; more likely, he preferred to receive the substance of Chinese support while avoiding the risks of total hostility to the Soviet Union. It was Peking, not Tirana, which initiated the rift with Moscow in June 1960; thereafter Hoxha had no choice but to declare his colors.

[135] For a detailed summary, see Jane P. Shapiro, "Albania and the Socialist Camp: Challenge to Soviet Leadership" (unpub. M.A. thesis, Russian Institute, Columbia University, 1962), pp. 31–48, and for a factual summary of political and economic developments, Tretiak, *op. cit.*

[136] This was when, during the visit of both in Tirana, Khrushchev reportedly offered support to Marshal P'eng Teh-huai in the latter's effort to force Mao to abandon his extremist position. See Charles, "The Dismissal of Marshal P'eng Teh-huai," *op. cit.*

CHAPTER TWO

The Soviet-Albanian Conflict Becomes Clear – 1960[1]

Unlike Sino-Soviet public polemics, Soviet-Albanian ones did not begin in full force on Lenin's birthday in April 1960.[2] The commemoratory Albanian speech on that occasion, delivered by Politburo candidate member Ramiz Alia, was (understandably) so strongly hostile to and concentrated on Yugoslavia[3] that it could with difficulty be interpreted

[1] Cf. J. F. Brown, "Albania, Mirror of Conflict," *Survey,* No. 40 (Jan. 1962), pp. 24–41, and "The Balkans," *ibid.,* No. 42 (June 1962), pp. 81–95; Stavro Skendi, "Albania," in Stephen D. Kertesz, ed., *East Central Europe and the World* (Notre Dame, 1962), pp. 197–228, and "Albania and the Sino-Soviet Conflict," *Foreign Affairs,* XL, 3 (April 1962), pp. 471–478; William E. Griffith, "An International Communism?" *East Europe,* X, 7 (July 1961), pp. 3–9, 41–45, and "Albania: An Outcast's Defiance," *Problems of Communism,* XI, 3 (May–June 1962), pp. 1–6; Harry Hamm, *Rebellen gegen Moskau* (Cologne: Verlag Wissenschaft und Politik, 1962); T. Zavalani, "The Importance of Being Albania," *Problems of Communism,* X, 4 (July–Aug. 1961), pp. 1–8; Lazitch, "Dossier du Parti communiste albanais," *op. cit.;* Wolfgang Leonhard, "Moskaus albanische Sorgen," *Die Zeit,* March 10, 1961; Viktor Meier, "Der Parteitag der albanischen Kommunisten," *Neue Zürcher Zeitung,* Feb. 20, 1961, "Der Alleingang der albanischen Kommunisten. Ein Problem für die Einheit des sozialistischen Lagers," *ibid.,* April 23, 1961, and "Albanien im Schatten Jugoslawiens," *Aussenpolitik,* XIII, 7 (July 1962), pp. 469–478; Anton Logoreci, "Albania: A Chinese Satellite in the Making?" *World Today,* XVIII, 5 (May 1961), pp. 197–205; Curt Gasteyger, "Das neue Schisma im Ostblock: Das sowjetisch-albanische Konflikt," *Europa-Archiv,* XVII, 7 (April 10, 1962), pp. 213–224. The thesis of Branko Lazitch, "Une rébellion imaginaire: Les désaccords du Parti communiste albanais," *Est et ouest,* XIII, 256 (April 16–30, 1961), pp. 14–18, has been disproved by subsequent developments.

[2] *Zëri i Popullit,* April 23, 1962. I have found no evidence concerning Albanian support of Chinese opposition to the Soviets in pre-April meetings of international front organizations. See, for the January 1960 meeting in Rome of the WPC presidium and the Cairo meeting of the Afro-Asian Solidarity Committee secretariat, Hudson, Lowenthal, and MacFarquhar, *op. cit.,* p. 13, ftn. 5a, and, for the mid-February Tunis meeting of the IUS Executive Committee, TANYUG Radio-Teletype in English to Europe, Feb. 18, 1960, 1851 GMT. Albanian contributions disappeared from *Problems of Peace and Socialism* after August 1960, Chinese ones since November 1959. An April 27 *Pravda* article by Hoxha was also unclear in tendency. It violently denounced revisionists, especially Yugoslav ones, and did not mention dogmatists, but it praised Krushchev's trip to the United States.

[3] More strongly, e.g., than B. Ponomarev, F. Konstantinov, and Yu. Andropov, "On Old Revisionist Positions," *Kommunist,* No. 8, May 1960, p. 48.

as an all-out attack against Khrushchev. It was in fact no stronger against Belgrade than other post-1957 Albanian statements, and, unlike the simultaneous Chinese attacks, it referred only to "revisionism" rather than to "modern revisionism." In addition, it included several almost ostentatiously friendly references to the Soviet Union. However, while always identifying revisionism only with the Yugoslav revisionists, the speech did make clear Albanian adherence to Chinese rather than to Soviet views on several points of the Moscow-Peking controversy. While endorsing peaceful coexistence, it declared that

> we must untiringly unmask . . . the aggressive policy of imperialism and its dangerous attempts to prepare for war . . . [and] impose the policy of peaceful coexistence upon the enemies of peace. . . .

It further denounced "the Yugoslav revisionists" for declaring that war depends upon "certain insane people like Hitler" rather than having its "source in the character of the capitalist regime." Continuing, Alia declared that "the Yugoslav revisionists" try to

> distract the vigilance of the people from the instigators of war, and to have the imperialist enemies quietly prepare for war . . . [and] pretend that in the conditions of coexistence capitalism can only develop peacefully toward socialism . . .

and ask that

> in détente conditions the working class of the capitalist countries should not put obstacles in the way of the rulers of the country. . . .

Finally, in a new formulation probably intended to refer to Khrushchev as well, Alia concluded:

> When the situation seems to be calmer . . . they [the revisionists] try to infiltrate . . . like the Trojan horse into the countries of socialism in order to undermine them from within and . . . to overthrow the Marxist-Leninist parties and the peoples' democratic regimes. . . . Above all, at present, when one can perceive symptoms of a détente in international relations, the danger of revisionism, of dissemination of illusions on the question of building socialism, on the class struggle, and on the problems of peace, becomes greater. . . .

The only available indication of Albanian moves between the Alia speech in April and the Peking World Federation of Trade Unions (WFTU) meeting in June was the statement in early May by the Albanian delegate to a Geneva meeting of the United Nations Economic Committee for Europe to the effect that Albania was willing to establish trade relations with capitalist countries.[4]

[4] *Zëri i Popullit,* May 5, 1960.

The first international Communist confrontation where the Sino-Soviet dispute and Albanian support for China publicly emerged was at the June 5–9 meeting in Peking of the General Council of the World Federation of Trade Unions, one of the most important international Communist-front organizations. There, by attempting to form an oppositional group, the Chinese decisively challenged Soviet organizational supremacy in international Communism, as in April they had challenged Soviet ideological leadership.[5] The Soviets were supported by the French, Poles, Czechs, East Germans, Italians, and Indians; the Chinese by the Albanians, Japanese, Burmese, North Vietnamese, Ceylonese, Sudanese, Somalians, Argentinians, Indonesians, and the representative from Zanzibar. This was the first major international "fractional" split resulting from the impact of the Sino-Soviet dispute on the international movement as opposed to ideological difference. The lineup it produced has remained largely the same to date.

The Peking WFTU meetings were notable for the re-emergence of the Communist "right wing": the Italians (PCI) and the Poles. This alignment, already clear in 1956, had some common causes: the common Catholicism and anti-Russian feelings of the Italian and Polish populations, plus the lack of any national or party antagonisms between them. On the contrary, the 1956–1957 events had produced a common front between them against Soviet, French, East German, and Czechoslovak Communist "dogmatism" or "centrism." Both had long wanted further autonomy for themselves from Moscow direction; neither desired to break away completely from Soviet support. Both Gomułka and Togliatti preferred moderate policies at home and abroad to Stalinist or Chinese extremism.

That the Italians expressed their "rightist" views more freely than could the Poles was also understandable. Not in power, they were far more dependent upon gaining popular support. Furthermore, they were anxious to remain on good terms with Nenni's left-wing Socialists (PSI), with whom they shared power in many municipal governments and in the trade-union federation (CGIL); the Italian WFTU delegation in Peking included Nenni Socialists as well as Communists. Finally, the already apparent swing toward the left of the Italian Christian Democrats, which in early 1962 led to the *apertura alla sinistra,* made the Communists even more aware of the necessity of a moderate position.

[5] The most complete analysis of this meeting is in Zagoria, *The Sino-Soviet Conflict,* pp. 320–325; the most complete documentation is in CB 620 and 621, June 22 and 27, 1960; see also Hudson, Lowenthal, and MacFarquhar, *op. cit.,* pp. 16–17, and the PCF documents on the November 1960 Moscow meetings, *Contribution de la délégation française à la conférence des partis communistes et ouvriers* (n.p., n.d. [Paris: PCF, Nov. 1961]) (JPRS 14610, July 26, 1962), pp. 33–34, 43–45.

As to the Poles, Gomułka had less experience and taste than Togliatti for maneuver on the international Communist stage. Yet he was anxious to reinforce his domestically deviant position, and the relative success of his post-1956 Polish "domesticism,"[6] plus Khrushchev's increasing acquiescence in it, made Gomułka concern himself less than he otherwise might have with Soviet sensitivity.

The most important reason for this "rightist" tendency, however, was the increased possibility for maneuver which the public emergence of Sino-Soviet differences gave to smaller Communist parties. China needed Albania; the Soviet Union needed the Polish and Italian Communists, both of whom could hope to exact a certain increased freedom of expression of their genuinely rightist views as a price for their support against China. Not surprisingly, therefore, the Italian Communists made particularly clear, as did, albeit less so, the Poles, their strong opposition to the Chinese. The final resolutions passed by the meeting represented an ambiguous compromise.[7]

At the WFTU meeting, the Albanian trade-union head, Gogo Nushi, implicitly condemned Khrushchev's desire for a summit conference:

> . . . the Albanian workers have never underestimated the possibility of U.S. provocations and warlike activities. . . .[8]

Aside from the brief available excerpt of Nushi's speech, the Albanian position was much illuminated in the days immediately before the meetings on the occasion of a state visit to China by Haxhi Lleshi, Albanian head of state. Lleshi was accompanied by Liri Belishova, soon to be purged and arrested by Hoxha as pro-Soviet. At a state banquet in Lleshi's honor, Liu Shao-chi, Chinese head of state and second only to Mao in the Chinese Communist hierarchy, repeated the anti-Soviet ideological formulations of the April Chinese articles. He also strongly endorsed the "correct line" of the Albanian Communist Party and pledged Peking's total support to Tirana:

> . . . China and Albania are closely united fraternal countries; our unity is based on Marxism-Leninism and proletarian internationalism and can never be split. . . .[9]

6 Brzezinski, *The Soviet Bloc*, pp. 52–53.

7 NCNA, June 9, 1960, in CB 621, pp. 22–37.

8 NCNA, June 7, 1960 in CB 620, p. 43.

9 NCNA in English to Europe and Asia, June 3, 1960, 1723 GMT in SCMP 2275, June 13, 1960, p. 31; cf. Liu's June 6 banquet speech, *ibid.*, June 6, 2040 GMT. See also Lleshi's speech on the same occasion, *ibid.*, 1810 GMT, and at the June 6 banquet, *ibid.*, June 6, 2142 GMT; the speech of P'eng Chen at a rally the following day, *ibid.*, June 4, 1960, 1502 GMT, and Lleshi's on the same occasion, *ibid.*, 1553 GMT, both in SCMP 2275, June 13, 1960, pp. 34–37. Lleshi, Belishova, and the other Albanian delegation members were received by Mao

Liu took a particularly strong position against Yugoslavia; his words revived those of the 1949 Cominform resolutions:

> . . . It is particularly worth mentioning that the Albanian Party of Labor and people . . . have continuously dealt blows against the provocations and subversive activities of the Yugoslav modern revisionists and thoroughly exposed the ugly features of the Tito clique as agents of imperialism. . . .

Lleshi's speech contained a mixture of pro-Soviet and pro-Chinese statements. Belishova's June 6 speech, on the other hand, not only included none of Liu's clearly anti-Soviet ideological formulations, but also contained some strikingly pro-Soviet passages:

> . . . I want to point out with emphasis that, on our way to your country, when we passed through the Soviet Union, we received a very heartwarming reception from our respected Comrade L. Brezhnev, Comrade E. A. Furtseva, and other Soviet comrades. . . .

She concluded by quoting from a poem by Aleks Çaçi, "a well-known poet of our country," which could hardly have made her pro-Soviet sympathies clearer:

> My country,
> What a host of friends you have!
> Listen!
> From the depths of the heart come these words which resound all over China:
> "China and Albania are marching along the same road,
> With the same ideal, like one man."
> Who is it that links us so closely on this road?
> The Soviet Union,
> This name is like a beacon in the night, brightening the world!
> To all who long for happiness, the Soviet Union is their foremost friend!

These passages in the NCNA text of Belishova's speech were omitted in the version published the following day in Tirana.[10]

Presumably she exceeded her instructions, thus resulting in the deletions. The Soviets probably encouraged her in Peking, or when she stopped in Moscow en route, hoping to shock and give pause to the Chinese. In any case, like Trotsky at Lenin's funeral, she picked a bad time to be away from home.

Tse-tung in Hangchow on June 7 (NCNA English, Hangchow, June 7, 1960, in SCMP 2277, June 15, 1960, p. 37). The Albanian delegation also visited North Korea and North Vietnam.

[10] *Zëri i Popullit,* June 7, 1960. Lleshi's speech was condensed neither from an anti-Soviet nor an anti-Chinese viewpoint.

Immediately after the Peking meetings ended, the Soviets launched a major counterattack against the open Chinese threat to Moscow's control over the international Communist movement.[11] Khrushchev was even more determined to force Hoxha to capitulate, or to remove him; to this end he undertook an obscure but potentially far more deadly maneuver.

In early June, just before going to the Romanian Party Congress at Bucharest, he received Sophokles Venizelos, the Greek left-wing political leader. According to Venizelos' account, Khrushchev listened to the latter's complaints about the Albanian treatment of the Greek minority in southern Albania (*graece* Northern Epirus) and his desire that the Greek population there be given at least cultural autonomy. According to Venizelos' stenographic record of the talks, Khrushchev replied:

> . . . The Albanians as well as the Greeks there are very good people. The Communist parties salute the idea that every minority should be autonomous in order to be able to develop its language and civilization in accordance with its wishes. . . . I can assure you that I will communicate these things to Comrade Enver Hoxha when I meet him in Bucharest. . . .[12]

As is clear from the furious Albanian references to this incident at Bucharest and thereafter,[13] Hoxha viewed this move by Khrushchev as an implicit threat to partition Albania — the overwhelming traditional fear of all Albanian nationalists. Khrushchev can hardly not have realized the effect this would have; one must therefore assume that Soviet-Albanian relations before Bucharest were already tense.[14] One Albanian report states that on March 16, 1960, Moscow proposed that the 1952 Soviet-Albanian student-exchange agreement be altered so as to lower the Soviet and raise the Albanian financial contributions, but that on June 6, two weeks before the Bucharest meeting, Moscow agreed to withdraw this request. If true, this may have represented an unsuccessful Soviet maneuver to prevent the Albanians from totally supporting the Chinese.[15]

[11] Zagoria, *op. cit.*, pp. 323–324.

[12] Quoted from Venizelos' account of his interview in *To Vima* (Athens), June 28, 1960; see also *Deutsche Zeitung* (Cologne), July 5, 1960; *Zëri i Popullit*, Sept. 3, 1960; the only detailed (and excellent) analysis, by the distinguished Greek statesman Panayotis Pipinelis, "Griechenland und die Balkanpolitik Moskaus," *Neue Zürcher Zeitung*, Mar. 21, 1961; cf. "Why Is Ranković Going to Athens?" *Zëri i Popullit*, May 2, 1961. The interview was not denied by any Soviet source until October, when Kuusinen denied it at the Twenty-Second CPSU Congress (*Pravda*, Oct. 28, 1961).

[13] E.g., in Hoxha's Nov. 7, 1961, speech (*Zëri i Popullit*, Nov. 8, 1961, and Document 14).

[14] True, Venizelos' account nowhere speaks of territorial changes, but, given Albanian sensitivity on the danger of partition, Hoxha's (and most Albanians') reaction was inevitable.

[15] "Slanders and Inventions without Foundations," *Zëri i Popullit*, Dec. 30, 1961

There remains the question of when and how the Albanians took their final decision totally to defy Khrushchev and ally with Peking. The first evidence of the decision having been taken was the total Albanian support of China at Bucharest at the end of June. Furthermore, Lleshi's indecisive speech and Belishova's pro-Soviet speeches in Peking may well indicate that at that time, in early June, the decision had not yet been taken in Tirana. Perhaps Belishova and Tashko still hoped, through Soviet pressure, to overcome if not overthrow Hoxha and Shehu. Instead, by the Bucharest meeting they had clearly lost. Mao's challenge to Khrushchev in April and a more serious one in early June, and the sharp Soviet riposte in the middle of June, presumably forced Hoxha to choose between Moscow and Peking. He probably wished to avoid having to choose, but, once he could do so no longer, his choice, given previous Albanian pro-Chinese pronouncements and the whole course of Hoxha's relations with Khrushchev, was clear — for China.

The most striking public evidence that Soviet-Albanian relations were in a very bad way was that the Albanian representative at Bucharest was not First Secretary Hoxha (all the other East European parties sent their leaders) nor even Prime Minister Shehu, but the number three man in the Albanian leadership, Hysni Kapo. Perhaps Hoxha and Shehu did not feel it safe to leave Tirana before they had finally disposed of Belishova and Tashko, whom they probably purged and arrested around this time; perhaps they wished to avoid personal entanglement with Khrushchev until later.[16]

The Bucharest Conference

The Romanian Party Congress in late June was used by Khrushchev as the occasion for a meeting of all parties represented at it. As we now know,[17] this meeting was the scene of the first violent debate between top-level Soviet and Chinese party leaders before an international Communist party (as opposed to Communist front) audience and thus another step in the intensification of the Sino-Soviet controversy. The debate was marked by a new height of mutually bitter invective; it resulted in sharpening the polarization within the movement.

The most striking element in the meetings was the violence of the Soviet counterattack against the Chinese. On June 21, Khrushchev be-

[16] Chief of delegation Hysni Kapo, third-ranking Politburo member and PPSh CC Secretary, also Sulejman Baholli, PPSh CC member, and Thanas Nano, deputy director of the Agitprop department of the PPSh CC (Bucharest, Agerpres Radioteletype in English to Europe, June 19, 1960, 0910 GMT, and *Zëri i Popullit,* June 21, 1960).

[17] Crankshaw, *op. cit.;* cf. Zagoria, *op. cit.,* pp. 325–327.

gan the meeting by distributing, apparently on only a few hours' notice,[18] a long circular letter[19] detailing the Chinese sins and restating the Soviet views on the foreign policy and ideological points at issue. The letter also stated that the recent Chinese attacks on destalinization obstructed the continuation of the process in several other parties. (One of them was almost surely the Albanian.)

Khrushchev's public speech at the Congress also implicitly made clear his opposition to Mao, and, one can assume, to the Albanians as well. He indirectly threatened the Chinese and the Albanians with a cut in Soviet economic aid, thus slowing their transition to Communism, and did so — for Hoxha a particularly enraging insult — by using Yugoslavia as an analogy. He also made clear that the U-2 incident and the subsequent collapse of the Paris summit conference would not result in a change in the Soviet foreign-policy line toward what the Chinese and Albanians desired. He implied that on the issue of thermonuclear war "only lunatics and maniacs" (i.e., like Mao and Hoxha) "can now come out with appeals for a new world war." Finally, he implicitly denounced Chinese (and Albanian) "dogmatic" interpretations of Marxism-Leninism. Significantly, of the above four points, the two last and most clearly anti-Chinese ones were not reproduced in the Tirana version of Khrushchev's speech.[20]

In his public speech[21] P'eng Chen, the Chinese representative, anticipated the relatively moderate Chinese policy positions expressed in August, but his references to the operations of "the Tito clique . . . serving imperialism" again demonstrated Peking's support of the defiant Albanians.

Kapo's public Bucharest speech, like Alia's in April, did not identify Albania with all the Chinese ideological attacks against Khrushchev; indeed, it contained some extravagantly pro-Soviet passages. On two issues, however, the struggle against imperialism and against the "Yugoslav revisionists," Kapo clearly took pro-Chinese and anti-Soviet positions. On the former his formulation quite shamelessly twisted Soviet views:

> . . . Following the example set by the Soviet Union and supporting it on every occasion, our party and government are struggling for peace, which

[18] Hoxha to the November 1960 meeting, as reported by Zorza in *The Guardian* (Manchester) and Floyd in *The Daily Telegraph* (London), June 9, 1961; for the contents, see Crankshaw, *op. cit.*

[19] *Deutsche Zeitung* (Cologne), Sept. 30, 1960; English translation in Zagoria, *op. cit.*, pp. 455–458, who considers it (p. 455) "generally accurate."

[20] *Zëri i Popullit,* June 23, 1960.

[21] Speech of June 22, 1960, in *Peking Review,* III, 26 (June 28, 1960), pp. 4–6, quoted from excerpts in Hudson, Lowenthal, and MacFarquhar, *op. cit.*, pp. 139-140.

> is needed by all mankind with the exception of the warmongering imperialists. We are conducting talks with them by always being vigilant, by never failing in our principles, by never making any unilateral concessions, by never endangering even for a moment the ideological and political struggle. . . .

On the latter he again repeated the essence of the 1949 Cominform resolution:

> . . . the Yugoslav revisionists . . . these hateful renegades of Marxism-Leninism and vile lackeys of American imperialism . . . have been converted into an agency of imperialism. . . .[22]

But the published speeches gave only a faint indication of the fury of the Sino-Soviet exchanges at the closed multiparty meeting. Khrushchev denounced Mao as "an ultra-leftist, an ultra-dogmatist, a left revisionist." P'eng, who apparently had not expected such a violent attack,[23] replied in equally violent terms, declaring that Khrushchev had arranged the meeting solely to attack China and undermine its prestige. Kapo's speech at the closed session was also anti-Soviet and pro-Chinese.[24] To date the Albanians, in accordance with their (and the Chinese) objections to Khrushchev's methods, have published only Kapo's objections to Khrushchev's method of attack against the Chinese.[25] One report even indicates that Kapo urged that a Yugoslav exile Communist party be set up.[26] In any case, from Khrushchev's viewpoint the Albanian representative was certainly, as Ulbricht later characterized the Albanian position, "dogmatist and sectarian."[27] Although the proceedings of the subsequent July 10–12 Albanian Central Committee Plenum[28] have remained unpublished and its communiqué was ambivalent and relatively unrevealing, two long Albanian attacks on Yugoslavia appearing shortly thereafter indicated that Tirana's position remained unchanged.

The public speeches at the Bucharest meetings also provided additional information on the lineup of the East European parties in the rapidly developing Sino-Soviet dispute. As Table 2.1 reveals, they all supported the Soviet Union except the Albanians, who sided totally with the Chinese. The Italian delegation sympathized strongly with the

[22] *Zëri i Popullit,* June 23, 1960.

[23] *Hindustan Times* (New Delhi), Nov. 14, 1960, quoting Indian Communist sources; cited in Hudson, Lowenthal, and MacFarquhar, *op. cit.,* p. 132.

[24] Crankshaw, *op. cit.*

[25] "Khrushchev Has Been Devoting His Time to Aggravating the Divergencies with Our Party and State Instead of Solving Them," *Zëri i Popullit,* March 25, 1962, and Document 26.

[26] Brzezinski, *The Soviet Bloc,* 2nd ed., p. 427.

[27] Ulbricht, *loc. cit.*

[28] Communiqué: *Zëri i Popullit,* July 13, 1960.

TABLE 2.1

Bucharest: Public Speeches in the Third Congress of the Romanian Workers Party

○: formal or weak
Ø: positive
●: emphatic

	SOVIET UNION[1] Khrushchev	ROMANIA[2] Gheorghiu-Dej	BULGARIA[3] Zhivkov	EAST GERMANY[4] Ulbricht	HUNGARY[5] Kádár	CZECHOSLOVAKIA[6] Novotný	POLAND[7] Ochab	MONGOLIA[8] Dugersuren	NORTH KOREA[9] Kim Chang-man	NORTH VIETNAM[10] Le Duan	ALBANIA[11] Kapo	CHINA[12] P'eng Chen
1. Nuclear war would be a disaster	●	Ø										
2. War can be prevented	●	●	●	●	Ø	Ø	Ø	Ø				○
3. "Peaceful coexistence" endorsed	●	●	●	●		Ø	○	Ø				
4. U.S.S.R. promotes policy of peace	●	●	●	●	Ø	Ø	Ø	●			○	
5. 1957 Declaration confirms peace policy	Ø	○	Ø		○			Ø				
6. Khrushchev praised		Ø	●	○			Ø					
7. CPSU "creative Marxism-Leninism" endorsed		○	Ø									
8. Dogmatism, "leftism" opposed		○			○							
9. Revisionism opposed		Ø			○			○	Ø			
10. Socialist camp "headed," "led" by U.S.S.R.		○	○	Ø		Ø		Ø	Ø	Ø	●	Ø
11. Friendship with U.S.S.R. proclaimed			Ø				○				●	
12. Need for strengthening socialist unity					○			Ø	Ø			●
13. "Contemporary"* revisionism opposed		○	○								Ø	●
14. Yugoslav revisionism attacked	Ø	○									●	Ø
15. Yugoslavia: agent of imperialism											●	○
16. U.S. imperialism prepares for war**	○			○					Ø	●	Ø	●

Russians and went even further than they in their rejection of the Chinese position.[29] Thus the Peking lineup of parties remained unchanged, and the Albanians were now isolated in Europe.

From Bucharest to Hanoi — June to September 1960

Sino-Soviet and Soviet-Albanian relations continued to worsen after the Bucharest meeting. The meeting itself had ended with an innocuous communiqué[30] stressing complete unity and agreement, but, unable to agree on the actual issues, had decided,[31] at Chinese insistence,[32] on another meeting in the autumn, not of bloc parties but of all 81. During the rest of the summer increased Sino-Soviet polemics on both sides were coupled with extensive Soviet economic and propaganda sanctions against the Chinese, including the Soviet withdrawal of their technicians from China.[33] Moscow and Peking also reportedly exchanged secret letters, in which the Soviets expanded and reiterated their previous charges. Yet, presumably in preparation for reaching a compromise at the forthcoming Moscow meetings, both Soviet and Chinese declarations also modified some of their previous ideological positions along lines which were later incorporated into the final version of the Moscow Conference statement.[34] By the next international Communist confrontation,

---

Sources for the table on the Third Congress of the Romanian Workers Party:

[1] Khrushchev: *Pravda,* June 22, 1960.
[2] Gheorghiu-Dej: *Scinteia,* June 21, 1960.
[3] Zhivkov: *Rabotnichesko Delo,* June 24, 1960.
[4] Ulbricht: *Neues Deutschland,* June 23, 1960.
[5] Kádár: *Népszabadság,* June 23, 1960.
[6] Novotný: *Rudé Právo,* June 23, 1960.
[7] Ochab: *Trybuna Ludu,* June 23, 1960.
[8] Dugersuren: *Scînteia,* June 24, 1960.
[9] Kim Chang-man: *Pravda,* June 24, 1960.
[10] Le Duan: *Pravda,* June 24, 1960.
[11] Kapo: *Zëri i Popullit,* June 23, 1960.
[12] P'eng Chen: *Jen-min Jih-pao,* June 23, 1960.

[29] "Promemoria della delegazione italiana alla commissione preparatoria della conferenza degli 81 partiti comunisti e operai," *Interventi della delegazione del P.C.I. alla Conferenza degli 81 Partiti comunisti e operai* (Rome: Sezione centrale di stampa e propaganda della Direzione del PCI, Jan. 15, 1962), (JPRS 12461, Feb. 14, 1962), pp. 3–44.

[30] Signed by the twelve bloc parties, June 24, 1960; text: *Pravda,* June 28, 1960; excerpts: Hudson, Lowenthal, and MacFarquhar, *op. cit.,* pp. 140–141.

[31] "Intervention de Maurice Thorez," *Contribution,* p. 29.

[32] In my view, Lowenthal (*op. cit.,* p. 19) overestimates how much the Chinese won through this.

[33] Zagoria, *op. cit.,* pp. 326–331. The Soviet position is made clearer, and the intensification of the rightist trend illustrated, in Togliatti's report to a PCI CC plenum (*L'Unità,* July 24, 1960) and in the PCI "Promemoria," *Interventi,* pp. 3–44.

[34] Zagoria, *op. cit.,* pp. 333–336, 459–461; Hudson, Lowenthal, and MacFarquhar, *op. cit.,* pp. 22–24.

the North Vietnamese Congress in early September, Sino-Soviet relations were clearly much worse than at the last one in Bucharest. The preparatory drafting committee for the 81-party congress was scheduled to meet that same month,[35] but in anything but an auspicious atmosphere.

The Albanians had burned their bridges at Bucharest. For them the all-important issue, Yugoslavia, was not yet publicly at stake. The summer's Sino-Soviet feelers toward compromise therefore were hardly interesting for Tirana. Soon after the Bucharest meetings the Albanians reiterated their defiance of Yugoslavia. They insisted that Yugoslavia was not socialist, but

> . . . a Hell where the darkest terror reigns and where a clique of traitors, fed on American imperialist dollars soaked in the blood of the workers, has been able by deceptive methods to seize power and to install for the first time in history a revisionist Trotskyite regime.[36]

> . . . a trained *agentura* of the imperialist bourgeoisie, . . . the Yugoslav revisionists . . . appear to support the foreign policy of the Soviet Union [but] . . . in fact . . . support . . . Western imperialist policy. . . .[37]

Soviet actions against the Albanian regime during the summer of 1960 were much more drastic and more difficult to unravel than were its moves against Peking — quite naturally so when one considers Albania's relative powerlessness and Khrushchev's determination, if he could not force Peking to retreat, at least to cow or destroy Hoxha. Kapo's unpublished speech at Bucharest had made clear that Hoxha, Shehu, and the majority of the Albanian leadership were determined to defy Khrushchev and that the Chinese supported them in it. Judging by the published speeches at Bucharest, the Albanians came by far the closest to total support of the Chinese — closer than any of the Asian parties except the Malayans and one fraction of the Burmese; and the Chinese, presumably already preparing for the subsequent Soviet attempt at Moscow in November to ban "fractionalism," needed a totally reliable ally; otherwise they had no "fraction."

In the summer of 1960, probably immediately after the Bucharest meeting, the Soviets and probably some or all of the East European satellites substantially cut their economic aid to Albania.[38] In the sum-

35 "Lettera della delegazione del P.C.I. al compagno N. S. Krusciov e alla delegazione del P.C.U.S. alla conferenza degli 81 partiti comunisti e operai," *Interventi,* pp. 74–77, at p. 75.

36 "Let the Plotters and Revisionists of Belgrade Be Unmasked Through and Through," *Zëri i Popullit,* July 17, 1960, and Document 2.

37 "Unmask Yugoslav Revisionism and Fight It to the End," *Zëri i Popullit,* June 29, 1960, and Document 1.

38 *The New York Times,* Mar. 19, 1961; Bernard Ullmann, "The Long Shadow

mer of 1960, Albania was suffering from a severe drought and a serious grain shortage. Moscow, the Albanians charged in 1962, delayed answering an Albanian request for assistance and finally rejected it, whereupon Tirana had to turn to "other socialist countries"[39] — i.e., China. (The Russians have declared that they sent Albania 30,000 extra tons of wheat in 1960.)[40] Despite their own famine the Chinese thereupon made good on their probable earlier promise of support to Hoxha[41] by buying wheat in France for foreign currency and having it shipped directly to Tirana.[42] Chinese and Albanian public statements and reciprocal visits of high officials made clear the close Sino-Albanian alliance. Chinese specialists were assigned to Albania.[43]

Khrushchev almost surely did much more than reduce Soviet economic assistance to Albania. He probably tried and failed to carry off a *coup d'état* in Tirana, overthrow Hoxha, Shehu, and their associates, and replace them with pro-Soviet members of the leadership — including Belishova and Tashko.[44] Hoxha has since declared[45] that Belishova and Tashko were involved in Khrushchev's attempt to unseat the Albanian leadership. The Albanians more recently have declared that the Soviet Embassy in Tirana

> began . . . to detach the [Albanian] leadership from its party and to turn the army cadres and other cadres which had studied in the Soviet Union against it. . . .[46]

There may have been Yugoslav involvement as well. Some aspects of the plot or plots were probably exclusively Albanian. In view of their later arrest, trial, and execution, it seems probable that the Albanian participants also included Teme Sejko, a Soviet-trained Albanian rear admiral, Tahir Demi, an ex-Albanian representative to CMEA in Moscow,[47] a general, and some other officials. Sejko, in Moscow in 1947–

---

of Mao Tse-tung," *The New York Times Magazine,* Apr. 16, 1961; "Khrushchev . . . ," *Zëri i Popullit,* Mar. 25, 1962, and Document 26.

39 "Khrushchev . . . ," *Zëri i Popullit,* March 25, 1962, and Document 26; Hoxha speech, Nov. 7, 1961, *ibid.,* Nov. 8, 1961, and Document 14.

40 Radio Moscow in Albanian to Albania, Mar. 4, 1962, 1500 GMT.

41 See Chinese-Albanian trade agreement, NCNA English from Peking Feb. , 1961 (SCMP 2435, Feb. 8, 1961, pp. 23–25).

42 *The New York Times,* Nov. 6, 1960; Radio Tirana, Oct. 10, 1960, 2100 GMT.

43 *The New York Times Magazine,* Apr. 16, 1961, p. 19; CPR greetings on Albanian National Day, Peking, NCNA in English to Europe and Asia, Nov. 8, 1960, 1523 GMT, in SCMP 2389, Dec. 2, 1960, pp. 30–31.

44 Hamm (*op. cit.,* p. 51) is more skeptical of Soviet involvement.

45 In his Nov. 7, 1961, speech, *Zëri i Popullit,* Nov. 8, 1961, and Document 14.

46 "Khrushchev . . . ," *Zëri i Popullit,* Mar. 25, 1962, and Document 26.

47 Robert F. Lamberg, "Albanien zwischen Moskau und Peking," *Osteuropa,* II, 1/2 (Jan.–Feb. 1962), pp. 66–72.

1949 and again in 1956–1958,[48] presumably had extensive official contacts with the Soviet submarine base at Sazan, the island off Vlorë. Demi had clearly been heavily involved with Soviet economic officials. (Hoxha at this writing maintains his February 1961 version that Sejko, Demi, and the others were agents for a joint Yugoslav-Greek-American attempt to overthrow the Tirana regime; only remarkable and rare regard for historical consistency, however, had presumably prevented him from revising this version of the plot and including all of them in what it probably primarily was: a Soviet attempt to change the Albanian leadership.)

The summer was also the scene of a concerted attempt by the Soviet leadership to round up support in other Communist parties against the Chinese for the pending "summit conference" in Moscow. The only details available are in the Albanian version of the communications exchanged between Moscow and Tirana. The political significance of this exchange was relatively low; Soviet-Albanian relations had probably already reached the point of no return before or during the Bucharest meetings, and the exchange was therefore more *pro forma* than genuine dialogue. On August 13, Moscow proposed that negotiations be held in order to assume "perfect unity" before the forthcoming November Moscow meetings, lest "the spark of misunderstanding . . . become a fire."[49] In their reply of August 27 the Albanians, in another instance of their (and of the Chinese) concentration on method, stated that it would be a "violation of elementary Marxist-Leninist norms" for two parties to begin "negotiations with the object of criticizing the general line of another Marxist party"[50] (i.e., China).

The only two known pro-Soviet members of the Albanian leadership, Liri Belishova and Koço Tashko, were probably purged and arrested in August or early September; their removal was announced on September 8.[51] Either then or later, according to Mikoyan at the Soviet Twenty-

48 Lazitch, "Dossier . . . ," *op. cit.,* p. 15.

49 "Khrushchev . . . ," *Zëri i Popullit,* Mar. 25, 1962, and Document 26. That there was a Soviet approach to the Albanians in August was stated by Khrushchev at the XXII CPSU Congress (*Pravda,* Oct. 29, 1961, and Document 11) and in Leonid Sergeyev, "How the Present Albanian Leaders Reject All CPSU Proposals to Solve Misunderstandings in a Comradely Way," Radio Moscow in Albanian to Albania, Feb. 8, 1962, 1500 GMT, and Document 23.

50 "Khrushchev . . . ," *Zëri i Popullit,* March 25, 1962, and Document 26.

51 PPSh CC communiqué, Sept. 8, 1960, in *Zëri i Popullit,* Sept. 9, 1960, and Document 3. On July 27 Belishova spoke at Vlorë on her trip to Asia (*Zëri i Popullit,* July 28, 1960); her removal must have occurred thereafter. It seems safe to assume, considering general PPSh practice, that both were arrested. However, published sources are somewhat contradictory: the communiqué stated Tashko was expelled from the party for "hostile" actions, while Belishova was only expelled from the CC (for "grave" errors vis-à-vis the party line). On th

Second Congress in October 1961,[52] Belishova's second husband, Minister of Agriculture Maqo Çomo, was also removed and arrested.

One of the major causal factors in the summer's worsening in Sino-Soviet relations was probably the contradictory Soviet and Chinese attitudes toward Albania. The Soviet and East European cut in economic aid to Tirana was not only a method of blackmail against Hoxha but also an open challenge to Peking. The Chinese had to decide whether they would preserve their gains in Albania by taking up the slack in economic aid or bow out of the game. Had they done the latter, the loss to their prestige within the world Communist movement would have been great, but an open conflict with Moscow could at least have been postponed. The Chinese had withdrawn before as a result of Soviet pressure: their 1958 abandonment of their ideological claims about the people's communes and their public silence in respect to Khrushchev's support of Marshal P'eng's opposition to Mao were the latest in a series of such retreats. But now, for the first time, the Chinese did not retreat. On a much more significant issue than the communes, Chinese support of the rebellion of an East European satellite clearly within the Soviet geographic sphere of influence, Mao decided to stand. When, as seems probable, the Soviets countered with an unsuccessful *coup d'état* to overthrow Hoxha, the Chinese must have been both infuriated at its perpetration and delighted at its failure.

The Hanoi Confrontation — Early September 1960

The Sino-Soviet confrontation in early September at the Hanoi Congress of the North Vietnamese party still further worsened the Sino-Soviet dispute.[53] At the Congress the North Vietnamese themselves took a neutral position between the Russians and the Chinese,[54] as did the Japanese and North Korean parties. The Albanians came out strongly in

---

other hand, Mikoyan stated at the XXII CPSU Congress (*Pravda,* Oct. 22, 1961) that Belishova was purged and suffered "repression," while he mentions Tashko as having been only purged. Hamm (*op. cit.,* pp. 50–51) was told in 1961 in Albania by PPSh cadres that Belishova and Tashko had made no secret of their pro-Soviet views, which they had maintained after the Peking-Tirana alliance had become the PPSh general line.

52 *Pravda,* Oct. 22, 1961. His arrest was first reported in a dispatch from Belgrade to *The New York Times,* Mar. 20, 1961.

53 Zagoria, *op. cit.,* pp. 336–338; P. J. Honey, "North Vietnam's Party Congress," *China Quarterly,* No. 4 (Oct.–Dec. 1960), pp. 66–75.

54 Subsequent Vietnamese declarations, in my view, have confirmed this and controverted Honey's original view (*op. cit.*) that they took a totally pro-Russian position; see Honey's subsequent article, "The Position of the DRV Leadership and the Succession to Ho Chi Minh," *China Quarterly,* No. 9 (Jan.–March 1962), pp. 24–36.

favor of the Chinese, the Indonesians less so. The delegates from Bulgaria, Czechoslovakia, East Germany, Hungary, Mongolia, Poland, Romania, France, and Italy took clearly pro-Soviet positions.[55] The Albanian delegate to the congress, Minister of Defense General Beqir Balluku, reflecting the intensification of the Sino-Soviet dispute and the Soviet attempt to overthrow Hoxha, took a much stronger anti-Soviet and pro-Chinese ideological position than had Kapo at the Bucharest meeting. He implicitly attacked Khrushchev's policy of détente toward ". . . American imperialism, . . . the most ferocious enemy of the peoples. . . ." He more violently denounced

> . . . the Yugoslav revisionists, who are nothing but agents in the service of imperialism . . . [who] for sixteen years in succession have plotted to realize their aim — to swallow Albania. . . .[56]

In addition, Balluku did not declare that war can be averted, made only a formal reference to the necessity to fight dogmatism, and did not mention Khrushchev.

From Hanoi to Moscow

The preparatory commission for the November 81-party meeting began its sessions in Moscow in September, under the chairmanship of Suslov,[57] with the consideration of a Soviet draft.[58] It met for more than a month, and, in view of what is known of the acrimonious debate in the month-long full meeting in November,[59] one may certainly assume that the discussions were long and bitter. This seems likely in view of the anti-Soviet character of the Chinese propaganda campaign in late September celebrating the publication of Volume 4 of Mao's *Selected Works*.[60] During this same period the increasing Albanian public divergence from Moscow became clear in late September and October at the United Nations General Assembly in New York. Alone among the East European first secretaries, all of whom came with Khrushchev on the *Baltika,* Hoxha did not attend. Shehu, who did, traveled on the *Queen Mary* and in New York was ostentatiously slighted by the other Communist leaders, while Khrushchev publicly embraced Tito, the Albanians' chief enemy. Shehu later made clear his opposition to Soviet-

55 Honey, *op. cit.,* p. 72.

56 *Zëri i Popullit,* Sept. 8, 1960.

57 "Lettera," *Interventi,* pp. 74–77, at p. 75; "Intervention de Maurice Thorez," *Contribution,* p. 5.

58 Crankshaw, *op. cit.*

59 For the lengths of the meetings, see Belgian CP Politburo statement, *Le Drapeau Rouge,* Feb. 22, 1962.

60 Zagoria, *op. cit.,* pp. 338–339; SCMM Oct. 18, 1960, pp. 1–20.

sponsored proposals for disarmament and troop control in the Balkans and elsewhere.

Initially Albania,[61] like Bulgaria, had supported Romania's echoing of Khrushchev's 1957 proposal for a Balkan "atom-free zone."[62] When at the end of 1959 Bulgaria extended this to provide for total Balkan disarmament except for frontier guards, there was at first no reaction. However, when Zhivkov revived the proposal at the autumn 1960 U.N. General Assembly,[63] the Albanians, by then on quite different terms with Moscow (which, they felt, was threatening them *inter alia* with giving southern Albania to Greece), initially indirectly registered their opposition.[64] The depth of the Albanian opposition did not become apparent until Shehu's speech to the Albanian Parliament on October 25, upon his return from New York. There he declared that "one can never accept" complete disarmament in the Balkans, an "absurd and dangerous idea . . . in flagrant contradiction with the interests of the security of our people," one "which may have been conceived in the mind of someone in the Balkans" (i.e., Zhivkov) and which "puts in danger" the independence of his socialist fatherland.[65] In the same speech Shehu also attacked (again without naming its author) the Gomułka proposal, made to the United Nations General Assembly on September 27, that the number of military bases on foreign soil be frozen;[66] in fact, the Albanians reportedly wanted Soviet atomic rockets.[67]

Just before the Moscow Conference met, the Soviets and the Chinese further developed their recent propaganda themes.[68]

The Moscow meetings of the 81 Communist parties opened in November and lasted several weeks; its final declaration was published in *Pravda* on December 6. All the sessions were secret. It was the initial

[61] *Zëri i Popullit,* June 16, 1959. In 1959 (interview with *Rabotnichesko Delo,* Aug. 10, 1959) Shehu supported an additional Bulgarian proposal to Greece for a mutual nonaggression pact. The Soviets have now declared (Nikolayev, "How the Albanian Leaders Sabotage Creation of a Balkan Peace Zone," Radio Moscow in Albanian, Jan. 22, 1962, 1900 GMT, and Medvedev, "From Dogmatism in Theory to Adventurism on Politics," *Izvestiya,* Feb. 4, 1962) that the Albanians opposed the Romanian 1957 initiative and the Bulgarian 1959 proposal (the latter as "absurd and dangerous").

[62] *Pravda,* May 27, 31, 1959.

[63] Zhivkov to the U.N. General Assembly, Sept. 28, 1960, *Rabotnichesko Delo,* Sept. 29, 1960.

[64] Shtylla to the U.N. Political Committee (Oct. 13, 1960, *Zëri i Popullit,* Oct. 13, 1960), stating that disarmament should take place "in all areas of the world simultaneously."

[65] *Zëri i Popullit,* Oct. 26, 1960; cf. Medvedev, *op. cit.*

[66] *Trybuna Ludu,* Sept. 28, 1960.

[67] Preben Henriksen in *Land og Folk* (Copenhagen), Dec. 20, 1961.

[68] Hudson, Lowenthal, and MacFarquhar, *op. cit.,* pp. 159–171, at p. 159.

Western view[69] that the meeting had resulted in some kind of *modus vivendi* between Moscow and Peking and that, as illustrated by the preponderance in the final statement of Soviet ideological and policy formulation, it represented substantially a Soviet victory. It is now clear that on the contrary, and despite the fact that Sino-Soviet ideological polemics declined thereafter sharply in quantity and aggressiveness, Sino-Soviet and even more Soviet-Albanian relations deteriorated steadily after the meetings.

Italian, French, and Belgian Communist documentation has made it possible to reconstruct something, although far from all, of the course of the meetings.[70] It increases still further one's estimate of the bitterness, the all-inclusiveness, and the lack of agreement which characterized this Sino-Soviet encounter. It demonstrates that the key issue, as the whole course of Communist history would a priori have enabled one to forecast, was the organizational one: the issue of "fractionalism." On this issue (the attempt to force the Chinese to accept as binding the decisions of a majority of the 81 parties, i.e., the Soviet view) the Soviets launched the main thrust of their counterattack against the Chinese efforts within the international Communist movement to thwart Moscow's policies and subvert its satellites. On the same issue the Chinese remained adamant. Since, as all Lenin's theories and actions so clearly demonstrated, the organizational issue is the decisive one in any bureaucratic élitist movement, it follows that on this key issue the Soviets were unsuccessful at the Moscow meetings, and the Chinese, although they did not win on it, succeeded in maintaining the *status quo ante*.

The above reconstruction also demonstrates the significance of the issue of Yugoslavia for the Albanians and for the Russians, Chinese, and Italians as well. Ever since the 1948 Soviet-Yugoslav break Moscow's

[69] E.g., Brzezinski, *The Soviet Bloc,* 2nd ed., pp. 427–429.

[70] *Interventi, op. cit.; Contribution, op. cit.;* several articles in the Belgian newspaper *Le Drapeau Rouge* by Jean Terfve, Jan. 5, 8, 9, 10, 11, 15–17, 1962 (JPRS 12759, Mar. 2, 1962); see also Terfve's 1962 pamphlet, "Le XXIIe congrès du Parti communiste de l'U.R.S.S. et les bases du 'renouveau,'" *Communisme* (Brussels), No. 2, May 1962, pp. 1–22 (JPRS 14548, July 23, 1962); by Ernest Burnelle, Jan. 19–29, 1962 (JPRS 12615, Feb. 23, 1962), both pro-Soviet; and the pro-Chinese one by Jacques Grippa and the pro-Soviet answer by the Belgian CP Politburo, Feb. 22, 1962 (JPRS 13314, Apr. 4, 1962, pp. 10–91); Edward Crankshaw in *The Observer* (London), Feb. 12, 19, 1961, and May 6 and 20, 1962; for his analysis, "Khrushchev and China," *Atlantic Monthly,* CCVII, 5 (May 1961), pp. 43–47; for a detailed reconstruction of the meetings, with bibliography, see William E. Griffith, "The November 1960 Moscow Meeting: A Preliminary Reconstruction," *China Quarterly,* No. 11 (July–Sept. 1962), pp. 38–57, to be reprinted in a forthcoming Praeger volume on polycentrism, edited by Walter Laqueur. The following brief summary is taken from the conclusion of the article.

attitude toward Belgrade has always been an integral part and a faithful reflector of its general foreign-policy general line. When it favors détente, it favors détente with Yugoslavia as well; when it intensifies tension, Soviet-Yugoslav relations also worsen.

Finally, the reconstruction highlights that the Moscow meetings themselves were more "polycentric" than initial reports indicated. The Italian position on such issues as the peaceful transition to socialism and on contacts with Yugoslavia demonstrated that even in 1960 the international Communist movement was not divided into a Chinese-Albanian "left" and a Soviet "right," but rather in a far more complex manner.[71] On policy issues the Soviets were in the center, the Chinese and Albanians on the far left, most of the other Asian parties close to the Chinese; several of the European parties (East German, Czechoslovak, French) also had leftist policy sympathies but submerged them in favor of organizational loyalty to Moscow, and some other European parties (Polish, Italian, and in part Hungarian) were to the right. On the organizational issue, which involves the degree of control by Moscow of other parties, the extent and kind of Chinese influence, and the degree of polycentrism in the international Communist movement, the Soviet party was completely supported by those parties which by tradition, leadership, financial support, or Soviet economic aid or military presence or threat have consistently been faithful to Moscow; it was strongly opposed by the Chinese, who aspire first to more influence and eventually to predominance in the world movement, and with the Chinese by its Albanian allies. Moscow was less strongly opposed, but still was not endorsed, by the "Communist neutralists": those Asian parties, in and out of power, which gain from balancing between the Communist giants. Finally, it was endorsed, but far from totally, by the right-wing parties, in particular the Polish and the Italian, which did not desire a break with Moscow but preferred more autonomy than they now have.

In short, then, the Moscow meetings confirmed and deepened the rifts and feuds which had become public in 1960. They were followed by a continuing decline in Sino-Soviet relations and within the year by the Soviet-Albanian break.

The meeting which occurred in Moscow between Khrushchev and Hoxha was more of an exchange of denunciations than of views. According to a probably correct later Albanian account,[72] the meeting, at Khrushchev's initiative, was scheduled for November 9. Immediately preceding it, however, with no previous warning to Hoxha, the Soviets,

[71] Cf. Dallin, *op. cit.*

[72] "Khrushchev . . . ," *Zëri i Popullit,* Mar. 25, 1962, and Document 26. As of June 1962, Moscow had not challenged this version.

in the words of the Albanian account, distributed to all the delegates a "long official document" which denounced the Albanian leadership, *inter alia* for "anti-Soviet policies and activities," and "undertook the defense of antiparty elements" (i.e., the pro-Soviet Belishova and Tashko, purged the previous summer). Even so, the Soviets still pressed for a meeting with the Albanians, which finally occurred on November 12. As might have been expected, and as Khrushchev later declared,[73] it came to nothing; according to the Albanians, the Soviet leader at its conclusion declared that he could reach a better understanding with Macmillan than with the Albanians.

On November 16 (after Teng but before Longo), Hoxha delivered a philippic against Khrushchev[74] which ended all chances of a reconciliation between Moscow and Tirana. His speech contained all the major themes of the Albanian attack upon Khrushchev which he made public a year later. Hoxha repeated the Chinese position on the ideological issues: the nature of the epoch, peaceful coexistence, and peaceful transition to socialism. On the organizational issue, he denounced Khrushchev for having accused the Chinese party at Bucharest on short notice and for having demanded that the other parties support him in this, a procedure to which the Albanians had properly objected. Hoxha generally approved of the draft declaration, except for the ban on fractionalism. He declared that "the cult of personality does not apply only to Stalin . . . who had worldwide renown and was the follower of Lenin." He was predictably violent against Yugoslavia. Khrushchev, he declared, had gone to Belgrade in May 1955 without informing the Albanians and had thereafter disregarded their protest. In 1956 he had spread "false information . . . concerning the physical liquidation of Yugoslav agents including a pregnant woman" (i.e., Liri Gega); Khrushchev's analysis of the political causes of the Hungarian counterrevolution and of the events had been wrong;[75] he and Suslov had had confidence in Tito in spite of the latter's desire "to coordinate the counterrevolution in

[73] Khrushchev to the XXII CPSU Congress, *Pravda,* Oct. 29, 1961.

[74] See ftn. 70, *supra.* The available official Communist documents concerning this Hoxha speech are the attacks on it in the first speech to the Moscow meeting by the head of the PCI delegation, Luigi Longo, "Primo intervento," *Interventi,* pp. 45–71, at pp. 48–51, and by Thorez, "Déclaration de la délégation du Parti communiste français," *Contribution,* pp. 38–40. There also exist three apparently reliable but incomplete summaries of the Hoxha speech; the most extensive is in BBC European Service C.R.U. Talk No. 2,098, June 9, 1961, from which all the following quotations are taken; see also Victor Zorza in *The Guardian* (Manchester) and David Floyd in *The Daily Telegraph* (London), June 9, 1961. "Primo intervento" and "Declaration" have largely confirmed these three, as has "Marxism-Leninism Will Triumph," *Zëri i Popullit,* Nov. 1, 1961. The report Hoxha made to the December 19–20 PPSh CC Plenum (*Zëri i Popullit,* Dec. 21, 1961) has remained unpublished.

[75] Cf. *Interventi,* pp. 45–71, at pp. 48–49.

Albania and Hungary. Khrushchev had incorrectly taken the sole initiative of intervening in Hungary. Only Czechoslovakia "has held a correct attitude toward the necessity of unmasking Tito."

Referring to Khrushchev's interview with the Greek leader,[76] Hoxha declared that "we have put Sophokles Venizelos in his place," that "we shall make no territorial concessions," and added:

> . . . We do not want a rectification of the Albanian-Yugoslav frontiers . . . but we demand the protection of the Albanian minority in Yugoslavia, one million strong. . . .

Hoxha's most violent charges against Khrushchev dealt with Soviet-Albanian relations: Khrushchev had in August 1960 sent a letter to the Albanian party members asking them to "join a bloc" against the Chinese party,[77] thus making themselves guilty of fractionalism. The Soviet Union had brutally intervened in the Albanian party in an attempt to force some of its leaders "to choose between the 200 million Russians and the 650 million Chinese"; Belishova had "capitulated to the dishonest threats of the Soviet Union." The Soviet ambassador in Tirana and his staff were continuing their pressure, which had gone as far as to precipitate a revolution in the army. Marshal Malinovsky had attacked Albania at a Warsaw Pact Chiefs of Staff meeting; Marshal Grechko had threatened to exclude Albania from the Pact; Khrushchev had threatened to expel Albania from the socialist camp, but this would not depend upon him.[78] Khrushchev had told Teng Hsiao-p'ing, "We shall treat Albania like Yugoslavia";[79] on November 6, Khrushchev had said, "Russia has lost an Albania; the People's Republic of China has gained an Albania." Hoxha then emotionally described the Soviet economic pressure on Albania:

> . . . Albania has suffered earthquakes, floods and a drought of 120 days and has been threatened by famine. Only 15 days' supply of wheat remained in stock. After a delay of 45 days, the USSR promised us 10,000 tons of wheat instead of 50,000 tons or — in other words — 15 days' supply of wheat to be delivered in September or October. These are unbearable pressures. The Soviet rats were able to eat whilst the Albanian people were dying of hunger; we were asked to produce gold.[80]

[76] *To Vima* (Athens), June 28, 1960.

[77] This has now also been alleged in "Khrushchev . . . ," *Zëri i Popullit,* Mar. 25, 1962, and Document 26.

[78] This is particularly interesting in view of the November 1961 statement by the Indonesian CP head Aidit in Djarkarta that membership in the camp is determined by whether or not a country is "objectively" building socialism, and therefore Albania cannot be expelled from it, since even Khrushchev admits she is building it (*Jen-min Jih-pao,* Dec. 1, 1961).

[79] Cf. "A Year of Historic Proofs," *Zëri i Popullit,* Dec. 6, 1961, and Document 15.

[80] Cf. pp. 46–47, *supra.*

But in his attack Hoxha added nothing to the known issues in dispute. He also reportedly attacked the Poles violently, declaring that Foreign Minister Rapacki, a PZPR Politburo member, was an imperialist agent.[81] A week later before the end of the meetings, Hoxha and Shehu, perhaps taking fright at their own boldness, precipitously returned to Tirana via Budapest,[82] although probably not, as an East German later alleged,[83] via Italy as well.

Sometime after Teng and Hoxha, Longo, the head of the Italian delegation, spoke. (The absent Togliatti, the old Comintern fox, was presumably far too experienced to participate personally in so potentially hazardous an international meeting.) In addition to the points of his speech which have previously been covered, Longo violently attacked the Albanians. "Words fail us," he said, "for proper denunciation"; the Hoxha speech was "beneath contempt" both as to content and to method.[84] Its method was that of "hypocritical doubletalk," its personal attack on Khrushchev and the Soviet leaders "dishonest and childish."[85] In a clear reference to Hoxha's denunciations of Khrushchev's cut in Soviet economic aid to Albania, Longo declared:

> . . . we cannot disguise the ideological and political dissension of which we speak as a dispute involving nothing but relations among certain socialist countries. We do not want to intervene directly in international relations, but we cannot refrain from pointing out that certain insulting insinuations made by the Albanian delegate in connection with the policies of the Soviet government struck our ear as an insult to the entire assembly . . . all the more offensive the more it is masked behind oily assurances of friendship and fraternity, with epithets and turns of expression that one can conceive of addressing only to a class enemy. . . .[86]

Presumably, most if not all of the other pro-Soviet party representatives denounced the Albanians. Reports of only three are available at this writing. The Spanish Communist leader Dolores Ibarruri ("La Pasionaria") called Hoxha's speech "provocatory and unfit to be uttered by a militant proletarian,"[87] and "contrary to Communism and Marxism-Leninism." Hungarian First Secretary Kádár declared that

[81] Brzezinski, *The Soviet Bloc,* 2nd ed., p. 432, ftn.

[82] *Pravda,* Nov. 26, 1960; Radio Budapest, Nov. 27, 1960, in BBC, *Summary of World Broadcasts,* Second Series, No. 501, Part II: Eastern Europe, p. 3 (summary x), Nov. 29, 1960.

[83] Peter Florin, "Zur abenteuerlichen Politik der albanischen Führer," *Einheit,* XIII, 3 (Mar. 1962), pp. 14–26, at p. 24.

[84] "Primo intervento," *Interventi,* pp. 48–49.

[85] *Ibid.,* p. 49.

[86] *Ibid.,* p. 50.

[87] *Ibid.,* p. 71.

> . . . each of us to whom our unity and the interests of socialism and freedom are dear can do only one thing: oppose these false views with principled impatience. . . .[88]

The Outer Mongolian First Secretary Tsedenbal later said that his party had warned the Albanians that

> . . . unless they seriously revise their incorrect position it is only logical that they may finally find themselves in the company of their former adversaries — the revisionists.[89]

The Chinese, however, refused to disavow or take exception to the Albanian tirade.[90]

One can deduce something of the positions of the other parties, however, from the texts of the greeting messages sent by them to Moscow on the anniversary of the October Revolution, the ostensible occasion for the 81-party meeting. From their formulations on the possibility of avoiding war it is clear that the Chinese, Albanians, North Koreans, and North Vietnamese did not explicitly endorse the positive Soviet line on this issue. The fact that they were the only ones who used the formula "the camp of socialism headed by the Soviet Union," as subsequent events made clear, did not indicate a pro-Khrushchev attitude but the opposite. (When one remembers that Mao insisted on this at the November 1957 Moscow meeting, *inter alia* to prevent the Yugoslavs from signing the declaration, one can realize that the phrase was perhaps even by then far from being pro-Khrushchev.) According to Crankshaw[91] only the Albanians, North Koreans, Indonesians, Siamese, North Vietnamese, Burmese, Malayans, and Japanese took pro-Chinese positions. In view of this and later developments one may assume that they at least did not attack the Albanians.

After the Albanians left, the Chinese continued to refuse to accept the Soviet formulations on "fractionalism" and on the Twentieth and Twenty-First CPSU Congresses.

During the last days of November the conference was in recess and a "drafting committee" at work, of which presumably the Soviets and Chinese were members. The only evidence concerning the contents of the draft statement at this stage is in a letter of the Italian delegation to Khrushchev.[92] From this it appears that what, if any, reference

[88] Quoted in Florin, *op. cit.,* p. 25.
[89] Tsedenbal to the II MPR CC Plenum, *Pravda,* Feb. 3, 1962.
[90] See the Belgian CP Politburo statement, *Le Drapeau Rouge,* Feb. 22, 1962.
[91] *The Observer,* May 6, 1962.
[92] "Lettera," *Interventi,* pp. 74–77, at p. 74. This PCI letter was written to Khrushchev so that he would receive it "before the end of the work of the drafting committee."

should be made to the Twentieth Congress (apparently the Twenty-First had already been eliminated) was still a matter of controversy; the Italians opposed "any compromise or any retreat on this point."[93] This letter also gives the only evidence, aside from Crankshaw's brief reference to the hostile Chinese attitude and Hoxha's philippic, on the Yugoslav issue. Since the Yugoslav issue was the primary cause of Albania's defection to Peking, it is therefore of significance for Soviet-Albanian relations. There probably were Soviet-Chinese differences roughly parallel to those between the 1948 and 1949 Cominform resolutions, but no evidence is available on this point. (The Italian letter reveals a significant element for the general position of the Communist "right wing": the Italian attempt to tone down the condemnation of Yugoslavia.)

The draft declaration had probably contained, to assist in a compromise with the Chinese, a somewhat stronger condemnation of Belgrade than Khrushchev himself would have wanted. Even so, the Italians submitted an amendment which, they maintained,

> . . . does not stray from the substance of the concepts expressed in the draft declaration. However, it is couched in less bitter and offensive terms. . . .[94]

The amendment, the Italian letter continued, would prevent the Yugoslav leaders from arousing public opinion against the declaration, was more realistic about Yugoslav influence, and, most importantly, would eliminate the provision that all Communist parties must "isolate Yugoslavia from the workers movement" — a provision which would implicitly condemn the Belgrade Declaration and stop all contacts with Yugoslav organizations (which the Italian party was intensifying), thus hindering rapprochement with other leftist organizations. (The December declaration did not contain this final provision; it follows that this Italian, and Soviet, initiative[95] toward deleting it was successful.)

The Moscow Declaration

The Moscow meetings make clear that the final statement, as Mr. Zagoria has written, was

> . . . not a real compromise of Soviet and Chinese views, but a collation of them. While the document in its broad outlines must be regarded as a Soviet "victory," its ambiguities and qualifications were so numerous that

93 *Ibid.*, p. 75.
94 *Ibid.*
95 That the Soviets also favored this is clear from Florin, *op. cit.*

> it could hardly serve as a guide for any of the Communist parties. Both Russia and China could and did derive different conclusions from it. The ostensible Soviet victory was thus bought at the very heavy price of an unworkable compromise which served clearly to demonstrate that the Russians were no longer able unilaterally to dictate law for the entire international Communist movement. . . .[96]

Mr. Zagoria's negative judgment of it was later confirmed by the Belgian Communist Politburo, which publicly referred to the statement as

> . . . so "loaded" . . . that it was possible to quote from it to support the statement, the defense, and the application of political views diametrically opposed, and often outrageously divergent. . . .[97]

On the fundamental question of authority and legitimacy within the international Communist movement no decision was reached. The final statement contains no reference to "fractionalism," but only to "jointly" reached decisions (i.e., there was no clear unanimous decision as to whether a majority vote was binding or a unanimous one was required) and to bilateral and multilateral discussions. But in an 81-party meeting, the only worldwide authority, the Soviets were bound to have a majority, as was the United States in the early days of the United Nations General Assembly. By 1960, Peking and Tirana were no more ready than either Moscow, Washington, or Pretoria has been since 1945 to allow their interests to be determined by a majority in a group many of whose members are even less powerful than Albania.

On all other issues the statement leaned strongly toward the Russian position but usually was sufficiently ambiguous so that the Chinese and Albanians could (and did) interpret it in their favor. Although the formulation on Yugoslavia was a compromise, and probably went farther than Khrushchev would have wished, it was far from an adoption of the Chinese-Albanian view. Nowhere did it include the 1949 Cominform formulation that the Yugoslav leaders had become an *agentura* of the imperialists. Nor did it even declare that "objectively" they aid the imperialists; their "subversive" operations were not ascribed to anyone's benefit. Furthermore, it did not declare that Yugoslavia was no longer a socialist country; it only said that "it is in danger of losing the revolutionary gains" (i.e., socialism). Finally, as we have already seen, it omitted any mention of "isolating" Yugoslavia from the international Communist movement.

[96] Zagoria, *The Sino-Soviet Conflict,* pp. 367–368. See *ibid.,* pp. 345–365, for a detailed analysis of the statement, on which the following is in part based.
[97] Belgian CP Politburo statement, in *Le Drapeau Rouge,* Feb. 22, 1962.

CHAPTER THREE

Prelude to the Break: Soviet-Albanian Relations — December 1960 to October 1961

The actual course of Soviet-Albanian relations from the November 1960 Moscow 81-party meeting to the October 1961 Soviet Twenty-Second Congress was very different from what it seemed to the West at the time.[1] Immediately after the meeting Sino-Soviet published polemics ceased and mutual news coverage became more favorable.[2] There were at first relatively few serious public indications that Soviet-Albanian relations were continuing to deteriorate. One of the few was the only public Communist criticism of the Albanians, Ulbricht's December attack on them for their "dogmatist and sectarian" line at the November 1960 Moscow meetings.[3] Nevertheless, a close study of Soviet and Albanian published ideological material indicates (as it might have then) that in fact relations were worsening.

Material released by Moscow and Tirana after the December 1961 diplomatic break now sets forth a much more detailed but often conflicting picture of the hitherto secret Soviet and Albanian actions during the period December 1960 to October 1961. Although Moscow-Tirana polemics ceased in April 1962 to include further new material on Soviet-Albanian relations during this period they may well resume doing so; therefore this account can have only provisional historical validity. It can, however, considerably enlarge the picture of Soviet-Albanian relations in this period. When one adds the newly available material to the Soviet and Albanian ideological articles published at the time, there emerges a remarkable illustration of the Marxist "unity of theory and practice"; each hostile Soviet action was accompanied by a veiled but clear Albanian ideological attack against Soviet policy positions.

This provisional historical reconstruction has two other purposes: first, to present a preliminary case study of an unsuccessful Soviet at-

1 An earlier version of this chapter was published as "Albania: Footnotes on a Conflict," *East Europe,* XI, 9 (Sept. 1962), pp. 14–23, and XI, 10 (Oct. 1962), pp. 18–24. For surveys of recent Albanian developments, see Ch. 2, ftn. 1.

2 Zbigniew Brzezinski, *The Soviet Bloc,* 2nd ed. (New York: Praeger, 1961), p. 429.

3 *Neues Deutschland,* Dec. 18, 1960.

tempt, in the context of the Sino-Soviet rift, to impose its will on a rebellious small Communist power, and second, to demonstrate the intimate and indissoluble link between Communist ideological pronouncements and political, economic, and military actions. The account itself throws much light upon Soviet strategy and tactics toward policy and organizational deviation[4] within the context of the Sino-Soviet dispute; the links between ideology and action offer methodological insights into the analytical techniques most useful in studying Soviet behavior on the basis of ideological declarations alone.[5] In order to enable the reader more easily to compare ideological pronouncements with the then unknown but now revealed Soviet and Albanian actions, the account of the latter is printed in italics.

According to the Albanian version,[6] *the Soviet chief engineer for the construction of the Tirana Palace of Culture (a 1959 gift by Moscow to Tirana) went to Moscow in October 1960, taking all the plans with him, and never returned. (Moscow has stated that the Albanians by April 1960 had so increased their demands for its size that its cost had risen two and one-half times.) In December 1960, Tirana's version continues, Soviet work on the palace slowed down.*

On December 21 the Albanian press clearly indicated that Soviet-Albanian relations were still far from repaired. On that day the birthday of the "inflexible Leninist" Stalin was celebrated ostentatiously in Tirana.[7] In the Tirana newspapers that morning the announcement of these celebrations, in a studied gesture of defiance toward Khrushchev, appeared on the front page, just below the Albanian Central Committee communiqué and resolution on the Moscow meetings.[8] While the resolution strongly praised the Soviet Union as the "vanguard" and "the most experienced and trained body" of the international Communist movement, its reference to the Moscow meeting's using "the method of consultation . . . for working out identical opinions," in the light of what we now know of its actual course, clearly indicated Albanian (and Chinese) opposition to the Soviet draft against "fractionalism" and

[4] The obvious comparison is to the 1948 Soviet-Yugoslav break; see Adam Ulam, *Tito and the Cominform* (Cambridge, Mass.: Harvard, 1951).

[5] This has been most recently, and very effectively, done by Zagoria, *The Sino-Soviet Conflict;* see especially his methodological remarks, pp. 24–38, and the excellent methodological analysis in Wolfgang Leonhard, *Kreml ohne Stalin* (Cologne: Kiepenheuer and Witsch, 1959), pp. 11–55.

[6] "Slanders and Fabrications Cannot Stand," *Zëri i Popullit,* Dec. 19 and 20, 1961, and Document 18.

[7] *Ibid.,* Dec. 21, 1960.

[8] Dated Dec. 20, 1960; text: *Ibid.*

Peking's demand that binding decisions be taken only unanimously.[9] The resolution also stressed the struggle against revisionism, fulsomely praised Hoxha, and referred to Moscow-Peking unity as "of special importance for the unity of the international Communist movement and for the unity of the whole socialist camp."

Only three days later Soviet Foreign Minister Gromyko, in his foreign-affairs speech to the Supreme Soviet, struck back at the Albanians by praising the Yugoslavs:

> Our relations with the Federal People's Republic of Yugoslavia can be described as good. They are developing normally. It should be noted with satisfaction that our positions on basic international issues coincide. The Soviet government hopes that cooperation between the two countries on questions of the struggle for peace and for a reduction of international tension will continue to develop successfully in the future as well. . . .[10]

According to the post-Twenty-Second Congress Soviet version,[11] *housing and transportation accommodations for Soviet specialists in Albania were cut in November and December 1960, around the time of Hoxha's premature return from Moscow. Later in December, after the Moscow meetings had concluded, the Soviets assert that they approached the Albanians with a proposal for "high-level economic talks," but the Albanians allegedly refused to participate.*[12] *The Albanians have recently declared, in a more documented version which seems closer to the truth, that on December 21, after the Albanian economic negotiator, Minister of Industry Spahiu, had been waiting in Moscow for two months for a decision, Soviet Deputy Foreign Trade Minister Semichastny declared that the trade and credit agreement under negotiation should be postponed for discussion "on a higher level."*[13]

A long theoretical article in the January 1961 issue of the Albanian

[9] See p. 52, *supra.*

[10] *Pravda,* Dec. 24, 1960; quoted from *CDSP,* XII, 52 (Jan. 25, 1961), pp. 10–16.

[11] Statement by Igor Ponomarev, a Soviet specialist in Tirana 1960–1961, in Radio Moscow in Albanian to Albania, Dec. 18, 1961, 1500 GMT, cited from British Broadcasting Corporation, *Summary of World Broadcasts,* Part I: USSR, (hereafter cited BBC/SU), second series, No. 826, Dec. 21, 1961, p. SU/826/A2/2; "The Truth about Soviet Specialists in Albania," *ibid.,* Dec. 26, 1961, 1100 GMT; and, for the Palace of Culture, "The Truth about the Palace of Culture in Tirana," *ibid.,* Dec. 24, 1961, 1500 GMT, both cited from BBC/SU/830/A2/1–2, Dec. 29, 1961; all three reproduced in Document 19.

[12] Leonid Sergeyev, "How the Present Albanian Leaders Rejected All CPSU Proposals to Solve Misunderstandings in a Comradely Way," *ibid.,* Feb. 8, 1962, 1500 GMT, in BBC/SU/867/A2/1, Feb. 10, 1962, and Document 23.

[13] "Khrushchev . . . ," *Zëri i Popullit,* Mar. 25, 1962, and Document 26.

party's theoretical monthly, like similar ones in Peking, appeared in part to present a unitary line; but it did not mention dogmatism or sectarianism, violently denounced the United States and Yugoslavia, and in other subtle ways echoed the April 1960 Chinese line.[14] There may have been some Albanian vacillation in early January 1961,[15] perhaps due to the first impact of the renewed Soviet economic pressure. Both Hoxha[16] and Shehu[17] fulsomely praised the Soviet Union, and the former denounced dogmatism and sectarianism as well as revisionism. Yet warm exchanges of telegrams between Mao and Hoxha[18] plus the departure on January 7 for Peking of an important Albanian economic delegation[19] make such an interpretation doubtful. In addition, neither the Soviet-Albanian exchange of New Year's greetings[20] nor the Soviet message of greeting on the occasion of the anniversary of the Albanian People's Republic[21] contained the phrase "dear comrades." Shortly thereafter the Albanian First Secretary was publicly referred to in Bulgaria as plain "Enver Hoxha," without the ritual prefix of "comrade."[22]

On January 6, according to later Albanian reports, the Soviet Embassy in Tirana, in a note to the Albanian government, reaffirmed Semichastny's statement in Moscow that only a meeting between Khrushchev and Hoxha could produce a new Soviet trade and credit agreement. Hardly by accident, the Albanian economic delegation left for Peking the next day. The Albanian Central Committee on January 14 refused to hold a Soviet-Albanian "summit meeting," declaring that it was unnecessary since the trade and credit agreement was already worked out and that the Soviet methods were "mistaken" and "unacceptable."[23]

Even so, during December, January, and February trade agreements were signed between Albania and the Soviet Union and the East European satellites, but only two satellites granted credit; the Soviet Union and the other satellites did not.[24] On January 26, in a greeting

[14] Agim Popa in *Rruga e Partisë,* VIII, 1 (Jan. 1961), pp. 11–23.
[15] Cf. Hamm, *Rebellen gegen Moskau,* p. 57.
[16] Hoxha to the Tirana city PPSh committee, *Zëri i Popullit,* Jan. 8, 1961.
[17] Shehu at Korçë, *ibid.,* Jan. 11, 1961.
[18] *Ibid.,* Jan. 13, 1961.
[19] *Ibid.,* Jan. 8, 1961.
[20] *Pravda,* Jan. 3, 1961.
[21] *Ibid.,* Jan. 11, 1961.
[22] *Rabotnichesko Delo,* Jan. 11, 1961.
[23] "Khrushchev . . . ," *Zëri i Popullit,* Mar. 25, 1962, and Document 26.
[24] Poland, Dec. 19, 1961 (*Bashkimi,* Dec. 20, 1960); USSR, Jan. 4, 1961 (TASS, Jan. 4, 1961); East Germany, Jan. 11, 1961 (credit) (*Zëri i Popullit,* Jan. 13, 1961); Romania, Jan. 13, 1961 (cited in Robert Schwanke, "Albaniens Aussenhandel 1948–1961," *Österreichische Osthefte,* VI, 2 (March 1962), pp. 130–136, at p. 133); Czechoslovakia, Feb. 2, 1961 (*Zëri i Popullit,* Feb. 21, 1961); Hungary, Jan. 23, 1961 (credit) (*Bashkimi,* Jan. 24, 1961); only Bulgaria was later, Apr. 29, 1961 (*ibid.,* Apr. 30, 1961). Altogether some $132–135 million

telegram sent by Albanian head of state Haxhi Lleshi to Ulbricht in return for the latter's telegram sent on the occasion of the fifteenth anniversary of Albania's national day, there appeared the phrase "the unity of the socialist camp headed by the Soviet Union."[25] However, in view of subsequent Albanian statements on this point,[26] as well as Albanian and Chinese use of the phrase thereafter,[27] it would appear that, in one of the many paradoxical turns taken by the Sino-Soviet Albanian dispute, in this context this ideological formula had become anti-Khrushchev. (The Chinese-Albanian use of this phrase emphasizes Soviet responsibility toward other Communist parties, defies Khrushchev's official abandonment of the phrase, and recalls Mao's insistence upon it at the November 1957 meetings, a move which in retrospect was in part intended — successfully — to wreck Khrushchev's policy of a rapprochement with Tito.)

In January 1961, the Albanians claim, Moscow stopped supplying building materials for the Tirana Palace of Culture. In that same month the Albanians (they claim) forwarded to the Soviet Embassy in Tirana a list of requests for technical assistance during 1961, including the extension of the stay of certain Soviet specialists. (This request was allegedly not answered by Moscow until April.)

On January 19 a new Soviet ambassador, Josif Shikin, arrived in Tirana.[28] Shikin was not just another Soviet ambassador. From 1945 to 1949 he had been head of the Main Political Administration of the Red Army; in 1949 he disappeared in the context of the purge of Zhdanov's followers subsequent to the latter's death.[29] He reappeared at the end of 1954[30] during Khrushchev's rise.

Immediately after his arrival a new crisis in Soviet-Albanian relations broke out. According to the Albanians, the Soviet Embassy in Tirana on January 20 abruptly informed the Albanian government that Moscow had decided to withdraw its oil specialists within the next week to ten

---

credits for the Albanian Third FYP has been scheduled: USSR, $83.75 million; CSR, $25 million; DDR, $10 million; CPR, $13.75 million. (See Theodor D. Zotschef, "Die wirtschaftlichen Probleme Albaniens," *Osteuropa-Wirtschaft,* VII, 1 [Mar. 1962], pp. 39–45.) Presumably the credits never materialized; see the Soviet declaration of April 26, 1961 (*infra*), in *Zëri i Popullit,* Dec. 6, 1961.

25 ADN, Jan. 26, 1961.

26 Most explicitly in "Deeper and Deeper into the Mire of Anti-Marxism," *Zëri i Popullit,* Jan. 9, 1962, and Document 22.

27 E.g., *ibid.,* Sept. 1, 1961.

28 *Ibid.,* Jan. 20, 1961. The appointment had been announced the previous November (*ibid.,* Nov. 25, 1960).

29 Robert Conquest, *Power and Policy in the U.S.S.R.* (New York: St. Martin's, 1961), p. 97.

30 Radio Moscow, Dec. 31, 1954, announcing the award to him of a medal for "length of service in the Soviet Army."

days. The Soviets, on the other hand, have declared that the Albanians ordered the oil specialists to leave the country within three days, and that on January 28, 1961, all Soviet specialists in the main directorate of geology were ordered by the Albanians to

> *. . . hand over the keys of their offices, filing cabinets, and desks; Albanian specialists and service personnel were present. When they returned to work the next day, specialists found that a secret search had been carried out at their place of work. . . .*[31]

The Albanians have replied that this was simply a regular security check and was participated in by Soviet specialists as well.

In any case — and this was the only public sign that a new Soviet-Albanian crisis had occurred — on January 20 a long ideological editorial appeared in the Albanian party newspaper.

In retrospect, particularly in view of what we now know of the details of the Sino-Soviet dispute, this editorial,[32] in addition to signaling a new Soviet-Albanian crisis, was the first detailed revelation of the main points at issue between Moscow and Peking (plus Tirana) in the Moscow November 1960 meetings. The editorial's contents have been confirmed by all later accounts of the Moscow meetings and by the continuation of the dispute thereafter.[33]

It began with a sharp and emotional reassertion of the primacy of the struggle against revisionism, the main danger. True, this formula had also been in the December 1960 Moscow Declaration; but the January 20 editorial never once mentioned dogmatism and sectarianism except to identify the struggle against them with the Yugoslavs. It also normally used the term "modern revisionism," an epithet which, as the course of the Sino-Soviet dispute has since made clear, is a peculiarly Sino-Albanian phrase often used by them so as implicitly to include Khrushchev as well as Tito.

The editorial asserted that the source of revisionism is "bourgeois ideology." On the other hand, at the October 1961 Twenty-Second Congress and thereafter the Soviets publicly developed the ideological thesis that the essence of both revisionism and dogmatism is "narrow nationalism" and have not stressed bourgeois influence as the origin of revisionism. One may therefore assume that at Moscow in November

[31] "The Truth About Soviet Specialists in Albania," cited in ftn. 11, *supra.*

[32] "The Struggle Against Revisionism as the Principal Danger in the International Communist and Workers Movement Is the Imperative Task of All Marxist-Leninist Countries," *Zëri i Popullit,* Jan. 20, 1961, and Document 5.

[33] E. Crankshaw in *The Observer* (London), Feb. 12, 19, 1961, the November 7, 1961, Hoxha speech (*Zëri i Popullit,* Nov. 8, 1961), and the Italian, French, and Belgian documents (cited in Ch. 2, ftns. 29, 5, 70, respectively).

1960 and generally during the Sino-Soviet dispute the Chinese and Albanians have maintained that revisionism is primarily a bourgeois rather than a nationalist deviation, and that the Soviets and their allies have maintained the contrary. This becomes even more probable in view of the fact that the epithets directed against the Yugoslavs in the January 20 Albanian editorial implicitly endorse (without mentioning) the 1949 Cominform resolution, which had declared that the Yugoslav leadership was not only right-wing nationalist deviationist (as the 1948 Cominform resolution had stated) but that, as its title indicated, the Yugoslav Communist Party was "in the power of murderers and spies."[34] The January 20 Albanian editorial refers to the League of Yugoslav Communists as the "traitorous revisionist clique of Tito" and as "traitors" carrying out the "special mission" of the imperialists, and to Yugoslavia as a *"place d'armes"* in the Balkans for the imperialists.[35]

The January 20 Albanian article's analysis of "Yugoslav revisionism" took a line which, seen in the context of subsequent statements made by Khrushchev and other Soviet leaders, often was directed against "right-wing opportunist" (i.e., Soviet) policy positions and particularly against Soviet policy toward Yugoslavia. This was followed by the assigning to "revisionism" of clearly Soviet views, and to its opponents ones of which the Soviets accused the Chinese and Albanians. The single most specific, and correct, charge against Khrushchev in this context was the implicit one that he considered Yugoslavia to be building socialism:[36]

> At the present time no Communist who holds firmly to the positions of Marxism-Leninism can say that the Tito clique is building socialism in Yugoslavia. . . .

Like the other Albanian charges against Yugoslavia, this represented one of the issues in dispute between the Soviets and the Chinese at the

[34] *For a Lasting Peace, for a People's Democracy!,* No. 28 (55), Nov. 29, 1949, p. 2.

[35] This attitude toward the Yugoslavs was nothing new for the Albanians or for the Chinese; beginning with the resumption of attacks against Belgrade in 1957, both have consistently maintained this position. See, e.g., "Modern Revisionism Should Be Combatted without Mercy until Its Complete Theoretical and Political Destruction," *Zëri i Popullit,* June 22, 1958, and "Let the Plotters and Revisionists of Belgrade Be Unmasked Through and Through," *ibid.,* July 17, 1960; and, for the CCP, "Modern Revisionism Must Be Criticized," *Jen-min Jih-pao,* May 5, 1958; Ch'en Po-ta, "Yugoslav Revisionism — Product of Imperialist Policy," *Hung Ch'i,* June 1, 1958; Hu Chi-pang, "Yugoslav Revisionism Viewed Through the Case of the Counter-revolutionary Nagy," *Jen-min Jih-pao,* June 18, 1959. English texts of the three Chinese articles: Vaclav Benes, Robert F. Byrnes, Nicolas Spulber, eds., *The Second Soviet-Yugoslav Dispute* (Indiana University Publications, Slavic and East European Series, Vol. 14, Bloomington, Ind., 1959, pp. 131–135, 170–180, 196–201. For analysis, see Zagoria, *op. cit.,* pp. 145–151.

[36] See his interview with C. L. Sulzberger, *New York Times,* Sept. 8, 1961, and *Pravda,* Sept. 10, 1961.

November 1960 Moscow meetings.[37] Furthermore, the article denounced what we can assume had been Khrushchev's position at these meetings, that the attacks against Yugoslavia should be toned down. It thus implicitly threatened Moscow with a serious deterioration in Sino-Soviet relations should it continue its insufficiently anti-Yugoslav line.

The editorial identified, and attacked as Yugoslav, policies which in fact were Soviet, for example, support of nonalignment. The editorial then insisted on the distinction between "real neutrality" and

> . . . the so-called "neutrality" of the Tito clique, which serves the most reactionary and warlike imperialist circles in order to divide the forces of peace. . . . There can be no common ground between the peaceful foreign policy of the socialist countries and that of the Tito clique. Whoever does not see this is blind.

The view expressed publicly by Gromyko the previous month that Soviet and Yugoslav foreign policy were essentially similar (one presumably also expressed by Khrushchev at the Bucharest and Moscow meetings) was thus violently denounced; on the contrary, the editorial declared, "the maneuvers of Tito . . . aim to divide and undermine the socialist camp and the international Communist movement. . . ." In a final passage in this section of the article "Yugoslav" became practically a synonym for "Soviet":

> In accordance with the Moscow declaration of 1960, the Albanian Party of Labor believes that it is necessary to fight modern revisionism, centered in Yugoslav revisionism, without mercy until its total defeat. Without unmasking revisionism it is impossible to unmask imperialism completely. It is necessary to unmask carefully and mercilessly the maneuvers of the Yugoslav revisionists, who under the pretext of fighting "dogmatism" attack Marxism-Leninism and under the pretext of fighting "leftist" deviationism deny the revolution; under the pretext of fighting against "sectarianism" and for a "flexible" policy, they preach unprincipled reconciliation with the middle class and capitulate before imperialism.

The accusation that Yugoslavia is an *agentura* of the imperialists was made most clear in respect to its receipt of United States aid, given because

> all the activities of the leaders of the Yugoslav revisionists serve the aims of imperialism . . .

because of the "Tito clique's"

> . . . active participation in the preparation and leadership of the counterrevolutionary coup in Hungary in 1956 . . .

and

[37] This has now been confirmed by *Interventi,* p. 75.

> . . . as a reward for Tito's visit to certain Asian and African countries, the aim of which was to alienate them from their friendship with the USSR and the other socialist countries and thus to weaken and disrupt the national liberation struggle of the colonial peoples and to assault and isolate the Communist parties in those parts of the world. . . .

The editorial concluded on a note of total defiance, foreshadowing the break the following October:

> . . . The Albanian Party of Labor is determined to pursue the struggle of principle against modern revisionism with firmness and consistency to the end, without any compromise.

The Fourth Albanian Party Congress, twice postponed,[38] met in Tirana from February 13 to 20.[39] Until it opened, only the January 20 Albanian editorial had indicated to the non-Communist world that serious differences with Moscow still persisted.[40] All the "fraternal parties" sent delegations.

Just before its opening, at a meeting on the evening of February 10[41] of the Chinese-Albanian Friendship Society, the militant mutuality of the Sino-Albanian ideological position and political support was starkly demonstrated.

The Albanian speaker, Abdyl Kellezi, declared:

> . . . the friendship between the Albanian and Chinese peoples is great and unbreakable. It is a close, fraternal friendship based on the immortal principles of Marxism-Leninism. It is a friendship steeled in our joint struggle for national liberation and for the sacred cause of building socialism and Communism in our two countries, in our joint struggle against U.S.-led imperialism and its lackey — the Belgrade Tito clique which

[38] *Zëri i Popullit,* Oct. 9, 1960 (postponed from November to December 1960), and *ibid.,* Dec. 21, 1960 (Dec. 1960 to Feb. 1961).

[39] For Albanian declarations at the congress, see *Zëri i Popullit* and Radio Tirana, Feb. 14–21, 1961, and "The Party's General Line Has Been and Will Always Be Correct," *Zëri i Popullit,* Feb. 17, 1961; cf. Zbigniew Brzezinski, "Albania Defies the Kremlin," *The New Leader,* XLIV, 13 (Mar. 27, 1961), p. 8.

[40] The proceedings of the PPSh CC Plenum on Feb. 6 were not published (*Zëri i Popullit,* Feb. 7, 1961). A February 8 *Bashkimi* article by Adil Çarçani, "The Albanian Party of Labor — the Glorious Leader of Our People," added nothing to previous Albanian pronouncements and was considerably less violent than the January 20 *Zëri i Popullit* one. However, although the congress slogans (*Zëri i Popullit,* Feb. 13, 1961) spoke of "the great socialist camp headed by the Soviet Union," this had become an anti-Khrushchev formula, and that day's *Zëri i Popullit* editorial, "The Congress of Great Victories and Prospects," referred to "the great Chinese people" but only to "the Soviet people." See also an account by Sepp Wodratzka (the Austrian Communist delegate) in *Weg und Ziel* (Vienna) XIX, 12 (Dec. 1961), pp. 799–802.

[41] *Zëri i Popullit,* Feb. 11, 1961.

> represents modern revisionism — and in our unswerving struggle for the defense of the purity of Marxism-Leninism.

The Chinese head of the society, Chiang Nan-hsiang, replied:

> . . . the heroic Albanian people have had a glorious revolutionary tradition under the correct leadership of the Albanian Party of Labor headed by Comrade Enver Hoxha, the long-tested Albanian leader. Guided by the slogan "with a pick in one hand and a rifle in the other," the Albanian people have been working at once for the defense of their sacred fatherland and for the building of their beautiful country, displaying their indomitable militant spirit and dauntless heroism. The Chinese people always have followed the accomplishments of the Albanian people with great joy and admiration. Your victories are our victories, the victories of the socialist camp. They are serious blows at the imperialist camp headed by U.S. imperialism and modern revisionism represented by the Tito clique of Yugoslavia, and are at the same time contributions to the cause of world peace and human progress. The Albanian Party of Labor is a militant Marxist-Leninist party. It always has remained true to the principles of Marxism-Leninism and proletarian internationalism, resolutely defending the unity of the socialist camp and the international Communist movement. It has always persisted in the stand defined in the Moscow declaration and statement, carried on an irreconcilable, stubborn struggle against modern revisionism represented by the Tito clique of Yugoslavia, and defended the purity of Marxism-Leninism. The Chinese and Albanian people will always stand together in their joint struggle against imperialism and for the building of socialism, supporting and encouraging each other and advancing shoulder to shoulder in their struggle.

The only Albanian speeches at the congress which provided new information and ideological and policy lines were those of Hoxha and Shehu on February 13;[42] all the other Albanian speeches and the final resolution[43] merely echoed them. The most important new material in Hoxha's speech was his announcement of the uncovering of a "criminal plot" against the regime carried on by

> . . . Yugoslavia and Greece, in collaboration with certain Albanian traitors, who are either in our country or have deserted to Yugoslavia, and in conjunction with the American Sixth Fleet in the Mediterranean. . . .

This "plot" was presumably the attempt in the summer of 1960, with probable Yugoslav and Soviet support, to overthrow Hoxha and Shehu, as a result of which Belishova, Tashko, and others were purged and arrested. Nevertheless, as of this writing Hoxha still officially maintains the Yugoslav-Greek-American version, although recent Albanian propa-

[42] *Ibid.*, Feb. 14, 1961.
[43] Feb. 20, 1961; text: *ibid.*, Feb. 22, 1961.

ganda output has been steadily edging toward alleging Soviet participation as well.

The primary objective of Hoxha's announcement of the "plot" was to give specific substantiation to his violently anti-Yugoslav line, thus gaining further popularity among the anti-Yugoslav Albanians and further defying Moscow. Hoxha's epithets against Tito were if anything stronger than ever, a sure indicator that relations with the Soviet Union were still worsening:

> . . . Tito's traitorous revisionist group . . . is the most aggressive and dangerous detachment of modern international revisionism, and a trained secret service agency of imperialism, chiefly of U.S. imperialism. . . .

His use of the term "agents of imperialism" and the designation in an authoritative Albanian editorial a few days later of the Yugoslavs as "a dangerous *agentura* of imperialism"[44] continued the complete Albanian return to the language of the 1949 Cominform resolution and indicated that this was presumably the Albanian and Chinese position on Yugoslavia at the Bucharest and Moscow meetings as well.

Much of Hoxha's attack against the Yugoslavs, however, was clearly directed against Moscow. (It also strikingly resembled the substance and often the very words of Khrushchev's charges against Hoxha in October 1961):

> . . . The Yugoslav revisionists have engaged in all sorts of attacks and calumnies against us, at times accusing us of being "nationalists," and at other times of being "dogmatists" and "sectarians," or people "who understand nothing of Marxism." This is a familiar tactic of the opportunists and revisionists of all periods in the fight against revolutionary Marxism.

Shehu used the same tactic even more clearly in his speech.[45]

Hoxha also, without so indicating, rejected several Soviet policy positions. Thus he declared that while the world balance of power has changed in favor of socialism, the Albanian party "has not underestimated the might of imperialism," which does not want peace. Therefore, "peace will not be assured by making concessions or showing flattery toward the imperialists" (again a jibe at Khrushchev). The Albanian party is in favor of summit talks, he continued, but

> . . . no international problem can be solved without the participation . . . of the Chinese People's Republic. . . .

44 "The Party's General Line Has Been and Will Always Be Correct," *ibid.*, Feb. 17, 1961.

45 *Ibid.*, Feb. 18, 1961.

(This was a position which Khrushchev clearly had not adopted.)

On peaceful coexistence, Hoxha's formulation and even more clearly the formulation of the final congress resolution were almost identical with the Chinese ones:

> . . . The principle of peaceful coexistence, formulated by the great Lenin, is defined in the Moscow Declaration of November 1960 as the only correct and reasonable principle in relations between states with different social systems under conditions of the division of the world into two opposing systems.
>
> The struggle to achieve peaceful coexistence is carried out through the struggle of countries of the socialist camp and other peace-loving countries to settle the concrete problems of present-day international life through negotiations, the struggle of the peoples for national liberation, and the struggle for peace. The peoples must impose this on the imperialists, who will not voluntarily renounce the "cold war," military blocs, and the arms race, just as they will not renounce intervention in the internal affairs of other countries, violation of the independence and sovereignty of peoples, and so forth.

With the exception of the first two sentences of the last quotation above, none of the quoted passages, and no reference at all to the plot, appeared in the *Pravda* version of the Hoxha speech.[46]

In view of what we now know of Soviet political and economic moves against the Albanians, Shehu's speech made even clearer than Hoxha's the Albanian determination to maintain their defiance in spite of these Soviet measures:

> The imperialists and the revisionists have done and will continue to do everything to convert this geographical encirclement into an economic blockade and political isolation against our socialist country. But they . . . will never achieve their aim. . . .

Shehu's prescription for those who impaired party unity was:

> For those who stand in the way of party unity: a spit in the face, a sock in the jaw, and if necessary, a bullet in the head. . . .[47]

The congress was also important for the speeches and messages of greeting by foreign delegates. It was the first occasion on which it was possible from published material (the speeches and messages of the "fraternal parties") to classify so many according to the issues they emphasized. In general the line-up, as shown by Table 3.1, was en-

[46] *Pravda,* Feb. 16, 1961.

[47] The report by an Albanian police defector (*Die Welt,* July 31, 1961) that 72 Albanian delegates to the congress were purged as pro-Soviet has not been confirmed.

tirely in accord with the evidence previously summarized from earlier occasions. The Chinese were completely on the side of the Albanians, and so apparently were the other East Asian parties: North Korean, North Vietnamese, Indonesian, Japanese, and Malayan. (Published evidence does not make it possible to classify them by the degree of their support.) All the other East European parties were on the side of the Soviets, as were the French and the Italians. But within this group there were clear distinctions. The French were almost frenetically pro-Khrushchev; their delegate's speech praised him six times by name, two more than Pospelov, the Soviet delegate, did.[48] Pospelov's speech was ideologically clearly, but not strongly, anti-Chinese, and anti-Albanian. The Polish delegate was Roman Nowak, in 1956 one of the pro-Soviet Natolin group, and demoted by Gomułka thereafter; the Polish leadership, in a nicely ironic gesture, had sent him to deliver one of the most clearly pro-Soviet (and implicitly anti-Albanian and anti-Chinese) speeches. Nowak declared:

> The supreme task for all our parties . . . is to fight to prevent the disaster of thermonuclear war. . . . Anything that can undermine the policy of peaceful coexistence . . . adherence to obsolete theses of the inevitability of war, may harm the cause of socialism and peace. . . .

He said that "the Leninist leadership of the CPSU, headed by Comrade Khrushchev," was "particularly worthy" in strengthening Polish-Soviet friendship, and that

> The successes of the socialist states — both internal and international — are based on . . . the Leninist ideas of the Twentieth Congress of the CPSU. . . . The world Communist movement, freed from the errors and distortions of the period of the cult of the personality . . . has entered a new phase of its development. . . . If one fails to understand this, one loses a sense of reality, lags behind, and divorces oneself from the world Communist army, which marches on. . . . Any attempt at opposing in practice the principles of equality and self-dependence of each Marxist-Leninist party to the principles of unity of action can do our cause irreparable harm and can only weaken the world forces of socialism. . . .[49]

The Italian delegate was quite as right-wing as the Polish. After fulsomely praising Khrushchev, he declared that dogmatism and sectarianism

[48] Speech by Gustave Ansart, *Zëri i Popullit,* Feb. 16, 1961. See also his interview "Sur l'attitude du Parti du travail," *France Nouvelle,* Nov. 15–21, 1961, summarized, with extensive quotations, in "Un communiste français au IVe congrès du Parti du travail albanais," *Est et ouest,* XIV, 284 (Sept. 16–30, 1962), pp. 15–18.

[49] *Ibid.,* Feb. 17, 1961; quoted from a briefer version in *Trybuna Ludu,* Feb. 19, 1961.

TABLE 3.1

Some of the Major Issues Disputed at the Albanian Congress

	Italian Party: Roasio	French Party: Ansart	USSR: Pospelov	Bulgaria: Velchev	Romania: Voicu	North Korea: Kum-chol	East Germany: Axen	Vietnam: Duy Trinh	Czechoslovakia: Barák	Poland: Nowak	China: Li Hsien-nien	Indonesian Party: Supit	Japanese Party: Yonehara	Malayan Party: Greeting	Hungarian Party: Ilku
War can be and should be averted	S	ER	ER	F	S	0	S	0	S	ER	F	0	0	0	0
Imperialism and war threat emphasized	0	F	F	0	0	S	0	0	0	0	S	0	F	0	0
Revisionism in general attacked	F	F	S	F	F	0	F	0	F	F	S	ER	F	ER	F
Yugoslav revisionism singled out	0	F	F	F	0	S	F	S	F	0	S	F	F	ER	0
Dogmatism attacked	F	S	S	F	F	0	F	0	S	F	F	0	0	0	0
The Twentieth CPSU "anti-Stalin" Congress endorsed	0	0	S	S	0	0	S	0	S	ER	0	0	0	0	0
Positive references to Khrushchev	1	6	4	1	2	0	2	0	1	2	0	3	0	0	1
Positive references to Hoxha	0	0	0	0	0	1	0	1	0	0	2	3	0	2	0
Praise of the "correct" leadership of the Albanian party	0	0	0	0	0	ER	0	ER	0	0	ER	S	0	S	0

CODE: ER — emphatic, repeated assertions; S — strong assertion; F — formal assertion; 0 — no mention.
SOURCE: A revised and expanded version of the chart in Brzezinski, *The Soviet Bloc,* second edition, p. 433, on the basis of the texts in *Zëri i Popullit,* February 15–19, 1961.

> . . . espouse the theory of passivity while waiting for the hour of decision. The Italian Communist Party always strives to enter as a decisive force into the new reality — the struggle for peace, democracy, and socialism. . . .

His organizational formula was the most right-wing of those expressed at the congress and reminds one of Yugoslav doctrines. He urged international solidarity among Communist parties

> . . . based on the reciprocal exchange of experience and critical cooperation. This international solidarity does not, however, exclude the transition to socialism along different paths for different countries. . . .[50]

The most striking speech to the congress was by the head of the Czechoslovak delegation, Rudolf Barák, then still a Politburo member and Interior Minister in Prague.[51] He identified "isolated" Albania's security entirely with Khrushchev:

> The Warsaw Pact, created on the initiative of the Leninist Central Committee of the CPSU, and Comrade Nikita Sergeyevich Khrushchev personally, guarantees . . . the security and defense of the Albanian People's Republic. . . .

He stressed the "great importance" of the Twentieth Congress, which

> . . . emphasized a peaceful policy and resolutely put an end to the harmful consequences of the cult of the individual.

He declared that the necessity for peaceful coexistence means that any attempt at narrowing the "front of peace-loving forces" would be a "sectarian mistake," and praised Khrushchev's performance at the Fifteenth United Nations General Assembly meeting the previous fall as having advanced the cause of peace. He stated that revisionism in general and Yugoslav revisionism in particular had "failed," thus deemphasizing the necessity of struggle against them. His attitude toward dogmatism, however, was implicitly more unfavorable, i.e., more anti-Chinese and anti-Albanian:

> In our days, confronted with the duty to mobilize all our forces in the struggle against imperialism, and for the prevention of war and the strengthening of peace, dogmatism and sectarianism could do great harm to our cause. Dogmatism does not wish to see, and cannot understand, the great changes which are taking place in the world. . . .

[50] Antonio Roasio, *Zëri i Popullit,* Feb. 17, 1961.

[51] *Ibid.,* Feb. 19, 1961. The version published the same day in *Rudé Právo,* although containing favorable general references to the XX CPSU Congress and to Khrushchev, did not include the specific passages quoted below; it seems likely their omission was an intentional anti-Barák move on the part of Novotný.

(After Barák's arrest in February 1962 for "anti-party" and "anti-state" activities,[52] Tirana[53] intimated that he had been trying, perhaps through Khrushchev's favor, to replace Novotný. Although Barák's Tirana February 1961 speech might be thought to add some credence to this hypothesis, it seems more likely that Novotný feared that Barák's popularity and his own difficult position might eventually result in Barák challenging him; he therefore preferred, by Barák's "prophylactic" removal, to run no such chances.)

The height of discord at the congress, the walkout of the Greek Communist delegation after the Albanians had refused to allow it to speak, became known from Greek and French Communist accounts only after the Moscow-Tirana diplomatic break.[54] *The draft Greek greeting message to the congress*

> *. . . spoke of the presence of gross deviations from Leninist norms and of the cult of the personality, which had grave consequences for our party. . . .*

The Albanians, however, "evidently thought this was directed at them" and, the Greek accounts continue, "decided to prevent its reading to the congress." Thereupon Shehu in the presence of all the foreign delegates

[52] KSČ CC Communiqué, *Rudé Právo,* Feb. 9, 1962; Novotný speech at Bratislava, Radio Prague, Feb. 22, 1962, 1800 GMT (BBC/EE/879/C3/4, Feb. 24, 1962), which was softened in the *Rudé Právo* version (Feb. 23, 1962) and removed entirely in the Prosecutor-General's interim report (*ibid.,* Mar. 25, 1962). (This softening was probably the result of second thoughts in the KSČ leadership, although Moscow may have played a secondary role in it. Cf. "Trial Splits Czech Communists," *The Sunday Telegraph* [London], Apr. 1, 1962.) Barák had been removed as Minister of the Interior the previous June (*Rudé Právo,* June 24, 1961). In 1956 he and Zápotocký, whom Novotný criticized after the 22nd CPSU Congress (*ibid.,* Nov. 21, 1961), were considered in Prague Communist circles as potential replacements for Novotný. See the excellent analysis by E.[rnst] H.[alperin], "Tschechoslowakischer Stalinismus," *Die Tat* (Zürich), Mar. 7, 1962; cf. another article by Halperin in *ibid.,* Feb. 10, 1962, and Ivo Duchacek, "Czechoslovakia: The Past Reburied," *Problems of Communism,* XI, 3 (May–June 1962), pp. 22–26, at pp. 24–25.

[53] "Rudolf Barák — Conspirator Unmasked," *Zëri i Popullit,* Feb. 16, 1962; cf. Blagoje Lazić (from Prague), "The Czechoslovak Public Still Has Not Been Told the Reasons for Barák's Replacement," *Borba,* Feb. 11, 1962.

[54] See account of an interview with the head of the Greek Communist delegation, Panos Dimitrious, "Greece Will Not Bow Her Head," *Literaturnaya Gazeta,* Nov. 11, 1961; an interview with the head of the French Communist delegation, Ansart, in *France-Nouvelle, loc. cit.;* the report of the Greek Communist delegation to the XXII CPSU Congress, delivered to the II Greek CC Plenum, in the Greek party's theoretical monthly *Neos Kosmos* (Bucharest), No. 12, 1961, and broadcast over the clandestine Voice of Truth in Greek to Greece, Dec. 14–17, 1961; "Deeper into the Mire of Anti-Internationalism and Disunity," *Neos Kosmos,* No. 2, 1962, broadcast over Voice of Truth, Feb. 4, 1962, 1735 GMT. For the Albanian version, see "Rudolf Barák — Conspirator Unmasked," *Zëri i Popullit,* Feb. 16, 1962.

"resorted to unprecedented provocations, insults, and threats," declared that the Greek representative, Dimitri Panayotis, was a spy of the Karamanlis government in Athens,[55] *and thus "obliged" him to leave the congress. The Greek Communist Central Committee immediately protested this, but the Albanians supported Shehu. According to the Greeks and French, the French, Czechoslovak, Romanian, East German, and "other" parties also protested. The Albanians have since declared that Andropov and Barák, the head of the Czechoslovak delegation, organized this "provocation."*

This incident primarily reflected nationalistic Greek-Albanian tension. The Greek party, released after 1948 from Yugoslav influence, thereafter opposed the incorporation of any of "Aegean Macedonia" (i.e., Greek Macedonia) into Yugoslavia,[56] and it may well also have taken a far from totally pro-Albanian attitude on the "Northern Epirus" question. As with the Venizelos incident, the Soviets were undoubtedly only too glad to utilize the anti-Albanian Greek Communist feelings in order further to infuriate the Albanians.[57]

As this Greek interlude shows, the atmosphere at the congress must have been tense indeed. *According to the French delegate (writing after the Soviet-Albanian break), most of the foreign delegations refused to applaud many of the Albanian declarations. The Italian delegate later stated that various delegations discussed leaving the congress in protest. In any case, many of them sent letters of protest, and apparently not only about the Greek episode.*[58]

On February 20, the day the Albanian congress closed, Pospelov, Andropov, and Shikin were received by Hoxha. The communiqué stated that the discussion was "very cordial and friendly."[59]

But, as the Soviets later told the story, just the contrary was the case. At the Soviet Twenty-Second Congress in October 1961, Pospelov said:

> *. . . during the last congress of the Albanian Party of Labor we encountered a number of glaring instances of direct anti-Soviet attacks by prominent Albanian officials, instances of a humiliating, hostile attitude toward*

[55] The Albanians later publicly declared this (*ibid*).

[56] R. V. Burks, *The Dynamics of Communism in Eastern Europe* (Princeton, 1961), pp. 91–106.

[57] In early March (*Pravda*, Mar. 12, 1961), Moscow (like Barák at the Conference) declared that Albania's "sovereignty and territorial integrity are guaranteed by the Warsaw Pact," but the Albanians deleted this passage from the *Zëri i Popullit* version on March 14. Cf. Ivan Ramos Ribeiro in the Brazilian CP weekly *Novos Rumos* (Rio de Janeiro, edition for Guanabara), No. 157, Feb. 9–15, 1962, p. 4.

[58] Roasio in *L'Unità*, Oct. 29, 1961; Ansart in *France Nouvelle, loc. cit.* (with text of PCF letter of protest, dated Feb. 20, 1961).

[59] *Zëri i Popullit*, Feb. 21, 1961 and Novotný in *Rudé Právo*, Feb. 23, 1962.

> *our specialists, geologists, and Soviet seamen. On behalf of the Central Committee, we handed the Albanian leaders the following protest and warning on Feb. 20, 1961:*
>
> *"The Central Committee of our party considers that such instances not only impede the development and strengthening of Albanian-Soviet friendship but also run counter to the interests of the entire socialist camp. If these abnormal phenomena are not stopped in good time, they may entail serious consequences."*[60]

On that same evening, Moscow later asserted:

> *. . . deputy director Skender Salija of the directorate of geology in Tirana, after removing the lock and seal from the doors to rooms occupied by Soviet geologist Lautin, searched the material in his desk and cabinet. . . .*[61]

From then on, the lives of the Soviet and East European specialists were far from easy; the Albanians harassed them constantly.[62]

The unity of theory and practice was operating, even if still temporarily concealed behind a facade of "socialist cordiality." At the beginning of March the Chinese again publicly declared their total support of Albania.[63]

In March, according to the Albanians, Khrushchev and Novotný informed Tirana that all Soviet and Czechoslovak economic aid to Albania would be cut off,[64] *presumably as a result of the events during the Albanian party congress.*

On March 19 a series of particularly detailed attacks against the Albanians began appearing in *Borba.* At the end of March, Hoxha was the only East European First Secretary who did not attend a Warsaw Pact meeting; Minister of Defense Balluku represented Albania instead.[65]

On April 13, according to Tirana, the Soviets canceled the unloading of materials for the Palace of Culture which had arrived in the harbor of Durrës on a Soviet ship. In any case, Moscow, in a note delivered April 25, 1961, informed Tirana that the Soviet specialists would be withdrawn because of Albania's "unfriendly attitude" and "pressure" toward them, and that Albanian-Soviet relations "henceforth" would be "on a new basis." In a letter dated April 26 and signed by Soviet First Deputy Premier Alexei Kosygin, Moscow, according to a 1962 Al-

[60] *Pravda,* Oct. 28, 1961; quoted from *CDSP,* XIV, 5 (Feb. 28, 1962), p. 20.

[61] "The Truth About Soviet Specialists in Albania," cited in ftn. 11, *supra.*

[62] Hamm, *op. cit.,* pp. 82–83.

[63] Lo Shih-kao, "The Victorious Struggle of the Albanian People," *Hung Ch'i,* No. 5, Mar. 1, 1961, pp. 17–24 (JPRS 8480, June 23, 1961).

[64] "Slanders and Fabrications Cannot Stand," *Zëri i Popullit,* Dec. 19, 1961, and Document 18.

[65] *Pravda,* Mar. 31, 1961; cf. Medvedev in *Izvestiya,* Feb. 4, 1962, and AP from Belgrade in the *New York Herald Tribune,* Mar. 31, 1961.

banian version, formally announced the cancellation of all economic aid to Albania:

> *After weighing all the circumstances, the Soviet Government is obliged to re-examine the question of future relations with the Albanian People's Republic. . . . The Soviet people and the peoples of the other socialist countries would not understand us if we, while depriving our country of material resources, should continue to satisfy the demands of the Albanian leaders who, to the detriment of the interests of the Albanian people, have trampled on elementary norms in relations with the USSR and its government. . . . It is understandable that the Albanian leadership cannot expect in the future that the USSR will help it as it has in the past, with aid from which only true friends and brothers have the right to benefit. The Soviet Union deems it necessary henceforth to establish its relations with Albania on a new basis, taking into account the unfriendly policy of its leadership toward the Soviet Union and the other socialist countries. . . . As concerns future relations between our countries, and USSR aid to Albania, these will depend entirely on the attitude adopted by the Albanian party. . . .*[66]

The Albanians maintain that some 50 Soviet specialists were ordered by Moscow to leave the very next day, and that all the others left "in the next few days."[67] *(None of this was known in the West until late summer of 1961.)*

On the same day, April 26, something did happen which was made public at the time but whose full significance (as a clearer albeit still esoteric warning by Moscow that it might favor Belgrade over Tirana) becomes clear only in the light of the immediately and hardly coincidentally preceding Soviet and Albanian moves: the announcement in Moscow and Belgrade of the forthcoming exchange of visits between the Soviet and Yugoslav Foreign Ministers, Gromyko and Popović, to begin the following month with a visit by Popović to Moscow.[68] (The visit in fact did not occur until July that same year.) Albanian attacks on Yugoslavia reached new heights.[69]

A new Soviet-Chinese trade agreement was finally signed on Apri 7,[70] but, in what could only have been interpreted in Moscow as a studied gesture of defiance and contempt, and in the first public indication that Sino-Soviet relations remained tense, Peking two weeks later signed a trade agreement with Tirana providing for Chinese credits o

[66] As quoted in "Khrushchev . . . ," *Zëri i Popullit,* Mar. 25, 1962, and Document 26.

[67] *Ibid.*

[68] *Pravda* and *Borba,* Apr. 26, 1961.

[69] "Another Act in the Long Chain of Hostile Activity by the Yugoslav Government Against Albania," *Zëri i Popullit,* Apr. 8, 1961, and Sofokli Lazri and Javer Malo, "Provocations to Cover Provocations," *ibid.,* Apr. 12, 1961.

[70] *Pravda,* Apr. 9, 1961.

112.5 million rubles ($123 million) during the next four years, roughly equal to the $132 to $135 million credits promised by the Soviet Union and the East European countries for the same period.[71]

In April the Chinese for about three million dollars bought 60,000 metric tons (2.2 million bushels) of Canadian wheat for Albania, where it was shipped the next month.[72]

There was only one public signal within the world Communist movement that a major turning point in Soviet-Albanian, and indeed in Sino-Soviet, relations was under way, one bound to renew the drift toward polycentrism within the world Communist movement. Appropriately and far from accidentally, the signal came from the father of polycentrism and the head of the Italian Communist Party, Palmiro Togliatti, in an article he published in April 1961 in the Italian Communist theoretical journal.[73] Careful as ever, Togliatti had held his hand until he was sure of Khrushchev's determination to force the Chinese to yield and of the Chinese refusal to do so. When he wrote the article, he must have known that Khrushchev had cut off Soviet economic aid to Tirana and was intensifying his relations with Tito, another tendency which Togliatti had long favored. Furthermore, the article's reference to Poland indicates that Togliatti was again (as in 1956) strengthening his relations with Gomułka, the bloc leader to whom his policy views were closest.

The Togliatti article was the second of the only two public criticisms of the Albanians by name (the first was by Ulbricht in the previous December)[74] which appeared anywhere in the Communist press until the Twenty-Second Soviet Party Congress. Togliatti's, however, was different from Ulbricht's. The latter had merely labeled the Albanians "dogmatic and sectarian." Togliatti put the matter on a different plane:

> When we had learned, for example, from our comrade who was present at the recent congress of the Albanian Party that at that congress questions of the life and internal debate of the party were posed in a manner which to us seemed erroneous and dangerous, we made known our opinion, but the direct responsibility and correction do not belong to us. . . .

Thus by not identifying in what way the Albanians' views were "erroneous and dangerous," and by making clear that this was not his but by implication their problem, Togliatti for the first time implicitly

[71] See Zotschef, *op. cit.*

[72] Statement by Canadian Minister of Agriculture Hamilton, in UPI dispatch from Ottawa, Aug. 9, 1961.

[73] Palmiro Togliatti, "A proposito di socialismo e democrazia," *Rinascita,* XVIII, (Apr. 1961), pp. 353–363, at p. 361; cf. *Nova Makedonija,* Apr. 7, 1961.

[74] *Neues Deutschland,* Dec. 18, 1960.

recognized the potential organizational community of interest between all small Communist parties, be they rightist or leftist in policies, which did not wish to be totally subservient to Moscow.

At the conclusion of the article, in another significant passage, Togliatti made clear that his views were to the right of Moscow's and close to the Poles':

> . . . it is interesting to us, at the end of our discussion, to underline the diversity and richness of the political and economic forms which, in those regimes, have been adopted in the work toward the solution of the most serious problems of socialism, such as those of the relationship between industrial development and that of agriculture and handicrafts, of the proper equilibrium between the output of producer and consumer goods, of the terms of collective management of the countryside, of the international division of labor on a socialist basis, and of the attitude to problems of coexistence and collaboration among various parties, of the activity of a parliament (the Polish one, for example) as an effective organ of direction and control over all economic life, etc., etc. They have already accumulated, in these diverse fields, enormous experience, which cannot be rejected, but which must be studied profoundly and attentively, because whether one wants it or not, it contains a precious contribution to the solution of the most grave problems which weigh on men in our advance toward the creation of a new society, liberated from the exploitation and the oppression of capitalism. . . .

In May 1961 a show trial opened in Tirana. In it Moscow-traine Rear Admiral Teme Sejko,[75] Tahir Demi (formerly Albanian repre sentative to CMEA),[76] and other officials were charged with involvemen in a "plot" organized by the Yugoslavs, the Greeks, and the America Sixth Fleet[77] to overthrow the Albanian regime. An Albanian genera who had fled to Yugoslavia in 1957, Panajot Plaku, was also implicated Belishova and Tashko were not tried; not until after Khrushchev's at tack on the Albanian leadership at the Twenty-Second CPSU Congres in October 1961 did Hoxha clearly imply that they had been plottin with Moscow against him.[78] The May trial was eerily reminiscent of th Rajk and Slánský trials in Hungary and Czechoslovakia in 1949 an 1952; the defendants all confessed and were found guilty, and in th same month (May 1961) four of them, including Rear Admiral Sejk were shot. The evidence at the trial stressed very strongly the maj

[75] Admiral Sejko had been trained in Moscow, 1947–1949 and 1956–1958; se Lazitch, *op. cit.*, p. 15.

[76] Lamberg, *op. cit.*

[77] *Zëri i Popullit* and Radio Tirana, May 16–26, 1961.

[78] In his November 7, 1961, speech (*Zëri i Popullit,* Nov. 8, 1961) and Doc ment 14.

cause of Hoxha's anti-Soviet policy, his fear of reabsorption into the Yugoslav sphere of influence:

> *Defendant:* . . . It was foreseen that northern Albania would become a zone of material or moral influence for the Yugoslavs, while southern Albania would pass under the material and moral influence of the Greeks. The Çamëria region would become autonomous under the Greek government. . . .

It again took a clearly anti-Khrushchev position on one of the major ideological issues between Moscow and Tirana:

> *Defendant:* . . . In fact, Yugoslavia is a capitalist state but they pretend that it is a socialist one. . . .[79]

With the exception of one probably inadvertent reference in the Bulgarian trade-union paper *Trud* on May 28, the Soviet and East European press and radio maintained complete silence on the trial until Khrushchev's October 1961 speech at the Twenty-Second CPSU Congress.[80]

In late spring 1961 signs again multiplied in Tirana that Soviet-Albanian relations were worsening.[81] In mid-May press dispatches from Belgrade[82] indicated that two Albanian Foreign Ministry officials had been executed as Soviet spies, but the next month Tirana declared them "monstrous fabrications,"[83] and it is still uncertain whether they were true. All Soviet diplomats and officials in Tirana were reportedly put under Albanian police surveillance, and all pictures of Khrushchev on public buildings were replaced by ones of Stalin.[84] At the end of May the Soviet submarines which since the war had been stationed at the naval base on the island of Sazan (Sasseno), outside Vlorë, were withdrawn.[85] (One wonders if the Albanians, presumably with Chinese

[79] Quoted from *Bashkimi,* May 20, 1961; cf. Khrushchev to Sulzberger, *New York Times,* Sept. 8, 1961, and *Pravda,* Sept. 10, 1961.

[80] Cf. *The Economist,* June 10, 1961, p. 1099. ADN mentioned it (probably by error); *Neues Deutschland* did not.

[81] These first became generally known in the West through the dispatches of West German correspondents who were allowed by Tirana to visit Albania in July and August. See especially the comprehensive articles by Harry Hamm, "Albanien auf Chinesischen Kurs," *Frankfurter Allgemeine,* Oct. 3, 1961; "Albanien unter dem Joch der Polizei," *ibid.,* Oct. 7, 1961, and his *Rebellen gegen Moskau,* and an article by an AP correspondent, Carl E. Buchalla, "Albanien wie es heute aussieht," *Stuttgarter Zeitung,* Sept. 30, 1961.

[82] *New York Times,* May 18, 1961; cf. Radio Athens, May 18, 1961, 1100 GMT.

[83] ATA, June 9, 1961.

[84] *The Observer* (London), May 21, 1961, quoting Belgrade dispatches and reports of "a Western legation in Tirana."

[85] Eight Soviet submarines and a tender spent eight hours at Gibraltar on the night of June 1 (Floyd in *The Daily Telegraph* [London], June 3, 1961, and Newell Hall in *ibid.,* June 5, 1961). The rumors from Polish and Austrian Com-

support, had successfully insisted upon their departure, or if the Soviets did this as another gesture of their displeasure and of the risks they would be willing to take. In any case, thermonuclear warfare and long-range missiles had diminished the base's value to the Soviet Union.)[86]

The Soviet and East European diplomatic missions in Tirana were drastically reduced. On July 6 (the Albanians stated in early 1962) the Albanian Central Committee in a letter to the Soviet Central Committee again reiterated its stand that bilateral talks were not possible as long as Moscow continued its political, economic, and military pressure on Albania.[87]

The Albanian regime printed only a brief summary of the new Soviet Draft Program.[88] Beginning in late June, Western monitors noted that Tirana was deleting from Radio Moscow Albanian-language broadcasts (relayed and rebroadcast by Radio Tirana) passages contrary to the Albanian general line, notably all references and quotations from Khrushchev and all statements concerning Soviet relations with and aid to underdeveloped countries.[89]

By May, Soviet and East European tourists had ceased to come to Albania.[90] During the summer Chinese technicians began to arrive[91] to replace the withdrawing Soviet and East European ones,[92] another assurance to Hoxha of the support which he could depend upon from Peking.

Denials by Tirana to the contrary,[93] it appears that Albania indirectly

---

munist sources that the Albanians kept some of the Soviet vessels behind remain unconfirmed. Cf. Hamm, *Rebellen gegen Moskau,* p. 66.

86 Philip Mosely, "Khrushchev's Party Congress," *Foreign Affairs,* XL, 2 (Jan. 1962), pp. 183–195.

87 "Khrushchev . . . ," *Zëri i Popullit,* Mar. 25, 1962, and Document 26.

88 *Ibid.,* Aug. 2, 1961.

89 "Uneasy Relations Between Tirana and the Soviet Bloc," BBC Overseas Service Central Research Unit, Background Note No. 711 (mimeo.), Sept. 30, 1961.

90 Hamm, *op. cit.,* p. 71. In June Tirana was refusing visas to Polish and East German tourists, and in July the official Polish tourist agency Orbis canceled all tours to Albania (Olsen from Warsaw, *New York Times,* July 19, 1961).

91 They staffed the copper refinery in Kurbnesh, the nickel and chrome mines at Pishkash, the fish-packing plant at Vlorë, and the harbor construction in Durrës (Buchalla, *op. cit.*). All East European specialists, presumably by Soviet instruction, left by August 31, in spite of Albanian efforts to keep them until their Chinese replacements could arrive (Hamm, *op. cit.,* p. 83).

92 In July 1961 a Vienna dispatch to a West German newspaper (*Stuttgarter Zeitung,* July 13, 1961) reported that in August 1960, a year before, Tirana had requested the withdrawal of the Czech nickel-mining experts, who were replaced by Chinese, some of whom had already arrived, and that in March 1961 the Albanians canceled nickel ore deliveries to Czechoslovakia, in spite of Soviet efforts to reverse the decision. This report is similar to the one in Hamm, *op. cit.* pp. 84–85.

93 ATA statement, *Zëri i Popullit,* Oct. 17, 1961, denying reports in *Ventiquatro*

approached Italy in late spring 1961 to expand trade between the two countries,[94] a proposal which, considering the large unfavorable Albanian trade balance with Italy, could only mean in effect Italian economic aid.

Perhaps the most significant public indication of the continued worsening of Soviet-Albanian relations was the early July (delayed) visit to Moscow by Yugoslav Foreign Minister Koča Popović. In the concluding communiqué he and Gromyko, in words which must have infuriated the Albanians still further, repeated the theme of Gromyko's previous December speech:

> The two sides noted with satisfaction that relations between the USSR and the FPRY were developing normally and that their positions on the main international questions were similar or identical. They expressed the hope that the two countries' cooperation in the struggle for peace and for reducing international tension would develop successfully in the future as well. . . .[95]

By late summer Soviet-Albanian relations were even more clearly getting worse. The Albanian press wrote of the necessity of Albania becoming self-sufficient in spare parts and generally in economic life.[96] In connection with the Moscow meeting of the Warsaw Pact powers on the German problem on August 3–5, Albania (which played down the conference in its progaganda media)[97] was the only country which published a separate and implicitly anti-Soviet declaration.[98] In spite of efforts on all sides to conceal the fact, it was clear, and the Soviets have now con-

---

Ore and *Il Giorno* as "a devilish provocation staged by certain reactionary circles and the Yugoslav revisionists."

[94] Marceau from Athens in *Le Monde,* July 29, 1961.

[95] *Pravda* and *Borba,* July 14, 1961 (quoted from *CDSP,* XIII, 28 [Aug. 9, 1961], p. 22); for Yugoslav editorial comment, see *Politika,* July 14, 1961.

[96] E.g., *Zëri i Popullit,* Aug. 23, 1961.

[97] Radio Tirana did not broadcast the text of the conference communiqué and deleted it from a Radio Moscow Albanian-language program which it rebroadcast on August 6. On Sept. 15, Sofia ceased relaying Albanian broadcasts to North America.

[98] *Zëri i Popullit,* Aug. 1, 1961. The declaration, although referring to the Soviet Union as the "essential and directing force" of the socialist camp, stressed such Chinese formulas as the camp's overwhelming strength, denounced Kennedy's "demagoguery" and his "furiously relighting the war psychosis," and declared that the West favors negociations only to avoid a solution. The statement's strong emphasis on signing a German peace treaty in 1961 did not at the time excite special attention. In retrospect, however, and in view of Hoxha's Nov. 7, 1961, statement (*Zëri i Popullit,* Nov. 8, 1961) that Khrushchev had been dilatory in signing such a treaty, the Albanian statement publicly opposed a Soviet policy position. As a further sign of the Albanians' anti-Soviet attitude on this point, the statement occupied the upper two-thirds of the first page of *Zëri i Popullit,* while the announcement of the space voyage of Major Titov was relegated to the lower third.

firmed,[99] that Hoxha was the only East European First Secretary who had failed to attend.[100] Thus, as the Soviets later stated, the Albanians and, presumably, the Chinese as well demonstrated to

> . . . the whole world that on this vitally important question they oppose the joint foreign policy of the socialist countries. . . .[101]

In mid-August the Albanian telegram to Moscow praising Titov's space flight,[102] alone among East European messages, did not congratulate or mention Khrushchev by name. The answering Soviet telegram sent three weeks later did not refer to the Albanians as "comrades."[103] Albania was also the only Communist country which did not congratulate Ulbricht on the August 13 erection of the wall between East and West Berlin,[104] and, on September 9, the only one whose delegation to the North Korean party congress was not mentioned by the Soviets as having been present in Moscow en route.[105] Greeting formulas used in Soviet-Albanian exchanges of messages clearly indicated continuing Soviet displeasure. Albanian (and Chinese) initial treatment of the September Belgrade neutralist summit conference was very negative[106] and remained so throughout its course in respect to Yugoslavia's role in it. By the end of August, in spite of Albanian requests for postponement, all Soviet and East European technicians in Albania had left.[107]

During the three months before the Twenty-Second Soviet Party Congress, Albania was absent from 18 out of 21 inter-bloc meetings (CMEA and otherwise) but did attend a plenary session of CMEA in September in Moscow.[108] Hoxha and his associates continued publicly to pledge their undying fealty to the Soviet-Albanian alliance and publicly to rec-

[99] Leonid Sergeyev, "How the Present Albanian Leaders Rejected All CPSU Proposals to Solve Misunderstandings in a Comradely Way," cited in ftn. 12, *supra.*

[100] The Moscow communiqué (*Pravda,* Aug. 6, 1961) spoke only of the "First Secretaries," but the Albanian press mentioned only "the representative" of the PPSh (*Zëri i Popullit,* Aug. 8, 1961).

[101] I. Medvedev, "From Dogmatism in Theory to Adventurism in Politics," *Izvestiya,* Feb. 4, 1962.

[102] *Zëri i Popullit,* Aug. 9, 1961; cf. *Daily Telegraph* (London), Aug. 16, 1961.

[103] *Zëri i Popullit,* Sept., 1, 1961, quoting an Aug. 28 Soviet telegram.

[104] Missing in texts printed in *Aus Der Internationalen Arbeiterbewegung* (East Berlin), Aug. 15–31, 1961. *Zëri i Popullit* for this period contained no congratulatory telegram, but a laudatory article appeared on August 16.

[105] *Pravda,* Sept. 9, 1961.

[106] E.g., *Zëri i Popullit,* Aug. 13, 1961.

[107] Hamm, *op. cit.,* p. 83.

[108] *Sovietskaya Rossiya,* Sept. 10, 1961, mentions Albania specifically as present; NCNA in English to Asia, Sept. 11, 1961, 1835 GMT, states that "all members attended." Albania was also represented at the seventh meeting of the CMEA transportation committee in Warsaw on Oct. 10 (TASS/ATA from Warsaw in *Zëri i Popullit,* Oct. 13, 1961). On Sept. 18 an Albanian-Czechoslovak cultural agreement was signed in Prague (*Zëri i Popullit,* Sept. 23, 1961).

ognize (more than, for example, Poland) Moscow as the head of the camp of socialism. In late August a new Albanian ambassador to Warsaw was appointed;[109] his post had been vacant for a year.

The Break Becomes Imminent

On August 19 Soviet Ambassador Shikin left Tirana;[110] he neither returned nor was replaced, and on August 21 Radio Tirana announced a new Soviet chargé d'affaires had been appointed.

Shikin's departure, as later Albanian documentation now indicates, signaled the total collapse of Albanian-Soviet relations. On August 24 the Soviet Central Committee, in apparently its final communication to Tirana, in a violent document which culminated in the assertion that the Albanian leadership had become "agents of foreign intelligence services," reiterated all its charges against Hoxha and his associates which Khrushchev made public the following October.[111]

Assuming, as seems probable, that such a Soviet charge actually was made, it was and remains one of the most significant indicators of the extent and depth not only of the Soviet-Albanian break but also of the Sino-Soviet rift, particularly when one remembers the significance of this same ominous formulation in the 1949 Cominform resolution. Khrushchev thus applied to the Albanians exactly the same charge that they and the Chinese levied against the Yugoslavs; that they were an *agentura* of the imperialists. Just as the Chinese and Albanian charges against the Yugoslavs implied that Khrushchev was consciously cooperating with an imperialist *agentura,* so this charge of Khrushchev's against the Albanians implied that the Chinese were doing the same.

Mutually favorable references in the Chinese and Albanian press and radio, coupled with esoteric slights to the Soviet Union and the East European states,[112] reached new heights. Both Soviet and Albanian propaganda treatment of the traditional September "Albanian-Soviet

109 *Zëri i Popullit,* Aug. 23, 1961.

110 According to the Albanian note to Moscow of Dec. 9, 1961, replying to the Soviet note of Dec. 3, 1961, severing diplomatic relations, *Zëri i Popullit,* Dec. 10, 1961, and Document 16.

111 "Khrushchev . . . ," *Zëri i Popullit,* Mar. 25, 1962, and Document 26. According to the Albanians, on August 26 all scholarships for Albanian students in the USSR were withdrawn by Moscow; "shortly after" the Albanian students were all expelled ("Crocodile Tears," *Zëri i Popullit,* Apr. 13, 1962, and "Slanders and Fabrications Will Not Stand," *ibid.,* Dec. 30, 1961, and Document 18).

112 On October 7 no official Albanian delegation attended the East Berlin twelfth anniversary celebrations of the founding of the DDR (*Zëri i Popullit,* Oct. 7, 1961). The Albanians did send a congratulatory telegram (*ATA,* Oct. 7, 1961), but at the meeting the Albanian ambassador, who sat on the platform, left after the speech by the head of the Chinese delegation (*Borba,* Oct. 9, 1961).

Friendship Month" made clear that Moscow-Tirana relations were seriously strained.[113] The September 1 *Zëri i Popullit* editorial spoke of the month only as strengthening the friendship between the Soviet and Albanian peoples, not between the state or parties. At the end of the month Moscow broadcasts in Albanian stressed the evils of the personality cult and the importance of the CPSU Draft Program (the full text of which, not having been broadcast by the Albanians, was broadcast to that country by Moscow) in counteracting abuses of "Leninist" norms in party and state activity.[114]

On September 5, in the course of a long interview granted to *The New York Times* foreign-affairs columnist Cyrus L. Sulzberger, Khrushchev declared: "Of course we consider Yugoslavia a socialist country." In this brief but very significant reference, apparently unnoticed in the West at the time, Khrushchev publicly revealed his position on an ideological issue which, as we have seen, was and remains a major point at issue between Moscow and Peking, and the one which concerned Tirana the most. It was a sign that a Moscow-Tirana break was imminent, and that all Soviet hopes of a reconciliation between the two had vanished. To infuriate the Albanians still further, Khrushchev added:

> . . . and should she [Yugoslavia] be attacked by an imperialistic state and appeal to us for help I think we would not turn down the request and would come to her help. . . .[115]

The obvious target of this rising Soviet pressure replied at the end of September. In a speech on September 30, Hoxha made clear, in a manner the significance of which was not then realized in the West, that Albania would not give in to Soviet pressure:

> The imperialists, the Belgrade revisionists, and all the enemies of our party and our people have tried by sword and fire, by means of various plots and blockades, to strangle our party and to subjugate our people.

113 There was less publicity for it in Tirana than in 1960 (although what there was — e.g., *Zëri i Popullit,* Sept. 1, 1961 — was entirely favorable) and practically none in Moscow. Contrary to 1960, no Soviet delegation arrived in Albania for it. Messages were exchanged only between the two friendship societies; Radio Tirana and the Albanian press gave no indication whether or not CPSU-PPSh messages were exchanged. The Sept. 1 speech by Hysni Kapo at the Tirana friendship rally (*Zëri i Popullit,* Sept. 2, 1961) included quotations from Lenin and Stalin but did not mention Khrushchev. For a vivid eyewitness account of one of the meetings, see Hamm, *Rebellen gegen Moskau,* pp. 44–46.

114 Radio Moscow, Sept. 28, 1961.

115 *New York Times,* Sept. 8, 1961, p. 11, and *Pravda,* Sept. 10, 1961. Khrushchev has not since publicly repeated the first statement, but he clearly inferred his continued adherence to it by declaring at the XXII CPSU Congress that Yugoslavia's revisionism "may ultimately lead to" imperiling her socialist construction (*Pravda,* Oct. 18, 1961) and in his speech at Varna, Bulgaria, on May 16, 1962 (*Izvestiya,* May 18, 1962, reprinted in *Zëri i Popullit,* May 18, 1962).

> These enemies think they can easily liquidate Albania because it is a small country. But they have miscalculated, they have failed, and they will fail shamefully because they have come up against and they will always come up against a rock-like impregnable fortress, heroically and gallantly defended by a brave people and party. Those who tried to dig a grave for Albania have fallen into the grave themselves. . . .
>
> . . . He who raises a hand against Albania will be struck down not only by this courageous land but also by all Communists of the world, all the peoples of the socialist camp, with the Soviet people at the head, and by all honest and progressive people. Let the enemies of our people and party remember that they will not take us by surprise. We are prepared for everything and we are ready to cope successfully with any situation. We know and understand their tricks, their plots, their machinations against our people and against our party. . . . We do not deceive ourselves with illusions and dreams; we are perfectly aware that the cares of mankind and our people cannot end before the extinction of imperialism and its agent — revisionism.[116]

Shehu re-echoed the same theme.[117]

At the same ceremony the Chinese Ambassador in Tirana, Lo Shih-kao, once again reaffirmed Peking's support of Albania:

> The industrious and courageous Albanian people, under the correct leadership of the Albanian Party of Labor and Comrade Enver Hoxha, have, by flying the banner of Marxism-Leninism, made an important contribution to the struggle against imperialism and modern revisionism, to the national and democratic movements in various countries, to peaceful coexistence, to the preservation of the unity of the socialist camp and the international Communist movement, to safeguarding the purity of Marxism-Leninism, and in other fields. They have also achieved great successes in the socialist revolution and socialist construction. . . .
>
> Although China and Albania are, geographically speaking, far from one another, our deep friendship grows stronger and develops constantly. Both in the struggle against common enemies and in the building of socialism our peoples always cooperate, support, and help one another. This friendship and unity rests on Marxism-Leninism and proletarian internationalism. They respond to the interests of the Chinese and Albanian peoples, to the interests of the socialist camp. This friendship and unity is invincible and will live forever.[118]

In the ten days before Khrushchev publicly attacked the Albanians, signs continued to multiply that tension between Moscow and Tirana was near the breaking point and that Peking continued completely to support Tirana. The first public indication of the suspension of Communist

[116] *Zëri i Popullit,* Oct. 1, 1961.
[117] *Ibid.,* Oct. 3, 1961.
[118] *Ibid.,* Oct. 1, 1961.

Party relations between Albania and the Soviet Union and its East European allies was the announcement on October 12 of the list of party delegations arriving in Tirana for the Fifth Congress of the Union of Albanian Women:[119] they were from China, North Vietnam, Indonesia, Japan, Brazil, and Algeria only; except for the last two, all were from parties which at the February Albanian Fourth Congress had clearly taken a pro-Albanian and anti-Soviet position.

On that same day, October 12, according to a 1962 Tirana account, the Albanian Central Committee approved the text of a letter to Moscow, written with the knowledge that no Albanian delegation had been invited to Moscow and that Khrushchev's attack was imminent, which called on the Soviet Central Committee to be elected at the Twenty-Second Congress to review and reject the actions of "N. Khrushchev and his group."[120]

Three days later an Albanian government decree lowered the price of consumer goods, probably a sign of Tirana's desire to acquire more popular support in view of events ahead.[121]

On October 16 the Chinese delegate to the Fifth Congress of the Albanian Women's Union spoke of the

> . . . correct leadership of the Albanian Party of Labor headed by their long-tested leader Comrade Enver Hoxha . . .

declared that Chinese-Albanian friendship

> . . . based on the principles of Marxism-Leninism and proletarian internationalism was unbreakable and no force could destroy it . . .

and asserted:

> . . . We assure you that we will always be with you, even in storm and stress. . . .[122]

The next day another meeting, the Twenty-Second Congress of the Soviet Communist Party, opened in Moscow, with no Albanian delegation present. In his opening speech[123] Khrushchev denounced the Albanians: the Soviet-Albanian dispute was now public.

[119] *Ibid.,* Oct. 12, 1961.

[120] "Khrushchev . . . ," *Zëri i Popullit,* Mar. 25, 1962, and Document 26. At the time the Albanian press did not mention this PPSh CC plenum. The letter was delivered on November 11 (*ibid.*).

[121] *Ibid.,* Oct. 15, 1961.

[122] Speech by Yang Yun-yu, NCNA from Tirana, Oct. 16, 1961 (SCMP 2604, Oct. 24, 1961, pp. 26–27).

[123] *Pravda,* Oct. 18, 1961.

CHAPTER FOUR

The Soviet Twenty-Second Party Congress[1] and the Soviet-Albanian Diplomatic Break

Khrushchev's and Chou En-lai's Twenty-Second Congress speeches made clear that the issues in dispute between the Soviet Union and China were as serious and unsettled as ever. The most serious challenge that the Chinese had issued to Khrushchev was on the organizational issue of "fractionalism." Peking's total support of Tirana in 1960 had made clear that the Chinese were claiming a worldwide hunting license within the world Communist movement. If China's only faithful ally had been, say, the Burmese or the Malayan party, it would have been less serious from Khrushchev's viewpoint; but Tirana had so clearly been within the Soviet sphere of influence and was so small and so totally dependent upon outside help that Khrushchev must have felt that the Soviet Union's prestige simply could not suffer successful Albanian defiance. For this reason he had to attack Hoxha and defy Mao in the process; as he said in his first speech, on a question of principle Moscow could not yield "either to the Albanian leaders or to anyone else."

With Khrushchev's attack on Albania at the Congress,[2] the "Albanian affair" suddenly exploded into an international sensation. As he had un-

[1] Mosely, *op. cit.;* Merle Fainsod, "The 22nd Party Congress," *Problems of Communism,* X, 6(Nov.–Dec. 1961), Special Supplement; H. T. Willett, "Khrushchev and the 22nd Congress," *Survey,* No. 40 (Jan. 1962), pp. 3–10; Boris Meissner, "Die Ergebnisse des 22, Parteikongresses der KPdSU," *Europa-Archiv,* XVII, 3 (Feb. 10, 1962), pp. 73–92; Brown, "Albania: Mirror of Conflict," *op. cit.;* Zagoria, *op. cit.,* pp. 370–383. For documentation, see Charlotte Saikowski and Leo Gruliow, eds., *Current Soviet Policies IV: The Documentary Record of the 22nd Congress of the Communist Party of the Soviet Union* (New York: Columbia, 1962), and Alexander Dallin and Jonathan Harris, eds., *Dissention in International Communism* (New York: Columbia, 1963). Unfortunately, neither of these documentary volumes was available to me during the writing of this book; they will be essential to students of the 22nd Congress and its aftermath in the international Communist movement. I have not found useful Peter S. H. Tang's "The Twenty-Second Congress of the Communist Party of the Soviet Union and Moscow-Tirana-Peking Relations" (Washington, D.C.: Research Institute on the Sino-Soviet Bloc, mimeo., 1962); cf. Thomas Perry Thornton, "On the Correct Handling of Contradictions," *World Politics,* XV, 1 (Oct. 1962), pp. 151–162, at pp. 153–157.

[2] In his first speech on Oct. 17 (*Pravda,* Oct. 18, 1961) and his second on Oct. 27, 1961 (*ibid.,* Oct. 29, 1961).

doubtedly intended, his attack required each Communist party to take a public position on the Albanian question, or, more accurately, to make more public the position it had been forced to take privately on it at the 81-party meetings the year before. The Soviet assault on Albania at the Congress may be divided into two categories of issues: organizational (the more important) and policy.

Khrushchev's main organizational charge against the Albanians was that they had defied an agreed decision of the world Communist movement, the universal validity given by the 1957 and 1960 declarations to the Soviet Twentieth Congress, and had conducted fractional activity within the movement against this decision, thus violating the agreed "international general line" and "proletarian internationalism." In addition, he declared, they had carried on specific anti-Soviet activity within Albania, including persecution of "Albanian friends of the Soviet Union." In the only note of — should one say pathos? — at the Congress comparable to Mme. Lazurkina's dream of Lenin telling her that he could not sleep quietly next to Stalin in the Kremlin tomb and therefore desired his removal,[3] Khrushchev denounced the Albanian leadership as the murderers of a pregnant woman:

> A few years ago the Central Committee of the CPSU interceded with the Albanian leaders over the fate of Liri Gega, a former member of the Politburo of the Central Committee of the Albanian Party of Labor, who had been sentenced to death along with her husband. . . . We were guided by considerations of humanity, by anxiety to prevent the shooting of a woman, and a pregnant woman at that. We felt and still feel that as a fraternal party we had a right to state our opinion in the matter. After all even in the blackest days of rampant reaction, the tsarist satraps, who tortured revolutionaries, could not bring themselves to execute pregnant women. And here, in a socialist country, they had sentenced to death, and they executed, a woman who was about to become a mother. They had shown altogether unwarranted cruelty.

With Jakova, Liri Gega was probably involved in the 1956 attempt to overthrow Hoxha and Shehu; Khrushchev's defense of her alone would have been bound to infuriate the Albanian leaders even more. But Khrushchev went still further:

> Comrades Liri Belishova and Koço Tashko, prominent figures in the Albanian Party of Labor, were not only expelled from the Party's Central Committee but are now being called enemies of the Party and the people. And all this merely because Liri Belishova and Koço Tashko had the courage honestly and openly to voice their disagreement with the policy of

[3] *Pravda,* Oct. 31, 1961.

> the Albanian leaders and took a stand for Albanian solidarity with the Soviet Union and the other socialist countries.
>
> People who today advocate friendship with the Soviet Union, with the CPSU, are regarded by the Albanian leaders as enemies.[4]

The cat was out of the bag: Like Hebrang and Žujović in Yugoslavia in 1948, Belishova and Tashko had gambled — and lost.

Having reeled off this catalogue of Albanian crimes, Khrushchev used them as justification of the most vulnerable part of his whole action — his making public the quarrel. After all, the 1960 Moscow Declaration had certainly implied the contrary:

> The Communist and workers parties hold meetings whenever necessary to discuss urgent problems, to share experiences, acquaint themselves with each other's views and positions, work out common views through consultations and co-ordinate joint actions in the struggle for common goals.
>
> Whenever a party wants to clear up questions relating to the activities of another fraternal party, its leadership approaches the leadership of the party concerned; if necessary, they hold meetings and consultations.[5]

Even so, there still remained the question of who would *decide* what was fractional, what was anti-Soviet, what was anti-Leninist. This dilemma made clear the true extent, the paradox, and the ultimate danger of Khrushchev's post-1953 attempt at a loosening of Soviet control over the East European satellites, and even more of the lesser degree of Soviet influence over China. As Molotov reportedly remarked in the July 1955 Soviet Central Committee Plenum, if Moscow had not broken with Yugoslavia in 1948, there would have been grave complications elsewhere in eastern Europe.[6] After Khrushchev in 1955 carried out his rapprochement with Tito, such grave complications certainly developed in Poland and Hungary. In his 1955–1956 rapprochement with Yugoslavia Khrushchev had gone very far toward recognizing the equality and autonomy of all parties and the doctrine of "various roads to socialism." But when Togliatti's "polycentrism" and the Poznań rising demonstrated its dangers, Khrushchev recoiled. After the Hungarian Revolution, with Chinese support, he retreated still further. Reluctantly, in part because he was pushed by the Chinese (and the Albanians), he condemned Yugoslavia while emphasizing that the international Communist movement had to have a "general line," and, while not abandoning the old Stalinist concept of the "leading role of

[4] Quoted from *CDSP,* XIII, 46 (Dec. 13, 1961), p. 27.

[5] Quoted from Hudson, Lowenthal, and MacFarquhar, *op. cit.,* p. 204.

[6] As reported in Seweryn Bialer, "I Chose Truth," *News from Behind the Iron Curtain,* V, 10 (Oct. 1956), pp. 3–15, at p. 13.

the Soviet Union," he gradually shifted to the less autocratic one of the "socialist commonwealth." Publicly during the 1956–1959 period only Gomułka (and he in a most subtle way) indicated that he was not entirely in sympathy with the Soviet "leading role."[7] The Chinese unpublicized challenge of 1957–1959 must in part have been on this organizationally essential point. In the 1960 Bucharest and Moscow context this emerged as the Soviet effort to force through a resolution forbidding "fractionalism," i.e., requiring the parties in the minority absolutely and permanently to accept majority decisions. The Chinese insisted upon their right to form a fraction in the international movement exactly as Lenin in 1903 had formed what at first was a minority fraction and only later became a majority. At the 1960 Bucharest and Moscow meetings the Chinese were in a relatively small minority; probably only the Albanians supported them completely. Clearly, since "fractionalism" is not mentioned in the December 1960 Moscow communiqué, the Chinese refused to accept the proposal to ban it; i.e., they refused to be bound by majority decisions. A "fraction" must be made up of at least two parties. Hence, in this context, the importance of Albania is evident.

Having thus committed himself to majority rule, Khrushchev then felt compelled formally to abjure any claim to a "leading role" for the CPSU. Whether or not he did this during the Bucharest meetings we do not know; but he did so during the Moscow meetings, and publicly at the beginning of January 1961.[8] This whole matter was confused both before and after the November 1960 meetings by the continued use by the Chinese and the Albanians of the phrase "the camp of socialism headed [or, sometimes, "led"] by the Soviet Union," but for them it had become an *anti*-Khrushchev formula.

To return, after this long but necessary excursus, to Khrushchev's October 1961 attack on the Albanians: How was he to explain his decision publicly to attack them, thus appearing to intervene in domestic Albanian party affairs and to violate the 1960 Moscow Declaration's formula for the handling of interparty controversies? He declared that intervention was justified because the Albanian leadership had persecuted "friends of the Soviet Union and had deliberately undermined Soviet-Albanian friendship." As to the apparent violation of the Moscow Declaration, he said that the Soviet party had tried and failed to hold fruitful discussions with the Albanians,[9] that the majority of fraternal delegates to the Congress had approved his criticism, that the Albanians,

[7] Brzezinski, *The Soviet Bloc, op. cit.*, p. 361.

[8] Khrushchev, *op. cit.*

[9] Aidit later declared (*Jen-min Jih-pao,* Dec. 1, 1961) that as far as he knew no such discussions had occurred.

while in 1957 and 1960 hypocritically supporting the Twentieth Congress decisions, had in fact long been sabotaging them, and that for all these reasons it was not only the right but the "internationalist duty" of the Soviet party to the world Communist movement publicly to condemn the Tirana leadership.

Chou En-lai and the Albanians quite naturally concentrated their attack on this last issue. The Chinese did not want a total break with Moscow and were probably surprised by the violence of Khrushchev's attack on Tirana; and, like the Albanians, they knew that the Soviets were most vulnerable on the precedural point. They therefore made clear from the beginning their opposition to Khrushchev's public attacks on the Albanians. Chou En-lai ostentatiously did not applaud them,[10] and within twenty-four hours Peking published[11] a speech, delivered several days earlier, by the Chinese delegate to the Tirana Women's Congress, declaring that

> The friendship between the Chinese and Albanian peoples, based on the principles of Marxism-Leninism and proletarian internationalism, is unbreakable and no force can destory it.[12]

When Chou spoke, two days after Khrushchev, he made quite clear Chinese dissent on the procedural issue:

> Our socialist camp, comprising 12 fraternal countries, from the Korean Democratic People's Republic to the German Democratic Republic, from the Democratic Republic of Viet Nam to the Albanian People's Republic, is a single entity. On the basis of independence and full equality we socialist countries and we Communist Parties of all countries support and cooperate with each other in a brotherly way. . . .
>
> We hold that should a dispute or difference unfortunately arise between fraternal parties or fraternal countries, it should be resolved patiently in the spirit of proletarian internationalism and on the principles of equality and unanimity through consultation. Any public, one-sided censure of any fraternal party does not help unify and is not helpful to resolving problems. To bring a dispute between fraternal parties or fraternal countries into the open in the face of the enemy cannot be regarded as a serious Marxist-Leninist attitude. Such an attitude will only grieve those near and dear to us and gladden our enemies. The Communist Party of China sincerely hopes that fraternal parties which have disputes or differences between them will unite afresh on the basis of Marxism-Leninism and on the basis of mutual respect for independence and equality. This, in my opinion, is

[10] *New York Times* Moscow dispatch, Oct. 18, 1961.

[11] NCNA in English to Europe, Oct. 18, 1961, 1818 GMT (SCMP 2604, Oct. 24, 1961, p. 23).

[12] NCNA in English from Tirana, Oct. 16, 1961 (SCMP 2604, Oct. 24, 1961, pp. 26–27). Cf. Zagoria, *op. cit.,* pp. 370–371.

the position which we Communists ought to take on this question. (*Applause*)[13]

After symbolically indicating Peking's opposition to the totality of Khrushchev's policies by laying a wreath with the inscription "to Josif Vissarionovich Stalin — the great Marxist-Leninist" on Stalin's tomb[14] on October 21 (only a few days before the dead dictator's body was removed), Chou precipitously left for Peking, thus in effect walking out of the Congress.[15] At Peking, in a striking gesture of endorsement and defiance, Mao personally met him at the airport.[16] In his closing speech Khrushchev ironically, almost sarcastically, replied:

> Comrade Chou En-lai, head of the delegation of the Communist Party of China, voiced concern in his speech over our having openly raised the issue of Albanian-Soviet relations at the Congress. As far as we can see, his statement primarily reflects alarm lest the present state of our relations with the Albanian Party of Labor affect the solidarity of the socialist camp.
>
> We share the anxiety of our Chinese friends and appreciate their concern for the strengthening of unity. If the Chinese comrades wish to apply their efforts to normalizing the Albanian Party of Labor's relations with the fraternal parties, it is doubtful whether there is anyone better able to facilitate accomplishment of this purpose than the Communist Party of China. This would really redound to the benefit of the Albanian Party of Labor and accord with the interests of the entire commonwealth of socialist countries.[17]

As to policy, the speeches of Khrushchev and other Soviet leaders levied two charges against Hoxha and his associates: "dogmatism and sectarianism" and "narrow nationalism and revisionism." Khrushchev asserted that Tirana's rejection of the Twentieth Congress had led to the rise of the personality cult, abuse of the leadership's authority, and consequent infraction of Leninist norms. As during the Congress the attacks against the antiparty group rose in volume and vehemence, so did those against Albania — another indication of the organic unity of domestic and foreign elements in Khrushchev's program for the Con-

[13] Quoted from *Peking Review,* IV, 43 (Oct. 27, 1961), p. 9.

[14] On Oct. 21 at 2:10 P.M.; Radio Tirana, Oct. 21, 1961, 2100 GMT.

[15] This becomes even clearer when one notes that the Soviet version of his departure (*Pravda,* Oct. 24, 1961) indicated he had left in connection with a meeting of the National Peoples Congress (which in fact met six months later, in March 1962), while the Chinese one (NCNA English from Moscow Oct. 23, 1961, in SCMP 2607, Oct. 27, 1961, p. 38) gave no reason. See Zagoria, *op. cit.*, pp. 370–371.

[16] NCNA in English to Asia, Oct. 24, 1961 (SCMP 2608, Oct. 30, 1961, p. 1). As Zagoria (*loc. cit.*) has noted, Mao had not met Chu Teh or Chou upon their return from the CPSU 20th and 21st Congresses.

[17] Quoted from *CDSP,* XIII, 46 (Dec. 13, 1961), p. 26.

gress. Suslov accused the Albanians of removing and subjecting to "repressions" Albanian friends of the Soviet Union, and termed their replies to Khrushchev's first speech "a mixture of hypocrisy and slanderous hints."[18] Speaking on October 26,[19] Otto Kuusinen, in age the senior member of the Presidium and the only one who had known Lenin and been a senior Comintern official, declared that Hoxha had arrested Albanians "who advocated friendship with the Soviet Union" (i.e., Belishova and Tashko), expelled Soviet specialists, and spread false rumors that Moscow had cut off grain shipments to Albania and supported Greek claims to "Northern Epirus." (The Soviets did cut off or at least greatly cut down grain shipments to Albania in the summer of 1960, and Khrushchev's interview with Venizelos certainly gave the impression, which the Soviets at the time did not deny, that Moscow was not totally opposed to the Greek claims.) In this same speech Kuusinen made one of the two specific references during the Congress from which one might infer a link between the antiparty group and the Chinese and Albanians.[20] He declared that Molotov was trying to fish not only in "domestic reservoirs" but also "perhaps in some foreign waters" in his attempt "to cook up a certain sectarian platform for his futher antiparty speculations."

Mikoyan introduced the main ideological theme:

> The actions of the Albanian leaders indicate that they are departing from internationalist positions and backsliding onto the path of nationalism. . . . Developments are showing that those who persist in revisionism and dogmatism arrive, even though from different directions, at one and the same thing — estrangement from Marxism-Leninism and from the socialist camp and the world Communist movement.[21]

In his second speech (after Chou's departure and the first Albanian reply), Khrushchev elaborated considerably on this and declared (for the first time publicly by any Soviet leader) that Hoxha and Shehu had not published the Soviet party's Draft Program, had removed and "subjected to repressions" Belishova and her husband, Minister Maqo Çomo,[22] and removed Tashko, had "repressed" Albanian students and sailors returning from the Soviet Union, and were "raising the cult of

[18] *Pravda,* Oct. 23, 1961.

[19] *Ibid.,* Oct. 27, 1961.

[20] The other was by Ignatov (*ibid.,* Oct. 25, 1961).

[21] Quoted from *CDSP,* XIII, 51 (Jan. 17, 1962), p. 15. According to *Trybuna Ludu,* Oct. 21, 1961, Mikoyan also quoted Shehu as having said that Stalin made only two mistakes: He died early, and before that he should have liquidated the entire present CPSU leadership.

[22] This was the first public indication that Çomo had been arrested; the Albanians never announced it.

Stalin." He added that at the February 1961 Albanian party congress Shehu had said that anyone disagreeing with the leadership would get "a spit in the face, a sock on the jaw, and if necessary a bullet in the head."[23]

Ponomarev[24] gave the most succinct and wide-reaching formulation of the identical results of dogmatism and revisionism, one which resounded thereafter from Soviet and pro-Soviet Communist sources:

> Beginning with loud, dogmatic statements to the effect that they alone are resolutely combating imperialism, they soon slipped into revisionist positions, repudiated in practice the basic tenets of the Declaration and the Statement, and counterposed their own narrowly nationalistic views to the common views of the Communist Parties.[25]

Pospelov[26] concentrated on the February 1961 Fourth Albanian Party Congress, to which, as to the 1956 Third Congress, he had been the chief Soviet delegate:

> We encountered a series of flagrant instances of overt anti-Soviet actions on the part of prominent Albanian functionaries, instances of a humiliating and hostile attitude toward our specialists, geologists, and sailors.[27]

He said that the Soviets had formally protested against those actions[28] but that thereafter the Albanians had only become more hostile.

There is little doubt that these Soviet charges against the Albanian leadership are true; but what, one may ask, of Ulbricht, Novotný, and Gheorghiu-Dej? True, Hoxha's blood purges had been more extensive and had lasted longer than theirs; but the principle was the same. Certainly Hoxha's personality cult was not as great, and his association with Stalin and Stalinism neither so long nor so bloody as Ulbricht's.

From Moscow's viewpoint the charge of "nationalism" and "revisionism" was more valid. Elaborated by Mikoyan, Ponomarev, Ignatov, and Pospelov, the essence of this charge was that by their defiance of the "general line" of the socialist camp and therefore their abandonment of "proletarian internationalism" the Albanian leaders were guilty of the deviation of "narrow nationalism." More significantly, the Soviet speakers declared that "narrow nationalism" was a symptom of revisionism as well as of dogmatism and sectarianism, and that the Albanians were therefore at least "potential" revisionists. "Objectively," they went on, the

[23] This was correct; see Shehu in *Zëri i Popullit,* Feb. 18, 1961.
[24] *Pravda,* Oct. 26, 1961.
[25] Quoted from *CDSP,* XIV, 3 (Feb. 14, 1962), p. 14.
[26] *Pravda,* Oct. 28, 1961.
[27] Quoted from *CDSP,* XIV, 5 (Feb. 28, 1962), p. 20.
[28] *Pravda,* Oct. 28, 1961.

Albanians already helped the imperialists, and inevitably they would be driven into becoming conscious agents of the imperialists.

Khrushchev, before attacking the Albanians, also denounced the "leaders of the Yugoslav League of Communists," who

> plainly suffer from national narrow-mindedness, [and] have turned from the straight Marxist-Leninist road on to a winding path that has landed them in the bog of revisionism.

But he gave two other indications that he was much less anti-Yugoslav than the Albanians and Chinese. One was his demand for

> . . . the determined struggle on two fronts — against revisionism, as the main danger, and against dogmatism and sectarianism.

(The Albanians and Chinese use the formula "struggle against modern revisionism and especially against Yugoslav revisionism.") The other indirectly confirmed his statement to Sulzberger that Yugoslavia was building socialism:

> The line they have adopted . . . plays into the hands of imperialist reaction, foments nationalist tendencies and may in the long run lead to the loss of socialist gains.

The moral he drew from all this, a veiled allusion to the issue of "fractionalism" and to his apparent refusal to discuss the Albanian issue in another 81-party conference, was clearly directed against Albania and China as much as against Yugoslavia:

> International conferences of Communists are one of the forms evolved by the fraternal parties that ensure their militant cooperation.
>
> The necessity for each party to observe joint decisions adopted collectively . . . [is] of tremendous importance.[29]

The Soviet charges against the Albanian leaders intensified markedly during the course of the Congress. While Khrushchev in his first speech only called on Hoxha and his associates to "abandon their mistaken views and return to the path of unity and close cooperation in the fraternal family of the socialist commonwealth," the Albanian and Chinese resistance so incensed the Soviet leader that in his second speech, on October 27, he in effect demanded that they be removed and punished for their Stalinist crimes — exactly the same demand that, according to Khrushchev, Stalin had so unwisely made toward Tito. Khrushchev blandly declared that

[29] Quoted from *CDSP,* XIII, 40 (Nov. 1, 1961), pp. 10, 32.

> The speeches by delegates and by representatives of the fraternal parties are convincing evidence that our party's Central Committee was absolutely correct in reporting to the Congress, openly and as a matter of principle, on the abnormal state of Soviet-Albanian relations.[30]

He failed to state that the Chinese had objected and that over thirty parties had neither criticized the Albanians nor taken any position at all on the Soviet-Albanian controversy.

Adducing further evidence for the correctness of Moscow's conduct, Khrushchev said that the Soviet Union in August 1960 twice unsuccessfully proposed a meeting with the Albanians, who then and at Moscow in November 1960 continued to reject negotiations; when, upon Soviet insistence, a meeting finally occurred, Hoxha and Shehu "disrupted it" and "made a deliberate show of walking out of" the conference, thereafter rejecting still another Soviet proposal for such a meeting.[31] Khrushchev kept his most extreme charge against the Albanians for the end:

> We do not recall an instance in which anyone shifted with such dizzying speed from protestations and vows of eternal friendship to unbridled anti-Soviet slander as the Albanians have done. Presumably they expect in this way to lay the groundwork for earning handouts from the imperialists. The imperialists are always willing to pay thirty pieces of silver to those who cause a split in the ranks of the Communists. But pieces of silver have never brought anyone anything but dishonor and shame.[32]

To return to the 1948 parallel, in his first speech Khrushchev was accusing Hoxha of being a leftist nationalist deviationist (the charge of the 1948 Cominform Resolution against Tito), while in his second he was accusing him of wanting to be, and destined to become, an imperialist agent (the charge of the 1949 resolution).

In conclusion Khrushchev in an ironic, if not indeed a sarcastic, tone made clear his disagreement with what Chou had said.

The final Congress resolution[33] was considerably less severe on the Albanians than Khrushchev's second speech. To attempt to analyze whether this, like other similar discrepancies, should be primarily explained by assuming that Khrushchev was unable to overcome opposition to his position would go beyond the scope and space of this volume; suffice it to say that in my opinion this seems unlikely.[34]

More probably it was a relatively conciliatory gesture vis-à-vis Peking. The resolution repeated the standard formula about dogmatism

[30] Quoted from *CDSP*, XIII, 46 (Dec. 13, 1961), p. 26.
[31] For the contrary Albanian version, see pp. 53–56, *supra*.
[32] See ftn. 30, *supra*.
[33] *Pravda*, Nov. 1, 1961.
[34] Cf. Mosely, *op. cit.*, and Fainsod, *op. cit.*

and revisionism of the 1957 and 1960 resolutions; both must be struggled against, and the latter is the main danger. As to the Albanians, the resolution, although strong, still offered them a way back:

> The Congress flatly rejects as unfounded and slanderous the attacks on the Communist Party of the Soviet Union and its Leninist Central Committee by the leaders of the Albanian Party of Labor. The actions of the Albanian leaders are at variance with the Declaration and Statement of the 1957 and 1960 Conferences of Representatives of Communist and Workers' Parties and can only be considered as being divisive, aimed at undermining the friendship and solidarity of the socialist countries, and as playing into the hands of imperialism. The Congress expresses the hope that the Albanian leaders, if they hold the interests of their people dear and really want friendship with the CPSU and with all the fraternal parties, will renounce their erroneous views and return to the path of unity and cooperation with all the socialist countries and with the international Communist movement.[35]

The Albanian Response — October to November 1961

The initial Albanian reaction to the Twenty-Second Congress was an editorial on October 18 praising the Soviet Union.[36] It was followed the next day by the full publication[37] of Khrushchev's first attack, along with Chou's Moscow speech. Perhaps encouraged by Chou's speech but more likely impelled primarily by their own fear-bred fury, the Albanians on the next evening broadcast a Central Committee statement[38] accompanied by a series of inspired messages and telegrams to the Central Committee by various individuals, groups, enterprises, and organizations.[39]

These Albanian documents are notable for their tone of extreme violence and defiance. A remarkable combination of traditional Balkan fury and left-wing Marxist-Leninist fanaticism, the Albanian anti-Khrushchev polemics were as violent as, and certainly more colorful than, anything in the "high Stalinist" period in the Soviet Union. They were certainly much more extreme than the relatively moderate, flowery, and above all "correct" language in which the Chinese Communists have normally couched their most icy blasts against Moscow. The Albanian invective probably caused much of the heightened fury of

[35] Quoted from *CDSP,* XIV, 7 (March 14, 1962), p. 25.
[36] *Zëri i Popullit,* Oct. 18, 1961.
[37] *Ibid.,* Oct. 19, 1961.
[38] Dated Oct. 20, 1961; text: *Zëri i Popullit,* Oct. 21, 1961, and Document 9.
[39] Texts: *Zëri i Popullit* and Radio Tirana, Oct. 20, *et seq.,* 1961; some samples: Document 10.

Khrushchev's second speech, and, since through January 1962 all important Albanian policy and ideological pronouncements were regularly reprinted in *Jen-min Jih-pao,* it served to exacerbate not only Soviet-Albanian but also Sino-Soviet relations. It seems doubtful that Peking initiated or even necessarily approved the intensity and extent of the Albanian verbal violence; but given their total alliance with Hoxha and the necessity for the Chinese of retaining the support of the other member of their "fraction," they quite possibly could not or did not feel it wise to restrain him.[40]

The Albanians called Khrushchev a "base, unfounded, anti-Marxist," "a plotter and common putschist," "a real Judas." They assailed "the anti-Marxist and anti-Albanian activities" of "Khrushchev and his group" and labeled Khrushchev's words as "demagoguery and hypocrisy . . . similar to the slanders of the imperialists and Tito."

The Albanian Central Committee statement immediately struck the main note which Tirana has consistently stressed:

> N. Khrushchev, by revealing to the enemies the differences which have long existed between the leadership of the Communist Party of the Soviet Union and the Albanian Party of Labor, brutally violated the 1960 Moscow Declaration, which stresses that differences arising between sister parties should be settled patiently in the spirit of proletarian internationalism and on the basis of the principles of equality and consultations.

By so doing, Khrushchev

> in fact began an open attack against the unity of the international Communist and workers movement, against the unity of the socialist camp.

It added that the Albanian party had "received with sympathy" Chou's statement criticizing Khrushchev's public attack.

The other note which the statement struck, one also to remain a major Albanian theme, was its total defiance of Khrushchev:

> The struggle which is being imposed upon our party and people will be long and difficult. But . . . our party and people . . . will . . . neither bend nor fall on their knees before the slanderous attacks, blackmail, and pressures of N. Khrushchev and his followers.

The full extent of the Albanian position, although foreshadowed in two *Zëri i Popullit* editorials,[41] was not revealed until Hoxha's November 7 speech.[42] This is a major documentary source not only for the past

[40] Cf. Brown, "Albania: Mirror of Conflict," *op. cit.*, pp. 29–30.

[41] "Marxism-Leninism Will Triumph," *Zëri i Popullit,* Nov. 1, 1961, and Document 12, and "The Name and Deeds of Josif Vissarionovich Stalin Live and Will Live for Centuries to Come," *ibid.*, Nov. 2, 1961, and Document 13.

[42] Hoxha, speech to the National Assembly, in *Zëri i Popullit,* Nov. 8, 1961, and Document 14.

and present of Soviet-Albanian relations but also for the Sino-Soviet dispute. The speech was characterized by fervent reiteration of friendship and alliance for the Soviet Union and the Soviet Communist Party; only "Nikita Khrushchev and his group" were totally defied. Referring to Khrushchev's charge in his second speech that the Albanians were preparing to accept "thirty pieces of silver from the imperialists," Hoxha declared that this

> . . . monstrous allegation can be believed only by fans of fables and detective stories. . . . We say to N. Khrushchev that the Albanian people and its Party of Labor will live on grass if necessary but will never sell themselves for 30 pieces of silver, because they would rather die on their feet with honor than live on their knees in dishonor.

The fact that Albania had powerful allies was constantly stressed, although Hoxha did not mention China by name; as the statement put it: "We shall win because we are not alone."

Hoxha repeated the theme that Khrushchev's public attack on them, as Chou had pointed out in Moscow, was a violation of the 1960 Declaration. Khrushchev, Hoxha continued, had unsuccessfully tried to dictate to the Bucharest and Moscow meetings in 1960 and was now returning to his "putschist methods" against Albania. This one-sided attempt to dominate the world movement, Hoxha declared, was Khrushchev's most serious offense. The ultimate essence of Hoxha's, like Mao's, defiance of Khrushchev was the defiance of Khrushchev's imperialism within the world Communist movement and Soviet insistence on the submerging of national views to Soviet policy. Like Mao's and Tito's position, Hoxha's professed to be "internationalist" but in fact, as the issue of fractionalism demonstrates, was nationalist. Both Mao and Hoxha insisted, like Tito, that even if they were in a minority of one, no majority, no matter how overwhelming, could force them to change their policies or actions.[43] "Narrow nationalism," as Ponomarev said, is indeed the common characteristic of the Chinese-Albanian left and the Yugoslav right deviations.

As to Khrushchev's statement that "all" other Communist parties supported him, Hoxha replied that

> Out of the 80 foreign delegations which attended . . . 34 . . . did not associate themselves with N. Khrushchev's slanders and the accusations against our party; they did not speak of the differences which exist between the Albanian Party of Labor and the Soviet leadership.

[43] See Frane Barbieri from Moscow, "The Simultaneous Game of Soviet Diplomacy," *Vjestnik* (Zagreb), Dec. 31, 1961, which alleges that these same charges are contained in a secret Chinese party letter circulated to other parties after the XXII CPSU Congress concerning Khrushchev's attack on the Albanians.

TABLE 4.1a
Issues in Speeches at 22nd CPSU Congress

○: Formal or weak
Ø: Positive
●: Emphatic

	1. ALGERIA[c] (24)*	2. ARGENTINA (25)	3. AUSTRALIA (26)	4. AUSTRIA (25)	5. BELGIUM (26)	6. BOLIVIA (29)	7. BRAZIL[b] (30)	8. BULGARIA (22)	9. BURMA[c] (30)	10. CANADA (25)	11. CEYLON (27)	12. CHILE (24)	13. CHINA[d] (20)
1. Urgency of action to prevent war	Ø	Ø	○	Ø	○			●	○	Ø			Ø
2. U.S. threatens world war	○	Ø					○		Ø	Ø			●
3. U.S. engages in imperialist intervention	○	Ø	Ø			Ø	●					●	●
4. Emphasis on national liberation movement	●	●	○			●	Ø	○	●		Ø	Ø	●
5. Praise of Soviet economic aid	○							Ø			●		○
6. Dogmatism oppósed							Ø	○			Ø		
7. Revisionism opposed							○	Ø					
8. Yugoslav revisionism attacked													Ø
9. Favorable reference to Khrushchev[e]	Ø2	●3		○1		Ø3	Ø2	●5	○1	Ø5	○1	Ø1	○1
10. CPSU the "vanguard" ("leading role") of socialism	●	Ø					○	●		○		Ø	
11. U.S.S.R. the "center"													
12. Reference to China	Ø[f]						○		Ø				
13. Socialist camp "headed by" U.S.S.R.													
14. CPSU "Creative Marxism-Leninism" praised						Ø		●			Ø		
15. CPSU 20th Congress endorsed	○	○		Ø	Ø	Ø	Ø	Ø		○	●	Ø	
16. Personality cult condemned		Ø					Ø	Ø			○	○	
17. Historical, international significance of 22nd Congress and Program	Ø	Ø	○	○		Ø	Ø	●		Ø	○		
18. "Joint" resolutions the basis of socialist unity							●						
19. 1960 Statement the basis of socialist unity								○	●				●
20. General attack on Albanian leadership (for:)		●		Ø		○	Ø	●			○	○	
21. — violating proletarian internationalism ('57; '60)		●					○	Ø			Ø		
22. — undermining socialist unity		○		Ø									
23. — deserting Marxism-Leninism		Ø						Ø					
24. — anti-CPSU 20th Congress		Ø		Ø									
25. — Stalinist methods								○					
26. — nationalism													
27. — political adventurism								○					
28. — objective aid to imperialism													
29. — acts leading to Albanian isolation								●					
30. — dogmatism and sectarianism													
31. — anti-Soviet actions													
32. — anti-peaceful coexistence													

18. CZECHO-SLOVAKIA[d] (21)	19. DENMARK (26)	20. DOMINICAN REPUBLIC (30)	21. ECUADOR (28)	22. EL SALVADOR (30)	23. FINLAND (24)	24. FRANCE (20)	25. GDR[d] (21)	26. GREAT BRITAIN (24)	27. GREECE (25)	28. GUADELOUPE (28)	29. GUATEMALA[a] (29)	30. HAITI (31)	31. HONDURAS[a] (30)	32. HUNGARY (21)	33. ICELAND (30)	34. INDIA (23)	35. INDONESIA (23)	36. IRAN (28)	37. IRAQ (25)	38. IRISH REPUBLIC[a] (30)	39. ISRAEL (28)	40. ITALY (21)
Ø	Ø	Ø	○			●	●	Ø			○			Ø	○				○	Ø	Ø	●
						○	○	○	○						Ø	●		Ø				
		Ø	Ø	Ø					Ø		○		Ø									
○		●	●	Ø						Ø	Ø	Ø	Ø		Ø	●	●	Ø	Ø	○	○	
Ø							○									Ø						
						○			○			○		Ø				○	●		○	○
	Ø					Ø			○					Ø			Ø	○	○		○	
																			○			
●5			○1		Ø2	Ø2	●7		●4		○1		○1	Ø3			○2	Ø2	Ø3		Ø3	Ø1
Ø						Ø					Ø		○						Ø		L.R. Ø	
																	●					
																	Ø					
●							Ø												Ø			
○	Ø				○	Ø	Ø		Ø					●		Ø		Ø	●			Ø
	○					○			○			○		●					Ø		Ø	○
●	○		○	○	Ø	Ø	●	○	Ø		○	○	Ø	Ø		Ø		Ø	Ø		Ø	
							Ø															
										Ø							Ø					
Ø			Ø	Ø	●	Ø	●		●			●		Ø				○	●		●	Ø
					Ø	○	●		●			Ø						Ø	Ø		Ø	Ø
Ø			Ø	Ø								Ø										
○			Ø		Ø				Ø			●							●		Ø	
																						Ø
												○										Ø
																			●		Ø	
						○																
														Ø								
						○						○										
					●		Ø														Ø	

TABLE 4.1b
Issues in Speeches at 22nd CPSU Congress

○: Formal or weak
Ø: Positive
●: Emphatic

	41. JAPAN (24)*	42. JORDAN (28)	43. LEBANON (27)	44. LUXEMBOURG[a] (29)	45. MALAYA[c] (30)	46. MARTINIQUE[c] (28)	47. MEXICO (27)	48. MONGOLIA (22)	49. MOROCCO (27)	50. NETHERLANDS (26)	51. NEW ZEALAND (28)	52. NICARAGUA[a] (30)	53. NO. KOREA (22)	54. NORTH VIETNAM[b] (22)	55. NORTHERN IRELAND[a] (30)
1. Urgency of action to prevent war	○	○		Ø		○		Ø		Ø		●	○		Ø
2. U.S. threatens world war	Ø				Ø		Ø				○	●	Ø		
3. U.S. engages in imperialist intervention	●	○	Ø			○	Ø				○		●	●	
4. Emphasis on national liberation movement	○	Ø	Ø		●	●	●	○	●	○			○	○	
5. Praise of Soviet economic aid							Ø	○						○	
6. Dogmatism opposed									○			○			
7. Revisionism opposed					○							○			
8. Yugoslav revisionism attacked															
9. Favorable reference to Khrushchev[e]	○1	Ø1	●3		○			●3	○1	○1			○2	○1	
10. CPSU the "vanguard" ("leading role") of socialism			Ø		Ø	Ø	Ø	○					Ø		
11. U.S.S.R. the "center"														Ø	
12. Reference to China													Ø	Ø	
13. Socialist camp "headed by" U.S.S.R.	Ø					Ø									
14. CPSU "Creative Marxism-Leninism" praised		Ø	Ø					Ø	Ø					Ø	
15. CPSU 20th Congress endorsed		Ø	○					Ø	●						
16. Personality cult condemned								○	○						
17. Historical, international significance of 22nd Congress and Program	○	○	Ø	○	○	○	●	●	Ø	Ø	○			○	○
18. "Joint" resolutions the basis of socialist unity															
19. 1960 Statement the basis of socialist unity	Ø				●		○						Ø	Ø	
20. General attack on Albanian leadership (for:)		Ø	Ø				○	Ø	○	Ø		Ø			
21. — violating proletarian internationalism ('57; '60)								Ø		Ø					
22. — undermining socialist unity			○				○					○			
23. — deserting Marxism-Leninism			Ø												
24. — anti-CPSU 20th Congress															
25. — Stalinist methods															
26. — nationalism								○							
27. — political adventurism										○					
28. — objective aid to imperialism												○			
29. — acts leading to Albanian isolation															
30. — dogmatism and sectarianism										○					
31. — anti-Soviet actions															
32. — anti-peaceful coexistence															

59. PARAGUAY[a] (29)	60. PERU (30)	61. POLAND (20)	62. PORTUGAL (25)	63. REUNION (30)	64. ROMANIA (21)	65. SAN MARINO[a] (29)	66. SENEGAL–AFR. IND.P.[a] (30)	67. SOUTH AFRICA[a] (29)	68. SPAIN (24)	69. SUDAN (30)	70. SWEDEN (30)	71. SWITZERLAND (28)	72. SYRIA (25)	73. THAILAND[a] (30)	74. TUNISIA (29)	75. TURKEY (30)	76. URUGUAY (26)	77. U.S.A.[c] (24)	78. U.S.S.R.: K-I (18)	U.S.S.R.: K-II (29)	79. VENEZUELA (26)	80. WEST GERMANY[d] (24)
	○	●	○		●	Ø			●		Ø	Ø	○				Ø	○	●	○		●
			○		○				●				○	Ø		●	○		Ø	Ø		
Ø	Ø							○					Ø	Ø	Ø	Ø	●	Ø	Ø	○	●	
●	Ø		●	●	○		Ø	●		Ø		Ø	Ø	○	●	○	●		●	○	Ø	
					○			Ø							○		Ø				Ø	
		○					○										○		●	Ø		
		○					○										○		●	Ø		
																			Ø	○		
	Ø2	●9		Ø4	●5			○2	●3	●2	●3	Ø1	Ø1		Ø1		○2	Ø1			Ø1	Ø2
		L.R. Ø	○										○	Ø.			Ø	Ø				Ø
																			Ø			
		Ø			●		○			●							○		●	○		
		●			Ø				●	Ø					Ø		●		●	●		
								○			●						Ø		●	●		
●	Ø	●	Ø		●	○		Ø	●	Ø	○	○		○	Ø	Ø	Ø	Ø	○			Ø
																			Ø			
				○				○						○						○	○	
	Ø	Ø	Ø	Ø	Ø	○			●	●			○		Ø	●	Ø	●	●	●	Ø	Ø
		Ø	○		Ø										Ø		Ø	●	Ø	Ø	Ø	Ø
	Ø				○					Ø							Ø			Ø	Ø	
		Ø							●											○		
		Ø							○	Ø					○				●	●		
																			Ø	●		
																Ø		●		Ø		
										Ø						Ø						
																●		Ø	Ø	●	Ø	

Here again Hoxha certainly had a point; Tables 4.1a and b indicate that 32 parties "abstained" at the Congress on the Albanian question, including the three "ruling" ones of China, North Korea, and North Vietnam, the only "ruling" parties in the Far East.

Hoxha then outlined his own policy position and his accusations against Khrushchev in far greater detail than he had done before Khrushchev's public attack upon him. Many general ideological aspects of his position coincide with and in large part reflect Chinese views. On the basic issue of "revising" Marxism-Leninism, Hoxha rejected Khrushchev's "creative" Marxism, which, he declared, led to "changes which banish the cause of the revolution" and remove the people "from the struggle for their national liberation." This was a clear reference to the Chinese-Albanian insistence that Khrushchev's policies in the underdeveloped areas have favored non-Marxist "national bourgeois" regimes (Nasser, Qassem, Nehru) rather than the indigenous Communist parties in these countries. It was also an indirect reference to the Chinese and Albanian feeling that the Soviets have given too much economic and technical aid to non-Communist underdeveloped countries like India and Egypt and not enough to Communist underdeveloped countries like theirs.[44]

Hoxha rejected Khrushchev's alleged belief in "a change in the nature of imperialism." He endorsed the Chinese view that peaceful coexistence can at best be a tactic but never a strategy rather than the

> . . . opportunist views of N. Khrushchev and his followers who consider peaceful coexistence the general line of the foreign policy of the socialist camp, the main road to the victory of socialism on a world scale, who, for the sake of peaceful coexistence, renounce the struggle to unmask imperialism and almost completely obliterate the ideological and political struggle against Yugoslav revisionism, under the pretext that on some

[44] This change was explicitly referred to by Longo (*L'Unità*, Dec. 23, 1961) as the basic cause of the Sino-Soviet dispute, as well as in the Belgian CP statement, *Le Drapeau Rouge, loc. cit.* See also Barbieri, *op. cit.*, which alleges that a secret Chinese letter on the Soviet attack on Albania contains *inter alia* this change.

NOTES to Table 4.1:

* The number in parentheses following the name of each country indicates the day of October 1961 on which the speech or message of greetings of its Communist Party appeared in *Pravda*.

a Message of greetings appeared in *Pravda* only, not read to 22nd Congress.

b Message of greetings read along with speech by delegate and included on chart.

c Speech plus unread message of greetings included on chart.

d Speech alone included on chart, although message of greetings appears in *Pravda*.

e When speech and message of greetings are both included on chart, the references to Khrushchev are counted from the speech only.

f Reference to China appears only in unread message of greetings.

foreign-policy issues Yugoslavia supports the Soviet proposals. Such a notion of peaceful coexistence is distorted and anti-Marxist because it leads to a repudiation of the class struggle.

He again rejected what he (incorrectly) alleged was Khrushchev's having made the peaceful transition to socialism "absolute."

Finally, he revealed another issue concerning which he (and presumably the Chinese as well) had been at odds with Khrushchev: Berlin. In the context of insisting on his complete support of the foreign policy of "the socialist camp headed by the USSR" against charges by Khrushchev that the Albanians were "adventurists and warmongers" or in favor of "rapprochement with the imperialists," Hoxha passionately denied that he was "afraid of imperialism" and "afraid to accept our responsibility in the settlement of important international problems," specifically concerning "the signing of a peace treaty with Germany and the settlement of the West Berlin problem." Asserting that Albania had always been in favor of signing the peace treaty and had always supported Soviet policy in this respect, Hoxha then strongly hinted (particularly when one remembers the previous Albanian statement on the question) that Khrushchev had deliberately and wrongly delayed its signing.[45]

Most of the issues on which we cannot be certain that Hoxha was expressing Chinese views as well as his own were geographical in character and limited to the Balkans. But on one, the question of Stalin, the Chinese, as evidenced by Chou's wreath-laying, share much if not all of the Albanian viewpoint.

This issue came up in the context of the organizational question of the Soviet right to impose their own views upon other Communist parties. Hoxha declared that

> The Soviet leaders consider as anti-Marxist, dogmatist, sectarian, and opposed to proletarian internationalism, and so forth, any party which is not of the same opinion as they on certain basic theses which were expounded at the 20th Congress.

This, he maintained,

> constitutes a brutal violation of the principles of equality and independence of Marxist-Leninist parties; it is in open contradiction to proletarian internationalism.

Specifically, Hoxha continued,

> The Albanian Party of Labor has been and is opposed to the criticism made of J. V. Stalin at the 20th Congress and repeated at the 22nd Congress.

[45] Cf. the attack on this in Florin, *op. cit.*

Hoxha was able very effectively to quote Khrushchev against himself:

> After all these actions, how hypocritical sound N. Khrushchev's words of January 1957 that "when it was a question of the revolution, of the defense of the interests of the proletarian class, in the revolutionary struggle against our class enemies, Stalin bravely and implacably defended the cause of Marxism-Leninism. . . . On the primary and fundamental issue — and the primary and fundamental issue for Marxist-Leninists is the defense of the interests of the working class, the cause of socialism, and the struggle against the enemies of Marxism-Leninism — on this primary and fundamental issue, may God grant, as the saying goes, that every Communist may struggle as Stalin struggled."

The Albanian (and the Chinese) case for Stalin and against Khrushchev's destalinization program was put even more effectively than in Hoxha's speech in an Albanian editorial appropriately entitled "The Name and Deeds of Josif Vissarionovich Stalin Live and Will Live for Centuries to Come":

> Stalin's name has found a secure and merited place in the history of mankind, in the hearts of the Soviet people and the peoples of the whole world. It is precisely because of this that he incurred the hatred of the enemies of socialism. There is not and will never be any force in the world which can uproot Stalin from the history and the hearts of the peoples of the world.
>
> By criminally denying and distorting Stalin's historic role in the struggle of the party and people of the Soviet Union for the cause of Lenin, N. Khrushchev . . . is now flying the banner of "anti-Stalinism," that tattered and discredited banner of the savage enemies of Marxism-Leninism and of socialism. Why are N. Khrushchev and his group doing this? He is doing so in order to broaden his prospects for the implementation of a revisionist, anti-Marxist policy. It is precisely for this that the enemies of socialism, the imperialists and their lackeys, the revisionists, have struggled all their lives and continue to struggle with all their strength. The open struggle against J. V. Stalin is a struggle against his immortal deeds, a struggle against Marxism-Leninism.

The amount of time Hoxha devoted to Yugoslavia, the violence of his tone, and the obvious sincerity of what he said demonstrated perhaps more clearly than ever before or since the decisive significance of the hatred and fear of Belgrade in Albanian thoughts and actions. Hoxha declared that the Albanian party

> . . . has also not agreed and does not agree with the Soviet leaders on the question of the attitude toward modern revisionism, and especially toward the traitorous clique of the Yugoslav revisionists. N. Khrushchev and his group used the issue of Stalin and the personality cult to prepare the

ground for the full rehabilitation of Tito's revisionist and traitorous clique, and to present it as a "victim" of Stalin's errors, thereby encouraging the revisionist renegades to initiate in all directions their activity against Marxism-Leninism under the demagogical slogans of "anti-Stalinism," etc.

He continued:

> The viewpoint of the Albanian Party of Labor was and continues to be that the conclusions of Stalin and of the Information Bureau concerning the revisionist renegade clique of Tito were and remain correct. These conclusions have been confirmed and continue to be confirmed both by the Yugoslav conditions at that time and by subsequent events down to the present time. The Yugoslav revisionists became the center of espionage and plots in the service of imperialism against the countries of the socialist camp.

In the text of the Hoxha speech broadcast by Radio Tirana and transmitted abroad in French by the Albanian press agency this statement referred only to the 1948 Cominform resolution, but the official Albanian text, in Albanian and in English translation, reveals that it referred to the 1949 Cominform resolution[46] as well. The validity of the latter had been a matter of subterranean but significant controversy among Stalinist and anti-Stalinist parties in 1955 and 1956;[47] and in fact, as first the Chinese[48] and later Khrushchev[49] revealed, the 1949 resolution was officially annulled, but the 1948 one never was. Hoxha's speech makes clear that the Albanian party had opposed the annulling of the 1949 resolution and still considered it valid; it is, therefore, further confirmation that, as indicated above, the issue of the validity, not of the resolution itself but of its contents (i.e., that Yugoslavia is an imperialist *agentura*), has remained a live one to the present day and one of the major points separating the Soviet and the Chinese-Albanian viewpoints. Hoxha declared that Khrushchev "unilaterally" threw "into

[46] "Communist Party of Yugoslavia in the Power of Murderers and Spies," *For a Lasting Peace, for a People's Democracy!*, No. 28 (55), Nov. 29, 1949, p. 2.

[47] See Walter Ulbricht, "Antwort auf eine Frage betreffend die Volksrepublik Jugoslawien," *Neues Deutschland*, Nov. 1, 1955; *Il Lavoratore* (Trieste), May 30, June 6, 1955, and *L'Unità*, June 1, 4, 1955, in *Ost-Probleme*, VII, 25/26 (June 24, 1955), pp. 991–993; Courtade and Fajon in *L'Humanité*, June 7, 8, 1955.

[48] *Jen-min Jih-pao*, May 5, 1958, reprinted in *Pravda*, May 6, 1958.

[49] Khrushchev to the VII Bulgarian CP Congress, *Pravda*, June 4, 1958, and to the 5th SED Congress, *Pravda* and *Neues Deutschland*, July 12, 1958. According to the Polish defector Seweryn Bialer, Khrushchev said this at the July 1955 CPSU CC Plenum. See also *Einheit*, No. 5, 1958; Novotný in *Rudé Právo*, June 18, 1958; "Modern Revisionism Should Be Combated without Mercy until Its Complete Theoretical and Political Destruction," *Zëri i Popullit*, June 22, 1958. Cf. for the above Zagoria, *The Sino-Soviet Conflict*, pp. 145–151, and Brzezinski, *The Soviet Bloc*, pp. 308–322.

the wastebasket" the Cominform resolution and rehabilitated Tito, thus making it

> . . . possible for the band of Yugoslav renegades to operate more freely against the world Communist and workers movement and against the countries of the socialist camp . . .

and leading to "the rehabilitation of all agents and their companions" in other Communist parties. This in turn made possible the "infamous role" of the Yugoslav revisionists in the Hungarian Revolution. In this connection Hoxha quoted a letter from Khrushchev to Tito dated November 9, 1956, agreeing with him that the question of the Yugoslav sheltering of Nagy after the Revolution should be dropped, apparently in return for Tito's support of Kádár, who, Khrushchev added, had been pushed by the CPSU as Rákosi's successor.[50] In spite of the "revisionist" activities of the Yugoslavs, Hoxha continued, Khrushchev in July 1958 and again during his 1959 visit to Tirana declared that the Yugoslavs should not be attacked lest it raise their importance and lower the still-existing possibility of a rapprochement with them.[51] Finally, Hoxha declared, in spite of the November 1960 Moscow Declaration's condemnation of the Yugoslav revisionists, Khrushchev had rehabilitated them still further by declaring to Sulzberger that "Of course we consider Yugoslavia a socialist country."[52] The Twentieth Congress, Hoxha went on, encouraged all revisionists and renegades, particularly the Yugoslavs, who plotted with Jakova, Spahiu, and Plaku in April 1956 to overthrow the Albanian leadership. Suslov and Pospelov had then tried to persuade him to rehabilitate Xoxe. When this failed, in 1957 Khrushchev offered asylum to Plaku. More recently, Khrushchev was silent about the "plot" of Sejko and others, recommended that other Communist parties take the same view, declared that the plot was invented, and now called its members "patriots and honest fighters."

Turning to Greece, Hoxha then made clear the major significance of Khrushchev's interview with Venizelos in exacerbating Soviet-Albanian relations. Khrushchev, he declared, had demanded that Albania adopt a policy of peaceful coexistence with Greece, had told Sulzberger[53] that American bases in Greece threaten Bulgaria but had never mentioned Albania, had "raised the hopes" of Venizelos for an "autonomous southern Albania," and, worst of all, had told Kennedy at Vienna that "relations between the Soviet Union and Albania have deteriorated."

[50] That this was true seems unlikely; the Soviets imposed Gerö upon the Hungarians. See Váli, *Rift and Revolt in Hungary,* pp. 236–240.

[51] This was correct; see *Pravda,* July 12, 1958.

[52] *New York Times,* Sept. 8, 1961; *Pravda,* Sept. 10, 1961.

[53] *Ibid.*

Finally Hoxha paid his respects to Togliatti, whose criticism of the Albanian party he called "irresponsible and slanderous," and whose 1956 thesis on polycentrism[54] he termed "anti-Marxist" and "a great service to the revisionist Tito."

Four days later, on November 11, the Albanians addressed a letter (approved at the October 12 Albanian Plenum) to the newly elected Soviet Central Committee which appealed to it to intervene against the "brutal anti-Marxist actions of Khrushchev and his group."[55]

The Soviet-Albanian Diplomatic Break

The elaborate, almost Habsburg ceremonial which requires Communist countries to accompany political anniversaries with long ideological pronouncements prevents them, even if they wished, from following Talleyrand's advice to diplomats: *"Et surtout, messieurs, pas trop de zèle!"* Hoxha had spoken on the occasion of the forty-fourth anniversary of the Bolshevik October Revolution, which coincided with the twentieth anniversary of the establishment of the Albanian party. The night before, at a meeting of the Chinese-Soviet Friendship Society in Peking celebrating the same anniversary, the Albanian ambassador and his staff had walked out, and the Chinese did not applaud,[56] when Soviet Ambassador Chervonenko had echoed Khrushchev's criticism of the Tirana leadership and, although reaffirming the international importance of the Twentieth and Twenty-Second CPSU Congresses, clearly disassociated Moscow from the whole range of Chinese policy and ideological views.[57]

The Chinese speaker, Wu Yu-chang, praised Stalin and implicitly reaffirmed the 1949 Cominform resolution.[58] More significantly, that morning *Jen-min Jih-pao* had reprinted the violently anti-Khrushchev Albanian editorial of November 1 along with the other favorable accounts of Albanian activities. On the next day, November 7, in an editorial devoted to the Albanian anniversary,[59] *Jen-min Jih-pao* made crystal-clear the Chinese support of Hoxha and their rejection, without mentioning them, of Khrushchev's charges against Hoxha. Peking praised Albanian foreign policy in phrases which were also a reiteration of Mao's own disagreements with Khrushchev:

[54] Palmiro Togliatti, "9 Domande sullo Stalinismo," *Nuovi Argomenti,* No. 20, June 16, 1956.

[55] "Khrushchev . . . ," *Zëri i Popullit,* Mar. 25, 1962, and Document 26.

[56] Hong Kong dispatch in the *New York Times,* Nov. 7, 1961.

[57] *Jen-min Jih-pao,* Nov. 7, 1961.

[58] *Peking Review,* IV, 45 (Nov. 10, 1961), pp. 8–10.

[59] The one on the Soviet anniversary (full translated text: *Peking Review,* IV, 45 [Nov. 10, 1961], pp. 5–6) was routinely pro-Soviet.

> Albania has all along pursued a peaceful foreign policy and struggled for defending world peace, for realizing peaceful coexistence among countries with different social systems, and for preventing imperialism from launching a world war. It resolutely opposes the U.S. imperialist policies of aggression and war, actively supports the struggle of the people of all countries in Asia, Africa, and Latin America against imperialism and colonialism, for winning and safeguarding their national independence, and supports all the oppressed people in the struggle for democracy.

The Chinese endorsement of the Albanian leadership could hardly have been more complete:

> The Albanian Party of Labor, headed by Comrade Enver Hoxha, the long-tested leader of the Albanian people, is a party taking Marxism-Leninism as its guide to action, a party long steeled in the flames of revolutionary struggle and a party which maintains close contacts with the masses. It has always been loyal to Marxism-Leninism and the principles of proletarian internationalism and to the 1957 Declaration and the 1960 Statement of the Moscow meetings. It has resolutely safeguarded unity with the Soviet people and the peoples of the other socialist countries and the unity of the international Communist movement.

After the Twenty-Second Congress the Soviet Union initially intensified its attacks on the Albanian leadership. They were frequently coupled with renewed blasts against the antiparty group, particularly Molotov, and they normally also represented implicit attacks against China. Moscow used the familiar and time-tested technique of presenting its most extreme charges, against both Albania and China, through the mouths of other than Soviet Communist leaders, thus not totally identifying itself with them but illustrating worldwide Communist support for the Soviet position.

Thus in mid-November *Pravda* reprinted a Danish Communist editorial repeating the general Soviet position, referring to "dogmatism and revisionism" instead of "revisionism and dogmatism," and calling peaceful coexistence one of the "decisive principles" of the "single line" of the Moscow 1960 statement, a veiled answer to Hoxha's denial that it or the Twentieth Congress represented the "general line" of the world movement.[60] Two days later *Pravda* reprinted Togliatti's speech to the November Italian Central Committee Plenum, which for the first time directly criticized the Chinese by name for their support of the Al

[60] "Albanian Leaders on a Dangerous Road," *Land og Volk* (Copenhagen), Nov. 13, 1961, reprinted in *Pravda*, Nov. 14, 1961. That same day's *Pravda* editorial, "The Victorious Banner of Marxism-Leninism," also contained esoteric criticism of the Albanian and Chinese position.

banians.[61] Two days later Moscow printed an article by Tim Buck, Secretary-General of the Canadian Communist Party, which made explicit the Soviet threat of expelling Albania from the socialist camp:

> The leaders of the Albanian Party of Labor well understand that in cultivating a hostile attitude to the USSR, they in fact are following the path of withdrawal of Albania from the commonwealth, one of the most important aspects of which is the Warsaw Pact.[62]

On Monday, November 20, the Albanian Embassy in Moscow took a step, certainly under orders from Tirana and probably planned for some time before but quite possibly precipitated by articles such as Buck's, which may well have been one of the most important immediate factors in causing Moscow to break off diplomatic relations with Tirana. It can best be described by quoting the only published source for it that I have been able to find, a Moscow *Agence France Presse* dispatch:

> *Moscow, Nov. 21 (AFP).* The Albanian Embassy in Moscow on Monday distributed to the diplomatic representations of the countries with which Albania has diplomatic relations documents concerning the history, geography, and cultural and economic life of Albania. They include three documents concerning Soviet-Albanian relations, the October 20 declaration of the Albanian Communist Party, the November 8 [actually 7] Hoxha speech, and a declaration of the Central Committee of the Albanian Communist Party concerning the discussions held in August of this year in Moscow by representatives of the Warsaw Pact states concerning a German peace treaty.
>
> The first two documents were both already published in Tirana. In the third the Albanians accuse Khrushchev of having damaged the world Communist movement by postponing the signature of a peace treaty for Germany contrary to the August agreements.[63]

The Soviets declared[64] that the Albanian Embassy also mailed these documents directly to the Soviet Union Republic Central Committees.

By this action, Moscow declared, the Albanians were deliberately informing capitalist governments of their anti-Soviet views, and secondly, in the third document, unilaterally publishing a declaration in respect to a Warsaw Pact meeting. (Subsequent Soviet and East European charges

[61] *L'Unità,* Nov. 11, 1961, reprinted in *Pravda,* Nov. 16, 1961, and *Jen-min Jih-pao,* Nov. 25, 1961.

[62] *Pravda,* Nov. 18, 1961.

[63] *Neue Zürcher Zeitung,* Nov. 24, 1961. A Yugoslav report indicates that at his Moscow reception on Nov. 8, the Albanian National Day, the Albanian Ambassador displayed a large bust of Stalin, thus incurring great Soviet displeasure (Barbieri from Moscow in *Vjestnik* [Zagreb], Dec. 11, 1961).

[64] Soviet statement on the Soviet-Albanian diplomatic rupture, Dec. 11, 1961, *Pravda,* Dec. 12, 1961.

indicate that the Albanians had begun an extensive program of distributing this material through their diplomats in the Soviet Union and East Europe.)[65] Next *Pravda* reprinted Gomułka's speech at the Polish plenum, which emphasized that

> Not one party disputed the fundamentally correct criticism addressed to the leadership of the Albanian Party of Labor.

Gomułka stressed the lack of support for the Chinese, and, referring to "such an important question as the general line of the foreign policy of socialist states," declared that "it is impossible to hide from the world the differences in the standpoints toward foreign policy."[66] Moscow hoped that such anti-Albanian statements, by such relative rightists as Togliatti and Gomułka, would have more effect throughout the world movement than ones by such obvious Stalinists and totally pro-Soviet figures as Thorez[67] and Novotný.[68]

For Khrushchev, already furious over Hoxha's post-Twenty-Second Congress conduct, the Albanian Embassy's distribution in Moscow of "anti-Soviet slander" may well have been the ultimate incentive to break off diplomatic relations with Tirana. It was certainly also a further move to force all Communist parties to declare themselves for the Soviets as against the Chinese. The activities of the Soviet Embassy in Tirana had probably been further restricted, as Moscow charged after the Twenty-Second Congress.[69] On November 25, Soviet Deputy Foreign Minister Firyubin transmitted two *notes verbales* to the Albanian chargé in Moscow. They announced the withdrawal of Soviet Ambassador Shikin from Tirana due to the restrictions which the Albanians had placed on his activity. In view of the Albanians' distribution of the "lies and ignominious slanders" of the Albanian Central Committee October 20 statement and the November 7 Hoxha speech "to enemies of the socialist camp" (obviously the incident referred to above), plus

65 They were doing the same toward the West; the Dec. 1961 issue of the *Tirana University Bulletin,* when it reached the West, included a "special supplement" (in plain-cover form, 5 by 7 inches) containing the complete English text of the Nov. 7, 1961, Hoxha speech.

66 Gomułka to the IX PZPR CC Plenum, in *Trybuna Ludu,* Nov. 23, 1961, reprinted in *Pravda,* Nov. 25, 1961; quoted from *CDSP,* XIII, 47 (Dec. 20, 1961), pp. 20–21.

67 *L'Humanité,* Nov. 8, 1961.

68 Novotný to the KSČ CC Plenum, Nov. 15–17, 1961, in *Rudé Právo,* Nov. 21, 1961.

69 For somewhat exaggerated Paris press dispatches re troop movements and alerts, evacuation reports, etc., from Tirana (presumably based on dispatches from the French legation there) which, however, most likely had some basis in fact, see *New York Herald Tribune,* Nov. 11, 1961, and an AFP dispatch in *Neue Zürcher Zeitung,* Nov. 11, 1961.

similar activities by various Albanian students in Moscow, they also demanded the recall of the Albanian Ambassador Nesti Nase. (These notes were not publicly known until published by the Albanians on December 10.)[70] The last remnants of Soviet-Albanian relations had collapsed.

Once having published Togliatti's and Gomułka's attacks on China, Moscow then felt free to cite also some stronger and also explicitly anti-Chinese statements by its more totally reliable subordinates Thorez and Ulbricht. On November 26 they quoted Thorez as declaring that

> the Chinese comrades were wrong in reproaching Khrushchev. . . . Their reproach was unjust.[71]

On November 29 they reprinted a stronger demand by Ulbricht that

> . . . the Chinese friends should in some form take a stand concerning the anti-Soviet sallies and violations of the Warsaw Treaty of the leaders of the Albanian party.[72]

On November 30, TASS transmitted a declaration by the Mongolian Second Secretary Tsend attacking Chou En-lai for opposing public discussion of the Soviet-Albanian dispute "without touching on the content of criticism."[73] (Needless to say, this is exactly what the Chinese did not intend to do.) That same day, in an article in *L'Humanité,* Thorez greatly widened the overt charges against the Chinese "leadership" by declaring them guilty of propagating "the erroneous theses of the Albanian leaders."[74]

The next day, December 1, was the first anniversary of the 1960 Moscow Declaration. It thus provided an opportunity for, and indeed practically required, both Moscow and Peking once again to publish comprehensive outlines of their political and ideological positions — in an editorial in *Jen-min Jih-pao*[75] and, on the following day, in a long article in *Pravda*[76] by Andropov, head of the Soviet Central Committee liaison section with Communist parties in power.

[70] Texts: *Zëri i Popullit,* Dec. 10, 1961, and Document 16.

[71] Thorez in *L'Humanité,* Nov. 22, 1961, and *Pravda,* Nov. 26, 1961.

[72] Summarized in *Pravda,* Nov. 27; text reprinted Nov. 29.

[73] The Nov. 30 *Pravda* text omits this passage.

[74] This was the first implicit reference to Mao, to whom "the leadership" (*la direction*) clearly refers. In the same article Thorez resumed the attack against Trotsky, ascribing to him such errors as the slogan "neither war nor peace," "adventurism," wanting to "stimulate revolution by war," and militarizing the trade unions — all clear references to Chinese ideological and policy considerations.

[75] "Holding Aloft the Marxist-Leninist Revolutionary Banner of the Moscow Statement," *Jen-min Jih-pao,* Dec. 1, 1961.

[76] Yu. Andropov, "The Twenty-Second Congress of the CPSU and the Development of the World Socialist System," *Pravda,* Dec. 2, 1961, and *CDSP,* XIII, 48 (Dec. 27, 1961), pp. 8–10.

The Chinese editorial was in form a restatement of the 1960 Moscow Declaration; in fact it emphasized, as had been done a year before, those passages which best justified its own ideological position, and in some respects it went even further. After fulsomely praising the unity of the socialist camp ("of 12 fraternal countries" — i.e., including Albania) and Soviet-Chinese friendship, and formally endorsing peaceful co-existence, it continued:

> Only when the imperialist and capitalistic systems are wiped off the face of the earth can mankind's great ideal of everlasting peace be really translated into reality.

Furthermore, its attacks on revisionism and particularly on Yugoslavia went considerably further than the Moscow Declaration, while it did not mention dogmatism or sectarianism. It again reiterated the theme of the 1949 Cominform Resolution. Its formulations on the nature of revisionism as the servant of imperialism were such as clearly to imply that Khrushchev was among its proponents, and that Peking foresaw a long struggle against it — and him.

The Chinese formulation of the relationship between proletarian internationalism and the equality and autonomy of individual parties again clearly revealed their refusal to submit to Soviet pressure and their continued insistence upon "unanimity through consultations" as a requirement for binding international Communist decisions.

In the same December 1 issue of *Jen-min Jih-pao* the Chinese also employed the Soviet tactic of pushing forward their own positions through the mouths of allied Communist leaders. On November 16 the Chinese had reprinted the full text of Hoxha's November 7 speech, and on November 8 they had published an original article by Shehu which stressed Hoxha's themes. They now published a statement by one of the most influential of their partial supporters, D. N. Aidit, the head of the Indonesian Communist Party. The Soviets would probably not wish totally to alienate Aidit, any more than they would Ho Chi-minh and Kim Il-sung, by attacking him in return. Aidit's article expressed what one can probably assume is Peking's real position on the question of the expulsion of Albania from the socialist camp, as well as, it may be, that of the Polish, Italian, and of other smaller Communist parties: that this is impossible as long as Albania is "objectively" building socialism. Aidit wrote:

> During and after the CPSU 22nd Congress imperialists, revisionists, Trotskyite elements, all reactionaries rejoiced at the criticism of Albania and the renewed criticism of Stalin and the anti-party clique. Concerning Albania they created an atmosphere as if the question had been raised

"who will leave the socialist camp." They were like a brothel master; from each one who withdrew they would draw profit. Actually, the question is completely different. This question and SEATO, NATO, and CENTO military alliances, organized according to treaty, are not the same. The socialist camp is organized from the socialist states. They did not do this according to treaty agreements. When a country genuinely achieves a socialist political, economic, and social system, although there are no treaty stipulations, and where there are opposing positions between this country and other socialist countries, this country is in the socialist camp. Adherence to the socialist camp is not decided by subjective reasoning but arises from objective fact: a country which is genuinely building socialism, one which does not have a society where man exploits man. Albania is a state which is building such a society. Comrade Khrushchev himself does not deny this.

Aidit's statement demonstrates Moscow's difficulty in attacking what Professor Brzezinski has called the "Jansenists"[77] — the extreme left wing — of the world movement. To maintain their centrist position and to prevent East European right-wing deviations, Khrushchev must maintain his condemnation of the Yugoslav "revisionists." The Albanians (and Chinese) thus find it easier to declare Tito an "imperialist agent" and Yugoslavia not to be a socialist country than do the Soviets in finding suitable ground for a counterattack against them. But for Khrushchev to declare that Albania (or China) is *not* building socialism would confront him with dialectical problems vis-à-vis the world Communist movement that he would find most difficult successfully to surmount.

In reprinting Aidit's article, the Chinese also implicitly endorsed his very strong formulations on the independent decision-making power of each individual Communist party (ones very similar to those of Gomułka, Kádár, and Togliatti), thus elaborating upon their own more cautious formulation in their December 1 editorial:

As I have repeatedly stated before (and this is in conformity with the contents and spirit of the 1960 announcement): The PKI is an independent Marxist-Leninist political party: it enjoys equal rights with other Communist parties; it does not accept leadership from other parties and of course does not lead other parties. The PKI determines its own policies, basing itself on Marxism-Leninism. The PKI is responsible to the Indonesian working class and laboring people, but at the same time, it is also responsible to the world workers movement. Therefore the people of the PKI, when faced with the fact of conflicts in the world Communist and workers parties, cannot adopt a negative attitude.

The anti-party clique which opposed the CPSU from within also constitutes an internal problem of the CPSU. Other parties have no right to

[77] "Deviation Control," *op. cit.*

> interfere because they cannot "deeply understand" its conditions and problems. We can only conclude that: the formulae for solving inner party opposition are determined to a large degree by the history, traditions, and conditions of the party concerned.
>
> As a consequence, each party has its own formulae when solving inner party opposition. The PKI does not intervene in the internal problems of other parties. In the same way, the PKI does not want other parties to intervene in its internal problems. This does not mean that the people of the PKI do not want to hear of the internal problems of the fraternal parties. However, the making of resolutions in regard to party internal problems is entirely the right of the Communist party concerned. It is only in this way that the friendship between the PKI and the other Communist parties and between the various Communist parties can be maintained and made more intimate. The intervention of one party into the internal problems of another party can only lead to splits and to unnecessary difficulties within the party which is the object of intervention.

The next Soviet riposte was in the Andropov December 2 *Pravda* article. Significantly, its title referred to the Twenty-Second Congress and not to the 1960 Moscow Declaration. The Andropov article was the most complete Soviet refutation up to then of the Albanian (and, *implicite,* the Chinese) case. Addressing itself to the Albanian charge that neither the Twentieth Congress nor any other purely Soviet event or pronouncement was *eo ipso* binding upon all other Communist parties, Andropov quoted the 1960 Moscow Declaration and the Albanian Third Congress to prove that the Twentieth Congress

> was warmly greeted by all the fraternal parties and was the beginning of a new stage in the international Communist movement.

Andropov then quoted a right-wing, "autonomist" leader, Gomułka, on the international significance of the CPSU Program:

> Although this program is that of one single party, the CPSU, . . . its significance and impact on developments will go far beyond the boundaries of the USSR. In a certain sense, it is a program for the entire international Communist movement and contains prospects for the development of all mankind.

He insisted that the CPSU Program "further develops Marxist-Leninist teaching, adapted to the new historic situation" as compared to the 1957 and 1960 Moscow Declarations — i.e., is "more equal" than they.

In conclusion he outlined the political and economic advantages for other Communist countries (and for Communist parties not yet in power) of supporting the Soviet (rather than the Albanian and Chinese) position:

> The mutual exchange of experience and the strengthening of cooperation between the socialist countries in all fields — economic, political, technical and cultural — is an objective necessity and is in the interests of each country and of the socialist commonwealth as a whole.[78]

The Andropov article was another signal that Moscow had decided to break diplomatic relations with Tirana. Only on December 10 did the world learn that on the day following the article, December 3, the Soviet Foreign Ministry transmitted another *note verbale* to the Albanian diplomatic personnel from the Soviet Union announcing the withdrawal of all Soviet diplomatic personnel from Tirana. Moscow gave as reasons the harassment of the Soviet Embassy and the Albanian demand that its personnel be cut to two-thirds.[79]

The first public Albanian response to this as yet unpublicized Soviet note was a long December 6 editorial[80] elaborating further on Hoxha's charges against Khrushchev. The editorial officially was in commemoration of the 1960 Moscow statement, which, it charged, Khrushchev had referred to shortly after its publication as "a compromise document of short duration." As an occasion for attacking Khrushchev, it chose the statement by the Soviet leader's son-in-law Adzhubei in the course of his interview with President Kennedy that "you Americans should be proud" of your President. "These matters," the editorial declared, "are not accidental" but rather comprise the entire opportunist line persistently followed by N. Khrushchev, who "called De Gaulle 'the pride of the French people,' " and declared that "Eisenhower 'sincerely desires' peace and the liquidation of the 'cold war,' " and now was spreading "throughout the world the illusion that Kennedy would . . . follow a peaceful policy."

After reiterating the main Chinese-Albanian policy lines and Hoxha's November 7 charges and declaring that the Italian Communist Party after the Twenty-Second CPSU Congress had "revived the revisionist theses on the 'degeneration' of the Soviet socialist system," the editorial, as usual, reserved its choicest epithets for the Yugoslavs. "The leaders of the League of Yugoslav Communists," it declared, "are subverters of the socialist camp and the international Communist movement and disrupters of the forces of peace." How, the article went on, can the statement's charges be reconciled with Gromyko's statement in his December 23, 1960, speech to the Supreme Soviet that "our positions coincide" with Yugoslavia's and with Khrushchev's statement to Sulzberger that, "Of course we consider Yugoslavia a socialist country"?

[78] Quotations from *CDSP,* XIII, 48 (Dec. 27, 1961), pp. 8–10.

[79] Text: *Zëri i Popullit,* Dec. 10, 1961, and Document 16. For the Albanian version, see p. 120, *infra.*

[80] "A Year of Historic Proofs," *Zëri i Popullit,* Dec. 6, 1961, and Document 15.

Fully aware of the attacks against the Italian Communist Party's "polycentrism" by Thorez, Gomułka, Novotný, and others, the editorial not only condemned Togliatti for having

> openly introduced the task of agreeing as much as possible with the Yugoslav Communists

but added the cryptic assertion:

> . . . the leaders of certain socialist countries in Europe started implementing this long ago by continually developing and expanding economic, commercial, cultural, political, and even party relations with the Yugoslav revisionists.

(The allusion presumably was to Poland, whose attitude toward Yugoslavia had remained considerably less hostile than Khrushchev's although more so than Togliatti's.)

Finally, in a clear forerunner of the diplomatic break, the editorial stated that "a few days ago" the Soviet Union and Hungary had canceled the consular agreement with Albania which permitted travel without visas by Albanians through those countries, necessary to get to China via the Soviet Union by air.

Replying in a brief note of December 4 and a much longer one of December 9,[81] both made public on December 10, the Albanians once again with even more bitterness and violence proclaimed their case against the "diabolical aims" of "N. Khrushchev and his group." As to cutting down the personnel of the Soviet Embassy in Tirana, they declared that they had only requested it be reduced to the same size as that of the Albanian Embassy in Moscow. They added that in any case Khrushchev had expected and intended that Shikin, who had spent only five months altogether in Albania, be withdrawn. As to the Soviet charges about the Albanian distribution of anti-Soviet material in Moscow, they countered with the statement that "for several years" the Albanian Embassy there had been full of microphones and all its visitors had been under police surveillance, that after the Twenty-Second Congress it had been forbidden to contact any Soviet citizens except the Soviet Foreign Minister, had been surrounded by Soviet police, and all Soviet citizens had been prevented from entering, and in any case the "pretext" that it had distributed anti-Soviet materials was "a shameful and provocative offense"; such materials as the Albanian October 20 Central Committee declaration and the November 7 Hoxha speech were

[81] Text: *Zëri i Popullit,* Dec. 10, 1961, and Document 16.

> inspired by feelings of eternal Albanian-Soviet friendship and based on the principles of Marxism-Leninism and the Moscow Declarations of 1957 and 1960.

After once again vowing the eternal friendship and gratitude of the Albanian people and party for the Soviet people and the Soviet Communist Party, the second note in language of almost apoplectic fury summed up Tirana's charges against Khrushchev.

These Albanian outbursts were not much more violent although much more specific than the simultaneous albeit esoteric anti-Soviet blasts from Peking. This was the period of the Adzhubei interview with President Kennedy and of the debate in the United Nations General Assembly on the admission of Communist China. Each alone was enough to arouse Peking's fury; but the blasts directed against them were in fact primarily aimed at Moscow, and their violence can undoubtedly be explained in part by the crisis and break in Moscow-Tirana diplomatic relations. In accordance with its firmly maintained policy of maintaining editorial silence on differences in the Communist camp, Peking did not comment on this latter issue directly, and in fact it did not publish the news of the break until December 15. However, the articles by the authoritative anonymous "Observer" in *Jen-min Jih-pao* of December 8 and 10[82] were the strongest Chinese statements for a year or more.

[82] "Observer," "Kennedy's Wishful Thinking," *Jen-min Jih-pao,* Dec. 8, 1961, and "Refuting Stevenson," *ibid.,* Dec. 10, 1961; English texts in *Peking Review,* IV, 50 (Dec. 15, 1961), pp. 5–7 and 7–10, respectively.

CHAPTER FIVE

After the Soviet-Albanian Break

The December 1961 International Confrontations

The first three weeks in December also saw two major international Communist-front gatherings, the Fifth World Federation of Trade Unions (WFTU) Congress at Moscow, December 4–15, and a meeting of the World Peace Council (WPC) in Stockholm, December 16–19. Both meetings were dominated by the Sino-Soviet dispute; in both the Albanians took a militantly pro-Chinese line, and in both the tripartite alignment (rightist, centrist, and leftist) became clearer and more pervasive. The Italian rightist offensive was the major new factor at both meetings; it must have made it more difficult for the Soviets to label the Chinese and the Albanians as the sole troublemakers.

In the WFTU debate[1] three complexes of issues were of significance for the Sino-Soviet dispute: the relative priority of the struggle for peace and of that for national liberation, joint action with non-Communist trade unions, and the degree of autonomy of national trade-union federations.

On the first issue, which was also the main point of Sino-Soviet dissension at the WPC meeting, the great majority of the delegates supported the Soviet position: absolute priority for the struggle for peace and for general and complete disarmament. The Chinese,[2] the Al-

1 For regular coverage, see TASS, NCNA, TANYUG, and especially the Moscow dispatches in *L'Unità* and *Avanti!* (TASS and NCNA coverages were each strongly slanted). For analysis, G. E. Lynd, "Workers Disunite," *Problems of Communism,* XI, 2 (Mar.–Apr. 1962), pp. 18–23; *International Organisations* (London, mimeo.), No. 131 (Jan. 1962), pp. 9–13, Kx. [Ernst Kux], "Kontroverse im kommunistischen Weltgewerkschaftsbund," *Neue Zürcher Zeitung,* Dec. 16, 1961; and Branko Lazitch, "Le travail 'fractionnel' des Chinois dans les organisations satellites internationales," *Est et Ouest,* XIV, 277 (Apr. 16–30, 1962), pp. 1–4. For a penetrating analysis of CGIL thinking, see Michel Bosquet (from Rome) in *L'Express,* Jan. 4, 1962, pp. 13–14; cf. Luciano Romagnoli in *Rinascita,* XIX, 1 (Jan. 1962), pp. 23–26.

2 Speech of Liu Chang-sheng, NCNA in English from Moscow, Dec. 8, 1961, 1942 GMT (*Peking Review,* IV, 50 [Dec. 15, 1961], pp. 24–27); see also his report on the WFTU Congress to a Chinese trade-union meeting, NCNA in English from Peking, Dec. 28, 1961 (SCMP 2651, Jan. 4, 1961, pp. 40–44), and the statement of the WFTU Chinese delegation, NCNA in English from Moscow, Dec. 13, 1961 (SCMP 2642, Dec. 19, 1961, pp. 34–36).

banians,[3] and most pro-Chinese Asian parties[4] opposed this; significantly, they were also joined by some African[5] and Latin American[6] delegations.[7] (Not surprisingly, on the issue of the overriding priority of anti-colonialism, the Chinese position exercised considerable appeal for underdeveloped countries.) The Chinese reportedly also demanded the deletion from the draft WFTU resolution of all references to the Soviet Twenty-Second Congress.[8] Both the Chinese and the Albanians, however, were careful at the meeting to moderate somewhat their polemics against Moscow. The fact that an Albanian delegation, led by the trade-union secretary Kocani, was present indicated that the Soviets did not as yet wish to allow the Soviet-Albanian break to cause unnecessary difficulties in international Communist-front organizations.[9] Kocani's speech followed the Chinese line. Far from attacking the Soviet Union, he praised it, although not as highly as he did China. However, in his speech he substituted "modern revisionism" (i.e., including Khrushchev) for the phrase "Yugoslav revisionism" in his prepared text.[10]

On the second issue the Soviets and their allies generally favored an extension of cooperation with non-Communist unions on certain specific issues, particularly the struggle for peace. The Italian delegation, which spearheaded the right-wing current, took an even stronger position in this respect.

On this issue and on the third, the question of national trade-union autonomy, the Italian delegation, led by Agostino Novella, WFTU chairman and head of the Italian trade-union federation (CGIL), which includes Nenni Socialists as well as Communists, arrived in Moscow with seventeen pages of amendments[11] to the draft congress resolutions. The

[3] The text of Kocani's speech is not in the Dec. 13, 1961, *Zëri i Popullit* report, but a Chinese broadcast (Radio Peking in Mandarin, Dec. 13, 1961, 1400 GMT) indicates it followed the usual Tirana line. The most revealing report on it is in Ferrara from Moscow in *L'Unità*, Dec. 13, 1961.

[4] The account in *Harian Rakjat* (Djakarta), Dec. 15, 1961, of the Moscow WFTU speech by Indonesian trade-union head Njono does not make it clear whether he took a pro-Soviet or a pro-Chinese position.

[5] E.g., Zanzibar (TASS in English to Europe, Dec. 10, 1961, 0655 GMT) and Nigeria (*ibid.*, Dec. 5, 1961, 0728 GMT).

[6] E. g., Roja Mendes of Brazil, *ibid.*

[7] According to Italian Communist reports ("Oggi in Italia" in Italian to Italy, Dec. 12, 1961, 2100 GMT, and Ferrara from Moscow in *L'Unità*, Dec. 14, 1961), the French delegation supported the Chinese and Albanians, *inter alia* by not applauding the Italian delegate Santi's speech; this is not clear from the French speeches.

[8] *Vjestnik* (Zagreb), Dec. 9, 1961.

[9] The Yugoslav "observer" stationed at the WFTU meeting also made it difficult for Moscow to exclude the Albanians.

[10] Ferrara from Moscow in *L'Unità*, Dec. 13, 1961.

[11] For the CGIL position and the preparation of the amendments, see a report by Luciano Romagna to the CGIL Executive Committee (*L'Unità*, Dec. 1, 1961)

amendments demanded a more extensive degree of cooperation with non-Communist trade-union organizations, particularly with such regional ones as the Pan-African Trade Union Federation, on an *ad hoc* basis and, if necessary, at the expense of organizational unity, rather than constant attacks on them and on imperialism; greater emphasis on convergence of WFTU aims with those "peoples struggling for their political and economic liberation"; and a major increase in the autonomy of national trade-union organizations affiliated with the WFTU.[12] (The amendments were thus clearly along the lines of previous Italian Communist right-wing pronouncements.) The Italians were guardedly supported by the Polish trade-union head Ignacy Loga-Sowinski[13] and by the Yugoslav observer Svetozar Vukmanović-Tempo.[14]

Loga-Sowinski stressed common action with non-WFTU members quite as strongly as did the Italians, while his formulations on worker participation in management, like many Italian Communist ones, were remarkably similar to Yugoslav views. One Italian report indicates that sympathy for the Italian position was also demonstrated by the Austrian, Swedish, Cypriot, Algerian, and Cuban delegations.[15]

On the issue of the WFTU's attitude toward such regional trade-union organizations as the Pan-African Trade Union Federation, its representative, the Guinean delegate, took the Italian position, stressing the importance of trade-union autonomy and of peaceful coexistence.[16] (This rightist attitude was just the opposite of the leftist, anti-Soviet one that the Guinean delegate took at the Stockholm WPC meeting; nationalism was the key common denominator in both.)

---

and the much more revealing article by Elio Capodaglio (*Avanti!,* Nov. 19, 1961), which includes comparisons of the WFTU draft program and the CGIL draft (published in *L'Unità,* Nov. 16, 1961), with quotations of both. The CGIL preliminary debate was in large part a reflection of the growing PCI-PSI polarization; see a statement by Novella (*L'Unità,* Nov. 16, 1961) and a letter to *Avanti!* (Nov. 15, 1961) by a group of PSI CGIL figures. It also reflected the post-XXII Congress PCI rightist trend.

12 For Novella's speech, see Ferrara from Moscow in *L'Unità,* Dec. 7, 1961; for Santi's *ibid.,* Dec. 13, 1961. There were also Japanese, Polish, Indonesian, Lebanese, and Spanish amendments submitted (*ibid.,* Dec. 8, 16, 1961).

13 See the text of his speech, *Głos Pracy,* Dec. 7, 1961 (cf. TANYUG from Moscow, Dec. 7, 1961), and his report on the WFTU meeting to the 15th Plenum of the Polish Central Trade Union Council, Dec. 30, 1961, in *Głos Pracy,* Jan. 2, 1962. The Poles also submitted some amendments; I have been unable to find any material about their contents (Moscow dispatches to *L'Unità* and *Avanti!,* Dec. 16, 1961).

14 See his speech in *Borba,* Dec. 12, 1961. Tempo went much further, stressing independence of national trade-unions and workers' self-management. One report (Radio Zagreb, Dec. 10, 1961) indicates that the Austrian delegate also supported the Italians.

15 Ferrara from Moscow in *L'Unità,* Feb. 13, 1961.

16 Habib Bah (TASS in English to Europe, Dec. 6, 1961, 0732 GMT); see Ferrara from Moscow in *L'Unità,* Dec. 7, 1961.

A clear indication of the extent of the rightist and leftist opposition to the Soviet-sponsored line was given when after the December 11 pro-Soviet speech by Benoît Frachon, the French representative, the delegations which neither stood nor applauded, according to an Italian report, included the Poles, Yugoslavs, Cypriots, and, on the presidium, the Indian and Chinese. Vukmanović-Tempo's speech the same day was not applauded by the Chinese and Albanians nor by some Latin American delegations.[17]

After long behind-the-scenes negotiations some of the Italian amendments were apparently accepted over strong Chinese, Albanian, and Southeast Asian opposition. However, the Soviet-led centrist majority, whose position was expressed in the speeches of Khrushchev,[18] the Soviet trade-union head Grishin,[19] the WFTU Secretary-General Louis Saillant (France),[20] and Benoît Frachon, prevented the Italians from winning their major points.[21] Even so, although the final resolutions were adopted all but unanimously (one Italian Socialist, Di Pol, voted against them), the Italian delegate Luciano Lama read a declaration clearly indicating CGIL dissatisfaction with the compromise reached.[22]

The December 16–19 Stockholm meeting of the World Peace Council[23] produced considerable additional evidence on the Sino-Soviet differences over political priorities. The Soviets, supported by an overwhelming majority of the delegates, insisted that the overriding priority of the world peace movement must be the struggle against atomic war and for the Soviet plan of general and complete disarmament, and that the peace movement must be broad rather than exclusive in its membership. The Chinese, Albanian, North Korean, North Vietnamese, Australian, and some African and Latin American delegates declared, on the contrary,

[17] Ferrara from Moscow in *L'Unità,* Dec. 12, 1961.

[18] *Pravda,* Dec. 10, 1961.

[19] *Trud,* Dec. 5, 1961. *Trud* did not publish the text of Novella's speech.

[20] TASS in English to Europe, Dec. 4, 1961, 0849 GMT.

[21] Radio Belgrade, Dec. 6, 1961.

[22] Text: *L'Unità* and *Avanti!,* Dec. 16, 1961.

[23] For running Communist coverage, see TASS and NCNA. The most revealing Communist source is the interview with one of the Italian delegates, Velio Spano, in *L'Unità,* Dec. 23, 1961. See the Austrian CP CC Resolution, Feb. 1962, rejecting the CCP position (*Volksstimme,* Feb. 10, 1962), an interview with an Austrian delegate, Dr. Scholl, in *ibid.,* Jan. 6, 1962; Terfve, *op. cit.;* for the Soviet attitude, *Pravda,* Dec. 26, 1961; for the Chinese, *Jen-min Jih-pao,* Dec. 23, 1961; for the North Vietnamese (stressing the Chinese position but with no indication of disagreements and essentially "neutralist"), Le Dinh Tham, chairman of the Vietnamese Peace Committee and head of the Vietnamese delegation at Stockholm, in *Nhan Dan* (Hanoi), Dec. 27, 1961. The most detailed summary of the WPC meeting is in *International Organisations,* No. 131 (Jan. 1962), pp. 1–8; for analysis, see Kx. [Ernst Kux], "Streit unter den kommunistischen 'Friedenskampfern,' " *Neue Zürcher Zeitung,* Dec. 31, 1961, and Lazitch, "Le travail 'fractionnel' des Chinois dans les organisations satellites internationales," *op. cit.*

that the first priority must be given to the struggle against imperialism and colonialism and for national liberation and that the peace movement must exclude those who did not agree with its political line.

The two senior Soviet delegates, Aleksandr Korneichuk and Alexei Surkov, stressed the danger of thermonuclear war and the consequent necessity for priority struggle for disarmament, a German peace treaty and a Berlin settlement, and the end of nuclear testing and demanded "broad" contacts, rather than a "sectarianism" which refused to recognize any but a single political viewpoint. They were supported by the French, Italian, Czechoslovak, Hungarian, Indian, and Japanese speakers. (The Japanese, who might normally have been expected to support the Chinese position, presumably could not avoid giving priority to the struggle against thermonuclear war in view of Japanese public opinion on this subject.)[24]

The Chinese speech by Liao Cheng-chih, head of the Chinese delegation,[25] was a renewed and intensified challenge to the general line of Soviet foreign policy. For him there were two priorities for the world peace movement:

> . . . to heighten our vigilance and continuously expose U.S. imperialism, the most vicious enemy of peace . . . [and to] support . . . the national liberation movement. . . .

For disarmament (he gave no credit to Khrushchev or the Soviet government for this; neither was mentioned in his whole speech),

> . . . it is necessary to wage an active and resolute struggle against the imperialist forces of aggression. . . .

His formulation on peaceful coexistence implicitly attacked the Soviet position on it. The Soviet view that peaceful coexistence must be the worldwide general line until the final victory of socialism was clearly rejected. Not only did Liao reject Khrushchev's desire to negotiate with Kennedy, who "does not have the slightest sincerity for negotiation," but he rejected the whole idea of two or a few great powers deciding the fate of all nations. This was a repetition of the Chinese position that they would not be bound by agreements to which they were not parties and also a direct appeal to the smaller Communist and left-wing representatives. On the other hand, Liao's violent attack on the United Nations would perhaps not appeal to them so much. By referring to the socialist camp as "composed of 12 countries," Liao clearly reaffirmed Chinese support of Albania.

[24] *Ibid.*
[25] Text: *Peking Review,* IV, 51 (Dec. 22, 1961), pp. 12–14.

The other Chinese speaker, Liu Ning-yi, flatly rejected the "erroneous and most harmful view" that disarmament was the priority task of the peace movement, which, he declared, must join hands with and support the national liberation movement and expose the true hostile nature of United States imperialism. As had Hoxha, Liu said that the latter, not West German militarism, was the primary danger to peace and that the primary task of oppressed nations was

> . . . the building and strengthening of their own armed forces . . . to defend themselves against imperialism and colonialism. . . .[26]

Liu's appeal to the smaller countries was not without success, particularly since the anti-colonial Chinese position was bound to appeal to the less developed and newly independent of them. Diallo Seydou, the Guinean representative, rejected the Soviet position on priorities just as flatly as the Chinese.[27]

The Albanian delegate took at least as extreme a position as the Chinese, demanding that the only item on the agenda of the forthcoming conference should be national independence. As summarized by the Communist Chinese news agency, the Albanian delegate Misha

> . . . pointed out that nobody has denied the importance of disarmament, but disarmament is not the only road. The wolf of imperialism cannot change into a sheep. . . . Even if it disguises itself as a sheep, it has the aim of making it more convenient for itself to eat sheep. The Kennedy administration is worse than the Eisenhower administration, he said. It poses a threat to the Soviet Union and the other socialist countries and uses the United Nations to attack the Congo. . . . Some people intend to take the path of concession to imperialism. In the past the peace forces had been far weaker than today, and at that time they dared to struggle, holding on and defeating imperialist attacks. At present, as the peace forces become ever stronger, why should they retreat? The people of Algeria, Angola, and the Congo are now resisting imperialism. No voting machine or "diplomacy in the lobby of the conference hall" can stifle their indignant voices, he said. In the past imperialist threats and intervention could not bar the victory of the Soviet people and neither can they bar the victory of the struggles of the peoples of these countries. . . . The Algerian and Cuban peoples cannot wait for disarmament by the United States and France. Thousands upon thousands of people suffer persecution by neocolonialism and are resisting it. At this juncture, how can one demand that they carry out disarmament? . . . The congress due to be held next year should be a congress of national independence, at which the true

[26] NCNA in English to Asia, Dec. 20, 1961 (SCMP 2647, Dec. 28, 1961, pp. 28–29; summary: *Peking Review,* IV, 52 [Dec. 29, 1961], pp. 13–14).

[27] NCNA in English to Asia, Dec. 19, 1961, 1704 GMT, SCMP, *loc. cit.*

features of U.S. imperialism, the enemy of peace, are thoroughly exposed. . . .[28]

An Albanian article in early March made the Albanian position clearer; at the Stockholm meeting, as at Moscow, they apparently did not attack the Soviets by name:

> . . . N. Khrushchev and the propagandists of his theses . . . carefully try to evade the resolute unmasking of American imperialism. . . . Indeed, even in articles written for occasions such as the Congress of the WFTU . . . or the gathering of the World Peace Council . . . it was not deemed appropriate to mention by name the main citadel of aggression and war in the world, monopoly imperialism of the United States of America.
>
> . . . In an article on . . . [the meeting of the WPC in Stockholm] which was published in the magazine *Za Rubezhom,* a bitter attack was made on the delegates who requested that the forthcoming World Peace Congress be a "congress of peace, national independence and disarmament." This article states: "These orators, using detestable methods, alleged that there are some people who consider total and general disarmament as the only task of the movement for the defense of peace and that they are, allegedly, weakening their support of the national liberation struggle of the peoples."
>
> . . . But . . . it was precisely the Soviet delegation which, with great obstinacy, refused to place on the agenda of the forthcoming congress of peace partisans the question of the struggle against colonialism and for national independence . . . and insisted that the agenda include only the issue of disarmament and peace. . . .
>
> . . . The position of the Soviet delegation on this issue provoked the righteous indignation of not only Communist revolutionaries, but also many non-Communist delegates, representing the peoples of Asia, Africa and Latin America. . . .
>
> . . . The Communist movement is familiar with the distorted view of N. Khrushchev that every "little war" is a threat to world peace, and that "every spark can set off a world conflagration." According to this logic, the conclusion emerges that every national liberation war is undesirable, since it may result in the eruption of a third world war. The position of the Soviet delegation at the World Peace Council in Stockholm was none other than the practical application of this anti-Marxist thesis of N. Khrushchev. . . .[29]

This Albanian article also elaborated on Liu's thesis that the United States, not West Germany, was the main threat to world peace and the

[28] *Ibid.,* Dec. 22, 1961, 1834 GMT.

[29] "Whom Do N. Khrushchev's Views and Actions Serve?" *Zëri i Popullit,* Mar. 2, 1962, and Document 25. See also the attack on the Albanian WPC delegation by Raymond Guyot in *L'Humanité,* Dec. 28, 1961, and the Albanian reply in *Bashkimi,* Dec. 31, 1961.

camp of socialism. (Presumably, the Chinese and the Albanians, neither directly involved in the Berlin crisis and both violently anti-American, considered Khrushchev's giving priority to Germany as being too pro-American.) As one of the Italian delegates later said,

> . . . a fundamental contrast was manifested between the positions of those who firmly believe in the possibility of averting war, in the existence of genuine conditions which today render possible the realization of general disarmament, bringing it down from the plane of the ideal to the plane of political reality, who . . . are convinced that in every country the struggle for peace ought to have its own particular line of development, and on the other hand those who have less faith in peaceful coexistence and disarmament and, therefore, place the accent on the basic struggle against imperialism, making their objectives for peace coincide with those for the liquidation of imperialism and colonialism in all its forms.
>
> It was soon evident . . . that any attempt at reconciliation would be quite useless . . .[30]

The same delegate made clear that the Italians had originally intended to introduce at this meeting much the same line that Novella and his associates had followed at the immediately preceding WFTU meeting.

Unprecedentedly, the agenda of the forthcoming 1962 World Peace Congress was not accepted unanimously. The Chinese and their Albanian, Asian, African, and Latin American supporters refused to accept the 1960 WPC presidium proposal that the congress would be only on peace and disarmament and that there would be another (undated) conference of African, Asian, and Latin American partisans of peace on the national liberation struggle, but supported the Guinean proposal that the congress should be on "peace, independence, and disarmament." Some 50 of the 250 delegates, perhaps disgusted by the controversy, left before the final vote, and 24 voted against the resolution on the subject.

Stronger Anti-Albanian Soviet Polemics

In mid-December two articles appeared in the Soviet press which further elaborated on the Soviet charges in the Andropov December 2 article. In some respects implicit replies to the Chinese articles already discussed, they reflected the increasing exacerbation of Sino-Soviet relations as a result of the WFTU and WPC meetings.

In a long article in the CPSU ideological journal *Kommunist* its

[30] Interview with Velio Spano, *L'Unità*, Dec. 23, 1961.

editor, Konstantinov,[31] charged the Albanian leadership with having published only a "truncated, falsified" version of the Soviet Draft Program, deliberately omitting "all that concerns criticism of Yugoslav revisionism and contemporary revisionism in general," passages which "give the lie" to Albanian anti-Soviet charges in this respect. Konstantinov compared Hoxha's and Shehu's "lawlessness" with Yezhov's and Beria's. Reviving the basic ideological charge made by Ponomarev at the Twenty-Second Congress, he declared that the essence of the Albanian affair is "nationalism." This, he said, was evidenced by the "inordinate demands" the Albanians made on the Soviet Union and other socialist countries, and was due to the fact that they "do not understand the role of the neutral countries in the struggle for peace," and to their "resentment of the aid given by the Soviet Union and the other socialist countries to underdeveloped countries of Asia and Africa," which "extends the anti-imperialist front." Echoing Khrushchev's main charge against the Chinese at the 1960 Bucharest and Moscow meetings, Konstantinov charged that

> . . . Hoxha and Shehu above all militate against the definition of our epoch given in the declaration of 1957, the statement of 1960, and the Program of the CPSU. . . .

This, he said, was particularly true in respect to peaceful coexistence, which the 1960 declaration had termed the general line but which the Albanians consider

> . . . merely a phrase, words which do not bind one, a clever tactical maneuver. . . .

There followed a passage clearly directed against Mao's famous declaration that imperialism in general, and the United States in particular, is only a "paper tiger":

> . . . The dogmatists Hoxha and Shehu do not want to realize that the imperialist tiger, while remaining a tiger, can no longer plunder with impunity, as . . . in the past, for he is now very much afraid of the socialist giant. . . .[32]

The other article, a December 14 *Pravda* editorial,[33] declared that Hoxha's deviation on peaceful coexistence is "a direct divergence"

31 F. Konstantinov, "The Schismatic, Anti-Marxist Activity of the Albanian Leaders," *Kommunist,* No. 17, 1961, pp. 38–53.

32 As an example of Chinese articles on this theme, see "He Who Cannot Kill a Tiger Cannot Be a Hero," *Kung-jen Jih-pao,* Sept. 12, 1961, quoting extensively on this theme from Vol. 4 of Mao's collected works.

33 "On a Dangerous Path," *Pravda,* Dec. 14, 1961 (quoted from *CDSP,* XIII, 50 [Jan. 10, 1962], pp. 23–25, 32).

from the principle of the 1960 Moscow statement. In a clear albeit explicit reply to the previous Chinese articles, it stated that

> . . . The question of peace and peaceful coexistence is the paramount question of modern times. Either peaceful coexistence or destructive world thermonuclear war — there is no other choice. It is quite clear, therefore, that those who oppose a policy of peaceful coexistence are playing into the hands of the most militant and adventurist circles of imperialism, which are preparing a new thermonuclear war. . . .

The article then repeated the charge that the Albanians had declared that Albanian-Soviet relations would be "on the basis of known principles of peaceful coexistence among states with different social systems" — a distortion of what the Albanians actually had said.[34]

Turning to the Albanian charge that the Soviets were trying to "impose" their views, contrary to the 1960 Moscow Declaration, the article stated that on the contrary the Soviet Communist Party had insisted that the formula "camp of socialism led by the Soviet Union" should be deleted.[35] In the course of a long diatribe against the lawless cult of the personality in Albania the article contained an interesting new twist in the constant attempt to equate dogmatism with revisionism and the Albanians (and Chinese) with the Yugoslavs:

> . . . The Albanian leaders crudely distort the heroic history of the CPSU and of the development of the Soviet state and try to equate the entire experience of the CPSU and of the Soviet people with the Stalin cult. Such fabrications have nothing in common with reality. It is not difficult to notice that at this point the Albanian leaders join hands with the revisionists. Both try to affix the cult of the individual to the Soviet social system. But, as the saying goes, horseradish is no sweeter than radish, and both points of view are equally alien to revolutionary theory. . . .

Declaring that Hoxha had deliberately sabotaged the resolutions of the 1948 and 1956 Albanian Party Congresses, the article asserted that

> . . . The actions of the Albanian Party of Labor's leaders on the question of the cult of the individual bear the distinct marks of a top-level antiparty conspiracy. . . .

The conclusion was a further step in building up the Soviet accusation that the Albanians were "objectively" serving the imperialists, in this instance citing as authority that presumably imperialist journal the *New York Post:*

[34] See *Zëri i Popullit,* Oct. 5, 1961.

[35] The reference was to Khrushchev, *op. cit.;* cf. Zagoria, *op. cit.,* pp. 346–347.

> . . . Under the smoke screen of shrill phrases about their "loyalty" to Marxism-Leninism and to the Declaration and Statement of the fraternal parties, the leaders of the Albanian Party of Labor in reality wage an open struggle against the general line of the world Communist movement. It is not surprising, therefore, that the imperialists have welcomed the present "separate" course of the Albanian leadership with undisguised approval. . . .

The Soviet Union's constantly increasing counterattack against Albania and China continued throughout December, January, and February. In a long, programmatic, and very strong ideological editorial on December 20, *Pravda*[36] strongly emphasized the importance for the whole world Communist movement of the new Program's declaration that the CPSU as the dictatorship of the proletariat in the Soviet Union had now been replaced by the CPSU as a "party of the whole people" — a thesis which represents Khrushchev's internal liberalization program in perhaps its most all-inclusive form. At the same time it made clear that a monoparty system is not "obligatory" — another indication of the extent of domestic autonomy which Khrushchev is willing to grant to Communist parties in power. After reiterating the "creative" importance of the Twentieth and Twenty-Second Congresses as a "new stage" for all Communist parties, the editorial once again indirectly reaffirmed the Soviet position on the issue of fractionalism by declaring that all Communist parties observe decisions arrived at "jointly" (i.e., in contrast to the specific Chinese reaffirmation of unanimity). Lastly, it emphasized the importance of

> . . . the development of the theory of scientific communism, the struggle for its purity, against revisionism, dogmatism, and sectarianism. . . .

Just as the most violent and complete attacks on the Soviet position came from the Albanians and not the Chinese, so the most complete of the December series of Soviet or Soviet-sponsored attacks on the Albanians and the Chinese came not from a Soviet leader but from the Hungarian First Secretary János Kádár. From Moscow's viewpoint Kádár must have seemed almost an ideal instrument for this purpose. Himself having some sympathy for the rightist, "autonomist" wing of the world Communist movement, he was, however, so weak internally, required as he was to balance between Nagyist revisionism and Stalinist extremism, and so dependent upon the presence, actual or potential, of Soviet power to support him, that he probably had no alternative but to accede to Soviet desires in the drafting of his contribution, which then

[36] "The Leninist Party Is the Leader and Organizer of the Nationwide Struggle for the Victory of Communism," *Pravda*, Dec. 20, 1961.

achieved the official Soviet imprimatur by being published in *Pravda* on December 26.[37]

Kádár began by a sharp refutation of the Chinese views on peaceful coexistence and the national liberation struggle, without (as throughout) mentioning the Chinese by name. (This aspect of his article may most probably be explained by the Chinese attack on the Soviet positions on these two issues at the meetings of the World Federation of Trade Unions and the World Peace Council earlier in December.) Kádár outlined and rejected any concessions toward the Albanian and Chinese position on peaceful coexistence. On the national liberation struggle Kádár again summarized, and somewhat distorted, the Albanian and Chinese position:

> . . . There are people who fail to realize the facts, or perhaps wishing to mislead others, who mix up three such fundamentally different notions as civil war, the liberation struggle against colonialists, and imperialist war.

He countered by declaring simply that "these cannot and must not be confused."

Turning to the increasingly important ideological question of the nature and origins of dogmatism, Kádár then developed more fully than the Soviets had done before the thesis that it, like revisionism, is a product of bourgeois nationalism. This was immediately followed by a sarcastic thrust clearly aimed at Mao (Hoxha, Shehu, and the Albanian leadership are far too young to be called "senile"):

> . . . We could, unfortunately, observe, that this disorder appears in some people as a "senile disorder," and in combination with power it can assume a harmful and revolting character.

Kádár then delivered a blast against the rightist theories of the Italian Communist Party (to whom he referred only as "the socialists who call themselves 'leftist' representatives of the workers' class in capitalist countries") and in so doing gave the most complete ideological refutation yet published of the revisionist thesis that Stalinism proves that something was wrong with "the socialist system":

> . . . The leading party of a socialist society itself reveals the errors that come up and hamper development, and the party itself corrects them, thus speeding up the rate of advance and setting free all the creative forces of society. After liberating itself from arbitrariness and the violation of legality connected with this arbitrariness, the social system of the Soviet Union and other socialist countries has consolidated and entered

[37] János Kádár, "Lenin's Ideas Will Triumph," *Pravda,* Dec. 26, 1961.

a new stage of development. . . . The builders of socialism reveal the shortcomings themselves. They overtly oppose the errors committed during the advance on untraveled roads in the building of a new society, and they overcome these shortcomings with the strength of their healthy young organism.

Kádár asserted that not only the overcoming of the cult of the personality but also the current "discussion among the Communists" are in fact signs of health, not of decay:

> . . . The imperialists would like to profit from the discussions and the differences in views between the Communist and workers parties and the Albanian leaders.
>
> They will now shout from each housetop: Look here, the Communists are quarreling, and there is a split in the Communist camp. Yes, there is indeed a discussion among the Communists. There were some even before, and there will be some even in the future. But none of our discussions eases the situation of capitalism. Communist discussions result every time in the consolidation of Marxist-Leninist ideas, and in the overcoming and elimination of erroneous views. The Communist parties and the entire international Communist movement represent a union of people with equal thoughts, and Marxism-Leninism is not a code of dead dogmas, but a living and steadily developing science.
>
> The struggle between new and old is going on in the ideological sphere as in any other sphere of life. As a rule, large-scale discussions in a revolutionary movement usually take place at turning points of its social development.

He then came to the gravest charge he made against the Albanians and by clear implication against the Chinese: "Trotskyism." This charge, one of the worst which any Communist can hurl, was framed in such a fashion as to be clearly within the context of the Sino-Soviet dispute and the Soviet-Albanian polemics on issues of foreign policy and of the transition to Communism:

> . . . After the victorious end of the civil war in 1921 . . . Trotsky asserted that it was impossible to build socialism in one country alone, and that a world revolution must come first. Trotsky refused to see that the revolutionary wave in the capitalist countries had ebbed. At the same time he did not believe in the possibility of building a socialist society in backward czarist Russia. He cloaked his disbelief in "leftist" phrases and demanded a "permanent revolution." . . .
>
> . . . Another discussion is now underway about how to go further. Regardless of the existence of capitalism in a great part on the world, history poses the question of a higher stage of society to be attained by mankind, a society without exploitation, of Communist building. The views

of Enver Hoxha and his stooges strikingly remind one in many respects of the views of the Trotskyites, who in the early twenties refused to make daily efforts to build socialism, and even resorted to adventurism and phrasemongering. As is known, this tendency of the Trotskyites suffered a shameful defeat, and at the present stage of its development the world Communist movement, having matured, dooms similar views to failure in advance. . . .

Kádár then approached his last and most tricky point: the question of authority within the international Communist movement. Here he clearly reaffirmed the Soviet position: "jointly" arrived at (i.e., majority) decisions, the Soviet party "marching in front of all" but all parties having "equal rights and responsibilities," with "neither one party nor . . . several parties either leading or being led." He rejected the Italian thesis of polycentrism, declaring that

> . . . only loyalty to the ideas of Marxism-Leninism as well as ideological and political mutual understanding can guarantee the unity of the international Communist movement. . . .

Thus he could only pose, not solve, the contradictory position in which Khrushchev had found himself: If only ideological unity remains, the Soviet Union no longer being the "leading party," who defines this ideology?[38]

It was now the turn of the Chinese and the Albanians. In a New Year's editorial *Jen-min Jih-Pao*[39] took a harder foreign-policy line than it had since the beginning of the Sino-Soviet dispute, and intimated that the dispute would worsen still further.

The Albanians were surprisingly silent from early December to early January, but apparently only because they were preparing another major editorial salvo. Appearing on January 9, it was an all-out attack on "N. Khrushchev and his group," appropriately entitled "Deeper and Deeper into the Mire of Anti-Marxism."[40] Although it added nothing basically new to the controversy, it expanded our knowledge of the policy differences between Moscow on the one hand and Peking and Tirana on the other by stating them more clearly than was done at the World Peace Congress. Summing up all its charges, the article declared that

> . . . N. Khrushchev and those who follow him . . . have revised the fundamental teachings of Marxism-Leninism on the reactionary and aggressive nature of imperialism, and on this basis they treat opportunisti-

[38] Ulbricht (*Neues Deutschland,* Dec. 18, 1960) said that exactly this question had been raised at the Moscow meetings.

[39] "New Year's Greetings," *Jen-min Jih-pao,* Jan. 1, 1962, and *Peking Review,* V, 1 (Jan. 5, 1962), pp. 6–9.

[40] *Zëri i Popullit,* Jan. 9, 1962, and Document 22.

cally the question of peace and peaceful coexistence, the national liberation struggle of enslaved peoples, the question of the paths of transition from capitalism to socialism, proletarian dictatorship, and so forth. They have seriously trampled on the principles of proletarian internationalism in relations between fraternal Communist and workers parties and between the socialist countries. . . .

Peaceful coexistence, the article declared, cannot be the "general line" of the foreign policy of socialist countries since relations between socialist states must be better than those merely of peaceful coexistence. The "dangerous . . . wrong, pacifistic, and bourgeois" views of Khrushchev on disarmament result in

> . . . the conclusion . . . that the national liberation struggle of enslaved peoples, the struggle against the various forms of colonialism and neocolonialism, and the revolutionary struggle of the working people to overthrow capitalist slavery are secondary problems which do not merit special attention and which depend entirely on the achievement of general and total disarmament. And this logical conclusion is and has been more confirmed each day by the practical acts of treason of N. Khrushchev and his group. . . .

But the achievement of total and general disarmament "demands a long time" because of the imperialist opposition to it; therefore,

> . . . it is erroneous and very dangerous to check the struggle of the enslaved peoples and the working people in the capitalist countries, and to compel them to endure untold suffering and pain, pending the achievement of general and total disarmament. . . .

In addition, the article maintained, Khrushchev

> . . . has intentionally ignored the necessity of struggling to unmask the warmongering activities of imperialism, especially of American imperialism. . . .

At the Twentieth Congress and thereafter Khrushchev had overemphasized the peaceful transition to socialism, had not told Communists "that they should simultaneously and concurrently prepare for both events," and had opportunistically identified peaceful with parliamentary transition.

Khrushchev's incorrect destalinization policy had led to the 1956 Hungarian events: it had

> . . . provided grist for the reactionary and revisionist elements and facilitated conditions for them to carry on their hostile activity. . . .

Furthermore,

> . . . Khrushchev, Mikoyan, Suslov, and other Soviet leaders[41] closed their eyes to the hostile activity of . . . Tito and the Imre Nagy group, together with the imperialists . . . and trusted and supported them. . . .

As to Stalin himself, the article declared that

> . . . Our party also firmly repudiates the efforts of N. Khrushchev's group to uncrown Stalin and to deny his great merits as a distinguished theoretician of Marxism-Leninism who resolutely defended Leninism from the attacks and distortions of Trotskyites, Bukharinites, and other enemies, and further developed it under new historic conditions. . . .

It returned again to the frequent Albanian charge that Khrushchev himself was developing a personality cult, this time citing as an example such "unworthy stupidities" as his pounding on the table at the United Nations General Assembly with his shoe.

As to the Soviet charges that the Albanian leaders had not carried out the resolutions of their party congresses against the cult of the personality and violations of socialist legality, the article declared that in 1948 it had been the Yugoslav agent Koci Xoxe who had been guilty and in 1956 it had been the "traitors Plaku, Jakova, Spahiu, Gega" and others,

> . . . certain revisionist elements of the Tito clique who, encouraged by the revisionist theses of the 20th Congress, unsuccessfully tried at the Tirana party conference in April 1956 to split the party, to overthrow its leadership, and to create in Albania a situation similar to the one which was later created in Hungary. . . .

The article then proceeded to link these, Tito, and the May 1961 "plotters" with the Greeks, Yugoslavs, and the American Sixth Fleet with "Khrushchev and his group":

> . . . It is this very scum of our society which N. Khrushchev and his supporters are protecting, while they present the correct activities of our party and our trials against the spies and agents of imperialism and its lackeys as terrorism, as violation of socialist legality, as consequences of the existence of the personality cult, and so forth. . . .

As to the question of authority and legitimacy in the international Communist movement, the article attempted to meet head-on the Soviet statement that the Twentieth Congress represents "a new stage in the international Communist movement" by maintaining that this "openly

[41] Note that the Albanians here made no distinction between Khrushchev and Suslov; if Suslov were the "Stalinist" that some Western observers often declare him to be, the Albanians would hardly have mentioned him in this context.

contradicts" the 1960 Moscow Declaration's statement about the equality of parties and that furthermore

> . . . the authors of the *Pravda* article, trying to justify their position, refer to the contents of the 1960 Declaration on the international significance of the Twentieth Congress. But it is known how this thesis was included in the Declaration. The Soviet leaders, contrary to the spirit of the Declaration on the independence and equality of sister parties, are using this thesis to impose on them the decisions of the Twentieth Congress, although at the Moscow meeting of November 1960 they solemnly stated that they would never interpret and use it with such intent. The true aims of N. Khrushchev and his comrades are now appearing more and more clearly. . . .

The article also presented an extensive but hardly totally convincing account of the controversy about the phrase "the camp of socialism headed by the Soviet Union," declaring that this is favored by Albania because the Soviet party is "the most experienced," but that it implies no directing powers. Khrushchev's "hypocritical and formal" abandonment of the phrase, on the other hand, was "an inadmissible concession to the revisionist elements," which only

> . . . encouraged them in their efforts to disrupt the international Communist movement, to spread their anti-Marxist views, and to isolate the Communist and workers parties from the historic experience of the Soviet Union and its Communist Party. Because of this, in certain Communist parties — for example, the Italian Communist Party — much propaganda has been made for "polycentrism," which, in fact, means to renounce the principle of the international solidarity of the Communist and workers parties as well as the general laws of the socialist revolution and the building of socialism, discovered by Marxism-Leninism and attested in practice and, above all, by the historic experience of the Communist Party of the Soviet Union. . . .

A sharper Soviet response to the renewed Chinese and Albanian assault followed in five articles by senior Soviet ideological spokesmen in the three most authoritative organs of Moscow's views: *Pravda, Kommunist,* and *Problems of Peace and Socialism.*[42]

[42] A. Popov and A. Sergeev, "Peaceful Coexistence — the General Line of Soviet Foreign Policy," *Kommunist,* No. 18, Dec. 1961, pp. 54–62, passed for the press Dec. 26, 1961, but appearing at the end of the month (*New York Times* Moscow dispatch, Dec. 31, 1961); A. Rumyantsev (its editor), "Our Common Ideological Weapon," *World Marxist Review* (English and Canadian edition of *Problems of Peace and Socialism*), V, 1 (Jan. 1962), pp. 3–12 (Russian edition passed for the press Dec. 22, 1961, but since printed in Prague, appearing in Moscow several weeks later — *New York Times* Moscow dispatch, Jan. 14, 1962); Jiří Hendrych (Czechoslovak Politburo member and CC Secretary), "The XXII Congress of the CPSU and the Development of the Socialist World System,"

The primary theme of these articles was peaceful coexistence. As a prelude to emphasizing its absolute necessity, they described the probable damage of thermonuclear war in terms which, although not explicitly reversing the post-Malenkov doctrine that only the imperialists would be totally destroyed by it,[43] still went much further than any previous Soviet declarations and were strikingly parallel to earlier Italian ones.

After quoting or paraphrasing[44] Khrushchev's statement at the Twenty-Second Congress[45] that the Soviet Communist Party, the camp of socialism, and the forces of peace had enabled war to be avoided, the articles made more clearly a point which Khrushchev had formulated at the Congress.[46] Peaceful coexistence was defined:

> . . . not only as the general foreign-policy line of the peace forces at the present moment, but *as the basic line that will remain in force until the social and political problems which now divide mankind are solved. . . .*[47]

Nevertheless, they stressed the importance of the "subjective factors" of struggle for peaceful coexistence:

> . . . *the slogan of excluding world war from the life of society is a militant slogan, a slogan for the mobilization of the masses. . . .*[48]
>
> . . . Peaceful coexistence does not exclude revolutionary changes in society but presupposes them, does not slow down the world revolutionary process but accelerates it, does not preserve the capitalist order but deepens the disintegration and collapse of imperialism. . . .[49] By dedicating their creative energies to the building of Communism, the peoples of the USSR and the other socialist countries are at the same time making a decisive contribution to the class struggle against the moribund capitalist system. . . .[50]

---

ibid., pp. 12–20; N. Inozemtsev, "Peaceful Coexistence — A Most Important Question of Our Times," *Pravda,* Jan. 17, 1962; P. Pospelov (head of the Institute of Marxism-Leninism), "V. I. Lenin and the Prague Conference," *Pravda,* Jan. 18, 1962; cf. Terfve, *op. cit.;* Vladimir Smolanski, "Peaceful Coexistence and the Class Struggle," Radio Moscow, Feb. 1, 1962, 1915 GMT, and I. Medvedev, "From Dogmatism in Theory to Adventurism in Politics," *Izvestiya,* Feb. 4, 1962. Although the Popov, Sergeev, Rumyantsev, and Hendrych articles appeared before the Chinese and Albanian ones, they are treated in this context because they form part of the same syndrome of escalating Soviet ideological pressure, primarily on the peaceful-coexistence issue.

43 Inozemtsev, *op. cit.*

44 Rumyantsev, *op. cit.,* p. 8; Popov and Sergeev, *op. cit.,* p. 61; Inozentsev, *op. cit.*

45 *Pravda,* Oct. 18, 1961.

46 Khrushchev, *loc. cit.*

47 Rumyantsev, *op. cit.,* p. 8 (italics in original); cf. Inozemtsev, *op. cit.,* Popov and Sergeev, *op. cit.,* p. 61.

48 Rumyantsev, *op. cit.,* p. 9 (italics in original).

49 Inozemtsev, *op. cit.* (italics in original).

50 Rumyantsev, *op. cit.,* p. 5; cf. Popov and Sergeev, *op. cit.,* p. 58.

Moreover, in reply to the Chinese-Albanian charge that the Soviet Union should give them aid, so their transition to Communism would be simultaneous with its transition rather than with that of non-Communist underdeveloped countries, one non-Russian author, Hendrych, clearly implied that China's and Albania's continued defiance of Moscow would slow down their transition still further.[51]

The articles then turned to an attack on the Chinese and Albanians, as usual without naming the former, but this time clearly connecting both with the antiparty group, who were accused of taking an "anti-Leninist" attitude on peaceful coexistence.

Although it seemed at the end of January 1962 that Sino-Soviet relations were continuing to deteriorate fairly rapidly, in February and early March this process appeared to be slowing down somewhat. Many observers had expected that in early March the Soviet Central Committee plenum would bring some major new intensification of the continuing anti-Chinese counterattack; the contrary was the case.

There was no immediate letup, however, in anti-Soviet Albanian polemics. After a brief lull in early February, on February 25 the opening of the Fourth Albanian Congress of agricultural cooperatives gave Shehu and Kapo the occasion to launch renewed denunciations of Khrushchev. In his opening speech Shehu,[52] after almost proudly describing Albania's plight of total geographical encirclement by capitalists and revisionists and of economic blockade by "Khrushchev and his followers," accused the Soviet First Secretary of using "fierce and unprincipled conspiratorial methods" against "socialist Albania." Kapo[53] denounced Khrushchev's concessions to imperialism, his reluctance, like that of the revisionists, to aid national liberation movements, ostensibly lest war might result but actually to aid imperialism, and the ever-increasing solidarity of Khrushchev and Tito:

> . . . N. Khrushchev and his followers . . . draw more and more closely to the Tito gang. The line and the aims which they pursue are identical. Palmiro Togliatti has publicly called for a greater rapprochement with "our Yugoslav comrades." . . .

Kapo reaffirmed Tirana's allegiance to Chou's Moscow doctrine against the public airing of party differences:

> . . . Our party never publicized these affairs outside our Communist family. Our party never gave the imperialist enemies weapons against the Soviet Union and the socialist camp . . . even when the hostile actions

[51] Hendrych, *op. cit.,* p. 17.
[52] *Zëri i Popullit,* Feb. 27, 1962.
[53] *Ibid.,* Feb. 28, 1962.

of N. Khrushchev and his companions in certain socialist countries and in Western countries were being speculated on by the entire world . . .

and concluded with the assertion that:

. . . It is not the leaders of the Albanian party who have sold themselves to imperialism, but the "marvelous" and "preferred" men of N. Khrushchev like Rudolf Barák and others who have sold themselves to imperialism for 30 pieces of silver. . . .

At the begining of March another new Albanian ideological declaration[54] further refined Tirana's classification of "N. Khrushchev." After describing and denouncing his manifold revisionist betrayals of Marxism-Leninism, the socialist camp, and international communism, it concluded by pointedly quoting Lenin:

". . . A man who 'sincerely' declares himself a Communist but who in reality, instead of conducting a clear-cut and ever resolute policy, a policy that is heroic and courageous to the point of self-denial (only such a policy is consonant with recognition of the dictatorship of the proletariat), wavers and appears afraid — such a man, because of his lack of character, his vacillation, and his indecision, commits treason no less than the out-and-out traitor. From the standpoint of personality, the difference between the traitor who acts from weakness and the traitor who acts from calculation and premeditation is very great. From the standpoint of politics, this difference *does not exist,* since politics involves in fact the fate of millions of people and this fate is not altered by the manner in which millions of poor workers and peasants are betrayed — whether by traitors who betray from weakness or by traitors who betray from self-interest. . . ." (V. I. Lenin, *Works,* Vol. 30, p. 404, Albanian ed.)

In early February, Suslov[55] reiterated the Soviet formula that revisionism was "the chief danger in present-day conditions" and stressed the continuing need for vigilance against revisionism and reformism as well as against dogmatism. However, he went on to say that "dogmatism is the most dangerous form of divorce of theory from practice" and, obviously referring to the Albanian claim to primacy in the struggle against revisionism, declared that

. . . Dogmatic and ultra-leftist distortions of Marxism nourish revisionism and create favorable, nutritious soil for it. One cannot fight successfully against revisionism or uproot it from Communist soil without first overcoming and outgrowing dogmatic distortions of Marxism.

[54] "Whom Do the Views and Actions of N. Khrushchev Serve?" *Zëri i Popullit,* Mar. 2, 1962, and Document 25.

[55] *Pravda,* Feb. 4, 1962; quoted from *CDSP,* XIV, 5 (Feb. 28, 1962), pp. 12–16.

Dogmatic positions are expressed in the most concentrated form by the leaders of the Albanian Party of Labor. . . .

At the end of January the Soviet line on peaceful coexistence was reaffirmed, with perhaps somewhat more emphasis on the continuing inevitability of revolution — be it peaceful or nonpeaceful — as a pre-requisite for the establishment of the dictatorship of the proletariat and socialism.[56] The Sino-Soviet greetings and celebrations of February 13–14, honoring the twelfth anniversary of the Sino-Soviet Treaty of Friendship, Alliance, and Mutual Assistance, were on both sides notably less cordial than those of the previous year yet did not indicate that the Sino-Soviet dispute had substantially worsened since the previous month.[57] The most significant element in Soviet propaganda output during this period was the intensification of emphasis on the "international significance" (i.e., the automatically binding force) of the Twenty-Second Congress and of the Soviet party program, and in general on the Soviet Union as the "center" of the international Communist movement. On February 21, *Pravda* devoted three pages to documenting this claim, carrying anti-Albanian statements by fraternal parties and their leaders demonstrating the international support given to Khrushchev against Hoxha by quoting their anti-Albanian statements. It then answered the Albanian and Chinese charge that imperialism is aided by publicizing interparty disputes, implying more clearly than before Moscow's duty to do so:

> . . . F. Engels criticized the idea that genuine revolutionaries should not unmask sham revolutionaries because the mutual recriminations would give comfort to the bourgeoisie. Engels said: "Any struggle has times when it is impossible not to give some comfort to the enemy if you do not want to do yourself positive harm." Fortunately we have advanced so far that we can give the enemy such private comfort if at this price we achieve real successes. . . .

These themes were made even more explicit in another major programmatic article on this same theme by Viktor Rudin in the February issue of the same magazine.[58]

The March 5 Soviet Central Committee Plenum, as announced, was devoted by Khrushchev primarily to agricultural problems. The Soviet

[56] G. Starushenko, "Peaceful Coexistence and Revolution," *Kommunist,* No. 2, Jan. 1962, p. 81 (passed for the press, Jan. 30, 1962).

[57] For anniversary editorials, see *Pravda,* Feb. 14, 1962, and *Jen-min Jih-pao,* Feb. 14, 1962 (in *Peking Review,* V, 7 [Feb. 16, 1962], pp. 6–7).

[58] Viktor Rudin, "Triumph of the Leninist Principles of Party Life," *World Marxist Review,* V, 2 (Feb. 1962), pp. 3–10.

First Secretary chose implicitly to attack the Chinese on the familiar theme that they wanted a kind of Communism of ascetic poverty:

> . . . Among the many responses to the new Party Program in foreign countries one also encounters those that express doubt about whether the Program is correct in laying special emphasis on the production of material benefits for the people. Some critics of our Party Program are trying to represent Soviet Communists almost like people who are inclined to picture Communism in the form of a table laden with good things.
>
> Such reproaches against Communists and Marxist-Leninists are not new. The opponents of scientific Communism, standing on idealist positions, have always tried to ridicule and discredit the sober and realistic approach of Marxist-Leninists to the people's vital needs, to the satisfaction of their material requirements. Our opponents have tried and are trying to represent the concern of Communists for the people's welfare in a vulgar and extremely distorted form.
>
> Marxist-Leninists have always exposed such attacks on Communism and waged a decisive struggle against them. . . .
>
> . . . Communism cannot be conceived of as a table with empty plates at which sit "highly conscious" and "fully equal" people. To call this "Communism" is like inviting people to eat milk with an awl. This would be a caricature of Communism. . . .[59]

In the winter and early spring of 1962, then, Sino-Soviet relations seemed to be worsening steadily. True, the Chinese had ceased in January 1962 to reprint all Albanian anti-Soviet speeches and articles, and they were also careful not to associate themselves publicly with any anti-Soviet Albanian acts. Nevertheless, direct Soviet-Albanian and esoteric Sino-Soviet polemics were clearly still intensifying.

SUAVITER IN MODO, FORTITER IN RE: *The Decline of Public Divergence*

Sometime in April 1962 these trends were reversed: There developed a definite surface improvement in Sino-Soviet and Soviet-Albanian relations.[60] Exchange of delegations began again between Moscow and Peking, the Soviets began reprinting some Chinese articles,[61] mutual em-

[59] *Pravda,* Mar. 6, 1962; quoted from *CDSP,* XIV, 8 (Mar. 21, 1962), p. 3.

[60] Cf. Roderick MacFarquhar in *The Daily Telegraph* (London), May 1, 1962; Harry Schwartz in *The New York Times,* May 6, 1962; Richard Rockingham Gill, "Der chinesisch-sowjetische Disput und der Kongress in Peking," *Hinter den eisernen Vorhang,* VIII, 5 (May 1962), pp. 1–6.

[61] Notably "Laying a Solid Foundation, Working Serenely and Going Forward Step by Step," *Jen-min Jih-pao,* Mar. 29, 1962, reprinted in *Pravda,* Apr. 3, 1962. A concerted and probably exaggerated attempt was made, presumably at Soviet initiative, by Communist correspondents in Moscow to demonstrate that this reprinting portended significant improvement in Sino-Soviet relations; see Pancaldi

phasis on the importance of Sino-Soviet unity increased, and a new albeit not extensive Sino-Soviet trade agreement was signed.[62] This surface improvement of Sino-Soviet relations was also reflected in the international front organizations: after a violent encounter at the February Cairo meeting of the Afro-Asian Writers Conference,[63] the late March Vienna session of the World Peace Council Executive Committee resulted in unanimous agreement on a communiqué and thus in some relaxation of Sino-Soviet ideological tension.[64] The June 1962 Budapest meeting of the WFTU Executive Committee also less clearly mirrored Sino-Soviet differences than at the WFTU Congress in Moscow the previous December.[65] Direct Albanian polemics by name against Khrushchev stopped as of April 13;[66] the Soviets ceased public condemnation of Hoxha and Shehu about the same time.[67] Hoxha in late May referred to this problem with Moscow only as "a number of existing difficulties, for which we are not to blame";[68] and Khrushchev at the end of April indicated a more hands-off Soviet attitude toward Albania:

---

from Moscow in *L'Unità* and Barbieri from Moscow in *Vjestnik* (Zagreb), both Apr. 4, 1962. For further Soviet reprinting, see Barbieri in *Vjestnik*, Apr. 19, 1962. He also (*Vjestnik*, Apr. 5, 1962) reported that Ho Chi-minh had mediated between Moscow and Peking.

62 NCNA in English from Peking, Apr. 20, 1962 (SCMP 2726, Apr. 27, 1962, pp. 38–39). Cf. Barbieri from Moscow, *Vjestnik* (Zagreb), Apr. 16, 1962. See also a new agreement on Sino-Soviet scientific and technical cooperation, *Pravda*, June 25, 1962.

63 TASS and NCNA, Feb. 12–14, 1962; "Wolves and Sheep," *Vjestnik* (Zagreb), Feb. 22, 1962. This had been preceded by a Sino-Soviet clash at the Dec. 9–11, 1961, Gaza meeting of the Afro-Asian Peoples Solidarity Organization. See the pro-Soviet speech by its secretary Yusuf as-Sibai (TASS, Dec. 11, 1961) and the pro-Chinese one by Liao Cheng-chih (NCNA, Dec. 11, 1961).

64 *International Organisations* (London), No. 123 (Apr. 1962), pp. 1–8; Barbieri from Moscow in *Vjestnik* (Zagreb), Apr. 5, 1962; Spano in *L'Unità*, Mar. 22, 1962.

65 See, for the Chinese, who took a very anti-Yugoslav line, NCNA from Budapest, June 5, 1962, 0055 GMT; for North Korea (pro-Chinese), KCNA in English to Asia, June 2, 1962, 1647 GMT; for Poland, PAP in English to Europe, June 3, 1962, 1727 GMT; for the USSR, *Trud*, June 1, 1962; for the peace and disarmament appeal, *ibid.*, June 5, 1962. Albanian coverage of the meeting (*Zëri i Popullit*, June 1, 3, 5, 1962) did not indicate whether an Albanian representative participated.

66 The last one was "Crocodile Tears," *Zëri i Popullit*, Apr. 13, 1962.

67 The last Soviet attack on Hoxha and Shehu by name was on Mar. 16, with the exception of one in Radio Moscow in English to Southeast Asia, May 10, 11, 12 1962, 1100 GMT. See also the attack on Hoxha and Shehu in Georg Kar, "The Socialist Revolution — Peaceful and Non-Peaceful," *World Marxist Review*, V 5 (May 1962), pp. 28–35, at p. 34, ftn. 10. The Soviets continued their polemics against the Albanians, but did not name their leaders; they remained considerably more critical of the Albanians than the latter did of Moscow.

68 In his strongly anti-Yugoslav and pro-Chinese election speech, *Zëri i Popullit*, May 31, 1962. For an earlier, more theoretical example, see "Lenin's Ideas Live and Triumph," *ibid.*, Apr. 22, 1962. For other Albanian attacks on Yugoslavia, see Albanian-Yugoslav disputes at the Warsaw international con

> . . . As far as Albania goes . . . we see certain matters differently from the leaders of the Albanian Party of Labor. We have been engaged in arguments with them over these matters, but the internal development of Albania is the internal affair of the Albanian people themselves, and we have been and are now adhering strictly to the principle of noninterference in the affairs of other peoples, including the Albanians.[69]

There were also a few other signs of a slight détente in Soviet-Albanian relations, notably the renewal of trade agreements between Albania and the East European states.[70] The significance of these agreements, though deriving more from the fact of their conclusion than from their content, was unclear. They probably reflected in part a minor Soviet gesture of conciliation toward China; and they perhaps also indicated a preference on the part of some of the East European leaderships (in particular, the Polish) to encourage a continuation of Albania's defiance whereby they would gain increased maneuverability vis-à-vis Moscow. Albania's relations with pro-Soviet Balkan Communist parties also appeared to improve. Albania had been excluded from a mid-March Sofia meeting of the Communist committee for mutual understanding and cooperation in the Balkans,[71] yet in late May the chairman of the Greek committee was cordially received on a visit in Tirana.[72]

But this surface improvement in Sino-Soviet-Albanian relations was both deceptive and short-lived. How or why it occurred remains unclear; a stage of declining Communist ideological polemics is far less revealing than one in which controversy is increasing. In retrospect, it probably represented an ebb in the cyclical pattern so characteristic of the "divergent unity" of Sino-Soviet relations.[73] It most likely resulted from a Sino-Soviet agreement, which the Chinese presumably then imposed upon the Albanians, that such violent and public controversy

ference of resistance historians (TANYUG in English to Europe, Apr. 19, 1962, 1104 GMT, and "The People Must Not Forget June 22nd," *Zëri i Popullit,* June 22, 1962) and at a Balkan medical conference at Bucharest (B. L., "The Delegate from Tirana at the Doctors' Gathering," *Borba,* May 19, 1962); see also "The Splitting Activities of the Traitorous Yugoslav Trade Union Leaders Should Be Firmly Denounced," *Puna,* Apr. 27, 1962.

[69] Interview with Gardner Cowles, *Pravda,* Apr. 27, 1962, in *CDSP,* XIV, 17 (May 23, 1962), p. 24.

[70] Poland, *Zëri i Popullit,* Jan. 20, 1962; Hungary, *ibid.,* Mar. 6, 1962; Bulgaria, *ibid.,* Mar. 7, 1962; Czechoslovakia, *ibid.,* Mar. 24, 1962; East Germany, *ibid.,* Apr. 1, 1962; Romania, *ibid.,* Apr. 10, 1962.

[71] See *Zëri i Popullit,* Mar. 16, 18; Nikolayev, "The Words and Actions of the Albanian Committee for Balkan Collaboration and Mutual Understanding," Radio Moscow in Albanian, Apr. 29, 1962, 1900 GMT.

[72] *Zëri i Popullit,* May 22, 1962.

[73] See Brzezinski, "Patterns and Limits of the Sino-Soviet Dispute," *op. cit.* For the Chinese anti-Khrushchev mood, see the revealing Peking dispatch by Jacques Marcuse in *The Sunday Times* (London), May 20, 1962.

was detrimental to the interests of both sides and only gave aid and comfort to the "imperialists."

Yet in retrospect it seems unlikely that the Soviets and Chinese agreed on much else. The massive esoteric Chinese polemics against Khrushchev's ideological and policy positions, which began with the February onslaught against Bernsteinism[74] and the March one against Kardelj[75] continued after mid-April; the late April one against Kautskyism[76] and the mid-May one against the Economists[77] were among the most extensive and extreme since the April 1960 esoteric exchanges;[78] and although Moscow did not immediately undertake anything so extensive in reply, Soviet and East European propaganda output also indicated that the ideological and policy difference between Moscow and Peking had not diminished.[79]

Chinese ideological and economic support of Albania showed no significant signs of lessening.[80] Nor did Albanian pronouncements indicate that Hoxha was giving way on any substantive issues: particularly vis-à-vis Yugoslavia they were quite as strong as ever. The most direct Albanian attack against Moscow during late spring 1962 was the official governmental protest[81] against its exclusion from the June Moscow meet-

74 Hsiao Shu and Ma Ch'un-ping, "On Bernsteinian Revisionism," *Hung Ch'i*, No. 3–4, Feb. 10, 1962, pp. 55–64 (JPRS 13347, Apr. 5, 1962, pp. 89–102). This and the three subsequent articles appeared only in Chinese; they were not carried in English either by NCNA or the *Peking Review*.

75 Wu Chiang, "Our Age and Edvard Kardelj's 'Dialectics,'" *ibid.*, No. 5, Mar. 1, 1962, pp. 17–37 (JPRS 13615, May 1, 1962, pp. 32–64).

76 Li Fu, Li Ssu-wen, and Wang Fu-ju, "On Kautskyism," *ibid.*, No. 8–9, Apr. 25, 1962, pp. 28–41 (JPRS 13903, May 29, 1962, pp. 76–120).

77 Pien Chung-yin, "Revolutionary Tradition of Political Parties of the Proletariat," *ibid.*, No. 10, May 16, 1962 (SCMM 317, June 12, 1962, pp. 7–16). The importance of these Chinese articles was not generally recognized in the West; see, however, the analysis by Harry Hamm in the *Frankfurter Allgemeine Zeitung*, Aug. 29, 1962.

78 Chou En-lai's speech to the March–April NPC meeting also indicated no CCP ideological concessions; see *Peking Review*, V, 16 (Apr. 20, 1962), pp. 3–7.

79 E.g., Ilichev on the Lenin anniversary, *Pravda*, Apr. 23, 1962; Boris Ponomarev re Dimitrov, "A Remarkable Marxist-Leninist," *Rabotnichesko Delo*, June 15, 1961.

80 E.g., NCNA-ATA agreement, *Zëri i Popullit*, Apr. 12, 1962, and NCNA in English from Tirana, Apr. 12, 1962 (SCMP 2722, Apr. 19, 1962, pp. 28–29) opening of Sino-Albanian joint shipping line, NCNA in English from Tirana, Apr 13, 1962 (SCMP 2722, Apr. 19, 1962, p. 29); exchange of May Day messages *Zëri i Popullit*, May 2, 1962; Yung Hai-po at 14th Congress of Soviet Komsomol reference to "12 socialist states" (i.e., including Albania), NCNA English from Moscow, Apr. 16, 1962 (SCMP 2725, Apr. 26, 1962, p. 35); Ch'en Yi at Hungarian reception in Peking ("12 socialist states"), NCNA in English to Asia, Apr. 4 1960, 1601 GMT. For North Korean economic support of Albania, see, e.g., the dispatch from Pyongyang to Tirana of three North Korean experts in rice cultivation (Pyongyang KCNA in English to Europe, Mar. 10, 1962, 1109 GMT).

81 *Zëri i Popullit*, June 6, 13, 1962, and Documents 27, 28.

ings of the Council for Mutual Economic Aid[82] and the political consultative committee of the Warsaw Pact powers.[83] This June CMEA meeting not only further underlined the economic, political, and military isolation to which the Soviet Union and the other East European Communist states had consigned Albania, but also, at a meeting where the Chinese reportedly refused to send observers,[84] marked the formal admission of Outer Mongolia to CMEA. The exclusion of Albania coupled with the admission of Outer Mongolia thus formalized on the economic level the political lineup[85] which since 1960 had characterized the Communist parties in power.

This ostentatiously anti-Albanian Soviet move did not, however, excite any extensive propaganda retorts in the Albanian press, with the exception of the formal protest noted above. The same curious Albanian reticence also marked Tirana's propaganda treatment of an even more hostile Soviet move: the intensified Soviet rapprochement with Yugoslavia. (For the Chinese, Khrushchev's offer of planes to India at a time of intensified Sino-Indian tension was its equivalent.)[86]

From its beginning the gradual Moscow-Belgrade improvement of state relations had characterized, in part arisen from, and intensified the Sino-Soviet dispute. By the spring of 1962 another factor became increasingly important in accentuating the Soviet-Yugoslav rapprochement: a common interest in combatting the discriminatory features of the Common Market.[87] Khrushchev probably hoped that he could increase his influence within all anti–Common Market neutralist countries through a rapprochement with the one of them, Yugoslavia, which is nearest to Moscow ideologically and is the most threatened economically by West European integration. For Yugoslavia, caught in the economic squeeze between the Common Market and CMEA and ideologically and politi-

[82] Communiqué, *Pravda,* June 9, 1962.

[83] Communiqué, *ibid.,* June 10, 1962.

[84] Barbieri from Moscow in *Vjestnik* (Zagreb), June 13, 1962, and Vuković from Moscow in *Politika,* June 18, 1962, who report the Chinese were offered but refused full membership. North Korea and North Vietnam also did not send observers. Observers from China, North Korea, and North Vietnam had been present at CMEA technical commission meetings as late as mid-May (7th meeting of CMEA commission for food and light industries, Prague, May 15–18, 1962, in ČTK in English to Europe, May 19, 1962, 1218 GMT).

[85] The Albanian edition of *Problems of Peace and Socialism* had ceased with the Feb. 1962 issue; instead (a new slap at Tirana) a Greek edition was added.

[86] See *Peking Review,* Apr.–June 1962, *passim.*

[87] Cf. Ernst Halperin in *Die Tat* (Zürich), May 24, 1962; C.[hristian] K.[ind], "Jugoslawien und die EWG," *Neue Zürcher Zeitung,* Apr. 29, 1962; "Between Brezhnev and the Six," *The Economist,* Oct. 13, 1962, p. 133. For an excellent general survey of the Soviet-Yugoslav rapprochement, see J. F. Brown, "A Soviet-Yugoslav Rapprochement?" *The World Today,* XVIII, 9 (Sept. 1962), pp. 365–372.

cally opposed to the political concessions which association with the Common Market would inevitably require, a rapprochement with CMEA and therefore with the Soviet Union seems less dangerous.[88] Internally, by the spring of 1962 Yugoslavia was again caught up in one of her recurrent economic crises. The 1961 liberalization had led to a rush to import from abroad and buy consumer goods at home which, with wages leaping ahead of productivity and a series of bad harvests, had seriously threatened the already passive Yugoslav balance of payments and inhibited capital investments. In May 1962 Belgrade reacted by a renewed retreat toward greater party influence and central economic controls.[89]

Nor did the mid-April decline in personalized Soviet-Albanian polemics appear to slow down or diminish the Soviet-Yugoslav rapprochement. Khrushchev thereafter made even more favorable gestures to Belgrade, and Peking and Tirana continued to attack the "Tito clique" as "agents of the imperialists." In April Soviet Foreign Minister Gromyko visited Belgrade; the concluding Soviet-Yugoslav communiqué reiterated the "fundamental identity" of Soviet and Yugoslav foreign-policy views.[90] During Khrushchev's visit to Bulgaria in late May he made the most pro-Yugoslav Soviet declaration since 1957:

> . . . There was a time when our relations with Yugoslavia were strained. Today we can note with satisfaction the improvement of relations with that country — one of the largest on the Balkan Peninsula. The peoples of Yugoslavia waged a heroic struggle against the German fascist invaders and earned great respect from the peoples by that struggle. Our relations with Yugoslavia are now normal; I would say more — they are good. On many international issues having to do with safeguarding and consolidating peace our positions coincide. We are sincerely eager to see our efforts in the struggle for lasting world peace and for the security of nations proceed in the same direction.

88 "Soviet-Yugoslav Trade Is Scheduled to Increase More than 30 Percent in 1962," *The Daily Telegraph* (London), May 24, 1962.

89 See Tito's speech at Split, *Borba,* May 7, 1962; Kardelj to the Škupština, *ibid.,* May 29, 1962; Eric Bourne from Belgrade in *The Christian Science Monitor,* May 17–19, 1962; C.[hristian] K.[ind] from Belgrade, "Disziplinaraktionen in der Partei Titos," *Neue Zürcher Zeitung,* May 19, 1962; on agriculture, Paul Underwood from Belgrade in *The New York Times,* June 10, 1962; "Belgrade's Moment of Disillusion," *The Economist,* June 9, 1962.

90 *Pravda* and *Borba,* Apr. 22, 1962. See also Gromyko's Supreme Soviet speech, *Pravda,* Apr. 25, 1962. The apparently anti-Yugoslav article by Rumyantsev, "Under Cover of Devotion to Principle," *World Marxist Review,* V, 4 (Apr. 1962), pp. 88–89, was less so than previous ones on the subject. However, a fact which must also have enraged the Albanians, there was no indication that the Yugoslavs would make decisive ideological concessions to Moscow; see, e.g., Puniša Perović, "Discussion on 'Polycentrism,'" *Review of International Affairs* (Belgrade), XIII, 289 (Apr. 20, 1962), pp. 10–12.

We also have good relations with Yugoslavia in the area of trade. We hope that mutually advantageous economic relations between the Soviet Union and Yugoslavia will continue to broaden. We are also prepared to strengthen and broaden relations between our countries in the areas of culture and science, in exchanges of delegations — in all spheres, since this is in the interest of the peoples, in the interest of the consolidation of peace.

The position of the Soviet people is that despite the difference in the way we see a number of political and ideological questions, we, as a country that is building Communism, are going to do all we can to bring about good cooperation with Yugoslavia and thereby help her peoples consolidate their socialist positions. And this will not only contribute to improved relations between the Soviet Union and Yugoslavia but will redound to the benefit of all countries that are building socialism and Communism. . . .[91]

Belgrade announced that the Soviet government had invited Tito to "spend his vacation" in the Soviet Union, a Yugoslav parliamentary delegation visited Moscow, and a new, increased Soviet-Yugoslav trade agreement was signed.[92]

The Albanian reaction to all this, although predictably sharp, did not at first include a return to polemicizing against Khrushchev by name, presumably because the Chinese would not let them. In a page-long editorial on June 30,[93] Tirana developed a new thesis:

. . . The Tito clique is the bridge between the revisionists and the imperialists, so long as this tie cannot be openly and directly established. . . .

For this purpose

. . . It is in the interest of the American imperialists and modern revisionists now to restore the red coloring to the faded mask of the Tito clique. . . .

Quoting but not identifying many of Khrushchev's laudatory phrases about Yugoslavia, the article concluded:

[91] *Pravda,* May 17, 1962; quoted from *CDSP,* XIV, 20 (June 13, 1962), p. 3. Cf. V.[iktor] M.[eier], "Chruschtschews Bulgarienreise," *Neue Zürcher Zeitung,* May 25, 1962; Wolfgang Leonhard, "Bulgarisches Gastspiel," *Die Zeit,* May 25, 1962. Peking (NCNA in English to Europe, May 20, 1962, 1820 GMT) and Tirana (*Zëri i Popullit,* May 18, 1962) repeated these remarks of Khrushchev's without comment.

[92] Zorza in *The Guardian* (Manchester), May 29, 1962.

[93] "The Rumpus over Tito's 'Reversal' and the Undeniable Truth," "by the editorial collegium," *Zëri i Popullit,* June 30, 1962, and Document 30. See also Hoxha's earlier, more moderate election speech, *Zëri i Popullit,* May 31, 1962, reprinted in *Jen-min Jih-pao,* June 9, 1962.

. . . "fruitful and comprehensive" collaboration has begun with the aim of rallying and consolidating the forces of modern revisionism in its struggle against Marxism-Leninism. This process is at the moment in full swing and will become more concrete in the future. . . .

The Soviet-Albanian Conflict Again Intensifies

The resumption of Albanian attacks on Khrushchev was not long in coming: in a long speech on July 16 which reiterated the Albanian ideological position, Shehu denounced "the present Soviet leadership headed by Nikita Khrushchev,"[94] and a few days later an Albanian Central Committee resolution referred to "the hostile activities of Nikita Khrushchev and his following."[95] In late August Ramiz Alia denounced "the slanders and counterrevolutionary public appeals of N. Khrushchev and his gang."[96] In late July, the Chinese Foreign Minister Ch'en Yi indirectly but clearly indicated that serious Sino-Soviet differences still persisted,[97] and in early August Peking resumed its attacks against Belgrade.[98] In reply, Khrushchev in late August (without naming their source) denounced[99] the Chinese attacks on the Economists, and indicated that Soviet-sponsored CMEA economic integration would continue without China and its allies, while Peking closed all Soviet consulates in China. In mid-September on the occasion of the state visit of Soviet Chief of State Brezhnev to Belgrade,[100] the Albanians[101] and the

[94] *Zëri i Popullit,* July 17, 1962. For another attack by Fadil Paçrami, see *ibid.,* July 18, 1962.

[95] *Ibid.,* July 22, 1962.

[96] In a speech on the 20th anniversary of the founding of *Zëri i Popullit* (*ibid.,* Aug. 25, 1962). The speech, less the personal attack on Khrushchev, was reprinted in *Jen-min Jih-pao,* Aug. 27, 1962. Three days later Abdyl Këllezi referred to the "wild blockade of Nikita Khrushchev and his followers," *Zëri i Popullit* (Aug. 28, 1962). See also the implicit Albanian attack on the CPSU Program's thesis of the "all-people's state," in Hulusi Hako, "The Dictatorship of the Proletariat and Socialist Democracy as Its Basic Model," *Rruga e Partisë,* No. 8 (Aug. 1962), pp. 33–46 (JPRS 15546, Oct. 3, 1962, pp. 30–63).

[97] Interview with *Sankei* (Tokyo), July 26, 1962.

[98] E.g., Liao Ching, "Yugoslavia's Economic Troubles," *Jen-min Jih-pao,* Aug. 4, 1962, and *Peking Review,* V, 33 (Aug. 17, 1962), pp. 11–13; Chen Mou-yi, "Economic Deterioration in Yugoslavia," *Hung Ch'i,* No. 17 (Sept. 1, 1962), abridged translation in *Peking Review,* V, 40 (Oct. 5, 1962), pp. 14–17, 23.

[99] N. S. Khrushchev, "Vital Questions of the Development of the World Socialist System," *Kommunist,* No. 12 (Aug. 1962), pp. 3–26 (passed for the press Aug. 24, 1962), and *World Marxist Review,* V, 9 (Sept. 1962), pp. 2–18. For the closing of Soviet consulates in China, see a Moscow dispatch in *The New York Times,* Sept. 21, 1962, and a Reuters dispatch from Hong Kong in the *Christian Science Monitor,* Oct. 4, 1962.

[100] See p. 155, *infra.*

[101] "Modern Revisionism to the Aid of the Basic Strategy of American Imperialism," *Zëri i Popullit,* Sept. 19, 1962, and Document 31.

Chinese[102] reacted with attacks which exceeded even their former level of fury, and the Chinese, North Koreans, and Albanians again refused to accept Soviet positions in international front organizations.[103] The Sino-Soviet rift and the Soviet-Albanian break were once again at least at the same level of hostility as in 1960 and 1961.

As these lines are being written (in late November 1962), it is still too early to venture a definite hypothesis as to the course and causes of what now seems to be the failure of the first serious attempt by Moscow and Peking to emphasize unity instead of divergence. Yet even now certain lessons can be drawn from it which may be useful in isolating and analyzing probable similar developments in the future.

First, the lowered intensity in Sino-Soviet and Soviet-Albanian polemics in the late spring and early summer 1962 was not only deceptive but far less significant than most Western observers thought at the time. True, there were during this period a series of surface signs that Sino-Soviet relations were improving.[104] Yet Soviet actions and Chinese words belied them. The Soviet rapprochement with Yugoslavia continued,[105] esoteric Chinese polemics against Soviet positions were published throughout the spring and (in a less detailed form) the summer;[106]

102 "See to What Depths the Modern Revisionists Have Stooped!" *Jen-min Jih-pao,* Sept. 17, 1962, and *Peking Review,* V, 38 (Sept. 21, 1962), pp. 12–15; Jen Ku-ping, "The Tito Group — An Army Corps of U.S. Imperialism in Its Grand Strategy of Counter-Revolution," *Jen-min Jih-pao,* Sept. 18, 1962, and *Peking Review,* V, 41 (Oct. 12, 1962), pp. 12–16. Contrary to the *Hung Ch'i* spring articles, these were broadcast extensively in English and Russian and published in English in *Peking Review.*

103 The Chinese abstained from voting on the resolution of the Seventh Congress of the World Federation of Scientific Workers in Moscow on Sept. 13–15, 1962; see for this and for the speeches of the Chinese and Albanian delegates, NCNA in English to Asia and Europe, Sept. 21, 1962, 1700 GMT.

104 The Soviet press regularly carried reports, albeit brief and superficial ones, on Chinese economic developments. Radio Moscow broadcasts to China emphasized Soviet friendship, aid, and support for the CPR in contrast to earlier ideological polemics, and meetings, social or otherwise, between ranking Soviet and Chinese officials took place. The Chinese press gave considerable publicity to Khrushchev's radio and television speech of July 2 (*Pravda,* July 3, 1962), which reiterated Soviet support for China on the question of Taiwan (SCMP 2775, July 11, 1962, p. 18).

105 The Soviets received a Yugoslav parliamentary delegation headed by Stambolić in late June and an economic delegation headed by Todorović in early July. On July 6 a Soviet-Yugoslav trade protocol was signed in Moscow envisaging a twofold increase in trade between 1960 and 1965 (*Pravda,* July 7, 1962). On July 11, *Borba* announced that Soviet chief of state Brezhnev would visit Yugoslavia in the autumn.

106 Chang Yu-yu, "The Futility of Bourgeois Parliamentary Democracy," *Hung Ch'i,* No. 13, July 1, 1962, pp. 20–27 (JPRS 14703, Aug. 2, 1962, pp. 46–67); Shao T'ieh-chen, "On Sophism," *ibid.,* No. 14, July 16, 1962, pp. 34–37 (JPRS 14827, Aug. 13, 1962, pp. 90–100); Hsiao Hua, "The Chinese Revolution and Armed Struggle," *ibid.,* No. 15–16, Aug. 1, 1962, in *Peking Review,* V, 32 (Aug.

Moscow broadcasts to Albania continued esoteric polemics against Tirana's ideological positions;[107] Sino-Soviet and Soviet-Albanian differences in the international front organizations, although less obvious, were still present;[108] and by early July the Soviets began to reply again, esoterically and indirectly, to the Chinese and Albanian polemics.[109]

Second, the September Albanian resumption of public attacks was only one part of a generally rising level of Sino–Albanian–North Korean polemics. As before, the Chinese blasts were ostensibly against the Yugoslavs, and Pyongyang this time demonstrated more clearly than before its support of Chinese positions.[110] The Chinese began again to reprint Albanian attacks against the Soviets,[111] although (as they had done since January 1962) omitting the direct attacks on Khrushchev by name; but Peking's September articles were stronger than ever before. They declared that Yugoslavia was no longer a socialist state but that

---

10, 1962), pp. 6–9 and 33 (Aug. 17, 1962), pp. 14–16; Li Yuan-ming, "Engels' Criticism of Von Vollmar and Others," *Jen-min Jih-pao,* Sept. 9, 1962.

107 E.g., Radio Moscow in Albanian, July 17, 1960, 0630 GMT (BBC/SU/999/A2/1, July 19, 1962); *ibid.,* July 29, 1962, 2130 GMT (BBC/SU/1015/A2/1, Aug. 8, 1962); *ibid.,* July 30, 1500 GMT (BBC/SU/1010/A2/1, Aug. 1, 1962); *ibid.,* Aug. 2, 1962. 1900 GMT (BBC/SU/1017/A2/1, Aug. 10, 1962); *ibid.,* Aug. 8, 1962, 1900 GMT (BBC/SU/1022/A2/1, Aug. 16, 1962); *ibid.,* Aug. 22, 1962, 1900 GMT (BBC/SU/1034/A2/1, Aug. 30, 1962); *ibid.,* Aug. 25, 1962, 2130 GMT (BBC/SU/1039/A2/1, Sept. 5, 1962); *ibid.,* Aug. 27, 1962, 2130 GMT (BBC/SU/1036/A2/1, Sept. 1, 1962).

108 See, e.g.,the speeches at the Moscow World Peace Congress by Khrushchev (*Pravda,* July 11, 1962), by Mao Tun (*Jen-min Jih-pao,* July 12, 1962, in *Peking Review,* V, 29 [July 20, 1962], pp. 5–13, and the abridged and clearly politically censored version of it in *Pravda,* July 10, 1962), and by the Albanian delegate, Dhimitër Shuteriqi (*Zëri i Popullit,* July 15, 1962). For Soviet-Albanian differences at the Helsinki World Youth Festival, see an article by the head of the Albanian delegation, Todi Lubonja, in *ibid.,* Aug. 31, 1962.

109 B. N. Ponomarev, "Champion of Peace and Socialism," *World Marxist Review,* V, 7 (July 1962), pp. 8–15, passed for the press June 20; N. P. Farberov, "The All-Peoples' State: The Logical Result of the Development of the State of the Dictatorship of the Proletariat," *Sovetskoe Gosudarstvo i Pravo,* No. 7, July 1962, pp. 14–24, passed for the press July 6; S. Titarenko, "Internationalism — The Banner of the New World," *Krasnaya Zvezda,* July 17, 1962; G. M. Shtraks, "On the Peculiarities of the Contradictions in Social Development," *Voprosy Filosofii,* No. 7, 1962, pp. 26–36, passed for the press July 18.

110 "The Sino-Indian Boundary Question Must Be Solved Peacefully," *Nodong Sinmun* (Pyongyang), Sept. 26, 1962; "The Tito Group Which Betrays Socialism and Serves Imperialism to Obtain Aid from the West," *ibid.,* Sept. 28, 1962; "The Consequences of Revisionist Economic Policy in Yugoslav Industry," *ibid.,* Sept. 30, 1962, "Yugoslav Agriculture in Capitalist Quagmire," *ibid.,* Oct. 3, 1962; "The Essence of the Self-Government of Enterprises Advertised by the Tito Group and Its Consequences," *ibid.,* Oct. 16, 1962. Hanoi was less pro-Chinese; it did, however, reprint the *Hung Ch'i* attack against Kardelj (cited in ftn. 75, *supra*), in *Hoc Tap,* No. 8 (Aug. 1962).

111 Excerpts from Shehu's July 16 report to the Albanian People's Assembly omitting the attack on Khrushchev appeared in *Jen-min Jih-pao,* July 30, 1962 (SCMP 2798, Aug. 14, 1962, p. 30).

"the revisionist line of the Tito group has led to the restoration of the capitalist system in Yugoslavia,"[112] while stressing that China "naturally has its own independent home and foreign policies."[113]

At the end of September the communiqué of a Chinese Central Committee Plenum[114] used a phrase the Soviets had also employed to press their own claims,[115] "the general line of our country is entirely correct," and, in a clear reference to Moscow, denounced "great-nation chauvinism."[116] Chou En-lai declared on September 30 that

> . . . the imperialists, the reactionaries of various countries and the modern revisionists . . . have continually, and in close collaboration, stirred up anti-Chinese campaigns in a frenzied attempt to isolate China and to compel China to change its just stand in international affairs. But . . . the Chinese people will never submit to any pressure, much less bargain away principles. . . .[117]

The plenum communiqué, describing more precisely the activities of these "imperialists, reactionaries, and modern revisionists," had declared that these included "subversion within our state [and] our Party."[118] The contrast with Brezhnev's statements and the subsequent Soviet-Yugoslav communiqué following his visit became more glaring than before.

Finally, in view of the true but only subsequently revealed course of Sino-Soviet and Soviet-Albanian relations,[119] still unknown political, economic, and perhaps even military moves on both sides presumably lay behind the resumption of ideological polemics. The large-scale Chinese attack launched on Indian border positions in late October[120] was probably a part of this ideological-political-military syndrome.

Indeed, it is probably in Soviet actions rather than Chinese and Al-

[112] Jan Ku-ping, *op. cit.*

[113] "See to What Depths the Modern Revisionists Have Stooped!" *op. cit.*

[114] *Jen min Jih-pao,* Sept. 29, 1962, in *Peking Review,* V, 39 (Sept. 28, 1962), pp. 5–8. The *Pravda* version of Oct. 1 deleted some of the most anti-Soviet passages.

[115] See p. 139, *supra.*

[116] Cf. in the CRP statement on the declaration of the Soviet government on relations among socialist states, Nov. 1, 1956, the use of the phrase "chauvinism by a big country" (Paul E. Zinner, ed., *National Communism and Popular Revolt in Eastern Europe* [New York: Columbia, 1956], pp. 492–495, at p. 494). Ch'en Yi made the same statements (*Jen-min Jih-pao,* Oct. 1, 1962, and *Peking Review,* V, 40 [Oct. 5, 1962], pp. 8–9).

[117] *Jen-min Jih-pao,* Oct. 1, 1962, quoted from *Peking Review,* V, 40 (Oct. 5, 1962), p. 6; cf. "Strive for New Victories in Our Country's Socialist Cause," *ibid.;* "The Rising Peoples' Forces Are Invincible," *Hung Ch'i,* No. 19 (Oct. 1, 1962), in *Peking Review,* V, 40 (Oct. 5, 1962), pp. 9–12.

[118] The communiqué also announced the dismissal from the CCP secretariat of two former associates of P'eng Te-huai (see Charles, *op. cit.*).

[119] See Ch. 3, *supra.*

[120] *New York Times,* Oct. 21, 1962.

banian words that one must search for the precipitating element in this new crisis. Moscow's continued intensification of its rapprochement with Yugoslavia was not only in itself a factor worsening Sino-Soviet relations but also an indicator that Moscow was generally pursuing a more anti-Chinese policy as well, indeed that Moscow had probably never calculated (as, most likely, neither had Peking) that a genuine Sino-Soviet reconciliation on the substantive issues was either likely or possible.

When one considers the continuing Chinese economic crisis[121] and the additional blow to Peking of the greatly decreased Soviet trade and aid,[122] the Soviet calculation was understandable. Nevertheless, despite a marked turn to the right in Chinese domestic policy,[123] their foreign-policy line continued extremist,[124] as evidenced *inter alia* by their continued support for Albania.[125] There were no indications that Albanian domestic reasons required Tirana to take a more conciliatory line toward Moscow; indeed, the open break with Khrushchev, Hoxha's and Shehu's previous narrow escapes vis-à-vis Belgrade, and the continuing Khrushchev-Tito rapprochement made it more likely than ever that Tirana's temporary moderation in the spring and early summer had only been under Chinese pressure and that Hoxha had only too willingly resumed all-out polemics against Khrushchev.

As so often before, the latest outbreak of Sino-Soviet and Soviet-

[121] Peter Schran, "Some Reflections on Chinese Communist Economic Policy," *The China Quarterly*, No. 11 (July–Sept. 1962), pp. 58–77.

[122] This decrease in trade is summarized in the following table:

USSR-CPR Foreign Trade 1959–1961
(Millions of dollars)

	Soviet Exports to China	*Soviet Imports from China*	*Total Volume of Goods Exchanged*
1959	954.45	1,100.25	2,054.70
1960	817.00	848.00	1,665.00
1961	367.33	551.44	918.77

(This indicates not only a severe contraction of trade but also heavy Chinese repayments on earlier debts.)

SOURCES: 1959–1960: *Vneshnaya Torgovlya SSSR za 1960 god* (Moscow, 1961), pp. 162, 168; 1960–1961: *Vneshnaya Torgovlya SSSR za 1961 god* (Moscow, 1962), pp. 179, 185.

[123] W. A. C. Adie, "Political Aspects of the National People's Congress," *The China Quarterly*, No. 11 (July–Sept. 1962), pp. 78–88.

[124] A. M. Halpern, "Communist China's Foreign Policy: The Recent Phase," *ibid.*, pp. 89–104.

[125] See, *inter alia*, the Chinese greetings to Lleshi and Shehu on the occasion of their election to office by the Albanian People's Assembly (SCMP 2786, July 26, 1962, p. 23); the speech of Hu Yao-pang at a mass meeting in Tirana in celebration of the 13th CPR anniversary (*Zëri i Popullit*, Sept. 30, 1962); and the Chinese greeting message of mid-October (*ibid.*, Oct. 16, 1962).

Albanian polemics was over Yugoslavia. Tito had politely refused the Soviet invitation to spend his vacation on the Black Sea[126] and this "hard-to-get" attitude on his part may have been an additional factor in Khrushchev's decision to have Soviet Chief of State Brezhnev return Tito's 1956 visit to the Soviet Union.[127] The visit[128] ended with a communiqué[129] couched in general terms which seemed to give the Yugoslavs more satisfaction than the Russians: The 1955 Belgrade Declaration (on "various roads to socialism") was specifically reaffirmed and the broad scope of the rapprochement (not excluding resumption of party relations) formally set forth. Quite as importantly for Belgrade, a simultaneous new Soviet-Yugoslav trade agreement indicated a further increase in the level of trade.[130] Tito's forthcoming visit to the Soviet Union (in December) was also announced.

A few days before the Brezhnev visit, the Peking *Jen-min Jih-pao,* using as a peg an interview given the month before by Tito to the American columnist Drew Pearson,[131] on September 17 and 18 printed two full-scale attacks against Yugoslav revisionism which if anything went further than their predecessors.[132] On September 19, in itself a clear indication that Tirana was following Peking's lead, a new Albanian blast appeared[133] — the first full-length Albanian editorial attack on Khrushchev since early spring.[134] In addition to repeating all the previous Albanian themes against Tito and Khrushchev, it heightened some of

[126] This was publicly stated by Tito in his interview with Drew Pearson on Aug. 7, 1962 (*Borba,* Aug. 12, 1962), but the refusal presumably occurred sometime earlier; the invitation was extended in May.

[127] *Borba,* July 11, 1962.

[128] For its course, see C.[hristian] K.[ind] from Belgrade in the *Neue Zürcher Zeitung,* Sept. 24, 1962 *et seq.* For Togliatti's favorable reaction, see his article in *Rinascita,* Oct. 13, 1962.

[129] *Pravda* and *Borba,* Oct. 5, 1962. The *Pravda* version of the communiqué was textually less reserved than the *Borba* one.

[130] *Ibid.* The Soviet-Yugoslav agreement signed on Feb. 15, 1962, envisaged a roughly $120 million yearly trade turnover for 1963–1965. The Soviet-Yugoslav trade protocol signed in Moscow on July 6 (after the Mikoyan-Todorović negotiations) said only that the increase over the February one would be "considerable." The October 4 protocol signed at the conclusion of Brezhnev's visit to Belgrade envisaged a $180 million turnover for 1963, thus doubling the 1960 volume and bringing the Soviet Union's share in total Yugoslav foreign trade close to the 1957 level.

[131] *Borba,* Aug. 12, 1962, and *Review of International Affairs,* XIII, 298 (Sept. 1, 1962), pp. 30–34.

[132] "See to What Depths the Modern Revisionists Have Stooped!" *op. cit.;* Jen Ku-ping, *op. cit.*

[133] *Zëri i Popullit,* Sept. 19, 1962, and Document 31. The Pearson interview was published in *Zëri i Popullit* on Sept. 18, 1962.

[134] For Soviet replies, see pp. 158 *et seq., infra.*

them and added some new ones; it was the most violent Albanian attack to date against Moscow.

In a clear indication of the lack of Albanian interest or belief in any Sino-Soviet efforts at rapprochement, the article declared that

> N. Khrushchev's revisionist group has never ceased its divisive and unfriendly activity against our unity. N. Khrushchev's beautiful words about unity are nothing but a bluff and demagogy, a mask which he needs to deceive, to gain time to conduct calmly his divisive activity, to undertake new measures even more dangerous against the unity of the socialist camp and the Communist movement.
>
> . . . On the question of the unity of the socialist camp and of the international Communist and workers movement, the line of the traitorous Titoist clique and that of N. Khrushchev's revisionist group are entirely at one end and . . . they both, in fact, serve the objectives and the plans of imperialism.

For the first time publicly, the article listed as one of Khrushchev's sins his support of India in the Sino-Indian border conflicts.[135] Finally, its attacks on Khrushchev's policy of peaceful coexistence culminated in the charge — the most violent one until that date — that

> . . . the line of rapprochement and fusion with imperialism . . . constitutes the core of the anti-Marxist concept of N. Khrushchev's group on peaceful coexistence. . . .

In this "rapprochement and fusion," the article continued, Tito was Khrushchev's "counsellor and mediator." Revealing another issue in the Sino-Soviet and Soviet-Albanian disputes, the article declared that Khrushchev's most recent declarations on "broad economic collaboration" with the Common Market[136] "also form part of the framework of reconciliation and rapprochement with imperialism." In fact, Moscow, urged by the Italian Communists,[137] did take a more conciliatory position toward the EEC.

A week after the Brezhnev-Tito communiqué, in a long editorial published on October 13,[138] *Zëri i Popullit* reached even greater heights in

[135] See Mikoyan and Indian Minister of State Krishnamachari in *Pravda,* July 26, 1962, reprinted in *Jen-min Jih-pao,* July 28, 1962.

[136] Khrushchev, *op. cit.;* see also the Soviet theses on the Common Market and capitalism, *Pravda,* Aug. 26, 1962. The Yugoslavs are also taking a less anti-EEC attitude (*Avanti!,* Sept. 18, 1962).

[137] See the PCI theses for its 10th Congress, *L'Unità,* Sept. 13, 1962; an article in *L'Unità,* Sept. 6, 1962; and Eugenio Peggio in *Rinascita,* Sept. 8, 1962. For the PCF-PCI controversy at the Moscow conference on the EEC, see André Delcroix in *France-Observateur,* XIII, 646 (Sept. 20, 1962), pp. 7–8.

[138] "A Great Betrayal of Marxism-Leninism," *Zëri i Popullit,* Oct. 13, 1962, and Document 32.

its denunciation of Khrushchev. Defining "the strategic fundamental questions uniting the Khrushchev group with the Tito clique" as

> . . . class conciliation between socialism and capitalism, political and ideological coexistence between them, peace and coexistence at any price, negation of all revolutionary movements, and the economic and political integration of the world . . .

the article declared that the Brezhnev visit

> . . . constitutes a link in the chain of N. Khrushchev's aims to achieve a rapprochement with the Yugoslav revisionists, to coordinate with them a new revisionist course to split the socialist camp and liquidate socialism. . . .

The key new element in the article was a declaration which appeared to call for the expulsion of "Khrushchev and his group" and all other "modern revisionists" from the international Communist movement:

> The preservation of the unity of the socialist camp and of the international Communist movement, as well as the further strengthening of this unity, requires firm opposition to modern revisionism, combating and unmasking it in all its forms and in all its domains in order to fix once and for all the demarcation line with revisionism. Revisionism is a sore point in the Communist movement. One must heal this wound as soon as possible in spite of the terrible pain which this operation may cause.
>
> . . . These Communists who are wading in the mud of N. Khrushchev and who have now the possibility of more or less seeing the betrayal to Marxism-Leninism must, from now on, find the energy and the courage of stopping and detaching themselves from the revisionists. They are faced with the alternative: either to fall in the abyss where the Khrushchev group leads, or to courageously and firmly react, uniting with the mass of the party and resolutely relying on the working masses, and deal a mortal blow to the revisionists. It is only in this way that one can help the party, the country, socialism, Communism, and peace.[139]

Only a few days later, in a message from Mao, Liu, and Chou to Hoxha, Lleshi, and Shehu, Peking declared that the Albanian Party of Labor

> . . . fights to maintain and strengthen the unity of the socialist camp and the international Communist movement and to keep the purity of Marxism-Leninism, and has made a great contribution of historic importance to mankind.[140]

[139] The article also declared that "the Bolsheviks of the Lenin party itself" also oppose "Khrushchev's revisionism"; this, however, was probably only a propaganda rather than a factual assertion.

[140] *Ibid.*, Oct. 16, 1962.

Whether or not this Albanian call for a split in the international Communist movement represented the actual (albeit unexpressed) Chinese position was not immediately clear, but that Sino-Soviet tension was greater than ever before seemed certain.

India, Cuba, and Albania

The mid-October worsening of Sino-Soviet and Soviet-Albanian relations was sharply intensified in the latter part of that month by the Sino-Indian border conflict[141] and the Soviet-American confrontation over Cuba.[142] As with so much else in this book, only a preliminary estimate of their significance can be sketched here. The October 20 Chinese attack on India[143] was in part an attempt to force Khrushchev to halt his arms shipments to Nehru and to abandon his favorable attitude toward the neutralist national bourgeoisie, one of the key issues in the Sino-Soviet dispute; it was primarily an effort to destroy the power and prestige of the only other Asian major power. China's initial military successes and the prompt American and British aid to India further decreased the likelihood of any concessions by Peking to Moscow. Initial Soviet reaction to the Sino-Indian conflict,[144] probably in part because of the Cuban crisis, was minimally pro-Chinese, but it failed to satisfy Peking, which adopted a violently anti-Nehru ideological line and began strong implicit criticism of Moscow's refusal to denounce Nehru.[145] After

[141] For the background of the Sino-Indian war, see CB 689, Sept. 19, 1962; for its course, see the Chinese press and radio and *The New York Times;* for analysis, Mark Mancall, "What Red China Wants," *The New Republic,* CXLVII, 20 (Nov. 17, 1962), pp. 9–12, and G. F. Hudson, "Behind the Himalayan War," *The New Leader,* XLV, 23 (Nov. 12, 1962), pp. 3–4.

[142] See the detailed chronological summary in *The New York Times,* Nov. 3, 1962.

[143] It was foreshadowed by the October 13 Albanian reference to Sino-Soviet differences over India and the mid-October recall of Chinese ambassadors in the Soviet Union and East Europe. See Hong Kong and Moscow dispatches in *The New York Times* and Belgrade and Washington dispatches in *The Times* (London), both Nov. 14, 1962.

[144] "In the Interests of the Peoples, in the Name of Universal Peace," *Pravda,* Oct. 25, 1962, advocating Indian acceptance of the Chinese proposal, which *Pravda* had printed the day previously. See the Chinese proposals in *Jen-min Jih-pao,* Oct. 25, 1962, and *Peking Review,* V, 43 (Oct. 26, 1962), pp. 5–6; "Fair and Reasonable Proposals," *Jen-min Jih-pao,* Oct. 27, 1962, and *Peking Review,* V, 44 (Nov. 1962), pp. 8–10. Cf. Kx.[Ernst Kux] "Moskau und der Krieg im Himalaya. Parteinahme für Peking," *Neue Zürcher Zeitung,* Oct. 27, 1962.

[145] "More on Nehru's Philosophy in the Light of the Sino-Indian Boundary Question," "by the editorial department of *Jen-min Jih-pao,*" *Jen-min Jih-pao,* Oct. 27, 1962, and *Peking Review,* V, 44 (Nov. 2, 1962), pp. 10–22, at pp. 11, 18, 20; see also "Observer," "India Sheds the Cloak of Nonalignment," *Jen-min Jih-pao,* Nov. 11, 1962. Excerpts of the Oct. 27 *Jen-min Jih-pao* article were reprinted in *Zëri i Popullit,* Nov. 1, 1962. For the identical Albanian attitude, see speech by

Khrushchev's retreat in the Cuban crisis Moscow took a completely "neutral" attitude on the Sino-Indian conflict,[146] perhaps even including, as Nehru indicated [147] and the Chinese reported without comment,[148] continuation of MIG fighter shipments to India.

The Indian defiance of China and the nationalist, anti-Chinese position taken by the majority of the Indian Communist Party (CPI), plus the arrest of pro-Chinese elements in the CPI leadership,[149] posed serious problems to Khrushchev. Concessions to the Chinese could hardly improve his position, while defiance of India would lose him world-wide neutralist and Indian Communist support. Moreover, the CPI's "nationalist" deviation was to the right (pro-Nehru) rather than, as the Albanian, to the left. Not only would each Communist party therefore have to declare its attitude toward the pro-Chinese minority and the pro-Nehru majority of the CPI,[150] but the issue posed by the CPI was not identical with the Albanian one. The rightist nature of the CPI's majority plus Moscow's increasingly neutral attitude meant that there might develop three potential Communist attitudes: pro-Soviet, pro-Chinese, and pro-CPI majority.

The Chinese attacked Indian border posts in force on October 20.[151] On October 22, President Kennedy declared a "quarantine" against further shipments of Soviet "offensive" guided missiles to Cuba and demanded the removal of those already there. (One of the factors in Khrushchev's putting them there was probably his desire, by a rapid,

Hysni Kapo in *ibid.*, Nov. 8, 1962, and Document 34. According to NCNA (English to Asia and Europe, Nov. 2, 1962, 1507 GMT) the full text was reprinted in *Nodong Sinmun* (Pyongyang) and in *Bao Tan Viet Ho* (Hanoi) and excerpts were printed in the JCP organ *Akahata,* all on Oct. 31, 1962. See also "Observer," "The Pretense of 'Nonalignment Falls Away,'" *Jen-min Jih-pao,* Nov. 11, 1962, and *Peking Review,* V, 46 (Nov. 16, 1962), pp. 5–7.

146 "Negotiation Is the Road to Settling the Conflict," *Pravda,* Nov. 5, 1962 (not reprinted or quoted in *Jen-min Jih-pao*). As late as November 2, Khrushchev reportedly informed Nehru he would not continue military aid to India (Rosenthal from New Delhi in *The New York Times,* Nov. 4, 1962).

147 Stanford from New Delhi in *The Christian Science Monitor,* Nov. 15, 1962.

148 *Jen-min Jih-pao,* Nov. 11, 1962.

149 See the CCP attack on the CPI majority leader S. A. Dange as a "self-styled Marxist" in "More on Nehru's Philosophy in the Light of the Sino-Indian Boundary Question," *Jen-min Jih-pao,* Oct. 27, 1962, and *Peking Review,* V, 44 (Nov. 2, 1962), pp. 10–22. Peking published on Nov. 12 (NCNA in English to Asia and Europe, 1820 GMT) the CPI Nov. 1 resolution entitled "National Emergency Arising Out of Chinese Aggression," presumably as a prelude to attacks against the CPI majority.

150 For the CPI majority's attempt to win world-wide Communist support, see a letter by Dange to other Communist parties, in a Reuters New Delhi dispatch in *The Christian Science Monitor,* Nov. 16, 1962, and in *The Statesman* (New Delhi), Nov. 16, 1962.

151 Peking has consistently maintained that the Indians attacked the Chinese (*Jen-min Jih-pao,* Oct. 21, 1962, *et seq.*).

cheap, and successful "facing down" of Washington, to change drastically the Soviet-American strategic power balance without war and thus *inter alia* to deprive Mao of one of his main arguments against Moscow.) At first the Cuban crisis appeared to improve Sino-Soviet and Soviet-Albanian relations; Peking[152] and Tirana[153] endorsed Soviet and Cuban actions, while Moscow's initial reaction to the Sino-Indian border conflict[154] was, in part because of the Cuban crisis, a minimal endorsement of the Chinese position. But Khrushchev's forced retreat on Cuba[155] and his subsequent less pro-Chinese attitude on the Sino-Indian border fighting[156] led to further sharpening of the Sino-Soviet and the Soviet-Albanian disputes. For Mao and Hoxha, and now for Castro as well, Khrushchev's withdrawal was "another Munich."[157]

The Chinese, probably with some success, urged Castro to defy Russian pressure to come to an accommodation with Washington,[158]

152 "Stop New U.S. Imperialist Adventure," *Jen-min Jih-pao,* Oct. 24, 1962; Chinese governmental statement, *ibid.,* Oct. 25, 1962, and *Peking Review,* V, 44 (Nov. 2, 1962), p. 5; "The People of the Whole World Should Be Mobilized to Support the Cuban People and Smash U.S. War Provocation," *Jen-min Jih-pao,* Oct. 28, 1962; "Defend the Cuban Revolution!" *ibid.,* Oct. 31, 1962, and *Peking Review,* V, 44 (Nov. 2, 1962), pp. 6–7; "The Heroic Cuban People Will Surely Win," *Hung Ch'i,* Nov. 1, 1962; note to Cuban government by Chinese Foreign Minister Ch'en Yi, *Jen-min Jih-pao,* Nov. 2, 1962; "The Fearless Cuban People Are the Most Powerful Strategic Weapon," *ibid.,* Nov. 5, 1962; Jen Ku-ping, "The Disgraceful Role of the Tito Group on the Cuban Question," *ibid.,* Nov. 12, 1962, and *Peking Review,* V, 46 (Nov. 16, 1962), pp. 7–9.

153 E.g., "U.S. Imperialists Threaten Heroic Cuba and Endanger World Peace," *Zëri i Popullit,* Oct. 25, 1962, and Albanian governmental declaration, *ibid.,* Oct. 26, 1962; "Kennedy Expresses and Represents the Aggressive Policy of U.S. Imperialism," *ibid.,* Oct. 30, 1962; "The Plots and Intrigues Against Cuba Will Fail, Cuba Will Win," *ibid.,* Nov. 2, 1962. Needless to say, Tirana endorsed the Chinese position totally; see "To Defend the Just Cause of People's China Is to Defend Peace and Socialism," *ibid.,* Oct. 23, 1962. The PPSh CC met from Oct. 26 to 28 but the Oct. 28 communiqué only stated that Hoxha, "in addition to agricultural problems, spoke about certain current international issues" (*ibid.,* Oct. 29, 1962).

154 See ftn. 144, *supra.*

155 His retreat first became public in the Soviet leader's letter to Kennedy of October 28 but was in fact apparently contained in his unpublished message of October 26. (See an apparently authoritative account of it by Robert Donovan in the *New York Herald Tribune,* Nov. 2, 1962; cf. "Reason Must Be Victorious," *Pravda,* Oct. 26, 1962).

156 See ftn. 146, *supra.*

157 *Kwang-ming Jih-pao,* Nov. 5, 1962. See also "The Fearless Cuban People Are the Most Powerful Strategic Weapon," *Jen-min Jih-pao,* Nov. 5, 1962 ("The attempt to play the Munich scheme against the Cuban people . . . is doomed to complete failure"), the clearly anti-Soviet speeches by P'eng Chen (*ibid.,* Oct. 29, 1962) and two speeches on the occasion of the 45th anniversary of the Bolshevik Revolution, by Wu Yu-chang (*ibid.,* Nov. 7, 1962) and Foreign Minister Chen Yi (*ibid.,* Nov. 8, 1962).

158 See *Jen-min Jih-pao,* Nov. 3, 1962, *et seq.,* and Jacques Marcuse from Peking in *The Sunday Times* (London), Nov. 11, 1962.

while Moscow and the pro-Soviet Communist parties took a theoretically equally pro-Castro position although in fact totally endorsing the Soviet retreat in Cuba, a move which Castro privately and publicly opposed.[159] On the other hand, the Cuban Communists, themselves divided into the leftist-radical *Fidelistas* and the totally pro-Soviet "old-line Communists,"[160] ostensibly remained on equally good terms with both Moscow and Peking; actually, Castro took as pro-Chinese an ideological position as his dependence upon Soviet economic aid permitted, while the old-time Cuban Communist leader Blas Roca remained totally pro-Moscow.[161] Factional struggles make strange and geographically isolated bedfellows. On November 6, Peking reported a striking example of Albanian-Cuban friendship:

> . . . Albanian Ambassador to China Reis Malile went to the Cuban Embassy [in Peking] yesterday to show his support for Cuba's struggle. The Albanian ambassador held the hand of Cuba's Chargé d'Affaires ad Interim Regino Pedroso Aldama and said: "Albania has been surrounded for 18 years, but it never yields or gives up the struggle. Today the Cuban people are in a similar situation. The Cuban people are a brave people!" In reply Pedroso said: "The Albanian people are also a brave people!" The two diplomats hugged each other in a warm embrace amidst applause.[162]

Soviet, Chinese, and Albanian general ideological polemics in October and November reflected the intensification of Sino-Soviet tension. In addition to repeating their previous positions on the 1960–1961 issues in dispute, they included new ideological formulas whose extent and seriousness, particularly if the latest Albanian declarations were added to them, might more justifiably than at any previous time be interpreted to indicate that for both Moscow and Peking the open break for which the Albanians had already called on October 13 was a possibility for

[159] See his references to Moscow-Havana differences in an interview, *Hoy* and *Revolucion,* Nov. 2, 1962, and Tad Szulc in *The New York Times,* Nov. 9, 1962.

[160] Ernst Halperin, "Kuba zwischen Moskau und Peking," *Die Tat* (Zürich), April 2, 1962; Theodore Draper, *Castro's Revolution, Myth and Realities* (New York: Praeger, 1962), pp. 201–211.

[161] See his speeches at the Nov. 1962 Bulgarian and Hungarian CP Congresses.

[162] NCNA in English to Asia and Europe, Nov. 6, 1962, 1846 GMT. There are other indications of Cuban sympathy for Albania: an Albanian cultural week opened in Havana on October 8, 1962, and a British journalist, reporting in late October 1962 on an interview with Che Guevara, wrote: ". . . When I asked Che Guevara, for instance, how Marxist-Leninist he considered the Poles, he shook his head slowly as if he wanted to say 'only middling.' For the Jugoslavs, however, there is little sympathy, chiefly disdain; for the Albanians, on the other hand, there is a certain respect, and it was not entirely based on the Albanian brandy which my Fidelista friend offered me and which — I hesitate to admit it — had a gentleness and a fine bouquet that came close to those of many of its better French competitors" (Henry Brandon, in *The Sunday Times* [London], Oct. 28, 1962).

which they must make systematic advance ideological preparation. However, the previous esoteric symbolism remained: The Chinese identified only the Yugoslavs (and not the Soviets), the Soviets only the Albanians (and not the Chinese), while the Albanians identified everyone and every party by name.

During the summer and early autumn Moscow had made only incomplete and esoteric references to the anti-Soviet Chinese and Albanian polemics.[163] By mid-October, however, a major Soviet counterstatement appeared as an editorial in the November issue of the Soviet-controlled international Communist monthly *Problems of Peace and Socialism.*[164] Besides reiterating the previous catalogue of charges against the "dogmatists and sectarians," explicitly against the Albanians and implicitly against the Chinese, the article set forth a new category of deviation (the counterpart of "modern revisionism"), "modern pseudorevolutionary dogmatism," and labeled the Albanians as Trotskyites whose unmasking helped the struggle against "modern dogmatism" (thereby implying that this might come to be true of the Chinese as well).

This editorial was written before but published during the Cuban crisis. After it, on the occasion of the anniversaries of the 1957 and 1960 Moscow Declarations, Ponomarev published an authoritative elaboration of Moscow's post-Cuban position[165] and launched a violent attack against the Albanians (and, by clear implication, against the Chinese) for their attitude concerning it. He prefaced it with the statement from the 1960 Moscow Declaration that, although

[163] A. P. Kositsyn, "The Historical Role of the Dictatorship of the Proletariat," *Voprosy Istorii KPSS,* No. 5, 1962, pp. 27–46 (passed for the press Sept. 10, 1962); "A New V. I. Lenin Document," *Pravda,* Sept. 28, 1962, and *Kommunist,* No. 14, 1962, pp. 3–14; L. F. Ilichev, "The Building of Communism and the Social Sciences," *Pravda,* Oct. 20, 1962; the reported Soviet judicial rehabilitation of Bukharin (see a Moscow dispatch to *Borba,* Oct. 16, 1962); D. Kondakov, S. Pertsova, and N. Gorbunova, "The First Party Conference after the October Victory — on the Publication of the New Edition of the Stenographic Report on the Seventh Extraordinary Congress of the Russian Communist Party (Bolsheviks)," *Pravda,* Oct. 21, 1962, and a Moscow report on the book's contents by P. Vuković in *Politika,* Oct. 11, 1962.

[164] "The Revolutionary Platform of the International Communist Movement," *World Marxist Review,* V, 11 (Nov. 1962), pp. 33–40 (passed for the press, Oct. 23, 1962); copies of the Russian edition, *Problemy Mira i Sotsialisma,* went on sale in Moscow on Nov. 4, 1962 (Topping from Moscow in *The New York Times,* Nov. 5, 1962). This article marked the Soviet return to direct criticism of the Albanians; in the Oct. 19 *Pravda* version of Ulbricht's report to the XVII SED CC Plenum (*Neues Deutschland,* Oct. 14, 1962), the passage criticizing the Albanians was omitted. As an editorial appearing in the only international Communist publication, the article at least in theory had greater validity than a mere Soviet pronouncement or a signed article in the journal.

[165] Boris Ponomarev, "The Victorious Banner of the World Communists," *Pravda,* Nov. 18, 1962.

> . . . the main danger in the Communist movement is revisionism, whose ideology has found fullest expression in the Program of the League of Communists of Yugoslavia . . . the documents of the conference also refer most forcefully to the danger of nationalism and national limitedness. Dogmatism, sectarianism, nationalism, and rigid adherence to the personality cult have proved to be the decayed breeding ground for the splitting activities of the leaders of the Albanian Party of Labor and their attacks upon creative Marxism-Leninism, on the socialist comity, and on the international workers movement. . . . The stand taken against the generally recognized vanguard of the world Communist movement, which, according to the definition of the Moscow conferences, has been and remains the CPSU, shouldering the heaviest burden in the struggle against imperialism and rendering great and effective support to all progressive liberation movements and trends, leads the Albanian bosses into camp with the anti-Communists. . . . Pseudorevolutionary phrases and slogans cannot conceal the main fact — the actions of the Albanian bosses harm the cause of socialism and Communism.

The Chinese attack on the Indian northern border was accompanied by two major mid-November Chinese ideological assaults on Moscow's position. For Peking, the Soviet retreat in Cuba and neutrality on the Sino-Indian border dispute were caused by cowardice before "American imperialism." These articles naturally reflected the most extreme Chinese view yet published. Insisting that "revolution is the locomotive of history" and that "the distinction of a Marxist-Leninist from a modern revisionist lies first of all in the attitude toward imperialism," Peking declared that "modern revisionists . . . have degenerated into the voluntary propagandists, political agents, and stooges of imperialism." In a clear reference to Khrushchev's Cuban retreat, one article stated:

> . . . Historical experiences show that the more resolute is the struggle against imperialism, the better will world peace be safeguarded. On the contrary, if one retreats, bows down, or even begs for peace before imperialism at the expense of the revolutionary people, one only encourages imperialism to carry out more aggressively its policies of aggression and war, thereby increasing the danger of a world war. As Comrade Fidel Castro has said: "The way to peace is not the way of sacrificing and infringing upon the people's rights, because that will be the way leading to war."

In a formulation strongly reminiscent of Stalin's on the sharpening of the class struggle during the transition to socialism, Peking asserted:

> . . . the nature of imperialism and the reactionaries will never change . . . they will never withdraw from the arena of history of their own

accord . . . the nearer they approach their doom, the more frenziedly they will struggle. . . .[166]

The other Chinese article identified dogmatism with the underestimation of the importance of "concrete forms" of socialism, such as that made by those (i.e., the Soviets) who "during the stage of the democratic revolution" (in the twenties and thirties) "wanted us to apply knowledge mechanically from books and the experience of other countries without any analysis." Finally, in a formulation particularly suggestive of possible Chinese advance ideological preparations for a Sino-Soviet break, it declared that

> . . . All Communists must work hard to raise their ability to distinguish Marxism-Leninism from revisionism, to distinguish the way of opposing dogmatism with Marxism-Leninism from that of opposing Marxism-Leninism with revisionism under the cover of opposing dogmatism, and to distinguish the way of opposing sectarianism with proletarian internationalism from that of opposing proletarian internationalism with great-nation chauvinism and narrow nationalism under the cover of opposing sectarianism.[167]

The November Bulgarian and Hungarian Party Congresses[168] were the first major international Communist Party confrontations since the Soviet Twenty-Second Congress in October 1961. Not only did they provide renewed confirmation that the lineup of parties on the Sino-Soviet and Soviet-Albanian issues had not significantly changed since 1960[169] and that the Sino-Soviet rift was again widening rapidly, but they also were characterized by a newer, more publicly antagonistic method of Sino-Soviet debate in the international Communist arena. At both congresses the Chinese delegate followed Chou En-lai's 1961 example[170] in attacking the speeches of other delegates censuring the Albanians. However, going farther than Chou, he identified the Albanians as the party involved, and he made clear (without naming Moscow) that Peking strongly differed with Khrushchev's policies on the United States, Cuba, and Yugoslavia.[171] His speeches were prominently

166 "Carry Forward the Revolutionary Spirit of the Moscow Declaration and the Moscow Statement," *Jen-min Jih-pao,* Nov. 15, 1962.

167 "Defend the Purity of Marxism-Leninism," *Hung Ch'i,* No. 22, Nov. 16, 1962.

168 *Rabotnichesko Delo,* Nov. 6, 1962, *et seq.,* and *Népszabadság,* Nov. 22, 1962, *et seq.*

169 Based on a survey of foreign delegates' speeches available to me as of Nov. 27, 1962.

170 See p. 93, *supra.*

171 According to a Western report (Underwood from Sofia in *The New York Times,* Nov. 9, 1962) at Sofia the Chinese delegate also criticized the Soviet withdrawal of missiles from Cuba.

reprinted in Peking,[172] but their esoteric criticism of Soviet policy and their explicit defense of Albania were usually censored in their Soviet and East European versions.[173] The Soviet, East European, and other non–East Asian delegates, on the other hand, defended Khrushchev's "policy of peace" in Cuba, attacked the Albanians, and condemned China's defense of them. Zhivkov and Kádár repeated the new Soviet line that China and India should make peace (while expressing no preference between them) and advocated the continued improvement of state relations with Yugoslavia[174] (while, like Ponomarev, registering condemnation of Yugoslav revisionism). Zhivkov[175] announced the purge of Yugov and Tsankov,[176] a step greeted with favor by Belgrade[177] and therefore with hostility by Peking and Tirana. The intensification of the Sino-Soviet and Soviet-Albanian struggles was also reflected in renewed dissension in international Communist front organizations on the Sino-Indian and Cuban issues.[178]

During late October and November, Tirana consistently followed

[172] E.g., his Sofia speech was given "considerable space and prominence" (Peking press reviews, NCNA in English to Asia and Europe, Nov. 10, 1962, 0216 GMT) in *Jen-min Jih-pao,* Nov. 10, 1962; also in NCNA in English to Asia and Europe, Nov. 9, 1962, 1301 GMT, and in *Peking Review,* V, 46 (Nov. 16, 1962), pp. 10–11.

[173] E.g., in *Rabotnichesko Delo,* Nov. 9, 1962. An initial survey of foreign delegates' speeches showed an unclear pattern in printing attacks on the Albanians and on the Chinese for having defended them (e.g., Zambrowski, the PZPR delegate, reportedly attacked the Albanians [Radio Belgrade, Nov. 8, 1962, 2100 GMT], but the Polish text of this speech [*Trybuna Ludu,* Nov. 9, 1962] does not refer to them).

[174] Yet the BCP Congress Resolution (*Rabotnichesko Delo,* Nov. 14, 1962) and Kádár still expressed reservations on the "revisionist concepts" of the LCY program; cf. the Ponomarev article (ftn. 165, *supra*) and the new Soviet CPSU history's favorable reference (as in its earlier editions) to the 1948 Cominform Resolution (Radio Zagreb, Nov. 14, 1962, 1830 GMT).

[175] *Rabotnichesko Delo,* Nov. 8, 1962 (not reprinted or quoted in *Jen-min Jih-pao*). Ulbricht, always a reliable bellwether, had also denounced the Albanians at the XVII SED CC Plenum (*Neues Deutschland,* Oct. 14, 1962).

[176] And the expulsion from the party of Chervenkov, who, if not the first two, had in 1959 showed signs of being pro-Chinese. See V.[iktor] M.[eier], "Säuberung in Bulgarien," *Neue Zürcher Zeitung,* Nov. 7, 1962.

[177] Statement by FPRY Foreign Secretariat spokesman Drago Kunc, *Borba,* Nov. 10, 1962.

[178] E.g., at the Oct. 29 Stockholm meeting of the WPC Presidium; see a letter by the Chinese delegate Cheng Shen-yu to *Dagens Nyheter,* Nov. 1, 1962, attacking the Indian delegate Diwan Chaman Lall, and the newspaper's comment on it. See also the speech of the Chinese delegation head at the Conakry Afro-Asian Lawyers Conference, NCNA in English to Asia and Europe, Oct. 18, 1962, 1956 GMT. According to *The Statesman* (New Delhi), Nov. 16, 1962, the CPI decided not to send a delegation to the November meeting in Colombo of the economic council of the Afro-Asian Solidarity Committee because it considered the host Ceylonese CP to be under Communist domination. See also the postponement of the scheduled Oct. 31 Leipzig WFTU meeting (Olsen from Warsaw in *The New York Times,* Nov. 23, 1962).

Peking's pro-Castro and anti-Indian line and made overt its esoteric anti-Soviet line.[179] In addition, the Albanians intensified their polemics against the Common Market and resumed attacks on the Italian Communist Party, this time with previously unparalleled detail and fury. (Like the Indian Communist refusal to follow either Moscow or Peking, the renewed role of the Italian Communists once again indicated the triple division of international Communism into right, center, and left tendencies.) On the day of Khrushchev's public retreat over Cuba, Tirana reported that "the Western press, especially the West German press, considers this move a victory for United States diplomacy."[180] In a speech on October 25 (printed only on November 4),[181] Hoxha repeated all the previous Albanian charges against Khrushchev and also condemned the Soviet and Italian theses on the Common Market and the Italian theses for the forthcoming PCI Congress.[182] He also declared that Khrushchev shared Soviet scientific advances with revisionists and capitalists rather than with socialist allies.

Hoxha's themes were made even more explicit and extreme in a subsequent speech by Hysni Kapo[183] and in a long ideological attack by *Zëri i Popullit* on the Italian Communists' theses for their forthcoming Tenth Party Congress.[184] Kapo repeated the October 13 Albanian call for the expulsion from the international Communist movement of all "modern revisionists" (explicitly including, in the Albanian definition, Khrushchev).

The Albanian attacks against the Italian Communists' theses in part resulted from Tirana's realization that the PCI's views offered a more complete and up-to-date program of "modern revisionism" than did the ideologically inactive Yugoslavs. The Albanians condemned the Italian views on war, on the importance of "national and historical peculiarities," on the substitution of "structural reforms" (within the Italian constitutional structure) for socialist revolution, and (recalling the Chinese

179 "Kennedy Expresses and Represents the Aggressive Policy of U.S. Imperialism," *Zëri i Popullit,* Oct. 30, 1962; "The Plots and Intrigues Against Cuba Will Fail, Cuba Will Win," *ibid.,* Nov. 2, 1962.

180 Radio Tirana, Oct. 28, 1962, 1900 GMT.

181 *Zëri i Popullit,* Nov. 4, 1962, and Document 33.

182 The resumption of Albanian polemics with the PCI reflected a further hardening of the PCI attitude concerning the PPSh, the LCY, and the EEC. See the PCI theses for its forthcoming congress in *L'Unità,* Sept. 13, 1962 (JPRS 15,679, Oct. 12, 1962), the CGIL position for an Oct. 31 WFTU meeting (Luciano Lama [a PCI CGIL leader] in *ibid.,* Oct. 14, 1962 [JPRS 15,986, Nov. 1, 1962, pp. 1–6]), and Eugenio Peggio in *Rinascita,* XIX, 21 (Sept. 29, 1962), pp. 12–13 (JPRS 15,786, Oct. 19, 1962, pp. 16–25).

183 *Zëri i Popullit,* Nov. 8, 1962, and Document 34.

184 "Concerning the Theses for the Tenth Congress of the Italian Communist Party," *Zëri i Popullit,* Nov. 17 and 18, 1962.

articles in the spring) their similarity to Bernstein, Kautsky, and the Economists. Kapo made most explicit this latest Albanian version of the makeup of the "modern revisionist" conspiracy and of the key role of Togliatti in it:

> . . . The modern revisionists are now coordinating their anti-Marxist views and their destructive activity everywhere; they are creating a united revisionist front. . . .
>
> The views spread by the revisionist leaders of the Italian Communist Party, headed by P. Togliatti . . . constitute . . . the intermediate link that unites into a single entity, into a unique code of modern revisionism, the views spread by Khrushchev at the 20th Congress . . . and thereafter about the so-called "peaceful" and "parliamentary" path of the transition to socialism with the openly opportunist and revisionist views of the traitorous and revisionist Tito clique. . . .

By late November, Sino-Soviet relations seemed to be moving toward — although not necessarily destined to reach — an open break.[185] It was still too early to determine whether the November Chinese cease-fire on the Indian border[186] would result in nothing more than a brief interruption of Sino-Indian hostilities or would improve Sino-Soviet relations.[187] In any case, Cuba and India had become more important irritants to Sino-Soviet relations than Albania, although Moscow's and Peking's attitude toward Tirana still remained one of the most important esoteric indicators of their true nature. Nehru and Castro were now at least as great obstacles as Hoxha to their improvement. Unlike them, however, Hoxha continued to profit from the renewed worsening in Sino-Soviet relations.

[185] Hong Kong reports indicated that Communist Chinese there were denouncing Khrushchev to Western journalists as a "traitor." See, e.g., a Hong Kong dispatch in *The Observer* (London), Nov. 18, 1962. Earlier refugee reports indicated these charges were being made against Khrushchev at CCP cadre meetings, (see a dispatch by its Hong Kong correspondent in *Avanti!,* Oct. 21, 1962) and after the 22nd CPSU Congress in meetings including non-party members (Oka from Hong Kong in *The Christian Science Monitor,* Nov. 17, 1962).

[186] CPR statement, *The New York Times,* Nov. 21, 1962. For analysis, see Joseph C. Harsch, "Peking Tries to Avert Western Chain Reaction," *The Christian Science Monitor,* Nov. 23, 1962.

[187] It did result in Moscow and pro-Moscow CP's endorsing the Chinese offer. See, e.g., Kádár's final speech at the VIII Hungarian CP Congress, *Népszabadság,* Nov. 25, 1962.

CHAPTER SIX

Albania Today

Albania and Her Neighbors[1]

The chief preoccupation of Albanian foreign policy since the break with Moscow has naturally been the further cementing of protective ties with Peking. From Communist China the Hoxha regime urgently needs continuing economic aid as well as political protection against a renewed Soviet attempt to overthrow it (either directly or via Yugoslavia) and support within the international Communist movement. It continues to receive both, although Peking's economic assistance is nowhere equivalent to the Soviet and East European aid it replaced.

But the Albanians have lived dangerously too long to relish the idea of having all their eggs in one basket. China, though distant enough to be a safe ally, is almost too far away to afford adequate protection against dangers closer at hand. Furthermore, China's own economic situation is so near disaster that its ability to continue adequate material assistance, less than the Soviets as it is, is not certain. Under these circumstances Hoxha would have to be foolhardy indeed not to see the wisdom and necessity of broadening Albania's sources of economic assistance and of trying, if not to come to friendly terms with its neighbors, at least to keep them divided.[2] He had to expect that Albania's traditional enemies would immediately explore any new opportunities created by the Soviet break with Tirana, but at the same time he had reason for hoping that they would no more be able to cooperate with one another in 1961 than they had in 1912 or 1920.

The Tirana regime has therefore been surveying the possibilities of fruitful diplomatic action. Vis-à-vis Belgrade and Athens, both historically Albania's enemies, they are obviously slim: Yugoslavia, Hoxha must with some reason believe, would only befriend Albania the better

[1] An earlier version of this section appeared in the author's "Albania: An Outcast's Defiance," *op. cit.*, pp. 4–6. Cf. the penetrating analysis by Viktor Meier, "Albanien in Schatten Jugoslawiens," *op. cit.*

[2] In this connection, Peking's rapprochement with Pakistan and Nepal offered Tirana a useful analogy.

to eat it up, and the immutable cornerstone of Greece's Albanian policy has been the Greek nationalist demand for annexation of "Northern Epirus." From Hoxha's point of view Italy is the least dangerous (because not geographically contiguous), the least unpopular, and at the same time the most able to provide economic aid. Moreover, Italy has always preferred an independent albeit weak Albania to one partitioned or controlled by Yugoslavia and Greece, and Rome also is anxious to expand its international influence.

Hoxha consequently turned first to Rome. He had already made a preliminary approach to the Italians in May 1961, and immediately after the Soviet-Albanian diplomatic break Tirana and Rome concluded a new agreement providing for a 50 per cent increase in Italo-Albanian trade.[3] (In view of the already large adverse Albanian trade balance with Italy, the new accord perhaps comes closer to being an agreement for aid than for a normal expansion of trade.) The official Italian airline Alitalia has opened a line from Rome to Tirana via Bari.[4] (A KLM Tirana stopover on its Amsterdam-Beirut flight[5] was maintained for only a few weeks.)[6] Now that the Albanians can no longer travel to Peking via Moscow, they have no alternative but to go via Italy, the Middle East, and the Rangoon-Kunming airline into China.

But Hoxha evidently does not intend to limit his efforts toward expanding Albania's Western contacts only to Italy. In a significant editorial published on January 9, 1962, *Zëri i Popullit* declared:

> We wish to establish diplomatic relations and to have good trade, cultural, and other relations with all capitalist countries which want them, especially with our neighbors, on the basis of vigorous respect for the recognized principles of peaceful coexistence. . . .

In line with this declaration Tirana has proceeded to reactivate trade relations with France, West Germany, the Near East and Africa,[7] to station a permanent ambassador in Vienna[8] (neutral Austria, once a

[3] *Bashkimi,* Dec. 8, 1961. According to the well-informed Swiss Balkan expert Viktor Meier (*op. cit.,* p. 476), the Italians have also sent experts to Albania, the Italian state oil company ENI has shown interest in Albanian oil, and there have been Italian-Albanian negotiations about the granting to Albania of Italian governmental and private credits.

[4] *Corriere della Sera,* Apr. 16, 1962.

[5] *Frankfurter Allgemeine Zeitung,* May 3, 1962.

[6] *Ibid.,* June 13, 1962.

[7] *Ibid.,* June 5, 1962, and Rolf Breitenstein, UPI, from Tirana in the *New York Herald-Tribune,* June 5, 1962. A protocol on exchange of goods between Albania and Ghana was signed in Accra on Feb. 16 (*Zëri i Popullit,* Feb. 18, 1962), with Egypt (*ibid.,* Mar. 25, 1962), and with Iraq (*ibid.,* Mar. 27, 1962).

[8] *Christian Science Monitor* (Boston), Jan. 24, 1962. Diplomatic relations at the ambassadorial level have also been established with Morocco (*Zëri i Popullit,* Feb. 13, 1962).

traditional protector of the Albanians against the Serbs and Italians, is now prosperous enough again to resume a similar role if it wished to do so), and to make moves towards better relations with Great Britain.[9] There are, however, no indications of any Albanian overtures for a rapprochement with Washington, and in view of Communist China's implacable hostility towards the United States this seems unlikely, at least in the near future.

There have even been some recent indications that Albania and Greece, despite their traditional enmity, may be moving toward an accommodation that would end the official state of war still existing between them. Notwithstanding the reawakening of Greek public interest in the "recovery of Northern Epirus" as a result of Moscow's abandonment of Hoxha, Greece at the same time does not wish to see Italy or Yugoslavia, or both, move into Albania first; indeed, it might even prefer Hoxha to a regime under Italian or Yugoslav control. Athens realizes, moreover, that its major NATO allies would hardly countenance any Greek military adventures in Europe's traditional Balkan tinderbox. As for the Albanians, now dependent solely on the protection of a remote Chinese ally, common sense dictates a desire to minimize the risks in their relations with their neighbors.

The Greek government has reportedly intimated its willingness to shelve the issue of Northern Epirus for the sake of a rapprochement with Albania.[10] Premier Karamanlis stated in the Greek parliament that Athens was prepared to end the state of war between the two countries if a suitable formula could be agreed upon.[11] For its part the Tirana regime has made an initial conciliatory gesture by permitting the repatriation of a number of Greeks who had been in Albania since the Greek civil war.[12] However, another Albanian feeler in late May 1962 reportedly came to nothing, again because of the "Northern Epirus" question; and in early September a visit of two Albanian parliamentarians to Greece also did not come off. Nevertheless, both Tirana and Athens appeared in the autumn of 1962 still to desire some improvement of relations.[13]

[9] AFP report from Belgrade, Jan. 13, 1962. An Albanian trade delegation arrived in London in Oct. 1962 (*The Observer* [London], Oct. 14, 1962).

[10] *The Economist* (London), Jan. 20, 1962; *The Times* (London), Jan. 23, 1962.

[11] *The Scotsman* (Edinburgh), Feb. 6, 1962. The pro-government Greek newspaper *Acropolis* (quoted in *Borba,* Jan. 3, 1962) reported that there has been "no other manifestation whatever on the part of Greece" with regard to the resumption of diplomatic relations with Albania.

[12] *Zëri i Popullit,* Jan. 1, 1962; *The Times* (London), Dec. 29, 1961; Radio Tirana, June 13, 1962, 1900 GMT.

[13] The proposal was made to Mercouris (see *supra*) by Albanian Foreign Minister Shtylla; for its unfavorable reception in Greece, see an Athens dispatch to *The Sunday Times* (London), June 3, 1962. For the failure of the Albanian parlia-

Of Albania's neighbors, however, Yugoslavia is certainly the one most involved in the new situation created by the Soviet-Albanian break. On the one hand, Tito is totally and permanently hostile to Hoxha, Shehu, and their group, and Belgrade's prestige still smarts from the Albanian Communists' 1949 execution of Xoxe as a "Titoist" and from the failure of Yugoslav-encouraged efforts in 1956 and 1960 to overthrow Hoxha. In addition, there is the problem of the Kosmet region which, with its hundreds of thousands of Albanian inhabitants, constitutes an Albanian irredenta within Yugoslavia's borders. On the other hand, Tito has too great an interest in preserving the Balkan *status quo* to be disposed to take any flagrant risks. It therefore seems highly unlikely that he will seek to exploit Albania's increased isolation by a new attempt at Hoxha's overthrow, whether by military force or even indirectly by a Belgrade-inspired *coup d'état.*

There are, indeed, signs in the contrary direction. Although diplomatic relations between Belgrade and Tirana remain minimal, Yugoslavia has not been content merely with repeated disavowals of any hostile intent towards Albania, but has officially indicated its readiness to normalize those relations and to resume trade exchanges between the two countries.[14] It has also announced a considerably increased degree of autonomy for the Kosmet,[15] presumably in order to counteract any potential tendency among its inhabitants, now that Albania is no longer a Soviet satellite, in favor of rejoining their independent and defiant brethren across the border. On the other hand, trials of alleged pro-Tirana conspirators in the same region have underlined Belgrade's determination to keep the Kosmet within the Yugoslav state.[16] Belgrade probably hopes that the rapidly increasing population and economic growth of the Kosmet will prove increasingly attractive to the Albanians to the south. One may well doubt, however, whether this "supranational" Yugoslav nationalism which Belgrade hopes to create in the Kosmet and make attractive to all Albanians can surmount the extreme ethnic nationalism so typical of any rapidly developing but still relatively primitive areas like the Kosmet or Albania itself.

Albania's revolt against Moscow has had the further side effect of reviving historic frictions among its neighbors. Perhaps the most striking evidence of this has been a renewed flare-up of Yugoslav-Greek polemics

---

mentary delegation's visit, see *Kathimerini* (Athens), Sept. 12, 1962; for general analysis, V.[iktor] M.[eier] from Athens, "Griechenlands Konflikte mit seinen nördlichen Nachbarn," *Neue Zürcher Zeitung,* Sept. 23, 1962, and his "Albanien im Schatten Jugoslawiens," *op. cit.,* p. 471.

[14] *Borba,* Jan. 13 and 20, 1962.

[15] TANYUG, Jan. 17, 1962.

[16] *Politika* (Belgrade), Sept. 15, 1961.

about Macedonia.[17] While in part this was instigated by overeager Macedonian nationalists in Skopje, and furthered by the Soviet-Yugoslav rapprochement, the reactions on both sides represent implicit mutual warnings not to disturb the *status quo* either on the Greek-Yugoslav frontier or in Albania.

Yugoslav-Bulgarian relations, although on the surface improving as a result of Soviet pressure, are far from good[18] (the Macedonian question alone makes any genuine rapprochement very difficult), and Albania may well hope to gain from this historic rivalry as well. These increasing Balkan rivalries, from which Tirana can well hope to profit, were perhaps one of the reasons why the initial Albanian soundings among its neighbors and the West appeared to diminish in early 1962. Hoxha can afford to wait; he is apparently receiving minimum necessary aid from Peking, and the renewal of Albanian economic relations with the East European states indicates that even Moscow has had second thoughts about its initial attempt at total economic blockade.

Albanian Internal Affairs

While Hoxha was executing such a complex minuet on the international parquet, the Albanian internal situation remained remarkably stable. There has been no reliable evidence of disunity in the Albanian leadership since the purge of Belishova and Tashko in late summer 1960; there has been no effective popular opposition since the war.[19]

Nor was the country's economic situation desperate; it seemed that the regime was quite capable of keeping it under control. Its very underdevelopment was in its favor; with the overwhelming majority of the population still engaged in subsistence agriculture, the replacement of Soviet and East European aid by Chinese[20] enabled most of the key deficit items (primarily industrial equipment and grain) to be met. Furthermore, trade increased with the West and with uncommitted areas.[21] The inevitable dislocations[22] resulting from such a rapid shift

17 *The Economist,* Jan. 13, 1962; *Borba,* Dec. 30, 1961. These polemics did not decline after the intensified Soiet rapprochement with Yugoslavia in the spring of 1962; see, e.g., "How the Macedonian Minority in Macedonia 'Has Disappeared,'" *Nova Makedonija* (Skopje), June 10, 1962.

18 See, e.g., an attack by *Borba* on Sept. 14, 1962, on an anti-Yugoslav Bulgarian book.

19 Cf. two articles by David Floyd, a British correspondent who visited Albania in late spring 1962, in *The Daily Telegraph* (London), June 5 and 15, 1962.

20 In 1959 China's share of total Albanian foreign trade was 2.7 per cent, in 1961 it had grown to 28.2 per cent, and for 1962 it has been projected as 59.1 per cent, higher than the Soviet Union's share ever was.

21 See pp. 160–162, *supra*.

22 Throughout 1961 the Albanian press reported "savings" arising from cuts in

in the foreign-trade pattern do not appear to have produced anything like catastrophic results. This was in part due to the resumption of trade with the East European countries, particularly with Czechoslovakia. Trade with the latter was scheduled to increase in 1962, presumably because of the resumption of Albanian chrome shipments to the plant in Slovakia.[23]

However, the country's relative freedom of choice in foreign-trade outlets is growing, the proportion of foreign subsidy to national income is decreasing, and the possibility of decisive foreign political influence, due to the increasing distance of subsidizing countries (China vis-à-vis the Soviet Union, the Soviet Union vis-à-vis Yugoslavia), is declining. Basically, the Albanian outlook is far from hopeless. Undoubtedly, capital investment and economic growth will proceed at a slower pace than before 1962. This has resulted in a definite decline since 1960 in the Tirana regime's popularity, both within and without the Communist party. It has also given rise to a fairly widespread feeling that, were Khrushchev, Hoxha, and Shehu to leave the scene, a renewed Albanian rapprochement with Moscow might be desirable. But such potential party and nonparty dissent does not reach to the Albanian Politburo level, and Hoxha's and Shehu's ruthless elimination of all dissent has produced a climate of terror which will probably inhibit any effective opposition in the near future to their anti-Khrushchev course.

Predictions regarding Balkan politics are best avoided — except perhaps for the one traditionally attributed to the British traveler returning to his London club after a Continental tour: "There'll be trouble in the Balkans in the spring!" The Balkan political scene does indeed appear somewhat more disturbed than usual as a result of the Soviet-Albanian break. However, the thermonuclear age tends to freeze national boundaries and to deter — to some extent — even local wars. All in all, the new situation in south-central Europe seems unlikely to erupt into serious armed conflict. On the contrary, provided Hoxha continues to obtain sufficient outside assistance and protection to keep his economy functioning and his neighbors quiet, the present Albanian regime and its policies bid fair to continue to surprise the world and disconcert the Kremlin.

---

imports — e.g., importation of oil pipes and drilling equipment was cut by 312 million leks, roughly the total annual import need (*Zëri i Popullit,* June 7, 1961); the tanning and leather-processing enterprise at Vlorë eliminated all imports and planned to produce steel axles, water pumps, etc. (*Bashkimi,* Apr. 12, 1961). The lack of any statistical data after 1959 (the last year covered by a published statistical yearbook) makes any more detailed analysis impossible.

[23] *Zëri i Popullit,* Mar. 29, 1962; *Statisticke Zpravý,* 1962, No. 1, pp. 24–25; *Tudomány és Technika* (Bratislava), Aug. 30, 1962.

Conclusion

As the Albanian affair has once again demonstrated, ours is indeed an age of nationalism — and not least so in the Communist camp. East and West are both having their difficulties with the diffusion of power so characteristic, it begins to appear, of the fifties and sixties of the twentieth century; Albania, like Yugoslavia, is an example of how badly Moscow can and does cope with the problem.

The Albanian affair is of course far from over, nor is it likely to be wound up soon, any more than one of its enabling factors, the Sino-Soviet rift. Any conclusions about it, therefore, must be more than usually provisional; they may well turn out to be premature. The fact that both Khrushchev and Mao are in their late sixties is the most significant potential factor for rapid change in the world, the Communist camp, and even in Albania.

Yet Albania has been more than just flotsam and jetsam driven by the torrent of Sino-Soviet discord: it has been and is now a factor, albeit a small one, on its own — a small but persistently irritating burr under the saddle in which Khrushchev and Mao are condemned to ride together, crowded, uncomfortable, each disputing the right to the reins, yet each knowing that if he falls off he will have no horse at all.

Small as the burr is, one may best begin with it. Certainly Albania's extreme nationalism has been the major cause for Hoxha and Shehu's defiance, quixotic as it first seemed to a postnationalist West, and for the popular support without which they could hardly have brought it off. Albania is underdeveloped, Balkan, and Moslem, more Middle Eastern than European, with extremist, violently nationalist, ruthless, Western-educated intellectuals and a mass of subsistence-level peasants traditionally susceptible to demagogic nationalism. Albanian nationalism, like Polish nationalism, is defensive: the country is small, poor, surrounded by hostile neighbors, always threatened by partition, absorption, or foreign control. In addition, the large Kosmet irredenta guarantees that its nationalism will be extreme. Finally, its élite and the country as a whole retain some memories of past Ottoman glories, when Albanians were among the chosen Moslem ruling group who looked down upon and oppressed the Slav *rayah;* like the Sudeten Germans in interwar Czechoslovakia, the Albanian élite after 1912 was a deposed élite, oppressed, they felt, by those they formerly ruled.

By 1960 thoroughly purged and loyal to Hoxha and Shehu, the Albanian Communist élite had the characteristics of its non-Communist predecessor: the typical ruthlessness of élites in underdeveloped areas and the extreme nationalism of a small, menaced ruling group. It was determined to unite and industrialize the country. It was also more internationalist as a result of a combination of the old Ottoman élite feeling with Western education and Marxist-Leninist ideology. As in Yugoslavia, this new internationalism reinforced rather than conflicted with new Albanian nationalism. Finally, the new Albanian Communist élite had all the pride and self-confidence that comes from having fought their own way to power rather than having ridden into Tirana behind Red Army tanks.

But by 1960 the Albanian Communist leadership also was suffused with a very special kind of desperation, not surprising in those who twice had nearly been slaughtered by their domestic and foreign Communist foes and therefore quite naturally and most strongly disinclined to run the same risks again. In 1948 Hoxha and Shehu had been saved from Tito's and Xoxe's firing squads only by Stalin's break with Belgrade; in 1956, almost as surely, they had been saved from removal by the Hungarian Revolution. Both times they escaped from the greatest danger that can befall a small state like Albania: a firm alliance between one or more of its rapacious neighbors and a major power under whose influence they already were.

From the Albanian view, Communist China continues to be as close to the ideal protector as a small, harassed Balkan country can ever expect to have. It is powerful but distant, hostile to the Soviet Union but yet not without influence over it, and therefore capable of maintaining Albania economically, willing to support her against Moscow, and perhaps able somewhat to restrain Moscow against Tirana. It is ideologically strongly anti-Yugoslav, and nothing ever unites an alliance like a common, furiously detested enemy. It is ferociously anti-American, as is Albania because of Washington's aid to Belgrade. Finally, it is far away, and its resources still so limited, that it could not, even if it seriously wished, restrain Albania in its search for secondary means of support among its neighbors near and far.

For China, Albania is cheap, its regime apparently stable, its loyalty to extremism unquestioned, its chances of reconciliation with Moscow minimal, its need for a powerful protector total, its possibility of finding another one equally small. Most importantly, perhaps, China cannot afford politically to drop Albania; it could not soon recruit another anti-Soviet ally again.

For the Soviet Union, the Albanian affair represents a loss the unmitigated nature of which is only partially concealed by the much more important but not, at least as yet, total Sino-Soviet rift. Moscow failed to prevent the Chinese rebellion; it failed to prevent Albania from joining it; it failed to overthrow Hoxha and Shehu; it failed to pressure or persuade China to abandon Albania to Moscow or Belgrade; it failed to beguile or compel the Asian "neutralist" Communist parties to condemn Albania; it failed, above all, to crush a country so small, so Balkan, so poor, so isolated, and to the world at large so nearly ridiculous that Moscow itself ever since has run the risk of being thought impotent. As with Yugoslavia, as differently with China, as again differently with North Korea and North Vietnam, Khrushchev has tried and failed to meet the problem: the rise to independent power in Peking of a major Communist party and state and the disruption such a development inevitably causes in the Soviet Union's scheme of "proletarian internationalism." Hoxha has been the first but hardly the last to profit from Mao's challenge; Khrushchev bids fair to continue the loser.

	1938	1939	1950	1951	1952	1953	1954	1955	1956	1957	1958	1959	1960
Total	1,343.8	2,145.9	1,426.7	2,435.5	2,243.5	2,550.8	1,838.4	2,791.3	2,890.4	4,117.3	5,390.8	5,965.3	—
Export	339.4	353.0	323.9	457.6	653.8	549.4	546.7	650.0	950.4	1,451.6	1,460.5	1,700.6	—
Import	1,004.4	1,792.9	1,102.8	1,977.9	1,589.7	2,001.4	1,291.7	2,141.3	1,940.0	2,655.7	3,930.3	4,264.7	—

Albanian Exports, 1938, 1950–1960, by Country, at Current Prices

	1938	1950	1951	1952	1953	1954	1955	1956	1957	1958	1959	1960
Soviet Union	–	203.1	241.1	373.6	264.5	268.3	270.8	429.6	748.6	682.5	763.3	1,251.1**
Bulgaria	–	8.5	18.2	21.5	26.3	38.3	35.1	29.6	25.8	57.5	33.9	–
Czechoslovakia	9.0	30.3	85.5	103.0	115.3	83.0	109.8	165.1	242.4	244.3	338.1	361.5**
East Germany	0.7	–	–	25.3	52.4	66.7	64.9	95.9	140.5	127.7	240.7	241.3**
Hungary	–	36.6	52.0	66.9	35.0	51.2	84.6	53.0	77.4	80.6	108.5	–
China	–	–	–	–	–	–	–	36.2	33.8	40.5	42.3	–
Poland	–	24.6	41.1	48.6	40.1	35.7	62.5	50.4	93.6	127.7	96.0	127.3**
Romania	–	20.8	11.7	14.9	13.8	3.2	1.5	33.7	28.1	25.4	25.0	47.7**
Italy	232.0	–	8.0	–	2.0	0.3	11.7	32.1	28.4	26.4	43.2	26.8**
Yugoslavia	2.5	–	–	–	–	–	2.5	4.5	21.9	47.0	6.1	–
Switzerland	–	–	–	–	–	–	6.6	15.8	3.8	–	2.7	–
Other	95.2	–	–	–	–	–	–	4.5	7.3	0.9	0.8	10.6**

Albanian Imports, 1938, 1950–1960, by Country, at Current Prices

	1938	1950	1951	1952	1953	1954	1955	1956	1957	1958	1959	1960
Soviet Union	–	409.9	1,170.3	685.3	1,061.2	535.7	782.9	835.0	1,299.4	2,234.9	2,401.4	2,137.2**
Bulgaria	–	17.6	21.3	93.3	73.2	104.7	120.6	41.2	66.2	115.2	193.8	–
Czechoslovakia	34.1	185.0	254.0	246.3	330.9	212.6	311.5	271.4	318.7	524.3	513.5	390.5**
East Germany	48.5	–	43.1	141.6	129.0	125.2	307.0	256.5	212.4	284.0	377.6	271.5**
Hungary	11.5	186.6	130.3	169.1	112.7	120.0	216.8	103.6	77.3	188.2	159.5	–
China	–	–	–	–	–	–	63.4	204.7	295.2	84.2	120.6	–
Poland	–	185.1	132.8	126.5	138.0	112.0	142.6	101.8	164.2	236.8	246.8	194.0**
Romania	10.0	118.6	209.2	120.9	133.1	70.2	131.8	70.5	84.5	136.0	74.4	120.5**
Italy	431.1	–	16.9	6.7	23.3	11.3	47.8	27.3	94.3	89.2	117.3	159.5**
Yugoslavia	99.9	–	–	–	–	–	9.9	7.7	19.8	26.4	23.2	–
Switzerland	–	–	–	–	–	–	5.6	15.8	8.7	0.4	3.9	8.2*
Other	369.3	–	–	–	–	–	1.4	4.5	25.0	10.7	32.6	156.3**

* Estimated, ** calculated.

SOURCES: For 1938, 1950, 1955–59, *ASRPSh* 1960, pp. 240–41; for 1951–54, *ESE* 1960, Ch. 6, p. 13; for 1960: Soviet Union, *Vneshnaya Torgovlya SSSR,* 1961, pp. 61, 65; East Germany, *Statistisches Jahrbuch der D.D.R.;* 1960–61, p. 574; Poland, *Rocznik Statystyczny* 1961, pp. 269–270, Romania, *Anuarul Statistic al R.P.R.* 1961, p. 315; Italy, Statistical Office of the European Communities, *Foreign Trade, Monthly Statistics,* Feb. 1961, No. 2, p. 30; Czechoslovakia, *Statisticke Zpravý,* 1962, No. 1, pp. 24–25.

TABLE 6.2

Principal Indicators of Albania's Industrial Production, 1938, 1950–60

Year	*Industrial Production* Total Production	Light Industry	Food Processing	Labor Force (thous.)	Electric Energy (thous. kwh)	Cement (tons)	Bricks and Tiles (thous.)	Lumber Productio (cu. meter
	(million leks)							
1938	1,387.0	398.0	607.6	. . .	9,315	9,000	4,045	3,165
1950	5,750.0	554.0	3,471.8	83.3	21,434	15,881	17,639	51,479
1951	8,262.7	1,556.6	4,737.8	98.7	24,154	18,205	19,679	59,677
1952	11,316.5	2,602.0	5,934.4	124.2	39,372	19,263	30,812	72,709
1953	13,231.8	3,374.5	6,609.5	138.8	49,844	13,159	57,027	90,247
1954	14,190.5	3,743.5	6,525.9	129.7	61,723	15,395	59,741	95,326
1955	15,900.0	4,212.8	6,944.7	138.3	85,266	44,549	76,087	106,561
1956	17,245.3	4,683.0	7,351.5	138.2	103,876	64,784	81,169	106,290
1957	21,712.3	6,132.4	8,753.4	150.8	124,976	70,221	87,482	124,530
1958	26,047.6	7,847.6	10,046.0	169.5	149,700	77,552	94,434	146,913
1959	31,170.2	9,103.6	12,273.9	194.0	174,998	74,157	147,725	157,424
1960	34,672.0	9,226.0	14,236.6	202.4	194,300	72,896	165,116	170,175

SOURCES:
1938, 1950–57: in leks, *ASRPSh* 1958, pp. 40–41; in physical units, pp. 44–45; labor force, p. 33.
1958–59: in leks, *ASRPSh* 1960, pp. 112–13; in physical units, pp. 114–15; labor force, p. 93.
1960: in leks, *Bashkimi,* Mar. 4, 1961, p. 2; in physical units, *Bashkimi,* Feb. 5, 1961, p. 1.

TABLE 6.3

Indicators of Albania's Production in the Mining Sector, 1938–60 (in tons)

Year	Bitumen	Coal	Crude Oil	Chromium Ore	Copper Ore	Blister Coppe
1938	17.1	3,686	108,116	7,000	. . . .	. . . .
1942	18.0	. . . .	230,300	35,910	. . . .	1,300
1948	11.8	12,000	. . . .	16,500	. . . .	. . . .
1950	26.3	40,860	131,763	52,191	14,207	938
1951	. . .	51,750	122,177	52,260	12,251	789
1952	36.0	78,909	149,352	60,247	24,373	1,254
1953	25.0	105,321	149,472	47,389	21,976	571
1954	17.0	149,344	175,427	100,321	21,395	656
1955	22.0	194,641	208,078	122,094	24,465	939
1956	23.0	224,112	265,748	132,173	27,880	576
1957	24.0	235,733	489,765	167,290	55,971	925
1958	32.2	255,677	403,197	201,300	87,460	946
1959	. . .	287,894	479,274	247,770	105,329	1,006
1960	. . .	281,220	727,538	289,148	. . . .	944

SOURCES:
1938: *ASRPSh* 1959, pp. 74–75; 1942–48: Skendi, *Albania,* pp. 173–189; 1950–57: *ASRPS* 1958, pp. 44–45; 1958–59: *ASRPSh* 1960, pp. 114–115; 1960, coal: *Shënime Për Agjitatorë* No. 10, May, 1961, pp. 16–21; 1960, crude oil: *Bashkimi,* Feb. 5, 1961, p. 1; 1960, chromiu ore: *Bashkimi,* Feb. 5, 1961, p. 1; 1960, blister copper: *Bashkimi,* Feb. 5, 1961, p. 1; bitume 1938–1958: L. V. Tyagunenko, *Razvitiye Ekonomiki Narodnoy Respubliki Albanii* (Develo ment of the Economy of the People's Republic of Albania), (Moscow: All-Union Institute Scientific and Technical Information of the State Scientific and Technical Committee of th Council of Ministers and of the Academy of Sciences and the Economic Institute of th Academy of Sciences, 1960), pp. 1–80 (JPRS 4568).

TABLE 6.4

Principal Indicators of Albanian Agricultural Crop Production, 1938–59 (in tons)

Year	*Wheat*	*Rye*	*Corn*	*Rice*	*Vegetables*	*Potatoes*	*Tobacco*
1938	38,570	3,080	143,750	640	31,302	3,600	1,950
1948	70,000	8,000	160,000	3,000	....	....	....
1950	85,303	7,860	108,615	3,002	53,734	26,457	1,651
1951	81,725	10,284	116,594	3,329	47,472	15,189	2,457
1952	81,754	8,146	97,150	4,738	39,286	13,275	2,000
1953	121,824	13,524	158,600	6,176	75,361	21,951	4,508
1954	108,769	11,465	127,246	8,229	89,014	24,523	3,930
1955	118,081	14,849	176,531	9,580	101,582	30,187	7,137
1956	93,964	13,314	177,932	5,177	98,924	19,239	7,043
1957	121,168	14,639	222,682	6,612	95,135	25,837	8,024
1958	96,678	8,585	167,481	4,906	70,889	15,619	7,954
1959	101,666	9,089	208,617	5,294	75,139	26,337	13,369

SOURCES:
1938, 1950–57: *ASRPSh* 1958, pp. 56–63, 1948, Skendi; *Albania,* p. 169.
1958–59: *ASRPSh* 1960, pp. 138–49.

TABLE 6.5

Indicators of Albanian Agricultural Development, 1938–60

Year	*Farm Credits (in thous. leks)*	*Members of Cooperatives*	*Cattle* (*in thousand heads*)	*Sheep*	*Goats*	*Mechanization of Agriculture*		
						Tractors	*Combines*	*Cultivators*
1938	....	....	391.2	1,573.9	932.3	28	..	..
1950	83,501	10,932	419.2	1,707.0	830.2	238	..	65
1951	113,440	11,423	403.3	1,558.5	800.2	272	3	85
1952	120,831	17,122	381.6	1,476.1	773.7	349	3	115
1953	135,571	22,382	388.8	1,602.0	871.0	493	13	313
1954	150,185	21,804	404.5	1,639.0	915.3	574	26	336
1955	338,560	28,507	421.9	1,734.3	1,014.1	916	108	349
1956	596,715	92,891	415.7	1,627.2	967.2	1,136	114	417
1957	559,200	162,380	405.4	1,612.1	1,029.3	1,308	138	533
1958	868,790	235,982	422.5	1,661.9	1,095.1	1,852	216	672
1959	1,041,314	252,035	418.7	1,615.0	1,162.3	2,220	259	692
1960	....	....	424.3	2,674.6		....	...	...

SOURCES:
1938–1957: *ASRPSh* 1958, pp. 55, 80–83, 90, 94.
1958–1959: *ibid.,* 1960, pp. 129, 131, 180–81, 281.
1960: *Zëri i Popullit,* May 3, 1961, p. 2.

Documents

DOCUMENT 1

"Unmask Yugoslav Revisionism and Fight It to the End, Zëri i Popullit, *June 29, 1960 (complete text).*

According to the Declaration issued at the meeting of representatives of Communist and workers parties of socialist countries held in Moscow in November 1957: *"The Communist parties believe that under present circumstances the most formidable danger is revisionism, that is to say, right-wing opportunism which, as a manifestation of bourgeois ideology, paralyzes the revolutionary energy of the working class and seeks the preservation or the restoration of capitalism."*

This conclusion, this extraordinarily just thesis, continues and will continue to make it necessary to fight without mercy against modern revisionism as represented by the Yugoslav revisionists. For life itself and practical activity, both in the ideological sphere and in politics, have shown that the most aggressive, the most formidable and most diabolical detachment of modern revisionism is Yugoslav revisionism — the revisionist clique of Tito and his collaborators.

There are many examples to prove that in the ideological and political spheres the revisionists have been transformed lately into an aggressive weapon of bourgeois ideology against the working class of every country; as traitors to Marxism-Leninism and the working class and as fierce enemies of socialist and Communist construction, they have become supporters of the restoration of capitalism and all the aggressive activities of U.S. imperialism and a docile and blind tool for the maneuvers of the warlike imperialists.

Innumerable facts prove that long ago Tito's revisionist clique became a trained *agentura* of the imperialist bourgeoisie, which tries to sow ideological confusion among the masses, to destroy the conscience of Communists and the working class, to split the iron unity of Communist and workers parties and of the international Communist movement, and to weaken and paralyze the anticolonialist national liberation movement of peoples fighting against the imperialist yoke, a movement which has now begun in all four corners of the globe.

Tito and his collaborators, as defenders of the interests of capitalism and the warmongers, deserve the same commendation and the same awards from capitalism as John Foster Dulles, Dwight Eisenhower, Chancellor Adenauer, McCarthy, and their like for their efforts to keep capitalism in the saddle.

With various writings and demagogic Marxist speeches and with their anti-Marxist program approved by the Seventh Congress of the League of Communists of Yugoslavia.[1] Tito's renegade group has not only tried to reject the fundamental principles of Marxism-Leninism as a theory of the class struggle, the socialist revolution, the dictatorship of the proletariat, and the leading role of the party; but also it has tried to sell these anti-Marxist ideas to other countries through Yugoslav "diplomats," "specialists," and "journalists" and to put them into practice wherever it might find even temporary support.

The Yugoslav revisionists will never be

[1] The Seventh Congress of the League of Communists of Yugoslavia (LCY) met April 22–27, 1958. For analysis and text of the LCY Program and the adverse reaction of the Communist bloc press, see V. L. Benes, R. F. Byrnes, and N. Spulber, eds., *The Second Soviet-Yugoslav Dispute* (Bloomington, Ind.: Indiana University Press, 1959). [Ed.]

able to disclaim their responsibility for the bloody events of the counterrevolution in Hungary. Not only did they prepare — ideologically speaking — the Hungarian counterrevolutionaries, those traitors to Marxism-Leninism and the working class, but they participated directly in their organization, urging them to take up arms against the people's government, to initiate a white terror against honest Communists. It was not coincidental that at the general staff of the 67th Infantry Division, which at the time of the counterrevolution was stationed at Subotica on the Hungarian frontier, one spoke openly of Titoism triumphing in Hungary, of its union with Yugoslavia which would then have had 25 million inhabitants, etc. The counterrevolution in Hungary bears the seal of the joint activity of U.S. imperialism, Yugoslav revisionism, and international reactionary circles.

The Yugoslav revisionists have pursued and continue to pursue toward our country and our people a criminal policy which, by acts of diversion, plots, dispatch of agents and spies for sabotage, and even attempts on the lives of militant members of the government and party, aims at liquidating the people's government and the independence of our people's republic. But all these attempts by the revisionists have failed and will fail shamefully, thanks to the heroic stand and struggle of our party and our glorious people.

In the past few years U.S. imperialism has suffered many and repeated defeats. The fight against U.S. imperialism has spread to the four corners of the globe. The policy of the countries of the socialist camp headed by the USSR has unmasked imperialism and its warlike plans. This has complicated matters for imperialism. Therefore, it has never had more need of devoted renegades, collaborators like the Yugoslav revisionists, to be utilized as "capitalism's watch dogs," or as a "Trojan horse" in the ranks of the peoples' revolutionary movement.

The attitude of the Yugoslav revisionists toward certain international problems on which, as a matter of form, they appear to support the foreign policy of the Soviet Union is nothing but a colossal bluff, a lie to hoodwink the Yugoslav and other peoples.

In fact — and this can be clearly seen in the attitude of the revisionists toward the U.S. provocation against the Soviet Union in the U-2 spy plane and the sabotage of the summit conference by U.S. imperialists — Titoist foreign policy is nothing but a form of support for Western imperialist policy.

There was a reason why Dulles loved Tito and his collaborators and why he gave him American dollars; there is also a reason why they are now loved by U.S. Under Secretary of State Douglas Dillon, who, as the Yugoslav ambassador in Washington stated, gave and is still giving his assistance to the Titoist clique. Tito's ambassador said: "After each interview with Dillon I feel like a new man." The most vicious enemies of Communism — like Dulles was and like Dillon now, who has not lost a single opportunity for wishing for the death of Communism and Communists — wholeheartedly support, encourage, and embrace the traitor Tito.

The Yugoslav revisionists have changed their mask many times. Depending on the time and situation they maneuver so as best to serve their imperialist bosses and, first and foremost, U.S. imperialism. They have never ceased their struggle against Marxism-Leninism, against socialism and Communism, against the Marxist-Leninist Communist and workers parties, against the socialist countries and against the unity of the socialist camp.

Modern revisionism, as the Moscow Declaration emphasizes, is still the most formidable danger today; that is why the primary task of all Communists is still the continuation — with even greater energy — of the fight against revisionism, particularly Yugoslav revisionism, which is socialism's and Communism's most dangerous enemy. The fight against Yugoslav revisionism must not be interrupted at any time; it must not be underestimated but must be continued until revisionism is completely uprooted. The uncompromising fight to unmask the Titoist renegades — those enemies of Marxism-Leninism — is also an international contribution to the betrayed Yugoslav people.

DOCUMENT 2

"Let the Plotters and Revisionists of Belgrade Be Unmasked Through and Through," Zëri i Popullit, *July 17, 1960 (excerpts).*

At the beginning of July this year, one of the most demented leading agents of imperialism, the executioner of the Yugoslav peoples Aleksandar Ranković,[1] made a speech at a big meeting in Sremska Mitrovica, Serbia. . . .

When A. Ranković, the organizer of plots against the independence of the Albanian people, referred to Yugoslavia's relations with its neighboring countries, he was so carried away by his spy's imagination that he viewed the Italian neofascist regime as "more democratic" than the regimes of the peoples' democracies in the Balkans. He said: *"While along the Italian-Yugoslav frontier we have millions of crossings both ways every year and thousands of persons freely cross the frontiers, along other parts of our frontier darkness prevails and one sees the barbed wire and hears the frontier guards' hobnailed boots."*

If millions of persons every year cross the Italian-Yugoslav frontier, as Ranković affirms, this shows that the regimes of Tito and the Italian neofascists are of a similar character and have a unity of aims and methods. As to the unveiled allusion made by Ranković to our frontier, this proves the diabolical desire of the Belgrade revisionists to conspire against our fatherland. How he would like our frontier to be open so he could send hundreds and thousands of spies to organize plots against our people and our homeland!

We tell Ranković, the plotter, that Albania is not a country where darkness reigns but a socialist stronghold where the people reign, the people who are determined to defend to the end the victories they have won with their blood. We are proud of our frontier guards who heroically and vigilantly watch over the inviolability of our fatherland's frontiers. No one knows better than our frontier guards the true nature of the Yugoslav revisionists, who resort to anything to overthrow our people's power and to wipe out the independence of our homeland. . . .

Our frontiers are open only to honest people, to those who are the friends of Albania, while they are closed to spies and provocateurs and will remain closed as long as plots are being hatched in Belgrade and along our frontiers. Our party, government, and people have never allowed and never will allow our frontiers to be touched or to be bargained over. The Albanian people welcome their friends with "bread and salt" and their enemies with bullets.

As to the cunning, cruelty, efficiency, and scale of their activities, the Yugoslav revisionists have exceeded all the imperialist agencies in plotting against the Albanian People's Republic. They are so zealous and so thoroughly trained in this respect that the imperialists primarily use the hands of the revisionists to do the bulk of the work directed at overthrowing the people's power and installing a capitalist regime in Albania.

The history of relations between our country and Titoist Yugoslavia is a history of plots aimed at liquidating our independence and transforming Albania into a part of the Titoist Hell, as well as a history of the heroic resistance put up by the Albanian people, of the uncompromising, arduous, and intricate struggle aimed at safeguarding the independence of our country against the ignominious plots

[1] Aleksandar Ranković, Vice President of the Federal Executive Council and Secretary of the Executive Committee of the Central Committee of the LCY, formerly Minister of Interior. [Ed.]

of the Titoists. He who does not know the history of relations between our country and Yugoslavia cannot fully and precisely appreciate the danger the Yugoslav revisionists represent.

The plotting of the Yugoslav revisionists against our country started with our struggle for national liberation; even then our party confronted the Yugoslav revisionists. In 1943 Tito tried under the guise of military cooperation to influence all the movements for national liberation in the Balkans, to assume leadership of them, and later under the guise of the "Balkan Federation"[2] to subjugate all the Balkan peoples. What a frightful thing for the Balkan peoples if these imperialist plots had succeeded! Our party has struggled with all its energy against the realization of the Titoist plots of the "Balkan general staff" and the "Balkan Federation."

In Sremska Mitrovica, Ranković alluded nostalgically to the days when the Belgrade revisionist leadership *"made great efforts to realize an armed military collaboration in the Balkan and Adriatic region,"* adding: *"Through the most difficult days of the history of the Balkans we looked confidently to the future and made the greatest political contribution to unity and close collaboration among the Balkan peoples."* It goes without saying that this "policy of unity and very close cooperation among the Balkan peoples" was a policy of subjugating the Balkan peoples behind the mask of Tito's Balkan Federation. Our Party of Labor resisted all these plots and since then the struggle between the Yugoslav revisionists and our Party of Labor has become even harsher.

The provocateur Ranković tried hard at Sremska Mitrovica to vilify the immortal name of G. Dimitrov[3] by implying that G. Dimitrov himself supported the "Balkan Federation." G. Dimitrov was an eminent Marxist-Leninist, a great personality of the international Communist movement, and a consistent revolutionary.

G. Dimitrov, in dealing with Tito's efforts to enslave the Balkan peoples behind the mask of the "Balkan Federation," declared on February 4, 1948, at the Second Congress of the Fatherland Front of Bulgaria that *"these states do not need a federation or a confederation or a customs union"* and that *"they need to strengthen and safeguard their independence and sovereignty by mobilizing and organizing the internal democratic forces of the people."*

After realizing that they could not subjugate the Balkan people by means of the idea of a "Balkan general staff" or a "Balkan Federation," the Titoists plunged openly into the struggle by organizing diversionary plots inside the parties and the socialist states of the Balkans. This is how they organized in Albania the plot to overthrow the people's power and to install in power the revisionists, led by the traitor Koci Xoxe. The Yugoslav revisionists organized similar plots in some other socialists countries. All these Titoist conspiracies were foiled by the Communist and workers parties concerned.

But the traitorous group under Tito does not give up plotting. The Yugoslav revisionists organized a counterrevolutionary plot in Albania in 1956 and placed at its head the enemies of the Albanian people, Liri Gega, Dali Ndreu, Tuk Jakova, Bedri Spahiu, and so on. They proposed to overthrow the people's power by means of this counterrevolutionary plot

[2] A Balkan Federation, comprising Yugoslavia, Albania, and Bulgaria, was a primary goal of postwar Yugoslav foreign policy; Soviet opposition in January 1948 brought a halt to steps in this direction. See Adam B. Ulam, *Titoism and the Cominform* (Cambridge, Mass.: Harvard, 1952), pp. 86-95, and Milovan Djilas, *Conversations With Stalin* (New York: Harcourt Brace, 1962). [Ed.]

[3] Georgi Dimitrov, Secretary General of the Executive Committee of the Comintern, 1935–1943; Chairman (later Secretary General) of the Central Committee of the Bulgarian Communist Party and Chairman of the Politburo, 1945–1949; and Prime Minister of Bulgaria, 1946–1949; died July 2, 1949. [Ed.]

and to install a revisionist government in Albania. But this time also our party and our people nipped the revisionist plot in the bud, thus saving the freedom of the fatherland and the socialist regime of Albania.

The Yugoslav revisionists organized a plot aimed at completely liquidating the Albanian population of Kossovo-Metohija by compelling the Albanians through terror to acquire Turkish citizenship, by forcibly sending to Turkey hundreds of thousands of Albanians, and by imprisoning and killing thousands and thousands of other Albanians. They tried to deceive the Kossovo-Metohija patriots by provocative organizations set up by the Titoist UDB[4] in order to attract the true Albanian patriots into these "patriotic" and "illegal" organizations to liquidate them later on through Ranković's UDB.

The Albanian people will never forget that the president of Yugoslavia, Josip Broz-Tito, during his meeting with the King of Greece in Corfu in 1956 discussed, at the latter's suggestion, the idea of dividing Albania between Greece and Yugoslavia.

Our party is profoundly convinced by its great experience acquired in the struggle against the Yugoslav revisionists that imperialism organized the counterrevolution in Hungary in 1956 essentially through the instrumentality of Josip Broz-Tito, A. Ranković, and the rest of the traitorous gang in Belgrade. We are profoundly convinced that if the revisionists were not in power in Yugoslavia and that if Yugoslavia were a socialist country, no imperialist attempts could have led to the bloody events of the Hungarian counterrevolution.

One of the chief aims of the Yugoslav revisionists' plots is to torpedo the national liberation movements of the Arab countries and of Africa and Asia, as well as of the Latin American countries, to liquidate the Communist and workers parties where these parties exist and to prevent their creation where they do not exist, and to attract these countries onto the path of imperialist subjugation, to sabotage their relations with the socialist camp. We are fully convinced that the Yugoslav revisionists are now more than ever hatching plots against the freedom of the Albanian people and the freedom of the other peoples of the socialist countries in the Balkans and against the unity of the socialist camp.

Today the relationship of forces in the international arena is in favor of socialism, and the socialist system is becoming stronger every day while the imperialist system is decaying. This is an objective law. For this reason international imperialism, chiefly the United States, feels more than ever that it is necessary to disrupt the unity of the socialist camp. And the best means, the most effective means, of attaining the goal required by imperialist interests of disrupting the unity of the socialist camp and the international Communist movement are the modern revisionists, particularly the Yugoslav revisionists.

Considering the existing balance of power in the international arena and its tendency to change continually in favor of socialism and to the detriment of imperialism, imperialism cannot militarily attack the socialist camp without necessary preparations. And these preparations consist primarily of the need to divide the socialist camp and the international Communist movement, to sweep away the elements of revolution and progress in its own rear lines, i.e., to liquidate the Communist and workers parties in the capitalist countries, etc., and also to continue the arms race and complete the complicated military preparations.

It is for these reasons, as stressed in the Moscow Declaration of 1957 of the Communist and workers parties of the socialist camp that " . . . *the Communist parties consider in present circumstances revisionism to be the main danger*." These are the reasons

[4] UDB, initials of the State Security Department, Yugoslav security police. [Ed.]

why today more than ever revisionism must be thoroughly unmasked in order to uproot it and wipe it out as an ideological trend; the struggle for socialism and the struggle for universal peace cannot be separated from the struggle against revisionism. The more we unmask the Yugoslav revisionists the stronger will be the unity of the socialist camp, the more impossible it will be for the imperialists to undertake aggressive actions, and the more peace will be ensured throughout the world.

For a very long time Titoist Yugoslavia has not been a socialist state; for a long time it has been a Hell where the darkest terror reigns and where a clique of traitors, fed on American imperialist dollars soaked in the blood of the workers, has been able by deceptive methods to seize power and to install for the first time in history a revisionist Trotskyite regime.

Our Party of Labor, faithfully guided along the Marxist-Leninist road by its Leninist Central Committee and led by Comrade Enver Hoxha, will continue without compromise to the very end the struggle aimed at completely unmasking the Belgrade revisionist plotters because it considers this to be its most elementary duty in order to safeguard the purity of Marxism-Leninism, the unity of the socialist camp, and the freedom and independence of our country and because in this manner we help our fraternal peoples in Yugoslavia who have suffered a terrible misfortune.

We shall do this because we are convinced that in this way we will bring our modest contribution to the struggle against imperialism and the preservation of world peace, and we shall never be diverted from this road for any reason whatsoever, by any force whatsoever, because our experience has convinced us that this is the best way to remain faithful to proletarian internationalism, to the Moscow Declaration, to socialism and Communism, to the peoples' aspirations to free themselves from capitalism and maintain peace throughout the world.

DOCUMENT 3

Communiqué of the Plenum of the Central Committee of the PPSh, Rruga e Partisë, *VII, 10 (October 1960), p. 3, and* Zëri i Popullit, *September 9, 1960 (complete text).*

The Plenum of the Central Committee of the PPSh convened under the chairmanship of the First Secretary of the Central Committee of the PPSh, Comrade Enver Hoxha, to review and approve the report of the Politburo of the Central Committee of the PPSh, "On Certain Organizational Issues of the Party," presented by Comrade Rita Marko, member of the Politburo and secretary of the Central Committee of the PPSh. The Plenum made the appropriate decision in the matter.

The Plenum of the Central Committee of the PPSh, after also reviewing the grave errors regarding the party line committed by Comrade Liri Belishova, member of the Politburo and secretary of the Central Committee of the PPSh, decided unanimously to expel her from the ranks of the Plenum of the Central Committee of the PPSh.

At this meeting the Plenum of the Central Committee of the PPSh elected to the post of secretary of the Central Committee of the PPSh Comrade Ramiz Alia, candidate of the Politburo of the Central Committee of the PPSh.

The Plenum of the Central Committee of the PPSh, at a joint session with the Central Auditing Committee, reviewed the hostile activity toward the party undertaken by Koço Tashko, Chairman of the Central Auditing Committee, and decided unanimously to expel him from the Central Auditing Committee and from the party.

The Plenum of the Central Committee of the PPSh in the course of its proceedings learned with sorrow the news of the death of the distinguished militant of the international Communist movement, Wilhelm Pieck, President of the German

Democratic Republic and dear friend of the Albanian people. The Plenum of the Central Committee honored his memory by holding a minute of silence.

The Plenum of the Central
Committee of the PPSh

Tirana, September 8, 1960

DOCUMENT 4

Communiqué, Zëri i Popullit, *December 21, 1960 (complete text).*

The Central Committee held a plenary meeting on Dec. 19 and 20, 1960, under the chairmanship of Comrade Enver Hoxha, First Secretary of the Central Committee of the Albanian Party of Labor.

The Plenum heard a report by Comrade Enver Hoxha on behalf of the Albanian Party of Labor delegation which participated in the meeting of the representatives of the Communist and workers parties held in Moscow in November 1960.

1. The Plenum discussed and unanimously approved Comrade Enver Hoxha's report and all the activities of the delegation of the Albanian Party of Labor during the proceedings of the meeting of the representatives of the Communist and workers parties, and passed the appropriate resolution.

2. The Plenum unanimously approved the Declaration and appeal of the Moscow conference addressed to the peoples of the world.

3. The Central Committee Plenum decided to convene the Fourth Congress of the Albanian Party of Labor on Feb. 13, 1961.

Signed: The Plenum of the Central Committee of the Albanian Party of Labor. Tirana, Dec. 20, 1960.

Resolution

The Plenum of the Central Committee of the Albanian Party of Labor, which met on Dec. 19 and 20, 1960, heard and discussed the report by Comrade Enver Hoxha, First Secretary of the Central Committee of the Albanian Party of Labor, who headed the delegation of the Albanian Party of Labor to the meeting of the representatives of the 81 Communist and workers parties in Moscow.

The Plenum unanimously approved the activities of our party delegation which participated in the Moscow conference, as well as the Declaration and appeal addressed by the conference to the peoples of the world.

The Plenum of the Central Committee of the Albanian Party of Labor notes that the Declaration of the 81 Communist and workers parties is a programmatic document for the Communist and workers movement which, on the basis of the immortal Marxist-Leninist teachings and the collective experience of all the Communist and workers parties, defines their principled positions on the most important contemporary problems and the tasks for their future struggle for peace, national independence, democracy, and socialism.

The correct Marxist-Leninist line, which our Party of Labor has always followed in regard to foreign policy matters — peaceful coexistence among nations with different systems, the struggle to defend peace, the construction of socialism in our country, defense of the purity of Marxism-Leninism, and strengthening of the unity of the socialist camp and the international Communist and workers movement — is fully reflected in the Declaration.

The Plenum noted that the conference of the 81 Communist and workers parties once more proved that meetings of the parties' representatives and mutual discussions on problems, through the method of consultation, are useful and indispensable for working out identical opinions and coordinating activities in the struggle for the common cause. Experience has proved that only such meetings as the two Moscow conferences in November 1957 and November 1960 serve this purpose and yield results.

The Declaration analyzes and correctly defines the characteristics of our epoch, the unity of the socialist camp and its role, the problem of war and peace, the breakdown of colonialism, the tasks of the Communist and workers parties, and matters connected with the international Communist movement. The Plenum of the Central Committee pointed out that our party will base all its activities on these principles and will faithfully implement the Declaration signed by the 81 Communist and workers parties in November 1960, just as it faithfully implemented the 1957 Moscow Declaration.

The Plenum of the Central Committee of the Albanian Party of Labor emphasizes that the Declaration's estimation of the role of the Soviet Union within the socialist camp and of the Communist Party of the Soviet Union — as the most experienced and competent body of the international Communist movement — expresses an objective fact and the feelings of the Albanian Communists. Our party has always viewed the CPSU as the acknowledged vanguard of the international Communist movement. The Albanian people consider the Soviet people their dearest friend, just as the Soviet people have in the Albanian people a faithful friend forever. This friendship, based on Marxist-Leninist teachings, was enshrined in the hearts of the Albanian people during the darkest days of the struggle for liberation and the struggle for building socialism. It has been forged by our party and its Central Committee headed by Comrade Enver Hoxha. There is no force on earth capable of marring it.

The Communist and workers parties guard their unity as their most precious possession and are strengthening it with each passing day, in accord with Marxist-Leninist principles and proletarian internationalism. The unity of the Communist and workers parties of the socialist countries — the unity of the socialist camp — is based on the unity of the international Communist movement. The unity of the two largest parties — the Communist Party of the Soviet Union and the Communist Party of China — and the two largest countries of the socialist camp — the Soviet Union and the Chinese People's Republic — has special importance for the unity of the international Communist movement and the socialist camp. The Plenum considers the Declaration of the 81 parties as the basic document for further strengthening the unity of the Communist and workers parties of all countries and the socialist camp. The Albanian Party of Labor will, in the future too, devote all its forces to ensuring our unbreakable unity.

The imperialist enemies have tried to split and speak about splitting the socialist camp and the international Communist movement. They dream of achieving this. However, the hopes of the imperialists, headed by the United States, are doomed to failure. The Moscow conference in November 1960 gave their plans a hard blow, a destructive blow. The Declaration is an important weapon for all world Communists in their struggle against imperialism and for the defense of peace. The conference of the 81 parties also condemned the Yugoslav form of international opportunism which has become the concentrated expression of the "theories" of contemporary revisionists. The Declaration reveals the true nature of the Yugoslav revisionists as traitors to Marxism-Leninism who are carrying out disruptive activities against the socialist camp and the international Communist movement. In this connection, the Plenum of the party Central Committee considers as very important the Declaration's conclusion on the need for further unmasking the leaders of Yugoslav revisionism, regarding this an indispensable task for the future, as well, for every Marxist-Leninist party.

The Plenum of the Central Committee of the Albanian Party of Labor advises all party organizations to study most attentively the historic documents of the conference of the Communist and workers parties held in Moscow in November 1960 and its Declaration and appeal addressed to all the peoples of the world, to widely propagate them among the masses during the campaign for the preparations for the party's Fourth Congress, and to support them in all their activities.

Signed: The Plenum of the Central Committee of the Albanian Party of Labor

DOCUMENT 5

"The Struggle Against Revisionism as the Principal Danger in the International Communist and Workers Movement Is the Imperative Task of All Marxist-Leninist Countries," Zëri i Popullit, *January 20, 1961 (complete text).*

One of the most important features in the development of the international Communist movement at present is the struggle against revisionism. Special attention was given to this problem in the Declaration issued by the Communist workers parties in 1957 and more fully in the 1960 Declaration. In the 1960 Declaration it is again stressed that revisionism, the essence of which is represented by Yugoslav revisionism, remains the main danger in the international Communist and workers movement.

The Albanian Party of Labor holds to its previous opinion — that modern revisionism, and particularly Tito's revisionist clique, is the main danger to the Communist movement and that the Communist and workers parties must not cease for a moment their principled struggle against it. Revisionism constitutes the main danger because it attacks the most vital issues of the international Communist movement and the present development of the world.

The contemporary danger of revisionism is closely connected with the principal characteristic of the present epoch which, as the Declaration emphasizes, is the transition from capitalism to socialism. V. I. Lenin stressed that in the age of imperialism, which is the threshold of the proletarian revolution, the danger of opportunism in the revolutionary movement of the working class greatly increases. This is proved by the history of the development of Marxism-Leninism and the international Communist movement. But this conclusion of V. I. Lenin must be emphasized even more now that the problems of the disintegration of capitalism, the transition to socialism through the socialist revolution, and the establishment of the dictatorship of the proletariat are to an even greater extent not merely theoretical questions but part of the daily struggle of the Marxist-Leninist parties and the working classes, a struggle which compels the middle classes, and especially the imperialist middle classes, to mobilize all their resources and to utilize every means to divide and destroy the revolutionary movement, to bar the road to revolution, and to protect and re-establish capitalism. In this activity capitalism makes use of revisionism precisely because the denial of the socialist revolution and the dictatorship of the proletariat is the basic content of modern revisionist theories and because the safeguarding and restoration of capitalism in the countries where it has been overthrown is their principal aim. The revisionists are endeavoring to paralyze the revolutionary drive of the working class now at a time when its revolutionary spirit must develop at all costs; they are trying to disarm the proletariat and its vanguard party — ideologically speaking — just at a time when it needs the correct Marxist-Leninist orientation as much as it needs air to breathe. They are trying to disorganize the working class and leave it without revolutionary guidance at the precise moment when it needs the Marxist-Leninist leadership of the Communist and workers parties more than ever in its fight for peace, democracy, national independence, and socialism. Have the revisionists perhaps renounced their plans and therefore ceased to present a serious threat to the Communist movement? The revisionists will continue to exist; they will continue to be a great and constant danger for the Communist movement; they will not renounce their designs until the total disappearance of capitalism from the face of the earth.

Revisionism has, moreover, a large social and economic basis and ideological roots which make it the principal danger for the Communist and workers revolutionary movement. In the capitalist countries the class roots of revisionism are the aristocracy of the working class, the petite bourgeoisie, and the peasant smallholders who form a milieu conducive to maintaining the influence of the bourgeoisie in the workers movement. In the socialist countries the internal source of revisionism lies in the influence of still-existing remnants of bourgeois ideology in the consciousness of people, which cannot disappear all at once even after the liquidation of the economic basis of the bourgeoisie. Capitulation before imperialist pressure is its external source. Ideologically speaking, the permanent sustenance of the revisionists is bourgeois ideology because revisionism is one of the forms of bourgeois ideology's influence on the proletariat — the reflection of bourgeois ideology in theory and practice. So long as the social and economic basis of revisionism has not disappeared and the means of penetration of bourgeois influence into the workers movements of capitalist and socialist countries have not been barred, the danger of revisionism and the pressure exerted by the bourgeoisie on the workers movement will not cease.

Now, when the ground is slipping from under the feet of imperialism and when the balance of power in the international arena is changing more and more in favor of socialism and to the detriment of imperialism, the imperialists, headed by American imperialism — the number one enemy of peace and socialism — while not giving up their attempts at organizing direct aggression against the countries of the socialist system, are making use of modern revisionism as their principal weapon — the traitorous revisionist clique of Tito in particular — to sap and divide the socialist camp and the international Communist movement. Marxism-Leninism and the facts of international life irrefutably prove that imperialism will not change its nature to its dying day and will in no way desist from attempts to undermine and destroy the revolutionary movement and the socialist camp; consequently revisionism, as its principal weapon in this context, remains the essential danger for the international Communist movement.

Today, when the Communist and workers parties are practicing a policy of multiple alliances with various social forces in the fight for peace, democracy, national independence, and social progress and when the socialist countries are following the line of peaceful coexistence between states with differing social systems, the danger of right-wing opportunism — the danger of the propagation of illusions damaging to the issues of the class war, the transition from capitalism to socialism, the struggle for peace, the attitude toward the Social Democrats and national bourgeoisie, etc. — is very great. It is precisely this opportunist tendency of the right which constitutes, under present conditions, the principal danger in the international Communist movement; this has been proved by the facts.

Finally, revisionism represents the principal danger for the Communist movement because its viewpoints are intermixed with and in many cases merge with bourgeois propaganda and the viewpoints of right-wing leaders of the Social Democrats, thus creating a common front hostile to Marxism-Leninism and socialism. Revisionism represents in this sense a serious danger, because it camouflages with Marxist and Leninist phrases its opportunist right-wing views, which are the expression of bourgeois ideology, and then proclaims them as the "creative development of Marxism under new conditions" in the fight against "dogmatism," "sectarianism," "adventurism," etc., as is done by the Yugoslav revisionists. This can deceive and mislead many people, even people who are honest but not sufficiently conversant with the ideological and political point of view, and this happens in the ranks of the Communist and workers parties as well as outside them. Moreover, revisionism, especially Yugoslav revisionism, now represents a serious danger because it provides weapons to the reactionary forces of the national bourgeoisie in colonial countries who, in order to deceive the popular masses in those countries, make use of "socialist" slogans and spread propaganda of a "socialist ideal," such as the "specific socialism" of Tito.

All this shows that, despite the severe blows it is suffering, modern revisionism has not been conclusively destroyed but, on the contrary, continues to exist and is an international phenomenon constituting a real and serious danger, the principal danger to the international Communist and workers movement. The fact remains that the revisionists are at the head of a whole state, Yugoslavia. Therefore, any relaxation of revolutionary vigilance, any weakening of the principled struggle against it, and any hesitation in this struggle lead inevitably to a recrudescence of revisionist tendencies which gravely damage our great cause.

The Declaration of the Communist and workers parties brilliantly confirms the viewpoint which our Party of Labor has held all along with the greatest resolve — that the traitorous revisionist Tito group constitutes a particularly great danger to the unity of the socialist camp and the international Communist movement, to the peoples' struggle for freedom against colonialism, and to the forces of peace.

The Yugoslav leaders betrayed Marxism-Leninism long ago. To the Moscow Declaration of 1957, which is a great Marxist-Leninist document of the international Communist movement, they counterpoised their own revisionist, anti-Marxist, and anti-Leninist program, in which the profoundly opportunistic "theories" of international modern revisionism are concentrated.[1] On the most important questions of our time Tito's traitorous revisionist clique has taken a stand which is in complete opposition to Marxism-Leninism and has proclaimed that its basic ideas on the socialist revolution and the dictatorship of the proletariat, on the nature of imperialism, on peace and war, on the struggle for national liberation, etc., are outdated.

By stubbornly carrying on their nationalist and antisocialist policy, the revisionist Yugoslav leaders have set the League of Communists of Yugoslavia against the entire international Communist movement. They have separated Yugoslavia from the socialist camp, and they have diverted it from the road to socialism and made it dependent on so-called aid from U.S. imperialism and other imperialists, thus creating conditions which endanger the revolutionary gains achieved by the heroic struggle of the Yugoslav people. At the present time no Communist who holds firmly to the positions of Marxism-Leninism can say that the Tito clique is building socialism in Yugoslavia.

The Albanian Party of Labor, holding firmly to the revolutionary positions of Marxism-Leninism and of proletarian internationalism, has always unmasked without mercy or compromise the divisive and subversive activities of the Yugoslav revisionists against the socialist camp and international Communism, stressing that this activity is precisely the "special mission" entrusted by imperialism to the traitorous Belgrade clique within the general capitalist offensive against socialism and the world revolutionary movement. The role of the Belgrade revisionists has been starkly demonstrated at all crucial times in international developments of recent years. The Marxist-Leninist parties can never forget the infamous program which the League of Communists of Yugoslavia brought to light in 1957 with a view to counterbalancing and neutralizing the effect of the Declaration of the Communist and workers parties and of uniting and organizing the international revisionist forces against the Communist movement

[1] See Document 1, footnote 1.

and the socialist camp. The peoples of the socialist countries, and our people in particular, cannot shut their eyes to the subversive and espionage activities continually carried on by the traitors of Belgrade. No Communist, no honest person, can remain silent in the face of Kardelj's mad and monstrous attacks[2] and the accusations of the Yugoslav press against the CPR and the glorious Communist Party of China. These accusations are aimed at the unity and cohesion of the two largest Communist parties and the two largest socialist countries — the USSR and the CPR, the CPSU and the Communist Party of China — which form the basis of the unity of the entire international Communist movement and of the entire socialist camp. No international Communist can or should remain indifferent in the face of the attacks and vicious activities of the Tito revisionist clique against a socialist country such as Albania and against the Albanian Party of Labor.

The Marxist-Leninist parties have waged a determined struggle to unmask the Titoist group as a vicious enemy of peace and of the freedom of peoples. The Belgrade revisionists talk a lot about peace and active, peaceful coexistence — to use their own words; they even pretend that they are the ones who resurrected the Leninist principle of peaceful coexistence, which, they claim, had been left "in oblivion" by the Communist and workers parties. An old popular maxim says that man must not be judged by his words but by his deeds. In fact, the Titoists completely distort the Leninist principle of peaceful coexistence; they distort it in a specific way which plays into the hands of the bourgeois imperialists. They link up peaceful coexistence with peace between the workers and the monopolists of the capitalist countries; they link up peaceful coexistence with peace between the enslaved peoples and the oppressing imperialists; they make coexistence depend on the renunciation of the political and ideological struggle against imperialism and its nerve-center, American imperialism, which, according to them, would result in an aggravation of international relations. This means, in other words, that to preserve peace one must cease unmasking the warlike actions of the imperialists and that the peoples must not fight to defend peace but must beg for it, bowing to the ground before American imperialism! Tito's group of traitors applies these "principles" strictly and tries with all its strength to conceal the true origin of wars — imperialism, especially U.S. imperialist circles — and to give the impression that everyone today — even the Government of the United States — is struggling for peace. At the same time it tries directly or indirectly to put the blame for the tension in international relations on the socialist countries. A glaring proof of this is the provocative attitude of the Belgrade traitors on the question of why the summit meeting in Paris failed last May, when Tito brazenly blamed the Soviet Union for it and absolved the truly responsible party, that is, the U.S. Government. One must also recall the accusations made by Tito, Kardelj, and the revisionist Yugoslav press that the CPR is against peaceful coexistence and constitutes a great danger to peace. It is no secret that these accusations have been and are still widely used by the U.S. Government to aggravate the international situation and justify the "cold war," the "position of strength" policy, and the unbridled arms race with the excuse of alleged "Communist aggression." These same charges were also used by the U.S. representatives at the 15th session of the U.N. General Assembly in order not to allow a debate on the restoration of the legitimate rights of the CPR in that organization.

The trump in the Titoist game is to

[2] Edvard Kardelj, Vice President of the Federal Executive Council, Secretary of the Executive Committee of the Central Committee of the LCY, and author of *Socialism and War: A Survey of Chinese Criticism of the Policy of Coexistence* (Belgrade: Kultura, 1960). [Ed.]

create an uproar over the so-called policy of "neutrality" and "nonalignment" which Yugoslavia supposedly follows and which the Yugoslav leaders unblushingly identify with the true policy of neutrality followed by the former colonial and dependent countries. By this they try, on the one hand, to conceal from the Yugoslav people and world public opinion the true nature of the traitorous Titoist group as an agency of American imperialism; on the other hand, by speaking about "the particularly great role" of the countries now engaged in the preservation of peace — and they put Yugoslavia at the head of these countries — the Yugoslav revisionists try to create distrust toward the peaceful policy of the Soviet Union and the other socialist countries and so divide the forces of peace.

However, all the attempts of the Belgrade renegades to hide their real nature as enemies of peace are useless; one cannot hide the sun with a sieve. Everybody knows that "neutral" Yugoslavia takes sides, that it is part of the Balkan pact, and that it is thereby tied up with the aggressive NATO and CENTO blocs headed by American imperialism. Tito's Yugoslavia is nothing more than a camouflaged American "place d'armes" in the Balkans; it is armed and continues to be armed, not because somebody threatens to attack it, but in order to attack the countries of the socialist camp at the right moment. The friends of revisionism do not give their aid and arms to the traitorous Belgrade group for no reason. The facts show each day that the military collaboration with NATO by the two members of the Balkan pact — Greece and Yugoslavia — is continually being strengthened despite the "vows" of denial of the Belgrade revisionist heralds. It is clear that the real neutrality practiced by the independent former colonial states, which is directed against imperialism and contributes to peace, has nothing in common with the so-called "neutrality" of the Tito clique, which serves the most reactionary and warlike imperialist circles in order to divide the forces of peace; what's more, there can be no common ground between the peaceful foreign policy of the socialist countries and that of the Tito clique. Whoever does not see this is blind.

All the activities of the leaders of the Yugoslav revisionists serve the aims of imperialism, which tries to divide and undermine the Communist movement and the socialist camp, strangle the revolutionary movement and wars of national liberation, and disorient and divide the forces of peace in the world. For these activities they are paid by the American imperialists and their partners with millions and billions of dollars. Everybody knows that after 1948 Yugoslavia received from the United States and other imperialist powers so-called "aid" amounting to the fabulous figure of more than three billion dollars. It is not by chance that the Tito clique received these billions of dollars just before or after services rendered to imperialism at certain crucial moments of international developments in recent years. Yugoslavia was paid hundreds of millions of dollars by the imperialists for its active participation in the preparation and leadership of the counterrevolutionary coup in Hungary in 1956, and for its attacks against the Soviet system. It received 300 million dollars when it came out with its revisionist program in counteraction to the Declaration of the Communist and workers parties of 1957. Yugoslavia received about 95 million dollars at the end of December 1958 as a reward for Tito's visit to certain Asian and African countries, the aim of which was to alienate them from their friendship with the USSR and the other socialist countries and thus to weaken and disrupt the national liberation struggle of the colonial peoples and to assault and isolate the Communist parties in those areas of the world. During the summer of 1960 Yugoslavia had visits from a succession of proven representatives of imperialism: the well-known warmonger Winston Churchill, U.S. Under Secretary of State Dillon, the director of the International Monetary

Fund, Jacobson, the former chief of the British Labor Party, Gaitskell, with whom Tito had several "cordial talks" in secret. It is significant that all these visits were made after Tito's pro-U.S. stand on the question of why the Paris summit meeting failed and before the beginning of the ferocious revisionist attacks by Kardelj and the Yugoslav press against the CPR attacks which were aimed at dividing the socialist camp and the international Communist movement. As a result, at the end of December 1960 it was announced officially that the imperialist countries, primarily the United States, had granted another 275 million dollars to Yugoslavia. Some may see in this "a mere coincidence," but it is not a matter of one or two cases.

It was in vain that Tito tried in his speech of December 26, 1960, before the Yugoslav People's Assembly, to refute what is stated in the Declaration of the Communist and workers parties on the Yugoslav revisionists. He said that the Communist parties had been unable to produce any facts proving that the Yugoslav leadership was revisionist and that they could not quote any statements rejecting Marxism-Leninism. What concrete arguments! As a popular saying goes, the snake never shows its feet. Circumstances compel the revisionists to masquerade as Marxists, to conceal their opportunist rot behind "Marxist" phraseology. It is the characteristic feature of revisionism, old and new. However, as Tito himself admitted, the views of the Yugoslav League of Communists completely contradict the entire contents of the Communist and workers parties' Declarations of 1957 and 1960, which vividly express the creative development of Marxism-Leninism under the new historical conditions of our time.

Communists must not be deceived by the maneuvers of Tito for a fictitious "rapprochement" with the socialist countries on the pretext that, allegedly, on certain basic foreign policy questions — that is, disarmament, the liquidation of colonialism, etc. — the Yugoslav position is identical with that of the socialist countries. This demagogical maneuver aims at deceiving the peoples, at ensuring the cessation of the ideological and political struggle against the Belgrade renegades and, if possible, at securing a loan from the East as well. But the crux lies elsewhere: under cover of this maneuver he carries on his work to divide and undermine the socialist camp and the international Communist movement. His special attacks on China and Albania are aimed at the same goal. All must unmask these maneuvers without mercy. There can be no illusions about the "good" intentions of Tito and his associates.

Tito once again repeated the old arguments: that the condemnation of Yugoslav revisionism in the Declaration is slander, interference in the internal affairs of Yugoslavia, an attack on the Yugoslav people, and other nonsense. The Communist and workers parties never have failed and never will fail to distinguish between the Yugoslav people and Tito's traitorous revisionist gang. This is already common knowledge.

The Declaration of the Communist and workers parties stresses that the further unmasking of the Yugoslav revisionist leaders and the active struggle to preserve the Communist movements from the Yugoslav anti-Leninist and revisionist ideas remain imperative tasks of the Communist-Leninist parties. In accordance with the Moscow Declaration of 1960, the Albanian Party of Labor believes that it is necessary to fight modern revisionism, centered in Yugoslav revisionism, without mercy until its total defeat, since without unmasking revisionism it is impossible to unmask imperialism completely. It is necessary to unmask carefully and mercilessly the maneuvers of the Yugoslav revisionists, who under the pretext of fighting "dogmatism" attack Marxism-Leninism and under the pretext of fighting "leftist" deviationism deny the revolution; under the pretext of fighting against "sectarianism" and for a "flexible" policy, they preach unprincipled reconciliation with the middle class and capitulate before imperialism. In the struggle against revisionism, especially against the Tito revisionist clique, our Party of Labor is guided by the immortal teachings of the great Lenin, who forcefully pointed out that **"any inconsistency or letup in unmasking those who act as reformists or 'centrists' means a direct increase in the danger of the overthrow of proletarian rule by the middle class, who tomorrow will utilize for the counterrevolution what today may appear to the shortsighted as merely a 'theoretical divergence'"** (*Complete Works,* Vol. XXXI, p. 66, Russian edition). Lenin's words of genius have been completely confirmed by the international events of these last few years. Our party regards them as a beacon guiding all its activity, its principled struggle against the revisionists. It is not a question of "stronger or weaker measures" in the struggle against revisionism nor a question of the particular work done by one or another party; "to preserve the purity of Marxism-Leninism," Comrade Enver Hoxha says, "is the main task of every party, of every Communist. The struggle against modern revisionism is the task of every Communist, wherever he may be, in every country of the world" (*Zëri i Popullit,* June 12, 1958). As for the Albanian Party of Labor, it regards the principled struggle without quarter and without compromise against revisionism, in particular against the traitorous revisionist clique of Tito, as an indispensable condition for the defense of the national interests of our country, for safeguarding the purity of Marxism-Leninism, for the uninterrupted strengthening of the unity of the socialist camp and the international Communist movement, for the struggle against imperialism, and for the preservation of world peace. It regards it as its lofty internationalist task, which the Moscow Declaration of 1960 has prescribed for the entire international Communist movement. The Albanian Party of Labor is determined to pursue the struggle of principle against modern revisionism with firmness and consistency to the end, without any compromise.

DOCUMENT 6

Hoxha report to the Fourth Congress of the PPSh (excerpts), Zëri i Popullit, *February 14, 1961, and* Kongresi IV i Partisë së Punës së Shqipërisë *(Tirana: N. Sh. Botimeve "Naim Frashëri," 1961), pp. 11–167* (excerpts).*

I. THE INTERNATIONAL SITUATION AND THE FOREIGN POLICY OF THE PEOPLE'S REPUBLIC OF ALBANIA

1. The consolidation of the world socialist system and the further decline of the world capitalist system . . .

Our Party of Labor has always regarded as its foremost duty and promoted with all its strength the preservation and the constant consolidation of the unity of the great socialist family on the basis of the Leninist principles of equality, noninterference, mutual respect, close cooperation, and fraternal, mutual assistance. In the most difficult moments when international reaction, headed by U.S. imperialism and utilizing all its agents, especially the Yugoslav revisionists, was attacking the Soviet Union and the unity of the socialist camp, our party and government have raised ever higher the banner of unity. They were, are, and always will be prepared to face any obstacles and fulfill to the end their international duty, just as the other fraternal countries will fulfill their duties toward our country if the need should arise. (*Stormy applause, ovations*) One for all and all for one. The banner of our unity is the banner of our victories, of the victory of peace and socialism in the world.

The Albanian people are rightly pleased that the People's Republic of Albania, guided by our Party of Labor, has also made and continues to make its modest

* Revised and edited from the official Albanian translation: Enver Hoxha, *Report on the Activity of the Central Committee of the Party of Labor of Albania* (Tirana: 1961). [Ed.]

contribution to this precipitous rise in the international authority of the world socialist system, to the ever-growing superiority of the forces of socialism over the forces of capitalism, and to the historic struggle for the victory of Communism.

But, while the world socialist system is precipitously advancing, developing, and flourishing and is daily demonstrating an ever-increasing and indisputable superiority, the world capitalist system is decaying and disintegrating and is daily demonstrating its reactionary and antisocial character, its inability to solve the social problems of its time. The death knell of capitalism is now tolling.

The collapse of the system of colonial enslavement under the impact of the national liberation movement is the heaviest blow to imperialism since the formation of the world socialist system. Approximately 1,250 million people have been liberated from the imperialist colonial system. A large number of newly independent states have emerged in Asia, Africa, and Latin America. The great impetus of the national liberation movement and its historic victories, aiming at the complete destruction of colonialism, have dealt a fatal blow to the rear-guard of imperialism. The disintegration of the imperialist colonial system is the direct result of the might of the peoples' struggle for national liberation, under the favorable international conditions created by the weakening of imperialism and by the strengthening of socialism. The facts refute the imperialist and opportunist claim that the colonial and semicolonial countries gained their political freedom through imperialist assistance and not through struggle and revolution. The liberation of the peoples from colonial enslavement has been achieved in different ways, but regardless of the manner, the basis of their liberation has been and remains the mass struggle of the peoples in its various forms. During recent years the national liberation struggle of the oppressed peoples under colonialism has been transformed into a revolutionary hurricane on a world-wide scale, which is rapidly bringing about the disintegration of the hated colonial system and bringing it nearer to its doom. It has become one of the most important phenomena of our epoch and the greatest victory over imperialism since the formation of the socialist camp. . . .

Our party and people, who have themselves experienced colonial exploitation and oppression, have supported and will always support without reservation the armed struggle for national liberation of the oppressed peoples. We consider this our internationalist duty. We express our solidarity with the brave and fraternal Algerian people, who for so many years on end have been fighting with exemplary heroism, and we are convinced that the day is not far off when we shall salute the Algerian Republic as a free, independent, and sovereign state, with which our people's state will be happy to maintain close friendly relations and cooperation. (*Applause*) We express our full sympathy with the courageous struggle being waged by the peoples of the Congo and Laos against the imperialist aggressors and their lackeys, and we demand an end to the criminal and dangerous imperialist intervention in these countries.

We think that the diabolical intrigues and plots of the colonialists to recapture their lost positions in the former colonies constitute a grave threat to these peoples and to peace in general. American imperialism in particular is openly emerging as the gendarme of international reaction, with the intention of suppressing the national liberation struggle, prolonging the life of the colonial system, and seizing the former colonies for itself. The peoples of Africa, Asia, and Latin America, who have gained much experience from their arduous struggle against imperialism and its lackeys, will no doubt know how to resist the American neocolonialists; they will no doubt be able to recognize and expose the true nature of those who, under the pay of American imperialism and the mask of friendship, conceal an axe under their cloak and deem it a duty to hamper and obstruct their just struggle for liberty and for the consolidation of their national independence, to sow the seed of discord among them, to isolate them from their natural internationalist supporters, from the countries of the socialist camp, and in effect to abandon them once again to the mercy of the imperialist jackals. We can see what is going on in the Congo and in Laos; we are witnessing the continuous American aggression against revolutionary Cuba, and we see that it is not accidental that the attacks of American imperialism tie in with the intrigues and attacks of the Yugoslav revisionists against the heroic people of Cuba and its revolutionary leadership. If the ugly plots and aggression of American imperialism against Cuba have failed and will fail in the future as well, this is due to the steadfastness of the Cuban people (*stormy applause, ovations*), to the solidarity of the countries of the socialist camp, and to the peoples of Latin America and the other peace-loving peoples. There is no doubt that the further expansion of the coordinated struggle of the peoples fighting for liberation and those who are already liberated, of the countries of the socialist camp and the other independent countries which are against colonialism, and of the Communist and workers parties in the imperialist and colonial countries as well as in other countries, the further strengthening of the front of the anticolonial forces in the world and the unmasking of American neocolonialism and the true nature of American imperialism will hasten the total annihilation of colonialism. Thus a new era will dawn for all those who have suffered so greatly under oppression, and the cause of peace in the world will be strengthened.

It is clear, comrades, that all these magnificent victories of the world socialist system and the national liberation movement of dependent and colonial peoples have decisively weakened the dominating position, the influence, and the prestige of the capitalist system and have at the same time sharpened on an unprecedented scale its all-round contradictions and general crisis.

The creation of the world socialist system and the disintegration of the imperialist colonial system have greatly narrowed the sphere of imperialist domination and, consequently, the sphere in which its laws are operative. This has sharpened all the contradictions which are gnawing at the capitalist system from within, both class and national, internal and external. The attempts to save capitalism from its irreconcilable contradictions, to preserve its decadent foundations through the militarization of the economy and the arms race are carrying the capitalist order toward its inevitable doom and further tightening the knot of its contradictions. The economy of the capitalist countries has entered a blind alley from which it cannot escape, and it is becoming more and more unstable. Not only have the periodic economic crises not disappeared, as the bourgeois ideologists and their revisionist colleagues maintain, but they are becoming more frequent and today seriously threaten many capitalist countries. The decay of capitalism is clearly evident in the most powerful capitalist country, the United States of America, where widespread unemployment has become chronic, production growth rates are declining, the arms race has assumed unprecedented proportions, the fascist and racist tendencies in everyday life are becoming more and more evident, and the military circles are increasingly determining the policy of the government.

All this clearly shows that the international situation is developing in favor of socialism and to the disadvantage of capitalism, that socialism is becoming stronger every day while capitalism is becoming weaker, that the socialist camp is much stronger than the imperialist camp. This is the principal characteristic of our times. The Moscow Declarations of 1957 and 1960 state that the main content of our time is the transition from capitalism to socialism, that our age is the age of the struggle between two opposing social systems, of the socialist and national liberation revolutions, of the breakdown of imperialism, of the liquidation of the colonial system, and of the triumph of socialism and Communism.

Our Party of Labor has always had and continues to have a correct Marxist-Leninist grasp of this question. But does this mean that the hands of the imperialists are already tied because the forces of socialism surpass those of capitalism? That we are now in a position to impose our will on them, whereas they are in a position to do nothing? That we are now in a position to guarantee peace, while they are not in a position to unleash war?

The Marxist-Leninist dialectical method and the materialist conception of history give us the correct answer: Both the overestimation of our forces and the underestimation of the enemy forces on the one hand, and the underestimation of our forces and overestimation of the enemy forces on the other, lead to grave errors. The first weakens vigilance and leads to adventurism, while the second leads to opportunist errors and attitudes. Therefore, our party has always stressed that the balance of power in the world has changed in favor of socialism, that the forces of socialism are stronger than those of imperialism, that the forces of peace are stronger than the forces of war; but at the same time it has not underestimated the forces of imperialism. The correct line of our party on this matter has found accurate expression in its attitude toward the problems of war and peace, toward imperialism, and so forth. Our party has always maintained that it is possible to prevent world war, that today world war is not fatalistically inevitable, but at the same time it has maintained that the danger of war exists, for as long as imperialism exists so too will the basis for aggressive war. On the one hand, we are concentrating all our efforts on strengthening the socialist camp, on preserving and tempering its unity, and on increasing its defensive power; on the other hand, while consistently following the Leninist policy of peaceful coexistence between states with different social systems, we have at the same time always unmasked imperialism and in particular American imperialism, its war preparations, and its aggressive nature. Hence our slogan: "Let us hold a pick-axe in one hand and a rifle in the other." (*Stormy applause, ovations*)

To view this problem differently means openly to contradict the Moscow Declarations of 1957 and 1960 and to pass over to the rightist positions of revisionism and opportunism.

We sincerely love peace, and we are striving to guarantee it, while the imperialists are doing everything in their power to prepare for a third world war. What do the facts show? Let us recall the American imperialist aggression against heroic Korea in 1950, the Anglo-French-Israeli aggression against Egypt in 1956, the Anglo-American armed intervention in Lebanon and Jordan in 1958. Let us look at the war of extermination waged by French imperialism and the NATO bloc against the heroic Algerian people and the brutal intervention of the American-Belgian imperialists in the Congo and of the United States of America in Laos. These are not minor and isolated events. If the imperialists unleash such aggressive local wars and derive calculated profits from them, then it is possible for them to launch a world war. The American imperialists, not unintentionally, obstruct the unification of Korea and Vietnam in the Far East. The southern parts of these countries have been converted by them into bridgeheads for aggression, into bases for launching a new war against the People's Democratic Republic of Korea and the Democratic Republic of Vietnam, against the People's Republic of China and against the Soviet Union.

The Albanian people, as well as the overwhelming majority of the peoples of Europe, still retain vivid memories of the innumerable crimes committed by the Hitlerite Nazis during the Second World War. But whereas the peoples rightly expected that this monster would never again raise its head, we see that West Germany, with the direct aid and encouragement of the American, British, and French imperialists, has once again been armed to the teeth. There German revanchist militarism has been revived. The same monopolist groups which brought Hitler to power, which built and equipped his aggressive war machine, are now in power; the same Hitlerite generals who, with torch in hand, set Europe ablaze and stained their hands with the blood of tens of millions of victims are now in command. Not only this but, in addition to the Bundeswehr troops, one finds concentrated in West Germany today large special forces equipped with the most modern arms of the aggressive NATO bloc and under the command of the Nazi criminals Speidel and Heusinger. In violation of the Potsdam agreements, Adenauer's Bundeswehr, which is as similar to the Hitlerite Wehrmacht as two drops of water, is being liberally equipped with atomic weapons and rockets by the American imperialists, and the most modern armaments are now being serially produced by West Germany itself.

Comrades, in France three successive generations have profusely shed their blood to defend their country from the attacks of the German imperialists. There is no village and no crossroad in France without a memorial with the names of the Frenchmen who have fallen for their fatherland in war against the German aggressors. Yet what do we see today? The German imperialists, during a time of peace and without firing a single shot, are comfortably establishing themselves on French territory, liberally bathed with the blood of the immortal Communards, of Gabriel Peri, and of millions of French patriots. And not only in France but in Italy, Greece, Spain, and other countries.

The military expansion of German militarism is taking place in capitalist Europe with the complicity of the ruling circles of these countries and with the approval of American imperialism. Not to see the purpose for which these bases are created, to close one's eyes and remain silent in the face of these developments, which are an integral part of the imperialists' plans for unleashing a world war, not only means to forget the lessons of history and to misunderstand the course of events, but it means to commit a crime against the peoples and the cause of peace.

The American imperialists have found their staunchest allies in the German militarists and revanchists. During recent years, despite numerous warnings from the Soviet Union and other peace-loving countries, the American imperialists have unscrupulously continued the rapid militarization of West Germany; and the threat to the peace and security of the peoples has increased. The Germany of Bonn has been converted into a dangerous base of aggression and West Berlin into a permanent den of provocation against the German Democratic Republic and the other socialist countries.

Here it is fifteen years after the end of the Second World War and German militarism is endangering peace in Europe and the world while the peace treaty with Germany has not yet been signed. Why do the United States of America and its partners systematically oppose the proposals repeated so often by the Soviet Union and the German Democratic Republic for the solution of the German problem? Why are they interested in prolonging as long as possible and even preventing the conclusion of the peace treaty with Germany? Is it not clear that they do this in order to have a free hand in their hostile activity against the socialist countries, to gain time to quietly prepare and unleash a war against us when they deem it fit to do so, when they are ready?

Our party has always firmly unmasked the revival of German revanchist militarism and has drawn the attention of our people to this real danger. We have supported all the proposals of the Soviet Union and the Democratic Republic of Germany for the peaceful solution of the German problem. We believe that in order to strengthen the security of the German Democratic Republic, of our camp, and of peace in general, it is high time to sign the peace treaty with Germany, with both existing German states. Should West Germany and its allies oppose this, our socialist countries, as well as other interested countries, will sign a separate peace treaty with the German Democatic Republic. In this way the plans of imperialism, with its tactics of prolongation and delay, will be disrupted, the problem of West Berlin will be solved as well, and a great step forward will be made on the road to peace and international security. The sooner this step is taken, the better it will be for the preservation of peace and for the democratic development of Germany.

In the aggressive plans of American imperialism in the Far East, Japan plays the role which West Germany plays in Europe. The Japanese-American security pact, which was imposed on Japan by the United States of America last year, marks an important step toward the rapid conversion of Japan into an aggressive imperialist bridgehead in Asia.

If the American imperialists are for peace, as they demagogically declare, then why do they reject the proposals of the Soviet Union and the other signatories of the Warsaw Pact for the conclusion of a nonaggression treaty between the members of the Warsaw Pact and the members of NATO and for the mutual renunciation of their opposing military pacts as well as the proposal of the Chinese People's Republic for a nonaggression treaty in the Pacific Ocean area with the participation of the United States of America; why, on the contrary, do they unceasingly strengthen the aggressive treaties of NATO, CENTO, and SEATO, transforming them into brutal instruments of their aggressive plans? Why do they maintain, expand, and continuously equip with nuclear weapons and rockets approximately 300 military bases built on foreign territory encircling our socialist countries? As is known, they are directed against the Soviet Union, the Chinese People's Republic, and the other peoples' democracies in Europe and Asia. The American imperialists do not conceal this. The American bases on foreign territories openly violate the sovereignty of the countries where they are located and are a means of pressure and continuous intervention in their internal affairs. In the event of imperialist aggression, they may invite fatal attacks upon the countries which have accepted them.

Let us mention another fact: the summit conference. The peoples had hoped that this meeting of the heads of the great powers would contribute to the relaxation of international tension, the removal of the war threat, and the solution of the German and disarmament problems. As is known, the American Government, by the aggressive, unparalleled, and premeditated act of sending the U-2 spy plane over the territory of the Soviet Union on the eve of the summit conference, torpedoed it. The U-2 incident is not an isolated aggressive act, committed only in this particular instance, but must be evaluated and dealt with as an expression of the entire policy of violation of sovereignty, brutal intervention in the internal affairs of other countries, and aggression on the part of American imperialism.

Our party and government are and always have been in favor of summit talks. They have their advantages, and they can make an effective contribution to the cause of peace and international cooperation. But for talks between the heads of governments and states to be effective, they must be accompanied by responsible mass action on the part of the peoples because, in the final analysis, it is the people who decide. (*Applause*)

Moreover, experience daily confirms that no international problem can be solved without the participation of a world power such as the Chinese People's Republic. The participation of the Chinese People's Republic in summit talks is also in the interest of peace and of the ultimate solution of the basic problems disturbing mankind. The participation of the Chinese People's Republic in such talks makes imperative the solution of the problem of restoring its legitimate rights in the United Nations Organization. (*Stormy applause*)

We all know that, in the context of its aggressive policy toward the whole socialist camp, American imperialism has relentlessly continued its markedly hostile activities toward the Chinese People's Republic. The loss of China was a mortal blow to imperialism. The United States of America has forcibly occupied Taiwan and other Chinese islands, thereby committing perpetual aggression against the great People's China; it continues its economic blockade, armed provocations, frenzied campaigns, and intolerable pressure; it organized the counterrevolutionary movement in Tibet; it obstructs the restoration of the legitimate rights of the Chinese People's Republic in the United Nations, where the seat of the great Chinese people is still held by the puppet Chiang Kai-shek.

It is clear that for the solution of outstanding problems through negotiations and for a summit meeting for this purpose, one of the major premises is that the United States of America be compelled to end this aggressive, shortsighted, and dangerous policy toward the Chinese People's Republic and that the Chinese People's Republic be allowed to take its proper seat in the United Nations Organization. Our party and government will always firmly support the legitimate rights and the consistently peaceful policy of our dear friend, the Chinese People's Republic. (*Stormy applause*) We are unshakably convinced that its participation in the United Nations Organization and in the summit talks will have great and beneficial impact on the cause of peace and international security. This must be considered as a battle which the forces of peace must win over the forces of war, as a battle to strengthen peace.

When the United Nations Organization was created, for the fundamental purpose of protecting the peoples from the horrors of a new war, the peoples pinned great hopes on it. And the truth is that if this organization had expressed the will of the peoples and had not been converted into an instrument of the foreign policy of the United States of America on many critical occasions, it could have played a large role in the service of peace and international security. It is worthwhile and gratifying to note that — thanks to the persistent struggle of the participating socialist countries as well as to the recent increase in the number of newly liberated countries, which contribute their valuable experience gained in the struggle for freedom and peace against colonialism and imperialism — the United Nations Organization is daily becoming an important platform for the defense of the rights of peoples and world peace. This was demonstrated by the last session of the General Assembly.

The People's Republic of Albania actively participates in its proceedings and, together with the other socialist and peace-loving countries, makes its contribution. But at the same time it must be emphasized that the absence of the Chinese People's Republic is an organic shortcoming of the United Nations Organization which greatly diminishes its capacity and authority. Moreover, the American imperialists still exercise great influence through the executive machinery of the Secretariat, which is wholly in their hands, as well as through the different branches of the Organization owing to the voting procedure. This negative influence often impedes effective decisions in favor of the freedom of peoples, as in the case of the Congo and Algeria, or in favor of peace and international security.

Let us look at the disarmament problem. Since 1946 and throughout the past 15 years, the Soviet Union, first and foremost, has submitted countless proposals relating to this vital issue, ranging from the solution of partial problems right up to general and complete disarmament. The People's Republic of Albania always has supported and will resolutely support these very important proposals. For many years in succession the General Assembly has conducted endless discussions on this problem; it has even passed a series of unanimous resolutions in favor of disarmament; but what has been substantively accomplished? Has a single concrete effective measure been taken? Has any tangible result been achieved? None. On the contrary, the arms race has been developing with the greatest intensity. The United States of America and its partners have relentlessly pursued a policy of tension and provocation, whereas, as is known, the Soviet Union, the Chinese People's Republic, and the other socialist countries have not confined themselves to advancing concrete proposals but have taken unilateral measures to ease the path to a solution of this key issue of our time.

It cannot be denied that the discussions within the United Nations Organization as well as outside it, in various conferences and organizations, have helped to make known the just and peaceful policy of the Soviet Union and the other socialist countries and, at the same time, to unmask the negative attitude of the Western powers. But it must also be pointed out that imperialist and revisionist propaganda has sought to utilize these prolonged and endless discussions in order to create illusions and vain hopes among the peoples, while the imperialist powers themselves have continually tried to extend such futile discussions as long as possible so that behind this empty talk they could promote as much as possible the arms race and prepare for aggression.

How then can peace be preserved and world war avoided? It is clear that imperialism does not voluntarily renounce war; it does not cast away its arms of its own free will. To believe in such a possibility is to deceive oneself. Therefore, we must make it impossible for the imperialists to unleash war, and this can be achieved by confronting them with the economic, military, moral, and political might of the socialist camp, the might of the international working class, of the national liberation movement, and of all countries which are opposed to war and all the forces in favor of peace. This is the way, and the only way, if we start from the positions of Marxism-Leninism. (*Applause*)

Peace cannot be ensured by making concessions to the imperialists or by flattering them. All the endeavors of the socialist countries in the field of international relations, the policy of peaceful coexistence with capitalist countries consistently followed by the great Soviet Union and the other socialist countries, and the permissible tactics and compromises on our side should help strengthen us and weaken the enemy in order to compel him to abandon the arms race, the production and testing of atomic weapons, the creation of military bases, and preparations for a third world war.

Imperialism, headed by the United States of America, confronts us as a serious threat to peace. It is aggressive and vicious despite the fact that it is no longer master of the world, as in the past. Imperialism has changed neither its skin nor its nature; it has not become lamblike. A wolf can never become a lamb, according to a popular saying. Likewise, warlike imperialism does not become peace-loving. As stressed in the Declaration of the conference of the 81 party representatives: "War is the permanent fellow-traveler of capitalism"; "Imperialism is a serious threat to all mankind"; "As long as imperialism exists, the basis for aggressive wars will also exist"; and "The main force of aggression and war is American imperialism." And this is so; this is what Marxism-Leninism teaches us.

Therefore, in the face of this savage enemy of all humanity, which is trying to plunge the world into another world war that would result in incalculable misery and ruin from the use of existing nuclear weapons, the socialist camp must be militarily as well as politically and morally prepared to deal with any kind of imperialist adventure. The popular masses throughout the world must rise to stay the hand of the imperialists, to unmask the intrigues of the imperialists and their lackeys — the revisionists — who are trying to sow discord among the peoples, to deceive them, and to catch them unprepared, by surprise. (*Fervent applause*) The peoples must strengthen their vigilance. This is the way, and the only way, to halt the imperialists and to make them incapable of unleashing war. The enemy cannot be trusted, and this is the case with imperialism — especially American imperialism.

The existence and the struggle of two opposing world systems determine the existence of two opposing lines in international politics; on the one hand, there is the peaceful and consistent policy of the glorious Soviet Union, People's China, and the other socialist countries, which daily finds ardent and ever-increasing support among the peoples of the whole world, and, on the other hand, there is the aggressive warmongering policy of the imperialist powers, chiefly the United States of America, which is endangering world peace. These two opposing lines in international politics have been clearly evident even in recent years.

To those who doubt our sincerity in the struggle for peace, who allege that socialism needs a world war in order to conquer everywhere, we reply that we repudiate this bourgeois propaganda charge of the so-called "export" of socialist revolution just as we resolutely oppose the imperialist export of counterrevolution. To those who think that socialist countries stand for peace because they are weak and fear for the fate of their system, we reply that there is no doubt whatsoever that should the mad imperialists, disregarding all consequences, unleash a third world war, it would result in the utter destruction of imperialism, in the liquidation of capitalism as a social system. (*Fervent applause*)

The struggle for peaceful coexistence between states with different social systems constitutes one of the fundamental aspects of the peaceful foreign policy of the socialist camp together with the consolidation of fraternal cooperation and mutual assistance among the socialist countries and the backing and support of the revolutionary anticolonialist and anti-imperialist struggle of the enslaved peoples.

The principle of peaceful coexistence, formulated by the great Lenin, is defined in the Moscow Declaration of November 1960 as the only correct and reasonable principle in relations between states with different social systems under conditions of the division of the world into two opposing systems.

The struggle to achieve peaceful coexistence is carried out through the struggle of the countries of the socialist camp and other peace-loving countries to settle the concrete problems of present-day international life through negotiations, the struggle of the peoples for national liberation, and the struggle for peace. The peoples must impose this on the imperialists, who will not voluntarily renounce the "cold war," military blocs, and the arms race, just as they will not renounce intervention in the internal affairs of other countries, violation of the independence and sovereignty of peoples, and so forth.

Fighting resolutely and consistently for peaceful coexistence, the Soviet Union, the Chinese People's Republic, and the other socialist countries have taken the initiative on numerous occasions to settle outstanding problems. The government of the Soviet Union as well as the governments of the other socialist countries have continuously made attempts to solve peacefully all the problems disturbing mankind. All these initiatives have had wide repercussions on world public opinion and enjoy the support of all peace-loving peoples because they offer the prospect of establishing lasting world peace. In their efforts to preserve peace the Soviet Union and the other socialist countries, members of the Warsaw Pact, have not only made proposals but they have taken concrete steps as well. But until now none of these efforts has borne the expected results because the peaceful policy of the socialist countries, supported by the other peace-loving countries as well, is confronted with the aggressive policy which the imperialist powers, chiefly the United States of America, are stubbornly pursuing in preparation for a third world war. The new President of the United States, Mr. John Kennedy, has announced that this is going to be his policy too. In his message to Congress he declared that he will pursue the same course of action as that of his predecessor — the Eisenhower course of the "cold war," the arms race, pressures, and blackmail. Following in Eisenhower's footsteps and expressing the feelings of the American monopolies and reactionaries, Kennedy declared in his message that he will pursue the policy of armaments, the reinforcement of the submarine fleet with "Polaris" missiles, the increase in rocket production, the strengthening of the air force for the purpose of arms and troop transportation, and so forth. The immediate rise in the value of war industry stocks in the United States the day after Kennedy's speech clearly shows in whose interest it was made. In addition, President Kennedy clearly defined his position toward the national liberation movement, toward Cuba, Laos, etc. He openly took under his protection the aggressors and oppressors of peoples. He did not even forget to "promise" the peoples living in the peoples' democracies their "liberation" from Communism (*laughter*), for which the new president will work in the future. It is clear that by "liberation" Mr. Kennedy means the restoration of capitalism, oppression, and exploitation, which our people shed their blood to liquidate. In his message Kennedy did not neglect to attack the policy of the Soviet Union and that of the Chinese People's Republic as well. But at the same time, in order to deceive naïve people, he also waved the olive branch (*hilarity*) and even spoke of peace and coexistence. Undoubtedly we are dealing here with a bluff "à la Kennedy" (*hilarity*), for if he were sincere in what he was saying, not only would he not have dreamed of the "liberation" of the peoples of Eastern Europe from Communism but he would have declared himself in favor of establishing diplomatic relations with the six socialist states of Asia and Europe with which the United States of America, with only itself to blame because of its "cold war" policy, still has no relations.

It is clear that the policy of the imperialist states continues, as in the past, to be a policy responsive to monopoly interests. Therefore, the peoples' vigilance should be increased and strengthened more and more each day. At the same time our socialist countries will consistently pursue their peaceful policy in order to undermine the imperialist plans for a new war. And forces do exist to prevent its outbreak. These forces are the peoples and their resolute struggle; as Stalin said, if the peoples take into their own hands the cause of the preservation of peace and defend it to the end, peace will be guaranteed and consolidated. (*Stormy applause, ovations*)

In this tense and complex international situation, in this struggle to keep the peace which has embraced all the peoples and peace-loving forces in the world, our party, successfully implementing its correct Marxist-Leninist line and the concrete tasks set by the Third Party Congress, has taken an active part; it has made a valuable contribution to the preservation and further consolidation of the unity of the socialist camp, to the unmasking and thwarting of the aggressive plans and policy of American imperialism and of all the enemies of peace and socialism, to the elimination of the menace of war, and to the preservation of peace in general. The Albanian Party of Labor will continue consistently to follow this path in the future as well. (*Stormy applause, ovations*)

2. The foreign policy of the People's Republic of Albania

In foreign policy, the government and the Central Committee of the party have resolutely and successfully carried out the tasks laid down by the Third Party Congress. The international position of the

People's Republic of Albania has been further consolidated. Our country is constantly expanding its relations with other countries and plays an active role on the international scene in favor of peace and cooperation among peoples, against the war policy of imperialism and its lackeys. The results achieved on the international scene by the People's Republic of Albania are a clear-cut confirmation of the correct Marxist-Leninist line pursued by our party in the field of foreign policy.

The People's Republic of Albania has become a factor for peace and progress in the Balkan and Adriatic area, a living reflection of the superiority of the socialist over the capitalist system, a real obstacle to the aggressive plans of American imperialism in this part of the world. The enemies of our party and people, the imperialists and revisionists, hate the sight of us. They abhor our strategic position and the great wealth of our fatherland. They are infuriated when they see in their rear a small country and heroic people fighting dauntlessly and persistently to defend its freedom and independence and building socialism successfully. (*Stormy applause, ovations*) They are infuriated by the magnificent achievements of our people, gained under the guidance of our party and government in all fields, by the fiery patriotism, by the high political awareness, by the preparedness and revolutionary vigilance of our people, and by the indomitable Marxist-Leninist line of our party, which never has and never will hesitate to defend Marxism-Leninism, to defend the cause of the people and socialism regardless of any sacrifice, and to face and overcome successfully all storms, even the fiercest and most violent. (*Stormy applause, ovations*)

Albania is the only country building socialism under conditions of hostile capitalist encirclement. Its development as a sovereign state, continuously repelling the relentless attacks of its enemies, testifies to the ability of our party and government, which are creatively applying Marxism-Leninism to the conditions of our country and pursuing a correct, peaceful, and vigilant policy, testifies to the strength and solidarity of the socialist camp, headed by the Soviet Union. (*Stormy applause, ovations*)

Albania, despite capitalist geographical encirclement, is not an isolated country of the socialist camp. She is a worthy member of this camp; she is a member of the Warsaw Pact; she has powerful and faithful friends — the countries of the socialist camp, headed by the Soviet Union — and she has as allies all the peace-loving peoples in the world and the mighty working class of the whole world. These factors form the basis of the might of our socialist fatherland, which is flourishing on the Adriatic shore. (*Applause*)

Friendship with the Soviet Union has been, is, and will always remain the cornerstone of the foreign policy of the new Albania. (*Stormy applause, ovations*) This friendship has been forged by our heroic party in the fire of the struggle for freedom and national independence, for socialism and peace; it has been sealed with the blood of our fearless partisans and the Red warriors of the glorious Soviet Army, which, by its historic victories over fascism in the Second World War, created the conditions for and contributed to the liberation of our fatherland from the fascist monster. Friendship with the Soviet Union will live through the ages like the majestic mountains of our fatherland, and there is no power on earth which can touch it (*stormy applause, ovations*); it is indestructible because it is based on the principles of Marxism-Leninism and proletarian internationalism. This friendship is expressed and tempered every day by the fraternal relations and general collaboration between our two countries, by the great internationalist aid given to our country by the Soviet Union for the construction of socialism, and by our common struggle for the cause of the peoples' liberation, peace, and socialism. The Albanian people, guided by the party, will temper and will safeguard forever as its most precious possession its love and gratitude for the great Soviet Union and its glorious Communist Party, the party of the immortal Lenin, whose teachings illuminate each step of our party and people on the path to socialism and Communism. (*Fervent applause*) The Albanian people will be eternally grateful to the fraternal Soviet people for their internationalist aid and assure them that just as the Albanian people have in the Soviet people a dear and cherished friend, so the Soviet people have in the Albanian people a faithful and resolute friend. (*Stormy applause, ovations*)

Friendship and fraternal cooperation with the Chinese People's Republic have been further consolidated on the basis of Marxism-Leninism, the common struggle for socialism and peace, and mutual fraternal aid and support. (*Applause*) Thousands of kilometers separate Albania from China geographically, but such is the power of Marxism-Leninism that we feel very near to us the friendship and exemplary solidarity of the great Chinese people of 650 million and its tested leadership, the glorious Communist Party of China, which is successfully building socialism under the victorious banner of Marxism-Leninism. (*Stormy applause, ovations*) Our party and people feel honored to have such a precious friend as the great and talented Chinese people. The Chinese People's Republic is a mighty bulwark and the pride of our socialist camp, a sure source of support for the cause of national liberation, peace, and social progress in Asia and in the world. (*Applause*)

With all the other socialist countries — Poland, Czechoslovakia, the German Democratic Republic, Hungary, Romania, Bulgaria, Korea, Mongolia, and Vietnam — our people are linked by indestructible friendship. They have consolidated and will consolidate still further their fraternal relations with them in the interests of socialism and peace. (*Stormy applause, ovations*)

The close collaboration of the socialist countries of Europe within the framework of the Council for Mutual Economic Assistance, as shown in the coordination of state plans, the cooperation and international division of labor, the close ties and mutual fraternal aid, and the continuously expanding cultural relations, have contributed greatly to the consolidation of the indestructible friendship among the countries of the socialist camp. They are a clear expression of the friendship and fraternal solidarity among our countries.

All the socialist countries are united in the mighty socialist camp which, as stressed in the Declaration of the 81 Communist and workers parties, "is a social, economic, and political family of independent and sovereign peoples, united by close ties of international socialist solidarity and by common interests and goals, peoples who are marching on the road to socialism and Communism."

The unity of the socialist camp, based on the immortal principles of Marxism-Leninism, has successfully thwarted and will always thwart all the intrigues and assaults of international reaction, headed by American imperialism and its lackeys. The Warsaw Pact is an important factor in behalf of security and peace at a time when the American imperialists and their partners are feverishly preparing to kindle the fire of a new world conflagration. The Albanian Party of Labor and our government have always considered that their main duty is to safeguard and continuously consolidate the unity and cohesiveness of the socialist camp, to further strengthen the Warsaw Pact.

The new Albania increasingly attracts the attention of the outside world. She is loved and respected by the international proletariat and peace-loving peoples for her heroic struggle against fascism, for the loyalty of her people and party to the socialist camp and Marxism-Leninism, for her active support of the national liberation struggles of oppressed peoples, for her consistent peaceful policy, and for her great revolutionary upsurge which has led our country from darkness to light, from poverty to the road to prosperity and happiness, the road to socialism. This gives us renewed strength to march forward along the road to socialism and Communism.

The People's Republic of Albania has always pursued and will pursue a policy of peace and friendship in its relations with other countries, a policy based on the well-known principles of peaceful coexistence between countries with different social systems. Peace is the fundamental condition upon which we can build a happy life for our people. The People's Republic of Albania will always be a resolute fighter in the battle for peace and will always oppose the aggressive policy of imperialism and all the plots of the enemies of peace.

Our party and government have always paid particular attention to relations with neighboring countries and especially to the situation in the Balkan and Adriatic area. Our policy has always aimed and still aims at the transformation of this area into one of peaceful and fruitful cooperation. The proposal advanced by the government of the Soviet Union and the People's Republic of Albania to transform the Balkans and the Adriatic area into a zone of peace, free of atomic arms and rocket bases, is directed toward this goal. The implementation of this proposal would at the same time be a contribution to the efforts for general and complete disarmament, within the framework of which even the disarmament of the Balkan countries would be acceptable and practicable. We must emphasize that the negative factors in the situation in this area are the Balkan Pact, an appendage of NATO, the installation of American rockets in Italy, Greece, and Turkey, and the frequent visits of the American Sixth Fleet to the ports of those countries and those of Yugoslavia.

The People's Republic of Albania has continued its efforts to develop relations with neighboring countries on the basis of equality, noninterference, mutual respect and benefit. On the initiative of our government, normal relations have been re-established with Yugoslavia. At its Third Congress, our party declared that despite the great damage caused by the hostile policy of the Yugoslav leaders, we were ready to establish correct and neighborly relations. And we have made sincere efforts to establish and develop normal good neighborly relations, trade, cultural, and tourist exchanges, and so forth. But the Yugoslav leaders have never abandoned their hostile policy toward our country and have continued their brutal intervention in our affairs, their attempts to liquidate our party, our people's power, our freedom and national independence. This is clearly demonstrated by the facts, the organization and activation of various groups of agents, the dispatch of whole gangs of saboteurs from Yugoslavia, and the endless provocations along our border. The Yugoslav leaders in their public speeches and press as well as through farcical legal proceedings, which have particularly increased of late, miss no opportunity to slander and attack our party, our government, and our people, but this mud falls on their own faces.

The tragic fate of the Albanian population living in Yugoslavia is familiar to all. Our party will continue to speak out against the persecutions, the deportations to Turkey, and the chauvinist extermination policy pursued in Yugoslavia toward our brothers in Kossovo, Macedonia, Montenegro, and the Dukagjini highlands. Our party considers this its lofty humanitarian duty, deriving from the principles of Marxism-Leninism, and will continue to do so as long as Yugoslavia has not guaranteed the Albanian population of one million inhabitants its full rights as a national minority, on the basis of the principles of international law. In the future, just as in the past, we will be for normal neighborly relations on the basis of peaceful coexistence and reciprocity. To this end, our People's Republic is prepared to continue developing normal relations, but on the condition that the Yugoslav government does not obstruct them and abandons without delay its hostile activities against the People's Republic of Albania.

In regard to our relations with Greece,

they have not changed at all owing to the reactionary and shortsighted policy of the Greek ruling circles, who have blindly submitted to the American imperialists and coordinate their hostile policy toward Albania with that of the ruling circles of Yugoslavia. We have made numerous attempts to normalize our relations with Greece, we have taken unilateral initiatives, we have given the Greek government sufficient opportunities to respond to our readiness and good will by the repatriation of Greek citizens sheltered in Albania, by the clearing of the Corfu Channel, by our proposals for the normalization of the border situation, of trade, and so on. But the Greek rulers have continued their policy of criminal provocations along the border, of insane campaigns on the so-called state of war between our two countries and their absurd claims to southern Albania, of plots against the territorial integrity of our fatherland. Naturally, they have received and will always receive the answer they deserve. While always maintaining a high level of vigilance, we shall also continue in the future our policy of normalizing relations with Greece on the above-mentioned principles, but of course much depends in this respect on the Greek government, which must abandon without delay its hostile activities toward the People's Republic of Albania.

We very much love and respect the fraternal peoples of Yugoslavia and Greece, and we will work relentlessly to strengthen the sincere friendship we feel for our fraternal neighbors. We are convinced that they do not and never will approve the criminal actions of their governments against a peaceful people who seek to live in peace and to maintain good neighborly relations with them. We appeal to the neighboring peoples of Yugoslavia and Greece to constrain their governments and to check them in their activities against our fatherland, because these actions may lead to the disruption of peace in the Balkans. We believe that the governments of Yugoslavia and Greece know full well the Albanian people and its people's power, and realize that if they should raise the sword against our outstretched hand, we would be certain to break that sword. (*Stormy applause, ovations*) In our time the old order in the Balkans has been overthrown just as it has been overthrown in the world. In the Balkans there exist and flourish three socialist states, Bulgaria, Romania, and Albania, which are as united as flesh and blood to one another and to the other countries of the socialist camp headed by the Soviet Union. (*Stormy applause, ovations*)

The vital interests of the peoples of this region strongly demonstrate to the socialist and nonsocialist countries the necessity for coordinating their joint struggle for the preservation of peace and cooperation between states on the basis of nonintervention, equality, and mutual interests. We sincerely favor a policy of good neighborly relations and are convinced that such a policy is in the interest of Albania as much as in the interest of the neighboring countries. But let the rulers of our two neighbors have no illusions that they may take Albania by surprise, that they may isolate Albania or have isolated her, as they fancy, or that they may soon be able to settle accounts with her. The Albanian people have suffered much throughout their history, and they are not easily lulled to sleep. They cannot be deceived by the Greek and Titoist bluffs.

The present Yugoslav state is not a "neutral" or "non-bloc" state, as Belgrade propaganda claims or as the professed or secret friends of the Tito regime try to present it. This "neutrality" and "extra-military bloc" attitude of the Yugoslav state bears no resemblance whatsoever to such neutral states as the United Arab Republic, India, Indonesia, Switzerland, or Austria. Present-day Yugoslavia is a state that participates in the aggressive NATO bloc through the Balkan Pact. The Balkan Pact, which binds together Yugoslavia, Greece, and Turkey, obliges NATO as well as Yugoslavia to come to the aid of one another at any time with all the means at their disposal. The Yugoslav leaders themselves have more than once declared that this treaty was signed because, allegedly, Yugoslavia was in danger of "being attacked" by the countries of the socialist camp. This has always been and will always be an absurd fabrication because the socialist countries have never had and never will have any intention of attacking Yugoslavia or any other country. But the reverse has been and remains true, that is, that the members of the Balkan Pact, closely linked to the NATO powers, are preparing for aggression, particularly against the socialist countries of the Balkans. It suits the policy of the Belgrade revisionist clique to claim today that the military articles of this treaty "have lost their value." This humbug can, of course, deceive no one except those who wish to be deceived and indirectly wish to deceive others in order to support Titoism.

On the basis of the Balkan Pact, military and operational plans are openly or secretly coordinated, especially those of Yugoslavia and Greece; both their armies are equipped with modern weapons openly given by American imperialism on credit and gratuitously; aggressive bases have been set up, and many times each year groups of top-ranking officers of the general staffs of these states meet to coordinate military plans and to attend maneuvers and war games conducted in their territories. Greece and Yugoslavia are feverishly making military preparations. American imperialism goes so far in these preparations as to finance the military highways which are being built in Yugoslavia. It is a crime against world peace, it is a crime against the socialist camp, it is a crime against the socialist countries of the Balkans, and in particular it is a crime against Albania to fail to unmask publicly the aggressive plans of the Titoists and to conceal them under a smokescreen of false "neutrality," under fallacious and anti-Marxist slogans alleging that the renegade Titoist clique is carrying on the construction of socialism in Yugoslavia. We have unmasked and will continue to unmask the diabolical and divisive role as well as the plots of the ruling Yugoslav group, the Titoist renegades, against peace, against the socialist camp, and against Albania, because we feel very deeply the responsibility we have toward the defense of peace, socialism, our camp, and our fatherland. (*Stormy applause, ovations*)

Titoist Yugoslavia is conspiring together with her ally Greece and in conjunction with NATO and the American Sixth Fleet in the Mediterranean against the freedom, independence, and sovereignty of our country. This is proven by the facts.

I can tell the Congress, the people, and the party that these two neighboring countries, Yugoslavia and Greece, in collaboration with certain Albanian traitors, who are either in our country or have deserted to Yugoslavia, and in conjunction with the American Sixth Fleet in the Mediterranean, some months ago organized an attack against Albania with the aim of liquidating the People's Republic of Albania. Their criminal plot failed completely. (*Stormy continued applause, lengthy ovations*) The conspirators and the facts are in the hands of the people's justice. This odious plot failed because our heroic party, our people, our army, and the state security forces were guarding, vigilantly as ever, the defense of our fatherland and people. (*Stormy applause, ovations*)

Our relations with Italy have been developing more or less normally, especially in the field of trade. The conclusion of an agreement on reparations is a step forward. But the installation of rockets on Italian soil must be mentioned as a negative factor. We cannot help but feel uneasy about the transformation of Italian territory into an imperialist base for aggression against our country and the other countries of the socialist camp. We are anxiously following the actions of the Italian government in this respect, and, as we have stated, we cannot stand by with our hands folded.

We think that trade, cultural relations, and communications between our two countries can be developed successfully and to our mutual advantage if the ruling circles of Italy show a more realistic understanding of these problems. We think that it would be in the interest of friendly relations between our two neighboring countries and in the interest of peace in this area if Italy should give up her role as a den for Albanian war criminals, for this does not conform to normal relations between two countries.

The Albanian people have always felt close to the Arab peoples, with whom they are bound by age-old historical traditions and many similar customs, by numerous wars fought side by side against common enemies, and by mutual aspirations for freedom, independence, and progress. Our people and government have supported and will support to the end the just struggle for the liberation and the consolidation of the national independence of the Arab countries. When the fraternal people of Egypt were viciously attacked by the imperialist aggressors in Suez in 1956, the entire Albanian people rose to their feet in protest against the invasion, and thousands of Albanians were ready to go as volunteers to the aid of the heroic Egyptian people. Our sympathy and solidarity have always been, at the most critical moments, with the peoples of Syria, Iraq, Tunisia, and Morocco, just as they are now with the brave and indomitable Algerian people, whose just cause has won the admiration of all peace-loving peoples and will most certainly be victorious. We have emphatically denounced the ruthless exploitation by the imperialist monopolies of the immense wealth of the Arab subsoil, especially the oil, and we firmly support the right of the Arab peoples to take these riches completely into their own hands, for they belong to them and should be contributing to the economic consolidation and prosperity of the Arab countries themselves. The People's Republic of Albania is resolved to extend further in the future its present friendly relations and collaboration with the Arab countries with regard to questions of direct mutual concern as well as the question of national liberation and of peace in the United Nations Organization. We have a common interest in the struggle to preserve the peace, which is being threatened by imperialism. We are united by the Mediterranean Sea. Let us act in such a way that our efforts, in close cooperation with other peace-loving countries, will convert this sea into a bridge of friendship and a source of prosperity for the inhabitants of its shores.

The same may also be said of many Asian and African countries, such as India, Guinea, Ethiopia, Afghanistan, Indonesia, Burma, Ghana, and so forth, which pursue a policy of peaceful coexistence. Conditions are gradually being created for the further extension of our contacts with these countries.

We have normal relations with Turkey, and negotiations are in process to extend them, primarily in the field of trade. We hope that our relations with General Gursel's government will favorably develop to the benefit of both countries and of peace in the Balkans.

We have normal relations with France, Austria, Finland, and a number of other countries. We desire to develop these relations further in the field of trade, cultural exchange, and tourism.

We recently established diplomatic relations and signed an economic and cultural agreement with the Republic of Cuba. The Albanian people, who have demonstrated their solidarity with the heroic and revolutionary struggle of the Cuban people, led by their distinguished son Fidel Castro, salute this event, which opens up the path of friendship and collaboration with the new Cuba that emerged from the revolution (*applause*) and which provides an opportunity for understanding and contact between our people and the peoples of Latin America.

Our party and government have always been in favor of normal relations with all countries which want to have such relations with us, on the principles of peaceful coexistence, equality, nonintervention, and mutual respect.

The People's Republic of Albania, a loyal member of the socialist camp and the Warsaw Pact, enveloped by the ardent love of the fraternal peoples, occupies a worthy place among the peace-loving countries and does not spare, nor will it ever spare in the future, any efforts to make a modest contribution to the cause of peace and general disarmament. This is confirmed by its activity in the United Nations Organization in behalf of peace and national liberation, in behalf of the just and peaceful solution of the central issues which disturb mankind today.

Our party and government, in close collaboration with the glorious Soviet Union, the Chinese People's Republic, and the other countries of the socialist camp, as well as with all the peace-loving countries, will always fight courageously for the cause of peace. May our fatherland become, here on the shores of the Adriatic, a firm bulwark of peace and socialism, a glorious example of the friendship which unites the countries of the socialist camp, an example of the transforming powers of socialism and the victorious ideas of Marxism-Leninism. (*Continued applause, ovations*)

[The following sections are omitted:

II. THE RESULTS OF SOCIALIST CONSTRUCTION IN OUR COUNTRY
III. THE FURTHER DEVELOPMENT OF OUR COUNTRY ON THE PATH OF SOCIALIST CONSTRUCTION
IV. CERTAIN PROBLEMS ON STRENGTHENING THE PARTY — Ed.]

V. THE STRUGGLE ON THE IDEOLOGICAL FRONT AND THE TASKS OF THE PARTY . . .

2. Let us strengthen our propaganda efforts on behalf of the fundamental principles of Marxism-Leninism and our struggle to safeguard its purity.

Today a bitter struggle for the conquest of men's minds is being waged in the world between Marxism-Leninism and bourgeois ideology and all its manifestations. Confronted with the magnificent achievements of the socialist countries and the dissemination of Marxist-Leninist ideas throughout the world, the imperialist bourgeoisie and the exploiting classes of all countries are conducting a furious propaganda campaign in order to spread by all possible means the ideology of anti-Communism, monstrously to distort Marxism-Leninism, to vilify the socialist order, and to falsify the policy and aims of the Communists. In these efforts of the imperialist bourgeoisie, a shameful role is being played by its helpmates, the leaders of right-wing social democracy, the revisionists of Marxism, and opportunists of all shades.

Under these conditions, particular importance must be given to the struggle in the ideological sphere for the defense of the purity of the victorious doctrine of Marxism-Leninism, for a correct and profound analysis of the problems of contemporary world development, and for the propagation of the fundamental principles of Marxism-Leninism and the correct line which the Albanian Party of Labor has followed and will continue to follow with regard to these questions.

Our party, in order to have a correct understanding of the social phenomena and the changes which have occurred and are now occurring in the world, has always started from the materialist conception of history, a class analysis of the correlation of forces, and a profound and objective study of the actual situation existing in the world today. Marxism-Leninism teaches that this is the only correct method; it is the method which protects one from errors in political action. Any deviation from this dialectical method leads to metaphysics and idealism, to revisionism and opportunism, and to a topsy-turvy appraisal of different events and situations.

The main characteristic of all opportunists and revisionists, former as well as present-day, is precisely their denial of these fundamental principles of Marxism-Leninism. Here too is to be found the source of all their distorted views, of all their hostile and pernicious activity in both theory and practice. The great Lenin said that at the root of all the revisionist views lies the idea of collaboration between classes with opposing interests. Revising the Marxist theory of classes and the class struggle, the revisionists say Marxism is outdated; they deny its fundamental principles, distort all the urgent problems of our time, relinquish the ideological and political struggle against the class enemy, and capitulate before him. Naturally, if they came out in the open, no one would believe their nonsense; so the revisionists try to disguise themselves by presenting their views as the last word in "creative" Marxism. But beautiful phrases can fool no one, much less Communists, Marxist-Leninists, who when judging parties or persons judge them not only by their words and appearance but chiefly by their deeds and work. They judge thusly: Whom do these views serve, and in the interest of which class are they? In this matter the Marxist parties and all Communists are guided by Lenin's teachings:

> People have always been and will always be the stupid victims of deceit and self-deception in politics until they learn to discern *the interests* of some class behind all moral, religious, political, and social phrases, declarations, and promises (Lenin, *Works,* Vol. 19, pp. 7–8, Russian edition).

The modern revisionists deny the chief contradictions of our time, at the root of which stand certain classes and social forces. Consequently, speculating with allegedly "Marxist" phrases, the revisionists spread dangerous illusions on many important questions of our time. Thus, for example, when they speak of our age, they present it as an era of general tranquillity and harmony in which "the capitalist social system in its classical form is a thing of the past," in which there is a possibility of the "general integration" of the whole world, even of the capitalists, into socialism, and in which problems such as the struggle between the proletariat and the bourgeoisie, between socialism and capitalism, between the forces of freedom and slavery, between democracy and reaction, and between the forces of peace and war have totally disappeared. (*Laughter*) And according to revisionist logic, this is all quite natural because they believe that as a result of the change in the correlation of forces in the international arena, capitalism and imperialism have undergone radical changes; neither are they exploiters and aggressors nor are they any longer a source of wars and oppression. Indeed, the revisionist Kardelj even "argued" theoretically that the danger of war emanates in fact from the socialist countries, and particularly from China and Albania! (*Laughter*) Look how far the enemies of Marxism have gone in their absurdities; look where their great zeal the better to serve their masters, the imperialist bourgeoisie, has brought them!

The modern revisionists, neglecting a class analysis of the situation and seeking to deceive the masses, speak demagogically of the policy of peaceful coexistence or even of the problem of war and peace. They see these problems in a topsy-turvy way, through anti-Marxist spectacles. They view the policy of peaceful coexistence, the fundamental principles of which were first formulated by Lenin, as a policy of conciliation with imperialism for the sake of which every form of class struggle must be relinquished, in accord with the maxim "Let us not antagonize the rich uncle" (*Laughter*) although he is already weakened and on the road to bankruptcy. According to the revisionists, the policy of peaceful coexistence applies not only to relations between countries with different social systems but also to relations between classes within the capitalist countries as well as between the oppressed peoples and their colonial exploiters. The revisionists preach that an ideological and political struggle should not be waged against imperialism in order to unmask the policy of war and aggression. These anti-Marxist conceptions, which are in flagrant contradiction to the interests of the working class and of socialism, are designed to impose upon the socialist countries and Communist parties an opportunist policy, a policy of entreaties and flattery, a policy of dangerous concessions and compromise, all of which will enable the enemies of socialism, the imperialists, and the reactionary bourgeoisie, to realize more easily their policy of war and terror, of oppression and exploitation. But the Communist parties and socialist countries follow not the revisionist concepts but the immortal and ever-triumphant teachings of Marxism-Leninism. Our Party of Labor has struggled and will continue to struggle in the future against the revisionist views on these questions and will always faithfully apply the illuminating doctrines of Marxism. (*Stormy applause, ovations*)

Deviating from the class position, the modern revisionists reject as "obsolete" the principal teachings of Marxism-Leninism on socialist revolution and the dictatorship of the proletariat as the indispensable condition for the transition from capitalism to socialism. The basis of all the opportunist reasoning of the modern revisionists is the allegation that the modern capitalist state is losing its class character more and more each day and that it can serve the bourgeoisie equally as well as the proletariat. According to revisionist logic, the system of bourgeois democracy can serve as "the juridical and political framework of the initial phases of socialist development." Starting from such conceptions, the right opportunists consider the peaceful transition from capitalism to socialism as an absolute, as the only possible path. They present this peaceful transition as evolutionary, as a simple change in government in which certain people are replaced by other people.

The Marxist-Leninists do not deny the possibility of a peaceful transition to socialism, but they do not by any means view it as a repudiation of the class struggle, as the mere process of securing a majority in the bourgeois parliament without radically smashing the old bourgeois state machinery and replacing it with the organs of proletarian dictatorship — suitable for carrying out a profound socialist transformation and prepared at any time to crush resolutely all possible resistance on the part of the bourgeoisie. The Marxist-Leninists are guided in this matter by the immortal teachings of the great Lenin, who said:

> The opportunist gentlemen, including the Kautskyites, as if ridiculing Marxist theory, "teach" the people the following: At first the proletariat should win a majority by means of their general right to vote; then, on the basis of such a majority vote, they should take over the state power and finally, on the basis of "consequent" (some call it "pure") democracy, organize socialism.
>
> On the other hand, we, on the basis of Marxist theory and the experience of the Russian revolution, say: First the proletariat should overthrow the bourgeoisie and secure for *itself* the state power, and then use this state power, i.e., the proletarian dictatorship, as a class weapon to win over the support of the majority of working people (V. I. Lenin, *Works*, Vol. 30, p. 294, Albanian edition). (*Fervent applause*)

In other words, the Marxist parties, as stated in the Moscow Declaration, by no means consider the peaceful path as the only possible path of the transition to socialism. On the contrary, they never for a moment forget that the ruling classes, as historical experience to date teaches us, never voluntarily relinquish their power; therefore, the Marxist-Leninist revolutionary parties prepare themselves equally and simultaneously for both the peaceful transition and the seizure of power through armed uprising, always keeping their arms loaded and their powder dry so as not to be taken by surprise in the event of bourgeois violence against the revolutionary uprising of the working class. Lenin's teachings on this matter are clear and precise:

> An oppressed class — he says — which does not try to learn to use arms, to possess arms, does not deserve anything better than to be treated as slaves (V. I. Lenin, *Selected Works,* Vol. I, p. 864, Albanian edition).

If you are well prepared for an armed uprising, you also create favorable conditions for the peaceful seizure of power. (*Stormy applause, ovations*)

This is the only correct Marxist-Leninist attitude on this question, which is so important and vital to the working class and all working people, and which our party always has and continues to maintain. The revisionist theories on "the evolutionary and peaceful transformation" of modern capitalism into socialism are designed to sway the Communist and workers parties from the correct revolutionary path, to detach the working masses from the struggle to overthrow the bourgeoisie; they are designed to preserve unscathed and to perpetuate the capitalist order.

The opportunist and defeatist theses of the modern revisionists with regard to the state and to socialist construction are also very dangerous and in flagrant contradiction to Marxist-Leninist teachings. While repeating the stale allegations that within the socialist state the dictatorship of the proletariat and democracy are two altogether incompatible phenomena, while accusing the socialist state of "bureaucratic despotism" and toying with the slogan of so-called "democratization," the modern revisionists preach the immediate "withering away," the liquidation, of the socialist state. To the Marxist-Leninist parties it is as clear as daylight that not merely the liquidation of the socialist state but even the slightest weakening of the organs of the proletarian dictatorship or its liberalization would be suicidal to our socialist countries at a time when they still confront imperialism, which never has and never will give up its furious designs and efforts to destroy the socialist order. This was thoroughly confirmed by the bitter experience of the counterrevolution in Hungary.

Marxist-Leninists do not have and cannot have the slightest doubt that the socialist state, as a dictatorship over the vanquished exploiting classes and all types of working class enemies and imperialist agents, ensures at the same time the broadest democracy for the workers, for the people. These are elementary principles of Marxist-Leninist theory. Our party has always considered that one of its permanent tasks is relentlessly to bring to perfection the socialist state order and to struggle against any kind of bureaucratic manifestation. But it does not forget for a single moment that, as long as there still exists the danger of imperialist aggression and subversive activity against our country and the socialist camp, it is by no means permissible on the pretext of "democratization" to weaken, be it ever so slightly, the organs of the proletarian dictatorship. On the contrary, they should always be held ready and waiting to liquidate any possible probes by internal or external enemies.

The experience of the Soviet Union and of all the other socialist countries has proved the correctness of Marxist-Leninist theory regarding the existence of a series of general laws which are indispensable for every country embarking upon the road of socialist development. The successes of our country, of the other socialist countries, and of the world socialist system as a whole have been achieved precisely because of the correct application of these general laws of socialist construction, while taking into consideration the concrete conditions and the historical peculiarities of each country as well as the interests of the entire socialist camp.

The revisionists of Marxism distort and deny these laws. The socialist state, according to them, must give up its economic and organizational functions; otherwise, "bureaucratic" tendencies emerge, and the state is converted into a force that stands "above society," etc. To avoid these dangers, they preach the decentralization of economic management, "producers' self-government." By preaching the constant weakening of the economic role of the socialist state, the revisionists repudiate a most important principle of socialist construction and socialist state organization — the principle of democratic centralism — and they try to replace it with the free and independent development of economic forces, i.e., with petty bourgeois spontaneity which gives free rein to anarchy in production.

Life and experience has refuted all these modern revisionist views which serve only the class enemies, which seriously damage the cause of socialist construction, and which create the danger of capitalist restoration. Our party has fought and will continue to fight firmly against all these views; it strictly adheres to the teachings of Marxism-Leninism on the construction of socialism, the correctness of which has been verified by the rich and many-sided experience of the Soviet Union, which is of universal significance, and that of all the other socialist countries. This experience is a treasured possession in the theory and practice of socialism, from which our party has learned and will continue to learn. (*Stormy applause, ovations*)

During the past few years our party and all the other Marxist-Leninist parties have been waging a successful struggle against the views of the modern revisionists as well as against their actions to divide the socialist camp and the international Communist movement. But in spite of all the crushing blows and defeats it has suffered, revisionism has not been ideologically routed; it has not been completely destroyed. As emphasized in the Moscow Declaration, revisionism — as one of the forms of bourgeois ideological influence upon the proletariat and as a reflection of bourgeois ideology in theory and practice — remains the chief danger to the international Communist movement.

Tito's traitorous revisionist group constitutes a serious threat to the unity of the socialist camp and the international Communist movement, as well as to the cause of peace and the liberation of the peoples; it is the most aggressive and dangerous detachment of modern international revisionism and a trained secret service agency of imperialism, chiefly of American imperialism. Our Party of Labor has always waged a firm struggle against the hostile views and actions of the Belgrade revisionists and has considered this struggle an indispensable condition for the protection of the interests of our fatherland, for the defense of the purity of Marxism-Leninism, for the consolidation of the unity and cohesion of the socialist camp and the international Communist movement, for the successful conduct of the struggle against imperialism, and for the preservation of peace. It has considered and continues to consider this struggle as its lofty internationalist duty. (*Fervent applause, ovations*)

The Yugoslav leaders are seasoned traitors to Marxism-Leninism and the working class. Their profoundly opportunistic views, as was stated in the Declaration of the 81 Communist and workers parties, were sanctioned by the infamous program adopted by the Seventh Congress of the League of Communists of Yugoslavia, which is the platform, the concentrated exposition, of the views of modern international revisionism.

Our party has had long experience in the struggle against the Yugoslav revisionists. It fully recognizes their true nature as anti-Marxists, chauvinists, and seasoned agents of imperialism. The entire history of the relations between our party and the Yugoslav leadership, between our country and Titoist Yugoslavia, is a history of continuous plots by the Titoist clique to subjugate our party and to liquidate the independence of our country; it is a history of the heroic resistance of the Albanian Party of Labor and our people against the diabolical designs of this clique, against all sorts of pressure and blackmail.

To defend themselves against our principled Marxist-Leninist struggle and to denigrate our party, the Yugoslav revisionists have engaged in all sorts of attacks and calumnies against us, at times accusing us of being "nationalists" and at other times of being "dogmatists" and "sectarians" or people "who understand nothing of Marxism." (*Laughter*) This is a familiar tactic of opportunists and revisionists of all periods in the fight against revolutionary Marxism.

It is the usual practice of the Yugoslav revisionists, in order to deceive their people and the simple-minded, to employ "Marxist" terms, to present themselves as resolute fighters and partisans of the liberation of the colonial peoples and of peaceful coexistence and as supporters of the Soviet disarmament proposals, and, finally, to swear repeatedly that they are building socialism. (*Laughter*) In the Moscow Declaration of the 81 Communist and workers parties it is emphasized that the Yugoslav revisionists are in fact neither for peace nor for socialism; and how can the Yugoslav revisionists be for peace and peaceful coexistence and against imperialism when, as stressed in the Declaration, they conduct subversive activities against the socialist camp and the international Communist movement, when under the pretext of a "non-bloc" policy they carry on activities designed to split all the peace-loving forces and countries, and when Yugoslavia participates in the Balkan military bloc which is connected with the aggressive imperialist blocs of NATO and CENTO? How can it be said that Yugoslavia is a socialist state and is building socialism when, as stressed in the Declaration, the Yugoslav revisionists have betrayed Marxism-Leninism, detached Yugoslavia from the socialist camp, and made it dependent on American and other imperialist charity, and when they have set the League of Communists of Yugoslavia against the entire international Communist movement and fight furiously to destroy this movement?

Our party firmly agrees with the position of the Declaration of the 81 Communist and workers parties, according to which the further unmasking of the Yugoslav revisionist leaders and the active struggle to defend the international Communist movement against the anti-Leninist ideas of the Yugoslav revisionists continue to be an indispensable duty of all Marxist-Leninist parties. (*Continous applause*) It believes that an uncompromising and resolute struggle should be waged against revisionism until its utter extinction. Any slackening of revolutionary vigilance or weakening of the principled struggle against it, any vacillation in this struggle under any pretext whatsoever, will inevitably lead to a revival and intensification of the revisionist tendencies which greatly harm our great cause. Without mercilessly unmasking revisionism, and chiefly the Belgrade revisionist clique, imperialism cannot be properly unmasked. Without clearly defining the boundary which divides the revisionist views from Marxism-Leninism, dogmatism and sectarianism cannot be successfully opposed from a correct position. This struggle for the complete ideological and political rout of this renegade gang is in itself an international service to the Yugoslav people.

While fighting resolutely against revisionism as the chief danger, our party has fought and will continue to fight against any manifestation of dogmatism and sectarianism, which is likewise a danger to the cause of socialism. In all its activity our party has kept and must keep this matter in mind, because only in this way will we be protected from any error in our great struggle for socialism and Communism.

The most important questions of contemporary world development and of the struggle on the ideological front have been extensively dealt with from the Marxist-Leninist point of view at the two Moscow meetings of Communist and workers representatives of 1957 and 1960 and have found their correct expression in the historic Declarations approved at these meetings. Our Marxist-Leninist party has fully approved these documents. It has resolutely fought to implement the principles of the Declaration of 1957 and to defend it from any distortion. In the future our party will also be faithful to the principles of the Declaration of 1960 and will fight courageously for its implementation and defense. (*Continued applause*) The Declaration of 1960 is a Marxist-Leninist document of great importance; it is a militant program for the entire international Communist and workers movement. The conclusions and the principles of the Declaration are a confirmation of the correct general Marxist-Leninist line, which our party has faithfully defended and put into practice.

The Moscow Declaration profoundly analyzes the most important questions of our time, such as the problem of the definition of the nature of our epoch; it makes a profound analysis of the change in the correlation of forces in favor of socialism in the present period, the development and the consolidation of the socialist system on the one hand and the decline and disintegration of the capitalist system on the other. It expresses the view of the Communists on mankind's most urgent problem, the problem of peace and war. The Declaration analyzes in detail the problems relating to the struggle against colonialism and the working class struggle in the capitalist countries, and it sets forth the tasks of the Communist and workers parties within the different colonial and capitalist countries, considering them the most consistent and resolute leaders in the struggle for freedom and independence, for liberation from national and social oppression, for democracy and socialism. An important part of the Declaration is devoted to problems regarding the roads to socialism, as well as to problems regarding the struggle for the purity of Marxist-Leninist ideology and for the consolidation of the unity of the international Communist and workers movement and of the socialist camp.

The Declaration is imbued with the spirit of revolution. Its cutting edge is directed against imperialism, especially American imperialism, which is characterized as the chief warmonger, as an enemy of the peoples, as a vehicle of war, an aggressor and international gendarme and exploiter, and against revisionism, which remains the chief danger, with Yugoslav revisionism as its most concrete and dangerous manifestation.

The clear and profound explanation of the problems and the chief tasks of the international Communist movement, which are embodied in the Moscow Declaration of 1960, constitutes one of the major points of orientation for the ideological-political work of our party.

Our party propaganda work, utilizing all the forms and means at its disposal, should organize the all-round explanation of these matters from the positions of Marxist-Leninist revolutionary theory. Not only the Communists but all the workers and the broad masses of people must be educated in the ideas and the spirit of the Declaration of the 81 Communist and workers parties.

Our Party of Labor is one of the militant detachments of the international Communist and workers movement. The Moscow Declaration assigns an important place to the problem of the further strengthening of the Marxist-Leninist unity of the international Communist movement, to the problem of the consolidation of international solidarity. The imperialists and the enemies of Marxism-Leninism have always failed in their struggle against the working class and the international Communist movement because, *inter alia,* the proletariat and the Communists have always been solidly united not only on a national but also on an international scale. The immortal slogan of the Communists, which was already used by Marx and Engels in the *Communist Manifesto* and which has now become the motto of the entire great army of the proletariat and of international Communism, is "Workers of the world, unite!" In these words is expressed the internationalist spirit of our movement, which is the irreconcilable enemy of any manifestation of chauvinism or bourgeois nationalism.

The Moscow Declaration and its principles constitute a concrete basis for the further consolidation of the unity of the international Communist movement, a real foundation for the strengthening of proletarian solidarity in the fight against the common enemy, world imperialism, and its lackeys of all shades.

In the Communist movement there are no "leading" and no "led" parties. As stressed in the Declaration, all parties are equal and independent. They themselves formulate their policy, guided by the principles of Marxism-Leninism in conformity with the historical conditions of their country. The Marxist parties are bound to one another as parties of a single class, a single idea, and a single purpose; for this reason they grant one another fraternal mutual assistance in the common struggle for the victory of the great cause of the proletariat and exchange their experience accumulated in this struggle.

Our Party of Labor has always with the greatest resolution fought for, and made its contribution to, the consolidation of the unity of the international Communist and workers movement on the granitelike foundation of Marxism-Leninism. Guided by the principles of proletarian internationalism, it has always been conscious of the fact that our successes also comprise the successes and gains of the struggle of the working class and the peoples of other countries, and that the solidarity and aid of the international working class, of the fraternal parties and the fraternal peoples, have been and remain for us a very important factor in the realization of our goals. For this, the Central Committee of our party and all the Albanian Communists are grateful to the international Communist movement, the working class, and the fraternal parties of the different countries and assure them that, in the future as hitherto, we shall on our part remain united and resolutely faithful to them. (*Continued applause*) Our party will always struggle, on the basis of the principles of the Moscow Declaration, for the further consolidation of the unity of the international Communist and workers movement and for the development of international solidarity and ties with all the fraternal parties. While fulfilling honorably and faithfully its internationalist duties here in Albania, in the farthest outpost of the socialist camp, our party will always hold high the banner of Marxism-Leninism, the banner of triumphant socialism. (*Fervent applause, ovations*)

With regard to these matters, one of the vital tasks of our party propaganda is that in the future too it should strive to enlighten the Communists and all the masses of people in the Marxist-Leninist principles of proletarian internationalism, in the spirit of fraternal friendship with the peoples of the Soviet Union and the other countries of the socialist camp, in the feeling of fraternal unity and solidarity with the struggle of the working class, the Communist parties, and the peoples of other countries.

Our party propaganda should make clear to the Communists as well as to the masses of people that, in our struggle for the construction of socialism, just as we rely on the support of the broad masses of people in our own country, so also in the international arena we rely on the aid and support of the socialist countries and on the solidarity of the working class, the Communist parties, and the peoples of other countries. Without the solidarity and the internationalist support of the revolutionary movement, the international workers movement, and the fraternal Communist parties, we cannot realize the great goals lying before us, the construction of socialism and Communism.

Comrades,

Our party has traversed a difficult but, at the same time, heroic path during the course of which it has matured and become stronger. On this difficult path, in this arduous struggle against numerous enemies, our party has become tempered, the unity of its ranks has become steel-like, and the party ties with the people have become indissoluble. During the course of this difficult path and arduous struggle, enlightened by the teachings of Marxism-Leninism and imbued with infinite loyalty to it, our party has formulated its correct general line and has gained the maturity to orient itself correctly even under the most difficult conditions, to display courage and resolution whenever there has been a question of protecting the interests of the fatherland and socialism, and to defend the purity of Marxism-Leninism.

Since its foundation, there have arisen against the party and its general line various opportunist and revisionist elements, defeatists and deserters, who have tried to impede our forward march, to reconcile our correct line with that of our enemies, and to endanger the destiny of our fatherland and people with their mistaken, opportunist, and anti-Marxist tendencies. Take a look at these elements, from Sadik Premte to Koci Xoxe, from Tuk Jakova to Panajot Plaku, from Liri Gega to Liri Belishova, and you will see a conglomeration of selfish and ambitious people, careerists and opportunists, some of whom have ended in betraying the people and fatherland, a group of people devoid of any principles or Communist morals.

The history of our party is a history of the struggle and victory over the internal and external enemies of our people; it is a history of the struggle and victory of our Marxist-Leninist party for the purity of Marxism-Leninism against internal and external opportunism and revisionism. Every Communist and worker in our country should know this history well. The study of our party history must be the focus of our party propaganda. It must clearly set forth the difficult, heroic, and glorious road traversed by the party by underlying the correctness of the line followed by our party at each stage of its development, its loyalty to Marxism-Leninism, and its resolute and courageous struggle against the imperialist enemies and their revisionist hirelings.

Our party has always triumphed and has scored great victories in all fields because it has always remained loyal to the people's vital interests and has resolutely defended them, because it has always relied on the people, on their power and creative abilities, and because it has established close ties with the people and has firmly united them around its correct line. (*Stormy applause, ovations*)

The people, the broad working masses, our working class in alliance with the peasantry, are the decisive force which carried out the great political and social transformations in our country and which liberated the fatherland and today are building socialism. It was the broad masses of people, the workers, working peasantry, youth, and people's intelligentsia, who waged the glorious war of national liberation. The party showed them that everything, the independence of their fatherland and a better future, was in their hands, and they arose as one man, filled the ranks of the army, and fought heroically. At that time the enemies could not understand the source of our party strength or how it could organize the liberation struggle, create a powerful army, and liberate the country.

Later on when Albania emerged from the war ruined, impoverished, and encircled, or "isolated" as our enemies preferred to say, the latter threatened us and jeered, saying: "Now what are you going to do, how are you going to support yourselves, how are you going to live?" (*Laughter*) But the enemies rejoiced prematurely and settled their accounts without prior consultation with the innkeeper, without taking into account our heroic people, who had taken their destiny into their hands and had become the masters of their own country. Under the wise guidance of their party, our people got down to serious work and, along with the achievement of radical socio-economic transformations, within a short time, by selflessly and insistently overcoming all hardships, they healed the terrible war wounds, completed the reconstruction of the country, and prepared the conditions for beginning on a large scale the construction of socialism in our country. (*Continued applause, ovations*)

It frequently happens that even friends who have visited Albania, or have followed with interest from afar the achievements of our country, wonder and ask: How could little Albania survive all those tribulations, how could she emerge victorious from an unequal war against fascist invaders and traitors, how can she withstand the innumerable threats and pressures from the imperialists, chauvinists, and the traitorous Titoist gang, how does she overcome hardships and score one success right after another in all fields of socialist construction? We reply that the decisive factor in the achievement of all our country's historic victories is the people themselves, their struggle and work, the correct line of the party which was able to heighten the consciousness of the masses and to mobilize them yesterday for the war of liberation and today for the struggle for the preservation of independence and the construction of socialism, and the unbreakable tie between the people and the party. (*Stormy applause, ovations*) We reply that another very important factor is the support, assistance, and friendship of the fraternal peoples of the socialist countries, the backing of the entire international proletariat. Our party has bound our people with indestructible love and friendship to the peoples of other countries, to the heroic peoples of the Soviet Union, People's China, and the other peoples who are building socialism. Our enemies have always tried to harm this sacred friendship, but it will remain forever immortal. (*Stormy and continued applause, ovations*) Let us take, for example, our friendship with the peoples of the great Soviet Union. This was instilled in the hearts of all Albanians by our party during the most difficult days, during the days when the Soviet peoples were engaged in the Great Patriotic War, during the time when Albania suffered under the fascist yoke. Our great friendship was steeled in battle and blood, in the comradeship of arms, in the struggle for life, for freedom, and for the future. This friendship was further strengthened and tempered during these last sixteen years following liberation. The Soviet Union, by its victory over fascism, created a real possibility for and contributed to the liberation of our people. The aid and the support of the Soviet Union have been one of the most important external factors in the achievement of our great successes in the field of socialist construction. In this great and indestructible friendship, which no power or intrigue in the world can weaken, and in the friendship of all the other peoples of the socialist camp our people will in the future also find support and inspiration for new victories in the struggle for socialism and Communism. (*Stormy applause, ovations*)

Our people are brave, industrious, freedom-loving, loyal, and progressive. Our party, enlightened by the doctrines of Marxism-Leninism, also embodies in itself these lofty traditions of our people. Rest assured, comrades, that with such a remarkable people and our party's indomitable loyalty to Marxism-Leninism and to proletarian internationalism and its close friendship with the fraternal peoples and fraternal parties of the socialist countries, our country will march forward, ever forward, for there is neither wave nor storm that can frighten it; there is no force in the world that can halt our victorious march to the triumph of socialism and Communism. (*Stormy and continued applause, ovations*)

DOCUMENT 7

Hoxha speech, September 30, 1961, delivered at the Embassy of the Chinese People's Republic, Zëri i Popullit, *October 1, 1961 (complete text).*

Dear Comrade Ambassador Lo Shih-kao, comrades, and gentlemen,

Twelve years ago the great fraternal

Chinese people proclaimed their People's Republic. The first of October has become in China a day of great rejoicing for the working masses, who, justifiably proud, set a high example of peaceful and creative effort with the splendid victories which they score from year to year. All the peoples of the socialist camp as well as the whole of progressive mankind rejoice with great China. The anniversary of the proclamation of the Chinese People's Republic is also a day of rejoicing for the Albanian people and the Albanian Party of Labor, the sincere and loyal friends of the fraternal Chinese people. Permit me, dear comrade Ambassador, in the name of the Central Committee of the Albanian Party of Labor, the Presidium of the People's Assembly, the government of the Albanian People's Republic, and the entire Albanian people to extend to you, and through you to all the Chinese people, the Chinese Communist Party, and the government of the Chinese People's Republic the most heartfelt fraternal congratulations on the occasion of your great day.

The proclamation of the Chinese People's Republic and the establishment of a proletarian dictatorship in a country comprising a vast territory and one-quarter of the world's population marked a decisive step forward in the development of forces throughout the world in favor of socialism and to the detriment of imperialism. They marked the acceleration of the further disintegration and collapse of capitalism. The liberation of the great Chinese people has given an incomparable impetus to the just liberation struggle of the peoples of Asia, Africa, and Latin America.

Under the wise guidance of their glorious Communist Party, led by their distinguished son, Comrade Mao Tse-tung, the heroic Chinese people have achieved in the years since the proclamation of the republic brilliant and historic victories in socialist construction. By creatively applying Marxism-Leninism, the glorious Chinese Communist Party is transforming the Chinese People's Republic into a mighty socialist country. The Chinese people are successfully implementing the three red banners: the general line of the party on socialist construction, the great leap forward, and the people's communes. They have displayed a high level of creative initiative in all realms of socialist construction. Thus in the industrial sector, during the three years of the great leap forward, China fulfilled ahead of schedule the main targets of the second five-year plan, created an extensive modern industrial base, and increased by several times the productive capacity of the main industrial branches. In the agricultural sector, land reclamation, construction, and a series of other projects have been developed on a large scale, thus creating favorable conditions for the further expansion of agricultural production. During the same period education and culture have rapidly progressed. There is no doubt that the brilliant successes achieved so far represent a very solid basis for further and more rapid progress.

These brilliant successes are the result of the colossal efforts of this great and talented people and of their invincible unity with the glorious Chinese Communist Party. These successes are an inspiration to other peoples still suffering under the savage yoke of capitalism in their struggle for freedom, independence, and social progress.

The Chinese People's Republic, consistently pursuing the wise Marxist-Leninist policy of the strengthening of friendship and unity with the Soviet Union and the other countries of the socialist camp, supports with all its strength the revolutionary efforts of the oppressed peoples in their struggle against imperialism and colonialism, and resolutely struggles against the imperialist policy of aggression and war.

As a mighty socialist country, China is playing an ever greater role on the international scene. It is making an important contribution to the triumph of the principles of peaceful coexistence between states with different social and political systems and to the settlement through negotiations of international disputes, while remaining steadfast in the front ranks of the struggle against imperialism, particularly American imperialism, and for the consolidation of friendship between peoples, for an international détente, and for the preservation of world peace.

The wise Marxist-Leninist peace policy of the Chinese People's Republic is greatly appreciated by all the peace-loving peoples who see in her, just as in the Soviet Union, a firm and consistent supporter of the freedom and independence of peoples, an unflinching fighter against all forms of oppression, exploitation, and injustice. That is why the correct policy of the Chinese People's Republic cannot be obscured by the accusations and vile slander of the United States imperialists and their allies, nor by that of the modern revisionists and, primarily, by the Yugoslav revisionists.

The Kennedy government with its Western partners, while hypocritically speaking about peace in order to deceive the peoples, is pursuing its old policy against peace, is stepping up in an unprecedented manner the arms race and its feverish preparations for war, and is thus creating a very tense international situation. The imperialist states, with the United States at the head, have continually sabotaged the talks on disarmament and the cessation of nuclear tests, proposed by the Soviet Union, and strongly supported by the Chinese People's Republic and all other socialist countries. While rejecting the constructive proposals of the Soviet Union and the just and legitimate measures of the German Democratic Republic regarding the peaceful settlement of the German problem and, on this basis, the question of West Berlin, the American imperialists and their allies, particularly the revanchist Bonn government, have lately launched a vast bellicose campaign; they have further increased their aggressive activities and provocations as well as their efforts to create a war psychosis.

The Albanian Party of Labor, our government, and our people have supported the decision of the Soviet government to proceed with nuclear weapons tests as well as the signing of a peace treaty with Germany and the normalization of the situation in West Berlin as a free and demilitarized city.

Events are increasingly and even more clearly exposing the aggressive nature of imperialism. Therefore in the present international situation the peoples must more than ever increase their vigilance. All the peace-loving forces must strengthen their unity in order to check the aggressive plans for the preparation and unleashing of war by the imperialists and particularly by the American imperialists, those vicious assassins of peace and sworn enemies of mankind. The bellicose and warmongering plans and activities of the imperialists must be opposed and assailed without mercy. The demagogical efforts of the imperialists and their revisionist agency, with the Belgrade revisionist clique at the head, must be unmasked without vacillation. The Marxist-Leninist parties have waged and will continue to wage a resolute principled struggle against modern revisionism, which represents the main danger to the Communist movement. In this struggle between Marxism-Leninism and revisionism, Marxism-Leninism will be victorious while revisionism is doomed to inevitable failure and destruction. The revisionists may succeed in duping some Marxists but not the overwhelming masses. The revisionists may deceive for a while but not for always. The conscience of Communists is not an object for bargaining which may be bought and sold on the market. The clear-thinking minds of Marxists cannot be easily muddled by the tricks of acrobats and charlatans. Marxism-Leninism is merciless when it comes to renegades. Therefore the revisionists, whatever their guise, are terribly afraid because they know the fate that awaits them.

The American imperialists and their allies, terrified by the growing authority of the Chinese People's Republic throughout the world, are pursuing their warlike policy and flagrantly trampling underfoot the most elementary rules of international law and the fundamental principles of the

United Nations Charter. They have tried by every possible means for twelve years to deny the Chinese People's Republic the restoration of its legitimate rights in the United Nations. They have invented the so-called "two Chinas" policy as a diabolical tactical maneuver to keep alive the political corpse of Chiang Kai-shek, whom the Chinese people ousted from their fatherland in their heroic struggle, and to perpetuate the occupation of Taiwan. But whether the American imperialists and their lackeys like it or not, there exists today only one China, one and indivisible, the great Chinese People's Republic, a mighty socialist state which is progressing and thriving with each passing year and without the participation of which no important international problem can be solved.

The Albanian people, the Albanian Party of Labor, and our government condemn with the greatest resolve the machinations of the United States imperialists and those of their lackeys aimed at denying the Chinese People's Republic its legitimate rights in the United Nations. They support without reservation the policy of immediately granting to the Chinese People's Republic its rightful seat in the United Nations. We consider Taiwan and the other neighboring islands as an integral part of the Chinese People's Republic; that is why we have supported and will continue to support in the future the issue of their complete liberation.

Dear comrades and gentlemen, the Albanian people and the Chinese people are bound to one another by everlasting fraternal friendship based upon the principles of Marxism-Leninism and proletarian internationalism. This great friendship, which deepens, grows stronger, and flourishes with each passing day, has been tempered by our common struggle for the preservation of the purity of Marxism-Leninism, for the resolute unmasking to the end of the warmongering American imperialists and their lackeys, the modern revisionists with the dangerous Belgrade clique in the lead, for our common goals and ideals, for the construction of socialism and the preservation of universal peace. The builders of this indestructible friendship are our Marxist-Leninist parties which are struggling resolutely and without hesitation, no matter what the obstacle or difficulty, for the implementation of the Moscow Declaration of 1960 and for the consolidation of the unity of the socialist camp, with the Soviet Union at the head, and the unity of the international Communist and workers movement, which the hirelings of imperialism and modern revisionism are vainly trying to disrupt.

The fruits of this great friendship between our peoples are perfectly reflected in the expansion and many-sided consolidation of contacts and fraternal cooperation between our peoples and our two socialist countries. We note with great pleasure that during the last few years, particularly during 1961, cooperation in all realms between the Albanian People's Republic and the Chinese People's Republic has assumed greater momentum in the interest of our two peoples and of the socialist camp. The Chinese People's Republic has given and continues to give to the Albanian people substantial and generous international aid for the construction of socialism in Albania. The Albanian Party of Labor, the Albanian government, and the Albanian people have always been and will always be grateful to the great Chinese people, to the glorious Chinese Communist Party, and to the government of the Chinese People's Republic for this fraternal and disinterested aid.

Comrades and gentlemen, the Albanian people, under the wise and brave guidance of the Albanian Party of Labor, distinguished by a spirit of fervent patriotism and self-denying industry, are resolutely marching forward and have already scored brilliant successes in the construction of socialism and the strengthening of the international position of the Albanian People's Republic and its defensive capacity, fearing neither geographical encirclement by the capitalists and revisionists nor the constant hostile probes of the imperialists and their tools against our fatherland.

The imperialists, the Belgrade revisionists, and all the enemies of our party and people have tried by sword and fire, by means of various plots and blockades, to strangle our party and to subjugate our people. These enemies think they can easily liquidate Albania because it is a small country. But they have miscalculated, they have failed, and they will continue to fail shamefully because they have come up against and will always come up against a rocklike impregnable fortress, heroically and gallantly defended by a brave people and party. Those who tried to dig a grave for Albania have fallen into the grave themselves. The new socialist Albania is marching valiantly forward, as befits a socialist country which lives and struggles in the great century of Leninism. Its body shows the scars of the wounds inflicted by the swords and bullets of its enemies, but its brow is clear and bright, with neither wrinkles nor blemishes, its eye is the eye of an eagle, and its heart is as pure and ardent as the revolution. It is for this reason that all the progressive peoples and Communists throughout the world love, respect, and defend Albania and its heroic party. It is for this reason that he who raises a hand against Albania will be struck down not only by this courageous land but by all the Communists of the world, by all the peoples of the socialist camp with the Soviet people at the head, and by all honest and progressive people. Let the enemies of our people and party remember that they will not take us by surprise. We are prepared for everything, and we are ready to cope successfully with any situation. We know and understand their tricks, their plots, their machinations against our people and against our party. Herein lies the strength and maturity of our people and our party. We do not deceive ourselves with illusions and dreams; we are perfectly aware that the cares of mankind and our people cannot end before the extinction of imperialism and its agent — revisionism. And since we are not afraid to face up to our cares and to abolish them forevermore, we reap successes constantly, while our enemies reap failures.

With indescribable enthusiasm, the workers of our country have mobilized all their forces as never before for the fulfillment and overfulfullment of the targets of the third five-year plan. This is best demonstrated by the brilliant successes achieved in the fulfillment of the plan for the first nine months of this year.

The historic decisions of the Fourth Congress of our party best reflect the correct and consistent Marxist-Leninist policy of the Albanian Party of Labor. Inspired by these decisions, the Albanian people, as a worthy and inseparable member of the mighty socialist family, will in the future work even more resolutely for the construction of socialism in our free and sovereign fatherland.

Our people are confidently advancing along the path of socialism because everywhere in the world they have the support of friends and sincere and loyal brothers, primarily the fraternal peoples of the Soviet Union, the Chinese people, and the other peoples of the socialist countries. An ardent, pure, sincere, and immortal friendship that will live through the centuries has been forged in the hearts of our party and our people for the Soviet Union and the glorious party of Lenin and Stalin. This is not to the liking and confuses the plans of the Belgrade revisionists, who brand us as anti-Soviet and as Pharisees. But the party says to the people: Let the dogs bark; concentrate on your glorious work because you are in the right, and strengthen this friendship because our friendship with the Soviet Union is the cornerstone of our present and of our even brighter future. Our party and people will, as ever, struggle with all their might to consolidate their fraternal friendship with the Soviet Union, the Chinese People's Republic, and all the other socialist lands. They will struggle further to strengthen the unity of the socialist camp and to defend the lofty interests of their fatherland and of socialism in the southwestern corner of our camp, on the shores of the Adriatic and Ionian Seas.

On this great festive day of indescribable rejoicing for the fraternal Chinese people, permit me to drink this toast:

To the great, heroic, and talented Chinese people;

To the glorious Communist Party of China, headed by the beloved Comrade Mao Tse-tung;

To the President of the Chinese People's Republic, Comrade Liu Shao-chi;

To the government of the Chinese People's Republic, and Comrade Chou En-lai;

To the unbreakable friendship between our fraternal peoples;

To the powerful socialist camp, headed by the Soviet Union;

To peace and friendship among peoples;

To your health, Comrade Ambassador.

DOCUMENT 8

Khrushchev's comments on Albania in his report on October 17, 1961, to the 22nd Congress, Pravda, *October 18, 1961 (excerpt from* CDSP, *XIII, 43 [Nov. 22, 1961]).*

. . . The policy of the 20th Congress encountered ardent approval from the international Communist movement, from the fraternal Marxist-Leninist parties. This was reflected in the decisions of Congresses and other materials of the fraternal parties and in the documents of the conferences of representatives of Communist and workers parties in 1957 and 1960.

Thus the statement of the Moscow conference of 1960 pointed out that "the historic decisions of the 20th Congress of the CPSU . . . initiated a new stage in the international Communist movement and contributed to its further development on the basis of Marxism-Leninism."

At the same time it should be noted that, as it later turned out, our party's policy of overcoming the harmful effects of the cult of the individual did not meet with due understanding from the leaders of the Albanian Party of Labor; indeed, they began to conduct a struggle against this policy.

Everyone knows that until recently the relations between the Soviet Union and the People's Republic of Albania and between the Communist Party of the Soviet Union and the Albanian Party of Labor were friendly and good. The peoples of our country gave Albania comprehensive, disinterested help in developing its economy, in socialist construction. We sincerely wanted and want to see Albania a flourishing socialist republic and its people happy and enjoying all the benefits of the new life.

For many years the Albanian leaders signified their complete unity of views with the Central Committee of our party and the Soviet government on all questions of the international Communist movement. They repeatedly declared their support of the 20th Congress policy. Enver Hoxha, First Secretary of the Central Committee of the Albanian Party of Labor, stated this in his speeches at the 20th and 21st Congresses of our party. At the Third Congress of the Albanian Party of Labor, held soon after the 20th Congress, the criticism of the cult of the individual as well as measures to overcome its harmful consequences were fully and completely approved.

We Soviet people believed the Albanian leaders and considered that mutual understanding and unity of views existed between our party and the Albanian Party of Labor.

The facts show, however, that recently the Albanian leaders, despite their former declarations and the decisions of their own Party Congress, sharply changed political course without any excuse and took the path of acute deterioration of relations with our party, with the Soviet Union. They began to depart from the commonly agreed line of the whole world Communist movement on the major questions of our times, something which became particularly manifest from the middle of last year.

Now the Albanian leaders do not conceal the fact that they do not like the course, taken by our party, of firmly overcoming the harmful consequences of the Stalin cult, of sharply condemning the abuse of power, of restoring Leninist norms of Party and state life.

Evidently the Albanian leaders in their hearts disagreed with the conclusions of the 1957 and 1960 conferences of fraternal parties, which, as everyone knows, approved the decisions of the 20th Congress and our party's policy of overcoming the harmful consequences of the cult of the individual. This stand of the Albanian leaders is explained by the fact that they themselves, to our regret and distress, are repeating the methods that occurred in our country in the period of the cult of the individual.

We are following events in Albania with a feeling of anxiety for the destinies of the heroic Albanian people. We are pained to see that rank-and-file Albanian Communists and the whole Albanian people, who are vitally interested in friendship and cooperation with all the socialist countries, are obliged to pay for the mistaken line of the Albanian leaders. We are deeply troubled by this situation and have persistently sought and are seeking ways of overcoming the differences that have arisen.

The course drawn up by the 20th Congress of our party is a Leninist course, and we cannot concede on this fundamental question to either the Albanian leaders or anyone else. To depart from the 20th Congress line would mean not heeding the wise instructions of Lenin, who discerned the danger of the appearance of the Stalin cult even when it was in embryo. It would mean disregarding the costly lessons of history, forgetting the price that our party paid for not having heeded in time the instructions of its great leader.

Now the Albanian leaders, opposing the 20th Congress policy, are trying to pull our party back to ways that they like but that will never be repeated in our country. Our party will continue firmly and unswervingly to carry out the line of its 20th Congress, a line that has withstood the test of time. No one will succeed in diverting us from the Leninist path! (*Stormy, prolonged applause*)

If the Albanian leaders hold dear the interest of their people and the cause of building socialism in Albania, if they really want friendship with the CPSU, with all the fraternal parties, they should renounce their mistaken views and return to the path of unity and close cooperation in the fraternal family of the socialist commonwealth, the path of unity with the whole international Communist movement.

As for our party, it will continue, in keeping with its internationalist duty, to do everything it can so that Albania may march shoulder to shoulder with all the socialist countries.

From the rostrum of the 22nd Congress we declare that purity of the Marxist-Leninist teaching and irreconcilability with any kind of distortions of its great principles are law for our party. (*Prolonged applause*) Communists hold the cause of the revolution, the cause of the people, above all else, and its leaders are worthy of the name only when they express the vital interests of the working people and follow the true path. Such leaders and chiefs are forged in the course of the struggle itself, they win authority by their service to the people, to the cause of Communism, they serve the people and should be under the people's control. (*Stormy applause*)

DOCUMENT 9

"Declaration of the Central Committee of the Albanian Party of Labor," Zëri i Popullit, *October 21, 1961 (complete text).*

N. Khrushchev attacked the Albanian Party of Labor publicly at the 22nd Congress of the Communist Party of the Soviet Union. The anti-Marxist slanders and attacks of N. Khrushchev serve only the enemies of Communism and the Albanian People's Republic — the various imperialists and the Yugoslav revisionists. N. Khrushchev, by revealing to the enemies the differences which have long existed between the leadership of the Communist Party of the Soviet Union and the Albanian Party of Labor, brutally violated the 1960 Moscow Declaration, which stresses that differences arising between fraternal parties should be settled patiently in the spirit of proletarian internationalism and on the basis of the principles of equality and consultations. By attacking the Albanian Party of Labor publicly, N. Khrushchev in fact began an open attack against the unity of the international Communist and workers movement, against the unity of the socialist camp. N. Khrushchev bears full responsibility for this anti-Marxist act and for all the consequences which may follow.

Guided by the interests of the unity of the international Communist movement and the socialist camp, the Albanian Party of Labor has, since the beginning of our differences with the Soviet leadership, tried with great patience to resolve them in the correct Marxist-Leninist way, the way emphasized by the Moscow Declaration. N. Khrushchev, however, chose the anti-Marxist path of aggravating them — the path of attacks and slanders, of pressure and threats, and of the public airing of our differences.

The Albanian Party of Labor received with sympathy the statement of Comrade Chou En-lai, head of the delegation of the Communist Party of China, at the 22nd Congress of the Communist Party of the Soviet Union, which pointed out that unilateral criticism and public airing of differences existing between fraternal parties before our enemies cannot be considered a serious Marxist-Leninist attitude. However, from the rostrum of the 22nd Congress of the Communist Party of the Soviet Union, even after this principled admonition by the representative of the Communist Party of China, the most vicious attacks and slanders against the Albanian Party of Labor and the Albanian People's Republic are being meted out by certain members of the Soviet leadership and by certain leaders of the Communist and workers parties of other countries. Thus they too are assuming a heavy historical responsibility as the disrupters of the unity of the international Communist and workers movement.

Under such circumstances — in view of the organized anti-Marxist assault of N. Khrushchev and his supporters, in view of the slanders and fabrications designed to discredit our party, and in view of the grave danger to the future destiny of the unity of the international Communist and workers movement and the socialist camp — the Albanian Party of Labor cannot remain silent. By means of facts and documents it will make known to the entire international Communist and workers movement and world public opinion the whole truth concerning the relations between the Albanian Party of Labor and the leadership of the Communist Party of the Soviet Union and on which side the truth lies, and will unmask the anti-Marxist and anti-Albanian activities of N. Khrushchev and his group.

The unity of the socialist camp and the international Communist and workers movement is being seriously endangered by the anti-Marxist activities of N. Khrushchev and his followers. In this situation, the Albanian Party of Labor, with a clear conscience, has assumed and will assume all responsibility before the international Communist and workers movement and before the Albanian people for any action which it may take to defend the lofty interests of the people, the fatherland, and their socialist victories and to safeguard the purity of Marxism-Leninism and the unity of the ranks of the Communist movement and the socialist camp.

The struggle which is being imposed upon our party and people will be long and difficult. But difficulties have never frightened our party and people. Our party and people have been tempered in the struggle against the slanders, attacks, and numerous and repeated plots of the various imperialist and Yugoslav revisionists. They will likewise neither bend nor fall on their knees before the slanderous attacks, blackmail, and pressures of N. Khrushchev and his followers. Our party and our people, with their steel-like unity, will as always march resolutely forward and will triumph on their correct road, the road of the triumph of Marxism-Leninism and the cause of socialism and Communism. We will win because we are not alone. With us, and with the great cause of Marxism-Leninism, are the Communists and the peoples of the Soviet Union, who are linked to us by an indestructible love and friendship which we will always preserve intact in our hearts regardless of storm or stress; with us are the Communists and the people of China, all the Communists of the world, and the peoples of the other socialist countries. The victorious banner of the party, the invincible banner of Marxism-Leninism, will always wave proudly in the new socialist Albania.

Signed: The Central Committee of the Albanian Party of Labor. Tirana, October 20, 1961.

DOCUMENT 10

Public telegrams sent in support of the Central Committee of the Albanian Party of Labor against Khrushchev's attacks at the 22nd Congress.

Telegram sent by the workers collective of the Enver Factory, *Zëri i Popullit,* October 22, 1961.

Dear Comrades:

We have never been more indignant and annoyed than when we read the shameless slanders and false accusations made by N. Khrushchev at the 22nd Congress of the Communist Party of the Soviet Union against our Party of Labor and its tested Marxist-Leninist leadership by Comrade Enver Hoxha — the founder and leader of the party.

N. Khrushchev accuses us of changing our course and of moving away from the Soviet Union, the socialist camp, and proletarian internationalism. These are the coarsest slanders, and we reject them with contempt and disdain. The means and manner in which he has chosen to fight against the Albanian Party of Labor are doomed to failure. There is no power and can be no power on earth capable of separating our people from the party. We are with the party, with our Central Committee, and with Comrade Enver. We are convinced that our path is just. It is precisely for this reason that we fully support with all our hearts the Declaration of the Central Committee of the Albanian Party of Labor, and will support it always in the future, through storm and stress, until the final victory.

We assure you, dear comrades, that, united as a single body and as strong as steel, headed by our beloved party, we shall always be mobilized and ready for this long and difficult struggle which N. Khrushchev and his followers are imposing upon our party and people. The Albanian people prefer to die on their feet [rather] than to live on their knees. This admirable trait of our people has been further strengthened by our illustrious party during these past 20 years. We are convinced that the final victory belongs to us, to glorious Marxism-Leninism, and to socialism and Communism.

Telegram sent by the participants of the meeting of Military Unit No. 3337 in Korçë, *Zëri i Popullit,* October 22, 1961.

Dear Comrades:

We soldiers, noncommissioned officers, and officers of Military Unit No. 3337 learned with profound indignation of the false accusations made by N. Khrushchev against the Albanian Party of Labor. We resolutely reject them. These unprincipled attacks serve only the enemies of socialism, who are trying to disrupt the unity of the socialist camp and the international Communist movement and to destroy the eternal friendship between the Albanian and Soviet peoples — a friendship which was sealed by the blood of our peoples in the heat of the struggle against the fascist invaders.

The glorious path followed by our party during these 20 years clearly proves that it has faithfully implemented the teachings of Marxism-Leninism and that it has always honorably fulfilled its internationalist duties. The great victory of our people's revolution and the brilliant successes achieved in the construction of socialism in Albania were achieved thanks to the correct Marxist-Leninist leadership of our party. There is no slander capable of obscuring this fact and undermining the steel-like unity of the people around the party and its Central Committee, headed by Comrade Enver Hoxha.

We, the soldiers and officers of Unit No. 3337, in reply to these attacks and accusations, once again assure the Central Committee that we shall always remain faithful to the teachings of the party, that we shall increase our revolutionary vigilance, that we shall further strengthen our military preparedness, and that we shall always stand ready to defend to the end the sacred boundaries of our beloved fatherland, the Albanian People's Republic.

Telegram sent by the workers collective of the sugar combine, "8 November," in Maliq, *Bashkimi,* October 29, 1961.

Dear Comrades:

Our anger over N. Khrushchev's new slanders and attacks against our glorious party and its Marxist-Leninist leadership is indescribable.

The history of our party attests to its uncompromising struggle against the imperialists and revisionists, its determined struggle to protect the purity of Marxism-Leninism, and its resolute struggle to strengthen the unity of the socialist camp and the international Communist and workers movement.

Since its founding 20 years ago, our party has never departed from the defense of the interests of the people and the interests of socialism. It is precisely for this reason that our party has been viciously attacked by the imperialists and Yugoslav revisionists. It is also precisely for this reason that today N. Khrushchev is attacking our party.

One must either be blind or else have decided to make common cause with the imperialists and Yugoslav revisionists in order to accuse our party of laying the groundwork for meriting the alms of imperialism. How repugnant are these accusations, which resemble like two drops of water the slanders of the imperialists and of Tito against our party and people. Who can believe such fabrications when it is well known by all how our party has struggled and is struggling against the imperialists and the Yugoslav revisionists? How ridiculous are those who repeat the lies which have long since lost their punch.

All those who speak this way, be it the imperialists, Tito, or even Khrushchev, know by now how our party has defended the interests and the honor of the Albanian people and the interests of socialism.

By acting in this manner, unprecedented for one who calls himself a Communist, Khrushchev is exposing to the whole world the face of an anti-Marxist, conspirator, and common putschist. He wants Albania to experience the same thing that Tito brought about in Hungary in October 1956. Everyone knows the tragedy which occurred at that time. Everyone knows who prepared it and how it happened. This will not happen in Albania. The plot which Tito had planned against Albania failed in 1956. The same thing will happen now with the plot of N. Khrushchev.

Never before in the history of the international Communist and workers movement has a leader of a Marxist-Leninist party attacked, prepared a putsch, and made a vigorous appeal for an uprising against a country which is building socialism and against a party which is struggling with all its strength and energy for the triumph of the great ideas of Marxism-Leninism, the triumph of socialism and Communism. Only the Yugoslav revisionists, who have nothing in common with Marxism-Leninism, have behaved in this manner, and now N. Khrushchev and his group are behaving in the same way.

Dear Comrades, profoundly angered by these new attacks and slanders, we pledge to you that the enemies of the party and the people will never make us yield. We tell the party: Hold high the banner of Marx, Engels, Lenin, and Stalin because, as always, we shall further strengthen our ranks around the party and its Central Committee, headed by Comrade Enver Hoxha, our most beloved son.

Excerpt from telegram sent by the workers of the clothing cooperative of Gjirokastër, *Zëri i Popullit,* October 29, 1961.

Dear Comrades:

We learned with deep indignation and hatred of the new and still more vile attack which N. Khrushchev made against our Party of Labor and our people in his closing speech at the 22nd Congress of the Communist Party of the Soviet Union.

It is now becoming as plain as day to every Communist and honest person in the world that N. Khrushchev, in his fight against our party and against Marxism-Leninism and the unity of the international Communist and workers movement, has gone beyond demagogy and hypocrisy and has exposed his true nature as a conspirator. His recent speech reminds us of the Christmas greetings issued by the presidents of the United States from the White House in which they shed crocodile tears for the fate of the Albanian people and call on them to overthrow the people's power. How sad it is that he has fallen so low! N. Khrushchev will enjoy the same success as Dulles and his associates. We assure him that he will gain nothing but our anger and curses.

N. Khrushchev has gone so far as to accuse the tested leadership of our party of deliberately guiding our party and our people away from the Soviet Union and the socialist camp in order to create a favorable basis for selling out the lofty interests of the fatherland and socialism for 30 pieces of silver, like Judas, and thus meriting the alms of the imperialists. How aggravating this slander is! Today everyone in the world knows that those who have sold their body and soul for 30 pieces of silver and who have merited alms from the imperialists are the Judas Tito and his associates, whom we have branded as traitors, while N. Khrushchev himself is openly defending them. Our party and our people have never bowed to imperialism, they have never held out their hand to beg, and this will never happen in the future either. We are convinced that Khrushchev knows very well from his own experience that the Albanian Communists and people are not for sale and that they will not live on alms. Our people and our party consider imperialism and revisionism the main threats to peace and to the unity of the international workers movement. Therefore, we have been and we shall continue to be uncompromising toward them. . . .

DOCUMENT 11

Khrushchev's speech on Albania and the Stalin Cult, delivered on October 27, 1961, to the 22nd Congress, Pravda, *October 29, 1961 (excerpts from* CDSP, *XIII, 46 [December 13, 1961]).*

. . . Comrades! The Central Committee's report and also speeches by delegates to the Congress have referred to the erroneous position of the leaders of the Albanian Party of Labor, who have taken the path of combating the line of our party's 20th Congress and undermining the foundations of friendship with the Soviet Union and other socialist countries.

The representatives of the fraternal parties have declared in their speeches that they share our alarm over the state of affairs in the Albanian Party of Labor and roundly condemn the dangerous actions of its leaders, which are prejudicing the fundamental interests of the Albanian people and the solidarity of the entire socialist commonwealth. The speeches by delegates and by representatives of the fraternal parties are convincing evidence that our party's Central Committee was absolutely correct in reporting to the Congress, openly and as a matter of principle, on the abnormal state of Soviet-Albanian relations.

We were obliged to do this because our repeated attempts to normalize relations with the Albanian Party of Labor have unfortunately borne no fruit. I should like to emphasize that the Central Committee of our party has shown a maximum of patience and has done everything in its power to restore good relations between our parties.

The members of the Presidium of the Central Committee of the CPSU have tried time and again to get together with the Albanian leaders and discuss the issues that have arisen. Back in August, 1960, we twice proposed a meeting to the Albanian leaders, but they avoided it. They were equally persistent in declining to have talks with us at the time of the Moscow conference of fraternal parties in November, 1960.

When, at the insistence of the Central Committee of the CPSU, such a meeting did take place, Enver Hoxha and Mehmet Shehu disrupted it and moved on to actions that can only be described as provocative. The leaders of the Albanian Party of Labor made a deliberate show of walking out on the November conference, indicating their refusal to defer to the collective opinion of the fraternal parties. To our subsequent suggestions that we meet, exchange views, and resolve our differences they again responded with a rude refusal, and they stepped up their campaign of attacks and slander against our party and its Central Committee.

There are no expedients that the leaders of the Albanian Party of Labor shrink from using in their efforts to hide from their people the truth about what our party and people are doing. Albania is the only country in the socialist camp in which the draft Program of the CPSU was not published in full. The Albanian press carried only sections of the draft, deliberately creating a distorted impression of our party's activities. This fact speaks for itself. After all, even Communism's adversaries were unable to pass over our Program in silence.

We can understand why the Albanian leaders are concealing the CPSU Program from their party and people. They fear the truth like the plague. The Party Program is something sacred for us, our lodestar in the building of Communism.

Had they published it in full, the working people of Albania would have been able to tell truth from slander, would have seen that all our party's activities, all its plans accord with the vital interests of the peoples, including the interests of the Albanian people, who are friendly to us. (*Prolonged applause*)

Our great party has more than once been subjected to bitter and filthy attacks from open and covert enemies of Communism. But it must be said outright that we do not recall an instance in which anyone shifted with such dizzying speed from protestations and vows of eternal friendship to unbridled anti-Soviet slander as the Albanian leaders have done.

Presumably they expect in this way to lay the groundwork for earning handouts from the imperialists. The imperialists are always willing to pay thirty pieces of silver to those who cause a split in the ranks of the Communists. But pieces of silver have never brought anyone anything but dishonor and shame. (*Applause*)

Clearly, the Central Committee of our party could not fail to tell the Congress the whole truth about the reprehensible stand taken by the leadership of the Albanian Party of Labor. Had we not done so, they would have gone on claiming that the Central Committee of the Communist Party of the Soviet Union was afraid to let the Party know of its differences with the leadership of the Albanian Party of Labor. Our party and the Soviet people should know how the Albanian leaders have been acting. And let the Congress, which is empowered to speak for the whole Party, state its attitude to this matter, pronounce its authoritative opinion.

It has been emphasized at our Congress that we are prepared to normalize relations with the Albanian Party of Labor on the basis of Marxist-Leninist principles. How have the Albanian leaders responded to this? They have lashed out at our party and its Central Committee with a blatant, mud-slinging statement.

Comrade Chou En-lai, head of the delegation of the Communist Party of China, voiced concern in his speech over our having openly raised the issue of Albanian-Soviet relations at the Congress. As far as we can see, his statement primarily reflects alarm lest the present state of our relations with the Albanian Party of Labor affect the solidarity of the socialist camp.

We share the anxiety of our Chinese friends and appreciate their concern for the strengthening of unity. If the Chinese comrades wish to apply their efforts to normalizing the Albanian Party of Labor's relations with the fraternal parties, it is doubtful whether there is anyone better able to facilitate accomplishment of this purpose than the Communist Party of China. This would really redound to the benefit of the Albanian Party of Labor and accord with the interests of the entire commonwealth of socialist countries. (*Prolonged applause*)

It is true, of course, that Communists should so frame their inter-Party relations as not to provide the enemy with the slightest opening. But unfortunately the Albanian leaders have grossly flouted this requirement. For a long time now they have been openly attacking the line of the 20th Congress, providing the bourgeois press with food for all sorts of speculation. It is they, the Albanian leaders, who have been shouting from the rooftops about having a position of their own, views of their own that differ from the views of our party and the other fraternal parties. This showed clearly at the Fourth Congress of the Albanian Party of Labor, and has been particularly clear of late.

Why did the Albanian leaders launch a campaign against the decisions of our party's 20th Congress? What treason do they see in them?

Above all, the resolute condemnation of the Stalin cult and its harmful consequences is not to the liking of the Albanian leaders. They are displeased that we should have resolutely denounced the arbitrary rule, the abuse of power from which many innocent people suffered, among them eminent representatives of the old guard who had been with Lenin in building the world's first proletarian state. The Albanian leaders cannot refer without vexation and rancor to the fact that we have put an end for good to the situation where one man at his own pleasure arbitrarily decided all-important questions relating to the life of our party and country. (*Prolonged applause*)

Stalin is no longer among the living, but we have thought it necessary to denounce the disgraceful methods of leadership that flourished in the setting of the Stalin cult. Our party is doing everything possible to prevent phenomena of this sort from ever again recurring.

One would have supposed that the Leninist line of the 20th Party Congress, which was supported by the fraternal parties, would have met with support from the leadership of the Albanian Party of Labor too, since the cult of the individual is incompatible with Marxism-Leninism. Actually, the Albanian leaders heaped encomiums on the Stalin cult and launched a violent campaign against the decisions of the 20th Party Congress, in an effort to make the socialist countries swerve from this sound course. This, naturally, was no accident. All that was reprehensible in our country in the period of the cult of the individual is manifested in its worst form in the Albanian Party of Labor. It is now an open secret that the Albanian leaders remain in power by resorting to force and arbitrary rule.

For a long time now there has existed in the Albanian Party of Labor an abnormal, evil situation in which any person objectionable to the leadership is liable to meet with cruel persecution.

Where today are the Albanian Communists who built the Party, who fought the Italian and German invaders? Nearly all of them are victims of the bloody misdeeds of Mehmet Shehu and Enver Hoxha.

The Central Committee of the CPSU has received more than one letter from Albanian Communists appealing to us to restrain the Albanian leaders from dealing savagely with the finest sons and daughters of the Albanian Party of Labor. The delegates to the Congress can form their own idea of the Albanian leaders' moral complexion by having a look at some of these letters.

The Albanian leaders reproach us with meddling in the internal affairs of the Albanian Party of Labor. I should like to tell you what form this so-called meddling took.

A few years ago the Central Committee of the CPSU interceded with the Albanian leaders over the fate of Liri Gega, a former member of the Politburo of the Central Committee of the Albanian Party of Labor, who had been sentenced to death along with her husband. This woman had for a number of years been a member of leading bodies of the Albanian Party of Labor and had taken part in the Albanian people's struggle for liberation. In approaching the Albanian leaders at the time, we were guided by considerations of humanity, by anxiety to prevent the shooting of a woman, and a pregnant woman at that. We felt and still feel that as a fraternal party we had a right to state our opinion in the matter. After all, even in the blackest days of rampant reaction, the tsarist satraps, who tortured revolutionaries, scrupled to execute pregnant women. And here, in a socialist country, they had sentenced to death, and they executed, a woman who was about to become a mother, they had shown altogether unwarranted cruelty. (*Stir in the hall. Shouts: "Shame! Shame!"*)

People of integrity today incur punishment in Albania just for daring to come out for Soviet-Albanian friendship, which the Albanian leaders are fond of talking about in such high-sounding and florid terms.

Comrades Liri Belishova and Koço Tashko, prominent figures in the Albanian Party of Labor, were not only expelled from the Party's Central Committee but are now being called enemies of the Party and the people. And all this merely because Liri Belishova and Koço Tashko had the courage honestly and openly to voice their disagreement with the policy of the Albanian leaders and took a stand for Albanian solidarity with the Soviet Union and the other socialist countries.

People who today advocate friendship with the Soviet Union, with the CPSU, are regarded by the Albanian leaders as enemies.

How is all this to be squared with the vows and protestations of friendly feelings for the CPSU and the Soviet Union that have been heard from Shehu and Hoxha? It is obvious that all their spouting about friendship is nothing but hypocrisy and deception.

This is the atmosphere that prevails in the Albanian Party of Labor, and this is why the Albanian leaders oppose the Leninist line of the 20th Party Congress. After all, to put an end to the cult of the individual would in effect mean that Shehu, Hoxha, and others would have to give up their key positions in the Party and government. And this they do not want to do. But we are certain the time will come when the Albanian Communists and the Albanian people will have their say, and then the Albanian leaders will have to answer for the harm they have done their country, their people, and the cause of socialist construction in Albania. (*Stormy, prolonged applause*)

Comrades! Our party will continue to combat revisionists of all shades as it has in the past. Steadfastly conforming to the principles of the Declaration and the Statement of the conferences of Marxist-Leninist parties, we have exposed and shall continue unremittingly to expose the revisionism that has found expression in the program of the League of Communists of Yugoslavia. We shall also constantly combat dogmatism and all other deviations from Marxism-Leninism. (*Applause*)

DOCUMENT 12

"Marxism-Leninism Will Triumph," Zëri i Popullit, *November 1, 1961 (complete text)*.

The 22nd Congress of the Communist Party of the Soviet Union has concluded its work. It has approved the draft of the new party program and defined the future objectives. The Soviet people now face the task of the construction of Communism, the banner of which bears the following inscription: "From Each According to His Ability, to Each According to His Needs." Communism, the dream of mankind, is now on the agenda. It is being built by the Soviet people, who were the first to break the shackles of capitalist slavery, the first to establish a regime of workers and peasants, and the first to embark upon the road to socialism.

During the past 44 years, since November 7, 1917, when the guns of the "Aurora" proclaimed a new era — the era of socialism and Communism — the Soviet people have achieved great successes. The Soviet Union is now the most powerful socialist state with a large and modern industry, a developed agriculture, and the most advanced science and technology in the world. The day is not far off when Lenin's fatherland will occupy first place in the world in over-all industrial output and in per capita production. The 22nd Congress of the Communist Party of the Soviet Union mapped out the road leading to the achievement of this historic task within as brief a period of time as possible.

The Soviet Union is also the most powerful state defending world peace. At the head of the socialist camp, it is fighting the imperialist schemes to unleash a new war. Its foreign policy of peace and friendship between peoples — its policy of peaceful coexistence between states with different social systems, of defending the freedom and independence of the oppressed and newly liberated peoples from the colonial yoke — is being endorsed and supported by all the peace-loving peoples. The 22nd CPSU Congress, which convened at a time when the international situation had become greatly aggravated, also assigned new tasks in the struggle against the diabolical imperialist plans in order to preserve world peace.

The achievements of the Soviet Union are of historic significance not only for the Soviet people but for all the people in the world. The Albanian people, who are linked to the Soviet people by eternal friendship, rejoice at these achievements as if they were their own. The Albanian Party of Labor and the Albanian people wholeheartedly greet the builders of Communism who, guided by the great party of Lenin, are marching forward to new victories.

Our party and people will in the future, as in the past, march beside the Communist Party of the Soviet Union and the Soviet people along the enlightened path of Communism and peace. There is not and will never be any force in the world which can divert our party and people from this path and from friendship with the Soviet Union. We wish the Communists and Soviet people new successes in the realization of the tasks set by the 22nd Congress of the Communist Party of the Soviet Union for the construction of Communism. We say to the Communists and Soviet people that we will never confuse the party and the fatherland of the great Lenin with the anti-Marxist and provocative attacks launched by N. Khrushchev and his group against our party and people, against Marxism-Leninism, and against the unity of the international Communist movement.

At the 22nd Congress of the Communist Party of the Soviet Union N. Khrushchev openly attacked the Albanian Party of Labor. In violation of the most elementary principles of the relations between Communist and workers parties, the principles of proletarian internationalism, and the 1957 and 1960 Moscow Declarations, he raised his hand and struck with a force and in language which he did not use even against the imperialists and their obedient lackeys — the Yugoslav revisionists.

The path that N. Khrushchev chose and the methods he used in his attack against the Albanian Party of Labor, against a party which has always resolutely defended the principles of Marxism-Leninism and proletarian internationalism, the party of a people eternally friendly to the Soviet Union, clearly unmask the aim of N. Khrushchev and his anti-Marxist group to turn the 22nd Congress of the Communist Party of the Soviet Union into a platform for his open attack on Marxism-Leninism, on the unity of the international Communist movement and of the socialist camp.

Along with the attack against the Albanian Party of Labor, his conspiracy against international Communism also came out into the open. Long ago N. Khrushchev began his attacks against Marxism-Leninism in order to revise its fundamental theses. For a long time he has been undermining relations between the Communist and workers parties and the countries of the socialist camp. For a long time he has been plotting against the Marxist-Leninist parties by relying on the support of revisionist elements, and then finally he came out into the open as a disrupter of the international Communist movement.

Neither demagogy nor intrigue can conceal this great truth. They cannot save N. Khrushchev and his group from being branded as disrupters and subverters of international Communism. Neither demagogy nor intrigue can absolve him from responsibility for the crime he committed in declaring war on the Albanian people, who are building socialism under the burden of geographical encirclement by capitalist states and the Yugoslav revisionists.

N. Khrushchev tried by all means to win the approval of the 22nd Congress of the Communist Party of the Soviet Union and the representatives of the Communist and workers parties at this Congress for his conspiracy against the international Communist movement and the socialist camp. What did he and the members of his group say against the Albanian Party of Labor?

The Albanian leaders are not in agreement with our 20th Congress, our struggle against Stalin, and our leadership; therefore, they cannot belong to the family of international Communism. This, in short, was the content of N. Khrushchev's accusations against the Albanian Party of Labor in his first report — amazing logic. According to this, the conclusion emerges that the decisions of one party, even when some of its positions are incorrect, are binding on all other Communist and workers parties, and that if someone disagrees with N. Khrushchev's revisionist theses, he ceases to be a Communist. Our party noted at the November 1960 Moscow meeting that some of the theses of the 20th Congress of the Communist Party of the Soviet Union have served not the Communist movement but rather its enemies, that the fight against the cult of Stalin, in the form that it assumed, benefited the revisionists and the open enemies of socialism, and that N. Khrushchev was using impermissible methods of pressure and conspiracy to subjugate our party.

These are the "faults" with which N. Khrushchev charged our party at the 22nd Congress of the Communist Party of the Soviet Union. These are also the "arguments" which were used to "convince" the delegates of the congress and the representatives of the fraternal parties of the "retreat" of the Albanian Party of Labor from the positions of Marxism-Leninism and proletarian internationalism, of its "fall" into positions of narrow nationalism, adventurism, and anti-Sovietism, and of its "passing" into the arms of imperialism.

However, it should be noted that he did not succeed in this. With the exception of the leading group, which followed N. Khrushchev in the fabrication of slanders and banal abuse against our party, the delegates of the 22nd Congress of the CPSU did not follow the path in which he sought to lead them. The same thing happened with many of the representatives of the fraternal Communist and workers parties at the congress, who did not speak against the Albanian Party of Labor. There were also representatives such as Comrade Chou En-lai, the representative of the Chinese Communist Party, who openly opposed N. Khrushchev's anti-Marxist act.

Of 71 representatives of the fraternal parties who spoke at the congress, 25 did not attack the Albanian Party of Labor, although they may have had reservations concerning our party since it cannot be excluded that a party may hold certain critical views regarding another party. But this is not bad; this is natural. It is the methods and means N. Khrushchev used to impose his own will upon our party, to subdue it, and to conspire against it that are deplorable.

Logically enough, after this defeat N. Khrushchev took the next step. Determined to pursue the issue to the end in order to achieve his aim of dividing the international Communist movement, in his concluding speech he abandoned questions of principle and turned to slander and unfounded allegations against the Albanian Party of Labor, which proves his complete lack of evidence and which shows what a pseudo-Marxist we are dealing with.

What did he say, precisely, when he furiously assaulted the party and the Albanian people? Such a reign of terror has been established in Albania that even pregnant women are shot. The Albanian Party of Labor is a party of terrorists and criminals, and the Albanian Party of Labor and the Albanian state are headed by foreign agents who work against the interests of the people. Therefore, the Communists and the people should rise up and overthrow this regime. This is the main substance of Khrushchev's accusations in his concluding speech. What is there of Marxism in this? How does it differ from what the imperialists and Belgrade revisionists are saying? All these charges are so petty that no man with brains and a clear conscience could believe them or, worse, could accept them as "proof" of the retreat of the Albanian Party of Labor from the positions of Marxism-Leninism. Needless to say, such fabrications cannot stand because they are false, because they are filthy lies taken from the imperialist anti-Albanian propaganda arsenal, because they are slander manufactured in Belgrade by the Yugoslav revisionists. They are data collected by the enemies of the Albanian Party of Labor and international Communism.

The answer which our people gave to the attacks and slanders and the open appeal of N. Khrushchev and his group for a revolt against the party to overthrow the people's power is now known to everybody. The numerous telegrams which we have published, and which are only a small part of the thousands of telegrams which have reached and are reaching the Central Committee from all over the country, show clearly what indignation and contempt they have caused throughout the country. Words are inadequate. The people are revolted — and rightly so — because they hear from N. Khrushchev's lips the same slanders they have heard for 17 years in succession from the enemies of socialism.

For 17 years now our people have heard the appeals of the United States State Department to "overthrow the Tirana terroristic regime." This appeal is also being made by the Titoist clique. The same thing is being said by the Greek monarcho-fascists. Karamanlis and Venizelos. The Italian neofascists are singing the same tune.

For 17 consecutive years, faithfully and courageously led by their Marxist-Leninist Party, our people have confronted and destroyed all the plots organized by these elements together or separately.

What can the Albanian Communists and the Albanian people say about N. Khrushchev when they hear that he has joined the chorus of their sworn enemies — the chorus of the enemies of socialism?

What too can the Albanian Communists and the Albanian people say when they know that the troops and supporters of the imperialists and the Yugoslav revisionists in their fight against our party and country were the traitors to the Albanian people, the spies, and the renegades from the party, and when they see that the hope of N. Khrushchev in his fight against our party and country are the traitors and renegades of the party? But this is not surprising. This is the inevitable result of the deviation of N. Khrushchev from the positions of Marxism-Leninism and his embarking upon the road of plots — a result which inevitably leads him to disaster.

At the 22nd Congress of the Communist Party of the Soviet Union, however, certain leaders of the fraternal Communist and workers parties who participated in this congress joined N. Khrushchev in his attacks on our Party of Labor and the unity of the international Communist movement. We are referring particularly to the representatives of the Communist and workers parties of the capitalist countries. They looked only at one side of the question. They do not know, in fact, how the relations developed between us and N. Khrushchev's anti-Marxist group. N. Khrushchev's workshop presented them with fabrications. For this reason, we tell these comrades that they did not weigh the matter properly. They unjustly accused our party.

It is clear then why N. Khrushchev began an open fight against our party and people. The purposes and the means to achieve them are also known. The end result is also certain: Marxism-Leninism will triumph. A fight was imposed upon our party and people which they did not want; now, however, they cannot avoid it. This is a difficult fight — it may be a long fight. The difficulties, however, have never frightened us and will never frighten us. The struggle against N. Khrushchev's designs, aimed at splitting the international Communist movement, at revising the fundamental principles of Marxism-Leninism, and at undermining the socialist victories achieved by the Soviet Union and the other countries of the socialist camp, is the struggle for Marxism-Leninism. This fight must be fought to the finish, until Marxism-Leninism is completely victorious over its enemies, the revisionists. This is the fight of all Marxist-Leninists throughout the world against revisionism. Our party and people will steadfastly struggle, along with all the Communists and the international Communist and workers parties in the world, for the triumph of Marxism-Leninism and for the unity of the international Communist movement and the socialist camp. Our party and people will also steadfastly struggle for friendship with the Soviet Union and for building socialism in our country.

Our party and people will also in the future fight against the imperialists' plans for unleashing a new war and the plots of the imperialists and their lackeys, the Yugoslav revisionists, who hate the sight of our country. N. Khrushchev referred to the alms of the imperialists. He should not expect us to accept such alms. He should look for that among his friends, the revisionists. The People's Republic of Albania has never accepted and will never accept alms from anyone, much less from the imperialists.

The attacks of N. Khrushchev and his group neither frighten nor shake the Albanian Party of Labor. There is no force on earth that could divert our party from the path of Marxism-Leninism. In this struggle, our people stand together with all the Communists in the world, even with the Communists of the Soviet Union. The Albanian Party of Labor and the Albanian people have been and will always be, to the end, with the party of the great Lenin and the Soviet people. Even at the present time — when N. Khrushchev has raised his hand and is savagely attacking us, as he is attacking the Communist Party of the Soviet Union and the Soviet people first of all and the whole of international Communism — our party and people stand by the Soviet Communists and the Soviet people. Dear comrades and friends, we are with you and will always be with you. Our just cause will triumph. This is what all the Albanian Communists and the Albanian people say.

This is not the first time that the enemies of socialism have attacked Marxism-Leninism. This is not the first time and will not be the last time that they will meet with disaster. We are convinced of this — we are fighting for it.

We learn from the history of Communism that its enemies do not have the courage to meet face to face with Marxism-Leninism. They try to muddle and to deceive the people with demagogy and pseudo-Marxist phrases and by professions of fidelity to Marxism-Leninism. For this reason, vigilance is necessary. We are convinced that the Communists and the Soviet people will reflect on the attacks which N. Khrushchev is making today against the Albanian Party of Labor and the whole international Communist movement; they will reflect on and see the great plot which N. Khrushchev began to put into operation a long time ago and which is now assuming greater proportions, and they will understand that if this plot is not unmasked and forcefully opposed, it will become dangerous and will cause great suffering.

Vigilance and courage to avoid being deceived by the plotters' intrigues and to pull the detonators from the mines which they have laid and which they are preparing to set off — these are needed by all Communists, all revolutionaries, and all those who dearly care for the great cause of Marx, Engels, Lenin, and Stalin — the cause of Communism, democracy, social progress, and peace.

DOCUMENT 13

"The Name and Deeds of J. V. Stalin Live and Will Continue to Live for Centuries to Come," Zëri i Popullit, *November 2, 1961 (complete text).*

J. V. Stalin, as a loyal pupil of Lenin, displayed great qualities throughout the whole history of the Communist Party of the Soviet Union in the struggle for the triumph of the great October Socialist Revolution and for the creation of the first socialist state in the world, in the struggle for the defense of the victories of the proletarian revolution and of the Soviet state against the attacks of the enemies within the country and abroad, in the struggle for the final triumph of socialism and the creation of the conditions for the building of Communism. Together with the great Lenin, Stalin was one of the leaders of the October Socialist Revolution, one of the founders of the first workers and peasants state in the world. J. V. Stalin was and remains a titanic figure in the history of mankind, in the history of the international Communist and workers movement, and in the struggle for the liberation of the peoples from imperialist subjugation. He was in the front ranks of those fighting for the creation of a revolutionary party of a new type. Together with Lenin he made a distinguished contribution to the formulation of the ideological, organizational, tactical, and theoretical bases of the Soviet Communist Party, forging it into a revolutionary party.

Current history knows J. V. Stalin as an indomitable revolutionary, a great theoretician, and a brilliant organizer. After Lenin's death Stalin, with competence, courage, and loyalty to Marxism-Leninism, led the Soviet party and people on the road to the construction of socialism under conditions of capitalist encirclement. The enemies of socialism, the enemies of the Soviet people and of the Communist Party, the imperialists and opportunists of all shades, tried their utmost to divert the Soviet party and people from the Leninist road, to split it from the inside, to divest the working class of its confidence in its strength and in the possibility of building socialism and Communism. J. V. Stalin, remaining loyal all his life to Leninism and to the advice of the great Lenin, courageously led the party and people in the fierce struggle against the traitors to the cause of socialism, in the liquidation of the Trotskyites, Bukharinites, Zinovievites, bourgeois nationalists, and other vicious enemies who had tried to disarm the party ideologically, to disrupt its unity, and to destroy the Soviet regime and the socialist revolution.

The Communist Party of the Soviet Union, led by its Leninist Central Committee headed by J. V. Stalin, always loyal to the teachings of Lenin, mapped out the monumental plan of socialist industrialization. The Soviet people, implementing this colossal program within a historically brief period, transformed a technically backward Russia into one of the world's most advanced industrial powers. During the five-year plans a sound basis for socialist construction was created, as were the giants of industry, the new branches of the heavy machine building industry, which played a decisive role both in the increase of the defensive capacity of the Soviet state and in all-round economic and cultural development. The world historic victory in the patriotic war would not have been assured and the present heights of economic, technical, and scientific progress which led to the conquest of the cosmos would not have been achieved without the party's Leninist line on socialist industrialization, resolutely implemented by the Communist Party of the Soviet Union led by the strong arm of J. V. Stalin, and the struggle against the Trotskyite-Bukharinite plotters and other opportunists, nor without the creative capacity of the Soviet people and the organizing power of the state of the proletarian dictatorship.

The Communist Party of the Soviet Union, headed by J. V. Stalin, successfully implemented the Leninist policy of the collectivization of agriculture. The complete victory of the kolkhozes guaranteed the triumph of socialism in the countryside and strengthened the alliance of the working class with the peasantry — the supreme principle of the dictatorship of the proletariat.

Under the leadership of the Communist Party of the Soviet Union during the years when it was headed by J. V. Stalin, the Soviet Union became the country of triumphant socialism, exploitation of man by man was abolished once and for all, and the Soviet Union became an example and an inspiration for all mankind.

In the days of the great patriotic struggle against fascism, the sworn enemy of mankind, the Soviet people and their glorious army performed deeds of legendary heroism under the leadership of the party and the supreme commander-in-chief, J. V. Stalin. Stalin was a great military leader, and, at the head of the party, he organized the victory over fascism. He set forth the task and led the Soviet people and army in the liberation of not only the Soviet homeland but also the homelands of other peoples who were suffering under the fascist yoke. Therefore, the peoples of Europe and of the whole world gratefully remember the decisive historic role of the Soviet people and of the Soviet army and its commander-in-chief, J. V. Stalin, in the annihilation of fascist Germany and the liberation of the subjugated peoples.

The present colossal victories of the Soviet people and their magnificent prospects on the road to building Communism have their origin in the great October and the wise leadership of the party, which advanced under the banner of Marx, Lenin, and Stalin.

The 44-year-old path traversed by the great Soviet people and the birth of the world socialist system are, therefore, closely bound up with the life and deeds of J. V. Stalin. These are historic facts which cannot be denied. J. V. Stalin devoted his whole life to the great cause of the revolution, to the liberation of the exploited, to the happiness of peoples, to socialism and Communism. Thus Stalin's name has found a secure and merited place in the history of mankind, in the hearts of the Soviet people and the peoples of the whole world. It is precisely because of this that he incurred the hatred of the enemies of socialism. There is not and will never be any force in the world which can uproot J. V. Stalin from the history and the hearts of the peoples of the world.

But N. Khrushchev imposed upon the 22nd Congress of the CPSU the decision to remove the coffin of J. V. Stalin from the mausoleum in Red Square where he was lying next to V. I. Lenin. In doing so, N. Khrushchev and his group committed another act in the process of "de-stalinization," which he began at the 20th Congress. All the revisionists and opportunists in the world, all the enemies of Marxism-Leninism, from Tito to Brandt and Spaak, from the ideologists of imperialism to the social democratic lackeys, are now using the banner of "anti-Stalinism" in their frenzied struggle against socialism, against the unity of the socialist camp and the international workers movement. By criminally denying and distorting J. V. Stalin's historic role in the struggle of the party and people of the Soviet Union for the cause of Lenin, N. Khrushchev as well is now flying the banner of "anti-Stalinism," that tattered and discredited banner of the savage enemies of Marxism-Leninism and of socialism. Why are N. Khrushchev and his group doing this? He is doing so in order to broaden his prospects for the implementation of a revisionist, anti-Marxist policy. It is precisely for this that the enemies of socialism, the imperialists and their lackeys, the revisionists, have struggled all their lives and continue to struggle with all their strength. The open struggle against J. V. Stalin is a struggle against his immortal deeds, a struggle against Marxism-Leninism. N. Khrushchev and his group are therefore taking upon themselves a heavy responsibility before history, before the Soviet people, before the international Communist movement, and before all the people in the world who love peace, democracy, socialism, and social progress.

DOCUMENT 14

Enver Hoxha, "Speech Delivered at the Celebration of the 20th Anniversary of the Founding of the Albanian Party of Labor and the 44th Anniversary of the Great October Socialist Revolution," Zëri i Popullit, *November 8, 1961 (excerpts). (Revised and edited from the English translation which appeared as a supplement, in plain cover, to the bulletin of the State University of Tirana,* Buletin i Universitetit Shtetëror të Tiranës, *4 [October–December, 1961]).*

[A brief introduction and section praising the role of the Albanian Party of Labor in the historic struggle for the national independence of Albania are omitted — Ed.]

. . . In the past our people had no firm and loyal support in the international arena with whose backing and assistance they could successfully withstand the aggression of the imperialists and liquidate the profound economic, social, and cultural backwardness into which Albania had been plunged by foreign invaders and the domination of the exploiting, reactionary, and backward-looking classes. Our people acquired such support with the triumph of the great October Socialist Revolution, with the birth of the first socialist state in the world, the glorious Soviet Union. (*Stormy applause*)

The triumph of the October Revolution opened a new epoch in the history of mankind, the epoch of the collapse of imperialism and the liquidation of the colonial system, the epoch of the triumph of socialism and Communism in the world. It gave a powerful impetus to the revolutionary struggle of the international working class against the capitalist system and to the liberation struggle of the oppressed peoples against the imperialist yoke. The Soviet Union became the powerful and sure support in the struggle for the liberation of the workers and of all the peoples. The balance of power began to shift with each passing day against capitalism and imperialism and in favor of socialism and the peace-loving peoples. Under the powerful, life-giving influence of the ideas of the great October Revolution, the anti-imperialist and democratic liberation movement acquired new impetus in Albania as well; the Communist and workers movement, on the basis of which the Albanian Communist Party was later created, took root and developed. Thanks to the aid of the glorious Soviet army, which smashed the war machine of Nazi Germany in World War II, it became possible to liberate our country from fascist slavery. The unstinting internationalist aid and support of the Soviet Union after the liberation of the country was the decisive external factor which enabled our country to stand firm as granite in the face of all the plots of the imperialists and their tools, to overcome all difficulties, and to advance with confidence on the road to socialism. Herein lie the roots of the profound, eternal, and indestructible friendship of our people with the glorious, fraternal peoples of the Soviet Union. (*Stormy applause*) This sacred friendship between peoples was forged by our party during the most difficult moment of the common struggle against the fascist scourge, when our country was groaning under the heel of the Italian and German fascist invaders, and when Hitler's hordes were at the gates of Leningrad, Moscow, and Stalingrad; it was sealed with the pure blood of the Albanian partisans and the heroic soldiers of the Soviet army; it was tempered and further strengthened in the common struggle for the construction of socialism and Communism and for peace in the world. Our Party of Labor and the Albanian people have cherished and will always cherish this sacred friendship with the glorious fraternal people of the Soviet Union as the apple of their eye, as their most treasured possession. Neither the maneuvers of the imperialists, the intrigues of the renegade Tito gang, nor the slanders, pressures, blackmails, and blockades of N. Khrushchev have been, are, or will ever be able to break this friendship. (*Applause*) The life-giving Albanian-Soviet friendship will live through the centuries! In celebrating the 44th anniversary of the October Socialist Revolution, the revolution which shook the old world to its foundations and laid the foundations of a new world, our party and our people convey their best wishes to the fraternal Soviet people and the Communist Party of the Soviet Union for new and ever greater victories, for the glory of the great Communist cause. (*Stormy applause*) . . .

[Omitted are comments on the founding of the Albanian Communist Party, the correct line and indestructible ties between the party and the Albanian people, and the role of the party during the wartime partisan struggle and the national liberation of Albania.]

On November 29, 1944, while the renowned Soviet army, routing Hitler's hordes, was bringing liberation to the Yugoslav and Bulgarian peoples and thus creating the objective conditions for the liberation of Albania as well, our valiant partisans completely liberated our fatherland from the invaders and traitors. (*Applause*) Tens of thousands of martyrs, Communists as well as nonparty patriots, gave their lives in this sacred and glorious struggle and with their pure blood prepared the way for our people to march forward toward a happy life, socialism, and Communism. . . .

[Comments omitted on the correct line of the Albanian Party of Labor regarding the postwar entry of Albania on the road to socialism.]

During this period, our party had to wage a bitter life-or-death struggle against the brutal intervention, the hostile activity, and the vicious attacks of the Tito gang on our party and country, as well as against the Trotskyite and subversive activity of Tito's tool Koci Xoxe and his associates, who had placed the party under the control of the security organs which he himself directed, which were flagrantly violating socialist legality and Leninist norms in the party, and which were preparing for the annexation of Albania to the Yugoslav Federal Republic. Our party emerged victorious from this difficult struggle, because it remained ever faithful to the principles of Marxism-Leninism and did not deviate from these principles in the face of the most rabid attacks, slanders, pressures, and blackmail of the traitorous Belgrade gang. The saving aid in this struggle was rendered to our party by the Central Committee of the Communist Party of the Soviet Union and by J. V. Stalin (*applause*), who, in publicized letters on the situation within the Yugoslav Communist Party, unmasked before the world the true nature of this gang of renegades. . . .

[Comments omitted are on the correct application of the principles of Marxism-Leninism in the construction of socialism, on the contrast between prewar and postwar economic, social, and cultural conditions, on the success of the Marxist-Leninist ideological education, and on the Fourth Congress of the Albanian Party of Labor, which marked the completion of the economic base of socialism and the proclamation of the third five-year plan.]

Realizing that our country finds itself geographically encircled by capitalism and revisionism, the party has taught our heroic people to be ever vigilant, to build socialism with a pickaxe in one hand and a rifle in the other and not to lay down the rifle as long as imperialism and its tools exist in the world. (*Stormy applause. All rise. Ovation*) Our party has always kept in mind the question of the defense of the freedom and independence of our country. It has always devoted special attention to the steady strengthening of the defensive might of our country, to the constant improvement of the military capacity and preparedness of our people's army, of the state security forces, and of the border guards. I am happy to inform the whole people that our glorious armed forces are fully in form and prepared militarily to defend the Albanian People's Republic successfully and to give a worthy rebuff to any enemy rash enough to violate the sacred boundaries of our beloved socialist fatherland. (*Applause. All rise. Ovation*)

For the defense of the liberty and independence of our fatherland, our Party of Labor has relied not only on the internal forces of the people but also on the united strength of the entire great camp of socialism. At the same time, as a worthy member of the Warsaw Pact, Albania has discharged and is honorably discharging its internationalist duty to defend the common interests of the socialist camp in the Adriatic and Mediterranean area against any possible imperialist aggression.

Dear Comrades,

Such, in broad outline, is the path traversed by our glorious party during the 20 years of its existence; such are the historic victories achieved by our people under the wise leadership of the party.

These victories can be ascribed first of all to the heroic struggle and efforts of our people, to their ardent patriotism, to their firm determination, to their creative abilities and their talents. This has been and remains the decisive factor in the liberation of our country and the construction of a socialist and Communist society in our country. These victories can be ascribed to the guidance of the Albanian Party of Labor, which at every stage and at every moment has followed a correct general line. Life itself and experience have demonstrated that our line is a Marxist-Leninist line which fully conforms to the vital interests of the Albanian people as well as to the common interests of the socialist camp and the international Communist movement, our great cause of socialism, the freedom of peoples, and peace.

Our party has always preserved its Marxist-Leninist line as pure as crystal and has defended it in bitter combat with various enemies and deviationists, from Anastas Lulo and Sadik Premte, Ymer Dishnica and Sejfulla Malëshova, to Tito and Koci Xoxe, Tuk Jakova and Bedri Spahiu, Liri Gega and Liri Belishova, etc., who have tried to divert our party from its correct path. But our party has always remained as firm as granite. In this struggle, it has maintained and strengthened with each passing day the ideological and organizational unity of its ranks, on the basis of Marxism-Leninism, as one of the most important factors accounting for our victories and for the strength and invincibility of our party in the face of every enemy. We shall preserve this unity with fanaticism, and we shall strengthen it still further.

Convinced from their own experience of the correctness of our party's line, our people have without reservation supported and upheld the party at all times and in all circumstances and have rallied around it in indestructible monolithic unity. In this unity lies the unyielding might of our party and our people, the firm guarantee of all past, present, and future victories of our people. This unity is the most severe blow to all the enemies of the party and the people, to the imperialists and revisionists of all shades. We, the party and the people, shall preserve this unity as the apple of our eye and shall strengthen it unceasingly with each passing day. (*Stormy applause. All rise. Ovation*)

The great historic victories achieved by our people in the struggle for the liberation of the country and for the construction of socialism in a new, independent, and sovereign Albania are due also to the internationalist assistance and support which the Soviet Union first of all and the Chinese People's Republic and the other countries of the socialist camp have given and are giving to our country. The party and the Albanian people will be forever grateful to them for their generous assistance. This assistance is a wonderful expression of the eternal friendship which binds our people to the glorious peoples of the Soviet Union, to the great Chinese people, and to all the peoples of the other socialist countries. We shall always cherish this sacred friendship as our most treasured possession, for therein lies our joint strength and the firm guarantee of our invincibility . . .

The world socialist system, which includes over a billion people with a great economic and military potential, a potential which is constantly increasing at an unprecedented rate, is today the decisive factor in the development of world history. It exerts a tremendous influence on the world; it has become a great attracting and revolutionizing force.

With each passing day the world socialist system is demonstrating more and more its indisputable superiority over the capitalist system. It has become the shield of all the progressive forces in the world, the invincible bulwark of freedom and peace, of democracy and socialism.

The development of socialism with its irresistible momentum and the rise of the national liberation struggle of the peoples to a higher level have inevitably led to the collapse of the imperialist colonial system of slavery. . . .

As a result of the creation and consolidation of the world socialist system and the collapse of the imperialist colonial system, the sphere of imperialist rule has been greatly narrowed, its general crisis has deepened, and all its internal and external national and class contradictions have been sharpened. Today imperialism is no longer the sole and all-powerful master of the world. It can no longer do as it pleases. Its laws do not operate everywhere in the world. The capitalist system, which is heading toward its inevitable doom, is confronted by the powerful and invincible world socialist system, around which all the anti-imperialist revolutionary forces which are fighting for national and social liberation have rallied and continue to rally more and more.

This is the reality of our time, and this reality convincingly shows that the balance of power in the world today has shifted radically and conclusively in favor of socialism and against imperialism. The forces of socialism, the forces of national liberation, peace, and democracy are superior to the forces of imperialism, colonialism, war, and reaction. All this has created a new situation in the world and conditions which are favorable to waging even more successfully the struggle against imperialism and for peace and the promotion of the socialist, national-liberation, and popular democratic revolutions.

The Albanian Party of Labor recognizes and understands the profound changes which have occurred in the world, the new conditions and phenomena which have appeared. But we reject all the attempts by the modern revisionists who, under the guise of "creatively interpreting Marxism under new conditions," are propagating their distorted and opportunist views and seeking to portray them as a further development of Marxism, while they quickly label as dogmatic, sectarian, or adventurous anyone who goes on record against those views. This is a familiar tactic. There is nothing new or original about it. All revisionists and opportunists, from Bernstein to Tito, have denied the basic principles of Marxism under the pretext of "changing conditions" and "new phenomena." As V. I. Lenin used to say, by always masking themselves behind the slogan of the fight against dogmatism, by utilizing "the appropriate little word: dogmatist," they rise up against Marxism.

Correct, revolutionary Marxist-Leninist conclusions must be drawn from the changes which have occurred in the world; conclusions must be drawn which will not create pacifist and reformist illusions, which will not weaken the struggle against imperialism but will strengthen ever more this just struggle. Conclusions must be drawn which will not postpone the cause of revolution but will bring it ever closer, which will not divert the people from the struggle for their national independence but will raise this struggle to an ever higher level.

Let us take the problem of war and peace. Can it be said that the change in the balance of power in favor of socialism has also brought about a change in the nature of imperialism, that imperialism has been bound hand and foot and can no longer do anything, that it can neither unleash wars nor undertake further aggressive action? Such a conclusion is not only erroneous but also very harmful. The underestimation of the forces of the enemy and the overestimation of our own forces result in a relaxation of vigilance and lead to dangerous adventures, just as the underestimation of our forces and the overestimation of the forces of the enemy lead to unprincipled concessions, errors, and opportunist positions. Proceeding from the actual situation of the balance of power existing in the world today, our party has always maintained and will continue to maintain that on the question of war and peace two possibilities should be considered and prepared for: the prevention of war as well as the unleashing of war by the imperialists. Our deep conviction that at the present time world war and the other aggressive wars unleashed by imperialism can be prevented is by no means based on the "good intentions" of the leaders of imperialism, but on the colossal economic, political, and military might of the powerful socialist camp, on the unity and the struggle of the international working class, on the resolute struggle of all peoples of the world against the imperialist warmongers, and on the unity and cohesion of all peace-loving forces. (*Stormy applause*)

Throughout the years of the existence of the people's power, the government of the People's Republic of Albania has resolutely and consistently pursued a foreign policy which fully corresponds to the interests of our people and fatherland, to the interests of the defense of national liberty and independence, to the interests of the entire socialist camp, and to the cause of peace and the progress of human society. The basis of the foreign policy of the Albanian Party of Labor has always been and remains the constant strengthening of the ties of friendship, fraternal cooperation, and mutual aid and support with the countries of the socialist camp, headed by the Soviet Union; the support of the anti-imperialist and anti-colonial national liberation struggle of oppressed peoples and nations and the revolutionary struggle of the workers in capitalist countries; all possible efforts to secure relations of peaceful coexistence between the People's Republic of Albania and the capitalist countries, especially with Albania's neighbors; all possible efforts to preserve and consolidate peace, especially in the Balkans and the Adriatic areas; and the unmasking of the policy of war and aggression, pursued by the imperialist powers, headed by the United States of America, and by their partners and tools surrounding our country, such as the Italian imperialists, the Greek monarcho-fascists and the Yugoslav revisionists.

In foreign policy, our party and government have always marched shoulder to shoulder with the other socialist countries in their efforts to preserve and consolidate world peace. They have always approved and strongly supported the general line of the foreign policy of the Soviet Union and all the other socialist countries for the settlement of the most important international problems. And this foreign policy of the Albanian People's Republic has always met with the full approval of the Soviet Union and the other socialist countries, which have always considered it a correct policy to the advantage of our common cause.

But recently N. Khrushchev and his companions have changed their tune and accuse us at times of being "adventurers and warmongers" and at other times of seeking a "rapprochement" with the imperialists. (*Laughter*) Apart from slander and fabrications, those who accuse us have no evidence, not a single fact, to prove that the foreign policy of the Albanian People's Republic has changed. Nothing has changed in our foreign policy. There has been no change in our stand on the question of war and peace, nor on that of our relations with other states, particularly with neighboring states, nor with regard to the struggle against imperialism and the unmasking of the Yugoslav revisionists.

The 20-year life and revolutionary struggle of the Albanian Party of Labor have refuted these base slanders and inventions, which have caused deep indignation and anger in our people who have fought and continue to fight heroically against imperialism and its lackeys. Those who accuse and slander the Albanian Party of Labor and its leadership are unable to present a single fact to prove their allegations, whereas we can present many facts and documents which clearly show their deviation from the positions of Marxism-Leninism and the struggle against imperialism. We have never had any illusions about our enemies, we have neither embraced them nor kissed them, we have not flattered them nor rubbed elbows with them, we have not bowed down before them. (*Stormy applause. All rise. Ovation*) Our party and government have always maintained a resolute, principled Marxist-Leninist stand toward the enemies of peace and socialism. They have sharply and continuously unmasked the imperialists and their policy of war and aggression, be they American or British, French or Italian; they have been implacable foes of the class enemies. They have been in solidarity with and have vigorously and without reservation supported the just cause of the peoples who have risen to struggle against imperialism. They have rendered all possible support to the fraternal peoples of Algeria, Cuba, the Congo, Laos, etc., in their sacred struggle against imperialism, resolutely condemning all the aggressive ventures of imperialism.

For all these "services" rendered to imperialism by our party during the past 20 years, it has been rewarded by imperialism and its tools with a savage and relentless fight against the Albanian People's Republic, waged by means of constant plots and provocations, by means of diversion, blackmail, and repeated slander.

We are accused of being afraid of imperialism (*laughter*), of being afraid to assume responsibility for the settlement of important international problems. The issue involved here is the signing of a peace treaty with Germany and the settlement of the West Berlin problem. The Albanian Party of Labor and the government of the Albanian People's Republic have never been and will never be afraid of imperialism, they have never been and will never be afraid of their responsibilities as a socialist country and member of the Warsaw Pact, and they have scrupulously and honorably discharged their international duties. (*Stormy applause*) The whole world knows the position of the Albanian Party of Labor and the government of the Albanian People's Republic on the German question; it has been stated in many well-publicized documents. The Albanian Party of Labor and the government of the Albanian People's Republic have always supported and continue firmly to support the efforts of the Soviet Union and the German Democratic Republic for a peaceful settlement of the German problem. We have been and still are for the earliest possible settlement of these problems because every delay only benefits our enemies. The declaration of the Central Committee of the Albanian Party of Labor on the German question publicly stated that "in time of danger we shall fight to the end alongside the Soviet Union and the other fraternal countries, under any circumstances, regardless of sacrifices; as always we will on every occasion show our solidarity with them to the end, and honorably discharge our duty." Such has been, and will remain, the position of our party and government. (*Stormy applause*)

Thus the question arises: Who is really afraid? Who is afraid of assuming responsibility for settling the German question? Who is prolonging the matter? Is it we, who are and have been for the earliest possible settlement, or is it our accusers, who have retreated on this question and have dragged it out from year to year?

Or let us take the issue of disarmament. It is common knowledge that our government has supported the Soviet Union's proposal for complete and total disarmament, because as long as arms exist and the arms race continues, and as long as total and complete disarmament has not been realized, peace will not be assured. The Soviet government, together with our government, advanced the proposal to convert the Adriatic and the Balkans into a zone of peace, free of atomic weapons and rocket bases. But the proposals of the Soviet Union and the socialist countries for complete and total disarmament and for the creation of zones of peace have been rejected by the imperialist powers. Under such conditions, our government has fully supported and continues to support the decision of the Soviet government to resume nuclear weapons tests as a very important and indispensable measure for the security of the Soviet Union and the entire socialist camp and for checking the imperialist forces, headed by the United States of America and the Bonn revanchists, who have intensified to the utmost the unbridled arms race and their mad preparations for a new world war. We realize that the disarmament problem is a difficult one which will require great effort for its solution, and that a resolute and uncompromising struggle must be waged by the socialist countries and all peace-loving forces in order to impose disarmament upon imperialism. But N. Khrushchev, instead of following this correct path, is seeking to disarm a socialist country such as the Albanian People's Republic, which is surrounded on all sides by enemies. By weakening the defensive strength of Albania, he has harmed not only the interests of our country but those of the entire socialist camp. And all this is occurring at a time when the American Sixth Fleet is cruising about the Mediterranean like a sea monster, when American rocket bases are being installed in Greece and Italy, when the NATO forces are feverishly continuing the arms race, and when the imperialists and West German revanchists are rattling their sabers and gravely endangering world peace. The Albanian government bears neither guilt nor responsibility for this. In any case, N. Khrushchev should by no means have gone to the point of openly inciting the imperialists and various reactionaries against a socialist country such as the Albanian People's Republic. However, the defense of Albania's borders is fully secured. (*Stormy applause. All rise. Ovation*)

In a world with states of different social systems, the only correct principle governing relations between them is the principle of peaceful coexistence, the principle defined by Lenin and implemented by Stalin. Our Party of Labor has always believed and believes that the policy of peaceful coexistence conforms to the vital interests of all peoples, of socialist as well as capitalist countries; it conforms to the aim of further strengthening the positions of socialism and world peace. Therefore, our party has made this principle the basis of the relations of our socialist state with other, nonsocialist states.

It is absurd to accuse our party and socialist state of opposing peaceful coexistence. This slander is refuted by all the practical activity of our state in the field of foreign policy. We are not opposed to the principle of peaceful coexistence, but we do not agree with certain opportunist views of N. Khrushchev and his followers who consider peaceful coexistence the general line of the foreign policy of the socialist camp and the main road to the victory of socialism on a world scale, who, for the sake of peaceful coexistence, renounce the struggle to unmask imperialism and almost completely obliterate the ideological and political struggle against Yugoslav revisionism, under the pretext that on some foreign policy issues Yugoslavia supports the Soviet proposals. Such a notion of peaceful coexistence, which assumes also the unmasking of imperialism and its policy of war and aggression, should promote the development of the struggle of the working class in the capitalist countries as well as the national liberation movement in the colonial and dependent countries. On the other hand, the revolutionary successes of the working class and the national liberation movement, by narrowing and weakening the positions of imperialism, strengthen the cause of peace and peaceful coexistence. Along with the struggle to impose the policy of peaceful coexistence on the bourgeois governments of their countries, the Communist parties in the capitalist countries are at the same time waging a class struggle to overthrow the bourgeois regimes and to bring about the transition to socialism according to the specific conditions in each country.

As for the forms of the transition to socialism, N. Khrushchev badly complicated this issue, too, at the 20th Congress and later. He almost raised to an absolute the peaceful path to the seizure of power by the working class, and the illusion was created that the working class could come to power only by securing a parliamentary majority. These theses pleased only the revisionists and the various opportunists who used them to justify their anti-Marxist views. We Albanian Communists have never been and are not a priori opposed to the peaceful path. But the teachings of Marxism-Leninism, historical experience, and contemporary reality teach us that, to secure the victory of the socialist cause, the working class and its party must prepare themselves simultaneously for both possibilities — the peaceful path and the nonpeaceful one. To orient oneself toward only one of these possibilities is to embark upon an erroneous path. Only by being well prepared, especially for the nonpeaceful path, do the opportunities increase for the peaceful path as well.

This is how we understand peaceful coexistence and its relation to the class struggle. This is how we understand and implement the policy of peaceful coexistence with other nonsocialist states, and above all with our neighbors.

It is strange that N. Khrushchev and his followers ask us to practice peaceful coexistence with our Greek neighbors. They accuse us of not going along with them on the proposals for the disarmament of the Balkan countries, they accuse us of not making efforts for a "Balkan understanding," and they join in the chorus of Tito and Karamanlis which alleges that we are the "warmongers of the Balkans" at a time when Greece continues to consider herself in a "state of war" with Albania, when she is advancing territorial claims on our country and is plotting to attack Albania, and when monarcho-fascist Greece has become a fortress, armed to the teeth by the American imperialists against our socialist countries. The accusations of our critics are baseless, since no one in his right mind can think that tiny Albania, surrounded by wolves which for 17 years in succession have tried to swallow her alive, does not want peace and disarmament.

Everybody knows and experience has shown how far monarcho-fascist Greece has disarmed and to what extent the hopes of those who believed in this have been fulfilled, but if we had failed to criticize N. Khrushchev (and we made this criticism in a comradely fashion) when he raised the hopes of Sophokles Venizelos for "the autonomy of southern Albania," it would have been treason on our part. N. Khrushchev did not like our just criticism. This is the least evil. But he twisted our criticism into a countercharge, accusing us of allegedly slandering the Soviet Union, which liberated us and defends us. This is, of course, Machiavellian. But later the devil again showed his horns. When the Americans, Greeks, and Turks were conducting large-scale military maneuvers along the Albanian and Bulgarian borders, N. Khrushchev said in a statement to the *New York Times* reporter, Sulzberger, on September 10, 1961: "You [Americans] have also established bases in Greece and from there you are threatening our ally Bulgaria." Has not monarcho-fascist Greece installed rockets against Albania too? When did N. Khrushchev decide that Albania should no longer be an ally of the Soviet Union? This is astonishing. Are these trifling matters? Is it permissible for the First Secretary of the Central Committee of the Communist Party of the Soviet Union and the Premier of the USSR even were he engaged in mortal combat with socialist Albania, to say openly to the Greek reactionaries that socialist Albania is not an ally of the Soviet Union and to inform President Kennedy that "relations between the Soviet Union and Albania have deteriorated"?

According to certain people, it is we who view things as "sectarian nationalists," while others, who are gambling with the interests of our people, are Marxists. Tomorrow these same critics may hold us responsible for the election defeat of the Greek Progressive Party, the EDA. (*Laughter*) Do these so-called Marxists think, perhaps, that we ought to hand over the keys to our country to the Greek monarcho-fascists so that their line of "peaceful coexistence" may triumph and the seizure of power in Greece "by peaceful and parliamentary means" may be realized? (*Laughter*) No, they should not expect that of us. These so-called Marxists should not forget that the Albanian Party of Labor and the Albanian people demonstrated their internationalism by saving tens of thousands of heroes of the Greek people and of the Greek Communist Party who certainly do not spit on the horse after they have crossed the river. (*Stormy applause*)

This is the foreign policy which our party and government have followed. These are our views on the problems of contemporary world development. It is precisely for these attitudes and views that we are criticized; it is for this that N. Khrushchev attacked us at the 22nd Congress of the Communist Party of the Soviet Union. On these grounds he first made public, in a unilateral fashion, our differences, thereby giving weapons to the enemy and assuming a heavy historical responsibility as the disrupter of the unity of the international Communist movement and of the socialist camp. Our Party of Labor has never aired our differences openly; it has spoken of them only at party meetings; but now that N. Khrushchev has made them public, our party is also obliged to state its views in public.

In attacking our party in his speech at the 22nd Congress of the Communist Party of the Soviet Union, N. Khrushchev said that Albanian-Soviet relations had deteriorated owing to the fault of the Albanian leadership. It is well known that the 20 years of our party's revolutionary activity have been 20 years of colossal effort to promote the friendship between the Albanian people and the Soviet peoples, to establish closer fraternal ties between the Albanian People's Republic and the Soviet Union; they have been 20 years of exemplary collaboration between our party and the glorious Communist Party of the Soviet Union. The 20 years of our party's activity have been 20 years of sincere loyalty, of great fraternal love for the great party of Lenin, which has been, is, and always will be for us a source of inspiration and guidance from which we have learned and will continue to learn how to work and to struggle for the welfare of our people and for the cause of socialism and Communism. The 20 years of our party's activity have been years of unstinting and all-round assistance by the Soviet Union to the Albanian people, fraternal internationalist aid which our party and government have utilized wisely for the economic development of our country, for the construction of socialism in Albania, and for the improvement of the living standards of the Albanian people.

Under such circumstances, it is absurd and incredible to claim that the Albanian leaders "without reason" and "with amazing speed" have altered their attitude toward the Soviet Union and the Communist Party of the Soviet Union. Equally incredible is the monstrous allegation that the Albanian leaders are linked with imperialism and have sold themselves for 30 pieces of silver. (*Laughter*) Such "revelations" can be believed only by fans of fables and detective stories but not by serious men, because any honest man, however little he may know about the 20-year history of our party, cannot fail to see that such slander is not justified by any stand of our party or any action of its leadership. Throughout its revolutionary history, the Albanian Party of Labor has always fought and is fighting with determination against imperialism and its agents. Never in the past, the present, or the future has Albania ever held out or will it hold out its hand to anyone for alms, much less to the imperialists and their allies. (*Stormy applause. All rise. Ovation*) From its friends and brothers in the countries of the socialist camp it has received and receives not alms but only internationalist aid in the form of credits, and it will continue in the future to accept aid only from those socialist countries which may wish to offer such aid. We seek alms from no one. If, for one reason or another, N. Khrushchev and his followers do not wish to help us, it is in vain that they expect us to go to the imperialists and their allies for "alms." Our people have friends and comrades in the socialist countries who have not left them and will not leave them in the lurch. (*Stormy applause. All rise. Ovation*) But apart from this, we say to N. Khrushchev that the Albanian people and its Party of Labor will live on grass if necessary but will never sell themselves for 30 pieces of silver, because they would rather die on their feet with honor than live on their knees in dishonor. (*Stormy applause. All rise. Ovation*)

Why then did Soviet-Albanian relations deteriorate? N. Khrushchev knows the reason perfectly well because he himself is the culprit. We shall limit ourselves to saying that the June 1960 Bucharest meeting was the starting point.

Even prior to June 1960 differences existed between our Party of Labor and the Soviet leaders on certain questions of an ideological and political nature; however, they exerted no negative influence on the relations between our two Marxist-Leninist parties.

The Albanian Party of Labor has always declared and declares now as well that the experience of the Communist Party of the Soviet Union, the lessons of its congresses, including the 20th and 22nd Congresses, have been, are, and will always be of great help on our road to the construction of a socialist and Communist society. However, our party has not been and is not of the same opinion as the Soviet leaders on certain specific fundamental theses of the 20th Congress of the Communist Party of the Soviet Union, just as it is not now of the same opinion regarding certain theses of the 22nd Congress or the new Program of the Communist Party of the Soviet Union approved by the 22nd Congress. Does our party not have this right? Is this not in keeping with the teachings of Marxism-Leninism and of proletarian internationalism? Can this be considered an anti-Soviet position, as our accusers claim?

The Soviet leaders consider as anti-Marxist, dogmatic, sectarian, and opposed to proletarian internationalism, and so forth, any party which is not of the same opinion as they on certain basic theses which were expounded at the 20th Congress. Indeed, the former member of the Presidium of the Central Committee of the Communist Party of the Soviet Union E. Furtseva went so far as to declare from the rostrum of the 22nd Congress: "How can those who do not accept the resolutions of the 20th Congress of our party call themselves Communists?" (*Laughter*) (Although we say that we do not agree with *some* theses of the 20th Congress, the Soviet leaders prefer to generalize and to claim that we do not agree with the entire 20th Congress.) This means, according to certain Soviet leaders, that the criterion of loyalty to Marxism-Leninism, to Communism and proletarian internationalism, is allegedly the position one takes on the 20th Congress of the Communist Party of the Soviet Union. Can this be Marxist logic? If all the Communist and workers parties of the world were to adopt the new criteria invented by Furtseva, then mere lack of agreement, let us say, with the many revisionist theses of the 8th Congress of the Italian Communist Party would plunge millions of Communists into misfortune and would create confusion among them, because they would not know to which address to surrender their party cards. (*Laughter*)

According to the Leninist principles governing the relations between Marxist parties, however important the congress of a party may be, however large and authoritative the party of a country may be, the decisions of its congress are binding only on its members. The Moscow Declaration states that in the international Communist movement all parties are equal and independent; they formulate their policies starting from the concrete conditions in their countries and guided by the principles of Marxism-Leninism. The attempt to transform the decisions of the congress of one party into international norms binding upon all parties constitutes a brutal violation of the principles of equality and independence of Marxist-Leninist parties; it is in open contradiction to proletarian internationalism. Therefore, it is not our party but the Soviet leadership, headed by N. Khrushchev, which has slipped from the positions of Marxism-Leninism and of proletarian internationalism by attempting to impose its own policy on other parties and by asking them to renounce their views and to yield and obey.

Whether or not our party stands on the positions of Marxism-Leninism can by no means be determined by its critical attitude toward certain theses expressed by leaders of some fraternal parties nor by the subjective evaluation that may be made of its line and activity by N. Khrushchev and his followers. The criterion of truth is to be found in life and in practice; therefore, as far as individuals and the various parties are concerned, they should be judged by the facts and by their practical activity. The path traversed by the Albanian Party of Labor, the line pursued by it since its founding and its 20 years of political activity are convincing facts which testify to its firm loyalty to Marxism-Leninism, to the vital interests of the Albanian people, to the great cause of socialism and Communism, and to the cause of world peace. (*Applause*)

Our Party of Labor has made its observations on certain basic theses of the 20th Congress and on certain positions of the Soviet leaders with which it did not agree through normal party channels, thereby observing the jointly established principles governing relations among fraternal parties. We have already stated our observations on foreign policy and the problems of contemporary world development. Let us now take up another important problem on which we have held and continue to hold an opinion different from that of the Soviet leaders. It is the question of the attitude toward J. V. Stalin and his work.

According to our party's point of view, N. Khrushchev first had to discredit J. V. Stalin and his work before he could expound his opportunist theses at the 20th Congress of the Communist Party of the Soviet Union and later propagate them. This he did in the special report, "On the Cult of the Personality and Its Consequences," presented to the 20th Congress. Our party did not and does not agree with the manner in which criticism of Stalin was voiced at the 20th Congress and later. (*Applause*)

N. Khrushchev, when slandering our party at the 22nd Congress and brutally meddling in our internal affairs, said that the Albanian leaders are against the criticism of the cult of the personality of Stalin because the methods of the personality cult allegedly flourish in our party and because terror and injustice allegedly reign in Albania. We shall not stop here to refute these slanders, but the fact that their author stooped so low that he utilized "arguments" borrowed from the most rabid enemies of socialism and Communism in order to mobilize public opinion against our party shows his sinister intentions. It is clear that, by linking at the 22nd Congress the unfounded attacks against the Albanian Party of Labor with the "struggle against the cult of Stalin and the antiparty group," N. Khrushchev intended to demonstrate the "similarity" between the alleged "Albanian Stalinism" and the "epoch of Stalinist crimes" in the Soviet Union in order to create the "atmosphere" he needed at the Congress and before world public opinion to make his slanders more credible.

The Albanian Party of Labor has always taken and continues to take into account the teachings of Marxism-Leninism on the role of the masses, the classes, the party, and the leaders. It has always considered and continues to consider the appearance of the personality cult as a phenomenon alien to Marxism-Leninism and harmful to a Communist and workers party. Our party has not hesitated, when the occasion has arisen, to criticize while in embryonic form the various manifestations of this kind in its own ranks, as it did at its Third Congress. Likewise, our party, when the occasion has arisen, has fought bravely against and has rooted out any violation of revolutionary legality and any abuse of power by anyone, as it did at its First Congress. Everybody knows the fate which befell the enemy of the party and the people, Koci Xoxe, and his associates, who, prior to 1948, incited by the Yugoslav revisionists and abusing the confidence of the people and the party, violated the laws of the state in order to dig a grave for the cadres of the party and the regime.

Neither the malady of the personality cult nor the violation of socialist legality exists in our party. But while guarding against manifestations of the personality cult, our party, in the correct Marxist-Leninist manner, teaches love and respect for its leaders; and while scrupulously respecting socialist legality, our party and people's power are severe toward the enemies of our People's Republic, toward all those who try to wipe out the historic gains of our people. (*Stormy applause*)

The Albanian Party of Labor has been and is opposed to the criticism made of J. V. Stalin at the 20th Congress and repeated at the 22nd Congress for still other basic reasons.

According to our party's point of view, J. V. Stalin, in all his theoretical and practical activity, was and remains one of the most distinguished leaders and personalities not only of the Soviet Union and the Communist Party of the Soviet Union but also of the international Communist and workers movement, one of the most ardent defenders and greatest theoreticians of Marxism-Leninism. (*Stormy applause. All rise. Ovation*) His great historic merit lies in the fact that for many years he was a faithful disciple and determined comrade-in-arms of V. I. Lenin in the struggle for the overthrow of tsarism and the triumph of the great October Socialist Revolution. After Lenin's death, as head of the Communist Party of the Soviet Union, he faithfully defended Leninism against the rabid attacks of the Trotskyites, Bukharinites, Zinovievites, and other enemies and smashed them ideologically and politically. As the head of the party, J. V. Stalin made a great contribution to the successful construction of socialism in the Soviet Union and to the successful conduct of the Great Patriotic War of the Soviet Union against fascism; he further developed Marxism-Leninism on a number of important questions relating to Soviet socialist society and the construction of socialism and Communism. He made an invaluable contribution to the strengthening of the socialist camp and the international Communist movement and to the unmasking of modern revisionism, as personified by Tito's traitorous revisionist group. In thus appraising J. V. Stalin's work, there can be no doubt that the errors he may have made in the last years of his life were partial and cannot serve as a criterion for giving a general appraisal of J. V. Stalin's person and his work. In a general evaluation of J. V. Stalin's activity, his great merits stand in the foreground: the struggle for the defense of Leninism, the struggle for the construction of socialism in the Soviet Union, the struggle for the creation and strengthening of the socialist camp and the consolidation of the unity of the international Communist and workers movement, the consistent struggle against imperialism, and his policy of defending peace and peaceful coexistence. These constitute his basic characteristics as a leader and as a Communist. Such has been and remains the unshakable position of the Albanian Party of Labor with regard to the evaluation of the work of J. V. Stalin. (*Applause*)

N. Khrushchev's erroneous position in criticizing J. V. Stalin lies in the fact that:

a) He greatly exaggerated Stalin's errors in a one-sided and tendentious manner, even going so far as to make base slanders against him. Stalin was portrayed almost as an "enemy" of the Soviet Union and of Communism; he was characterized as "brutal," "capricious," "despotic," "murderous," "bloodthirsty," and "criminal" toward party cadres and loyal and tested revolutionaries; as a "dupe" of the imperialists and fascists (*laughter*); as a man who committed great "follies" in practice and theory, who "had no idea" of what was going on in the Soviet Union, who showed "a lack of respect for Lenin's memory," and many other charges of this kind. Isolated statements made at the 20th Congress and afterwards to the effect that Stalin remains an outstanding Communist, and so forth, are entirely formal and were made in order to mitigate the bad impression and the righteous indignation which these accusations against Stalin aroused among Communists throughout the world. In fact, neither at the 20th

Congress nor to this day have the leaders of the Communist Party of the Soviet Union made any positive appraisal, even in their propaganda, of the theoretical legacy of J. V. Stalin for the purpose of showing his positive sides and his contribution to the defense and further development of Marxism-Leninism. This inhuman attitude reached a culmination at the 22nd Congress of the Communist Party of the Soviet Union, where not only were the accusations of the 20th Congress repeated, this time publicly, but also a special resolution was adopted to remove Stalin's embalmed body from the mausoleum. Unable to denigrate Stalin by means of arguments over basic principles in the realm of practical and theoretical activity, Khrushchev, in order to fight Stalin, is reducing the matter to the level of the security police and is taking measures to liquidate Stalin's corpse. After all these actions, how hypocritical sound N. Khrushchev's words of January 1957 that

> . . . when it was a question of the revolution, of the defense of the interests of the proletarian class, in the revolutionary struggle against our class enemies, Stalin bravely and implacably defended the cause of Marxism-Leninism. . . . On the primary and fundamental issue — and the primary and fundamental issue for Marxist-Leninists is the defense of the interests of the working class, the cause of socialism, and the struggle against the enemies of Marxism-Leninism — on this primary and fundamental issue, may God grant, as the saying goes, that every Communist may struggle as Stalin struggled. (*Laughter*)

b) At the 20th Congress of the Communist Party of the Soviet Union and in Soviet propaganda following the Congress, N. Khrushchev treated the question of the personality cult in a one-sided manner, forgetting the Leninist doctrine on the relations between the masses, classes, parties, and leaders. In his brilliant book *Left-Wing Communism, an Infantile Disorder,* the great Lenin spoke of the necessity of creating in each Marxist party a more or less stable directing group, composed of the persons with the most authority, influence, and experience, and these are called leaders. Without such a stable leadership, the struggle of the working class and its Communist Party cannot be crowned with success. At the 20th Congress, under the pretext of the struggle against the cult of the personality, and in contradiction to the clear teachings of Lenin, mass democracy was opposed to the function of the leaders. It is a good idea for us to recall what V. I. Lenin wrote in this connection:

> . . . To reach the point . . . of opposing in general the dictatorship of the masses to the dictatorship of the leaders is a ridiculous absurdity and idiocy. It is particularly ridiculous to see *young leaders* who speak worthless nonsense replace (under the slogan: "Down with the leaders!") older leaders who have humane views on simple questions (V. I. Lenin, *Works,* Vol. 31, p. 31, Albanian edition).

N. Khrushchev and his group used for their own anti-Marxist aims — and this is becoming clearer with each passing day — the so-called "principled criticism" of the personality cult of Stalin. It is none of our business how and for what reason he used it on the domestic level (in the Soviet Union and within the Communist Party of the Soviet Union); only the Communist Party of the Soviet Union can judge this. Nevertheless, we cannot help noting that, in fact, N. Khrushchev, by speaking of the "crimes" committed during the Stalin era — the "murder of innocent people," the "elimination of thousand of cadres" through "sham" trials, the reign of "terror," which is described with the greatest zeal in the darkest colors — by making these things known to world public opinion, is rendering a very great disservice to the Soviet Union and pleases only the imperialists and all the enemies of Communism. N. Khrushchev, alleging that the Albanian leaders "are throwing mud at the Soviet Union," has rebuked the leadership of our party for the correct criticism it made at party meetings of certain unworthy moves against our country. But what shall we say of his unrestrained zeal to darken a whole glorious epoch, the epoch of the construction of socialism in the Soviet Union, to discredit the glory of the Soviet Union in the eyes of the whole world by portraying it as a country where terror and murder have reigned, just as the reactionary bourgeois press has described it and is describing it in its propaganda? Is it not he himself who is discrediting the Soviet Union by his actions? Is he not gravely sullying the heroism of the Soviet peoples, who, in the struggle against internal and external enemies and in the struggle against countless difficulties and obstacles, under the leadership of their Communist Party headed by Stalin, laid the foundations of the socialist and Communist society in the Soviet Union, when he proposes that a memorial to the "victims" of the personality cult be erected in Moscow? Some call these actions "bold self-criticism." Let us probe this more deeply to see how much good and evil this kind of "bold self-criticism" has brought to the Soviet Union and the Communist movement!

In speaking of the "inequities" and the "victims of the period of the personality cult" and in declaring the various trials to have been shams, N. Khrushchev, irrespective of the errors which may have been committed during this whole struggle, remains consistent in his anti-Marxist concepts regarding imperialism and its lackeys. In fact, he has rendered a service to imperialism by portraying it as harmless to the countries now building socialism; he is weakening the vigilance of the peoples in their struggle against the agents of imperialism, who have carried on and are carrying on vicious activity against the socialist camp. N. Khrushchev also adopted the tactic of silence toward the plot organized by the Yugoslav revisionists, the Greek monarcho-fascists, and the American Sixth Fleet which was unmasked here a few months ago. Moreover, after recommending this tactic to certain other fraternal parties, he spread the word that the plot was a fabrication, that participants in this plot were "patriots and honest fighters," whom he later took under his protection in his closing speech to the 22nd Congress of the Communist Party of the Soviet Union. Therefore, according to his logic, whoever fights against imperialism, whoever fights against its agents, whoever fights to defend the freedom and independence of a socialist country is an agent of imperialism. And, on the other hand, whoever rises up against the people's power and against the party, whoever serves the enemies of socialism is a "martyr," a "good patriot," and is taken under the protection of the leader of the Communist Party of the Soviet Union. They will even erect monuments to such men.

N. Khrushchev used the issue of the cult of Stalin to dethrone Leninism, to lay the groundwork for the revision of Marxism-Leninism, and to propagate his opportunist views on the most important questions of contemporary world development and the international Communist movement. This action and this tactic of his are neither new nor original. Trotsky also used the same tactic in his fight against Leninism. J. V. Stalin stated:

> In his works Trotsky also made an attempt (an attempt!) to pave the way for the substitution of Leninism by Trotskyism. Trotsky had to discredit at all costs the party, the cadres who made the revolution, so that by discrediting the party he might also discredit Leninism. It was necessary to discredit Leninism in order to smuggle in Trotskyism as the "only proletarian" ideology. (This is no joke). All this was done of course (oh, of course!) under the banner of Leninism so that the process of smuggling might be carried out "without any harm whatsoever" (J. V. Stalin, *Works,* Vol. 6, p. 361, Albanian edition).

N. Khrushchev had also used the Stalin question to strike a blow at the sound

Marxist-Leninist elements in the leadership of the Communist and workers parties of various countries, to intimidate, and in the case of resistance, even to liquidate anyone who dares to oppose him, to silence the other parties and the various leaders who do not support his revisionist views and policy. In brief, the question of the personality cult is used as a bogey to put pressure on other parties and to liquidate leaders who are not to the liking of N. Khrushchev. These designs, which until yesterday he concealed under the guise of "principled" and "Marxist" phraseology, he revealed publicly at the 22nd Congress of the Communist Party of the Soviet Union. In his speech he said, "To put an end to the personality cult means essentially that Shehu, Hoxha, and others must give up their leading posts in the party and state." And he added, "They do not want to do that."

If one takes into account that in the same speech, as mentioned above, he takes under his protection and considers as patriots antiparty elements and agents of imperialism, participants in the plot organized by imperialism against the Albanian People's Republic, then one clearly understands the "principled" struggle of N. Khrushchev against the personality cult in Albania — his great concern! He wants to liquidate the present leaders of our party and replace them with antiparty elements and any plotter and agent of imperialism.

That N. Khrushchev is seeking, under the pretext of the struggle against the personality cult, to dethrone Leninism in order to pave the way for revisionism is also shown by the fact that he is not at all concerned with the just and principled Marxist-Leninist struggle against the personality cult. If this were not so — his demagogical words notwithstanding — he could not have failed to note that at present in the Soviet Union one sees each day more and more manifestations of the cult of the personality, indeed often of his own person and in the most flagrant and exalted forms. Thus one can find hardly an issue among illustrated Soviet periodicals without photographs of Khrushchev; the pages of the Soviet press are filled with quotations from his speeches, everywhere and on any question it is he alone who speaks, and a full-length film has been made on his life and other films have been made on his travels to the various countries of the world; his praises are sung in speeches and articles, attributing to him personally the greatest achievements of the Soviet peoples in the fields of industry, science, and technology. Great efforts are being made, in all haste, to present Khrushchev not only as a "great military strategist" but also almost as the "architect" of the victory over fascism in World War II. (*Laughter*)

Where then are those principles of N. Khrushchev regarding the struggle against the manifestations of the personality cult which he advertises so loudly in his unprincipled fight against other fraternal parties and their leaders?

This is the reason, comrades, why our party has not been and is not now in agreement with the Soviet leaders on the matter of their criticism of Stalin.

Our Party of Labor has also not agreed and does not agree with the Soviet leaders on the question of the attitude toward modern revisionism, and especially toward the traitorous clique of the Yugoslav revisionists. N. Khrushchev and his group used the issue of Stalin and the personality cult to prepare the ground for the full rehabilitation of Tito's revisionist and traitorous clique and to present it as a "victim" of Stalin's errors, thereby encouraging the revisionist renegades to initiate in all directions their activity against Marxism-Leninism under the demagogical slogans of "anti-Stalinism," etc.

It is known that Tito's revisionist clique was openly condemned in publicized letters of the Central Committee of the Communist Party of the Soviet Union, signed by J. V. Stalin and V. M. Molotov, as well as in the resolution of the Information Bureau of Communist and workers parties of June 1948, "On the Situation in the Communist Party of Yugoslavia," which was later supported by all the Communist and workers parties in the world. Later, in November 1949, the second resolution of the Information Bureau appeared in which it was demonstrated that Tito's clique had finally degenerated into an agency of imperialism, that it had liquidated the gains of the revolution in Yugoslavia, that it had diverted Yugoslavia from the road to socialism and from the socialist camp and had made it economically and politically dependent on imperialism, that the Titoist gang was engaged in wide-scale espionage activities and plots against various socialist countries, that in different ways it was supporting the imperialist policy of war and aggression, and so forth.

The viewpoint of the Albanian Party of Labor was and continues to be that the conclusions of Stalin and of the Information Bureau concerning the revisionist renegade clique of Tito were and remain correct. These conclusions have been confirmed and continue to be confirmed both by the Yugoslav conditions of that time and by subsequent events down to the present time. The Yugoslav revisionists became the center of sabotage and plots in the service of imperialism against the countries of the socialist camp. Under their direction, Koci Xoxe's gang operated in Albania and tried to destroy the Albanian Party of Labor and liquidate the people's power. From Tito's Yugoslavia hundreds and thousands of agents and provocateurs, spies and saboteurs, were illegally smuggled into the socialist countries to carry out missions of terror, sabotage, and plots against socialism in these countries. Since 1948 Tito's revisionist clique has placed itself more and more openly in the service of American imperialism, to which it is linked by the millions and billions of dollars given to Yugoslavia in the form of economic and military aid; it is linked through participation in the Balkan Pact, which is nothing but an appendage of the North Atlantic Treaty; it is linked through the policy of sabotage and plots against the socialist countries and against the national liberation movement of peoples recently liberated or still suffering under the yoke of colonialism.

Until 1955 all the Communist and workers parties were unanimous in condemning the Yugoslav revisionist leadership and in waging a firm and principled ideological and political struggle against it. However, precisely at this time, N. Khrushchev declared that a great injustice had been done to Yugoslavia and her leaders, that "under the influence of the agent Beria" baseless accusations had been made against them, and that on the Yugoslav question, too, J. V. Stalin had seriously erred. And immediately he took the initiative, went to Belgrade, where he called Tito "dear comrade," unilaterally threw into the wastebasket the resolution of the Information Bureau, and loudly proclaimed that Yugoslavia was a socialist country and that the Yugoslav leaders, though somewhat irresolute, were in general Marxist-Leninists.

What does experience show; what does life show? Experience and life, both before and after 1955, show that in their assessment of the Yugoslav question Stalin and the Information Bureau were right, because their assessment was based on objective facts, on the teachings of Marxism-Leninism. On the other hand, practical experience and life show that with regard to their stand on Tito's revisionist clique N. Khrushchev and his followers were wrong, because their action was based on subjective views and was contrary to the teachings of Marxism-Leninism, contrary to objective reality.

Let us look at the facts. What were the results of the efforts to rehabilitate Tito's clique? The Yugoslav revisionist leaders have renounced neither their anti-Marxist views nor their hostile activities against the socialist camp and the fraternal Communist and workers parties. The most obvious result of N. Khrushchev's efforts was the fact that after 1955 it became possible for the band of Yugoslav renegades to operate more freely against the world Communist movement and against the countries of the socialist camp under the mask of "persecuted comrades," exploiting in this manner even the patronage of the First Secretary of the Central Communist Party of the Soviet Union. The rehabilitation of the Yugolsav revisionists brought with it also the rehabilitation of all their agents and companions in certain fraternal parties where, under the mask of "correcting errors," a real campaign against sound party cadres was begun as well as the activation of antiparty elements. This happened in certain parties of the socialist countries in Europe as well as in certain parties of the capitalist countries. Most typical in this connection are the events in Hungary, where the activation of revisionist elements, headed by Imre Nagy, with the support and overt encouragement of the Yugoslav revisionists, led to the outbreak of the counterrevolution which endangered the very existence of Hungary as a people's democratic state.

Nevertheless, N. Khrushchev, constantly and with great confidence in Tito and his companions, has stubbornly followed a policy of rapprochement, of flattery, and of caresses toward the Yugoslav revisionists. The events in Hungary showed this stand even more clearly. When the counterrevolution broke out in Hungary, it was clear to everyone that the Yugoslav revisionists were playing an underhanded role in the Hungarian developments. This was apparent in their influence on the counterrevolutionary discussions of the "Petöfi" Club; this was apparent during the counterrevolutionary uprising and in the enthusiasm expressed by the Yugoslav revisionists at that time; and it was still more apparent in the fact that the traitor Imre Nagy found asylum in the Yugoslav Embassy in Budapest following the collapse of the counterrevolution. Instead of mercilessly unmasking the Belgrade renegades as the direct inspirers of the counterrevolutionary coup in Hungary, N. Khrushchev tried in every way to mitigate their responsibility, to minimize it, and finally to absolve them of it entirely. L. I. Krylov, then Soviet Ambassador to Albania, informed the Central Committee of the Albanian Party of Labor of the letter which N. Khrushchev sent to J. B. Tito on November 9, 1956. In this letter, N. Khrushchev wrote to Tito, among other things, the following:

> . . . The Central Committee of the Communist Party of the Soviet Union has examined your recent letter. We consider it possible to agree with your view that no particular importance should be given now to the question of whether or not the Yugoslav Embassy in Budapest acted correctly in giving asylum to Imre Nagy and his companions. We note with satisfaction that, since the Brioni talks, you have been in full agreement with our attitude toward comrade János Kádár as a distinguished personality with revolutionary authority in Hungary, capable of heading a new revolutionary government in these difficult times and conditions. . . . You were fully satisfied with the fact that in connection with the removal of Rákosi, the Central Committee of the Communist Party of the Soviet Union has, since the summer of this year, endeavored that Comrade Kádár should become First Secretary of the Central Committee of the Hungarian Workers Party.

Any comment on this letter is superfluous. This letter shows quite clearly that the First Secretary of the Central Committee of the Communist Party of the Soviet Union, trampling under foot every rule governing relations between fraternal parties, went so far as to interfere even on a question of such importance and of such markedly internal party character as the appointment of this or that person to the position of first secretary of a fraternal party. This also shows that N. Khrushchev has long been in full agreement with J. B. Tito and that it seemed logical to him to consult with Tito — that enemy of socialism and the very inspirer and organizer of the counterrevolution in Hungary — on everything, even on the "appointment" of the first secretary of another party.

From this it is clearly understandable and entirely logical why N. Khrushchev tried to silence the question of Yugoslav intervention in the Hungarian events: because he could not do two things at the same time — consult with Tito and unmask Tito.

Following Tito's notorious speech at Pula in November 1956, the struggle of the Communist and workers parties against Yugoslav revisionism was revived and the Yugoslav leaders were criticized for their stand. However, Tito's traitorous group not only did not make any self-criticism or take any positive step toward the Communist movement, but in 1958 it even deemed it suitable to formulate and sum up its revisionist ideas in the program of the League of Communists of Yugoslavia, which was published as a counterbalance to the Moscow Declaration of Communist and workers parties of November 1957. It now seemed that there was no room for the slightest illusion since Tito and his group had openly declared in this program what they had concealed for years under demagogical pseudo-Marxist and pseudo-socialist slogans. But what happened? At first N. Khrushchev, who felt uncomfortable before public opinion and the international Communist movement, took a halfhearted stand against the Yugoslav revisionists. But this did not last long. With amazing speed and contrary to the most elementary logic, at the Fifth Congress of the Socialist Unity Party of Germany in July 1958 he recommended silence regarding the Yugoslav revisionists, saying:

> In the struggle for our common cause we should not pay more attention to the Yugoslav revisionists than they deserve. They wish to seem important, and everyone to think that they are the center of the world. . . . We will not contribute to the kindling of passions and the exacerbation of relations. Also, given the situation which has been created in our relations with the League of Communists of Yugoslavia, it will be useful to preserve a spark of hope and to seek common ground on some questions.

He stressed this again during his visit to Albania in May 1959. At the same time, with ever greater frequency, the word began to circulate on "Comrade Tito"; propaganda commenced once again that "Yugoslavia is a socialist state," that between the Soviet Union and Yugoslavia "there is mutual understanding on many questions of foreign policy."

It is appropriate for us to recall that in his time V. I. Lenin waged an irreconcilable struggle not only against opportunism but also against those who preached "unity" with the opportunists.

The revisionist group of Yugoslav leaders, being left unmolested in their traitorous, antisocialist, and conspiratorial work, continued with greater intensity its activity to disrupt the Communist movement and to undermine the national liberation and anti-imperialist movement of the peoples who are fighting for liberation or who have recently achieved national liberation. With each passing day the Yugoslav revisionists revealed themselves as enemies of Communism and the freedom of peoples. It is precisely because Tito's gang is of this nature that the representatives of the 81 fraternal Communist and workers parties resolutely condemned the Yugoslav revisionist leaders in the 1960 Moscow Declaration. As is known, the Declaration points out that the Yugoslav leaders, after betraying Marxism-Leninism, withdrew their country from the socialist camp and made it dependent on the so-called "aid" of the American imperialists and other imperialists, thereby endangering the revolutionary gains achieved through the heroic struggle of the Yugoslav people; that the Yugoslav revisionists are undermining the socialist camp and the international Communist movement; that under the pretext of the policy of nonalignment with blocs they are engaging in activities which harm the cause of unity of the peace-loving forces and nations. Finally, the Declaration points out that a constant struggle must be waged to unmask completely the group of Yugoslav leaders.

Nevertheless, after November 1960 the

Soviet leaders forgot these correct theses of the Declaration in the majority of cases. Indeed, as if to encourage Tito's revisionist clique and to "appease" its anger, the Soviet leaders deemed it reasonable to address warm official statements to the Yugoslav "Comrades." Thus, on December 23, 1960, only a few days after the Declaration of the 81 fraternal parties was issued, A. Gromyko, a member of the Central Committee of the Communist Party and Foreign Minister of the Soviet Union, declared in the Supreme Soviet of the Soviet Union that on certain basic issues the foreign policy of the Soviet Union is in complete harmony with the foreign policy of Yugoslavia. N. Khrushchev himself, in an interview granted to Sulzberger, the commentator of *The New York Times,* which was published in *Pravda* on September 10, 1961, stated: "Of course we consider Yugoslavia a socialist country." Is such a statement not contrary to the Declaration of the 81 fraternal Communist and workers parties? Does it not seem that the First Secretary of the Communist Party of the Soviet Union intended by this statement to "appease" the anger of the Yugoslav revisionist leaders and to inform them publicly that what is written in the Moscow Declaration or in some other document of the Communist Party of the Soviet Union is a matter of form, whereas he has other views?

Why is this happening? Why is such good will being so persistently displayed toward a band of renegades from Marxism-Leninism who have sunk up to their necks into the mire of revisionism and treason and, at the same time, are savagely attacking Communist and workers parties which have always been faithful to the revolutionary doctrines of Marxism-Leninism and to the cause of socialism?

The Albanian Party of Labor could not and cannot agree with such an opportunist stand toward Tito's dangerous revisionist gang, which is an *agentura* of imperialism and an enemy of socialism and Communism, of the Albanian Party of Labor and the Albanian people. In the struggle against modern revisionism, particularly against Tito's revisionist clique, our Party of Labor has always taken and continues to take account of the invaluable teachings of the great Lenin, who emphatically stated that opportunism constitutes a serious danger to the very existence of the socialist order.

Because our party has experienced at its own expense the meaning of Yugoslav revisionism not only in theory but also in practice, it understands very well these important teachings of Lenin. The fact is that never once did Tito's clique, either before 1948 or after 1955, renounce its plots and diversionary action against the Albanian People's Republic and the Albanian Party of Labor but, on the contrary, increased them. Therefore, the struggle of the Albanian Party of Labor against Yugoslav revisionism is not only an important internationalist duty of our party, as a Marxist-Leninist party, but it is also a sacred duty to defend our socialist fatherland against the designs and plots of the Yugoslav revisionists. Certain Soviet leaders did not like this attitude of the Albanian Party of Labor because it opposed and obstructed their schemes to approach and embrace the Titoist clique. Word began to go around that "the Albanians are hotheaded," that they "are narrow-minded and fight against the Yugoslav leaders from a position of nationalism," that "the Albanians want to seize the banner of anti-revisionism," and that "they are helping to raise the prestige of Tito's clique," etc., etc. But our party did not deviate from its principled position and continued to wage a consistent and uncompromising struggle against the Yugoslav revisionists. This action of our party has never been to the liking of N. Khrushchev and is one of the reasons for his vicious stand against the Albanian Party of Labor and its leadership.

The position of N. Khrushchev's group toward Yugoslav revisionism is, in fact, a position which differs not only from that of the Albanian Party of Labor but also from that of the entire international Communist and workers movement and from the position taken in the Moscow Declarations of 1957 and 1960, in which revisionism is declared to be the main danger of the international Communist and workers movement and Yugoslav revisionism the subverter of the socialist camp and the forces of peace. Therefore, it is clear that the Soviet leadership is trying to weaken the struggle against opportunism and revisionism in the Communist movement. Here too lies the source of the attempts to distort by all kinds of maneuvers the clear-cut thesis of the two Moscow Declarations on revisionism as the main danger to the Communist and workers movement and to bring into the foreground the struggle against dogmatism. Each day it becomes clearer to our party that by paying lip service to the necessity for fighting against revisionism while not, in fact, doing so, N. Khrushchev and his followers, under the pretext of the struggle against dogmatism, are fighting against Marxism-Leninism and attempting to repudiate the fundamental theses of the revolutionary doctrine of the proletariat, just as Tito attempted before him and just as all kinds of opportunists and revisionists have attempted in the past.

What have been the results of the propagation of the various opportunist views, of the unprincipled struggle against J. V. Stalin, and of the policy of reconciliation with Tito's traitorous revisionist clique which N. Khrushchev and his group have so persistently practiced? Although they shout to the skies "the marvelous results" allegedly obtained from the "criticism of the personality cult of J. V. Stalin" and the "normalization of relations with Yugoslavia," and although they present the matter as though the 20th Congress initiated a new era in the development and further strengthening of the world Communist movement, the facts directly contradict this. These distorted views and actions became a signal for the opportunist and revisionist elements in many countries to launch a revisionist attack against the Marxist-Leninist parties. This happened in the Communist parties of the United States, Denmark, the Netherlands, Italy, France, and England, etc. Under the influence of the opportunist views voiced by N. Khrushchev at the 20th Congress, revisionism revived and spread widely in many Communist and workers parties, thereby seriously endangering the entire international Communist movement. It is precisely under the slogans of the struggle against "Stalinist despotism," borrowed from the "secret" report "On the Cult of the Personality and Its Consequences," which, strangely enough, fell into the hands of reactionary circles in the West and was reproduced by the ton, that imperialist reaction and modern revisionism, especially the revisionist renegades of Belgrade — the enemies of socialism, of the Soviet Union, and of the peoples of all the countries of the socialist camp — organized the counterrevolutionary activities against the socialist order in Poland and the counterrevolutionary coup in Hungary. It is precisely under the cover of those opportunist theses, of the attacks against Stalin and the conciliatory attitude of N. Khrushchev toward the Yugoslav revisionists, that Tito's renegade band revived and was given a free hand to carry on its undermining activity against the socialist camp and the international Communist movement on a broad scale.

It is perfectly clear to us that such an interpretation is not acceptable either to N. Khrushchev or to his followers. But it is logical for us to ask: Why was it precisely after the 20th Congress that the renegades and revisionists immediately revived in the ranks of the Communist and workers parties of the various countries, the Yugoslav revisionist clique raised its head once again, and they jointly launched a frontal attack against Marxism-Leninism? Why did not the theses of, let us say, the 19th or the 18th Congress of the Communist Party of the Soviet Union become their banner? There is only one explanation: Certain theses advanced at the 20th Congress had an opportunist character and therefore provided ideological food for the renegades and revisionists in their struggle against Marxism-Leninism; furthermore, the position taken toward Stalin and the Tito clique were anti-Marxist, and that is why they were therefore utilized so successfully by the enemies of Marxism and socialism for their purposes.

These bitter consequences were also felt in Albania. In our country, opportunist elements of the Tuk Jakova and Bedri Spahiu type, as well as many other elements expelled from the party for antiparty activities, were activated and, under the direct instigation of the Yugoslav revisionists, organized the plot at the Tirana Party Conference in April 1956. It is known that a major role in this plot was played by the traitor Panajot Plaku, a Yugoslav espionage agent of long standing, who fled from Albania to Yugoslavia and to whom N. Khrushchev even offered political asylum in the Soviet Union in 1957. The slogans of these traitors were the demagogical slogans of the "liberalization and democratization of the dictatorship of the proletariat," "the normalization of relations with Yugoslavia," "the rehabilitation of Koci Xoxe and other antiparty elements earlier condemned," etc. It is very significant that precisely at that time, in April and May 1956, the Soviet leadership, through M. Suslov and P. Pospelov, tried to persuade our party to rehabilitate the traitor Koci Xoxe, the enemy of the party and the Albanian people and agent of Tito's clique, who had been shot for his hostile activity designed to liquidate the party and the people's power and to transform Albania into the seventh republic of Titoist Yugoslavia.

N. Khrushchev's anti-Marxist position on the above-mentioned questions has, therefore, rendered great harm to our common cause of socialism and Communism.

Nevertheless, the international Communist and workers movement has been able to withstand successfully the assault of the revisionist renegades. The ranks of the Communist and workers parties have been strengthened owing to the might and resolution of the fraternal Communist and workers parties and to the vitality of Marxist-Leninist ideology. And so it shall always be. Marxism-Leninism is the banner of victory; therefore, its enemies, the revisionists and opportunists, have failed and will always fail shamefully. (*Applause*).

From what has been said above, it is clear that the nature of our differences has been entirely ideological and political and that our party has not been in agreement with certain opportunist views and actions of N. Khrushchev on certain vital questions of contemporary world development and the international Communist and workers movement — views which are contrary to some of the basic principles of Marxism-Leninism and constitute a serious violation of the Declarations of the Communist and workers parties of 1957 and 1960. But the existence of these distorted views among the Soviet leaders is only half the evil. The greatest evil is that they are trying at any price to impose their opportunist concepts on all the Communist and workers parties, without refraining even from the most brutal pressure, blackmail, and attacks against fraternal parties and their leaders who do not agree with the revisionist theses of N. Khrushchev and who oppose them and resolutely defend Marxism-Leninism. Herein lies the greatest evil, and herein lies also the source of the tension in the relations between our country and the Soviet leadership. Realizing that his manifold efforts to bring the Albanian Party of Labor to its knees and to impose upon it his anti-Marxist views failed before the indomitable Marxist-Leninist stand of our party, and wishing to justify his impermissible and hostile activity against the Albanian Party of Labor and the Albanian People's Republic before his party and the international workers movement, N. Khrushchev has resorted to savage public slanders, such as those which he and other Soviet leaders made at the 22nd Congress of the Communist Party of the Soviet Union.

The fact that he chose the rostrum of the 22nd Congress of the Communist Party of the Soviet Union from which to pass "judgment" on our party, and the fact that he hoodwinked the representatives of certain fraternal parties into taking an unfriendly stance toward our party in their greetings to the Congress of the Communist Party of the Soviet Union, throws light on his "putschist" methods, on his surprise tactics aimed at unilaterally imposing his desires on the international Communist and workers parties, and on his disregard for the basic principles governing relations between fraternal Communist and workers parties and jointly established and defined in the Moscow Declarations.

Only an international forum, an international meeting of Communist and workers parties can examine the actions of a Communist and workers party and judge whether or not it stands on correct positions — and only after the arguments of the party in question have been heard in detail. But N. Khrushchev was afraid to convene such a meeting because he was convinced that he would not achieve his aim of condemning our Party of Labor. For this reason also he did not invite our party to the 22nd Congress, because the Albanian Party of Labor would have disclosed the truth about Albanian-Soviet relations, would have unmasked his anti-Marxist views and actions, and would have completely refuted his baseless slanders and accusations.

The method used by the First Secretary of the Communist Party of the Soviet Union in his unilateral attack on our party is known to the international Communist and workers movement. He used these tactics in Bucharest as well, where he tried to bring Marxist-Leninist parties to their knees by fallacious and one-sided accusations and to compromise representatives of fraternal parties by sudden pronouncements which were neither well founded nor carefully thought out. But in spite of his endeavors, he did not achieve his aim. On the contrary, N. Khrushchev was compelled to accept the convening of the Moscow conference of November 1960, where correct debates took place and where it became clearly evident that his views did not meet with the enthusiastic support of the participants — a fact which is also expressed in the very documents approved by the representatives of the 81 parties which N. Khrushchev is brutally violating in everything he does. Therefore, in order to attack our party and since he was afraid to convene an international meeting, he resorted to his putschist methods and used the 22nd Congress for this purpose.

In this manner, N. Khrushchev has effectively sabotaged any future international meeting because, by publicly and unilaterally attacking our party, he has placed the Albanian Party of Labor in a position of inequality.

At the 22nd Congress N. Khrushchev and his followers accused our party of allegedly "destroying the unity and disrupting the socialist camp and the international Communist movement" by its actions. Only one who has lost all sense of responsibility and gravity can say such a thing. Who is, in fact, undermining our unity, the Albanian Party of Labor or the leaders of the Communist Party of the Soviet Union headed by N. Khrushchev? Our party, which has always observed the principle of settling differences in the party manner and on the basis of the principles of the Moscow Declarations of 1957 and 1960, or the Soviet leadership, which has trampled these principles under foot and has embarked upon the anti-Marxist path of pressures and blackmail, even going so far as to openly call for counterrevolution in socialist Albania? The Albanian Party of Labor has never spoken publicly of our differences; it has openly and courageously criticized the mistaken views and actions of the Soviet leaders only in the party manner and at party meetings, while N. Khrushchev was the first not only to speak publicly from the rostrum of the 22nd Congress of the existence of our differences but also to spout forth venom and to slander in broad daylight our party and people's power by depicting it as "a reign of terror where prisons and firing squads abound right and left," thus using the language of Ranković, who said that "barbed wire and the boot of the border guard reign in Albania." Our party stands for unity, and for its further consolidation, but for a sound and steel-like unity, not for an anemic and unsound unity. It is precisely because it stands for the steel-like unity of the international Communist and workers movement and of the socialist camp that it has courageously and in the party manner criticized the anti-Marxist manifestations and actions of N. Khrushchev which weaken this unity. (*Applause*)

We greatly regret the fact that certain leaders of the fraternal parties have associated themselves with the erroneous views of N. Khrushchev. We do not want to seek the causes which compelled them to take such a position (we understand quite well the difficult position they were in), but can one call their unilateral, a priori position correct when the majority of the representatives of the fraternal parties knew nothing of the development of relations between our party and the Soviet leadership? Or must new principles be established in the Communist movement according to which the great are to be heard but not the small; the great are right but the small are always wrong? In our opinion such reasoning is incorrect and does not conform to the Leninist norms of relations between parties. Such a position does not contribute to the strengthening of the unity of the international Communist and workers movement, to the strengthening of the socialist camp, but rather weakens it and will later cause great complications.

In spite of all this, N. Khrushchev was not supported at the 22nd Congress of the Communist Party of the Soviet Union by all the representatives of the fraternal Communist and workers parties. Out of the 80 foreign delegations which attended the proceedings of the Congress and spoke or addressed greetings in writing, 34 representatives of the fraternal parties did not associate themselves with N. Khrushchev's slanders and accusations against our party (*stormy applause*); they did not speak of the differences which exist between the Albanian Party of Labor and the Soviet leadership. Of course, many of them may have their own views concerning the activity the Albanian Party of Labor, but during the 22nd Congress of the Communist Party of the Soviet Union, which was the congress of a particular party, they considered it improper to discuss a matter which concerns the entire international Communist movement and thereby maintained a correct Marxist-Leninist position. It should also be said that the majority of domestic delegates at the 22nd Congress did not express themselves on the Soviet-Albanian differences. They did not speak against our party, and did not support N. Khrushchev in his attacks and slanders against the Albanian Party of Labor. Out of the 88 delegates who participated in the discussions of the congress, only 14 spoke against our party, and all of them were members of the Soviet leadership.

For their principled and correct stand, our Party of Labor thanks both the representatives of fraternal Communist and workers parties who did not support N. Khrushchev in his unilateral attack on our party and the delegates of the glorious Communist Party of Lenin who, faithful to the Bolshevik tradition and the Leninist principles of objective judgment on all questions, did not support N. Khrushchev in this anti-Marxist act. (*Applause*)

Among the many slanderous accusations launched from the rostrum of the 22nd Congress, the First Secretary of the Central Committee of the Communist Party of the Soviet Union also spoke about the alleged lack of democracy in our party and of the alleged violations of Leninist norms in the internal life of the party. This is, of course, open interference in the internal affairs of our party; however, we can say to these "defenders" of democracy: Better mind your own business because it is not in the Albanian Party of Labor but in your parties that scandalous violations of the most elementary rules of democracy exist. When Dimitri Polyansky attacked the anti-party group, and in particular Kliment Voroshilov, he naturally neglected to reveal in detail the entire behind-the-scenes preparations which he and his companions organized at the time of the plenum of the Central Committee of the Soviet Union in the summer of 1957. Polyansky concealed all these things from the congress, but he told them to their "friend" Liri Belishova, who reported them to our party. Let us take another example. When the Tirana tribunal delivered the well-deserved sentence to the agents of American imperialism, Yugoslavia, and Greece, Teme Sejko and his associates, from the entire press of the countries of the peoples' democracies in Europe only the newspaper *Trud,* the organ of the Bulgarian working class, reported on the trial accurately. But immediately, that very day, in the most "democratic" fashion (*laughter*), it was announced that the president and two secretaries of the Central Council of the Bulgarian Trade Unions were removed from their posts, and this was because the revisionist Tito that very day lodged a serious protest with the Bulgarian Government in connection with the report on the Tirana trial given by this newspaper. Finally, speaking of those who talk of internal democracy and respect for party norms — and here we are referring in particular to Palmiro Togliatti — how can he consider his behavior at the 22nd Congress as democratic and in accord with the rules when he spoke and condemned our party? He did not know what had gone before and how the relations between our party and the Soviet leadership had developed. At least our party did not give the Italian Communist Party any material. The Central Committee of the Italian Communist Party did not previously adopt any decision to denounce our party and thereby authorize its representatives to condemn our party. At least we know of no such matter. What kind of democracy then are these leaders talking about when they are scandalized without reason over the fate of one person, while, when the fate of a party, of 50,000 Communists and an entire people, is involved, they make statements which are insulting, totally irresponsible, and in flagrant contradiction not only to the elementary rules of party democracy but also to those of simple logic and human conscience? Palmiro Togliatti pronounced the Roman anathema against us, accusing us of disrupting the unity of the international Communist movement. On what grounds was Togliatti acting when, only a few years ago, he publicly attacked the Soviet socialist system and preached polycentrism and zones of influence within the international Communist movement? He does not and will not have any evidence against us, but with his own anti-Marxist theses he rendered a great service to the revisionist Tito. It is strange, however, that no one came out against Togliatti's revisionist views.

N. Khrushchev, who talks so much about democratic methods, patience, and internationalism, has employed the most anti-Marxist methods against our country — methods thoroughly alien to relations between socialist countries. In order to subdue the Albanian Party of Labor, to prevent it from having its own view, and to impose upon it his anti-Marxist views, he and his followers have not refrained from any measures, not only regarding relations between our parties but also regarding relations between our socialist states. We do not wish today to go into details and to dwell at length on these issues, since they are concretely illustrated by many facts and countless documents. But we will mention that as a result of the anti-Marxist methods used by the Soviet leaders to settle existing differences, and as a result of the repeated pressures in the economic, political, and military spheres, the relations between our country and the Soviet Union have been greatly aggravated. This process began in the second half of last year, that is, after the Bucharest meeting. Since then, N. Khrushchev, instead of agreeing to settle patiently the ideological and political differences between our party and the Soviet leadership, made them public and even extended them to state relations.

Thus in the economic field all the credits granted by the Soviet Union to our country for the third five-year plan were suspended, and this was done in order to sabotage the economic plan of our country; all the Soviet specialists who were working in Albania, whom our economy greatly needed, and whom we had officially asked to remain were unilaterally withdrawn and for no reason whatsoever; by issuing an ultimatum that, beginning with this year, we repay old credits (although, according to existing documents, this should begin after 1970), the Soviet side has broken off almost all trade relations on a clearing basis; scholarships have been cut off from all the Albanian students, civilian and military alike, who were studying in the Soviet Union. Pressures and restrictive measures in the military field accompanied economic pressures.

On the other hand, everyone well knows that the press of the Albanian People's Republic writes constantly on the life and successes of the Soviet Union in the construction of Communism and openly supports the various proposals of the Communist Party of the Soviet Union and the Soviet government concerning various international questions, whereas, for the past year and a half, the Soviet press has maintained a blockade of strict silence on Albania. While it never misses an opportunity to write about the slightest positive word that may by chance have been said by some English lord, the Soviet press has not written a line about Albania — let alone about the Albanian Party of Labor — as though there did not exist on the face of the earth either the Albanian People's Republic or the Albanian people, who are building socialism and struggling for peace, with the wolf at their door, surrounded as they are on all sides by the imperialists and their tools. The curtain of silence was raised only at the 22nd Congress of the Communist Party of the Soviet Union by N. Khrushchev, but he did so only to slander and to spout venom against the Albanian Party of Labor and the Albanian People's Republic.

Certain leaders of the socialist countries of Europe have also followed N. Khrushchev in these anti-Marxist and hostile actions toward the Albanian people. Altogether they are doing their utmost to isolate Albania economically, politically, and militarily by creating a "cordon sanitaire" around her. N. Khrushchev forgets that in the century of the triumph of Leninism there can be no "cordon" that can isolate a people and a party which are fighting resolutely for the triumph of socialism and Communism. There is no "cordon," however well organized and powerful, that can withstand the truth of Marxism-Leninism. Any "cordon" will be smashed, and its organizers will fail shamefully. (*Stormy applause. All rise. Ovation*)

The First Secretary of the Central Committee of the Communist Party of the Soviet Union and Chairman of the Council of Ministers of the Soviet Union did not confine himself to this. Seeing that all his pressures, blockades, and blackmail did not produce the result he desired — did not bring our party and people to their knees — he openly issued from the rostrum of the 22nd Congress an appeal for a counterrevolutionary coup to overthrow the leadership of the Albanian Party of Labor and to liquidate the party, something which he refrains from doing even in the case of the governments of capitalist countries because he considers it interference in their internal affairs. He said:

> . . . To put an end to the cult of the personality would in effect mean that Shehu, Hoxha, and others would have to give up their key positions in the party and government. And this they do not want to do. But we are certain the time will come when the Albanian Communists and the Albanian people will have their say (*laughter*), and then the Albanian leaders will have to answer for the harm they have done their country, their people, and the cause of socialist construction in Albania.

The Albanian people and the Albanian Communists have given their answer to N. Khrushchev in hundreds and thousands of telegrams and letters, a few of which have been published in our press. (*Stormy applause. All rise. Ovation*)

Our party and people have heard constantly, for 17 years in succession, appeals for the overthrow of our people's power and for the liquidation of our party and its leadership. They have heard them and continue to hear them every year from the State Department of the United States, from the American, British, and other imperialists, from Franco's radio "Nationalist Spain," from Tito's traitorous revisionist gang, from the Greek monarcho-fascists, and so forth. All these have even organized plots to achieve their aims. Now we hear such an appeal even from N. Khrushchev, who, in fact, is joining them in their hostile activities against the Albanian people and their Party of Labor. Upon whom have the imperialists and their tools relied in their activity against our people's power and party in our country? Their army has been the scum of our society, the degenerate and antiparty elements, the people who have sold themselves to the foreign intelligence services of the imperialists, whom our people recall only with a feeling of deep hatred, contempt, and revulsion. This will also be the army of N. Khrushchev. (*Laughter*) It cannot be otherwise. All our people, young and old, all the decent and patriotic persons in our country, whether party members or not, have rallied today more than ever before around our glorious party and its correct Marxist-Leninist line, which expresses the vital interests of our people and conforms to the common interests of our great cause, socialism and Communism. (*Stormy applause. All rise. Ovation*) The hostile activity and brutal intervention of N. Khrushchev will fail shamefully in the face of the steel-like unity of our party and people, in the face of this invincible force, just as all the hostile activity and all the plots undertaken by the imperialists, the Yugoslav revisionists, the Greek monarcho-fascists, and other enemies against the Albanian people and its Party of Labor have failed in the past and will always fail.

At the 22nd Congress of the Communist Party of the Soviet Union, N. Khrushchev accused our party and its leaders of being anti-Soviet, labeling any critical comment on his anti-Marxist views and actions, made at party meetings and according to Leninist rules, as an attack on the Soviet Union and the Soviet peoples. This is a monstrous slander and distortion. For 20 years in succession our party and people have been educated in the spirit of boundless love and indomitable loyalty toward the glorious Soviet Union and the Communist Party of the Soviet Union. They have demonstrated this love and loyalty by their deeds in the common struggle against fascism, by their joint efforts in the construction of the socialist and Communist society and for peace and the freedom of peoples; they have demonstrated them through their principled and resolute struggle against our common enemies — the imperialists and modern revisionists, particularly after the 20th Congress of the Communist Party of the Soviet Union and the Hungarian counterrevolution, when the enemies of socialism launched savage attacks and slanders against the Soviet system and stabbed the Soviet soldiers in the back. The sacred Albanian-Soviet friendship which our party and people have forged and strengthened constantly through 20 years of heroic struggle and untiring efforts cannot be so easily liquidated by a few unfounded accusations and base slanders. Albanian-Soviet friendship has deep roots and will live for centuries, the wishes and attempts of our critics notwithstanding. (*Applause*)

Who is in fact defending the Soviet Union and its prestige? N. Khrushchev, who with his unprincipled attacks and slanders against J. V. Stalin has discredited the glorious Soviet Union by depicting it as a country where the most savage terror reigned, as in the case of Hitler's Germany, or the Albanian Party of Labor, which has defended and is defending the Soviet Union from the savage attacks of imperialist and revisionist propaganda, which N. Khrushchev has furnished with weapons? Who is defending the Soviet Union and its prestige? N. Khrushchev, who by his anti-Marxist activities, attacks, pressures, and blockades against the Albanian People's Republic has given weapons to the imperialists with which to defile the Soviet Union before world public opinion, or the Albanian Party of Labor, which has shown and is showing that his anti-Marxist actions have nothing in common with the internationalist principles and traditions of the glorious Soviet Union and the great party of Lenin, that they are an unfortunate and temporary affliction on their healthy body?

Our party has listened patiently to what was said about it at the 22nd Congress. And now we are giving our view on these matters. The Albanian Party of Labor, with a clear and pure conscience, appeals to the Communist Party of the Soviet Union, appeals to the new Central Committee elected by the 22nd Congress, to judge with Leninist equity, with objectivity and composure and not in a unilateral manner, the situation which has been created in the relations between our two parties and our two countries. Our party has always been ready, for the sake of the unity of the Communist movement and of the socialist camp, for the sake of the interests of our two countries, to settle existing differences. But it has always been and remains of the opinion that these questions should be settled justly and in the Marxist-Leninist manner, on the basis of equality and not of pressure and dictation. (*Stormy applause*) We place our hope and confidence in the justice of the Communist Party of the Soviet Union.

Our party and people, regardless of the attacks, slanders, and hostile actions directed against them, will hold intact in their hearts the pure feelings of friendship for the fraternal peoples of the Soviet Union. Our party has taught us to love the Soviet Union, the fatherland of the great Lenin and Stalin, both in good times and in bad. For us the glorious Soviet Union, the Soviet peoples, and the great party of the Bolsheviks have been, are, and remain our most cherished friends, our liberators from the fascist yoke, and our loyal and resolute allies in the struggle for the construction of socialism in our country. We have been and will be bound for life with the Soviet Union, with the Soviet peoples, with the Communist Party of the Soviet Union. (*Stormy applause*) Our party and people have followed and are following with particular satisfaction the endeavors and glorious successes which the Soviet workers, led by their glorious Communist Party, have won in all fields of Communist construction and consider them as victories of the Albanian people as well in our joint struggle for the triumph of the great cause of socialism and Communism. We are firmly convinced that the objectives and tasks set forth by the 22nd Congress of the Communist Party of the Soviet Union will be, as always, successfully realized for the good of the peoples of the Soviet Union and of the entire socialist camp, for the benefit of the sacred cause of socialism and Communism and of the peace and freedom of all the peoples in the world.

Our party and people will fight as always for the cause of socialism and Communism, for a united socialist camp, alongside the fraternal peoples of the Soviet Union, alongside the fraternal Chinese people, alongside all the peoples of the countries of the socialist camp.

Comrades!

The entire life and activity of our party over 20 years, as well as the facts of contemporary reality, clearly show that our party has always had a correct general line, that in connection with the vital contemporary questions preoccupying the international Communist movement, particularly in connection with the question of Albanian-Soviet relations, it has taken a correct Marxist-Leninist and internationalist stand.

Deeply convinced that they are right, our people and party, united as a single body, with a clear and pure conscience and with firm determination, will in the future as well follow unswervingly their correct path. And on this path they will win. (*Stormy applause. All rise. Ovation*)

The guarantee of this is our heroic and

indomitable people and our glorious party, the party of the people's revolution; the party which in the course of 20 years has conquered fascism and has liberated our people and fatherland, which has triumphed over backwardness, hunger, and ignorance and has set our country on the road to socialism, progress, and culture; the party which, as a devoted offspring of our heroic people, has thwarted every provocation and plot designed to bring back slavery and poverty to our homes. The guarantee of our future victories will be our support and friendship with the Soviet peoples, with the Chinese people, with all the friendly peoples of the countries of the socialist camp, and with others with whom our party, as a party loyal to the principles of proletarian internationalism, has bound our small but heroic people in eternal and indestructible friendship.

We are experiencing some temporary difficulties because not only must we face the attacks and intrigues of our sworn enemies, the American and other imperialists, together with their allies and lackeys — the Yugoslav revisionists — but we must also repel new slanders and attacks against us. But difficulties have never frightened or daunted our party or our people. By closing our ranks behind the party, by strengthening our vigilance, and by increasing our efforts to achieve successfully the tasks for the fulfillment of the state plan in all fields — and to do this better than ever before — we shall emerge triumphant. (*Stormy applause. All rise. Ovation*) We are convinced that in this struggle and in these efforts we shall have the support of all our friends, of all the peoples of the socialist countries including first and foremost the Soviet people, of all the Communists of the world including first and foremost the Soviet Communists, who sooner or later will realize that the fist which is pointed at our party and people is wrongly aimed and is dangerous for all the Communists in the world. (*Applause*)

It is with confidence that we celebrate the great holiday of the 44th anniversary of the October Socialist Revolution and the great holiday of the 20th anniversary of the founding of our glorious party. It is with confidence that, with the revolutionary banner of victorious Leninism, the banner of our heroic party, unfurled, we Albanian Communists, together with our entire patriotic and fighting people, will advance with sure steps toward new victories for the glory of Marxism-Leninism, for the glory of Communism, and for the glory of our socialist fatherland. (*Stormy applause. All rise. Ovation*)

Long live the 44th anniversary of the great October Socialist Revolution!

Long live the 20th anniversary of the Albanian Party of Labor!

Glory to victorious Marxism-Leninism, the banner of the victories of our party and people!

Long live our heroic and indomitable people!

Glory to the Albanian Party of Labor! (*Stormy applause. All rise. Ovation*)

DOCUMENT 15

"A Year of Historic Proofs," Zëri i Popullit, *December 6, 1961 (complete text)*.

A whole year has elapsed since the publication of the Declaration of the meeting of the representatives of the 81 Communist and workers parties. The great historic significance of the Declaration lies in the fact that it is a collective document which, starting from the revolutionary positions of Marxism-Leninism, generalizes the common experience of all the Communist and workers parties on the fundamental problems of contemporary world development, such as the definition of our epoch and the analysis of the balance of power in the world, the problem of peace and war, the struggle against colonialism, the problems of the working class struggle in capitalist countries, the paths and forms of the transition to socialism, the struggle against revisionism and dogmatism, relations between the socialist countries and between fraternal Communist and workers parties, and so forth. Along with the 1957 Moscow Declaration, the Declaration of the 81 Communist and workers parties of 1960 is the fighting banner and guide to action of the entire international Communist and workers movement. It is the irreplaceable revolutionary program in the struggle for socialism, national liberation, peace, and democracy. The historic importance of the 1960 Declaration lies also in the fact that it forms a firm Marxist-Leninist base for the defense and further consolidation of the unity of the international Communist and workers movement and the socialist camp. Therefore, to respect it and to implement it consistently is the great task of all the Communist and workers parties in the world.

The year that has elapsed since the publication of the Declaration was a year of historic proofs which convincingly confirmed the correctness and vitality of its theses and principles on a number of fundamental questions regarding the contemporary development of the world and the international Communist movement.

It was a year of further changes in the balance of power in the international arena in favor of socialism and the freedom-loving, peace-loving, and democratic forces and against imperialism and colonialism and the forces of war and reaction.

The magnificent successes of the Soviet Union in all areas of building Communism and of People's China and the other people's democracies in building socialism, which prove the indisputable superiority of the socialist system over the capitalist system, the further development of the economic, political, and military forces of the great socialist camp, and the increase of its influence in the international arena — all these clearly prove the thesis of the Declaration that with each passing day the world socialist system is becoming the decisive factor in the development of human society and the main force in contemporary international life.

The further development of the powerful struggle of the broad working masses, headed by the working class, against the capitalist monopolies and for peace and democracy, better living conditions, and socialism; the onward rush of the national liberation movement of the enslaved African, Asian, and Latin American peoples against the imperialist colonial yoke; the winning of national independence by other peoples during 1961; the ignominious failure of U.S. aggression against revolutionary Cuba; and the failure of the efforts of the imperialist colonialists to crush by fire and sword the peoples who have arisen to fight for freedom — all these clearly prove that imperialism has become further weakened. They show that imperialism is incapable of imposing its will on the world or of stopping the wheels of history.

During the past year the process of the deterioration and disintegration of the world capitalist system and the further aggravation of its economic class, national, and international contradictions became more strongly evident. The unbridled militarization of the economy of many capitalist countries, which gravely damages a country's economy and burdens the working people; the chronic unemployment in the most advanced capitalist countries (including the United States — that bulwark of contemporary world capitalism which counts about 6 million unemployed); the powerful wave of strikes during 1961 in the United States, Britain, France, Italy, Japan, the Latin American countries, and in many other capitalist countries; the further aggravation of disagreements among the imperialist powers on the problems of the Congo, the "European Common Market," and other important matters — all are facts which clearly prove this.

However, the past year also clearly proved that although the balance of power has changed in favor of socialism and the freedom-loving and peace-loving people and against imperialism, the aggressive and reactionary nature of imperialism has not changed and will never change until its dying day. The year 1961 brilliantly confirmed the teachings of the Declaration that American imperialism is the main force of aggression and war, the chief bulwark of world reaction, and an international gendarme — the savage enemy of the peoples of the world.

What was the world situation following the assumption of power by President Kennedy's administration in the United States? Life, facts, and the international events of 1961, sooner than could be expected, dispelled as the sun dispels the morning mist the illusions spread by bourgeois propaganda and the modern revisionists that, upon the assumption of power by the new American president, millionaire John Kennedy, "great grounds for hope would emerge" and "brilliant prospects would open up" for easing international tension, normalizing relations between nations, and securing a lasting peace in the world.

Facts show that imperialism, headed by U.S. imperialism, has not renounced in the least its policy of war and aggression. Armed intervention in Cuba, the events in the Congo, Laos, South Korea, and South Vietnam, and the efforts to drown in blood the liberation struggle of the heroic peoples of Algeria, Angola, Oman, and elsewhere; the strengthening of the aggressive blocs, military bases, and the arms race; the revival of revanchist militarism in West Germany and Japan; the rejection of the constructive proposals made by the Soviet Union and other socialist countries; the brandishing of arms and threats of war in connection with the question of West Berlin; U.S. intervention in Latin American affairs; increased U.S. penetration in the Afro-Asian countries through the so-called "Peace Corps" and other means; the intensification and further development of espionage and diversionary activities against the socialist countries; the persecution of the Communist Party of the U.S.A. and other such activities — all clearly demonstrate the designs and real intentions of the imperialist powers, headed by the United States of America.

Times have now changed. Imperialism is no longer the all-powerful master of the world. The further change in the balance of power in 1961 on the international scene has naturally created more favorable conditions and greater possibilities for the prevention of another world war and other aggressive wars on the part of imperialism. This does not mean, however, that the danger of war no longer exists nor that the imperialists, headed by the American imperialists, have renounced their warmongering aggressive activities. War can be prevented if the peoples, above all the peoples of the socialist countries, remain vigilant and are prepared, militarily and spiritually, to halt the imperialists from starting another war and, as noted in the Declaration, in case the mad imperialists should start a war, to wipe capitalism off the face of the earth and bury it. The danger of war may well increase if the people relax their vigilance and cease carrying on an active struggle against the plans and aggressive activities of imperialism, and if they are militarily and spiritually unarmed in the face of heavily armed imperialism. "Our profound conviction that, at the present time, a world war and the other aggressive wars started by imperialism can be prevented," Comrade Enver Hoxha stated in his speech delivered on the occasion of the 20th anniversary of the Albanian Party of Labor and the 44th anniversary of the October Revolution, "is in no way based on the 'good intentions' of the leaders of imperialism, but on the colossal economic, political, and military might of the powerful socialist camp, on the unity and struggle of the international Communist and workers movement and the resolute struggle of the peoples of the world against the imperialist warmongers, and on the unity and solidarity of all the peace-loving forces."

The year which has elapsed since the publication of the Declaration clearly proved the correctness of its important conclusion that revisionism remains the chief danger for the international Communist movement. Revisionism has not been fully annihilated. On the contrary, recently, as a result of the relaxation of the struggle against it, revisionism has revived in many Communist and workers parties and is thus becoming an increasingly serious danger. This is shown by the example of some Communist and workers parties, especially the Italian Communist Party, which, following the 22nd Congress of the Communist Party of the Soviet Union, revived the revisionist theses on "polycentrism," on the "degeneration" of the Soviet socialist system, and so forth. Under the guise of the struggle against Stalinism, dogmatism, or nationalism, the revisionists are trying to bury the revolutionary spirit of Marxism-Leninism, to reject its fundamental principles, and to undermine the unity of the socialist camp and the international Communist movement. The Declaration's appraisal of Yugoslav revisionism as the concentrated expression of contemporary international opportunism and of the leaders of the League of Communists of Yugoslavia as traitors to Marxism-Leninism, subverters of the socialist camp and the international Communist movement, and disrupters of the forces of peace was also proved correct.

Profiting from the relaxation of the struggle against the Titoist clique by the leaders of some Communist and workers parties, and fully aided by imperialism, the Titoist clique has intensified its hostile activities. This is shown in its efforts to divert the conference of nonaligned countries from the struggle against imperialism, headed by the United States, and to disrupt the forces of the national liberation struggle, especially in Africa; it is shown as well in its vicious attacks against the Chinese People's Republic and in its direct participation in the organization of the plot against the Albanian People's Republic, and so forth. For its role in the service of imperialism, in addition to the more than 3 billion dollars received previously, the Titoist clique received during 1961 more than 197 million dollars from the United States and the other imperialist powers. All this proves the importance and timeliness of the Declaration's thesis that "the further unmasking of the leaders of Yugoslav revisionism and the active struggle to protect the Communist and workers movement from the anti-Leninist ideas of the Yugoslav revisionists continue to be indispensable tasks of the Marxist-Leninist parties."

Our Party of Labor has been rigorously faithful to the 1960 Declaration of the 81 Communist and workers parties and has made it the basis of all its ideological and political activities, just as it has been faithful to and has fully implemented the Declaration of the Communist and workers parties of 1957. But those who slander our party, who attack it and accuse it of thinking and acting in opposition to the Declaration are the ones who have trampled and are trampling on this collective document of the entire international Communist movement which N. Khrushchev, even before it was published, called "a compromise document of short duration." The events of the year which has elapsed clearly prove who violated and who is violating the principles of this Declaration.

Let us consider the question of the attitude toward imperialism. Was it not N. Khrushchev and his followers who, before the ink had dried on their signatures to the Declaration and before Kennedy had come to power, began to propagate throughout the world the illusion that Kennedy would, so to speak, follow a peaceful policy? In complete contradiction to the Declaration, which points out that American imperialism is the main force of aggression and war and the savage enemy of the peoples in the world, they believed the beautiful words of Kennedy about "peace," the words of this worthy representative of American imperialism. However, these illusions dissolved like salt in water as a result of the facts regarding the brief but intensive activity of the Kennedy government, which we have briefly summarized. And in the face of all these facts, according to the news agencies, A. Adzhubei, member of the Central Committee of the Communist Party of the Soviet Union, immediately after his interview with Kennedy, declared to American journalists: "You Americans should be proud" of your President! These matters are not accidental; they comprise the entire opportunist line persistently followed by N. Khrushchev and his group. Was it not N. Khrushchev who once solemnly and "in all sincerity" declared before all the Soviet people, the government, and the Communist Party of the Soviet Union that Eisenhower "sincerely desires" peace and the liquidation of "the cold war"? And was it not he who called De Gaulle the "pride of the French people"?

Those who today accuse our party of being afraid to assume its responsibility in the settlement of the German problem are, in fact, the ones who prolong the settlement of this problem by making concessions to the imperialist powers. They are precisely the ones who, pursuing their opportunist policy in flagrant contradiction to the Declaration, have almost completely halted the struggle to unmask American imperialism, hoping, it seems, that in this way the imperialist government of the United States would become peaceful.

Our Party of Labor, which is faithfully guided by the teachings of Marxism-Leninism on classes and the class struggle and by the two Declarations of the Communist and workers parties, has never had any illusions about Eisenhower, Kennedy, Macmillan, De Gaulle, Adenauer, or any other imperialist leader. They cannot be for peace as long as they represent the interests of the most reactionary and most warmongering circles of the great capitalist monopolies. On the contrary, our party has been faithfully guided by the Leninist teachings of the Declaration that as long as imperialism exists there will be a base for aggressive wars. For this reason, it has always kept high the vigilance of our people and resolutely unmasked the warmongering, aggressive activities of imperialism and its lackeys. It was precisely because it maintained and continues to maintain a resolute, vigilant attitude that our party was capable of unmasking and liquidating in time the plot organized against the People's Republic of Albania by the revisionist leadership of Yugoslavia and the Greek monarcho-fascists, in cooperation with the American Sixth Fleet.

The violation of the Declaration by N. Khrushchev and those who follow him in his opportunist line and his unprincipled attacks against the PPSh is also clearly apparent in their attitude toward the revisionist clique of Tito. On December 6, 1960, *Pravda* published the Declaration, signed on December 2, 1960, which points out that "the Yugoslav revisionists are pursuing subversive activities against the socialist camp and the international Communist movement" and that, "under the pretext of an extrabloc policy, they are engaging in activities which endanger the cause of the unity of all the peace-loving forces and countries." Yet, on December 23, 1960, A. Gromyko, member of the Central Committee of the Communist Party of the Soviet Union and Foreign Minister of the Soviet Union, in connection with Yugoslavia declared to the Supreme Soviet of the Soviet Union: "We note with satisfaction that our positions on basic international issues coincide." This statement is not only in flagrant contradiction to the Declaration of the 81 Communist and workers parties, but is also a serious offense against the consistent, peaceful policy of the Soviet Union. To put in the same category the foreign policy of the Soviet Union, which serves the great cause of peace, freedom, and friendship between peoples, and the disruptive foreign policy of the renegade clique of Tito, which serves the oppressive and bellicose aims of American imperialism, means to render a poor service to the Soviet Union and to the cause of peace. They seek to convince the simple-minded that Titoist demagogy and lies are a "positive side" of this *agentura* of imperialism.

In open contradiction to the Declaration, N. Khrushchev and his followers, under the pretext of implementing the policy of peaceful coexistence, ended the ideological struggle against Yugoslav revisionism and proclaimed Yugoslavia a socialist country. N. Khrushchev himself said in his interview with the *New York Times* commentator, Sulzberger, which was published in *Pravda* September 10, 1961: "Of course we consider Yugoslavia a socialist country." The matter reached the point where Togliatti, at the Plenum of the Italian Communist Party devoted to the decisions of the 22nd Congress of the Communist Party of the Soviet Union, openly introduced the task of agreeing as much as possible with the Yugoslav Communists, while the leaders of certain socialist countries in Europe started implementing this long ago by continually developing and expanding economic, commercial, cultural, political, and even party relations with the Yugoslav revisionists.

At the same time, under the guise of the struggle against "dogmatism," an unprincipled struggle, full of slanders and frenzied pressures, is being carried on against the Albanian Party of Labor, which has defended and is resolutely defending Marxism-Leninism and the interests of the great cause of socialism from the attacks and undermining activities of the Belgrade revisionist gang.

These anti-Marxist stands and activities of N. Khrushchev and his group have consequently brought about the revival of revisionist views and trends in quite a number of Communist and workers parties. Not only have these views and trends not been unmasked with sufficient vigor but, on the contrary, every effort is being made to cover them up. But no matter how they are concealed, the Marxist-Leninist truth will triumph, and then the defenders of revisionism will find themselves in a tough spot. They will be subjected to a Marxist judgment by the masses of their own parties and will fail shamefully.

In view of these facts, it is by no means sheer coincidence that the renegade Tito enthusiastically welcomed, along with the furious attacks and slanders against the PPSh, the "new course" taken by N. Khrushchev at the 22nd Congress of the Communist Party of the Soviet Union. In a speech delivered at Skopje on November 13, 1961, Tito said among other things:

> In the work of the Congress we also saw a positive course which has now begun to be effectively mirrored in further developments, not only within the Soviet Union but also in the other socialist countries. For this reason, I believe that this Congress has had and will have great significance for further progress toward true democratic and progressive development, not only in the Soviet Union but also in other parts of the world in general. I cannot now go into problems of an economic nature, and I cannot speak about the prospects of the development of Communism, that is, its realization in this or that year. I do not want to take up this problem because it is a matter for study. I can only say that we welcome a course such as the one which was taken at the 22nd Congress.

See now what concerns and pleases the revisionist Tito: it is not the path and the brilliant prospects of the building of Communism in the Soviet Union, but precisely the "positive" ideological and political course which manifested itself at the 22nd Congress, and precisely the furious attacks against Stalin and against the PPSh! This, in fact, should make certain people wonder why such a renegade from Marxism and such a seasoned agent of American imperialism as Tito should praise them in this way.

Insofar as our Party of Labor is concerned, it has been and remains loyal to the important conclusions of the 1960 Declaration of the Communist and workers parties on the danger to the international Communist movement of revisionism, especially Yugoslav revisionism; and it has waged and will steadfastly wage an unyielding, principled fight to preserve the purity of Marxism-Leninism from revisionist distortions and to unmask the renegade Titoist clique as the sworn enemy of socialism and an agency of American imperialism.

The 1960 Moscow Declaration clearly defines the principles and the criteria of relations between socialist countries and Communist and workers parties on the basis of Marxism-Leninism and proletarian internationalism. Proletarian internationalism demands, on the one hand, the resolute defense of the unity of the international Communist movement and the socialist camp on the basis of the principles of Marxism-Leninism and the prohibition of any activity which may undermine this unity and, on the other, rigorous respect for the principles of equality, independence, and mutual assistance in relations between the socialist countries and fraternal Communist and workers parties and the settlement of any disagreement which may arise among them by means of comradely consultations on the basis of equality. The period which elapsed since the proclamation of the Declaration of the 81 Communist and workers parties has irrefutably demonstrated that violation of these principles seriously harms the unity of the international Communist movement and the socialist camp. Experience and facts have also proved that these principles have been violated and are being brutally transgressed by N. Khrushchev and his followers in their relations with the Albanian Party of Labor and the Albanian People's Republic.

From the beginning of June 1960, when the PPSh expressed at the Bucharest meeting a view different from that of N. Khrushchev and refused to approve his anti-Marxist actions, and especially after the November 1960 Moscow meeting of the 81 Communist and workers parties, where our party openly expressed its view and courageously criticized the opportunist views and the anti-Marxist actions of N. Khrushchev at an official conference of international Communism, N. Khrushchev and his followers began in their views on the Albanian People's Republic brutally to violate, with respect to the Albanian People's Republic, the Marxist-Leninist principles on relations between the socialist countries. Many economic and political pressures have been exerted and are being exerted upon the PPSh, the Government of the APR, and the Albanian people in order to make them yield. This is proved by numerous documents in the hands of our party and government. All the assistance and credits anticipated in the agreements signed with the governments of the Soviet Union and the other socialist countries in Europe have been withdrawn, and a strict economic and political blockade has been applied against a fraternal country which is building socialism under conditions of geographic encirclement by capitalists and revisionists. The state of affairs has gone so far that a few days ago the governments of the Soviet Union and the Hungarian People's Republic unilaterally annulled even the consular agreement which has existed between our countries for years, according to which no transit or visitor's visa for the citizens of our countries traveling among our countries was required from the respective governments. What can these anti-Marxist acts have in common with the explicit principles of the Declaration on cooperation and fraternal mutual assistance between the socialist countries?

Now, in order to justify these unheard-of anti-Marxist actions before public opinion, N. Khrushchev and his followers unscrupulously slander our party and people, saying that we deny the aid given by the Soviet Union to Albania for the building of socialism, are ungrateful for it, and other such things. Where did Maurice Thorez learn that about which he so confidently speaks? It is only slander, and slander cannot be evidence. Any honest man who wants to find out the truth should scrutinize the press of our party, and he will see that our party and all our people, both before and after the aggravation of our relations by the present Soviet leadership headed by N. Khrushchev, have always expressed and continue to express their deep gratitude for the generous and internationalist aid given by the Soviet Union to our country. They have considered and still consider this aid one of the important factors in the building of socialism in Albania. As for the pressure and the blackmail exerted on our country during the past one and a half years by N. Khrushchev and his group, they have nothing in common with the fraternal feelings which the Soviet people cherish for our people. They have nothing in common with the glorious internationalist traditions of the Soviet Union and the Communist Party of the Soviet Union.

N. Khrushchev and his group have brutally violated and are violating the principles of the Declaration on the relations between the fraternal Communist and workers parties, the principles of equality, independence, and equal comradely consultations with one another.

And when the anti-Marxist attempts to make the Albanian Party and the Albanian people yield, to impose upon them the distorted views of N. Khrushchev by means of pressure, blackmail, and impermissible blockades, failed utterly in the face of the determination and the Marxist-Leninist principles of our party, N. Khrushchev, followed by certain other people, publicly and slanderously attacked our party from the platform of the 22nd Congress. This anti-Marxist act, which is a serious blow to the unity of the socialist camp and the international Communist movement, is being extensively propagated by N. Khrushchev and his followers as the "apogee of Leninist principles." What hypocrisy and what mockery of Lenin! These people who are now boasting so much of this brand of "principle," which immensely pleased the sworn enemies of Communism and which gave them weapons with which to fight us, until yesterday were furiously attacking with the most offensive epithets the Albanian Party of Labor and its leadership, because it expressed its views about our disagreements in an honest, open, and principled way and without cunning and diplomatic dealing. It expressed them not publicly but at a meeting of the fraternal Communist and workers parties.

At the 22nd Congress and afterward, N. Khrushchev and his followers accused, and continue to accuse, our party of not agreeing with the line of the 20th Congress of the Communist Party of the Soviet Union, and from this they derive the absurd conclusion that our party has betrayed Marxism-Leninism and has landed in the lap of imperialism. It is true that our party has neither agreed nor agrees now with certain opportunist theses of the 20th Congress. But are the decisions of one party binding on all the Communist and workers parties? This is in flagrant contradiction to the 1960 Moscow Declaration, which clearly points out that "all the Marxist-Leninist parties are independent and equal, and that they formulate policies according to the concrete conditions in their own countries and on the basis of Marxist-Leninist principles."

With the aim of justifying his anti-Marxist action of publicizing our disagreements, which gave ammunition to the imperialists and revisionists all over the world, N. Khrushchev stated at the 22nd Congress that he had done everything possible to "bring into line" the leaders of the Albanian Party of Labor and that, with all possible means exhausted, he had no course other than to condemn publicly the Albanian Party of Labor and its leadership. After the 22nd Congress, this formula was repeated and is being reiterated by Maurice Thorez and certain other leaders of the European Communist and workers parties. Yes, N. Khrushchev and his group have made and are making many moves in the direction of our party and country. Immediately after the notorious Bucharest meeting, pressure, blackmail, and blockades in the economic and military fields commenced against them. In October 1960 N. Khrushchev stated that he would treat Albania the same as Titoist Yugoslavia, while at the end of March 1961 he and Novotný stated that they would cut off all assistance to the

Albanian People's Republic. This anti-Marxist pressure was repeated in many documents sent to the Central Committee of the Albanian Party of Labor by the Soviet leadership and the leaderships of some other socialist countries in Europe. Thus the letter sent to the Council of Ministers of the Albanian People's Republic by the Soviet Government on April 26, 1961, said, among other things, that "the Albanian leadership cannot expect that the Soviet Union will assist it any longer on the previous basis. This assistance is only for friends and true brothers."

What can there be in common between the appeal of N. Khrushchev and his followers for counterrevolution to overthrow the PPSh and to destroy our party, and Marxism-Leninism, international proletarianism, and the principles of the Declaration? What kind of discussions can there be, and how can our disagreements be settled when the first condition is that our party should abandon its views, and when unprecedented acts and pressure are resorted to against a Marxist-Leninist party and a socialist country, and when it is demanded that our party should subject itself at any cost to the ideas and anti-Marxist activities of N. Khrushchev?

In fact, it was of such "efforts" that N. Khrushchev spoke at the 22nd Congress, and about which the leaders of some Communist and workers parties in Europe are now sounding off in their parties. Anyone can understand that they have nothing in common with genuine efforts to solve the disagreements on the basis of the Moscow Declaration's principles of equality, independence, and consultations. N. Khrushchev has substituted for these principles the principle of dictation and pressure, in order to dominate other parties which disagree with his opportunist and revisionist views, and to make them yield.

These are the facts, and they clearly show who has remained faithful to the Declaration of the 81 Communist and workers parties, and who has trampled and is trampling upon it. They show who is resolutely defending the unity of the international Communist movement and the socialist camp, and who is destroying it. They show who has remained and is remaining faithful to the fundamental teachings of Marxism-Leninism, and who has deviated and is deviating from them in the direction of opportunism and revisionism. On its part, our party will in the future as well faithfully implement this great document of the international Communist movement, and it will firmly oppose any deviation from it, in accord with the great Lenin's teaching which maintains that sound unity is possible only on the basis of Marxist principles.

The party and all our people are deeply confident that the temporary difficulties which the international Communist movement is undergoing will be successfully liquidated, and that, united as never before, it will march ever forward, enlightened by the great ideas of the Declaration, toward the final triumph of our great cause — socialism and Communism, freedom of the peoples, and world peace.

DOCUMENT 16

"New Hostile Acts of N. Khrushchev's Group toward the Albanian People's Republic," Zëri i Popullit, *December 10, 1961 (complete text).*

We are publishing here the verbal notes of the Ministry of Foreign Affairs of the USSR delivered to the acting Chargé d'Affaires of the APR in Moscow as well as the notes of the Ministry of Foreign Affairs of the APR, directed to the USSR Embassy in Tirana, concerning the recall of the personnel of the Soviet Embassy in Tirana and the demand of the Soviet Government for the departure of the personnel of the Albanian Embassy in Moscow.

The contents of the verbal note presented on November 25, 1961, by Deputy Minister of Foreign Affairs of the Soviet Union, N. Firyubin, to acting Chargé d'Affaires of the Albanian People's Republic in the Soviet Union, Gac Mazi, in connection with the recall of the Soviet Ambassador, J. Shikin, from Albania:

The Ministry of Foreign Affairs of the USSR has been authorized, according to a recommendation made by the Soviet Government, to declare the following:

The Albanian Government, by following a course of further aggravation of its relations with the Soviet Union, especially since the 22nd Congress of the CPSU, has created an intolerable situation for the normal activity of the Soviet Ambassador in Tirana and the other Soviet diplomats. The Soviet Ambassador has been put in a position where he cannot carry out in normal fashion the recommendations of his Government. In fact, the USSR Embassy is in an isolated position, and the most elementary norms of international law are being violated with regard to it. By way of provocation, the Albanian authorities are slanderously accusing the members of the USSR Embassy of engaging in hostile activities against Albania. In addition, in the past few days the Albanian Government has taken an unprecedented step in the reciprocal relations between socialist countries, demanding without foundation a reduction of the staff of the Soviet Embassy by nearly three times.

In view of the fact that the Albanian authorities have intentionally created conditions which deprive the Soviet Ambassador to Albania of the possibility of performing his diplomatic functions, the Government of the Union of Soviet Socialist Republics is compelled to make the decision to recall the USSR Ambassador Extraordinary and Plenipotentiary, Comrade J. V. Shikin, from Albania.

The Ministry of Foreign Affairs of the USSR requests that the Albanian Government be informed without delay of this decision of the USSR.

The contents of the verbal note presented on November 25, 1961, by Deputy Minister of Foreign Affairs of the Soviet Union, N. Firyubin, to the acting Chargé d'Affaires of the Albanian People's Republic in the Soviet Union, Gac Mazi, in connection with the departure of the Ambassador of the Albanian People's Republic in the Soviet Union, Nesti Nase:

The Ministry of Foreign Affairs of the USSR has heard that the Embassy of the Albanian People's Republic in Moscow has lately been trying to distribute in an intensive manner all kinds of anti-Soviet material, containing zealous fabrications against the CPSU and the Soviet Union. Among these are the texts of the hostile declaration of the CC of the PPSh, dated October 20, the report by Hoxha of November 7 of this year, and other material containing all manner of falsehoods and base slanders against our party, the Soviet Government, and the decisions of the 22nd Congress of the CPSU. Thus, the situation has reached the point where the Embassy turned over these slanderous materials to enemies of the socialist camp.

One cannot fail to draw attention as well to the fact that Albanian citizens in the Soviet Union are widely exploited for hostile designs toward the Soviet Union. While abusing the sincere desire of the Soviet Union to help train highly qualified specialists for work in the Albanian national economy, the Embassy mobilizes the Albanian students for the dissemination of anti-Soviet propaganda. Thus Jukniu, a candidate of the Moscow Power Engineering Institute; Gurakuqi and Gjipali, students of the Moscow Technical Institute of Light Industry; Meçaj and Prillo of Moscow State University; Hajdar and Haxhimihali of the Institute of Chemical Technology; Reshati of the Moscow Institute of Chemical and Gas Industry and Paçma of the Leningrad Institute of Technology of Industrial Refrigeration have attempted to distribute anti-Soviet documents among Soviet and foreign students and have spoken slanderously on questions of Soviet-Albanian relations.

All these actions against the USSR cause righteous indignation among the Soviet people inasmuch as they have but one aim — to aggravate and worsen still further the relations between our countries and our parties with a view to destroying the unity and cohesion of the countries of the socialist camp.

The Ministry of Foreign Affairs has repeatedly drawn the attention of the Embassy of the Albanian People's Republic in Moscow to the fact that it is forbidden to distribute anti-Soviet material in the Soviet Union and to mobilize for this work Albanian citizens who are in the USSR. However, the Albanian side did not take any measures to end the distribution of this material. As if this were not enough, the Albanian Embassy, as the facts cited testify, has recently been trying to promote the distribution of material hostile to the CPSU and the Soviet Union, which is incompatible with the performance of the normal functions of any diplomatic mission, much less that of a country which claims to be a member of the socialist camp.

The Ministry of Foreign Affairs protests vigorously to the Albanian Embassy in Moscow in this respect, and it no longer considers it possible for the Ambassador of the Albanian People's Republic, Nesti Nase, to continue his stay in the USSR. Simultaneously, the Ministry of Foreign Affairs of the USSR has been authorized to demand the immediate suspension of the distribution of anti-Soviet material by the Albanian Embassy in the USSR and of the dissemination of propaganda hostile to the CPSU and the Soviet Union.

The contents of the verbal note of December 3, 1961, delivered by the Deputy Foreign Minister of the Soviet Union, N. Firyubin, to the acting Chargé d'Affaires of the Albanian People's Republic in the Soviet Union, Gac Mazi, in connection with the recall of the staff of the Embassy of the Soviet Union and the Soviet commercial representation in Tirana and the demand for the departure of the staff of the Embassy of the Albanian People's Republic and the Albanian commercial counselor in the Soviet Union:

The Ministry of Foreign Affairs of the USSR on the recommendation of the Government of the Union of Soviet Socialist Republics states the following:

The Albanian Government, in pursuing a course of further aggravation of Albanian-Soviet relations, particularly since the 22nd Congress of the CPSU, has unleashed in Albania a slanderous and hostile campaign against the USSR. It engages in measures deliberately designed to obstruct the normal activity of the Embassy and commercial representation of the USSR in Albania. The Soviet diplomats in the APR are isolated and even deprived of the possibility of maintaining official contacts with Albanian institutions and organizations.

By way of provocation, the Albanian authorities slanderously accuse the members of representative Soviet institutions of allegedly promoting hostile activity against Albania. The most elementary norms of international law are violated with regard to the Soviet Embassy and other Soviet institutions in Albania.

The Soviet side has repeatedly drawn the attention of the Albanian Government to the impermissible actions of the Albanian authorities toward the Embassy of the USSR in Tirana. The Albanian Government, however, has not only failed to take any measures, but it is complicating conditions more and more for the personnel of the Soviet institutions in Albania.

The groundless demand of the Albanian Government for the reduction of the staff of the Soviet Embassy to almost one-third its present personnel is an unprecedented step in relations between states, especially between socialist states.

The Ministry of Foreign Affairs of the USSR is authorized to reject emphatically the altogether impermissible demand of the Albanian Government regarding the reduction in the staff of the Soviet Embassy in Tirana. It is known that international law does not recognize the right of a country to limit in an arbitrary and unilateral manner the size of foreign diplomatic missions accredited to it. It is appropriate to recall, in this regard, that Albania, at several international conferences not long ago, was opposed to attempts to legalize the incorrect practice by which a state that accepts a diplomatic mission in its country fixes its numerical composition. Yet the Albanian Government is presently resorting to the methods of capitalist countries which use them to render difficult at any cost the diplomatic activity of the countries of the socialist camp.

Naturally, the Soviet side cannot remain indifferent to the intolerable situation created by the Albanian authorities for the members of the Embassy of the USSR and the commercial representation in Tirana. The Government of the Soviet Union, taking all this into consideration as well as the shameless allegation of the Albanian side that Soviet diplomats no longer have anything to do in Tirana, has decided to withdraw the entire personnel of the Soviet Embassy and the commercial representation from Albania. Three technical functionaries will remain to guard the buildings and other materials of the Embassy and the commercial representation of the USSR in Tirana.

The Albanian side will be informed at a later date which state the Soviet Government will charge with the protection of the interests of the Soviet Union and its citizens in Albania.

The Soviet side considers that, in view of the fact that the Albanian Government is deliberately further aggravating relations with the Soviet Union by utilizing its diplomatic mission in the USSR for anti-Soviet objectives, the continued stay of the staff of the Albanian Embassy and the commercial counselor of Albania in Moscow is pointless.

In this connection the Soviet Government demands that the entire personnel of the Embassy and the commercial counselor of Albania in Moscow leave the territory of the Soviet Union.

Note of the Ministry of Foreign Affairs of the Albanian People's Republic presented to the Embassy of the Soviet Union in Tirana on December 4, 1961:

To the Embassy of the Union of Soviet Socialist Republics, Tirana:

The Ministry of Foreign Affairs of the Albanian People's Republic, by order of its Government, and in connection with the verbal communication delivered on November 25 by Deputy Minister Firyubin to the acting Chargé d'Affaires of the Albanian People's Republic, has the honor to present to the Embassy of the USSR in Tirana the following, with the request that it be transmitted to the Soviet Government:

I. The Government of the Albanian People's Republic received with surprise and deep regret the notification concerning the decision of the Government of the USSR to recall its Ambassador to the Albanian People's Republic, Shikin, on the groundless and fabricated charge that conditions had been created for him which allegedly deprived him of any possibility of performing his diplomatic functions.

The Government of the Albanian People's Republic most emphatically rejects this false accusation, which is but another slander in a long chain of slanders and unfriendly acts, undertaken in a relentless and systematic manner by the Soviet leadership against the Albanian People's Republic, and which have but one aim — the aggravation and further deterioration of the fraternal relations between our two friendly peoples and our two friendly countries.

The allegations fabricated in order to justify the recall of Ambassador Shikin are completely groundless and tendentious. The Soviet Ambassador has never been obstructed in his work. On the contrary, he has always been given every opportunity to perform his mission as an Ambassador. The truth — and the only motive in the matter — lies in the fact that the authors of this grave and extraordinary act have adopted an unfriendly policy toward the Albanian People's Republic, and, in pursuit of this course, they are resorting to ever more reprehensible anti-Albanian and anti-Marxist actions.

It should be noted that, among other things, the history of the beginning, the duration, and the end of Ambassador Shikin's activity in the Albanian People's Republic makes one think that from the moment he was sent to Albania, the Soviet Government intended to recall him within a short time. He remained in Albania only five months, and one cannot but mention the fact that for the first time in the history of diplomatic relations between two countries, and precisely at a time when the sphere of normal activity of the Embassy had been considerably reduced owing to the fault of the Soviet side, an Embassy counselor with the rank of minister plenipotentiary was sent along with Ambassador Shikin. This was an act which could be understood only within the context of the predetermined recall of the Ambassador.

II. It is with surprise and the most profound indignation that the Government of the Albanian People's Republic received the notification of the Government of the USSR that it considers impossible the further stay in the Soviet Union of the Ambassador Extraordinary and Plenipotentiary of Albania, Nesti Nase, under the completely fabricated and unwarranted pretext that the Embassy of the Albanian People's Republic in Moscow has recently been distributing material hostile to the Communist Party of the Soviet Union and the Soviet Union. The Government of the Albanian People's Republic rejects with the greatest firmness this unfounded accusation and the protest of the Soviet Ministry of Foreign Affairs which was delivered on this occasion. The decision of the Soviet leadership concerning the departure of Ambassador Nesti Nase is an integral part of its unfriendly policy toward a socialist country, a friend, and a brother of the Soviet people, as is the Albanian People's Republic.

The Ambassador of the Albanian People's Republic to the Soviet Union, Comrade Nesti Nase, has always fulfilled his tasks conscientiously as a diplomat, as an Albanian, and as a Communist, respecting with the greatest rigor the laws and the rules operative in the Soviet Union. He has worked vigorously to strengthen and temper further the eternal friendship between our fraternal peoples and our socialist countries.

It is appropriate to say that in the performance of his honorable mission as a socialist diplomat, not only did he not have proper assistance, but he was obstructed by the Soviet authorities by all possible means, even the most impermissible, including concealed and overt surveillance. In fact, it is known that for years the Embassy of the Albanian People's Republic in the Soviet Union has been under constant surveillance by means of a special technical apparatus installed in the building at the time of its construction and that even to this day it is under obvious police control. Three members of the militia are permanently posted in front of the Embassy, and they inspect every person who enters the Embassy, thus obstructing the normal functioning and the regular performance of the diplomatic tasks of the mission and violating the most elementary norms which ought to be observed with respect to a foreign legation and, in particular, to that of a friendly and allied country.

The Government of the Albanian People's Republic protests most vigorously this decision of the Soviet Government by which it demands, without reason, the departure of the Ambassador of the Albanian People's Republic from the Soviet Union, a decision which is profoundly unjust and unjustifiable and in open contradiction to the fundamental principles of international law and of relations between socialist countries and which lays a heavy responsibility upon the Soviet Government for all the consequences that shall follow in relations between the Albanian People's

Republic and the Soviet Union.
Tirana, December 4, 1961

Note of the Ministry of Foreign Affairs of the Albanian People's Republic to the Embassy of the Soviet Union in Tirana, December 9, 1961:

To the Embassy of the Union of Soviet Socialist Republics, Tirana:

With the authorization of the Government of the Albanian People's Republic, the Foreign Ministry of the Albanian People's Republic kindly requests the Embassy of the Union of Soviet Socialist Republics in Tirana to transmit to the Government of the Union of Soviet Socialist Republics the following:

Since its creation, following the triumph of the national liberation war over the Nazi-fascist invaders and native traitors and the triumph of the people's revolution, the cornerstone of the foreign policy of the Albanian People's Republic has been the indestructible and eternal friendship with the Soviet Union. This friendship was forged during World War II and further strengthened by the Albanian Party of Labor after liberation. Its roots lie in the blood shed in common by the glorious Soviet Army of Liberation and the valiant Albanian partisans in the war against the common enemy. It is based on the eternal principles of Marxism-Leninism. The Albanian people, educated by their Party of Labor, have always considered the Soviet Union their liberator and dearest friend. The Albanian Party of Labor and the Albanian Government have considered it a duty of the first rank to preserve and to strengthen ever more this friendship and to nourish and strengthen ever more in the hearts of the Albanian People love and loyalty toward the great fatherland of V. I. Lenin and the Communist Party of the Soviet Union.

In the years following the liberation of Albania, the relations between the Albanian People's Republic and the Soviet Union were, for a long period, broadened and developed in all fields on the basis of the Leninist principles of equality, mutual respect, close cooperation, and fraternal mutual assistance. The Albanian people will always be grateful to the fraternal Soviet people for the internationalist aid given our country during this period, which has been an important factor in the construction of socialism in Albania.

During these years, the Albanian People's Republic, a loyal member of the socialist camp and of the Warsaw Pact, has at all times and under all conditions strengthened its unity with the Soviet Union, stood with the greatest resolution at the side of the Soviet Union against every attack and every slander on the part of the enemies of the fatherland of the Soviets, defended without vacillation the peaceful policy of the Soviet Union, and done its utmost to contribute to its triumph. The close relations of cooperation in the economic, political, cultural, and military fields and the fraternal friendship between our two countries have created truly internationalist and indestructible ties between our two peoples. And, as they have always demonstrated by their consistent attitude and actions, the Albanian Party of Labor and the Government of the Albanian People's Republic have been and remain resolute fighters for the preservation and further strengthening of the friendship and unity between our two countries and our two parties on a correct and inviolable Marxist-Leninist foundation.

Unfortunately, of late — and definitely since the second half of 1960 — relations between the Albanian People's Republic and the Soviet Union have not been what they once were. They have been damaged and embittered by N. Khrushchev and his group because, at the June 1960 Bucharest meeting of a number of Communist and workers parties and thereafter, the Albanian Party of Labor has not agreed with the anti-Marxist views of N. Khrushchev, has not yielded to Khrushchev's dictates on important ideological issues, and has resolutely defended and defends Marxism-Leninism. Unable to tolerate this principled position of the Albanian Party of Labor, N. Khrushchev and his group have brutally violated the principles upon which relations between socialist states are founded as well as the Moscow Declarations of 1957 and 1960, and because of the ideological differences with the Albanian Party of Labor, he has resorted to unilateral state measures — each of which has been more arbitrary and grave than the one preceding — against the Albanian People's Republic, with the aim of exerting pressure and forcing capitulation.

During this period N. Khrushchev and his group have consciously tried all possible means to force the Albanian people, the Albanian Party of Labor, and the Albanian Government into capitulation and to aggravate Soviet-Albanian relations on the state level as well, and, in doing so, have trampled on proletarian internationalism and every norm of international law and of relations between states. Suffice it to say that N. Khrushchev, unilaterally and with the sole aim of obstructing the building of socialism in Albania, canceled the credits granted by normal agreement to the Albanian People's Republic by the Soviet Union for the third five-year plan, 1961 to 1965, arbitrarily violated and annulled the 1961 trade agreement, unilaterally withdrew Soviet technicians, liquidated in fact the agreements on cultural cooperation, expelled on false grounds a number of Albanian students and cadets from the Soviet Union, canceled the agreement on the granting of scholarships to Albanian students and cadets studying in the Soviet Union, violated the military agreements, and organized a strict economic, political, and military blockade of the Albanian People's Republic.

N. Khrushchev, by publicly revealing at the 22nd Congress of the Communist Party of the Soviet Union the disagreements existing between the Albanian Party of Labor and the present Soviet leadership, and by distorting the truth and slandering in the most banal manner a fraternal people and a Marxist-Leninist party — as are the Albanian people and the Albanian Party of Labor — has not only incited imperialism and its lackeys against Albania, but has also dared to summon the Albanian people to counterrevolution. In so doing, he acted in the same way as the vicious enemies of the Albanian people, the Albanian Party of Labor, the socialist camp, and Communism. The Albanian people responded to this unprecedented provocation by consolidating their ranks around the Albanian Party of Labor and Government, by steeling their determination to build socialism, and by strengthening their vigilance for the defense of the achievements of their socialist fatherland.

On November 25, 1961, the Soviet Government, at the command of N. Khrushchev, withdrew its Ambassador, J. Shikin, from Albania under the false pretext that he "had been placed under conditions which prevented him from carrying out normally the orders of his government," and that this situation had become "intolerable," "especially since the 22nd Congress of the Communist Party of the Soviet Union." A pretense of this kind is absurd and is used only for malicious purposes. In fact, it is well known that the most favorable conditions were always, from the very beginning, created for the Embassy of the Soviet Union in Albania and for all its personnel, from the ambassador to the simplest worker. The Soviet representatives in Albania have always been treated not only as the diplomatic representatives of the most cherished friend and ally of the Albanian people — as the Soviet Union was and remains — but also as comrades and true brothers to whom not only the doors of the offices and the work and production centers but also the hearts of the Albanian people have been opened. As has also been pointed out previously by the Albanian Government, all the conditions necessary for performing his functions were created for Ambassador Shikin. However, Ambassador Shikin, since he first came to Albania 11 months ago, has been in the country only five months in all. Even more surprising is the allegation that his position became "intolerable following the 22nd Congress of the Communist Party of the Soviet Union," since it is well known that Ambassador Shikin left August 19, 1961, that is, two months before the convening of the 22nd Congress of the Communist Party of the Soviet Union.

The real reason, therefore, lies not in the so-called abnormal conditions but in N. Khrushchev's intention further to aggravate relations between the People's Republic of Albania and the Soviet Union. Thus, on the same date, the withdrawal of the Ambassador of the Albanian People's Republic to the Soviet Union, Nesti Nase, was requested on the pretext that, according to the Soviet side, the Albanian Embassy was trying to distribute anti-Soviet materials by using even Albanian students in the Soviet Union. The Soviet leadership includes among such materials the Declaration of the Central Committee of the Albanian Party of Labor of October 20, 1961, and also the speech delivered in Tirana by Enver Hoxha, First Secretary of the Albanian Party of Labor, on November 7, 1961. This was not all. Obstructive and discriminatory measures were taken against the Albanian Embassy in Moscow. The Foreign Ministry of the Soviet Union officially informed the Embassy of the Albanian People's Republic that the Albanian Embassy and the Albanian diplomats in the Soviet Union were forbidden to have direct relations or contact with Soviet institutions, with the exception of the Soviet Foreign Ministry. Furthermore, groups of militiamen surrounded the Albanian Embassy in Moscow, as if the two countries were in a state of war. They began to inspect every visitor to the Embassy and to prevent any Soviet citizen from entering the Albanian Embassy, including technicians sent by the Soviet office of diplomatic service. It is surprising that, while the Soviet side itself took unprecedented measures to isolate and restrict the Albanian Embassy and diplomats in Moscow, the Soviet Deputy Foreign Minister, Firyubin, in his verbal note of December 3, 1961, pretended in an openly slanderous manner that "the Soviet diplomats in the People's Republic of Albania were isolated and even prevented from maintaining official contacts with Albanian organizations and institutions."

The Embassy of the Albanian People's Republic in Moscow has always respected the regulations of the Soviet Government on the distribution of propaganda materials in the Soviet Union and has never violated them. The Government of the Albanian People's Republic rejects as a shameful and provocative offense the pretense that the Albanian Embassy ever distributed anti-Soviet materials. All the materials distributed by it — in accord with the regulations in force — have always been inspired by feelings of eternal Albanian-Soviet friendship and based on the principles of Marxism-Leninism and the Moscow Declarations of 1957 and 1960. It is really regrettable that, on such an unfounded pretext, the withdrawal of the ambassador of a socialist country from the Soviet Union was requested while the diplomatic representatives of the capitalist states in Moscow are freely distributing many materials. Also unfounded is the accusation regarding the Albanian students in the Soviet Union, who have been educated by the Albanian Party of Labor to harbor boundless love for the Soviet Union and who have always set an example of good behavior and respect for the laws and regulations of the country. But, as shown by the facts, these imaginary accusations were needed by N. Khrushchev's group to expel the Albanian students from the Soviet Union and to break off any contact between the Soviet people and Albanian citizens.

It is clear that the group of N. Khrushchev, in opposition to every internationalist principle and every norm of international law, unilaterally violated and annulled all agreements in force and cooperation between the Soviet Union and the Albanian People's Republic, and thus with conscious, premeditated, and hostile intent cut off all relations between the Soviet Union and Albania. In this situation, when, owing to the fault of N. Khrushchev, relations between the two countries were restricted to the utmost, it was clearly unnecessary for the Soviet Union to maintain a staff of about 80 people. For this reason, the Albanian Government rightly and on the basis of reciprocity proposed that the Soviet Embassy in Tirana maintain the same number of officials as the Albanian Embassy in Moscow.

In line with his anti-Albanian and anti-Marxist policy, N. Khrushchev went much further along the road of the deterioration of relations between the Soviet Union and Albania. On Sunday, December 3, 1961, Soviet Deputy Foreign Minister N. Firyubin, on the basis of vile and provocative slanders regarding the attitude of the Government of the Albanian People's Republic toward the Soviet Union and toward the Soviet Embassy in Tirana, informed Gac Mazi, Chargé d'Affaires of the Albanian People's Republic in the Soviet Union, that the Soviet Government had decided to withdraw the entire staff of the Soviet Embassy and the Soviet commercial representative in Tirana and, at the same time, he requested the withdrawal from Soviet territory of the entire staff of the Embassy and commercial counselor of the Albanian People's Republic in Moscow. At the same time, he stated that the Soviet Government would later make known to the Albanian side the country which would be charged with the protection of the interests of the Soviet Union and of Soviet citizens in Albania.

The Government of the Albanian People's Republic rejects with contempt and indignation the revolting and unfounded slanders and fabrications presented in the verbal communication by Firyubin as evidence to justify this hostile act, unprecedented in the history of the relations between socialist states. The unilateral decision of N. Khrushchev's group to close the Soviet Embassy and the commercial representation in Tirana, as well as the Albanian Embassy in Moscow, expresses not only his intention to cut off all relations between the Soviet Union and the Albanian People's Republic, but brutally violates the principles upon which relations between socialist countries are based as well as the glorious tradition of friendship always observed by the Soviet Union toward the other socialist countries and toward all the countries in the world. In fact, this decision is another manifestation of the pressure exerted on the Albanian People's Republic. It is an integral part of the anti-Albanian and antisocialist policy pursued with unprecedented ferocity by N. Khrushchev against the Albanian people and the Albanian People's Republic. This can please only the sworn enemies of the Albanian and Soviet peoples, of socialism, and of Marxism-Leninism — the imperialists and their lackeys, the Yugoslav revisionists. However, neither this new act of hostility toward Albania nor the threats and pressures of every sort used by N. Khrushchev can ever destroy Albanian-Soviet friendship. They will not be able to separate Albania from its friends, nor will they ever be able to frighten the true defenders of the unity of the socialist camp and Marxism-Leninism. All the attempts and the anti-Marxist designs of N. Khrushchev and his group will suffer complete failure.

One cannot pass over in silence the fact that N. Khrushchev decided to undertake this action to aggravate further the relations between the Soviet Union and the Albanian People's Republic — which is an allied socialist state and permanent member of the socialist camp, a member of the Warsaw Pact and of the Council for Mutual Economic Assistance, and which is led by a Marxist-Leninist party, the Albanian Party of Labor — at a time when he is making all possible efforts to strengthen relations with the member states of the aggressive North Atlantic Pact and with Tito's revisionist group, the sworn enemies of the Soviet Union and socialism.

The Albanian Government deeply regrets that a time has come when in the leadership of the Soviet Union, the first socialist state in the world, and the glorious Communist Party of the Soviet Union, founded by V. I. Lenin, there are people like the N. Khrushchev group who attack the best friends of the Soviet Union and do their utmost to harm the immortal cause of the socialist camp and Communism. This new, hostile act of N. Khrushchev will not only fail to further his diabolical aims, but it will have a totally opposite effect. The Albanian people will understand even better how correct and wise the Marxist-Leninist line of the Albanian Party of Labor has always been and remains, and they will further strengthen their unity around the party and the government. Moreover, the sympathy and solidarity with the Albanian people and the Albanian People's Republic will grow among all the honest people of the world.

The Albanian people, regardless of these successive hostile activities of N. Khrushchev and his group, will always hold intact their love and friendship for the fraternal Soviet people and the fatherland and party of Lenin. They are convinced that all the anti-Albanian and anti-Marxist attempts and designs of N. Khrushchev and his group will fail completely, since the truth will finally emerge victorious and Marxism-Leninism will triumph. The Albanian People's Republic will firmly continue on its correct path and will successfully build socialism and Communism.

As always, the Government of the Albanian People's Republic will, in the future as well, defend the foreign policy of the Government of the Soviet Union on all issues which are in the interest of the preservation of peace and struggle for general and complete disarmament, as well as the efforts to settle the German problem by concluding a German peace treaty and turning West Berlin into a free, demilitarized city, and will resolutely fight to preserve and consolidate the unity of the countries of the socialist camp on the basis of the principles of Marxism-Leninism and proletarian internationalism.

The Government of the Albanian People's Republic, emphatically protesting the Soviet Government's unilateral decision to close the Embassy of the Soviet Union in Tirana and the Albanian Embassy in Moscow, states that the entire responsibility for this grave hostile act falls on N. Khrushchev and his group. It expresses its full conviction that sooner or later the Soviet people and the Communist Party of the Soviet Union will condemn this criminal act and all N. Khrushchev's hostile activity toward a fraternal, friendly, and allied country like the Albanian People's Republic, which is building socialism and firmly fighting imperialism and modern revisionism by always holding high the banner of friendship and unity with the Soviet Union and the other fraternal countries, the banner of Marxism-Leninism.

Tirana, December 9, 1961

DOCUMENT 17

"A Soviet Specialist's Impressions of Albania," Radio Moscow *in Albanian to Albania, December 18, 1962, 1500* GMT *(excerpt from a talk by Igor Ponomarev, a Soviet building materials specialist, formerly in Albania,* BBC/SU/*826/A2/2, December 21, 1961*).

. . . Unfortunately, during the final period of my stay in Albania, the behavior of government officials, in particular at the Ministry of Construction, changed markedly. It was obvious that pressure was being exerted on all who openly expressed their sympathies for the Soviet Union. Not everybody, therefore, had the courage openly to express friendly feelings towards us, the Soviet specialists. Some Ministry of Construction officials delayed, without any reason, decisions on technical matters, obstructed our efforts to give technical aid, and hindered us in acquiring technical documentation. During the last stage, we were forced to refer even the most trivial technical matters to Albanian leaders. Effectual contacts with Albanian workers were deliberately made difficult. The Ministry officials made no attempt to hide their hostility towards us. . . .

DOCUMENT 18

"Slanders and Fabrications Cannot Stand," Zëri i Popullit, *December 19, 20, and 30, 1961* (*complete text*).

The Truth on the Affair of the Specialists

The anti-Marxist and anti-Albanian attacks which N. Khrushchev and his group launched from the rostrum of the 22nd Congress of the Communist Party of the Soviet Union against the Albanian Party of Labor, the Albanian People's Republic, and the Albanian people also included slanders and fabrications concerning the Soviet specialists who were working in our country. Thus O. Kuusinen, member of the Presidium of the Central Committee of the Communist Party of the Soviet Union, engaged in slander when he said that "the Soviet specialists in Albania, invited there by the Albanian Government itself, were expelled by the latter from Albania." P. Pospelov, former alternate member of the Presidium of the Central Committee of the Communist Party of the Soviet Union, went even further. He lied when he said: "During the last Congress of the Albanian Party of Labor we encountered a number of glaring instances of direct anti-Soviet attacks by prominent Albanian officials, instances of a humiliating, hostile attitude toward our specialists, geologists, and Soviet seamen." Since the 22nd Congress the same tune, that the Soviet specialists were, so to speak, expelled by the Albanian leaders, has been played by the propagandists of N. Khrushchev, who expect to gain something from these slanders.

To set the record straight, we are compelled to refer to certain facts relating to the course of events.

On December 21, 1960, Comrade Abdyl Këllezi, deputy chairman of the Council of Ministers of the Albanian People's Republic, forwarded to S. A. Skachkov, chairman of the State Committee for Foreign Economic Relations of the Soviet Council of Ministers, the following letter:

Very honorable Comrade Chairman:

> On December 14, 1960, a list of matters on which the Government of the Albanian People's Republic requests technical assistance from the Government of the USSR for 1961 was delivered to the economic attaché in the Embassy of the Union of Soviet Socialist Republics. I kindly ask you to study this request of the Government of the Albanian People's Republic so that the organs of the USSR can act on it at the most favorable time.

The list of items on which the Government of the Albanian People's Republic asked the Soviet Union for technical assistance for 1961 included branches of the Ministries of Industry, Mines and Geology, Construction, and so forth. The list defined the kinds of technical specialties and the number of specialists needed. It also specified the duration of their stay in Albania and requested that the term of stay in Albania for certain specialists be extended.

However, while the Government of the Albanian People's Republic was awaiting a positive reply to its request, on January 20, 1961, A. Pikalov, acting economic attaché in the Soviet Embassy in Tirana, at his own request, met Comrade Adil Çarçani, APR Minister of Mines and Geology, and officially notified him that

> the State Committee for Foreign Economic Relations of the USSR Council of Ministers has decided to withdraw, within a period of 7–10 days, the Soviet specialists working in the oil network in Albania, because the agreement of November 22, 1957, has been fulfilled.

Naturally, the Soviet leadership had the right to refuse to extend the term of the Soviet specialists in Albania, as requested by our government. But it neither had nor has any right to distort the facts relating to this question by trying to blame the Albanian Government for the withdrawal of the specialists.

In connection with the withdrawal of Soviet specialists from Albania on February 24, 1961, the APR Foreign Ministry sent the following note to the Government of the USSR:

> As is known to the Government of the Soviet Union, on December 21, 1960, Abdyl Këllezi, deputy chairman of the Council of Ministers of the Albanian People's Republic, forwarded to S. A. Skachkov, chairman of the State Committee for Foreign Economic Relations of the USSR Council of Ministers, the request of the Albanian Government for technical assistance from the Soviet Union for 1961, including the extension of the term of the Soviet oil specialists.
>
> While our government was awaiting a positive reply to this request, on January 20, 1961, A. Pikalov, acting economic attaché in the Soviet Embassy in Tirana, met Adil Çarçani, Minister of Mines and Geology of the Albanian People's Republic, and officially notified him that the State Committee for Foreign Economic Relations of the USSR Council of Ministers had decided to withdraw, within a period of 7–10 days, the Soviet specialists working in the oil network in Albania. The Soviet oil specialists in fact did leave Albania.
>
> The withdrawal of oil specialists by the Soviet Government at a time when the Albanian Government had officially requested an extension of their stay harmed an important sector of the Albanian economy, the oil sector.
>
> The Government of the Albanian People's Republic, in noting the above-mentioned, expresses deep regret at this unilateral measure of the Government of the Soviet Union.

With the aim of misleading public opinion, distorting the truth, and shifting the responsibility for everything to the Albanian side, the Soviet leaders remembered after two months to announce through their representatives in Tirana that the Albanian authorities were "the culprits" in the withdrawal of the Soviet oil specialists, not the Soviet authorities! In this connection, the Soviet Embassy in Tirana, in its note of April 24, 1961, points out:

> The allegation in the note of the foreign ministry of the Albanian People's Republic that the withdrawal of the 26 Soviet oil specialists from Albania in February by the Soviet Union was the result of the unilateral action of the Soviet Government is completely fabricated. The Government of the APR was informed in due time that the Soviet Government, despite the fact that the term of the Soviet oil specialists in Albania had expired, had instructed the appropriate Soviet organs to consider the request of Albania and to let the Soviet oil specialists remain in Albania. But the Albanian administration of the oil combine, acting on instructions from the APR Ministry of Mines and Geography, ousted the above-mentioned Soviet specialists by telling them to leave the oil combine within three days.

Obviously, everything is shamelessly reversed. But the facts mentioned above, such as the Albanian request for the extension of the terms of the Soviet oil specialists in Albania, directed to S. A. Skachkov, on which there has been no positive answer, and the official statement A. Pikalov made to Comrade Çarçani, January 20, 1961, on the withdrawal of the Soviet oil specialists, refute the "arguments" made in the belated note from the Soviet Embassy in Tirana.

It is obvious that the Soviet Embassy note had another purpose. It was meant to prepare the ground for the future withdrawal of all Soviet specialists in Albania. In fact, the note of April 24, 1961, attempted to make it seem that the Albanian authorities of the Central Directorate of Geology were behaving badly toward the Soviet specialists and were hindering them in their work. To "prove" this, it was said that the offices of the Soviet specialists were searched and the documents on the tables or in the drawers subjected to inspection. Finally, it was alleged that the Albanian Geological Directorate had temporarily obstructed the work of Soviet specialists who dealt with the drafting of the all-inclusive geological map of Albania.

These "arguments" are completely fabricated. In fact, according to the known security regulations of our state administration, in the Geological Directorate, as in all other institutes, regular inspection to maintain the security of secret documents has been carried out, be they in the offices of Albanian workers, or in those of Soviet specialists, whose names are Konstantin Briyantsev, Semen Pograbinsky, and Vladimir Kurochkin, and who displayed a spirit of complete cooperation in this matter.

As for the second "argument," that the specialists who were drafting the geological map were allegedly left for some time without work, this is completely absurd and needs no refutation. Suffice it to say that the Albanian authorities, who were paying wages to the Soviet specialists for this purpose, were eager for the completion of the map as early as possible. Therefore, there was no reason why there should have been any obstructions, as the Soviet note maintains.

The real purpose of the above "arguments" on the Soviet side is quite obvious in the April 24, 1961, Soviet Embassy note itself, the last paragraph of which points out:

> In view of the foregoing, we cannot help concluding that in the aide-mémoire and the note of the Foreign Ministry of the Albanian People's Republic willful attempts have been made to deny the indisputable facts regarding an unfriendly attitude toward the Soviet specialists. They reveal the unwillingness of the Albanian authorities to take the necessary measures to create normal conditions for the work of our specialists.
>
> This can be explained only by the fact that the Albanian side, it appears, not only is not interested in assisting the Soviet specialists, but through its unfriendly acts toward them is indirectly trying to exert pressure on the Soviet side to force us to recall the Soviet specialists to the USSR.
>
> Under the circumstances, the Soviet side considers it impossible to send new Soviet specialists to Albania. Nor could it extend the term of stay for the specialists who are now working there.
>
> The Embassy of the USSR in the Albanian People's Republic takes this occasion to reiterate to the Foreign Ministry of the APR its respect.

And without waiting for the reply of our government to this note, which was delivered to our Foreign Ministry April 25, 1961, about 50 Soviet specialists were immediately ordered by the Soviet Embassy in Tirana on April 25, 1961, to quit their work and to leave Albania at once. Some of these specialists had only two hours in which to serve notice to their work headquarters before their departure. Thus almost all the Soviet specialists departed on that day. This included even those whose term of stay in Albania had not yet expired. The other specialists still in the Albanian People's Republic departed within the next few days.

This is how the truth stands on the departure of the Soviet specialists from Albania. They were withdrawn by the Soviet leadership with the intention of harming our people's economy, on the one hand, and undermining Albanian-Soviet friendship on the other. The fabrications about the so-called "unbearable atmosphere" and the allegations that "the presence of Soviet specialists in Albania is a burden to Albania," and the like, whose aim is to shift onto our government the responsibility for the ugly act committed by the Soviet leaders against our country are really deplorable. They are fabrications and serious affronts to the feelings of fraternal love, deep respect, and cordiality of the Albanian people toward the Soviet people, as well as to the feelings of the Soviet people who have lived and worked in Albania.

Those who invent such tendentious

fabrications do not understand the reality of the indestructible ties by which the Albanian and Soviet peoples are united. Just as the blood shed by Albanian partisans was mixed with the blood shed by the glorious Red Army in the struggle for the liberation of Albania from fascist occupation, so was the sweat of the Albanian workers and specialists mixed with the sweat of Soviet workers and specialists in the struggle to build socialism in Albania.

Whatever attempts may be made and whatever "arguments" may be fabricated, they cannot justify the incorrect decision of the Soviet Government to withdraw the Soviet specialists from Albania. The best witnesses of the feelings toward the Soviet people and of the attitude toward them and their treatment on the part of the Albanian people and their party and government, the best witnesses of our correct stand, are the Soviet citizens themselves, the specialists and the military personnel who have been in our country and every Soviet citizen who has chanced to meet, in Albania, the Soviet Union, or any other place, any citizen of our people's republic.

The withdrawal of the Soviet specialists from Albania was decided upon by the Soviet Government itself for specific purposes, alien to the character of the relations between socialist countries, harmful to Albanian-Soviet friendship, and contrary to the principles of the 1960 Moscow Declaration of the 81 Communist and workers parties. At the same time, it invented a series of fantastic and unfounded fabrications against the Albanian Government.

Our party has persistently and invariably instilled in our people feelings of the deepest love and respect for the Soviet people, whom it has considered friends and brothers. Everyone in our country feels it a serious personal offense when he learns how the Soviet leadership is now engaging in slander and making much of the so-called "unbearable atmosphere" for Soviet citizens in Albania.

Documents can be fabricated and speeches made against our country. By now we have seen and heard many such slanders and allegations, and often we have not even had time to listen to all of them. But if one tells an Albanian that he does not respect or that he offends the Soviet people, he will never forgive that person and will consider it nothing but a most low and insolent provocation.

The Truth on the Affair of the Palace of Culture

Recently certain Soviet propagandists who have assumed the task of sowing enmity between our two friendly and allied countries, our fraternal peoples, have recalled, among many other calumnies, the affair of the Palace of Culture. They present the facts connected with this affair upside down. They fabricate shamelessly, declaring that it was the Albanian leadership which, through "maneuvers" designed "to discredit the Soviet Government, unilaterally refused this present."

But let us look at what the documents and the facts show concerning the truth about the Palace of Culture.

According to the January 1956 decision of the Central Committee of the Communist Party of the Soviet Union, a Palace of Culture was to be constructed in Tirana, as a gift from the Soviet Union to the Albanian people. The construction of the palace was to have been completed during the years 1959–1962. From March through April, 1959, representatives of the Soviet party arrived in Albania, and the main conditions for undertaking the construction of the Palace of Culture by the Albanian enterprise N.Sh.N. "21 Dhjetori" were discussed.

In April 1960 Soviet architects brought to Albania some modifications of the plan for the palace. The plans were brought by the director of "Mosprojekt," A. A. Osmer, and the author of the plans, V. A. Butuzov. These modifications were widely discussed in the Technical Council of the Ministry of Construction, and in the end the blueprint on which the Soviet architects insisted was approved. This blueprint was also approved by the State Committee for Construction of the USSR Council of Ministers, by the GKIS [State Committee for Foreign Economic Relations — Ed.], and by the Council for Urban Architecture of Mosprojekt. The protocol approving the plan was signed by the Albanian Minister of Construction, Josif Pashko, on April 23, 1960, and handed to the director of Mosprojekt, A. A. Osmer. In May 1960 the Albanian Government approved the principal plans for the construction of the Palace of Culture. In this protocol the Albanian side made certain observations, which the Soviet architects considered just. These observations concerned essentially the architectural implementation of the project and demanded a very small increase in the size of the structure on two points: the addition of five or six rooms to the club and two halls to the theater. Further, at the end of this protocol it was stated: "All the above-mentioned modifications and additions must be made for the sake of a more rational apportionment of the various parts of the Palace of Culture."

On May 29, 1960, the laying-out of the building began; on June 6, 1960, the construction began; and on July 14, 1960, the first concrete was poured. The Albanian side had taken all the necessary measures, and during the second trimester of 1960 the pace of work was very rapid. The plan was overfulfilled. The work was being carried out according to a plan approved by representatives of those who had awarded the contract and the N.Sh.N. "21 Dhjetori" of Tirana.

From the month of December onward, work slowed down, and in January 1961 the Soviet side completely suspended the supplies for the construction of the palace, both as far as the plans and as far as the materials were concerned, although until that time only a small part had been sent. The fact that the plans and the materials were not sent resulted in the nonfulfillment of the plan for the first four months of 1961, which was completed by only 52 per cent, and prevented to a great extent the rational exploitation of labor and machines, resulting in a loss of 975,000 leks to the enterprise N.Sh.N. "21 Dhjetori." The Albanian side spent approximately 48 million leks for the construction of the palace from the beginning of the project until the end of April 1961.

In October 1960, the head of the representatives of those who had awarded the contract, engineer T. M. Shtoll, went to the Soviet Union on the pretense that he would try to get all the plans for the project as well as send the materials and the equipment. Actually, he did not return again to Albania, and neither the plans nor the materials were sent.

Under these circumstances the enterprise N.Sh.N. "21 Dhjetori" repeatedly requested the vice president of the Soviet representation, engineer N. Knyazev, to intervene in order to obtain the plans and the materials. The latter replied that they were expected any day.

In view of the construction situation on the Palace of Culture, the Minister of Construction of our government, Josif Pashko, in a letter addressed April 11, 1961, to the Soviet ambassador to Tirana, J. V. Shikin, stated:

> With regard to the shortcomings in the construction of the Palace of Culture, I have the honor to inform you of the following:
>
> Since the end of December 1960 the pace of construction on the Palace of Culture, which is being built in Tirana with the help of the Soviet Union, has progressively fallen off and is not developing along the lines of the plan drawn up. This arises essentially from the lack of plans and certain materials.
>
> During frequent meetings which have taken place at the palace, the Albanian engineers charged with the execution of the project have mentioned to the representative of the Soviet party on this project, engineer Nikolai Stefanovich Knyasev, the above-mentioned obstacles. He has continually promised them that the plans and materials would arrive soon. Toward the end of January of this year the Albanian engineers working

on the project saw that, as a result of the lack of plans and certain materials, the plan was not being fulfilled and the specialized labor force and machines were not achieving the planned output. They reported this to the ministry so that the latter might intervene and so that the Soviet party might expedite the dispatch of plans and materials. To this effect, I personally, on February 5, 1961, called in the representative of the Soviet party, engineer Nikolai Stefanovich Knyasev, and asked him to intervene in order to speed up the dispatch of the plans and certain materials which were obstructing work.

During February, owing to the lack of plans and certain materials, work became even more limited. The necessary plans did not arrive. In view of this situation, and on my own recommendation, the Deputy Minister of Construction, engineer Kiço Glozheni, on February 28, 1961, officially called to the ministry Comrade Tukhtinov, representative of GKIS in Tirana who dealt with the construction of the Palace of Culture, and in the presence of engineer Knyazev, representative of the Soviet party for the construction of the palace, asked once again that they intervene for the dispatch of the plans.

In view of the fact that even after this appeal we had received no reply whatsoever, on March 3, 1961, the representative of GKIS, Comrade Beklechov, was once again officially called to the ministry, where the Deputy Minister of Construction, Comrade Rahman Hanku, after describing the serious situation created at the site because of the lack of plans and certain materials, asked him to intervene to ensure their speedy dispatch and requested a reply within 10 days.

Comrade Beklechov, who turned up at the meeting like someone who had just assumed his functions and who had not been brought up to date by his men on the situation at the palace, nevertheless promised Comrade Rahman Hanku that he would make an effort to settle the questions which had been brought up and reply to them on time. Following this meeting, however, not only were the plans and materials not dispatched, but a reply was not even received. On March 23, 1961, in communication No. 150 sent to the GKIS in Tirana by this ministry, the request for intervention for the dispatch of the plans and materials was reiterated, but this letter, too, has so far not been answered.

As I explained above, because of the failure to receive plans and materials, and especially because of the absence of any reply from the Soviet side, the enterprise charged with the project has retained for this long period of time the labor force and the specialists as well as the machines, which have been used very little.

Under these circumstances I have given orders to decrease the labor force and the machinery, and if the arrival of the plans should still be delayed, so as not to disrupt work completely and to leave this great project in the center of the capital at its present stage, I will take measures for Albanian engineers to draw up plans which, on the basis of the agreements approved by the Albanian Government and by the Soviet Government, should have been done entirely by the Soviet side some time ago.

In submitting to you what has been said above, I ask you to take urgent measures for the speediest possible dispatch of the plans and materials for the continuation of the construction of the Palace of Culture in accordance with the plan. I close, Comrade Ambassador, with the expression of my high consideration.

The Soviet side not only did not reply to these urgent requests, but on April 13, 1961, when the Soviet ship "Vostok" arrived in the port of Durrës carrying in its cargo, along with other merchandise for Albania, the materials destined for the Palace of Culture, it withdrew these materials on the pretext that they had been loaded by mistake and that these were not the materials destined for Albania. The truth is that these materials were in fact destined for the Palace of Culture in accordance with invoice No. 180, with their destination listed on the crates. In addition to this, on April 26 and 27, 1961, the Soviet side unilaterally withdrew all Soviet specialists engaged in the construction of the Palace of Culture.

In view of this situation, when work had been interrupted through the fault of the Soviet side and when so large a project in the center of the capital had remained with open foundations, gravely offending the deep feelings of friendship of the Albanian people toward the fraternal peoples of the Soviet Union, the Government of the People's Republic of Albania, on May 5, 1961, rightfully adopted decisions on the financing of the construction of the palace and the preparation of the relevant designs by our drafting organizations.

Not until three months and three days after the letter of the Albanian Minister of Construction on July 14, 1961, did a memorandum arrive in reply from the Soviet Government, carrying only the date and the month of the year 1961. It is no accident that it did not contain any details, any facts about the progress of work or about the questions raised by the letter of our Minister of Construction on the subject of the situation at the Palace of Culture in 1961. The memorandum of the Soviet Government stated that

> In the letter of the APR Minister of Construction, J. Pashko, dated April 11, 1961, a series of demands are presented which show that the Albanian side did not desire to discuss in a reasonable manner the questions arising in connection with the construction of the Palace of Culture, as is the custom in the relations between socialist countries.

Now, having read the letter from the Minister of Construction, you can see clearly in what a slanderous manner the Soviet Government treats the question, on the instigation of N. Khrushchev, when it says that in our letter of April 11, 1961, *"demands were presented showing that the Albanian side did not desire to discuss the questions in a reasonable manner."* The letter of our minister merely expresses one desire: *the fulfillment of the urgent need for the normal continuation of work on the Palace of Culture.*

The actions of the Soviet Government, such as the failure to dispatch the materials and plans, the withdrawal of the specialists, and the silence maintained for more than three months in reply to our letter, show the lack of desire on the part of the Soviet Government and, moreover, violate the agreement by the Soviet Government concerning the construction of the Palace of Culture.

The hostile efforts of N. Khrushchev to exert pressure by every means on the PPSh and the Albanian people are also revealed in this affair. It emerges clearly from the memorandum of the Soviet Government where, in a slanderous manner, it shifts to others its thoughts and its bad intentions. Here is what it says, among other things:

> On May 5 of this year the Albanian Government adopted a decision according to which it appears that it has taken over the task of completing all the work on the plans and the construction of the Palace of Culture.
>
> Naturally, such an action on the part of the Albanian Government cannot but cause legitimate astonishment, since it involves unilateral actions with regard to the Soviet-Albanian agreement of July 3, 1959, on the construction of the Palace of Culture. It is now quite clear that on this occasion the Albanian Government has pursued fully premeditated aims, which do not contribute in any way to an improvement in relations between our countries. It is no secret that now in Albania the character of the Soviet Union's disinterested aid to the Albanian people is being distorted in a most irresponsible manner, including the aid for the construction of the Palace of Culture.

These base fabrications do not merit comment.

This is the truth. These are the facts. Here facts, slanders, and fabrications are at issue. Now the question arises: Who in fact has exploited a humanitarian gesture, a gift, as "anti-Soviet propaganda"? Who attempts to undermine the traditional friendship between our countries — the Albanian Government, which was obliged to take measures to avert the shame and black mark, which the Soviet Government has brought upon itself, by allocating funds for the construction of the Palace of Culture at a time when these funds were not anticipated in the plan, or the Soviet Government, which at N. Khrushchev's instigation violated its promise to the Albanian people and violated the agreement, signed by the Soviet Government itself, by leaving the foundation of the Palace of Culture as an open tomb in the middle of town?

Our people, and especially the population of the capital, have given a just reply to this question by mobilizing all their forces to construct the Palace of Culture themselves.

The Truth on the Affair of the Students

When speaking at the 22nd Congress of the Communist Party of the Soviet Union, A. Mikoyan, according to the role prescribed for him, had the task of presenting the "theoretical arguments" in support of N. Khrushchev's appeals for a counter-revolution in Albania. His main argument was the affair of the students and the other Albanian citizens who were studying in the Soviet Union. He made out the following case:

> *A short while ago the naval students who were studying here returned to Albania. In conversations among themselves they were asking with surprise: What is the reason for the sudden deterioration in the relations between Albania and the USSR? For asking this, many of them were thrown into prison.*
>
> *The Albanian students who had been studying here returned home on vacation, and afterwards many of them were not given permission by the Albanian authorities to continue their studies in the USSR. Naturally, this caused discontent among them, and many of the discontented suffered reprisals.*
>
> *The Albanian leaders are, on the one hand, hounding those who wish to safeguard the friendship between our peoples, and, on the other hand, they organized a Soviet-Albanian friendship month in order to deceive the people. This happened in September.*
>
> *They may say these are their internal affairs and we should not interfere. But we are faced here with reprisals and measures against Albanians who are defending the traditional friendship with the Soviet Union. Inasmuch as this concerns us directly, we cannot remain indifferent, and we are obliged to express our opinion.*

Following the 22nd Congress, certain Soviet propagandists and their supporters continued the slanders over the affair of the Albanian students who had been studying in the Soviet Union.

A. Mikoyan is apparently alarmed at the "imprisonment" of many naval students. He is apparently pained because many Albanian students "were not given permission" by the Albanian authorities to continue their studies in the Soviet Union. He is apparently frightened by the "reprisals" suffered by many disgruntled students. He is apparently revolted by the measures taken against "friends" of the Soviet Union in Albania. These "matters" apparently are not an internal concern of the Albanian Party of Labor, the Albanian People's Republic, and the Albanian people, but of direct concern — we repeat, direct — to N. Khrushchev's group. We cannot say that such an attitude and such an opinion are surprising because, according to the logic of N. Khrushchev's followers, nothing is surprising, nothing is unexpected. To assert that such an attitude and such a point of view are repugnant, that they rest from beginning to end on slanders, is nothing novel because in their activities slander is their customary weapon. Therefore, name-calling aside, let the facts and documents speak for themselves, and they will throw full light on the truth about the affair of the Albanian students who were studying in the Soviet Union. They will show who drove them out, who subjected them to provocations and blackmail, and who closed the doors of the universities on them on the very eve of the new session.

During the 1960–1961 academic session, on the basis of the agreement of July 5, 1952, between the governments of the Soviet Union and the Albanian People's Republic whereby the Soviet Union paid 60 per cent of the scholarships and the government of the Albanian People's Republic 40 per cent, 1,213 citizens of the Albanian People's Republic were pursuing studies regularly in the Soviet Union.

During the 1961–1962 academic session, on the basis of the plan for cultural cooperation signed by the two countries in Moscow on February 8, 1961, an additional 100 students were selected and made ready to pursue studies in the higher institutions of learning in the Soviet Union.

In August 1961, after spending their vacation in the fatherland, the older students returned to the Soviet Union to continue their studies, and the younger students were ready to depart.

But at this time, on August 26, only four or five days before the beginning of the 1961–1962 academic year, the Soviet Government, pursuing at the instigation of N. Khrushchev a policy of pressure and blackmail, a policy of blockades and isolation in many fields, toward the Albanian Party of Labor, the Albanian People's Republic, and the Albanian people, went so far as to deprive Albanian citizens of the right to continue their studies in the universities and institutions of higher learning in the Soviet Union.

In a note from the Ministry of Foreign Affairs, the Soviet Government informed the government of the Albanian People's Republic that

> Effective as of September 1, 1961, the procedure common to all socialist countries in Europe regarding the accounts for the education of students and aspirants in the Soviet Union, whereby scholarships are paid by the country sending its citizens to the Soviet Union for study, will be applicable to Albania.

The purpose behind this unilateral cancellation of the intergovernmental agreement of July 5, 1952, was to make the training of the cadres of the Albanian People's Republic more difficult and thus to impair the building of socialism in Albania. It was an unjust decision, taken by N. Khrushchev to avenge himself on the Albanian Party of Labor, which had expressed correct Marxist-Leninist viewpoints, in accordance with the party rules, on a whole range of ideological and political questions about contemporary world developments, particularly the international Communist and workers movement—viewpoints which were incompatible with his anti-Marxist, opportunist theses.

Faced with such a situation, with the Soviet Government arbitrarily altering the conditions for Albanian students in the Soviet Union and suddenly creating great difficulties for our country, as has been pointed out, only four or five days before the start of the new session the Albanian students were obliged to return to Albania.

What reason, or rather what pretext, was fabricated by the Soviet Government at the command of N. Khrushchev for no longer permitting the Albanian students to continue studies in the Soviet Union?

The Soviet Government and the Government of the Albanian People's Republic, as is known, had concluded an agreement in July 1952 on "the education of citizens of the APR in public institutions of higher learning in the Soviet Union," which provided (in Article V) that:

> The Government of the Soviet Union shall pay the costs of upkeep and tuition for citizens of the Albanian People's Republic in the institutions of higher learning in the Soviet Union

and in Article VI:

> The government of the Albanian People's Republic shall pay to the government of the Soviet Union 40 per cent of the expenses specified in Article V of this agreement.

The agreement was an expression of the fraternal internationalist aid that the Soviet Union offered to the Albanian People's Republic for the training of the necessary cadres for the development of our national economy and culture.

Subsequently, on March 16, 1960, the Soviet Government requested a modification of the agreement and the conclusion of a new agreement on different bases and conditions from those of 1952.

The Government of the Albanian People's Republic, taking into consideration the fraternal relations and close cooperation between the two countries, the concrete conditions existing in the Albanian People's Republic, the urgent need for trained cadres, and the financial burden that would follow from a change in the conditions of study, advised the Ambassador of the Albanian People's Republic in Moscow, Nesti Nase, to request through the USSR Ministry of Foreign Affairs that no change be made in the conditions of study of Albanian students in the Soviet Union.

On June 6, 1960, in reply to the request of the Albanian Government, Soviet Deputy Foreign Minister N. P. Firyubin verbally informed our ambassador that

> The Soviet Government has examined once again its proposal on modifying the agreement on the conditions of reciprocal study of students and aspirants in public institutions of higher learning and scientific research institutions. It has given consideration to the Albanian request and has decided that the conditions of the 1952 agreement should remain in force.

Thus, the problem was considered solved, and the matter closed.

The Albanian Government, as always, appreciated this just decision of the Soviet Government as a friendly act, and for this very reason, as usual, during the 1960–1961 academic session, a considerable number of Albanian students were sent to institutions of higher learning in the Soviet Union and continued their studies in accordance with the earlier conditions until August 1961.

The Soviet Government, however, at the instigation of N. Khrushchev, as another repressive measure against the Albanian People's Republic, and with the aim of creating difficulties for our country even in the training of cadres, repudiated the official promise made to our government on June 6, 1960. That is evident from the Soviet note of August 26, 1961, which again raised the question of the conditions of study of Albanian citizens in schools of the Soviet Union. That note, completely ignoring the official communication of June 6, 1960, says:

> As a result of the negotiations which have taken place between the governments of the USSR and other European socialist countries, with the exception of Albania, new agreements have been concluded on the basis outlined in the note of the USSR Ministry of Foreign Affairs dated March 16, 1960. Although a year and a half has passed since the note of the USSR Ministry of Foreign Affairs was delivered to the Albanian Embassy in Moscow, the Albanian Government has not replied to the Soviet note in writing.

Note carefully: The Albanian Government's only fault was that it did not "reply to the Soviet note in writing." Since when are the verbal communication of our ambassador to the Soviet Ministry of Foreign Affairs and the verbal communication of the Soviet Deputy Minister of Foreign Affairs of June 6, 1960, no longer considered official documents? N. Khrushchev's concept of the official value of written and verbal communications is intriguing. N. Khrushchev insists on a "written reply" from our government to its note of March 16, 1960, while he himself verbally informs our government of a matter the importance of which need not be stressed, namely, the closing by the Soviet Government of the Soviet Embassy in Tirana and the demand for the closing of the Albanian Embassy in Moscow.

When the chargé d'affaires of the Albanian People's Republic in Moscow asked N. P. Firyubin to put his notification of the recall of the staff of the Soviet Embassy in Tirana and the departure of the personnel of the Albanian Embassy in Moscow in writing, Firyubin, on behalf of the Soviet Government, replied that any verbal or written communication by an official representative is considered an official act; therefore, there was no need to put it in writing. In other words, it boils down to this: "Do not what I do, but what I say."

One can easily understand the falseness of the pretext on which the Soviet Government nullified the intergovernmental accord of 1952 on the training of Albanian citizens in the Soviet Union.

Very significant also is the fact that on the same day — August 26, 1961 — that the Soviet Government made known its decision to curtail the scholarships of the Albanian students studying in the Soviet Union (about 60 per cent of the cost), the Soviet Ministry of Foreign Affairs sent the Embassy of the Albanian People's Republic in Moscow a note which alleged:

> The Ministry of Foreign Affairs of the USSR continues to receive reports that some Albanian students and Albanian auditors who attend Soviet institutions of higher learning have spread fabrications and various slanders regarding Soviet-Albanian relations and that they have tried to drag Soviet and foreign students into provocative conversations.

It states further:

> By making known the facts concerning the unworthy attitude of the Albanian students in the Soviet Union, the USSR Ministry of Foreign Affairs draws attention to the fact that their anti-Soviet views undoubtedly have a premeditated character.

The note concludes:

> The Ministry has been authorized to declare that, in the event of anti-Soviet outbursts on the part of the Albanian students, they will be asked to leave the USSR.

N. Khrushchev's group, the authors of the note, need slanders and fabrications in order to realize their malevolent schemes and to deprive our country of the possibility of training cadres in Soviet schools. Those who slander Albanian students have sunk pretty low! For it is well known that their devotion and respect for the Soviet Union and the Communist Party of the Soviet Union have become one of the best character traits of the citizens of the new Albania. The Soviet professors and students themselves can testify to the noble feelings of their Albanian comrades and students. The allegation that Albanian students used anti-Soviet expressions is a slander and an offense which the Soviet side deliberately practices to discredit the Albanian students and to justify the unjust measures taken against them.

Taking the Soviet note into account, one may ask: Who lies, the note of the Foreign Ministry, which presents the Albanian students as "anti-Soviet," or A. Mikoyan, who at the 22nd Congress described the Albanian students as "friends of the Soviet Union" who "suffered reprisals in Albania"? It is clear that in both cases we are faced with slanders to justify the malevolent schemes against the APR and the PPSh.

In the first case, the note of the Soviet Ministry of Foreign Affairs, slander is needed to justify the departure of the Albanian students from Soviet schools. In the second case, Mikoyan's statement, slander is necessary in order to have "reasoned evidence" of the conditions of "terror and insecurity" which exist in Albania, and thus to realize the appeal launched by Khrushchev for counterrevolution and to deceive world public opinion with regard to the real situation in our country.

According to A. Mikoyan and certain other Soviet propagandists, "terror, imprisonment, murder, and assassination" reign in Albania; sailors and students have been jailed in Albania, and so have "all honest people who favor friendship with the Soviet Union" — briefly, everyone has been jailed in Albania!

These monstrous slanders, which have rightly aroused feelings of legitimate hatred and disgust toward their authors have incensed our people. The slanderers look ridiculous in their eyes and have emerged as enemies in the same dock with the imperialists and the Yugoslav revisionists, because they bring just as much evil, because they represent just as great a danger with their appeal for counterrevolution.

Their intention to create difficult situations and troubles cannot be concealed with the veil of "their creative Marxism," which smells of pure revisionism.

The Albanian people, guided by their party, have endured many storms and stresses; they have survived many snares and intrigues; they have been steeled and have become stronger than ever in order to foil the plans of enemies, whatever the watchword with which they present themselves.

The Central Committee of the Albanian Party of Labor, the Government of the Albanian Republic, and all the Albanian people have appreciated and will appreciate the great internationalist aid given by the Soviet Union, the Communist Party of the Soviet Union, and the Soviet Government to the Albanian People's Republic in training Albanian cadres in the Soviet Union. Our sons and our daughters who have studied in higher Soviet institutions of learning and who have become acquainted with Soviet science and culture, the most advanced in the world, have brought back the knowledge and the extremely valuable experience of the Communist Party of the Soviet Union, of the builders of Communism in the Soviet Union. Educated by the Albanian Party of Labor, they have made and are still making a great contribution to strengthening Albanian-Soviet friendship.

As for the case of the "many jailed students," which so grieves Khrushchev and his followers that they cannot sleep, these students enjoy good health and are studying at the State University of Tirana and other higher institutes in our country or in other universities in the fraternal socialist countries.

DOCUMENT 19

Aleksandr Nikolayev, "The Truth about the Palace of Culture in Tirana," Radio Moscow *in Albanian to Albania, December 24, 1961, 1500* GMT (*excerpt* in BBC/SU/*830/A2/ 1–2, December 29, 1961*).

Material published on December 20 in *Zëri i Popullit,* with directly anti-Soviet aims, falsifies the truth about the building of the Palace of Culture in Tirana. The Albanian leadership took this step in order further to aggravate Albanian-Soviet relations. *Zëri i Popullit* claims that the Soviet Government unilaterally stopped fulfilling its obligations to build this project. As is known, early in 1959, guided by the desire to help strengthen Albanian-Soviet friendship, the Soviet Government decided to build the Palace of Culture in Tirana as a gift from the peoples of the Soviet Union to the Albanian people.

On July 3, 1959, an agreement on this matter was reached between the governments of the Soviet Union and of the Albanian People's Republic. This provided for the Palace of Culture to be built in the period 1959–1962. The Soviet Government did everything possible to begin the construction of this project as early as possible. In June 1959, before the signing of the agreement for the building of the Palace of Culture, the Soviet organizations in charge of the drafting of the project presented the plans for it to the Albanian Government for examination. The Albanian side expressed the wish for the project to be further expanded, and later it several times made changes in the plans. Patiently taking into account the proposals of the Albanian side, the Soviet Government sent its architects to Tirana. They drew up the final version of the project on the site together with the Albanian architects and builders. Furthermore, without awaiting final approval for the project, the Soviet side began work and by January 1960 had sent to the Albanian People's Republic a group of specialists of high qualifications, as well as the necessary technicians.

The Soviet expenditure on the project and the construction of the Palace of Culture had at that time reached nearly 4 million rubles (old currency). The development of the project and the beginning of the work on the Palace of Culture in Tirana, therefore, are the best proof of the care which the Soviet Government has taken to satisfy the wishes of the Albanian side. In April 1960 the Albanian side expressed its approval in principle of the latest architectural version of the Palace of Culture, but again made a number of suggestions which, if put into effect, would have resulted in a great increase in the initial volume of work. By now the cost of the palace had risen by two and a half times. In this way, the Albanian side made the construction of the palace considerably more difficult, and put the Soviet organizations in effect in the position of having to draft new plans. It was clear that this matter could be solved only through talks at the governmental level between our two countries, and that time was needed for this.

However, after the Moscow meeting of Communist and workers parties, the Albanian leaders assumed a hostile attitude towards the Soviet Union, and began to spread slanderous fabrications which intentionally distorted the internationalist character of the fraternal aid given by the Soviet Union to the Albanian people, and which included the Tirana Palace of Culture affair. Instead of discussing the matter of the Palace of Culture in a concrete way and in a businesslike atmosphere, the Albanian side, with provocative intentions, decided to take steps to force the Soviet side to continue the construction of this project.

On April 13 of this year a letter from Josif Pashko, Minister of Construction of the Albanian People's Republic, was handed to the Soviet Embassy in Tirana. It demanded, in the form of an ultimatum, that the Soviet Union send the missing part of the plans and the necessary building materials for the Palace of Culture in Tirana. . . . With obviously anti-Soviet intentions, the Albanian leadership spread a slanderous fabrication alleging that the Soviet Government was trying to exert economic pressure on Albania over the Palace of Culture. All this was done to fan Albania's anti-Soviet propaganda, in keeping with the present line of the Albanian leadership.

In connection with this arbitrary action of the Government of the Albanian People's Republic, on July 14 the Soviet Embassy in Tirana handed the Albanian Foreign Ministry a memorandum which said: "Since this humanitarian action of the Soviet Government — the building of the Palace of Culture in Tirana, a gift from the Soviet peoples to the Albanian people — is being exploited for anti-Soviet propaganda and for aggravating Soviet-Albanian relations, the Soviet Government is compelled under these circumstances to divest itself of the responsibility for proceeding any further with its construction." Accordingly, the entire history of the affair of the construction of the Soviet Union's Palace of Culture in Tirana shows that the Albanian leadership is vainly trying to saddle the Soviet Union with the responsibility, and necessarily brings to light the truth underlying all that has occurred.

DOCUMENT 20

Aleksandr Nikolayev, "The Truth about the Soviet Specialists in Albania," Radio Moscow *in Albanian to Albania, December 26, 1961, 1100* GMT *(précis with excerpts in* BBC/SU*/830/A2/2–3, December 29, 1961*).

"On December 19 of this year, the newspaper *Zëri i Popullit* published reports about certain matters affecting Albanian-Soviet relations and in particular the recall of Soviet specialists from Albania. In the course of this, the newspaper succeeded in distorting obvious facts in a shameless and provocative way."

As is known, the Soviet Union and other

socialist countries have given Albania extensive economic and technical aid. Specialists assisted in prospecting for oil, copper, chromium, and other ores and in building and modernizing the industrial plant. Their assistance gave Albania its first electric power, oil, timber, textile, and food industries. During 1950–60 the Soviet Union assisted in the planning, construction, or reconstruction of nearly 80 industrial enterprises. It gave Albania an oil refining plant which made possible a fourfold increase in its oil production.

The Albanian leaders used to acknowledge this assistance, but lately they have tried to disparage it. "Local party and government bodies were incited to spurn their [the Soviet specialists'] advice and recommendations and to create intolerable conditions for their work. Measures were taken against the Soviet specialists which were incompatible with the honor and dignity of Soviet men. . . . At the beginning of this year, the Albanian side began to take concrete steps to get rid of the Soviet experts. Here are some examples of the intolerable attitude of the Albanian authorities. . . . On January 28, 1961, all the Soviet specialists in the Central Directorate of Geology were invited to a certain place under the pretext of a meeting, and there the deputy manager, Skender Salija, asked them to hand over the keys of their offices, filing cabinets, and desks; Albanian specialists and service personnel were present. When they returned to work the next day, they found that a secret search had been carried out at their place of work." The display case with photographs illustrating Soviet successes was taken down. On the pretext of taking inventory, the Albanian authorities broke seals and locks on the Soviet geologists' doors and searched their filing cabinets. In February one Soviet expert had the seals on his door removed during his absence. During the night of March 20 the deputy manager himself removed the seals from the doors of another Soviet geologist and searched his desks. As of May 3, 1961, the five Soviet geologists who remained in Albania were not given the documents to enable them to complete their work.

"We could quote you dozens of examples like this. Besides creating intolerable working conditions for the Soviet experts, the Albanian administration has frequently broken the Soviet-Albanian agreement with regard to the conditions on which Soviet specialists were to be sent and their accommodations and living conditions." Thus, in November 1960, on the order of the Albanian Council of Ministers, regulations were issued which fixed low standards for the accommodations, living conditions, and transportation of foreign specialists. In December 1960 the management of Rubik geological enterprise decided that the Soviet specialists should vacate half their accommodations. When one comrade who worked in Durrës went home on leave, his belongings were moved from his flat and put in storage and his flat was taken over by the manager's chauffeur. There were instances of Albanian local authorities putting limitations on the Soviet specialists' consumption of electricity.

Under these circumstances the Soviet Government was compelled to recall all its specialists. Even after their departure, the Albanian authorities tried to belittle what they had done. Nevertheless the truth cannot be concealed, however much the Albanian leaders try to disclaim responsibility for their departure.

DOCUMENT 21

"This Is the Truth," Radio Moscow *in Albanian to Albania, January 9, 1962, 1500* GMT *(complete text,* BBC/SU/*841/A2/1–2, January 11, 1962).*

Dear friends, the newspaper *Zëri i Popullit* published on December 30 material relating to the so-called question of the Albanian students who formerly studied in the Soviet Union. Our correspondent learned the following from the

USSR Ministry of Higher and Specialized Education:

The Soviet Union has granted Albania considerable aid in training specialists with higher qualifications. During the last 10 years, 663 Albanian students have received diplomas from Soviet higher education establishments. In addition, 12 young Albanian scientists have completed postgraduate studies. They have all returned as valuable specialists, highly qualified technological engineers, geologists, doctors of medicine, pedagogical and scientific workers. As is already known, the new Albanian specialists educated in the Soviet Union have become the main force in the people's economy and in the development of their country's culture. It is interesting that the Albanian Telegraph Agency has recently published a report with statistics showing how well-equipped with technological engineers and experts in husbandry the people's economy of the country is. Certainly the Albanian people, which for 17 years have been advancing on the road to socialism, can be proud of these figures, but nobody denies the fact that this victory reflects the friendly and unselfish aid which the Soviet Union has afforded the Albanian people.

According to the agreement concluded in 1952 on facilities for Albanian citizens studying in Soviet institutions of higher education, the Soviet Government assumed the major share of the expenses connected with such studies. The Albanian share of such expenses was lower than that borne by any other socialist country whose students studied or are still studying in the Soviet Union. But if we go beyond the literal meaning of the agreement, we see that the Soviet state in practice met all expenses for the maintenance and tuition of the Albanian students, that is to say, it granted scholarships, paid the salaries of teachers, and met all other expenditures on food and economic needs. It is not necessary to point out that the living conditions of the Albanians in the Soviet Union were favorable from every point of view. For instance, they enjoyed a more privileged position than Soviet students, although the agreement spoke of equal rights with Soviet students.

The question arises as to why the Albanian students had to give up their studies in the Soviet Union. The Albanian press is now trying to prove that the Soviet Government refused to train Albania's specialists in Soviet institutes of higher education, alleging that it demanded large sums in payment for their studies. But such an assertion is merely a slander against the Soviet Union and the Soviet people. In reality the situation was as follows: the Albanian leaders gave their own and rather original interpretation to the principles of friendship and mutual aid between socialist countries. According to their views, it was quite permissible to receive material aid from other socialist countries without compensation even in part. But this of course could not go on forever. This was the reason why the Soviet Government had to raise with the Albanian Government the question of its assuming a real share of the expenses incurred by its students, as was done by all other socialist countries whose students were studying in the Soviet Union.

On August 26 of last year, Albania was informed that from September 1, 1961, the general regulation on the settlement of accounts in connection with students following postgraduate courses, applicable to all European socialist countries, would also apply to Albania. This just demand by the Soviet Government was in no way an act of discrimination on the part of the Soviet Government toward Albania, as the authorities concerned are now trying to demonstrate, because the citizens of all the other socialist countries are still studying in the Soviet Union. However, even before the Soviet Government presented this demand, the Albanian Embassy in Moscow informed the Ministry of Higher Education of the Soviet Union that nearly 300 students, that is to say, the main contingent of the Albanian students in the Soviet Union, would not return to the Soviet Union to continue their studies.

These activities by the leaders of the Albanian Government once more demonstrated how far they had gone in their adventurist policy of separating themselves from the Soviet Union and the socialist camp. It is precisely this which is the main reason for the interruption of the studies of the Albanian students in the Soviet Union.

DOCUMENT 22

"Deeper and Deeper into the Mire of Anti-Marxism," Zëri i Popullit, *January 9, 1962 (complete text).*

Since the 22nd Congress of the Communist Party of the Soviet Union, the N. Khrushchev group has furiously continued its campaign of attacks against the Albanian Party of Labor and the Albanian People's Republic. It is significant that this campaign is becoming more intense and more insulting at a time when Soviet newspapers are not only giving great publicity to the utterly reactionary and warlike interview with Kennedy but, surprisingly, are also finding space to say good words about him, and at a time when N. Khrushchev and his followers are taking one step after another to get as close as possible to the revisionist and traitorous Belgrade clique.

What strikes one's eye is that the authors of this campaign are as afraid of facts as they are of fire. Therefore, they avoid them and use instead bombastic generalizations which are frequently contradictory, and vile insults and offensive remarks such as N. Khrushchev and his comrades have never used against even the most enraged imperialists and colonialists.

Another fact which leaps to the eye is that N. Khrushchev and his supporters are trying by all possible means to avoid discussing the essence of the ideological differences of principle which are at the root of the differences between our party and the N. Khrushchev group. They transfer the problem to another terrain, and degrade themselves to the level of hurling the meanest and most banal lies against our party and country. Moreover, when they do feel compelled to deal with our ideological differences, they distort the position of our party, fabricate, attribute alien views to it, and afterward the authors of these fabrications themselves, starting from "an irreconcilable position of principle," begin to fight and to refute them.

Why is such an uproar being made over so-called Albanian "dogmatism"? Why is N. Khrushchev's group trying with such uncontrollable zeal to distort the position of the Albanian Party of Labor and to discredit it before international public opinion? It is obvious to every reasonable person that the main issue here is not the question of unmasking so-called Albanian "dogmatism." Nor is it a question of warning of "the great threat" it poses to the international Communist movement. The deafening clamor against the Albanian Party of Labor is in fact needed by N. Khrushchev and his group for something else. First, they need it, among other things, to attack certain fundamental theses of the revolutionary Marxist-Leninist doctrine, which is defended by the PPSh and true Marxist-Leninists in all countries, and secondly, to attract the attention of international public opinion to Albanian "dogmatism" as a smoke-screen behind which they can more easily and quickly spread their own revisionist views in the international Communist and workers movement.

To conceal their deviation from the positions of Marxism-Leninism, the authors of the anti-Marxist articles and speeches against our party maintain that the leadership of the Albanian Party of Labor radically altered its political line on the fundamental questions of contemporary international developments and its attitude toward the Soviet Union and the other socialist countries — or, as someone put it, has made a "political death leap." It is really curious how the political line of our party has altered completely, when the same people who say this call us "dogmatists," i.e., people who cannot abandon previous views. Furthermore, these very people were, until yesterday, congratulating us and viewing the policy of our party as a Marxist-Leninist line, which now emerges as "dogmatic" and radically altered. No, the policy of the PPSh and the APR Government remains what it was. Our attitude has not changed at all, neither toward imperialism and revisionism nor toward the Soviet Union and the other socialist countries. Neither has it changed toward the national liberation movement, nor toward the cause of peace, peaceful coexistence, and so forth. On the contrary, the only thing that has changed is the attitude toward our party and country and toward the fundamental teachings of Marxism-Leninism of N. Khrushchev and those who follow him. They have revised the fundamental teachings of Marxism-Leninism on the reactionary and aggressive nature of imperialism, and on this basis they treat opportunistically the question of peace and peaceful coexistence, the national liberation struggle of enslaved peoples, the question of the paths of transition from capitalism to socialism, proletarian dictatorship, and so forth. They have seriously trampled on the principles of proletarian internationalism in relations between the fraternal Communist and workers parties and between the socialist countries.

N. Khrushchev stated his opportunist views on these questions at the 20th and 22nd Congresses of the Communist Party of the Soviet Union. Certain of these theses constitute the ideological and political platform of all his anti-Marxist activity. He is, therefore, trying to impose these views on all the fraternal parties and to make them compulsory norms for the entire international Communist movement. N. Khrushchev, presenting the decisions of the 20th and 22nd Congresses as the quintessence of Marxism-Leninism and the attitudes taken toward them as positive criteria for judging whether this or that party does or does not stand on the positions of Marxism-Leninism, labels as "anti-Marxist," "nationalist," "dogmatic," and the like any party or person who opposes his opportunist theses expressed in the decisions of these Congresses. In this way, for example, he acted against the PPSh, which, as is known, neither agreed nor agrees with certain opportunist theses and certain anti-Marxist attitudes that appeared at the 20th and 22nd Congresses. Why are the Marxist-Leninist Communist and workers parties of all countries supposedly obliged to see the Marxist-Leninist truth through N. Khrushchev's revisionist glasses? Fortunately, fundamental Marxist-Leninist principles do exist, clearly set forth in the classic writings and proved by life itself and the experience of the entire international Communist movement. These principles cannot be replaced by the decisions of the 20th and 22nd Congresses, nor by the reports and speeches of N. Khrushchev. It is these principles, and not the 20th and 22nd Congresses of the Communist Party of the Soviet Union, which are sound criteria for judging whether this or that fraternal party stands or does not stand on the revolutionary positions of Marxism-Leninism. But N. Khrushchev is seeking to replace the classic writings of Marxism-Leninism and the Marxist principles formulated in the two Declarations of the Communist and workers parties in 1957 and 1960 with his revisionist platform. He wants to replace revolutionary Marxism-Leninism with opportunism and revisionism. This is also seen clearly in the article published by *Pravda* on December 14, 1961, under the heading "On a Dangerous Path." *Pravda* says, among other things: "When one refers to the line of the 20th Congress of the Communist Party of the Soviet Union, one does not simply mean the decisions of one party but a new stage in the international Communist movement." In this way, N. Khrushchev seeks to make the decisions of one party compulsory for all the fraternal parties, and to make the international meetings of Communist and workers parties and their collective documents completely useless and formal. Such an attitude openly contradicts the well-known thesis of the 1960 Declaration, which maintains that the fraternal Communist and workers parties "are independent and equal, and that they formulate their policy by starting from the concrete conditions in their own countries, under the guidance of Marxist-Leninist principles."

The authors of the *Pravda* article, trying to justify their position, refer to the contents of the 1960 Declaration on the international significance of the 20th Congress. But it is known how this thesis was included in the Declaration. The Soviet leaders, contrary to the spirit of the Declaration on the independence and equality of fraternal parties, are using this thesis to impose on them the decisions of the 20th Congress, although at the Moscow meeting of November 1960 they solemnly stated that they would never interpret and use it with such intent. The true aims of N. Khrushchev and his comrades are now appearing more and more clearly.

After all this, it is obvious how hypocritical and formal was N. Khrushchev's proposal, proudly recalled by the authors of the *Pravda* article, to exclude from the 1960 Declaration the thesis "the socialist camp headed by the Soviet Union."

The Albanian Party of Labor, as is also shown by the Moscow protocols of the November 1960 Moscow meeting, has been and continues to be of the opinion that the thesis "headed by the Soviet Union" is a correct and useful thesis. When we say that the Soviet Union stands at the head of the socialist camp, we by no means want to imply that the Soviet Union and the Communist Party of the Soviet Union are the "supreme authorities" which lead and direct, and the other socialist countries and the other Communist and workers parties are minor authorities which obey and subordinate themselves to the former. They are in no way like this. By this thesis we mean that the Soviet Union, as the first country which opened and is opening the road to socialism and Communism, and the Communist Party of the Soviet Union, as the great party of Lenin and Stalin and as the most experienced party in the international Communist movement, are, by their historical experience, pointing out for the other socialist countries and other Communist and workers parties the general Marxist-Leninist path toward the victory of the socialist revolution and toward the building of a socialist and Communist society. (This glorious experience does not begin with the 20th Congress. It is a reflection of the more than 50 years' struggle and efforts of the Communist Party of the Soviet Union. Moreover, the opportunist theses introduced by N. Khrushchev at the 20th and 22nd Congresses contradict the entire record and historical experience of the Communist Party of the Soviet Union and also contradict the facts of contemporary international life.) For this reason, the experiences of the Soviet Union and its Communist Party are of world-historic importance, including a considerable number of the theses of the 20th, 21st, and 22nd Congresses and of the new Program of the Communist Party of the Soviet Union.

In fact, by proposing to remove the thesis "headed by the Soviet Union," N. Khrushchev made an inadmissible concession to the revisionist elements and encouraged them in their efforts to disrupt the international Communist movement, to spread their anti-Marxist views, and to isolate the Communist and workers parties from the historic experience of the Soviet Union and its Communist Party. Because of this, in certain Communist parties, for example, the Italian Communist Party, much propaganda has been made for "polycentrism," which, in fact, means to renounce the principle of the international solidarity of the Communist and workers parties as well as the general laws of the socialist revolution and the building of socialism, discovered by Marxism-Leninism and attested in practice and, above all, by the historic experience of the Communist Party of the Soviet Union. It means to slip into the revisionist position and to preach the so-called "specific national road" to socialism, and the like. A picture has been painted that is truly curious: When we defended the thesis "headed by the Soviet Union," N. Khrushchev and some others attacked us and vehemently objected to this thesis; and now these very same people are attacking our party because it is allegedly following an "anti-Soviet" policy and "is disrupting the Communist movement and has strayed from Marxism-Leninism," and all this merely because it is not in agreement with certain theses of the 20th and 22nd Congresses of the Communist Party of the Soviet Union!

Simultaneously with his efforts to impose on other parties the decisions of the 20th Congress, N. Khrushchev has organized a whole campaign to impose the new Program of the Communist Party of the Soviet Union on them. While we do not deny the historic importance of this document as a program for building a Communist society in the Soviet Union, it nevertheless remains the program of a single party. For this reason, it cannot be imposed on other parties and cannot replace the joint documents of the Communist movement — the Declarations of 1957 and 1960. Our party is not in agreement with certain opportunist theses contained in the new Program of the Communist Party of the Soviet Union, particularly on questions of contemporary world evolution, which are in direct opposition to the two Declarations of the Communist and workers parties. But it greatly appreciates those parts of the program which present in a correct manner the valuable historic experience acquired by the Communist Party of the Soviet Union in the socialist revolution and in the building of socialism and Communism. As in the past, our party will study this experience with great care and will make use of it in the struggle to build a socialist and Communist society in our fatherland. This line of our party cannot be changed. It is futile to try to accuse us of trying to change our line.

The accusation that the PPSh did not fully publish the Draft Program of the Communist Party of the Soviet Union, which is constantly repeated by N. Khrushchev and his supporters, is absurd and baseless. The article against our party published in *Kommunist,* No. 17, 1961, points out that even some bourgeois newspapers were forced to publish the complete text of the program. We are not interested in what the bourgeois newspapers have published. If they have published the program, it seems that they had their own reasons for doing so. Insofar as our party is concerned, it is well known that it published the *draft* of the Program of the Communist Party of the Soviet Union in condensed form, and when this, with relevant modifications, was approved by the 22nd Congress of the Communist Party of the Soviet Union and became its program, our party published it in its entirety in the form of a pamphlet, along with the new statutes of the Communist Party of the Soviet Union, so that every worker in our country could buy and read them. The slanderous accusations that the PPSh is allegedly afraid to publish these documents because of the Albanian people, that it distorts the point of view and positions of the Communist Party of the Soviet Union, and that it lies about it evaporate automatically. It is also general knowledge that our press published in its entirety the accusations made against the PPSh at the 22nd Congress of the Communist Party of the Soviet Union. Why, then, do N. Khrushchev and his group not publish in the Soviet press the materials of our party, since they say that they are not afraid of the truth?

The authors of the articles in *Pravda, Kommunist,* and other organs which write against our party and country, shamefully distort the positions of our party in connection with certain questions of principle concerning contemporary world evolution. By struggling against the so-called "anti-Marxist," "dogmatic," and similar theses of the PPSh (which they have distorted in this way), they aim at justifying and at spreading the opportunist theses of N. Khrushchev. The main point is to make his revisionist pill more acceptable by covering it with the luster of the struggle against "Albanian anti-Marxism."

Let us consider the question of peaceful coexistence, which is repeatedly referred to in the *Pravda* and *Kommunist* articles. Faithful to the teachings of Marxism-Leninism and the Moscow Declarations of Communist and workers parties, the PPSh has based and always will resolutely base its foreign policy on the Leninist thesis: In the conditions of the division of the world into two systems, the policy of peaceful coexistence is the only correct and reasonable policy in the *relations between nations of different social systems,* in accordance with the acknowledged principles of complete equality, respect for territorial integrity, national independence and sovereignty, noninterference in the internal affairs of others, and cooperation based on mutual interest.

But in this world we not only have the problem of the relations between nations of different social and political systems; there is also the problem of relations between the socialist countries, as well as the problems of the struggle of the peoples against imperialism and colonialism and the struggle of the working people to overthrow the capitalist yoke. As a result, *besides peaceful coexistence between nations of different social systems,* which is one of its basic aspects, the foreign policy of the socialist countries has two other features: relations among the socialist countries, based on the principles of friendship, cooperation, and fraternal aid and assistance, and based on the principle of socialist internationalism; and support for the national liberation struggle of the enslaved peoples for national independence against imperialism, and the revolutionary struggle of the working class in the capitalist countries to overthrow capitalism and transfer power to the people.

Such is the clear Marxist-Leninist position which was also defined by the Moscow Declarations and to which the PPSh faithfully adheres on matters of foreign policy. Just the same, the afore-mentioned *Pravda* article alleges that the PPSh is against the Leninist principle of peaceful coexistence because it opposes the anti-Marxist thesis of N. Khrushchev which states that peaceful coexistence between nations of different social and political systems is *the general line* of the foreign policy of the socialist countries. This is really an amazing and illogical conclusion, which puts its authors in a difficult position.

It is known that N. Khrushchev himself has more than once declared to the world that the principles of peaceful coexistence are not enough for relations between the socialist countries, because the essence of their relations is to be found in the principles of cooperation, aid, and mutual, fraternal assistance in the spirit of socialist internationalism. This is also clearly noted in the 1957 Declaration of Communist and workers parties. How can this be reconciled with the thesis that peaceful coexistence is the general line of the foreign policy of the socialist countries? Does this mean that N. Khrushchev and his supporters prefer to take the side of the capitalist countries against the fraternal socialist countries for the sake of peaceful coexistence with this or that capitalist country?

N. Khrushchev's columnists refer to V. I. Lenin to find arguments in support of their distorted theses. Yet, it is known that V. I. Lenin never confined the foreign policy of the Soviet state merely to matters of the struggle for peaceful coexistence, in spite of the fact that the Soviet Union was then the only socialist country and was surrounded by the merciless storms of the capitalist world. It seems that the authors of the *Pravda* article have forgotten that the great Lenin has more than once emphatically stated that the Soviet socialist state, along with the efforts for peaceful coexistence with capitalist countries, must powerfully and by all possible means support the liberation struggle of the peoples enslaved by imperialism and the revolutionary struggle of the working people against the capitalist order. This is the lofty internationalist task of every socialist country. Or do they, perhaps, mean that, for the sake of peaceful coexistence with this or that capitalist country, the socialist countries should renounce such support?

The absurdity of the attitude of the originators of the attacks on the PPSh emerges even more clearly when, falsifying most crudely a *Zëri i Popullit* editorial, they accused our party of advocating relations of peaceful coexistence with the Soviet Union. (!) What should we believe? The accusation that the PPSh is against the Leninist principle of peaceful coexistence, or the accusation that the PPSh advocates relations of peaceful coexistence even with the Soviet Union?

It is childish to think that the PPSh, the party of a small socialist country surrounded by capitalist countries, is allegedly against peace and peaceful coexistence. N. Khrushchev and those who follow him presently in attacks on the PPSh, until yesterday welcomed and fully supported the foreign policy of our party and government, which, as is known by all, has not changed at all even with regard to our relations with neighboring countries. Now, according to the authors of the *Pravda* article, the responsibility for aggravating Albanian-Greek relations falls on our party and government, which are alleged to be against peaceful coexistence with Greece. This is a vile falsification of the position of our party and a service to the reactionary circles of Greece, which, as is known, is a member of the aggressive NATO bloc. The Albanian Party of Labor has never stated that it is against peaceful coexistence with Greece but has stated and continues to state that normalization of relations between Greece and the Albanian People's Republic is prevented by the absurd pretensions of the Greek Government that it is in a state of war with Albania and that it has territorial claims on the southern districts of Albania, an attitude which is in direct opposition to the recognized principles of peaceful coexistence. Or should we, perhaps, for the sake of peaceful coexistence, make concessions to the Greek chauvinists in their territorial claims on southern Albania, as N. Khrushchev did during his talk with Venizelos? The Albanian Party of Labor and the Government of the APR, faithfully following the principles of peaceful coexistence, have been ready and continue to be ready even today to establish diplomatic relations with Greece if the Greek Government renounces the baseless claims which prevent neighborly relations between our two countries. We wish to establish diplomatic relations and to have good trade, cultural, and other relations with all capitalist countries which want them, especially with our neighbors, on the basis of rigorous respect for the recognized principles of peaceful coexistence. The N. Khrushchev group, pursuing its anti-Marxist designs for the political and economic isolation of the Albanian People's Republic, vainly tries to accuse our party and government of being against peaceful coexistence. In vain he tries to besmirch our party and to slander it by alleging that "it is drawing closer to imperialism" whenever the Government of the APR tries to put into practice the principles of peaceful coexistence in its relations with its neighbors.

Let us consider the question of disarmament. The struggle to impose relations of peaceful coexistence and disarmament on the imperialists is one of the great problems of our time. The Albanian Party of Labor and the Government of the Albanian People's Republic have supported and resolutely support the efforts of the Soviet Union in this direction, including the Soviet proposal for total and complete disarmament.

The attitude of our party and government toward this question is crystal clear and leaves no doubt. Nevertheless, N. Khrushchev and his group are making a great clamor, accusing the PPSh of being against total and complete disarmament. This is nothing but a smoke screen to hide the distorted pacifist-bourgeois views of N. Khrushchev on general and total disarmament.

What are, in fact, the dangerous views which N. Khrushchev tries to impose on the international Communist and workers movement concerning general and total disarmament?

First, that general and total disarmament is the only real way to ensure peace; that it represents the primary and most urgent task of the hour, on which depend all other tasks and all other problems of the international Communist movement and contemporary world development. According to N. Khrushchev and his followers, all the fundamental questions that preoccupy the peoples today, such as national liberation and others, can be settled only as a result of total and complete disarmament, and the creation of a world without arms, armies, and wars. The enslaved peoples will automatically be freed from imperialism, because the imperialists will no longer have arms to keep them under their yoke, and the working people in all capitalist countries will be able to take over power peacefully, because the bourgeoisie will no longer have arms to maintain their domination. From this, the conclusion inevitably emerges that the national liberation struggle of the enslaved peoples, the struggle against the various forms of colonialism and neocolonialism, and the revolutionary struggle of the working people to overthrow capitalist slavery are secondary problems which do not merit special attention and which depend entirely on the achievement of general and total disarmament. And this logical conclusion is and has been more confirmed each day by the practical acts of treason of N. Khrushchev and his group. But it is clear to Marxist-Leninists that, as pointed out by the Moscow Declaration of 1960, total and general disarmament is a difficult problem and its achievement demands a long time because of the determined opposition of the imperialist powers headed by U.S. imperialism. Therefore, it is erroneous and very dangerous to check the struggle of the enslaved peoples and the working peoples in the capitalist countries, and to compel them to endure untold suffering and pain, pending the achievement of general and total disarmament. The colonial peoples do not want to wait until total and general disarmament is achieved. They want to be liberated as soon as possible, and the sure way of liberating them is the resolute struggle against imperialism. The peoples who have recently won their freedom, and who are in constant danger of imperialist aggression, can consolidate the freedom and independence which they have won, not by appealing for disarmament at a time when the imperialists are ready at any time to swallow them, but by increasing their vigilance and defensive might. The working peoples in the capitalist countries want to overthrow the capitalist yoke as soon as possible. They do not need to wait for this until general and total disarmament is achieved since the road to their liberation is the road to the completion of the socialist revolution and the establishment of the proletarian dictatorship by peaceful or nonpeaceful means. Historical experience has proved that the peoples who have already liberated themselves from the colonial yoke, and the working people who have overthrown the capitalist order and have embarked upon the road to socialism, have achieved it without total and general disarmament, thanks to their resolute struggle.

Secondly, N. Khrushchev hopes to achieve universal and total disarmament solely by issuing a general appeal for disarmament and has intentionally ignored the necessity of struggling to unmask the warmongering activities of imperialism, especially of American imperialism, which not only prevents disarmament by every means possible, but actually intensifies the unbridled arms race daily. Experience has shown, however, that the beautiful words of Kennedy and the other imperialist leaders about "peace" and their "desire for negotiations" are completely false and demagogic. For this reason, it is entirely impermissible and very dangerous to deceive oneself and others, and to lull the vigilance of the peoples with talk about the "purposes and good intentions" of the imperialists, as N. Khrushchev and his people are doing. Disarmament, whether general and total or local and partial, can be achieved only if the socialist countries and all the peoples and all the partisans of peace carry out a resolute struggle to impose it on the imperialist forces of aggression and war, especially on the imperialists of the United States.

It is clear that the pacifist bourgeois concepts of N. Khrushchev benefit not the peoples but imperialism and colonialism. This is also confirmed by the fact that, while N. Khrushchev and his group do not breathe a word against American imperialism but make efforts to "watch" it with care, they do not avoid using the most reactionary and banal calumnies to accuse our party of being against peace, peaceful coexistence, and complete and total disarmament. What is the purpose of spreading such slander against a socialist country? Do they mean to say that the danger of war comes from certain socialist countries and specifically from Albania? (!) If this is so, we must say they are not original at all, because a thesis of this kind, proposing to aid American imperialism, has been propagated for a long time by the reactionary bourgeois press and the revisionist renegade Kardelj.

No one can find, in any of our party's documents or materials, or in any speech or article in our press, even the smallest pretext to accuse the PPSh or the Government of the Albanian People's Republic of being against the Soviet proposal for general and complete disarmament. All we are dealing with here is a clumsy falsification, concocted deliberately and with pernicious intent to sling mud at our party and to discredit it before world public opinion. It is true that our party has, and justly so, condemned and severely condemns the unilateral and profoundly anti-Marxist action undertaken by N. Khrushchev and his followers to the detriment of the defensive capacity of the Albanian People's Republic and the entire socialist camp in the Mediterranean zone. But what has this got to do with the Soviet disarmament proposals? Do they want to convince us that N. Khrushchev undertook his hostile actions, which harm the defensive capacity of our socialist country, within the framework of action for general and complete disarmament? (!)

The allegation that the PPSh is now opposed to the proposal to transform the Balkans and the Adriatic area into a zone of peace without atomic weapons and rockets, a proposal which was made by the governments of the Soviet Union and the Albanian People's Republic in 1959, is also a malevolent calumny. In regard to this question, the position of our party and government has not changed at all. However, our party and the people neither can nor do agree with certain other proposals, made in 1960, to create a zone free of atomic weapons and rockets as well as complete disarmament down to the level of border guard units in the Balkans. Are these people not aware that the U.S. Sixth Fleet, armed to the teeth, has for a long time been plying the Mediterranean, that it is not cruising there merely for the sake of tourism but is a dangerous, aggressive weapon against the socialist countries? Could it be that they have forgotten that Italian imperialism, which is now being equipped with American weapons and rockets and which is a member of the aggressive NATO bloc, in the course of a few decades has committed aggression several times against our country and other countries in the Balkans? We are forced to refresh the memory of certain people that it was N. Khrushchev himself, and no one else, who during his spring 1959 visit to Albania, before the whole world and several times in succession, seriously drew the Italian Government's attention to the dangerous step it was undertaking by utilizing Italian territory for the establishment of bases for American rockets, which are directed mainly against the socialist countries in the Balkans. On our part, we have not changed our attitude at all. But perhaps N. Khrushchev has now changed his opinion and abandoned the 1959 proposal. If this is so, let him admit it openly. We would only like to note that this is a shortsighted policy toward the aggressive plans and activities of American imperialism and of other imperialist countries.

F. Konstantinov, the author of the article published in *Kommunist,* No. 17, 1961, complains that the PPSh has distorted the theses of the 20th Congress by allegedly accusing the leadership of the Communist Party of the Soviet Union of standing only for the peaceful form of transition to socialism. We will point out that Konstantinov has completely oversimplified and vulgarized the question (perhaps he has done this for "economy of thought"!). Our party has expressed criticism of the manner in which Stalin's road to socialism was presented at the 20th Congress of the Communist Party of the Soviet Union.

First, at the 20th Congress of the Communist Party of the Soviet Union, as in all the propaganda of the Soviet leadership since that Congress, the emphasis was mainly on the peaceful road, and the possibilities of such a road have been overrated up to the present time. This does not correspond to reality at all. Konstantinov cites the resolution of the 20th Congress. The resolution says, among other things: "There is no doubt that for a number of capitalist countries where capitalism is still strong and *where it has a colossal military and police apparatus at its disposal* an intensification of the class struggle is inevitable" (our emphasis). We now put the question: Under the present conditions of an unbridled arms race, feverish attempts to establish fascist dictatorship and unprecedentedly inflated military and police apparatus — under these circumstances, can suitable conditions be created in the capitalist countries for the peaceful seizure of power? In the United States, France, Spain, West Germany, and Greece, perhaps?

Second, at the 20th Congress N. Khrushchev really oriented the Communist and workers parties in capitalist countries to prepare *either* for the peaceful road *or* for the nonpeaceful one. But he did not tell them that they should, *simultaneously and concurrently,* prepare for both eventualities, so that they could be ready *at any moment to exploit all possibilities* for seizing power either by peaceful or nonpeaceful means. Our party believes that if there is good preparation for an armed uprising, favorable possibilities for seizing power by peaceful means are also created. Now to prove the thesis that on this question the 20th Congress of 1956 allegedly took a correct stand, F. Konstantinov cites materials from the 22nd Congress of 1961 which contain the words of Lenin, who said that the working class should, "without exception, resort to *all the forms* or types of social action." It should be ready to change, "quickly and fearlessly, from one form to the other." We rejoice at such an interpretation and consider it a step forward. But why was it necessary to wait over five years to recall these teachings of the great Lenin, and why is the PPSh, which has been faithful and remains loyal to these teachings, being attacked?

Third, at the 20th Congress N. Khrushchev identified, in an opportunist way, the seizure of power by peaceful means on the part of the working class as the winning of a parliamentary majority in countries with bourgeois parliaments, thus completely bypassing the fundamental teachings of Marxism-Leninism on the absolute need to destroy the bourgeois state apparatus and to replace it by the dictatorship of the proletariat. (At least let them read Lenin's classical work, *State and Revolution.*)

Further on, F. Konstantinov alleges that the PPSh views socialist revolution not as the result of internal developments in capitalist countries but as something imposed from abroad. In other words, he accuses our party of holding the anti-Marxist view of exporting revolution, and jumps to demolish this erroneous theory. We would like to tell him that, owing perhaps to philosophical stupor, he has mistaken the address and is vainly knocking on the wrong door. In none of our party's materials, in no article of our press, can F. Konstantinov or anybody else find even a single word which could raise the slightest suspicion concerning the position of our party in this connection. (In fact, F. Konstantinov is satisfied with one generalization and does not mention anything concrete at all.) The Albanian Party of Labor has firmly condemned and condemns the anti-Marxist theory of exporting revolution as well as the attempts of imperialists and their revisionist tools to export counterrevolution. It has always considered and considers socialist revolution the result of the internal contradictions in capitalist countries and the struggle of the working class in these countries. At the same time, the PPSh, consistently guided by Lenin's teachings, strongly emphasizes the imperative need for firm support by the socialist countries of the revolutionary struggle of the working class and of all the workers in capitalist countries, so that they may overthrow capitalist slavery and ensure the triumph of socialism. But perhaps it is precisely these teachings of Lenin that F. Konstantinov considers "exporting revolution"? (!)

In view of this, the position of N. Khrushchev and his group is obscure and contradictory. N. Khrushchev and his propagandists, who consider peaceful coexistence the general line of the foreign policy of the socialist countries, are, on the one hand, endorsing the support of revolutions by socialist countries and, on the other, overestimating *the external factor.* They have made almost absolute the importance of the external aspect and have presented the question in such a way that the victory of socialism on a world scale will occur *only* as a result of the policy of peaceful coexistence pursued by the socialist countries, the economic race between the socialist and capitalist orders, and the successes achieved by the countries of the socialist camp in building socialism and Communism.

It is known that our party always noted and continues to note the great support and internationalist aid given to the Albanian people by the Soviet Union. It has considered and still considers it a very important external factor for the liberation of our country from fascist slavery and for the building of socialism in Albania. But the Soviet leaders, headed by N. Khrushchev, in their recent material on Albania do not say even a single word about the role played by the Albanian people, under the guidance of the PPSh, in the struggle for the country's liberation and the victory of the people's revolution in Albania, or about the building of socialism here. Rather, they stress in a one-sided manner *only the external factor*—only the aid of the Soviet Union. How can we regard such an attitude? Does it not lead to the anti-Marxist theory of exporting revolution? Let "theoretician" F. Konstantinov explain this to us.

To find a way out of the embarrassing position in which they have placed themselves because of the policy of reconciliation and cooperation with the Tito clique, N. Khrushchev and his followers shamelessly distort our party's appraisal of the counterrevolutionary events in Hungary in 1956.

The Albanian Party of Labor has clearly expressed its attitude in connection with the 1956 counterrevolution in Hungary. It has pointed out and it states now that it was organized by the imperialists, chiefly by the American imperialists, in close cooperation with the internal reactionary forces, and also with Tito's revisionist clique and the Hungarian revisionist and traitorous elements of the Imre Nagy type, and his associates. It was organized within the framework of the frontal attack unleashed by the imperialists and the revisionists against the socialist camp and the international Communist movement after the 20th Congress of the Communist Party of the Soviet Union. For their ends, they also exploited certain errors of the former Hungarian leaders. This is a very clear and understandable phenomenon. Therefore, it is not necessary to speak about it any longer.

At the same time, our party expressed its critical attitude toward N. Khrushchev and his group concerning their attitude toward and appraisal of the counterrevolutionary events in Hungary. Our criticism on this issue consists of the following main points:

First, the counterrevolution was prepared and launched by the imperialists and the other counterrevolutionary elements under the slogans of "anti-Stalinism," borrowed from N. Khrushchev's "secret" report at the 20th Congress of the Communist Party of the Soviet Union. In fact, the unprincipled attacks against Stalin at the 20th Congress, his destalinization line, provided grist for the reactionary and revisionist elements and facilitated conditions for them to carry on their hostile activity. The so-called "Stalinist" misdeeds of the former Hungarian leaders were exaggerated. This enabled the traitorous and revisionist elements, like Imre Nagy and his associates, freely to execute their counterrevolutionary activity and to conceal it by presenting it as "a people's revolution."

Second, at the time when the Tito and Imre Nagy group, together with the imperialists, were feverishly preparing the counterrevolutionary coup in Hungary, N. Khrushchev, Mikoyan, Suslov, and other Soviet leaders closed their eyes to the hostile activity of these traitors and trusted and supported them. The fact that the Soviet leaders believed Imre Nagy's hypocritical "self-criticism" and kept it in their files to convince the others that Imre Nagy was a good man (!) cannot in any way be justified. It is also completely unjustifiable that N. Khrushchev believed so fully in the Yugoslav renegade and revisionist clique that he went to Brioni time after time for secret meetings with Tito, and was even deciding with him whom to appoint as First Secretary of the Hungarian Workers Party Central Committee. (!) (Moreover, this was impermissible interference in the internal affairs of a fraternal party.) This activity — surprising, to say the least — on the part of the First Secretary of the Central Committee of the Communist Party of the Soviet Union, is sufficiently proven by documents in the possession of our party: e.g., the letter which N. Khrushchev sent to J. B. Tito, on November 9, 1956, which was quoted in the speech by Comrade Enver Hoxha on November 7, 1961. To remove any doubt, we quote from this letter the passage in which N. Khrushchev addresses Tito in the following words: "You were in complete agreement with the fact that the Central Committee of the Communist Party of the Soviet Union, since this past summer, has been trying — with regard to the departure of Rákosi — to ensure that Comrade Kádár becomes First Secretary of the Central Committee of the Workers Party in Hungary." This requires no comment.

Third, even after the counterrevolutionary group in Hungary had failed, thanks to the blood of thousands of heroic Soviet soldiers and Hungarian Communists and patriots which flowed like a river in the streets of Budapest, N. Khrushchev, instead of unmasking — in addition to the imperialists — the traitorous clique of Tito as well, which was one of the main organizers of the Hungarian counterrevolution, "thought it possible" to conceal its activity. Thus in the above-mentioned letter of November 9, 1956, N. Khrushchev wrote to Tito: "We think it possible to agree with your point of view on not ascribing particular importance now to the question of whether the Yugoslav Embassy in Budapest did right or wrong in sheltering Imre Nagy and his companions."

Now N. Khrushchev and his men shun these facts and pass over them in silence, and in order to divert attention from them, they distort the position of our party, saying that it allegedly supports imperialist reaction, that it tries to minimize its responsibility in the Hungarian counterrevolutionary coup, and that it presents the coup solely as a consequence of the criticism of Stalin made at the 20th Congress of the Communist Party of the Soviet Union. We do not intend to enter into polemics with a certain Yu. Andropov, who, at the very moment of the counterrevolutionary events of 1956, was Soviet ambassador to Hungary. We simply want to point out that it is very difficult to convince people with such gross and banal accusations. It is not the PPSh but N. Khrushchev and his group who, by overestimating the role of the "Stalinist" errors of the former Hungarian leaders and by presenting them as the major cause of the counterrevolutionary events in Hungary, in fact underestimate the role of the imperialists in these events and completely conceal the hostile activities and the responsibility of imperialism's *agentura* — the Titoist revisionist clique. If the anti-Stalin campaign of N. Khrushchev and his opportunist attitude toward the clique of Tito, Imre Nagy, and their companions made it easier for the imperialists, revisionists, and reactionary forces to organize a counterrevolutionary uprising in Hungary, the responsibility does not in any way rest on the Albanian Party of Labor and its leadership.

N. Khrushchev and his supporters madly attack the PPSh and its leadership and accuse them of opposing the Marxist-Leninist teachings on the urgency of not permitting manifestations of any kind of the cult of the individual. To make these slanders more credible, they continue to create a great uproar over the "most ugly manifestations of the cult of the individual," which supposedly flourishes in Albania.

The Albanian Party of Labor and its leadership have been and continue to be faithful to the Marxist-Leninist teachings regarding the masses, the classes, the party, and the leadership. They have never been and they are not against the struggle to uproot any manifestation of the personality cult and have never hesitated to criticize, when the occasion demanded it, any manifestations of this kind in their ranks. Our party, however, does not agree and has never agreed with the manner in which this criticism has been and continues to be made against the person of J. Stalin on the part of N. Khrushchev's group since the 20th Congress of the Communist Party of the Soviet Union. It does not agree and never has agreed with Khrushchev's anti-Marxist aims, according to which he is using the criticism against Stalin in order to impose his revisionist views on the Communist and workers parties of other countries.

It is impermissible for our party or any Marxist-Leninists to tolerate the unprincipled attacks by N. Khrushchev against J. V. Stalin and the depiction of the entire period of his leadership as a time when, allegedly, murder, terrorism, persecution, and injustice held sway in the Soviet Union. Such altogether unprincipled "criticism" has greatly pleased the imperialist and revisionist enemies and provided them with an opportunity to throw mud at the Soviet socialist system and at Communism. At the same time, this "criticism" has put the Communist and workers parties in the capitalist countries in a difficult position in their struggle against the mad attacks of the reactionary bourgeois propaganda which, in propagating its slanders, refers primarily to N. Khrushchev's attacks on J. V. Stalin at the 20th and 22nd Congresses of the Communist Party of the Soviet Union. N. Khrushchev and his propagandists now try, in vain and with completely muddled logic, to accuse our party of having allegedly linked the personality cult with the Soviet system. It is publicly known that the PPSh, along with the other Marxist-Leninist parties, has waged and continues to wage a resolute principled struggle against the propaganda of the bourgeoisie and the modern revisionists, who are trying to discredit the Soviet order and Communism. This venomous weapon was not given to the imperialists and revisionists by our party, but by N. Khrushchev and his group. Let them also assume the responsibility before the Communist Party of the Soviet Union and the Soviet people for these hideous activities.

Our party also firmly repudiates the efforts of N. Khrushchev's group to uncrown Stalin and to deny his great merits as a distinguished theoretician of Marxism-Leninism who resolutely defended Leninism from the attacks and distortions of the Trotskyites, Bukharinites, and other enemies, and further developed it under new historical conditions. Portraying J. V.

Stalin as a "dogmatic" person detached from life, N. Khrushchev and his supporters try to conceal their revisionist views and to present them as the cream of the "creative development" of Marxism.

And now every person who is not in agreement with such an attitude toward J. V. Stalin and his work is proclaimed by N. Khrushchev and his group as a "dogmatist," an "enemy of Marxism-Leninism," a "terrorist," an "agent of imperialism," and so forth. (!)

Our party has not the slightest doubt that N. Khrushchev and his group criticized J. V. Stalin from malevolent intentions and not in the least from the principle of struggling against manifestations of the personality cult. It is impossible otherwise to explain the fact that the present Soviet leadership is frantically promoting the cult of the personality of N. Khrushchev, which is something everyone can see if only from the lavish propaganda disseminated about him. Things have even reached the point where certain unseemly stupidities committed by N. Khrushchev, which bring discredit to the Soviet Union — such as, for example, when he took off his shoe in the U.N. General Assembly — are slavishly elevated to the level of theory and presented as a "brilliant example of a Marxist attitude." Amazing as it may seem, A. Adzhubei, in his speech to the 22nd Congress of the Communist Party of the Soviet Union which was published in the Soviet press, called this gesture something "truly wonderful!" Has this also been done within the framework of the struggle against the personality cult? (!)

After having attempted by anti-Marxist methods to uncrown J. V. Stalin and his work, N. Khrushchev and his supporters have now launched base attacks and calumnies against the PPSh and its leadership, whom they accuse of grave violations of socialist legality and Leninist norms in the life of the party, of establishing a reign of terror, and so forth. What are the "facts" and "arguments" which they advance? The *Pravda* article of December 14, 1961, said, among other things: "As early as 1948, the First Congress of the PPSh resolutely criticized the serious errors committed in the political activities of the PPSh, pointing out that four years after the liberation of the country and the establishment of the people's power, the party had no statutes, program, or press organ, and that 'military and police methods' flourished in it. . . ." The most deplorable thing was that the "military and police" regime within the party was "under the control of the state security organs," and that "police informing" flourished.

Yes, the First Congress of our party severely condemned these negative manifestations in the life of the party, which resulted from the brutal intervention by the Tito clique in the internal affairs of our party and from the hostile and pernicious activity by the agent of this clique, Koci Xoxe. Koci Xoxe and his companions were severely condemned by our party during its First Congress for markedly hostile activity in the service of the Tito clique, for grave violations of party democracy, for putting the party under the control of the state security forces (Koci Xoxe was Minister of Interior and, at the same time, secretary of the party in charge of cadres), for grave violations of socialist legality, and for preparing the physical liquidation of party Secretary General Comrade Enver Hoxha, Comrade Mehmet Shehu, and other sound cadres of our party who, in fact, in one way or another, were isolated or eliminated from the leadership of the party. And if the party successfully braved this grave situation and in a short time liquidated the alien manifestations and established Leninist norms in the life of the party, special merit for this is due to the Secretary General of the party himself, Comrade Enver Hoxha. All this is documented in the resolutions of our party.

These are the facts, but the authors of the afore-mentioned *Pravda* article write something else. They say: *"We do not intend to enumerate the malefactors of* this terror against the honest Albanian Communists." Let us merely point out that *Hoxha* has been Secretary General of the party since then. (Our emphasis) Why is it that N. Khrushchev's publicists "do not intend to enumerate the malefactors" but slanderously attack Comrade Enver Hoxha? Why do they so zealously try to conceal the hostile activities of the traitorous clique of Tito and its agents, Koci Xoxe and his associates? Why is it that they protect a rabid traitor and enemy of our party and people like Koci Xoxe? To remove any doubt, we shall state that as early as 1956 N. Khrushchev, through M. Suslov and P. Pospelov and through Liri Belishova, exerted pressure on behalf of the rehabilitation of Koci Xoxe, but our party resolutely withstood it.

Later, *Pravda* points out that in the party conferences which took place before the Third Congress of the PPSh "a severe principled criticism was made of the Albanian leadership for violating Leninist norms of the internal life of the party," for "repression" of party cadres, and so forth. This is a deliberately distorted allusion to the efforts of certain revisionist elements of the Tito clique who, encouraged by the revisionist theses of the 20th Congress, tried unsuccessfully at the Tirana Party Conference in April 1956 to split the party, to overthrow its leadership, to create in Albania a situation similar to the one which was later created in Hungary — a fact which was stated by Vidić, Under Secretary of State for foreign affairs and former Yugoslav Ambassador to the Soviet Union. It is very clear to all Albanian Communists that the organizers of the revisionist attack against our party and its leadership at the Tirana Party Conference were such traitors as Panajot Plaku, Tuk Jakova, Bedri Spahiu, Liri Gega, Pajo Islami, Vehip Demi, Dhora Leka, and other degenerate elements unmasked as the agents of the Titoist UDB. (The Central Committee of our party has documents which prove with indisputable facts that these traitors were linked to the Tito clique and, acting under its direction, plotted to overthrow the people's power in Albania.) Why do the propagandists of Khrushchev speak with so much fervor and assurance in favor of the activity of these antiparty elements? In this, one sees clearly a link between the Khrushchev group and the Titoist gang and its agents at the Tirana conference.

The Tirana trial against the agents of the Greek and American secret services — Teme Sejko, Tahir Demi, and their associates, who received the punishment they deserved as traitors to the fatherland — confirmed through facts that they, too, were organizers of the antiparty activity which raised its head at the Tirana Party Conference. It is this very scum of our society which N. Khrushchev and his supporters are protecting, while they present the correct activities of our party and our trials against the spies and agents of imperialism and its lackeys as terrorism, as violations of socialist legality, as consequences of the existence of the personality cult, and so forth.

In *Kommunist,* F. Konstantinov writes that "The leaders of the PPSh make arrests and persecute the Albanian specialists, military men, and civilians who have studied in the USSR." Let us pass over the fact that this is a deplorable accusation which rightly disgusts all the citizens of the Albanian People's Republic. Let us say only that this is an extraordinarily absurd accusation because, according to this accusation, the majority of the Albanian intelligentsia (which is composed mostly of elements who have studied in the Soviet Union) is apparently imprisoned or detained. (!) And then, F. Konstantinov, resorting to amazing acrobatics, writes that "the violations of legality and arbitrary actions are committed by Hoxha and Shehu *in great secrecy.*" (!) At the same time, in an article in *Pravda* published the same day, one reads the opposite: "At present in Albania police methods and violence are *openly* applied against those who defend friendship with the USSR." (It would seem that these two papers have forgotten to check with each other.)

According to the authors of the articles and speeches against the PPSh, the violation of the Leninist norms of party life and the violation of socialist legality, the persecution of honest Communists, and so forth, have been carried on in Albania for a long time. It is amazing that N. Khrushchev and his companions, who raise a great clamor about their "high Leninist principles," did not say these things earlier. On the contrary, until 1960 they used to eulogize our party and its leadership. (!)

We do not want to start refuting one by one all these slanders and fabrications, because they are so banal and vile that they do not deserve to be mentioned. We only wonder why certain people like F. Konstantinov, a philosopher and former member of the Central Committee of the Communist Party of the Soviet Union who was discharged from this position at the 22nd Congress, has changed his trade and shifted from philosophical studies to the field of base fabrications? In so doing, does he think he will somehow strengthen his position and make his career?

One thing is very clear to our party and to all Albanian Communists and citizens of the Albanian People's Republic: The clumsy fabrications about the "Stalinist terror" in Albania have been concocted by N. Khrushchev and his propagandists not so much for the Albanian Communists and our people as to discredit our party and its leadership in the eyes of the people of other countries. Our people cannot be deceived by such rot. Albania is a small country where one cannot hide even the head of a pin. In Albania there are no distant regions such as the Virgin Lands and Siberia. Therefore, any arrests become known immediately. If N. Khrushchev hopes, by supporting certain loathsome traitors, enemies of the party and the people, and agents of the Titoist clique and of the imperialist secret services, to disorient and disrupt our party and people, he is making a serious mistake. The protection given to the Titoist clique and Albanian traitors only reveals more openly the nature of N. Khrushchev as a traitor to Marxism-Leninism and as an enemy of our party and people who slanders and brutally interferes in our internal affairs. This unmasks him as a man who tramples with both feet on the principles of the Declarations of the Communist and workers parties.

Seeking arguments to make more credible their absurd attacks against the PPSh and the Albanian People's Republic, N. Khrushchev and his men have been unable to find a better way than to ask for assistance from the reactionary bourgeois papers whose reports they apparently consider the highest criterion of truth. (!) We would rather not answer them by the same means and hence begin to quote articles from bourgeois papers, which, taking advantage of the fact that N. Khrushchev publicized our differences at the 22nd Congress, began to inflate them and to use them to disrupt the Communist movement and the socialist camp (although many reactionary papers have closely supported "Khrushchev's line"). Our party is not contemplating falling into the positions taken by the reactionary bourgeois papers and thus playing their game in disrupting Communist and workers parties and those of the socialist countries, as N. Khrushchev and his supporters are, in fact, doing. However, we would like to point out that N. Khrushchev's group has become the workshop where material in the interest of imperialist reaction against the APR is being formulated. Things have gone so far that the most vile types of provocations are used. N. Khrushchev's group prepares and gives for publication to Western bourgeois papers articles full of slanders against the PPSh and its leaders, and then reprints them on the pages of its official press with the tendentious aim of discrediting the Albanian leaders "through facts taken from reliable sources." (!) Let the readers judge for themselves how "Marxist" these actions are.

This is how things stand. The enraged attacks of N. Khrushchev and his supporters against the PPSh and the Albanian

People's Republic are further testimony to the way N. Khrushchev's group wallows even deeper and deeper into the mire of its anti-Marxist campaign. N. Khrushchev, by unscrupulously exploiting the authority of the Soviet Union and the Communist Party of the Soviet Union, has managed to influence certain personages in the international Communist movement to follow him in the unprincipled fight against the PPSh. He tries to create the impression that *the whole* international Communist movement follows him in "condemning" our party and its leadership and, on the other hand, tries to sow dissension between the Communist and workers parties of other countries and our party. But he will never manage to draw our party into a trap by such provocations. Our party will resolutely continue its principled struggle against N. Khrushchev's group, fully convinced that even the most authoritative sources, which today are attacking us from the Communist and workers parties of other countries, will, sooner or later, begin to think and comprehend the dangerous blind alley into which N. Khrushchev is leading them by his anti-Marxist activities. How can we blame, for example, Comrade K. Sylvestre, Secretary General of the Communist Party of Martinique, for having written in *Pravda* on December 17, 1961, about "brutal violations of socialist legality and merciless and criminal repressions against Albanian workers and activists"? It is clear that, being in Martinique, on the other side of the Atlantic Ocean, he knows nothing about the situation in Albania. He wrote a priori, believing the slanders of N. Khrushchev. He may even have written for the sake of the authority of the Soviet Union, even if he was not convinced that he was right. Amazing as it may sound, someone has, in fact, declared: "We are with N. Khrushchev, even when he is wrong." (!)

Our party and people do not doubt that the recent hostile and anti-Marxist action of N. Khrushchev against our country — the closing of the Soviet Embassy in Albania and the expulsion of the Embassy of the APR from the Soviet Union — did not even have the approval of N. Khrushchev's close friends in the Communist and workers parties of the other countries. This is not because they are particularly sympathetic toward the PPSh and its leadership, but because such an unprecedented act in the relations among socialist countries is an open violation of the principles of the Moscow Declarations of 1957 and 1960. It discredits the Soviet Union in the eyes of international public opinion and places the Communist and workers parties in a delicate position, especially in the capitalist countries. It provides imperialist reaction with ammunition to fight us. It gravely prejudices our common cause of socialism and Communism.

With his wild attacks on the PPSh and the Albanian People's Republic, N. Khrushchev is preparing for actions and designs still more ignoble, to the detriment of the unity of the socialist camp and the international Communist movement, to the detriment of our great cause. But let him be sure that any such action will be fatal to him; the powerful organization of the world Communist movement will heal the revisionist wounds which N. Khrushchev has inflicted on it. The revisionist elements which have become active in the ranks of the Communist and workers parties, as a result of the anti-Marxist activity of N. Khrushchev and his group, will be isolated and overcome, thanks to the resolute struggle of the true Communists, faithful to the great revolutionary doctrine of Marxism-Leninism. This is a clear and inevitable process. The truth of Marxism will triumph.

DOCUMENT 23

"Albanian Leaders' Refusal to Discuss Differences," Radio Moscow *in Albanian to Albania, February 8, 1962,*

1500 GMT (edited from commentary by Leonid Sergeyev, BBC/SU/*867/ A2/1, February 10, 1962*).

After August 1960 the CPSU Central Committee twice approached the Albanian leaders with a proposal to meet and discuss the misunderstandings which had arisen, but Hoxha and Shehu firmly rejected such talks, declaring in a provocative way that they would raise the whole matter at the Moscow meeting. When this meeting finally took place . . . they showed their complete unwillingness to reach a settlement of the problem at a higher level. Notwithstanding the provocative conduct of the Albanian delegation . . . the CPSU Central Committee continued its efforts to reach agreement. . . . In December 1960 the Soviet Government proposed . . . high-level talks on economic matters. Again they received a negative reply. In February 1961, during the visit to Albania of the CPSU delegation invited to the Fourth Congress of the Albanian Party of Labor, talks were again proposed to Hoxha and Shehu. Again the Albanian leaders replied with a rejection. As can be seen, the CPSU Central Committee has shown a great deal of patience in the hope that Hoxha and Shehu would change their minds and sit down at a table with the Soviet leaders and that everything would be clarified in an atmosphere of serious effort, in a businesslike way, as befits Communists. Hoxha and Shehu, however, . . . strove to undermine the friendship between the CPSU and the Albanian Party of Labor and between the Soviet and Albanian peoples. At the same time, it became apparent that the Albanian leaders were unwilling to take up contacts . . . with the leaders of other parties in the fraternal countries. When in March 1960 it was decided to hold an extraordinary meeting of the Political Consultative Committee of the Warsaw Pact countries at the highest level, neither Hoxha nor Shehu came to Moscow, pretending to be ill. . . . In August of last year, the first secretaries of the central committees of the Communist and workers parties of the European socialist countries met in Moscow to discuss matters connected with the conclusion of a peace treaty with Germany. An invitation was also sent to Hoxha as First Secretary of the Central Committee of the Albanian Party of Labor, but he treated this invitation with the same lighthandedness. As in March, the Albanian leaders evaded a meeting with the leaders of fraternal parties. . . .

How else is the position of the Albanian leadership to be explained but by complete indifference toward the collective opinion of the other parties . . . ? Evasion of direct responsibility, pleading illness as an excuse, outright refusal — these are characteristic of Hoxha's and Shehu's attitude. Nevertheless, in the report of the CPSU Central Committee to the 22nd Congress, the CPSU's readiness to normalize relations with the Albanian Party of Labor on Marxist-Leninist principles was stressed. In their reply the Albanian leaders let themselves go in a bombastic declaration in which they attacked the CPSU and its Central Committee. They prepared the speech made by Hoxha on November 7, which, with its anti-Soviet and slanderous character, can be listed among the worst examples of reactionary propaganda, and they launched in their country an unrestrained and slanderous anti-Soviet campaign. . . .

For more than a year the Albanian leaders have categorically refused to have any kind of contact with the CPSU Central Committee and have revealed themselves as open violators of the Moscow Declaration. . . . The endeavors of the Albanian leaders, who, without foundation, accuse the CPSU of a policy opposed to the principles of the Moscow Declaration, are in themselves nothing but filthy slanders against the CPSU. . . .

DOCUMENT 24

"Nepotism in Albania," Radio Moscow *in Albanian to Albania, Febru-*

ary 10, 1962, 1500 GMT (*excerpts from* BBC/SU/*869/A2/1–2, February 13, 1962*).

As you see, dear friends, the leaders of the Albanian Party of Labor have criticized mistakes in the work of the party with "courage." But this criticism was simply an effort to deal with minor cases of nepotism and to hide the rotten system by which party and government leading cadres are selected. It was an effort to avoid the blow coming to them and, by using high-sounding phrases, to deceive the people.

Was there any change after these speeches in the system of the selection of party cadres? None whatever. The leadership of the Albanian Party of Labor has agreed secretly that the selection of cadres is to be made on the basis of family relationships and nepotism. How petty the example of nepotism in the Librazhd cooperative, cited by Enver Hoxha to the Third Congress, now appears. Compare it with the situation in the Central Committee of the Albanian Party of Labor, in the party apparatus, in the Council of Ministers, and in many ministries. . . . Leading cadres of these organs have been selected by the Hoxha-Shehu group only on the basis of nepotism and of personal relationships. Half, or more, of the 53 members of the Central Committee of the Albanian Party of Labor are related. First, we have four couples: Enver Hoxha and his wife Nexhmije Hoxha; Mehmet Shehu and his wife Fiqrete Shehu; Hysni Kapo and his wife Vito Kapo; and Josif Pashko with his wife Eleni Terezi. The wives of Manush Myftiu, Politburo member, and of Pilo Peristeri, candidate-member of the Politburo, are sisters. Kadri Hasbiu, candidate-member of the Politburo and Minister of Internal Affairs, is the husband of Mehmet Shehu's sister. The brother of Hysni Kapo's wife is Piro Kondi, also a member of the Central Committee. . . .

Hoxha, Shehu, and Kapo set the example in this matter. Hoxha's wife is the head of the party Central Committee's culture and science department. . . . She is at the same time a member of the Presidium of the Albanian Women's Union and a Deputy in the People's Assembly. Peti Shamblli, Minister of Agriculture, Shefqet Peçi, Chairman of the State Control Commission, and Zoi Themeli, Deputy Minister of Internal Affairs, are related to Hoxha. Skender Xhuhlini, Director of the Geology-Topographic Organization, is Nexhmije Hoxha's brother. Haxhi Lleshi, Chairman of the Presidium of the People's Assembly, is also related to Nexhmije Hoxha.

Mehmet Shehu's family has also its share in the organs of the party and the state. His wife is Second Secretary of the Tirana Party Committee, Deputy to the People's Assembly, and member of the Presidium of the Albanian Women's Union. His brother works in counter-espionage for the security services. Shehu has put his friends and relations in all administrative organs, and above all in the Ministry of Internal Affairs, in which he serves as Minister.[1]

Vito Kapo, Hysni Kapo's wife, also occupies important positions. She is a Deputy to the People's Assembly, member of the Presidium of the People's Assembly, and Chairman of the Albanian Women's Union. Hysni Kapo's uncle, Bedri Hoxha, is chief of the Security Department; another relation of his is departmental head in the party Central Committee. The other members of the Politburo are doing as well as Hoxha, Shehu, and Kapo. In December 1960 Beqir Balluku's brother was appointed chief of police in Tirana. Muhamet Prodani, army corps commander, is married to the sister of Petrit Dume, Politburo candidate member and a General Staff Commander; Petrit Dume's brother, Hasan, is deputy Dean of Tirana University.

The leaders of the Albanian Youth Organization follow in the steps of their seniors. The children of A. Çarçani, Polit-

[1] Shehu was replaced by Kadri Hasbiu as Minister of Internal Affairs in July 1954, when he became Premier of Albania. [Ed.]

buro member, and of Zoi Themeli, Deputy Minister of Internal Affairs, were elected members of the Central Committee of the Union during its Fourth Congress. . . .

This system of selection for the organs of the party and the state creates the disease of nepotism and makes office a family gift. Customs totally alien to the principles of Marxism are rife in the organs of the party and the state. . . . How does the poor Librazhad cooperative compare with this. . . ? Striving to keep power in their hands, and to control the organs of the state and the party, the Albanian leaders do their best to keep out of these organs people whom they do not like. Such a system of cadre selection, alien to Marxist parties, has resulted, as far as the Albanian Party of Labor is concerned, in the violation of other Leninist party norms.

In these circumstances it is impossible to speak of the development of party democracy, of respect for the principles of party centralism, of the development of criticism and self-criticism. The Albanian leaders avoid all this as they avoid fire. They crush the creative initiative of party members. In such conditions a feeling of collegialism cannot exist in that party; and this principle is the highest principle of party management. How can one speak about collective leadership when all important decisions are taken by the Albanian leaders secretly and in a close family circle?

This rotten atmosphere of family interest has given rise in the Albanian Party of Labor to phenomena alien to the Communist parties such as immoderate praise, flattery without reserve, servility and self-adulation. This is the basis on which the shameful Hoxha cult has developed. Hoxha's wife shows great zeal in praising her husband; the same is true of Shehu's wife, Fiqrete. Nexhmije Hoxha, who has lost all modesty, in every speech she makes stresses her husband's merits, and to this end makes visits throughout Albania. . . . Everything is done on the basis of nepotism. You praise me; I will praise you. This makes the workers in the party and the state self-centered; they praise themselves continuously; they become swellheaded; they believe that they are irreplaceable, and they think they are incapable of making mistakes. It is not by chance that the Albanian leaders, who have no shame, declare that the Albanian Party of Labor has never made mistakes, and will never make any. They consider themselves as having a monopoly on the correct interpretation of Marxism-Leninism, and say this even after the Communist and workers parties have unanimously condemned their mistaken position as alien to Marxism-Leninism and designed to destroy the unity of and to split the world Communist movement.

In conclusion, I want to mention a point which characterizes the real mentality of the Albanian leaders. As we know, they talk much about their close unity with their people. But this is not true. You know very well that your leaders live on an estate in Tirana where no workers are allowed. This quarter and the entrance to it are guarded by sentries armed with automatic weapons. For example, the villa where Rita Marko, member of the Central Committee, lives is guarded every night by five or six guards with automatic weapons; the only thing missing is barbed wire. One might ask: Whom do the Albanian leaders fear, against whom do they protect themselves? If these protective measures and the practice of rotten family influence and nepotism are signs of close ties with the people, how is one to describe separation from the people?

DOCUMENT 25

"Whom Do N. Khrushchev's Views and Actions Serve?" Zëri i Popullit, *March 2, 1962* (*complete text*).

"In policy," said V. I. Lenin, "it is of no importance *who* directly defends this or that view. It is of importance *whom these views,* these proposals, and these measures *serve*. . . . Have no faith in words; rather, find out in whose interest they are" (Volume 19, p. 33, Russian edition). Each passing day shows ever more clearly whom the views and activities of N. Khrushchev and his group serve and confirms the grave danger which they represent and the great harm which they are causing to the world revolutionary movement, the cause of socialism, the freedom of peoples, and world peace.

Everyone who closely follows the activity of N. Khrushchev can readily see that his views and activities are not detached, isolated, and fortuitous errors. On the contrary, they bear witness to an entirely self-consistent opportunist line. They show that N. Khrushchev is deviating more and more from the revolutionary positions of Marxism-Leninism and that he is sinking more and more deeply into the mire of anti-Marxism.

The basic criterion as to whether a party or a leader stands on revolutionary Marxist-Leninist positions is his position toward the class enemy. It follows that the only correct policy is one which starts from a class position. In our time the main enemy of the international working class and of all peoples is imperialism, and above all its head, the center of world reaction — U.S. imperialism.

What, however, is the position of N. Khrushchev and his men on this fundamental question? Facts show that his position is not at all firm and principled but utterly contradictory, vacillating, and opportunist.

It is now no secret to anyone that N. Khrushchev and his men have acquired the habit of propagating harmful illusions about the chiefs of imperialism, and in particular American imperialism. In the beginning, such illusions were spun around the former President of the U.S.A., Dwight Eisenhower, presenting him as a person who "enjoyed the absolute confidence of his people" and who "sincerely loved peace." Yet, some time after the U-2 spy plane provocation, N. Khrushchev made a complete reversal of 180 degrees and called Eisenhower by his real name — warmonger. This strong reversal was followed by illusions concerning Eisenhower's successor, John Kennedy. His assumption of power was proclaimed by N. Khrushchev and his propagandists as an event of great significance, which would bring about essential changes for the consolidation of peace in the policy of the U.S.A. However, even this legend about President Kennedy was drowned out by the burst of arms at the Playa Giron in Cuba and the boom of guns in the forests of Laos. It was obscured by the brandishing of arms in West Berlin and the astronomical figures of the American military budget. After these and many other incidents, N. Khrushchev, in a speech delivered on May 6, 1961, in Yerevan, reprimanded those who had illusions about the Kennedy government. This was nothing more than a demagogical maneuver to conceal his tracks. His authorized messenger and diplomat-journalist, A. Adzhubei, disclosed what N. Khrushchev tried to hide. During the interview granted to him by President Kennedy on November 25, 1961, he told Kennedy "frankly": ". . . Your election to the high post of President of the United States was received with great hopes by public opinion in our country" (read: "by the group of N. Khrushchev" — Ed.).* Indeed, following this interview, he declared to American journalists that Americans should be proud of their president. (!) He made this statement only a few days after the Kennedy government had begun its persecution of the Communist Party of the U.S.A.

In two historic documents of the contemporary international Communist and workers movement — the Moscow Declarations of 1957 and 1960 — it is stressed that American imperialism is the main force of aggression and war, the international gendarme, and the most vicious enemy of the peoples in the whole world. However, it seems that Khrushchev's spokesman, A. Adzhubei, does not go along with this appraisal. After his second

* I.e., the editor of *Zëri i Popullit*. [W.E.G.]

"cordial" meeting with President Kennedy, Adzhubei said to American journalists on January 31: "We do not believe that the United States wants war." We would like to ask N. Khrushchev and his spokesmen: Since when has American imperialism rejected its policy of war and become peace-loving? Is Lenin's thesis that imperialism is the source of wars and aggression obsolete? If so, where does the danger of war come from? Who threatens the peace? Does such a danger no longer exist and can the peoples sleep peacefully?

N. Khrushchev and the propagandists of his theses, wishing to conduct an "elastic policy" for the sake of negotiations or some diplomatic machination, carefully try to evade the resolute unmasking of American imperialism. In many basic articles on international affairs, the Soviet press does not even mention American imperialism. Indeed, even in articles written for occasions such as the Congress of the WFTU, the international organization of the working class, or the gathering of the World Peace Council, which is an organ designed to organize and arouse the peoples to struggle against the warmongers for the preservation of peace, it was not deemed appropriate to mention by name the main citadel of aggression and war in the world, monopoly imperialism of the United States of America. What concepts guide N. Khrushchev and his followers in their attitude toward American imperialism? Can it be that by ignoring American imperialism, by not unmasking it, it becomes more virtuous, wiser, and peace-loving? What does this have in common with the classical Marxist-Leninist concept of imperialism? How can the position of N. Khrushchev be reconciled with the task laid down in the Moscow Declarations of the necessity of unmasking the American imperialist policy of war and aggression and of increasing the vigilance of the peoples toward the designs and pernicious actions of the imperialist warmongers?

Now N. Khrushchev and those who are propagating his theses try to create the impression that the main danger to peace in our time is not American imperialism but West German revanchism. This is putting the cart before the horse. The revanchist militarism of West Germany is no doubt a great danger to peace, a dangerous hotbed of war in the heart of Europe. It is the aggressive NATO bloc's chief striking force against the socialist countries. But is that any reason to conceal or minimize the danger represented by American imperialism as the head and main force of world reaction and the greatest enemy of peace and of the peoples of all countries? Everybody knows that the American imperialists are the chief support of the revanchists in West Germany. It is through their direct instigation and aid that militarism has revived there, that the Wehrmacht is being equipped with weapons of mass extermination and with rockets and is threatening the German Democratic Republic, and the other socialist countries.

We are expected to believe that all this is being done in order to strengthen peaceful coexistence, to lower international tension, and to preserve peace, and that these positions and activities allegedly correspond to the interests of all peace-loving peoples. This is in vain. It is difficult to convince people that peace can be preserved and strengthened by concealing the warmongers and still less by propagating pacifist illusions about imperialism and its chiefs. On the contrary, the propagation of such illusions endangers peace because vigilance is thus lulled and a free hand is given to the imperialists, above all to the American imperialists, feverishly to pursue the arms race and their preparations for a new world war.

However, according to the logic of N. Khrushchev and his followers, there is nothing wrong with this. In fact, if we forget about formal statements and if we consider the facts of their practical activities, they do not ascribe much importance to the struggle of the peoples for peace and consider the talks and meetings (especially the personal and even "intimate" talks and meetings) with the governments of the imperialist powers and their leaders as the primary factors for ensuring peace. Yes. Talks and meetings are necessary. However, they can yield positive results only if they are based on the resolute struggle of the peoples to settle international problems, to bind the hands of the imperialist warmongers, and to compel them to enter into serious discussions.

Today, great changes have taken place in the balance of power in the world. The positions of imperialism have contracted and become considerably weakened. With each passing day the world socialist system is increasingly becoming the decisive force in the development of human society. As a result of these changes, better conditions have been created for the struggle against imperialism. There is a real possibility of preventing a new world war and the other aggressive wars started by imperialism. The correctness of this conclusion, as also pointed out in the Moscow Declaration, has been confirmed by life. But there is no doubt for Marxist-Leninists that as long as imperialism exists, there will always be a basis for aggressive wars. To stress this is not to deny the possibility of preventing war nor to terrify the people with the threat of war. On the contrary, to deny it or to forget it, to speak one-sidedly in an undialectical manner only of the possibility of preventing war, as N. Khrushchev and the propagandists of his theses do, is dangerous and increases the threat of war because it lulls the people's vigilance and weakens their active struggle against the imperialist warmongers. The Declaration of the 81 Communist and workers parties correctly points out that Communists must neither underestimate the possibility of preventing a world war nor underestimate the danger of war. Only the victory of socialism in the whole world will conclusively remove the social and national causes for the outbreak of any kind of war.

Falsifying the Moscow Declaration of 1960, A. Rumyantsev, member of the Central Committee of the Communist Party of the Soviet Union, expressed the opinion in one of his latest articles that in order to remove *war* from the life of society (meaning *all kinds of war* because he does not make any distinction between them) it is by no means indispensable to destroy capitalism completely and to achieve the victory of socialism on a world scale, or at least in the major imperialist countries (he says nothing about that), since it suffices "first, to increase the might of the socialist camp in all directions; secondly, to strengthen further the independence of the countries which have been liberated from the colonial yoke; . . . and, finally, to increase further the cohesion of the peace-loving forces." Again, in the article "Peaceful Coexistence and Revolution," published in *Kommunist,* No. 2, 1962, the opinion is expressed that, under present conditions, it is possible to remove *war* from the life of society and that the realistic procedure for this is the implementation of the principle of peaceful coexistence. Later, the same article quotes one of the messages of the Soviet Government to the U.S. Government which points out that peaceful coexistence "is possible only if countries with different social systems observe international law and *regard the preservation of peace in the world as their highest goal*" (our emphasis). What does this mean? It means either that imperialism has changed its nature and is no longer aggressive and warlike, that it has renounced its war aims, and that it is ready to recognize as its highest goal the securing of world peace, or that imperialism is so weak that it is not capable of undertaking any aggressive action. None of this corresponds to reality. This is irrefutably proved by the entire development of contemporary international life. The worst thing about this is that these views seriously endanger the people's struggle for peace and against imperialism.

In his article, A. Rumyantsev also writes that, as was stressed at the 22nd Congress of the Communist Party of the Soviet Union, "peaceful coexistence — and only peaceful coexistence — is the best and only acceptable way of solving the vital issues *confronting society*" (our emphasis). How is this to be understood? Let us take such basic issues confronting contemporary society as the liberation of the oppressed peoples from the imperialist yoke or the liberation of the working class and all workers from capitalist exploitation. What is, in the final analysis, the real way to settle these vital problems?

Naturally, peaceful coexistence, correctly understood and put into practice, in the spirit of the Moscow Declaration of 1960, is not at all in contradiction to the national liberation movement of the oppressed peoples and the revolutionary struggle of the working class. On the contrary, as was also pointed out in the Declaration, under conditions of peaceful coexistence, favorable opportunities are created for furthering the class struggle in the capitalist countries and for developing the national liberation struggle of the peoples of the colonial and dependent countries, while the successes achieved by the latter help to strengthen peaceful coexistence. Communists do not and cannot hold the opinion that in order to achieve complete liberation of the enslaved peoples and the victory of socialism in all countries it is necessary to wage a third world war. They are the most resolute opponents of a world war and supporters of the strengthening of peace in the world.

Does this mean, however, that peaceful coexistence will automatically solve the problem of liberating the enslaved peoples and of achieving the triumph of socialism in the world? According to the teachings of Marxism-Leninism, as has already been confirmed and is being confirmed each passing day by life and facts, and as was pointed out in the two Declarations of the Communist and workers parties of 1957 and 1960, the only correct and possible path to the liberation of the enslaved peoples is their resolute struggle for national liberation against the imperialist colonizers, while the path to the overthrow of the capitalist order and the transition to socialism is the class struggle and the achievement of the socialist revolution in one or another form. But, according to A. Rumyantsev, the only correct and permissible path is peaceful coexistence. If that were so, should not the enslaved peoples perhaps renounce their national liberation struggle, and should not the working class and the workers in all capitalist countries renounce their class struggle for revolution and await liberation as a gift of peaceful coexistence?

We are not dealing here with some erroneous formula which A. Rumyantsev has accidentally advanced, but a clear expression of the opportunist line which N. Khrushchev and his group are obstinately following on the question of peaceful coexistence. What N. Khrushchev does not dare say aloud is unequivocally proclaimed by his zealous propagandists. In fact, the formulation of A. Rumyantsev reveals the essence of N. Khrushchev's known revisionist concept — already criticized by our party — on peaceful coexistence as the general line of the foreign policy of the socialist countries.

N. Khrushchev's revisionist concept on peaceful coexistence as a magic wand which can solve all problems has been delineated on many occasions and has found concrete expression in N. Khrushchev's stand and practical activities regarding a series of problems and important events on the international scene.

Let us consider, for example, the stand of the Soviet delegation at the gathering of the World Peace Council in Stockholm. In an article on this gathering, which was published in the magazine *Za Rubezhom*, a bitter attack was made on the delegates who requested that the forthcoming World Peace Congress be a "congress of peace, national independence, and disarmament." This article states: "These orators, using detestable methods, alleged that there are some people who consider total and general disarmament as the only task of the movement for the defense of peace and that they are, allegedly, weakening their support of the national liberation struggle of the peoples." But regardless of the efforts of N. Khrushchev's propagandists on the editorial board of *Za Rubezhom* to justify the anti-Marxist attitude of the Soviet delegation in Stockholm, they cannot alter the fact that it was precisely the Soviet delegation which, with great obstinacy, refused to place on the agenda of the forthcoming congress of peace partisans the question of the struggle against colonialism and for national independence on the part of the enslaved peoples, and insisted that the agenda include only the issues of disarmament and peace. What, then, does *Za Rubezhom* consider "detestable methods"? Is it a bad thing to request a discussion at the peace congress of the problem of the peoples' struggle for their national liberation, to ask that the struggle for peace not be separated from the peoples' struggle for freedom and national independence? This is an entirely just and legitimate demand which true Marxist-Leninists cannot but support without reservation. The position of the Soviet delegation on this issue provoked the righteous indignation of not only Communist revolutionaries but also many non-Communist delegates, representing the peoples of Asia, Africa, and Latin America, who are making many sacrifices in their struggle against imperialist oppression in order to win freedom and independence.

How is the position of the N. Khrushchev group on a question as vital as the national liberation of the enslaved peoples to be explained? Does he think that general and complete disarmament will automatically solve the problem of national liberation, and that the enslaved peoples should sit with their arms folded while awaiting the achievement of disarmament? Or does he think that the peoples' national liberation movement is a threat to peace and may cause a world war and that, therefore, the enslaved peoples should remain quiet lest they "provoke" imperialism? Or, perhaps, the one as well as the other? In fact, the Communist movement is familiar with the distorted view of N. Khrushchev that every "little war" is a threat to world peace and that "any spark can be transformed into a world conflagration." According to this logic, the conclusion emerges that any national liberation war is undesirable, since it may result in the eruption of a third world war. The position of the Soviet delegation at the Stockholm meeting of the World Peace Council was none other than the practical application of this anti-Marxist thesis of N. Khrushchev.

Whatever it may be, such a position only favors the imperialist colonizers; it is to the detriment of the peoples oppressed and enslaved by imperialism, to the detriment of the cause of peace and socialism, and in open contradiction to the Declaration of the 81 Communist and workers parties, which declares that the national liberation movement is one of the major forces of our time for the preservation of peace and that its victories reinforce the cause of peace and peaceful coexistence.

When one listens to N. Khrushchev and his followers, they appear to acknowledge the two paths of the transition to socialism: through arms and without arms, peaceful and nonpeaceful. But in fact they overestimate and attribute an almost absolute character to the peaceful path; they interpret it in a reformist and opportunist fashion, and they place all their hopes for the transition to socialism on general and total disarmament and on economic competition between the two systems. This is confirmed by many facts. Does not even A. Rumyantsev's article testify to this when he says that peaceful coexistence is the only correct and acceptable way to solve all the vital issues confronting society?

The N. Khrushchev group has also badly confused the issue of revolution and counterrevolution. At a press conference in Brazil on February 8, A. Adzhubei stated: "Revolution as well as counterrevolution are *no longer* exportable articles today" (our emphasis). It is clear that Adzhubei puts revolution and counterrevolution on the same level: On the one hand, he says that *it is only today* that revolution is not an article for export, while it seems that it still was so yesterday; on the other hand, *it was only yesterday* that counterrevolution was an article for export, while it is no longer so today. Accordingly, the danger of the export of counterrevolution by imperialism no longer exists. This serves imperialist reaction as a weapon for discrediting the socialist camp and the Communist movement and for lulling the people's vigilance. Indeed, what were the events in Hungary in 1956, the intervention of the American imperialists and their hirelings in Cuba in 1961, or the plot of the Yugoslav revisionists and the Greek monarcho-fascists in cooperation with the American imperialists against the Albanian People's Republic? The Moscow Declaration of 1960, in complete contradiction to Adzhubei's words, clearly points out that: "The Communist parties, guided by Marxist-Leninist doctrine, *have always been* opposed to the export of revolution. At the same time, they *resolutely struggle* against the imperialist export of counterrevolution. They consider it their internationalist task to appeal to the peoples of all countries to unite, to mobilize all their internal forces, *to participate actively, and,* by basing themselves on the power of the world socialist system, *to halt or to strike a fatal blow to imperialist intervention in the affairs of the people of any country which has risen in revolutionary war*" (our emphasis).

It is known that one of the fundamental theses of Marxism-Leninism, which was also emphasized in the two Declarations of 1957 and 1960 of the workers and Communist parties, is that the transition from capitalism to socialism can be realized only under the leadership of the working class and its revolutionary party, and by establishing the dictatorship of the proletariat. Yet this basic thesis has lately been neglected and studiously avoided by the propaganda of the N. Khrushchev group, by the Soviet press, and in the documents of the Communist Party of the Soviet Union, especially when it concerns the perspectives for the development of countries which have won their independence and have been liberated from the colonial yoke of imperialism. Thus, for example, in the new Program of the Communist Party of the Soviet Union, approved by the 22nd Congress, where reference is made to the noncapitalist path of development of former colonial countries, nowhere is it stressed that, for those countries to develop along this path, the guidance of the working class by its Marxist-Leninist party and the establishment of the dictatorship of the proletariat in some form are absolutely necessary. On the contrary, it is implied that the noncapitalist development of these countries can also be achieved under the guidance of other classes and other parties, that in these countries the transition to socialism could even be effected without the overthrow of the capitalist power and without replacing it with the dictatorship of the proletariat.

The fundamentally opportunist views of N. Khrushchev and his group on the question of revolution, as well as their views, positions, and activities on the question of imperialism, of war and peace, of peaceful coexistence and disarmament, do not in the least serve the working class, the toiling masses, and the peoples, but, on the contrary, greatly harm the cause of the victory of socialism. Indeed, they paralyze the revolutionary energies of the workers; they postpone the victory of the socialist revolution; they lengthen the life of capitalism; they condemn the workers of the capitalist countries to prolonged suffering under the heavy yoke of capitalism. The heroic Cuban people were a thousand times correct when they stressed in the second Havana Declaration that "to hasten the liberation of Latin America, be it only by one year, would mean saving millions of children and millions of minds for cultural development, and would mean saving the peoples from severe and innumerable sufferings." This is how these things are viewed by the peoples and the true revolutionaries.

N. Khrushchev has caused and continues to cause great harm to the cause of socialism, to the unity of the socialist camp, and to the international Communist movement by his unprincipled attacks against J. V. Stalin and his work, by his policy of rapprochement and reconciliation with Tito's revisionist clique, and by his hostile actions against the PPSh and the people of Albania.

N. Khrushchev and his group demagogically exploit the slogan of the struggle "against the personality cult and its consequences" for the purpose of discrediting the ideas of Stalin-Leninism, of revising certain fundamental teachings of Marxism-Leninism and propagating their opportunist views, of attacking and liquidating the healthy Marxist-Leninist elements in the leadership of the Communist and workers parties in different countries by activating and supporting to this end their own elements within these parties, and of rehabilitating the living and the dead traitors and enemies of Marxism-Leninism and socialism. N. Khrushchev and his followers, especially at the 22nd Congress and thereafter, publicly began and are still continuing a furious campaign of attacks and slanders against J. V. Stalin by presenting him as a wild despot, terrorist, murderer, and criminal and characterizing the period of Stalin's rule as a time of great errors, crimes, and grave violations of socialist legality. In so doing, they have given weapons to the imperialist reaction and joined with it in its efforts to discredit the Soviet Union, the dictatorship of the proletariat, and the socialist order in general, in order to defile the ideas of socialism and Communism.

Under the mask of the struggle against "dogmatism" and "sectarianism" and under the pretext that revisionism today has allegedly been unmasked and demolished, N. Khrushchev and his group have renounced the struggle against revisionism, which remains the main danger to the international Communist and workers movement, and they are drawing ever nearer to the traitorous Yugoslav revisionist clique. There is no need to refer again to the question of N. Khrushchev's scandalous attitude toward Tito's traitorous group in connection with the 1956 counterrevolutionary coup in Hungary and with other facts regarding the rapprochement with the Yugoslav revisionists. It is sufficient to mention that, following the 22nd Congress, meetings, talks, the exchange of delegations, and all-round relations with Yugoslavia were extended and are increasing day by day. N. Khrushchev and his followers are more and more frequently making statements to the effect that Yugoslavia is a socialist country, that its foreign policy coincides with that of the Soviet Union, and so forth. In this spirit of conciliation and rapprochement, a Komsomol delegation was even sent to Yugoslavia recently to "exchange experiences." (!) Facts reveal that such a policy of reconciliation with the revisionists is reviving the revisionist elements and views in the ranks of the Communist and workers parties. It is giving encouragement and a free hand to the Yugoslav revisionists to assault Marxism-Leninism and the unity of the Communist movement and to engage in hostile and disruptive activities against the socialist countries.

Have the hostile attitudes and actions of N. Khrushchev toward the PPSh and the Albanian People's Republic served, perhaps, the Communist movement and the cause of socialism, as N. Khrushchev and his spokesmen maintain? On the contrary, the anti-Marxist activities of N. Khrushchev and his group, such as the extension of ideological differences to the field of state relations, the organization of economic and political blockades and pressures, even reaching the point of actually breaking off diplomatic relations with the Albanian People's Republic, the one-sided public airing of our differences at the 22nd Congress of the Communist Party of the Soviet Union, the brutal intervention in the internal affairs of our party and country, slanders to the effect that among us there flourish the cult of the individual and a reign of terror, the protection of traitors and enemies of our party and people and the open calls for counterrevolution, for the overthrow of the leadership of the party and our people's power — all of these do not serve our socialist and Communist cause, but do great harm to it. It is clear to every honest and reasonable person that they have caused and are causing grave harm to the unity of the socialist camp and the international Communist movement, that they discredit the prestige and the foreign policy of the Soviet Union as well as relations among the socialist countries and among the Communist and workers parties, and that they give the imperialists weapons with which to fight us.

No matter how N. Khrushchev and his men try to justify their hostile anti-Marxist activities against our party and against our people and to mislead public opinion by alleging that they have made all possible efforts to normalize relations with the PPSh and the Albanian People's Republic, facts remain facts. We shall return to this question to supply documentary proof that N. Khrushchev not only has done nothing to improve relations between our two parties and between our two countries, but that, on the contrary, he has done everything possible to aggravate them. It is the PPSh, and not N. Khrushchev, which has, in fact, made sincere efforts to settle differences and to improve Soviet-Albanian relations in a Marxist-Leninist and an internationalist proletarian manner.

In order to conceal the fact that it has deviated from the Marxist-Leninist line and that it has violated the Moscow Declaration of 1960, and in order to justify its opportunist policy of capitulation, the N. Khrushchev group is furiously attacking the correct and principled position of the Albanian Party of Labor, be it on the meaning and implementation of the policy of peaceful coexistence, on disarmament or the many other problems of peace and war, on the paths of transition to socialism, and so forth. In fact, the truth is quite another thing. The Albanian Party of Labor is faithfully applying the teachings of Marxism-Leninism and the Moscow Declaration concerning these problems. This can be proved even by a quick comparison of the fabrications of N. Khrushchev's group and the official statements, attitudes, and activity of our party.

Let us take the question of peaceful coexistence. The propagandists of the N. Khrushchev group, in slandering the Albanian Party of Labor, write:

> The leaders of the Albanian Party of Labor, especially Enver Hoxha and Mehmet Shehu, assert that the policy of peaceful coexistence cannot be the general line of the policy of the socialist countries. In this connection, they assert that the principle of peaceful coexistence allegedly implies a refusal to support the national liberation movement. Outwardly, this way of presenting the question seems to be prompted by concern for the fate of the peoples of the colonial countries, but, in reality, they ignore the fact that the peoples of the colonial countries want to secure their freedom peacefully, without bloodshed. Peaceful coexistence responds precisely to this aspiration; in particular, it presupposes noninterference in the internal affairs of other countries and recognition that the peoples should solve all the problems of their existence independently (Radio Moscow, February 15, 1962).

Let us now briefly analyze this.

First, according to N. Khrushchev's propagandists, the Albanian Party of Labor, by opposing peaceful coexistence as the general political line of the socialist countries, is against peaceful coexistence in general. However, N. Khrushchev's propagandists forget that the Moscow Declaration does not consider the principle of peaceful coexistence as the general political line of the socialist countries, nor does it interpret it as a magic wand by which "each country can solve the problems of its own existence" but as the only correct and reasonable principle in relations between countries with different social systems. The Moscow Declaration notes that the foreign policy of the socialist countries is also guided by certain other principles: the principle of proletarian internationalism and fraternal mutual assistance in relations among socialist countries; and, with regard to the national liberation movement and the revolutionary struggle of the working class and the working masses, the principle of solidarity with them, and of assistance and support for the rights of the peoples for freedom, independence, and national and social liberation.

The slander by the N. Khrushchev propagandists that the PPSh is allegedly against peaceful coexistence is refuted by the official documents of our party and our government and by all their practical activities. The speech delivered by Comrade Enver Hoxha at the meeting devoted to the 20th anniversary of the PPSh and the 44th anniversary of the great October Socialist Revolution notes:

> The basis of the foreign policy of the Albanian Party of Labor has always been and remains the constant strengthening of the ties of friendship, fraternal cooperation, and mutual aid and support with the countries of the socialist camp, headed by the Soviet Union; the support of the anti-imperialist and anticolonialist national liberation struggle of oppressed peoples and nations and the revolutionary struggle of the workers in capitalist countries; [and] all possible efforts to secure relations of peaceful coexistence between the People's Republic of Albania and the capitalist countries, especially with Albania's neighbors. . . .

Our party and our government have consistently implemented the principles of peaceful coexistence. It is not necessary to enlarge upon the diplomatic relations which our country maintains with 17 capitalist and independent countries. Likewise, it is not necessary to speak of the efforts made by the Government of the APR and the readiness it has always displayed to improve relations with neighboring countries. We will only mention the trade relations which our country maintains with capitalist countries because the N. Khrushchev group has now begun to slander our party in this respect, thus contradicting its own revisionist conception of peaceful coexistence. The Albanian People's Republic has had, in the past as well, commercial relations with 12 nonsocialist countries. Until yesterday N. Khrushchev accused us of not making sufficient efforts to develop trade on the basis of mutual profit, on the basis of peaceful coexistence with capitalist countries. As has been the case in the past, this year the APR, faithfully following its correct policy, is developing commercial relations with nonsocialist countries such as Italy, Ghana, Egypt, Iraq. However, N. Khrushchev has now started the lie that the Albanian leaders allegedly are "orienting themselves toward the West," that they are "establishing intensive political, economic, and other relations with certain NATO countries." In short, it seems that his "genius" for invention is being fulfilled, namely, that the PPSh and the APR are selling themselves to imperialism for 30 pieces of silver. Fairy tales spun in broad daylight! N. Khrushchev is enraged because the Albanian Party of Labor and the Albanian Government, by pursuing a firm and consistent policy in their relations with capitalist countries in the spirit of Marxism-Leninism and the Moscow Declarations, are thwarting his efforts to isolate the APR and to establish a blockade against it.

Secondly, according to the propagandists of the N. Khrushchev group, the PPSh is denounced because, since it is against the thesis of peaceful coexistence as the general line of the foreign policy of the socialist countries, it is also against the desire of the oppressed peoples to win freedom peacefully, without bloodshed, and it is therefore against the vital interests of these countries.

We are dealing here with a transparent distortion of the position of our party and our government, which in their entire policy and in all their activity have supported and are supporting the just struggle of the peoples to win and to consolidate their freedom and national independence. Thus, the report of the Central Committee of the PPSh delivered to the Fourth Party Congress, states:

> Our party and our people, who have themselves known exploitation and colonial oppression, have supported and will always support without reservation the national liberation struggle of the oppressed peoples. We consider this our internationalist task.

In their great eagerness to slander the PPSh, the propagandists of the N. Khrushchev theses involuntarily betray his utterly anti-Marxist opportunist position regarding the question of the paths of liberation of the enslaved peoples. According to their logic, it appears that the only correct path for the liberation of the peoples from the colonial yoke is the peaceful path, and that if one accepts and supports at the same time the other path, the path of an armed struggle for national liberation, this would mean opposing peaceful coexistence. Therefore, according to this logic, the peoples of Algeria, Angola, Oman, the Congo, Laos, and so forth must renounce their armed struggle and take the peaceful path, for this path alone is in accord with the policy of peaceful coexistence. Thus one may accuse all those peoples who are waging an armed struggle for national liberation of being warmongers and against peace. Thus, we find ourselves again returning to N. Khrushchev's well-known thesis that all wars without exception should be prevented in order to safeguard peace and peaceful coexistence, because a single spark can set the whole world on fire. It is clear to everyone whom these views of N. Khrushchev serve and to whose benefit they are.

N. Khrushchev's propagandists also treat the question of the transition to socialism exactly in the same spirit. In attempting somehow to justify the opportunist views of N. Khrushchev and his group on this issue, and to slander the PPSh and to distort its position, Khrushchev's spokesmen said in a recent commentary: "The Albanian leaders, by denying the peaceful forms of the victory of the working class, are making common cause with the bourgeois propaganda which contends that war is allegedly the only means of achieving the victory of socialism throughout the world." Naturally this is merely slander, which is not worth refuting. Our party has never denied the possibility of the peaceful transition to socialism; still less has it believed that a world war is indispensable for the victory of socialism in all countries. In his speech on November 7, 1961, Comrade Enver Hoxha noted clearly that:

> We Albanian Communists have never been and are not a priori opposed to the peaceful path. But the teachings of Marxism-Leninism, historical experience, and contemporary reality teach us that, to secure the victory of the socialist cause, the working class and its party must prepare themselves simultaneously for both possibilities — the peaceful path and the nonpeaceful one. To orient oneself toward only one of these possibilities is to embark upon an erroneous path. Only by being prepared, especially for the nonpeaceful path, do the opportunities increase for the peaceful path as well.

However, the "logic" of the N. Khrushchev spokesmen is interesting. According to them, it appears that if one accepts simultaneously the peaceful and the nonpeaceful paths of revolutions, as we are taught by Lenin and enjoined by Marxist dialectics, it means that one is in favor of world war. Therefore, to be in favor of peace, one should renounce the nonpeaceful way and accept only the peaceful path to the victory of socialism. (!) On this basis, the bourgeoisie and its lackeys can denounce as warmongers and as opponents of peace the working class and the Communist Party of any country where the latter envisage a transition from capitalism to socialism by nonpeaceful means. Let the readers judge for themselves who aligns himself with bourgeois propaganda on this question.

Equally as absurd as the afore-mentioned accusations and slanders regarding the policy followed by the PPSh and the APR are N. Khrushchev's accusations and slanders regarding the policy of our party and our government on the problems of war and peace. Irresponsibly and utterly turning the facts upside down, N. Khrushchev's propagandists lie when they allege that:

> . . . the Albanian leaders distrust the strength of the socialist camp, overestimate the capacities of imperialism, capitulate before imperialism out of fear, and thus abandon to the imperialists the solution of the question of whether or

not there will be a war. In fact, a stand of this kind leads to a lack of faith and perspective; it causes the people to lose their faith in their ability to consolidate the peace. By such admissions, the Albanian leaders let the struggle for peace develop spontaneously, disarm the peoples, and thus weaken their efforts in the struggle to defend peace (*Radio Moscow,* February 7, 1962).

The line of our party on the question of war and peace was and remains most clear. Therefore, we consider it superfluous to deal with this problem at length, to refute with the aid of many facts and documents the gross slanders of the N. Khrushchev group. We will mention only a part of the report of the Central Committee of the PPSh, presented at the Fourth Party Congress, which expressed the correct attitude of our party, in the spirit of the Moscow Declaration of 1960:

> The Marxist-Leninist dialectical method and the materialist conception of history give us the correct answer: Both the overestimation of our forces and the underestimation of the enemy forces on the one hand, and the underestimation of our forces and overestimation of the enemy forces on the other, lead to grave errors. The first weakens vigilance and leads to adventurism, while the second leads to opportunist errors and attitudes. Therefore, our party has always stressed that the balance of power in the world has changed in favor of socialism, that the forces of socialism are stronger than those of imperialism, that the forces of peace are stronger than the forces of war; but at the same time it has not underestimated the forces of imperialism. . . .
>
> . . . Our party has always maintained that it is possible to prevent world war, that today world war is not fatalistically inevitable, but at the same time it has maintained that the danger of war exists, for as long as imperialism exists so too will the basis for aggressive war.

In view of this, where is the fault or the error of the PPSh? Does it lie in the fact that it fails to appraise the forces of imperialism and war along with a correct appraisal of the forces of socialism and peace? Does it lie in the fact that, along with its belief in the possibility of preventing a world war, it also points out the danger of war and the possibility of the initiation of aggressive wars on the part of imperialism? What does N. Khrushchev's group want? Can it be that it wants us to follow its path of illusions concerning the transformation of the character of imperialism, to maintain that imperialism allegedly does not now constitute a threat to peace and that it has now allegedly been bound hand and foot and is in no position to do anything at all? What could please the imperialists better than the propagation of these illusions?

Life itself has repudiated these illusions of N. Khrushchev. What do the imperialist acts of aggression against Korea, Vietnam, Egypt, the Congo, Cuba, and other countries show? No doubt the fact that these hotbeds of war have been extinguished and prevented from erupting into a world conflict clearly demonstrates the existing possibility of halting the aggressive wars of imperialism. But they also demonstrate that imperialism has not renounced its aggressive actions and that it is still in a position to undertake such actions, and all the more so when all sorts of pacifist illusions are being created about it, when the peoples' vigilance is being lulled, and when the people are not properly mobilized with firm determination to stay the hand of the imperialist aggressors.

To mention only the possibility of preventing war and not to speak of its danger, not to unmask the imperialist policy of war and aggression, as is being done by the N. Khrushchev group, means to trample on the Moscow Declaration with both feet, to lull the vigilance of the peoples, to weaken their struggle for peace, to disarm the peoples, and to give a free hand to the imperialists to carry out their aggressive plans.

Other slanderous activities by N. Khrushchev and his group against our country are contained in the accusations and inventions regarding the policy and attitude of the PPSh and the APR toward the question of disarmament. They portray matters as though the PPSh and the APR "were displaying deep mistrust toward the possibility of achieving disarmament in our time and basely falsifying the Soviet proposals." To justify this slander, the N. Khrushchev group gives as its only evidence "the fact" that "the leaders of the PPSh have set no example and have made no practical contribution to the achievement of the disarmament program," that allegedly "they opposed the proposal to create an atom-free zone in the Balkans and the Adriatic," and that allegedly "they spoke against the proposals of the Romanian Government for reducing tensions in the Balkans and for the creation of conditions for peaceful coexistence in this region."

Our party and government have always considered disarmament one of the major questions of our time for safeguarding peace, and they have considered and continue to consider that through the joint efforts of the socialist countries and the peace forces of the world, it is possible to impose disarmament on imperialism and to achieve concrete results in this direction. Throughout its existence the government of the APR has struggled shoulder to shoulder with the other socialist and peace-loving countries to solve the problem of disarmament and to make its contribution to this question. It has firmly supported the many proposals of the Soviet Union, in particular, as well as those of the other socialist countries for the solution of limited problems on the question of general and complete disarmament. The many documents of our party and government and all their practical activities in the international arena clearly testify to this.

N. Khrushchev accuses the PPSh and the APR of taking a stand against the proposal for the transformation of the Balkans and the Adriatic into a zone free of atomic arms and rockets. What is the truth? This proposal was advanced for the first time by the Government of the USSR and the Government of the APR in their joint declaration of May 30, 1959. This declaration states:

> The Government of Albania and the Soviet Government consider that the creation in this region of a nuclear-free zone would correspond to the interests of the people of the Balkan Peninsula and the Adriatic. Renunciation by the countries of this region of the installation of atomic and rocket bases on their territory would be a great contribution toward the transformation of the Balkans into a zone of peace and tranquillity.

The use of slanders and fabrications has led N. Khrushchev to such absurdities as to accuse the PPSh and the APR of opposing their own proposal. Have the PPSh and the APR changed their attitude toward this proposal? Not at all. They were and are determined to achieve the realization of this proposal. N. Khrushchev and his group are unable to cite a single fact to substantiate their slanders, because such facts are nonexistent.

If the reference is to the proposal of T. Zhivkov in 1960 regarding the disarmament of the Balkan countries (excluding Italy, where NATO rocket bases had already been established), down to the level of frontier guards, our party and government have rejected and reject this proposal as a dangerous and fruitless diplomatic step.

With regard to the attitude of the PPSh and the Government of the APR toward the proposal of the Romanian Government for a meeting of the heads of government of the Balkan countries to improve and develop relations among them, the truth here also refutes the slanders of the N. Khrushchev propagandists, who reproach the leaders of the PPSh and of the APR for having allegedly taken a stand against this proposal:

As early as September 19, 1957, only a week after the Romanian proposal, *Zëri i Popullit* published the reply of the Chairman of the Council of Ministers of the APR, Comrade Mehmet Shehu, to the then Chairman of the Council of Ministers of the Romanian People's Republic, Chivu Stoica, in which the Albanian Government declared itself ready to contribute to the improvement and development of relations among the Balkan countries. The letter said:

> The Albanian Government, appreciating the conclusion arrived at by the Romanian Government that the basic interests of the Balkan peoples necessitate broad, collective cooperation among the Balkan countries, and taking into consideration the real significance of this matter, approves the proposal of the Romanian Government that in the course of the year 1957 a conference of the heads of state of the governments of Albania, Bulgaria, Greece, Turkey, Yugoslavia, and Romania be held in the capital of Romania, or the capital of a country participating in this conference.

Later, too, the Government of the APR expressed this attitude. On June 16, 1959, *Zëri i Popullit* also published the declaration of the Government of the APR in support of the declaration of the Romanian Government which launched an appeal for a meeting of the heads of government of the Balkan states to safeguard peace in the Balkans. "The Government of the APR," states this declaration, "supports without reservation this proposal of the Government of the RPR and declares itself ready to participate in such a meeting."

Thus it can be clearly seen that we are dealing here with a clumsy lie. But this does not surprise us in the least, because falsifications and slanders have become the chief means of N. Khrushchev's group in its unprincipled struggle against the Albanian Party of Labor and the People's Republic.

Who is served by all these slanders and fabricated accusations against the policy of the PPSh and the APR, against a socialist country like the APR and against the Albanian people, who are fighting heroically for the cause of socialism and peace? These can only benefit the enemies of the Albanian people, the common enemies of all the socialist countries. Through these slanders and attacks against the PPSh and the APR, N. Khrushchev zealously serves the imperialists and reactionary forces in the world, and seriously harms the cause of unity of the socialist camp and the international Communist movement, the cause of socialism and peace.

Such is the true nature of N. Khrushchev and his group. The consistently anti-Marxist views, attitudes, and actions of N. Khrushchev can only be characterized as treason to the socialist camp and the international Communist and workers movement, to the great cause of socialism and Communism, to the liberation of the peoples, and to world peace. Forty-two years ago the great Lenin wrote:

> A man who "sincerely" declares himself a Communist but who in reality, instead of conducting a clear-cut and ever resolute policy, a policy which is heroic and courageous to the point of self-denial (only such a policy is consonant with recognition of the dictatorship of the proletariat), wavers and seems afraid — such a man, because of his lack of character, his vacillation, and his indecision, commits treason no less than the out-and-out traitor. From the standpoint of personality, the difference between the traitor who acts from weakness and the traitor who acts from calculation and premeditation is very great. From the standpoint of politics, this difference *does not exist* since politics involves in fact the fate of millions of people and this fate is not altered by the manner in which millions of poor workers and peasants are betrayed — whether by traitors who betray from weakness or by traitors who betray from self-interest (V. I. Lenin, *Works,* Vol. 30, p. 404, Albanian edition).

Our party, faithful to the vital interests of our people and the workers of the whole world, to Marxism-Leninism, and to the cause of socialism and Communism, will resolutely continue its correct principled struggle against the anti-Marxist, revisionist, and traitorous views and activities of N. Khrushchev and his group, deeply convinced that justice will triumph.

DOCUMENT 26

"N. Khrushchev Has Been Devoting His Time to Aggravating the Divergencies with Our Party and State instead of Solving Them," Zëri i Popullit, *March 25, 1962 (complete text)*.

Roughly six months have passed since N. Khrushchev publicly attacked the Albanian Party of Labor. It is clear now that this attack was in fact directed against Marxism-Leninism, against the unity of the socialist camp and the international Communist and workers movement. It is precisely for this reason that Communists, people in other countries, and the Soviet people have been asking since the 22nd Congress: Why attack the PPSh; why drag into the open the differences existing within the international Communist and workers movement; why not solve them patiently in the Marxist-Leninist way; in whose interest is all this? Neither at the 22nd Congress nor since, despite the resolutions, speeches, and numerous articles which have been and are still being written to justify the position of the Soviet leadership, has N. Khrushchev's group been able to justify itself and to give a reply to these legitimate questions which continue to be asked throughout the world.

Despite this, N. Khrushchev and his intimates have spared no efforts to find a justification for their anti-Marxist attitude toward the PPSh. With this purpose in mind, they produced the story that allegedly the Soviet leaders "were forced to act in this way [to publicly take issue with the PPSh] because all efforts to normalize relations with the PPSh were to no avail and an open struggle was the only possible solution." Thus "every effort was made but it was to no avail," and "an open struggle was joined because it was the only solution." These are the two "arguments" which N. Khrushchev and his intimates have advanced. And with these "arguments" [which, as we shall see later on, are completely false and unfounded — Ed. note] they are seeking to convince the world "that this entirely justifies" their unprincipled struggle based on the most vile slanders, blockades of every kind, and unbridled pressure by the leaders of a large state against the Marxist party of a small people. With these same fabricated "arguments" they are also seeking to justify their appeals for counterrevolution and their breach of diplomatic relations with a socialist country such as Albania.

N. Khrushchev and his group, in acting with such viciousness against the PPSh and in advancing appropriate "arguments" to justify themselves, no doubt anticipated that people would believe them because the rights of the PPSh would be eclipsed by the indisputable authority of the glorious Soviet Union and the great party of Lenin. Of course, such a concept is anti-Marxist, but that is all one can expect from a Marxist-Leninist revisionist. N. Khrushchev is trifling and speculating with the prestige and the authority of the Soviet Union. The peoples and Communists throughout the world are beginning to understand more and more the true nature of N. Khrushchev and his group; they are realizing more and more that N. Khrushchev's attack on the PPSh, his appeals for counterrevolution in Albania, and the breaking off of diplomatic relations with Albania are actions which cannot be justified by any fabricated "argument," actions which cannot be concealed behind the authority of the Soviet Union and its Communist Party. These anti-Marxist actions befit only those who have betrayed the cause of socialism and Communism. The peoples and Communists of the world are gradually realizing and will realize even more clearly that N. Khrushchev and his group are dividing the international Communist and workers movement, are acting like incorrigible opportunists and revisionists, and are helping only the enemies of socialism and Communism by their actions.

Before the Bucharest meeting, differences on certain ideological questions had never cast a shadow on the fraternal relations of our two parties.

Since the N. Khrushchev group comments so much on the "efforts" it allegedly made to normalize relations with the PPSh, we shall dwell on this question in this article. The "efforts" of N. Khrushchev to normalize relations, or, more precisely, the procedures he chose to settle the ideological differences which have appeared between the PPSh and the Soviet leaders — procedures which have consisted in extending these differences to the realm of state-to-state relations through economic, political, and military pressures, through threats and blockades, while seeking to impose his own views on the PPSh and the Albanian state — have resulted in the deterioration of relations, in their exacerbation, which culminated in the public attack launched against the PPSh from the rostrum of the 22nd CPSU Congress, and in the *de facto* breach of diplomatic relations with the Albanian People's Republic by the Soviet Government. The Bucharest meeting in 1960 was an about-face in the attitude of the Khrushchev group toward the PPSh and the Albanian People's Republic, which has resulted in the exacerbation of Soviet-Albanian relations. Before this, there existed between our two parties and our two countries fraternal and warm relations which served as a veritable model of proletarian internationalism. Until then the leadership of the CPSU and the Soviet Government maintained toward our country a friendly internationalist attitude, and had granted to Albania much aid in all realms of socialist construction, for which our party and our people are and will forever be grateful to the glorious CPSU and to the fraternal Soviet people. Our party has always correctly appraised, and now correctly appraises, the importance of this internationalist aid. "The experience of socialist construction in the USSR," said Comrade Enver Hoxha in a speech on November 28, 1959, at a solemn meeting devoted to the 15th anniversary of the liberation of our homeland, "and its very considerable aid have been and remain for us two important sources which have helped us successfully accomplish the tasks which have so far faced us in the great transformation of our economy and culture. Therefore, our people have always nourished and will nourish even further their affection and their devoted and sincere friendship for the great country of the October Revolution, the Soviet Union. Our friendship is a friendship between peoples, a friendship resting on the immortal teachings of Marxism-Leninism and proletarian internationalism, on the lofty and noble ideals of the triumph of socialism and the preservation of peace in the world, and therefore this friendship will live forever."

One should emphasize that our fraternal relations have never been tarnished, although between our party and the Soviet leadership headed by N. Khrushchev differences on certain important questions have existed for a long time. It is known, for instance, that our party is not in agreement with the criticism made of Stalin, with the manner in which it was made, and with the aims pursued through that criticism by N. Khrushchev and his group at the 20th CPSU Congress and after it. Our party has not been in agreement with the conciliatory and opportunist attitude of N. Khrushchev and his group toward the revisionist clique of Tito. It was not in agreement with the course set by N. Khrushchev on the question of peace and war and with the opportunist aims he sought to attain through it. It was not in agreement with his revisionist concept of the peaceful and nonpeaceful transition to socialism, etc. It is known, on the other hand, that N. Khrushchev has, on different occasions, spoken directly or indirectly against our party line, because of its principled stand regarding the Yugoslav revisionists and other problems. He has tried to exert pressure on our party to put an end to the just and principled criticisms against the Belgrade revisionists and to rehabilitate traitors to our party and our people, such as Koci Xoxe, Panajot Plaku, and their associates. All this is documented. In spite of this, our party has constantly tried to settle these disagreements over the correct Marxist-Leninist path, by means of negotiations and comradely criticism, while rejecting N. Khrushchev's propositions regarding the question of the Yugoslav revisionists and the rehabilitation of Albanian traitors in the service of Tito's clique. It is a fact that in spite of the above-mentioned misunderstandings, *until the middle of 1960* our party's relations with the Soviet leadership, especially the state-to-state relations between our two countries, never became strained. On the contrary, they followed the normal path of friendship and fraternal and international cooperation.

But during this time, N. Khrushchev saw that the PPSh was staunchly upholding its principled positions and making no concessions. He saw that our party was not inclined to follow his revisionist course. He became even more convinced of this at the Bucharest meeting, where our party firmly opposed the anti-Marxist procedures he utilized to attack Marxist-Leninist parties by surprise. Thus it was N. Khrushchev who first *decided on and then initiated* an offensive at Bucharest by harshly attacking the PPSh and its leadership.

As is known, at the Bucharest meeting and later at the Moscow conference in November 1960, the PPSh expressed its view on certain questions of contemporary world development and of the tactics and strategy of the Communist and workers international movement. It criticized certain opportunist views of N. Khrushchev and some of his anti-Marxist attitudes regarding relations among fraternal Communist and workers parties. This criticism was made in the correct way from party to party, during a conference of parties, and in complete accord with the principles of proletarian internationalism, which prescribes that fraternal Communist and workers parties should base their relations on equal rights and achieve unity of views and action through comradely criticism and consultations in a Marxist-Leninist manner, and in the spirit of proletarian internationalism. While at the Bucharest meeting the PPSh remained calm and dealt with the question of the correct way of settling differences which, as appeared in Bucharest, existed not only with the PPSh but also with other parties, N. Khrushchev, on the contrary, was already entering a mistaken anti-Marxist path. In reaction to the correct criticism by the PPSh, he had recourse to a method which is alien to Communist and to Marxist-Leninist parties, to the method of counteroffensive, replacing comradely criticism with brutal interference in other people's internal affairs and openly and harshly trampling on the principles of consultation, equality of rights, and proletarian internationalism, which should govern relations among Communist parties and socialist countries.

Immediately after the Bucharest meeting, and especially after the Moscow meeting, the "efforts" of N. Khrushchev to normalize relations with the PPSh assumed an even more concrete form: Credits granted to the Albanian People's Republic for its five-year plan were cut; Soviet specialists in Albania were recalled; all Albanian students in the USSR were sent back, etc. N. Khrushchev's "efforts," nicely portrayed by his propagandists, resemble the actions of the host who, having double-bolted his door and released his hounds, tells you: "Please come in." This "effort," this "sincere desire," is clearly expressed in a *Pravda* editorial of February 21, 1962, entitled "The Banner of Our Era." There one reads: "This criticism [*Pravda* is referring to N. Khrushchev's attack against the PPSh at the 22nd Congress — Ed. note] was addressed to the common sense of the Albanian leaders. It was intended to bring them back to positions of proletarian internationalism." How hypocritical this sentence is! According to the *Pravda* editors, N. Khrushchev's attack is comradely "criticism" which "makes an appeal to the common sense of the Albanian leaders!" Actually it appeals for a counterrevolution to overthrow the leaders of a Marxist-Leninist party of a socialist country. (Let us recall what N. Khrushchev said at the 22nd Congress; "But we are certain the time will come when the Albanian Communists and the Albanian people will have their say, and then the Albanian leaders will have to answer for the harm they have done their country, their people, and the cause of socialist construction in Albania.") N. Khrushchev's attack was aimed at restoring the Albanian leaders to positions of proletarian internationalism! Such is the cynicism of N. Khrushchev's group, which, by shedding crocodile tears over the "fate" of the Albanian people, reminds one of a person who stabs you in the back and then weeps over your demise.

To dispel any illusions about the "efforts" N. Khrushchev has allegedly made to normalize relations with the PPSh, let us turn to the corespondence between our two parties and to the main events which occurred after the Bucharest meeting. Numerous facts and documents are in our party's possession, some of which will be used in this article to show that, in his alleged "efforts" to settle differences with the PPSh, N. Khrushchev was always seeking our party's capitulation; he sought to dictate unacceptable anti-Marxist terms and to place the PPSh in a position of inequality and inferiority.

As is known, at the Bucharest meeting N. Khrushchev, without any warning but not without premeditation, endangered the unity of the international Communist and workers movement. He tried to make the different parties submit to his viewpoints and to his erroneous anti-Marxist acts by trampling — through arrogant and patriarchal methods — on the Leninist principles of consultation, of equal rights, and of proletarian internationalism in relations between fraternal parties. At the Bucharest meeting N. Khrushchev did everything he could to make our delegation approve his acts, to make it approve his opportunist and divisive views. But our party maintained a resolute and principled attitude. It denounced N. Khrushchev's assertions and anti-Marxist positions and expressed its own views on the correct way to settle the differences which had arisen in the socialist camp and the international Communist movement. At this meeting, the head of the Albanian delegation, Comrade Hysni Kapo, said:

> This important question, which Comrade N. Khrushchev has presented to us without warning and without previous study, should be studied and discussed in a proper and prudent manner, with great care and composure, and in a spirit of comradeship, according to Leninist norms and the Marxist-Leninist way, as our parties commonly do in such cases.

Such was the position of our delegation in Bucharest. The Central Committee of our party, through its representative, denounced N. Khrushchev's putschist methods and defended the idea of settling differences according to Leninist norms at the meeting in November 1960. N. Khrushchev did not appreciate the principled stand of our party's delegation, which opposed his anti-Marxist views and efforts to destroy the unity of the socialist camp. He was "hurt" by the correct criticism made from party to party, made by a small party, and he did not hesitate to call this criticism an "offense" against the leadership of the CPSU; and because of this "offense," he initiated pressures and vindictive acts against our party and country, which had the Marxist courage to obstruct the split in the socialist camp that N. Khrushchev deliberately set out to bring about.

Pressures and efforts to involve the PPSh in Khrushchev's plot against the unity of the socialist camp and the Communist movement.

Immediately after the Bucharest meeting a radical change became evident in the attitude of the Soviet leadership toward the PPSh and our country. The CPSU leadership based its policy and its position regarding the PPSh, not on attempts at settling differences, but on the idea of making us submit at any price and of taking revenge on our party because of its resolute stand.

From words they passed to deeds. N. Khrushchev refused and, what is more, remained silent a long time before refusing the urgent request of the Albanian Government for the purchase of a certain quantity of wheat from the USSR, at a time when our country was short of food due to the severe drought of 1960. Our country was forced to secure food by applying to other socialist countries. This constitutes overt pressure upon the PPSh.

On the other hand, the personnel of the Soviet Embassy in Tirana, acting on N. Khrushchev's instructions regarding a radical change of policy toward Albania, began feverishly to attack the Marxist-Leninist line of the PPSh, to divide our party and to sow panic and confusion in its ranks, to detach the leadership from its party, and to turn the army cadres and other cadres which had studied in the Soviet Union against it. All these "efforts," these pressures and brutal interventions were designed to make our party depart from the principled stand it maintained at the Bucharest meeting, and to oblige it at the November 1960 conference to support the opportunist and divisive views of N. Khrushchev and to assault with him the unity of the socialist camp and the international Communist and workers movement, and to assault the revolutionary teachings of Marxism-Leninism. With this in mind, on August 13, 1960, N. Khrushchev sent a letter to the Central Committee of the PPSh requesting negotiations, not for the purpose of settling the differences between the PPSh and the Soviet leadership but in order to place the PPSh in the same ranks as the Khrushchev group against a third party and thus to split the socialist camp. The letter proposed: "We feel it is important that the PPSh and the CPSU go to the forthcoming November conference with absolute unity of views. The CPSU Central Committee believes that, with this in mind, it would be reasonable to organize a meeting of representatives of our two parties before that conference." And out of the blue N. Khrushchev launched the threatening admonition: "Let us extinguish the spark of misunderstanding before it becomes a fire."

The point was therefore that the PPSh should go to the Moscow meeting "in agreement" with N. Khrushchev's anti-Marxist views, that the PPSh should renounce the correct principled position which it had defended at the Bucharest meeting and which did not please N. Khrushchev. This was to be the purpose of the meeting. This was "the first sincere effort," as it were, of N. Khrushchev to resolve existing misunderstandings and to normalize relations with the PPSh. And if the PPSh did not accept this solution, i.e., submit, then the "spark" ignited at Bucharest would turn into a "fire." Is it not clear that N. Khrushchev's group already foresaw and consciously prepared, as early as August 1960, the "fire" which was to break out at the 22nd Congress? Is it not clear what N. Khrushchev's group understands by "efforts" to settle differences with the PPSh — either submit or there will be a "fire"?

The Central Committee of the PPSh, in its letter dated August 27, 1960, gave a worthy reply to this ill-starred attempt. After pointing out that the differences which came to light in Bucharest were the result of N. Khrushchev's unjust attacks against a third party, and that consequently "to go to the forthcoming meeting with perfect unity of views" would amount to saying that our two parties had established a common attitude against a third Marxist-Leninist party, the letter stated:

> Marxism-Leninism also teaches that it would be a violation of the elementary Marxist-Leninist norms governing relations between Communist and workers parties if two parties should begin negotiations with the object of criticizing the general line of another Marxist party. It goes without saying that such an action would not be correct, that it would not make a contribution to the cause but would do it harm.

It was absolutely logical and natural for the PPSh, in spite of N. Khrushchev's threats, to refuse a meeting which would so oppose the most elementary rules of

Marxism-Leninism and which could give no positive result.

Let us continue with the "sincere efforts" of N. Khrushchev to negotiate with the leadership of the PPSh on settling differences and normalizing Soviet-Albanian relations: On November 9, 1960, at the conference of the 81 parties in Moscow, the Soviet leadership proposed that the First Secretary of the Central Committee of the PPSh, Comrade Hoxha, who had gone to Moscow as head of the Albanian delegation to the conference, meet with the First Secretary of the Central Committee of the CPSU, N. Khrushchev, for talks concerning relations between our two parties. Comrade Hoxha received this invitation with satisfaction and was preparing to go to N. Khrushchev. A few moments before Comrade Hoxha left for this meeting, however, our delegation received from the Soviet party an important official CPSU document distributed to all delegations participating in the Moscow conference, a document which made no mention of the existence of Albania as a socialist country, which slandered the PPSh, which undertook to defend antiparty elements in our country and which accused the PPSh leadership of settling party questions contrary to the rules of democratic centralism and of engaging in anti-Soviet policies and activities. These cowardly calumnies against the PPSh were revealed to the whole world Communist movement by the Soviet leadership before they were made known to our party. It is perfectly clear: The Soviet leadership, on the one hand, was inviting the First Secretary of the PPSh Central Committee for discussions while, on the other hand, it was simultaneously distributing materials filled with calumnies against our country for the obvious purpose of discrediting our party. Can one speak, therefore, of the "desire" of the Soviet leaders to settle differences? Can one speak of N. Khrushchev's "desire" for talks? N. Khrushchev, for the sake of appearances, was asking for negotiations to begin while in fact he was torpedoing them by making them contingent on preliminary conditions. "Admit the slanders which have been made public to the whole Communist movement, then come to an understanding with us" — this was in effect "the serious effort" made by N. Khrushchev and his group to come to an understanding with the PPSh. Do we not have here a deceitful, arrogant, insensible, and discriminatory attitude? Is this not an ultimatum — either submit or "fire" awaits you? Such an attitude has nothing in common with the "Marxist-Leninist method of negotiations, and the equalitarian, fraternal, and internationalist relations which should exist between fraternal parties. This is simply the attitude of an overlord, the attitude of the chauvinist, of a great state toward a small party. It was logical that under these abusive conditions the proposal for a meeting was rejected by our party with justified disgust.

Despite this, and motivated always by the desire to settle differences and normalize relations between our two parties and our two countries in the interest of the socialist camp and the international Communist movement, the PPSh delegation to the Moscow conference, after receiving new proposals from the Soviet leadership, agreed to start negotiations on November 10 and 11, 1960, with the leaders of the CPSU, and on November 12, 1960, the entire delegation, led by Comrade Hoxha, met N. Khrushchev and a group of Soviet leaders. All through these meetings it was clear that the Soviet leaders were not seeking a way to settle differences, but a means of forcing the PPSh to accept the views of N. Khrushchev's group and of persuading it to renounce its Marxist-Leninist principles. The fact is that the document slandering our party, distributed on November 8 and 9 to all the representatives of the parties in Moscow, was not regarded as a mistake by the Soviet leadership, that the pressures against our party and the disruptive activities of the personnel of the Soviet Embassy in Tirana were described as matters of no importance. Finally N. Khrushchev went to the extreme of declaring that he was better able to understand Macmillan than the leaders of the PPSh. The fact that he can reach understandings with Macmillan, Eisenhower, Kennedy, and the lackey Tito through compromises, concessions, and flattery is a personal merit envied by no one. But to force the PPSh to follow his revisionist course is something which has not happened and will never happen. Thus the "negotiations" yielded no results due to the fault of N. Khrushchev and his followers. This was N. Khrushchev's "second sincere effort" to settle differences and normalize relations with our party. But in reality it was the second serious effort to divert our party further from the positions of Marxism-Leninism and to subjugate it to his chauvinist domination.

After this setback, as could be expected, N. Khrushchev resorted to threats. He cynically declared that henceforth he would base relations with Albania on other foundations. This was no sooner said than done. N. Khrushchev went from words to deeds. Ideological differences were transferred to the realm of interstate relations. All credits were cut. All Soviet specialists in Albania were recalled suddenly and unilaterally. Commercial and military agreements were trampled upon.

With great patience, the PPSh Central Committee tried to safeguard the good relations which had existed between our countries, but with incredible insistence N. Khrushchev and his group endeavored to undermine them. Facts and documents prove this. Thus, our economic delegation, headed by the Minister of Industry, Xhafer Spahiu, which had gone to Moscow to sign an agreement for the period 1961–1965 and to sign an agreement on USSR credits to Albania for the mechanization of agriculture, was obliged to wait in vain for 64 days. While the conference of the 81 parties and the meetings between the two parties were taking place, the Soviet Ministry of Foreign Trade and the State Committee for Economic Relations, acting on N. Khrushchev's instigation and example, created all kinds of difficulties for our economic delegation — prolonged the meetings while waiting for "instructions from above," etc. This went on until December 21, 1960, when Semichastny, USSR deputy minister of foreign trade, during a conversation with members of the delegation, finally declared:

> The ministry is instructed to announce to the Albanian side that it would be advisable to postpone the matter of signing a long-term commercial agreement for 1961–1965 and the agreement on credits to Albania, in view of the need to discuss this question on a higher level.

And when the Government of the Albanian People's Republic was preparing to send Comrade Koço Theodhosi, Vice President of the Council of Ministers and candidate member of the Politburo, to conclude the agreements, the Soviet Government revealed on January 6, 1961, through a note from the Soviet Embassy in Tirana, that it did not accept this proposal of the Albanian Government and declared that economic questions "could only be discussed at the highest party and state level." In practice this meant that the Soviet Government was linking negotiations on economic questions and the conclusion of the agreements to its efforts to make our party submit to the views of N. Khrushchev's group.

This becomes even clearer when one realizes that on the basis of the top-level negotiations conducted in Moscow in December 1958 between representatives of the parties and governments of our two countries, these questions were concluded and the relevant agreements signed respectively on April 3 and July 3, 1959. Therefore it is clear that the Soviet leadership was exploiting the question of economic aid as a means of exerting pressure on the PPSh on the eve of its Fourth Congress, which was to be held in February 1961, in order to force it to renounce its Marxist-Leninist positions. It would seem that this was the "third sincere effort" made by N. Khrushchev to settle differences, to normalize relations, with the PPSh and the Albanian People's Republic.

The PPSh Central Committee, on January 14, 1961, again explained in a letter, with discretion and patience, where the truth lay, and declared its readiness to settle the differences in the correct Marxist-Leninist manner. The Central Committee stressed in particular:

> We are rightly astonished at the position adopted recently by the Soviet Government on these matters, and we cannot understand on what grounds it is asking unilaterally for a review of the aforesaid questions, discussed and decided at the highest level and settled conclusively. The Albanian party and Government have regarded and always will regard with satisfaction meetings of delegations of our two parties and our two governments at the highest level, or at any other level, for our party, our people, and our country are linked by eternal and unbreakable friendship with the CPSU, the Soviet people, and the USSR, but in view of the conditions under which the Soviet Government presents the questions, the PPSh does not consider it reasonable or opportune to send a top-level delegation. First because, as stated above, the matter at hand has been discussed and conclusively settled by the two parties, in full agreement and at the highest level, and, secondly, because the Soviet Government is raising these issues in an incorrect manner, which contradicts the spirit of relations between socialist countries and is thus unacceptable to us.

Time has shown that the PPSh fully understood N. Khrushchev's aims, his plans to make our party submit through economic pressure, to make economic aid contingent on approval of his opportunist line. It is clear that the Soviet leaders intended negotiations not to solve the economic questions at hand but to dictate the conditions for our party's submission. This is shown by the Soviet Government's letter to us on April 26, 1961, signed by First Deputy Premier Kosygin, which said in particular:

> After weighing all the circumstances, the Soviet Government is obliged to reexamine the question of future relations with the Albanian People's Republic. . . . The Soviet people and the peoples of the other socialist countries would not understand us if we, while depriving our country of material resources, should continue to satisfy the demands of the Albanian leaders who, to the detriment of the interests of the Albanian people, have trampled on elementary norms in their relations with the USSR and its government. . . . It is understandable that the Albanian leadership cannot expect in the future that the USSR will help it as it has in the past, with aid from which only true friends and brothers have the right to benefit. The Soviet Union deems it necessary henceforth to establish its relations with Albania on a new basis, taking into account the unfriendly policy of its leadership toward the Soviet Union and the other socialist countries. . . . As concerns future relations between our countries and USSR aid to Albania, these will depend entirely on the attitude adopted by the Albanian party.

The PPSh has made sincere efforts to put an end to differences with the Soviet leadership in a Marxist-Leninist manner.

Whoever studies the development of Albanian-Soviet relations, either through the excerpts we are reproducing or the correspondence exchanged between our two parties, will note that since the Bucharest meeting N. Khrushchev's group *has had the sole aim of making the PPSh capitulate* in order to impose its own views on it. In every letter from the Soviet leadership, in every "sincere effort" to improve relations, conditions are stipulated and pressure is exerted with regard to our party. This also is revealed in the excerpt of the letter we have just quoted.

On the other hand, the Central Committee of the PPSh and the Albanian Government have acted calmly and patiently, in the hope of barring the way to what N. Khrushchev and his intimates were deliberately preparing. This can be seen from the reply addressed by the PPSh Central Committee on July 6, 1961, to the CPSU Central Committee. In this letter our party expressed its opinion on the method of resolving differences between our parties, taking into account the objective concrete situation existing at this time:

> Certainly [states the reply] we are aware that to resolve these differences time and patience are needed on both sides as well as major efforts in order to create the conditions necessary to liquidate the negative phenomena which appeared a year ago in the friendly, fraternal, and, we can say without a shadow of doubt, more than exemplary relations previously existing between our two parties, countries, and fraternal peoples. First it is necessary to renounce the extension of the ideological differences existing between our two parties into the interstate domain, be it in the economic realm or in the political and military realm.
>
> Our party and government have never refused to begin bilateral talks on any questions. But we have noted and we note that for this the necessary conditions must be created, conditions of equality for both sides.

Nevertheless, the Soviet leadership headed by N. Khrushchev continued its dangerous practice of placing the PPSh in a position of inequality, of discrediting and discriminating against it, until at last, on August 24, 1961, it sent the PPSh Central Committee a new letter which closed all roads to negotiation and settlement of differences. Through this letter N. Khrushchev and his group embarked upon the road of the basest provocations and subversion. N. Khrushchev and his group transferred the ideological differences between the two parties to another realm, that of the security police, even going to the extreme of calling the leaders of the PPSh "agents of foreign intelligence services." This letter is in fact a prologue to what was said to the 22nd Congress, where N. Khrushchev made public before our enemies the disagreements in the socialist camp and in the international Communist and workers movement.

This was N. Khrushchev's "fourth sincere effort" to settle the differences with the PPSh, an effort which later at the 22nd Congress was made more explicit by his appeal for a counterrevolution in Albania. Therefore N. Khrushchev has consciously aggravated relations to the ultimate, leaving no way out. Nevertheless, the Central Committee of the PPSh, paying no attention to N. Khrushchev's provocations and monstrous calumnies, and realizing the great harm N. Khrushchev's actions were causing to the Communist movement in general, to the socialist camp, and to the friendship between the Albanian and Soviet peoples in particular, sent a new appeal to the CPSU to "examine calmly the situation which had been created." The response, approved at the Plenum of the PPSh Central Committee on October 12, 1961, addressed to the CPSU Central Committee which was to be elected by the 22nd Congress (and delivered to the Soviet Embassy in Tirana on November 11, 1961), states:

> Deeply concerned by the undesirable and extremely grave state of Albanian-Soviet relations at this moment, which originated in the brutal anti-Marxist actions of N. Khrushchev and his group, the PPSh and its Central Committee request the Central Committee of the CPSU to examine the situation which has been created and to take the necessary measures for its normalization. The plenum of the PPSh Central Committee is of the opinion that to cure this dangerous illness the urgent intervention of the CPSU Central Committee is necessary, a body in which the PPSh has had and still has unshakable confidence.

In this spirit, Comrade Hoxha in his speech of November 7, 1961, stated:

> The Albanian Party of Labor, with a clear and pure conscience, appeals to the Communist Party of the Soviet Union, appeals to the new Central Committee elected by the 22nd Congress, to judge with Leninist equity, with objectivity and composure and not in a unilateral manner, the situation which had been created in the relations between our two parties and our two countries. Our party has always been

ready, for the sake of the unity of the Communist movement and of the socialist camp, for the sake of the interests of our two countries, to settle existing differences. But it has always been and remains of the opinion that these questions should be settled justly and in the Marxist-Leninist manner, on the basis of equality and not of pressure and dictation. We place our hope and confidence in the justice of the Communist Party of the Soviet Union.

If the unity of the international Communist movement and the socialist camp were dear to N. Khrushchev and his group, if they were guided by the desire to settle differences and not to aggravate relations to the breaking point, if logic were to triumph over the runaway passion of the person who wants to have his way in everything, then one would stop to think. It is said that no one is so deaf as he who will not hear. And that is just what happened: Not only was the sound and sincere appeal of the PPSh not heeded, despite all that was said at the 22nd Congress of the CPSU, but things went even further — very much further — as far as the unheard-of act of breaking *de facto* diplomatic relations, which can be explained only by the logic of one who says: "I am everything, I do what I want, and I don't ask anybody's advice." The misfortune is that today this "I" finds himself at the head of the CPSU and at the head of the Soviet state, and his revisionist views and actions do harm which is immensely costly to the Communist movement in general, the socialist camp, and all mankind.

Numerous facts concerning N. Khrushchev's anti-Marxist positions toward our party and our country clearly indicate that he is acting deliberately against the PPSh and the Albanian people, against Albanian-Soviet friendship. But despite his vicious attacks and his anti-Marxist actions, N. Khrushchev and his group could not shake, even slightly, the granitelike foundations of the sacred friendship of our country with the glorious Soviet Union. Despite his unrestrained attacks, our party has always maintained a correct and principled attitude toward friendship with the Soviet Union, while in the USSR not a word can be read about our people's successes in the construction of socialism, as if there were nowhere on the face of the earth such entities as the Albanian People's Republic and the Albanian people. Instead there are cowardly attacks and the most banal calumnies against our party and our country. (Since the 22nd Congress some 150 different items have appeared in the central organs of Soviet propaganda attacking the PPSh.) In the Albanian press items are constantly being written about the successes of the fraternal Soviet people in the construction of Communism. The Fourth PPSh Congress was another clear indication that our party's line toward Albanian-Soviet friendship has remained steadfast and principled. "Friendship with the Soviet Union," states the resolution of the Fourth PPSh Congress, "has been, is, and always will be the cornerstone of our foreign policy." Our heroic party has forged it in the fire of the struggle for freedom, socialism, and peace. It rests on the principles of Marxism-Leninism and proletarian internationalism. Friendship with the Soviet Union will be further strengthened, and there is no force in the world which can undermine it. In the Soviet people and the CPSU our people have a cherished friend, just as the Soviet people have a loyal friend in our people and the PPSh. In the future as well our party will guard as a treasured possession our people's friendship with the fraternal Soviet people. It will struggle with all its might to strengthen it. Our unshakable conviction is that eternal Albanian-Soviet friendship will always triumph over the anti-Albanian actions of N. Khrushchev and his men.

The anti-Marxist positions of N. Khrushchev against the PPSh are the inevitable consequence of his abandoning the positions of Marxist-Leninist theory.

The facts indicate that all N. Khrushchev's "efforts" concerning the PPSh were and are aimed not at the settlement of differences but at the exacerbation of Albanian-Soviet relations. N. Khrushchev and his group, especially since the Bucharest meeting and thereafter, tried systematically and with ever-growing insistence: *first,* to align our party with their opportunist line and their anti-Marxist-Leninist attitudes toward the socialist camp; *next,* to silence it to prevent it from raising its voice against the anti-Marxist views and actions of N. Khrushchev; *then* to force the PPSh through pressures to submit; and *finally* to liquidate it or, failing this, at least to isolate it. Each of these stages has had its own methods and forms of struggle, which have also revealed the methods by which N. Khrushchev and his group seek to impose on others. The methods N. Khrushchev has employed and is employing in the struggle against the PPSh are the inevitable consequence of his desertion of the theoretical positions of Marxism-Leninism. They are the other side of the coin, a fact which better illustrates his opportunist and anti-Marxist activity.

Khrushchev's anti-Marxist attitude toward the PPSh is by no means accidental — it is *a link* in the chain of his activities against the socialist camp and against the international Communist and workers movement, which he is trying to push on to a profoundly opportunist and revisionist road, the dangerous road of unprincipled concessions to imperialism and bourgeois pacifism. With his views and his vehemence he has provoked great confusion in the ranks of some Communist and workers parties, and this has weakened their positions. This course discredits and compromises them. To achieve his anti-Marxist aims, N. Khrushchev, regardless of the consequences, stops at nothing and deliberately commits grave crimes which have caused and are causing very great harm to the entire world Communist movement, to the great cause of socialism and of Communism. In fact he is splitting the socialist camp and the international Communist movement. A striking proof of this is his unprecedented behavior toward the PPSh and the Albanian People's Republic. Only men who have lost all common sense can pretend that actions by N. Khrushchev and his group such as economic and political pressures and blockades against a socialist country like Albania — they went as far as to break diplomatic relations with the Albanian People's Republic — allegedly serve to consolidate the unity of the socialist camp and of the Communist movement! But does N. Khrushchev maintain such anti-Marxist attitudes solely toward the PPSh? Not at all. The anti-Marxist group of N. Khrushchev has committed many acts of blackmail against the PPSh. But does he direct these solely against our party? Is it solely against our party that he has committed blackmail and applied pressure through lobbying behind the scenes?

Each day N. Khrushchev and his anti-Marxist group are traveling further along a dangerous path. He is preparing new crimes, even more serious, against the socialist camp and the Communist movement. Our party, as is the case with Marxist-Leninists in all countries, is fully conscious of and concerned with the serious danger which threatens the cause of socialism as a result of the anti-Marxist views and actions of N. Khrushchev's revisionist group. While assuming full responsibility before the Albanian people and international Communism, the PPSh regards it as its lofty and principled task to wage, within the limits of its strength and capacities, a determined struggle for the defense of the purity of Marxism-Leninism and the solidarity of the socialist camp in a Marxist-Leninist manner, and only in a Marxist-Leninist manner. Only by a determined and principled struggle is it possible to defend Marxism-Leninism from revisionist attacks by N. Khrushchev and his group. Only thus is it possible to defend the Declaration of the 81 Communist and workers parties, which the supporters of N. Khrushchev now contemptuously regard as a document of "limited clauses" which "cannot have the desired universal value" (in other words, "a compromise and worthless document," as N.

Khrushchev called its draft in October 1960). Only thus can one defend the unity of the socialist camp and the international Communist movement, which is being trampled upon and seriously harmed by the anti-Marxist Khrushchev group. In vain do N. Khrushchev and his propagandists try, in a slanderous manner, to accuse our party of anti-Soviet feelings. Our party does not confuse the anti-Marxist group of N. Khrushchev with the great Soviet Union and the fraternal Soviet people. To be and remain a loyal friend of the Soviet Union does not mean to close one's eyes and blindly follow the anti-Marxist road of N. Khrushchev, when one knows that it leads toward an abyss and does great harm to the Communist movement, the socialist camp, and the interests and prestige of the Soviet Union itself. By struggling against the anti-Marxist views and actions of N. Khrushchev, the PPSh is struggling to defend Albanian-Soviet friendship. It is only on a rainy day that one gets to know one's friends, says an old proverb. Our party and our people have shown not only in words but in deeds, throughout their struggle, that they are faithful friends of the Soviet Union and the fraternal Soviet people, that they have been and will remain at the side of the Soviet Union, under all circumstances, whether pleasant or unpleasant. Such has been, is, and will be our unshakable attitude.

N. Khrushchev's propagandists seek to justify the attack launched at the CPSU 22nd Congress and all subsequent actions of the present Soviet leadership against the PPSh. But this is in vain. It is not a question of justifying but of explaining, because the people, Communists the world over, justifiably want to know: "Why is the PPSh being attacked so viciously? Why is N. Khrushchev provoking a split in the socialist camp and in the international Communist movement? Who benefits from it?" N. Khrushchev's group, instead of engaging in futile justifications, should have the Communist courage and Communist bravery, which only Marxist-Leninists have, to admit fully and to condemn publicly his anti-Marxist actions which bring harm to the PPSh, the international Communist and workers movement, the socialist camp, and the great cause of socialism and Communism.

DOCUMENT 27

Enver Hoxha's speech to his constituents, Zëri i Popullit, *May 31, 1962 (excerpts on international affairs).*

. . . What does the actual contemporary world situation indicate? To what do the facts and the course of events testify?

The forces of socialism, peace, progress, freedom, and true democracy are confronting the forces of darkness, war, oppression, and slavery — the forces of imperialism. In the forefront of the former stands the invincible, ever triumphant, and glorious socialist camp headed by the Soviet Union, while in the forefront of the forces of war, oppression, and reaction stands American imperialism, the head of world capitalism and the gendarme and enslaver of the people, and around it are all the forces of the reactionary bourgeoisie of the world — the forces of world capitalism. The latter are feverishly preparing a third world war, an atomic war. We must stay the hand of these forces before they commit this crime against mankind, and, should they initiate this crime, we must be fully in a position to bury them, so that they may disappear forevermore, leaving neither name nor trace behind. (*Stormy applause*)

We Albanian Communists, united with our people as a single body, are resolutely against war; we are resolutely for world peace. However, we believe that the imperialists are not seeking peace, because war is in their blood, because war is their motto, and because they are trying to kindle a war. Therefore, there is no sense in begging for peace. We must fight to win it. One cannot beg for peace; it must be won.

When we say that world peace is endangered, this means that someone is endangering it. Therefore, the one who is endangering it must be mercilessly unmasked. Accordingly, American imperialism, which is endangering peace, and all the warmongers of the world around it must be ideologically and politically unmasked without mercy. The imperialists are trying by all possible means to avoid this fatal unmasking, because this tears away their disguise, upsets their warmongering schemes, and obstructs them in their war preparations, and because it arouses the masses, increases the vigilance of the people, points out the evil, eliminates fatalism, demolishes the false slogans and illusions intended for the naive, increases the revolutionary drive of the masses and peoples who are fighting for freedom, and multiplies the might and the unity of the world proletariat in the struggle for its political, ideological, and economic rights. Any concession in this direction is a gain for the warmongers. The imperialists must not be permitted, even for a single moment, to step on green grass. We must see that the earth under their feet is scorched. Why should we make concessions in this respect? Neither Marx nor Engels, Lenin nor Stalin ever taught us such a thing, but rather the contrary. They have given the best example, crowned with success, of the merciless unmasking of capitalism and imperialism as well as of implacable opposition to revisionist, opportunist, and chauvinist theses, at a time when the world Communist movement was not as strong as it is today. Or should we, because we are now stronger, moderate our principled struggle, preserve the snake within our breast, and become generous toward the enemies of peace and Communism who are preparing a third world war, directed chiefly against the socialist camp? No. This is not permitted by Marxism-Leninism. This is not taught by the Moscow Declarations of 1957 and 1960. This is not permitted either by the present — which has been won — or by the future of socialism.

The Albanian Party of Labor and the Albanian people will resolutely march along the path pointed out by Marxism-Leninism because this is the only correct path. The might of the socialist camp, of which Albania too is a worthy member, is colossal. The forces of the world peace movement are so great that they are in a position to stay the hand of the imperialist aggressors and also fully to unmask them, ideologically and politically.

War is not made with flowers, but with arms; therefore, to avoid war, arms must be abolished. The Albanian people and the Party of Labor, united as a single body and standing resolutely for peace and against rapacious war, favor disarmament, the complete liquidation of nuclear weapons, the suspension of atomic tests, and the use of atomic energy — the great discovery of the century — only in science and for the good of mankind. It is for these reasons that we have supported and will support the correct proposals of the Soviet Union on this question. We have said and continue to say that general and complete disarmament, for the realization of which we should exert all our efforts, is the ideal of socialism. However, the achievement of complete and general disarmament is certainly not a job which can be easily and quickly done, because our enemies, the imperialist warmongers headed by the American imperialists — who do not wish to disarm — not only reject all the peaceful proposals of the Soviet Union and of our socialist camp, but they are increasing their armaments each day. This, of course, is being done in order to unleash war.

It is known that the countries of the socialist camp, despite the fabrications of imperialist propaganda, have never attacked nor will attack other people by armed force. However, it is clear to us that the imperialists are actually arming to attack and to destroy us, and not for defense, as they put it. Confronted with such a situation, is it permissible for us to be off guard or unarmed, or to allow modern Yugoslav revisionism to disrupt our unity and to becloud problems which are so clear, or to permit our doctrine to be distorted, or to indulge in hysterical appeals and flatter and caress the enemies? We think that these things not only must not be permitted but must be *fought against,* as well. The imperialists and their leaders, such as Kennedy and his associates, not only have not become more reasonable and have not given an inch, but, on the contrary, they are making furious assaults, are accelerating their armament, and are converting their countries to fascism and training fascist cadres of the Hitlerite type — such as the murderers of the OAS. They are preparing fascist coups against the Communist and workers parties in their countries to drive them underground and to destroy them, to strike at the democrats and patriots, and to prepare finally to ignite a war. The people, and chiefly the Communists, are aware of this. The American imperialists and their allies are being armed to the teeth. They continue the atom bomb tests, they will not accept either disarmament or the suspension of atomic tests, they have fully armed West Germany and their other partners, they have established military and atomic bases everywhere around the socialist camp, and their fleets, equipped with atomic rockets, are plowing the seas and oceans. Oppressive colonial war is going on in Laos, South Vietnam, South Korea, the Congo, Latin America, and many other countries of the world; indeed, in certain countries armed hot war is raging, while in other countries it is ready to start and only a spark is needed. The question of a German peace treaty and the conversion of West Berlin into a free, demilitarized city drags on year after year owing to the fault of the imperialists.

Thus everything attests to the feverish preparations of the imperialists, headed by American imperialism, to plunge the world into the wholesale slaughter of an atomic war. However, they will fail in all their plans because they are confronted by the invincible strength of the socialist camp and the world peace movement, which is vigorously acting to stay their hand.

It is for this reason that we, as all the other socialist countries, have kept and will always keep our powder dry so as to to be a position to thwart completely any attempt at aggression and any imperialist plot directed against our countries, peace, and freedom.

Dear comrades, Socialist Albania, a worthy and heroic member of the socialist camp and the Warsaw Pact, is a peace-loving and freedom-loving state, and through its struggle, efforts, and correct political positions, participates in and contributes to the strengthening of the socialist camp and the preservation of peace. Albania is a small state which is respected by the socialist, democratic, and progressive states and by all the simple and honorable people of the world, and they do this not without reason. The malefactors of the world, the imperialists and modern revisionists, hate the sight of Albania. But this hostility toward our people and our republic raises even higher the respect and increases the admiration of the people of the world for our country. This situation is linked to the fact that the balance of power in the international arena has radically changed since the victory of the great October Socialist Revolution, since the founding of the glorious Soviet Union. Now, with the formation of the socialist camp which includes 12 states within its bosom, socialism has been transformed into a world system extending from the Adriatic to the Pacific Ocean.

The mighty socialist camp has become the shield and the hope of all the progressive forces in the world, the bulwark of freedom and peace. Thrones and tyrants have been shattered, capitalist and reactionary regimes have been overthrown, fascist dictatorships have been destroyed, and colonialism is being demolished. All these transformations are such that imperialism today no longer rules the world, and can no longer do as it pleases. The crisis of capitalism is deepening with each passing day. Capitalism is being gnawed by great and inextricable contradictions. The establishment of the world socialist system, the disintegration of the colonial system, and the national liberation struggle of the people, which is spreading throughout the four corners of the globe, have deprived and are depriving imperialism of fabulous privileges and profits and are narrowing its sphere of influence, restricting its markets for speculation, and increasing and aggravating the internal and external class distinctions within the capitalist system. Opposed to this rotten system, which is heading toward an abyss and toward extinction from the face of the earth, stands the socialist system, which is daily and in every way being strengthened. It is flourishing, and it is being supported, defended, and embraced by the peoples of the world, the many millions of revolutionary throngs who are fighting for their national and social liberation. The epoch of imperialism has passed. World capitalism is in its death throes. But before its certain end, it is gnashing its teeth and, enraged, is threatening a third world war. Imperialism wants one of two things: either to force the progressive world, the socialist camp, the international working class, and the individuals and peoples who are struggling for freedom to submit to it and to the law of the jungle, or to unleash a war with the hope of re-establishing its savage domination on top of the ruins and the rivers of blood. But it is no longer as powerful as it was some 45 years ago, or even 23 years ago. Today there exists a force which can and which must stay its criminal hand. Under these conditions, it is entirely possible and logical, if done correctly, to stop the imperialists' plundering wars from becoming fatal. The peoples now possess colossal forces to prevent the unjust, aggressive wars of the imperialists. Therefore, the peoples must fight with all their strength to prevent the outbreak of war and to struggle for peace.

We Albanians do not view the struggle for peace as a struggle based on frozen, stereotyped formulas, and we are not the only ones who view it this way. We believe that the struggle for peace should arouse all the peoples in the world by applying all the great experience of the revolutionary struggle of the international workers movement and of the national liberation movement of the oppressed peoples against capitalism, against colonialism, and against fascism and for national and social liberation. We favor the struggle for peace and disarmament at the United Nations; we favor the struggle for disarmament and for the banning of nuclear weapons tests at Geneva. But we, and — together with us — billions of peoples in the world, cannot be satisfied with this much, especially when we see that the American imperialists and their lackeys are endlessly dragging out discussions in order to gain time in which to arm themselves to the teeth and to plunge the world into catastrophe. To allow the struggle for peace to come to the pitiful pass of discussions and meetings alone, and to expect the peoples to fold their hands and not to struggle with all their strength for their freedom and liberation, is neither just nor permissible. The struggle for peace is a complex and many-sided struggle. Why did the heroic Algerian people fight for seven years against the French colonialists? For their freedom, for their land, for their usurped rights, for their ancient culture. By destroying the French colonialists, heroic Algeria also made a worthy contribution to peace in the world. The Algerian people were forced by the imperialists to pass through this difficult road of untold misery; therefore, they deserve the respect and the greatest assistance of all the peoples who are struggling for peace. (*Strong applause*). The heroic feats of the fraternal Cuban people, led by the valiant Fidel Castro and his companions, who overthrew with their arms the hateful dictatorial regime of Batista, established the people's power by their heroic struggle and are successfully building socialism, thwarted the American armed intervention, and buried in the grave the counter-revolutionary bandits at Playa Giron, successfully and proudly resisted the terrible blockade of American imperialism, and have given a good lesson to the revisionist Escalante, who tried to undermine the revolution — are not all these a powerful contribution to the weakening of imperialism and the frustration of its plans? Are these not a priceless contribution to the strengthening of world peace? Fidel Castro and his companions did not and could not wait until they settled theoretically with the revisionists the question of whether to take power through violence or through peaceful means, until American imperialism was in the mood to disarm and Batista ready to give up his arms in order to give the Cuban people their freedom. The Latin American peoples and the Communist and workers parties of this continent will undoubtedly follow the example of heroic Cuba in their effort to take power in their own hands to throw off the chains of the Yankees and their lackeys, and to defend peace and mankind. (*Stormy applause, ovations*) Very significant was the act of the military fascist junta of Argentina, which did not show the slightest regard for the elections, the president, the parliament, or the political parties, but rather one morning eliminated them, liquidated them, and established a vicious military regime. The example set by Argentina will surely serve as a good lesson, although the examples of Hitler and Adenauer, who by one stroke of the pen and the sword made the German Communist and progressive parties illegal, are still fresh.

Is not the heroic liberation struggle of the fraternal peoples of South Korea and South Vietnam, who were savagely severed from their northern brothers and who are being savagely oppressed and bled by American imperialism and its lackeys in these countries, a great contribution to the defense of world peace? Is there some Leninist theory which prohibits the peoples from fighting for their freedom and their rights when the conditions are ripe in their countries? Is there some Leninist theory which tells the peoples who rise in revolt against a savage enemy armed to the teeth, such as American imperialism and world capitalism, to keep quiet, to disarm, and not to grieve or to annoy imperialism, "because we are now strong, because victory will sooner or later be ours, and the fig will ripen of itself and fall into our laps"? (*Laughter in the hall*) Is there a Leninist theory which separates and isolates the struggle of the peoples for disarmament and peace from their struggle for liberation, from strikes and demonstrations — such as those of the heroic Spanish people against fascist Franco and of the French workers against the presidential regime of De Gaulle and the fascist bands of the OAS — and from mass sabotage against the imperialist military preparations? No. Such Leninist theories do not exist.

To pass judgment and to make decisions on great international problems demands above all the energetic contribution of all individuals and peoples in the world, while the decisive role always rests with the socialist camp and its colossal economic, political, and military might. The unity of the socialist camp is and must continue to be the chief preoccupation and concern of the Communist and workers parties and peoples of the 12 socialist countries. This unity must become steel-like; it must be based on the principles of Marxism-Leninism and proletarian internationalism, full equality and independence of the socialist countries, and mutual fraternal assistance among them. This unity must be tempered in the struggle for the purity of Marxism-Leninism, because this unity is the foundation of our invincible might.

Fully convinced of the correctness of its line, our party is defending the sound unity of the socialist camp and the international Communist movement, the purity of Marxism-Leninism, the cause of socialism, peace, and the national and social liberation of the peoples, and the cause of the freedom and independence of our fatherland and the building of socialism in Albania. (*Stormy applause and ovations*)

It is very clear to Communists that modern revisionism is today a venomous weapon in the hands of world imperialism and capitalism in their efforts to harm triumphant socialism, to create splits, to undermine and weaken the socialist camp and the international workers movement, to prolong the life of capitalism, and to facilitate for imperialism the path of the struggle against socialism and Communism and against the peoples who are struggling for their liberation. The revisionists of the world are converging and are moderating the contradictions among themselves. The Marxist-Leninists cannot but take into consideration the activities of several years' duration of the traitorous and renegade Belgrade group and its close ties with American imperialism; they cannot forget their plots and innumerable diversions against the countries of the peoples' democracies and the Communist and workers parties of these countries and of the whole world. The Belgrade renegade group, in addition to other things, formulated its plan of global action in accordance with the program of the League of Communists of Yugoslavia, and this program has become the guiding line of modern revisionism in its struggle against Marxism-Leninism. Tito's declared intention is to liquidate "the camps," which, in fact, means to liquidate the socialist camp and to disrupt the unity of the Communist and workers parties of this camp. Under this tattered banner, all the renegades have thrown themselves against the socialist camp and against its unity and are anticipating the degeneration of the immortal, ever triumphant theory of Marxism-Leninism. Modern revisionism has, however, a shallow foundation. It is the irreconcilable enemy of Communism and of the broad masses of the peoples who support Communism and the Marxist-Leninist parties; therefore, its life is short. It is an infectious abscess, which will be eliminated by the surgeon's knife, and this surgeon, who will not allow the wound to become gangrenous, has sure and strong hands for such operations. This experienced surgeon is Marxism-Leninism. (*Stormy applause*)

The Communists of the world are acting in a revolutionary manner against this dangerous disease — revisionism — and will not allow this disease to infect our healthy body, because we have historic responsibilities to the peoples who base their hopes on the Communists. We have great tasks to fulfill, regardless of the sacrifices. In this struggle, we have laws defining our correct line — the laws of Marxism-Leninism, and the laws formulated by the Moscow Declarations of 1957 and 1960.

The righteous peoples of the world clearly understand that the modern revisionists aim at extinguishing the revolutionary vigilance of progressive mankind in the face of the dangerous threat of imperialist atomic war. They aim at disrupting the international Communist movement ideologically and politically, at checking the victorious momentum of the revolution, and at weakening the national liberation struggle of the peoples by diverting them from the correct path of the anti-imperialist struggle. This is what the Yugoslav revisionists have attempted for a long time and will always continue to attempt. The Titoist group has not only been unmasked before the world for its pro-imperialist policy, but it has lost out as well in its attempt to pose as the "leader of the neutralist group." Nor is the Belgrade group faring any better in its domestic affairs. To exonerate himself from the economic and political catastrophe of his "specific road to socialism," Tito has not hesitated to make threats, to chastise, and to appear as though he were going to act against those responsible for this internal catastrophe. But everyone knows who the culprit is and who is responsible. It will not be surprising in the least if one of these days the demagogical Titoist group should reveal more facets, indeed, of a more "dramatic" kind, by singling out one or two individuals as alleged culprits, and by sending these "culprits" temporarily into "golden confinement." The revisionists need sensational lies, because they believe that only thus do they present arguments to explain, with "sound reasons," the "positive" reversal of the Titoists.

By basing themselves firmly on the Moscow Declarations, the Communist and workers parties in the world and the Communists of the world will continue to unmask with still greater energy modern revisionism, which is the main danger to the international Communist and workers movement; they will rip off the mask of the Belgrade revisionist group and its master, American imperialism, and will burn all their cards in their hands.

Dear comrades,

The Albanian people are not alone on their glorious road, and they will never be alone. Albania has firm and faithful friends, the peoples of the Soviet Union first of all, the peoples of the Chinese People's Republic, and those of the countries of the peoples' democracies. This is an unbreakable friendship which will live through the centuries, and nothing can weaken it. (*Applause*) The Albanian people and their party have loved and defended, and will love and defend with all their strength, their friendship with the Soviet Union, their glorious liberator. (*Applause*) Our party teaches us to love the Soviet Union with ardent affection in happy times as well as unhappy times. The peoples of the Soviet Union know that it is the custom of the Albanian people never to betray a friend but to remain loyal to him to death. The peoples of the Soviet Union feel this warm and pure love, which with each passing day is more and more instilled in our country by the party. The Albanian people always identify themselves with the gigantic struggle of the Soviet peoples to build Communism, and they are daily studying their rich and manifold experience. Our love for the Soviet Union and the Communist Party of the Soviet Union, despite a number of existing difficulties for which we are not to blame, is at the core of our existence. Nothing has changed in this respect in our country. The victories of the Soviet Union are the victories of our people, who always rejoice at these victories. Let us march forward in this direction because this is the only correct road and the only internationalist road in the interests of socialism and Communism, in the interests of our two countries. (*Applause*)

Our people and party also feel great love for all the fraternal peoples of the socialist camp and heroic Cuba. We are bound to them as flesh to bones, and there is no force on earth which can separate us. The hostile forces which are acting against this alliance will be destroyed and will have no success. The final victory will be ours. This victory will be achieved by our Marxist-Leninist parties: the Communist Party of the Soviet Union, the Chinese Communist Party, the Albanian Party of Labor, and the other Communist and workers parties of the socialist camp and of the whole world — thanks to the correct implementation of Marxism-Leninism and the resolution of the disagreements existing between us through the Marxist-Leninist way alone and with Bolshevik methods. We are fully confident of this.

The socialist camp is now a powerful reality. It is the sun which illuminates, nourishes, and develops the revolutionary forces of the world for a better and more prosperous life, and the sun which scorches and burns and turns into dust and ashes the old world of misery, poverty, and ignorance, the hateful world of the warmongering, oppressive, and bloodthirsty imperialists and capitalists.

The Albanian people and the Albanian Party of Labor have very dear and loyal friends, in happy times and in unhappy times, in the great Chinese people, the glorious Communist Party of China, and comrade Mao Tse-tung. (*Stormy applause and ovations*) This boundless friendship, based on Marxism-Leninism, is flourishing and will be strengthened through the centuries in the interests of our two peoples and parties, in the interests of the socialist camp and international Communism, and in the interests of world peace. How ridiculous and shortsighted are all these imperialists and revisionists who measure the great influence of China on international problems by its number of atomic bombs, and the immortal and life-giving friendship between our two countries by the distance existing between us. In the century of Leninism, the distance which separates Albania and the Chinese People's Republic does not play a large role. Distances are no longer an obstacle since the triumph of Marxism-Leninism in a number of small and large countries in the world, the creation of the glorious camp of socialism, and the creation and the consolidation with each passing day of the international Communist movement.

The Chinese People's Republic is one of the decisive factors for world peace and the liberation of the peoples. The imperialists are denying the great People's China of over 700 million people its legitimate rights in the United Nations. But this does not minimize the great influence of China in the international arena. The Chinese People's Republic will take its seat in the United Nations because — as everyone says — "nothing can be resolved in the world, none of the international issues confronting mankind can be settled properly, without the participation of China." This fact is more than true. Then to whom must we turn to realize this great truth, whose denial has become a habit and a routine which is repeated like a sacred rite year after year from the rostrum of the United Nations and, as soon as the annual meeting of this organization is over, the same steps are taken as before? Should we turn perhaps to the American imperialists and the Yugoslav revisionists, who accuse the Chinese People's Republic of being a "warmonger" and "yellow menace" which "wants to overrun and dominate the world," and other shameless fabrications?

However, matters go even further than this. The American imperialists and their satellites in Asia are feverishly preparing for war against the great People's China and the Korean, Vietnamese, and Laotian peoples and against all the other peoples of Asia and the world. They are engaged in military build-ups around these peace-loving socialist states; they have occupied territory in these states; they are causing the blood of the peoples of South Korea and South Vietnam to flow; they have plundered Taiwan — the territory of China; they have established and are continuing to establish military bases; they are increasing their battle fleet, strengthening their military pacts, and so forth. The defense of China's rights is one of the greatest and most sacred struggles in which progressive and peace-loving mankind should presently engage. We Albanians, in sincerely loving and defending People's China, are championing a great, clear-cut, and urgent cause. In so doing, we are discharging our lofty internationalist duty toward a fraternal socialist country. World peace, which is being gravely endangered by the imperialists, cannot be defended without simultaneously fighting with resolution and without balking or hesitation to secure and defend the rights of the great Chinese people in the international arena.

However, the great and glorious China could not care less about the imperialist threats and the revisionist slanders. It is rapidly marching forward in the construction of socialism by holding high the Three Red Banners. Led by its glorious Communist Party, headed by Comrade Mao Tse-tung, it is firmly defending the purity of Marxism-Leninism, championing and aiding the liberation of the peoples from enslavement, and striving for the happiness of its people, for the defense of peace, for disarmament, and for the strengthening of the socialist camp and the international Communist and workers movement. (*Applause*) The Albanian people are grateful to and cordially thank the Chinese people and their Communist Party for the great aid they are rendering to them in the successful building of socialism.

The Albanian people have many friends in the world who sympathize with, love, defend, and assist them. This is a great and valuable mainstay for a small people who have never committed evil against anybody and who respect others as they wish to be respected in return. The policy of our party and government has been and remains unchanged — friendship with all the peoples of the world and good and correct relations with any state which desires to have such relations with our state. We neither want to interfere in their internal affairs nor permit others to interfere in our internal affairs. We want to live in peace with them provided they desire to do the same. We want to live as good neighbors, to have normal diplomatic and trade relations with our Balkan neighbors and with Italy, and to live with them on the basis of peaceful coexistence. We are convinced that this is in the interest of all and not only in our own interest. We enjoin our neighbors to cease their hostile activity against our country, because they have not had and never will have any success. If anyone thinks that he can impose upon little Albania because of the size of his state or his military strength or through blackmail and threats, he is committing a grave error and will suffer great disillusionment.

In the past, Bismarck, the so-called Iron Chancellor, could easily reject the just claims of the "ignorant shepherds in the wild Albanian mountains who were living in caves or thatched huts"; as he put it, he could with one blow of his sword sever from our country a part of its body, Kossovo, and give it to others. But now, in the century of Leninism, the sword of the chancellors has been broken and will be broken if they should raise it again. (*Stormy applause*)

The Albanian people harbor great love for all the freedom-loving and peace-loving peoples. They have particular respect for the Arab people, the peoples of Latin America, and Asian and African peoples who are selflessly fighting for freedom, independence, and the consolidation of their victories against colonialism and neocolonialism, against every intrigue of the American imperialists and their partners and lackeys. Our people wholeheartedly sympathize with all the European peoples who are fighting against fascism and war and who are struggling for peace, freedom, and democratic rights. They are developing friendly relations with them, and they will spare no efforts to develop these relations further.

On all international issues, the Central Committee of our party and the Government of the Albanian People's Republic have never failed to maintain a correct position, and they will firmly continue to maintain their correct position in the interests of socialism and world peace. (*Applause*) . . .

DOCUMENT 28

Albanian governmental statement on CMEA meeting, Zëri i Popullit, *June 6, 1962 (complete text).*

According to reports from press agencies, an agreement has been reached among the other member states of the Council for Mutual Economic Assistance to "hold a meeting" in Moscow June 6, 1962, to "discuss economic cooperation" among the member countries of this council.

The Government of the Albanian People's Republic, despite the known fact that the Albanian People's Republic is a founding and effective member of the Council for Mutual Economic Assistance, has received no official notification of this meeting and has not been invited to attend.

The Council for Mutual Economic Assistance was set up by the governments of eight European socialist states, including the Albanian People's Republic, in order to develop economic cooperation among themselves "based on the principles of complete equality, respect, sovereignty, national interests, and mutual benefit and fraternal assistance." This, as the Charter of the Council says, "contributes to the development of the people's economy as rationally as possible, to the improvement of the people's living standard, and to the strengthening of the unity and cohesion of these countries."

The Government of the Albanian People's Republic has always remained faithful to the aforesaid aims and principles, and has spared no efforts to implement them. The Council for Mutual Economic Assistance is a joint organization of the eight European socialist countries, and any council meeting should take place with all member countries participating. Article 6 of the Council Statutes states explicitly:

"The Council Session includes *delegations from all member countries* of the Council." Furthermore, the rules of procedure (Rule No. 23) state that "the Council Session can exercise judicial power only if attended by *delegations from all member countries* of the Council."

The June 6, 1962, meeting, which has the character of a Council Session and which is being held without the participation of the Albanian People's Republic, has been convened in open contradiction to the indisputable clauses of the Council for Mutual Economic Assistance Charter and its procedural rules. By acting in this way, the organizers of this meeting have consciously violated the Charter of the Council and the basic principles of the relations among socialist states.

The Government of the Albanian People's Republic, noting this arbitrary action which has nothing in common with socialism, states that the meeting of the Council for Mutual Economic Assistance, to be held in Moscow June 6, 1962, without the participation of the Albanian People's Republic, is unlawful and that whatever decisions it may adopt under the circumstances will not be binding on the Albanian People's Republic. The entire responsibility for these unjust actions and this open violation of the Council Charter and the principles of relations among socialist countries rests with the governments of those member countries in the Council for Mutual Economic Assistance which commit such actions.

The Council of Ministers of the Albanian People's Republic
Tirana, June 6, 1962

DOCUMENT 29

Albanian governmental statement on Warsaw Pact meeting, Zëri i Popullit, *June 13, 1962 (complete text).*

It has been publicly made known that the Political Consultative Committee of the Warsaw Pact held a meeting in Moscow on June 7, 1962, without the participation of the Albanian People's Republic. The German problem and that of West Berlin were examined at this meeting.

The Government of the Albanian People's Republic, as noted on previous occasions, points out that lately separate meetings have been convened within the framework of the Warsaw Pact without the extension of an invitation to the Albanian People's Republic, which is a member with full and equal rights in this organization.

The Warsaw Pact is a pact of friendship, cooperation, and mutual assistance, concluded among the eight European socialist states having equal and sovereign rights, whose lofty aim is the common interest, based on correct principles. The Albanian People's Republic, as all the other member states, is a contracting party to this pact. The third article of this pact explicitly states that "the contracting parties, guided by the desire to consolidate peace and international security, will consult among themselves on all important international issues relating to their common interests." For this purpose "and in order to examine questions regarding the implementation of this pact, as stated in Article 6, a Political Consultative Committee is to be formed in which *each member state of the Pact will be represented by a member of the government or by another specially appointed representative.*" On the other hand, neither any article nor the spirit of the Warsaw Pact gives any one state or a group of member states the right to call meetings of the Political Consultative Committee or of any other organ of the Warsaw Pact without the participation of all the contracting parties.

Under the circumstances, the meeting of the Political Consultative Committee of the Warsaw Pact held in Moscow on June 7, 1962, without the participation of the Albanian People's Republic constituted a brutal violation of the Warsaw Pact and of the sovereign rights of a member state, the Albanian People's Republic. Acts of this kind are impermissible and unprecedented in the relations between states in general and among contracting parties, especially among socialist states, of such an important pact in particular. They show that in the eyes of the leaders of certain member states of the Warsaw Pact, the agreements and treaties binding these countries to socialist Albania, which has been and will remain ever faithful to the great cause of the socialist camp and Communism, can be ignored and unscrupulously violated.

The Government of the Albanian People's Republic declares the meeting of the Political Consultative Committee of the Warsaw Pact, held in Moscow on June 7, 1962, without the participation of the Albanian People's Republic, and any other meeting which may be held in the future within the framework of the Warsaw Pact without the participation of the Albanian People's Republic, to be illegal because it is in flagrant contradiction to the Warsaw Pact itself and also to the principles of the relations among socialist states. It is a grave act, consciously and maliciously carried out not only against the Albanian People's Republic but also against the interests of the Warsaw Pact organization itself and the entire socialist camp. The responsibility for this most grave action and the decisions taken at the separate Moscow meeting rests with its organizers and with the governments which participated in the meeting.

The Albanian people, who suffered and made severe sacrifices during their struggle against the Nazi German invaders, are directly and very much concerned about a correct solution of the German problem and that of West Berlin. The Government of the Albanian People's Republic and the Albanian Party of Labor have expressed very clearly their position on these problems at the regular legal meetings of the Political Consultative Committee of the Warsaw Pact, where it was jointly decided that all the member states of the pact would take a coordinated stand on the solution of these problems in harmony with the interests of the socialist camp, the interests of the German people, and the security of Europe and the world. This principled and consistent attitude of the Albanian People's Republic has been expressed, *inter alia,* in the statements of the representatives of the Albanian Government and of the Albanian Party of Labor at the meeting of the Political Consultative Committee held in Moscow in March 1961 and at the meeting of the Communist and workers parties of the Warsaw Pact countries held in Moscow in August 1961, as well as in other known statements. The Albanian Government and the Albanian Party of Labor know nothing of the talks which have been held, or which are being held, among the various governments on the German problem and that of West Berlin, and they bear no responsibility for these talks. However, they are always in favor of settling these problems in harmony with the above-mentioned principles and interests.

The Government of the Albanian People's Republic resolutely protests against the separate meeting of the Political Consultative Committee of the Warsaw Pact, held in Moscow on June 7, 1962, without the participation of the Albanian People's Republic, and declares that the entire responsibility for this illegal meeting and these repeated unfriendly actions toward the Albanian People's Republic rests with the governments of the other member states of the pact which organized this meeting and consciously commit such reprehensible acts against the Albanian People's Republic, against the Warsaw Pact itself, and against the unity of the socialist camp.

The Council of Ministers of the Albanian People's Republic
Tirana, June 12, 1962

DOCUMENT 30

"The Rumpus over Tito's 'Reversal' and the Undeniable Truth," Zëri i Popullit, *June 30, 1962 (complete text).*

The recent rumpus over a certain "reversal" by Tito has again raised the question in the West "of guarantees to ensure the independence of Yugoslavia against world Communism." However, to one who has attentively followed American policy regarding Yugoslavia and the maneuvers of Tito's clique in its role as splitter of the socialist camp and the international Communist movement, it is clear that in fact there has not been and cannot be any "reversal." Nonetheless, American senators, who do not know everything known to the State Department, have insisted upon new "guarantees." Indeed, there was talk that a decision was made, presumably by the American Senate, to cease aid to Yugoslavia, and that Kennedy himself subsequently intervened to have this decision rescinded. Quite a comedy.

Just the same, there was no lack of "guarantees." Koča Popović, Yougslav secretary for foreign affairs, made an official visit to Washington, where he was cordially received by the State Department's chief, Dean Rusk, and by President Kennedy himself. The news agencies reported that these "agreeable and interesting talks," as Popović termed his talks with Dean Rusk, dealt with the European Common Market, Berlin, and all the matters and relations between West and East, United States aid to Yugoslavia, and, perhaps, the possibility of a visit of Marshal Tito to Washington at the end of this year. In a word, the watches were set, and other guarantees for the future were offered and accepted.

According to the Yugoslav news agency TANYUG, American Ambassador to Belgrade George Kennan, who is no second-rate person but is known as a "first-rate American specialist on Eastern affairs," declared that "there was no reason to doubt that Yugoslavia was a completely independent nation and that it would continue in the future as well to maintain this position."

In the end, "guarantees" were given by Kennedy himself. At his press conference June 7, he defended his government's policy regarding Yugoslavia, describing the aid to Tito's clique as being "in the national interests" of the United States. In this situation one could not hope for more. A word to the wise is sufficient.

It is therefore clear that the fuss over a certain "reversal" by Tito, which began after his Split speech when for purposes now known he implied that allegedly certain "changes in Yugoslav policy" were taking place, was only a sleeping pill for those who close their eyes and ears to the fact that this was nothing but a diabolical maneuver.

Belgrade, as well as Washington, speaks with pride about the alleged "independence" of Tito's clique. Lies from beginning to end! When one realizes that for the imperialists the dependent and enslaved countries are the socialist countries, while Taiwan, South Korea, South Vietnam, and so forth are proclaimed champions of independence, it is not difficult to draw the conclusion that Yugoslavia is as independent as these classic examples of imperialist enslavement. Nobody envies such "independence."

However, this is nothing new. The words "independence" or "socialism," which recur frequently in talk about Yugoslavia, are nothing but masks used by the Belgrade revisionists and their friends to conceal the truth. Here everything is clear: If these masks fell, the Yugoslav revisionists would become useless.

Close American-Yugoslav collaboration in all fields is so vast and obvious that it cannot be concealed. The history of American-Yugoslav relations speaks eloquently of the "independence" of Yugoslavia and the role entrusted it. For this, it is enough to mention only a few facts of recent years. Tito stated at the Seventh Congress of the League of Communists of Yugoslavia:

> We received economic and military aid from America at a time when this aid was most needed, i.e., during the time Stalin was exerting political, economic, and propaganda pressure against our country. This aid greatly helped us to overcome the great difficulties which we were encountering then.

Let us assume for a moment that it was only for a certain period that the Yugoslav revisionists received economic and military aid from the United States. Why was it, then, that the American imperialists granted this aid to Yugoslavia at that time? The "aid" given by the American imperialists to Yugoslavia may be considered about as disinterested as the "aid" given to the monarcho-fascists to oppress the Greek people and the present "aid" given to the reactionary cliques in the Far East. History does not disclose any cases in which the imperialists gave any disinterested aid. American aid has always and everywhere been aimed at placing the countries which receive this aid in economic and political dependence on American imperialism. Yugoslavia could not be an exception.

It is known that United States political, military, and economic aid to Yugoslavia does not relate to a certain period only, but has been continuous and has assumed ever greater proportions.

According to the November 27, 1961, issue of *U.S. News and World Report,* Yugoslavia received $3,500,000,000 in military and economic aid from the United States from 1948 to the end of 1961. The world press and various periodicals do not fail even to publish tables listing the years when this "aid" was accepted, and the amounts according to the categories in which the "aid" was given, sometimes openly and in many other cases not so openly, sometimes directly in dollars, at other times in surplus agricultural products, and in many cases in arms. Conclusions as to why this "aid" was given in specific circumstances are not lacking either. Thus, for example, during the counterrevolution in Hungary, in the organization of which the Yugoslav revisionists actively participated, and after Tito's speech at Pula in which he furiously and slanderously attacked the Soviet Union and all other socialist countries, Tito's clique received large sums of dallars. On November 3, 1956, an agreement to furnish surplus American agricultural products valued at $98,300,000 was signed between Yugoslavia and the United States, and at the end of December of the same year the American Government delivered to Yugoslavia a check for nearly 6,000,000 dinars.

In 1957, when the League of Communists of Yugoslavia refused to sign the Moscow Declaration of Communist and workers parties of socialist countries and instead promulgated its revisionist program, as a counterweight to the whole international Communist and workers movement, the United States gave to Yugoslavia another large loan. A report from AFP, dated November 22, 1957, said: "There have been clear indications that the Yugoslav position [the reference is to the Moscow Declaration] has caused great interest in the State Department. The impression reigns in Washington that the Yugoslav president, Marshal Tito, has once again insisted on showing his independence of the Communist bloc." And a few days later, on December 8, 1957, Tito received James Riddleberger, then U.S. Ambassador to Yugoslavia. On the following day *The New York Times* wrote that "Tito regarded Yugoslavia's refusal to sign the Declaration as a further proof of its continued independence." These are not simple coincidences. But this is not all.

On June 15, 1958, Tito made his infamous speech in Labin, the chief aim of which was to defend the revisionist nature of the LCY program, which had been scornfully rejected by all the Communist and workers parties in the world, and to give a new tone to the slanders against the Communist and workers parties of the socialist countries. The speech was applauded by the imperialist camp, and only three days after Tito spoke, on June 18, President Eisenhower praised him because he was endeavoring to "create centrifugal forces" within the socialist camp and expressed at the same time his readiness to strengthen ties with Yugoslavia.

At this time, on June 19 to be exact, Robert Murphy, then Assistant Secretary of the State Department, said: "He [Tito] has never wavered in his determination to protect the independence of Yugoslavia from interference into the internal affairs of his country." Certainly, after all these declarations, dollars should be forthcoming. And so it happened. On June 18 a Yugoslav military mission paid a visit to the U.S. Defense Department and asked for a speedier delivery of military equipment. *Newsweek* magazine wrote at the time that the United States had decided to give Yugoslavia "political priority with regard to American aid, as well as a loan." Further on it stressed: "The United States will give Yugoslavia 10 to 15 million dollars in special aid, as well as 80 to 90 million dollars' worth of surplus agricultural products, and is, in addition, considering the question of direct arms sales to it."

What does this prove? Total harmony between Yugoslav and imperialist policies is by no means accidental. This policy pursued consistently by Belgrade is enthusiastically approved and accepted by the imperialist camp. Indeed, the Yugoslav leaders, assisted by this sort of "aid," have been hastening along this path step by step. "In reality," *The New York Times* wrote, "the flexibility shown by the United States in the past in connection with its aid to Yugoslavia was reasonable as far as our interests are concerned."

The year 1959, like other years, did not pass without American aid to Yugoslavia. It is a matter of public knowledge that in that year it amounted to $156,300,000.

But it was in 1960 that the catastrophic consequences of the economic policy of the Yugoslav revisionists were clearly evident. It was at the time when the Yugoslav leadership was preparing to proclaim a new system of foreign trade and rate of foreign currency exchange which would open wider horizons to American capital in Yugoslavia. At that time, the revisionists declared that they were in need of $350,000,000 to meet the difficult payments situation. Owing precisely to this situation, the American State Department sent Under Secretary of State Douglas Dillon, who is one of the most powerful members of the New York Stock Exchange, to Belgrade. After his talks with the Yugoslav leaders, Dillon declared: "The United States has, for a number of years, tried to help Yugoslavia in order to strengthen it as an independent state. . . . Yugoslavia and the United States have reciprocal, constructive relations, which are reflected in economic collaboration and in the ever increasing exchange of persons and of joint programs for technical development." Later he said: "We are continually looking for fields of collaboration in which our common efforts will contribute to increasing the standards of living and the security of our peoples." The extent of improvement in the well-being of the Yugoslav people as a result of American-Yugoslav collaboration is better known to Dillon. This was made clearer by Tito's latest speech in Split. But it has also been previously made clear by the American press. On December 26, 1961, UPI, the American news agency, gave the following picture of the Yugoslav situation:

> The past years have seen changes in Yugoslavia which have pleased the West, but, on the other hand, they have displeased the Kremlin. Forcible collectivization has been practically eliminated by the Tito regime. The economy is adapting itself more and more to Western trade. Some aspects of free trade in industry have begun to appear on the scene. . . . The government is encouraging travel inside the country and abroad. Some Yugoslavs still have "a Marxist consciousness." They still like to show (and this only pro forma) that they are good socialists and that they are against the capitalist system. This is why they often join the leaders of the Afro-Asian bloc in their differences with the United States and Western imperialism.

After all this, is it possible to say that American aid has been poured into Yugoslavia without economic and political concessions?

But we were speaking of Dillon's visit. As expected and as happened on other occasions when American personalities visited Belgrade, Tito's clique received some more dollars. This is a fact. It is also a fact that the Belgrade revisionists then took on other commitments to the "generous uncle." Why all this generosity?

"Why is it that the government of the United States, while trying to fight other Communists throughout the world, is helping to strengthen the Communist regime in Yugoslavia? Why is the United States ready to help a so-called 'determined Marxist' in Europe, but breaks off relations with the government of Cuba?" Thus asked the *U.S. News and World Report* in one of its issues last year. It replied: "Americans should ask: Do Tito's interests coincide with our interests? Thus considered, our policy toward Tito is correct." So there. Everything is clear. But as was said at that time, this article was written to calm a few nearsighted people in America who, having heard Tito's phraseology, suspected that he might be a real Communist. These people, it will be recalled, raised their voices over the 130 fighter planes which the Kennedy administration was going to give to Yugoslavia, and over the training of Yugoslav pilots at American military bases. Some went so far as to say that the Kennedy administration would re-examine American policy toward Yugoslavia. But these voices were soon silenced. On October 18 of last year, Dean Rusk said at a press conference that he "did not have the slightest doubt that the policy of American military aid to Yugoslavia has helped it to preserve its independence vis-à-vis the Soviet bloc" and that "since 1948 Yugoslavia not only has preserved its independence but has also been a source of division within international Communism." Moreover, desiring to remove any doubts concerning the position maintained by the Yugoslav revisionists at the conference of nonaligned countries in Belgrade, the chief of American diplomacy deemed it necessary to declare that "the position taken by the Yugoslav delegation at the conference of nonaligned countries does not indicate that Yugoslavia has departed from its independent path."

The various speeches and declarations of Rusk, in spite of being camouflaged in diplomatic language, well reveal the services which the Yugoslav revisionists render to American imperialists, especially their divisive role in the international Communist movement and their undermining activity in the national liberation movements. Very significant also, in this connection, is another declaration of Rusk on February 5 of this year. Polemicizing with Senator Paul Kitchin, chairman of a special House committee,* the Secretary of State said: "American aid given under Eisenhower and Kennedy strengthened Yugoslav independence and made Tito an important example of a successful withdrawal from Soviet imperialism." He clarified this statement further when he said that "the Kennedy administration is convinced that Yugoslavia does not participate in the international Communist plot to undermine the independence of other countries."

Rusk called "the first decision" to aid Yugoslavia "very imaginative and daring" and concluded by saying that "the results exceed our expectations." Or, as his assistant Harlan Cleveland said recently, while speaking of the aid given by the United States of America to Yugoslavia: "It seems to me that we have been well rewarded for our money."

The facts that we have cited speak for themselves. They show that Tito's clique has put itself entirely at the service of American imperialism. This has been proved not only by the aid, statements, and praise which the American imperialist chiefs have lavished and are lavishing to sustain and encourage the Belgrade revisionist clique, but also by the revisionist policy and activities of the Yugoslav leadership, which always pursues the same aim: to divide the socialist camp and to prolong the life of imperialism. This is proved by its adherence to the Balkan

* Reference is to Representative A. Paul Kitchin of North Carolina. [W.E.G.]

pact which links it to NATO. This is provided by Tito's unconcealed attacks against the socialist camp, which he compares with the imperialist bloc, and by countless slanders against the Soviet Union and the socialist system. It was Tito who described the decision of the Soviet Government to resume nuclear testing as "something that alarms the entire world to a very great degree" and the Council for Mutual Economic Assistance as "a serious obstacle" to economic cooperation, comparing it with the Western Common Market. This is proved by the way in which the capitalist system is enhanced and gilded, and by the preaching of revisionist views on war and peace, coexistence, revolution, the nature of imperialism, and so forth.

In whose service and favor the policy and activities of the Yugoslav revisionist leaders are developing is clearly shown by their hostile attitude toward the struggle pursued by the oppressed people to liberate themselves from the American imperialists and other colonialists as well as toward the revolutionary struggle of the working class against the capitalist exploiters. Is this not proved by the attitude of the Yugoslav revisionists toward the Congolese struggle for independence, where they considered American intervention in the Congo as a "factor contributing to stabilization of the situation," as a very important and valuable factor? Is it not solely to the benefit of the American imperialists and to the detriment of the struggle for freedom of the Latin American peoples that the Yugoslav revisionists glorify Kennedy's plan for subjugation through the so-called "Alliance for Progress," and preach that American imperialism "has begun to understand that times are changing" and that it is allegedly "ready to straighten out and correct its errors"? Was it not to the benefit of the American imperialists and to the detriment of the struggle for liberty by the patriotic Laotian forces that the Yugoslav revisionists lauded the efforts of Washington to settle the Laotian problem because American imperialism "is really concerned over Laotian peace and neutrality"?

The Tito clique does not, in fact, differ from the other allies of the United States except for the "socialist" or "neutral" mask which it is forced to wear and the special role it plays, as the "Trojan Horse," to split the socialist countries and the international Communist and workers movement. One thing is true: If Rusk and the other American statesmen are forced to admit some elements of the truth to calm those who do not know what is known to the State Department, a thousand other activities are carried on to preserve this mask.

In the present situation, when the Yugoslav revisionists have suffered a complete fiasco in their economic and political system and when their activities have been greatly unmasked on the international plane, Tito's group must maneuver with cunning and find new methods to split the socialist camp and the international Communist and workers movement. Today it is in the interest of the American imperialists and modern revisionists to restore the red tint to the faded mask of Tito's clique. This is what they are doing. While on the one hand Koča Popović goes to Washington to strengthen ties with the United States and coordinate Yugoslav policy with that of the American Government, on the other hand Tito in his Split speech pretends that he is making "socialist" corrections in Yugoslavia. These maneuvers are an integral part of the great international plot of imperialist reaction, now commonly known, which is directed against socialism and peace.

Thus to weaken one's vigilance in the face of the danger represented by the Yugoslav revisionists and, even more, to have illusions about them, believing that they are, so to speak, correcting themselves and again taking the right road, that socialist elements in Yugoslavia are being strengthened, that socialism is being built there, etc., is to do great harm to the socialist camp and the international Communist and workers movement.

The international Communist and workers movement has emphatically stressed that it is the duty of Communists throughout the world to unmask consistently and to the very end the activities of the Yugoslav revisionists. This is the first condition for consolidating the unity of the socialist camp and international workers movement and strengthening the anti-imperialist front, peace, and socialism.

But what is in fact happening? Whereas the facts undeniably confirm that not only is socialism not being built in Yugoslavia but, on the contrary, an extensive and all-round degeneration toward capitalism is in process, the modern revisionists are using all their power to prove the contrary. However, allegations that "Yugoslavia is a socialist country," that "Yugoslavia is building socialism," and so forth, are only a bluff which does no harm to the capitalists but enables modern revisionists of all shades to embrace Tito and justify this after a fashion in the eyes of the others. In brief, Tito's clique is the bridge which links other revisionists with imperialism as long as this cannot be done openly and directly. Attempts to hide this truth are useless, even though different "arguments" are used to explain, on the one hand, why the imperialists help "socialist" Yugoslavia and, on the other, why the revisionists are strengthening their ties with the traitorous Tito clique. If "socialism is being built in Yugoslavia," how does one explain the help given by the imperialist Americans to the Tito clique? According to this logic, either the imperialists are not imperialists any longer but have begun to take an interest in the building of socialism, or socialism is not being built in Yugoslavia and the imperialists are in fact helping to restore capitalism. One or the other. The modern revisionists categorically deny the second; therefore they accept the first. Then, let them say so.

If "Yugoslavia is a socialist country," then one is entitled to ask: How many kinds of socialism are there in the world? According to the logic of the modern revisionists, there must be two kinds of socialism: a socialism which is the enemy of capitalism and against which the imperialists fight with all their savagery, and a socialism which is harmless to capitalism, which the imperialists aid without reserve. "Yugoslav socialism" is therefore harmless to capitalism; otherwise the imperialists would not help it. The truth is that Tito's "socialism" assisted by American imperialism has nothing in common with socialism. The Tito clique uses it only as a mask. It would be the same if we said that there were two kinds of imperialism: one bad, the enemy of the working class and all workers, an exploiter, and bellicose, and the other good, concerned with the well-being of the working class and all workers, a liberator of peoples and peace-loving. However, for Marxist-Leninists there are not two kinds of socialism, just as there are not two kinds of imperialism.

Modern revisionists find it difficult to justify why they so generously offer a hand to Tito. To befriend him they must trample upon the 1960 Moscow Declaration, which qualifies Yugoslav revisionists as traitors to Marxism-Leninism. But recently the modern revisionists let it be understood that they have decided to do even that. After all, did they themselves not say the day after the signing of the 1960 Moscow Declaration that this historic document, written and signed by representatives of 81 Communist and workers parties, was a compromise document? Here now are the consequences. Compromises do not last long. The revisionists have therefore trampled upon the 1960 Declaration, even on the point considered most essential: the position on Yugoslav revisionism.

Naturally those who oppose what was jointly decided and clearly written in the 1960 Moscow Declaration need to do some more maneuvering.

Of course, this is only a question of tactics. At the present state, the modern revisionists are forced to "keep their distance" from the Tito group, which has been seriously compromised by its obvious ties with imperialism. However, this "keeping their distance" does not change anything essential, that is, the ideological conciliation which unites revisionists in their struggle against Marxism-Leninism. This "keeping their distance" does not stop the mutual and noisy declarations of love and collaboration. On the other hand, the Belgrade revisionists are not such simpletons as not to understand "the necessity" of this "keeping of distance." This is what the "Trojan Horse" was waiting for: Make a breach in the wall, and the rest follows. That is what happened in 1956. However, events in Hungary, where Tito's clique was caught with its hands in the bag organizing the counterrevolution with the American imperialists, somewhat complicated the situation. One learns lessons from errors. The job has now begun on the basis of a broader plan.

Thus, under the guise of "peaceful coexistence" and "normal state relations," the process of fusion has begun. Statements regarding "normal relations" have been succeeded by those regarding "good relations," which, in turn, have been followed by countless exchanges of delegations, the expansion of economic and cultural relations, and so forth. In a word, "fruitful and many-sided" collaboration has begun with the aim of uniting and consolidating the forces of modern revisionism in their struggle against Marxism-Leninism. This process is at the moment in full swing and will become more concrete in the future.

"The fig leaf" which is still being used to pretend that "we have conflicting ideological views with Yugoslavia" is torn away by other slogans on "socialist Yugoslavia" and affirmations of "a unity of views on the most important questions of international policy." What remains to be done is the total conciliation not only in politics but also in ideology and objectives.

Recently one hears another "reason" for extending a hand to Tito. It is said that the American imperialists are trying to exploit present economic difficulties in Yugoslavia and organize a "counterrevolution" there. This argument continues: It is therefore right and in accordance with Marxism that in the face of such a danger, regardless of what was said in the 1960 Moscow Declaration, a policy of rapprochement be adopted toward Tito in order to "save" him from the "danger" emanating from imperialism. Thus one hears a very pleasant story: The imperialists are going to overthrow Tito. Why? In order to restore socialism? That is all that now remains to be said, and everything comes out into the open. However, it is still early for this. Besides, there is no reason for saying everything. The revisionists especially take great care not to say everything.

How long this will continue is of no great importance for the moment. The clear and determined position of the international Communist and workers movements toward the Tito clique is an obstacle with which the modern revisionists cannot fail to reckon. However, the revisionists have not calculated the consequences of their reconciliation with Tito. Simple logic leads to the conclusion that as long as the Tito clique is tied up with the imperialists, reconciliation with it is a step toward reconciliation with the imperialists. Whatever the modern revisionists do, whether they make up completely or still keep some "distance," whether they speak of "differences" on certain questions or even make certain "comradely criticisms" in the direction of the "Yugoslav comrades," it does not change at all what was said by the 1960 Moscow Declaration: The Yugoslav revisionists are traitors to Marxism-Leninism, and their further unmasking is the indispensable duty of the Marxist-Leninist parties.

For this reason Comrade Enver Hoxha was fully justified when he stated in his speech to his constituents that the "international Communist and workers parties, all the Communists in the world, basing themselves firmly on the Moscow Declarations, will continue with still greater force to unmask modern revisionism, to tear off the mask of the renegade group of Belgrade and its master, U.S. imperialism, and to burn all their cards in their hands."

DOCUMENT 31

"Modern Revisionism to the Aid of the Basic Strategy of American Imperialism," Zëri i Popullit, *September 19 and 20, 1962 (excerpts).*

On August 7, 1962, the head of the Yugoslav revisionists, Tito, granted an interview to the American journalist Drew Pearson, of the *Washington Post.* In this interview, which was published in our issue of September 18, 1962, Tito once more reveals his true nature as a renegade from Marxism-Leninism and a lackey and seasoned agent of American imperialism in the struggle against Communism, against the national liberation movement, and against world peace, as the imperialist intermediary attached to the revisionist group of N. Khrushchev.

Each day facts and events clearly show that imperialism, headed by American imperialism, is becoming increasingly aggressive and belligerent. Recently American imperialism, through the agency of Kennedy, Rusk, and others, once more proclaimed as its "basic strategy" the liquidation of the socialist countries and the revolutionary national liberation movement of the peoples and the establishment of the world hegemony of American imperialism. To attain this basic objective, it is feverishly struggling by every means and in every direction — economic, political, military, and ideological.

In all their attitudes and all their activity, the modern revisionists — first and foremost the traitorous revisionist Tito clique — contribute greatly to the realization of this strategic plan of imperialism, headed by American imperialism. Tito's recent interview testifies to this.

Tito denies the division of the world into two opposing systems, makes no distinction at all between them, and expresses regret at the deterioration of the "unity" of the capitalist world and the creation of the world socialist system, which he identifies as a military-political bloc. Tito openly denies the fundamental contradictions of our time — between socialism and capitalism, between the proletariat and the bourgeoisie, between oppressed peoples and imperialism, between the forces of peace and those of war, between the forces of democracy and those of reaction. Thus he preaches the renunciation of any war against imperialism and reaction, the renunciation of all revolutionary and national liberation movements. In this interview Tito frankly exposes the supreme aim of the revisionists: the integration of socialism with capitalism, the establishment of the complete domination of imperialism over the world.

On the one hand Tito preaches the transformation of the aggressive and belligerent character of imperialism and declares that the leaders of imperialism have become "sensible" and "peaceable" and that they "express the aspirations of humanity"; he openly undertakes to defend the policy of war and aggression of the imperialist powers, in particular American imperialism, and greatly concerns himself with the prestige of the U.S.A.; thus he recommends to them that in order to heighten this prestige, they take the initiative in banning atomic weapons. He praises the economic potential of the U.S.A. to the skies, etc. On the other hand, Tito slanders the peaceable foreign policy of the Soviet Union and the other socialist countries by representing it as a militarist policy allegedly formulated by military circles; he puts the economic and political organizations of the socialist countries and those of imperialism on a par and underplays the magnificent successes of the Soviet Union.

Playing the part of a "Trojan horse," Tito tries in his interview to drive wedges into the unity of the socialist camp, in particular the friendship uniting the Soviet and Chinese peoples.

As the leading spokesman of the views and goals of the modern revisionists, Tito also openly shows in his recent interview the objective toward which the revisionists should now be advancing. People have not forgotten the speech he made at Pula in November 1956. At that time he was the first to call on the modern revisionists, on those who openly declare themselves as such and those who disguise themselves, "to come out of their shells" and to engage in a more active struggle to bring about the triumph of the revisionist line, to carry the struggle against "Stalinism" and "dogmatism" through to its conclusion, and to liquidate courageously the consequences of the "personality cult." This was the path Tito recommended to all modern revisionists. The N. Khrushchev group and its followers have resolutely followed this path, never hesitating to use every means and method, from demagogy and intrigue to plots, interference, pressure, blackmail, and open threats.

This was the first step. In his recent interview, Tito urges the revisionists courageously to take the second step, to advance boldly toward rapprochement and open reconciliation with the imperialists, toward "economic and political integration" with the capitalist world, in other words, to follow the path of submission to imperialism. In his interview Tito frankly tells the revisionists that "our expectation is economic integration" and that "after economic integration comes political integration." He also tries to provide a "theoretical" basis for this revisionist path.

It is interesting to see that in his interview with the American journalist, Tito takes on the role of interpreter of the views and opinions of N. Khrushchev to the imperialists. He presents N. Khrushchev as a pacifist who is firmly, and with every means, supporting rapprochement and friendship with the American imperialists. He expressly told the American journalist that he knows Khrushchev well; that he knows his opinions; that he has more or less the same point of view, the same goal, and the same tactics; that they understand each other; and that he was convinced that a rapprochement could be achieved with him. Tito therefore recommended that the American imperialists be patient and not "dramatize things" because the devil is not as black as he is painted.

It is also interesting to note that the N. Khrushchev group has not replied to Tito's interview, that it has not contradicted Tito's interpretation of N. Khrushchev's opinions, tactics, and aims. This is significant. It means that N. Khrushchev and his group approve of what Tito said in his interview. This attests once again to the fact that they are in complete agreement with the views and actions of this seasoned agent of imperialism.

It is thus important that we should dwell in greater detail upon the analysis of the revisionist views expressed in Tito's interview, linking them closely with all the points of view and concrete actions of the modern revisionists.

1. *Champions of the imperialist policy of war, aggressions, and oppression*

The chief preoccupation of the revisionists has been and remains to convince Communists and peoples that imperialism has changed its nature as oppressor, exploiter, and aggressor; to convince Communists and peoples that they should renounce revolutions and national liberation struggles and thus justify their opportunist and pacifist policy which in no way serves the interests of the peoples but brings grist to the mill of bourgeois imperialism. . . . This revisionist line has found striking expression in Tito's recent interview. In this interview he said in particular:

> Why is it necessary for people to fight at present; over what issues? . . . In his time Hitler had the crazy idea of dominating the world. But among sane persons, among persons who are conscious of the aspirations of mankind, I see no grounds for such a concept of struggle. The world has outlived the period when one went to war because of economic problems. History has known a long series of wars, from looting by highwaymen to colonial conquests. But at present the countries of Asia and Africa are no longer colonies; they are no longer territories over which the great powers would quarrel for a share, because former colonies have now become independent countries. Productive forces have reached a high level of development in the advanced countries. So for them it is no longer a question of oc-

cupying a country in order to ensure for themselves the means of production, because they can produce them themselves and in sufficient quantity. . . . Further, wars hinder the integration in the world. . . . Thus war is an absurdity for which there is absolutely no need. But it looms on the horizon today because people are armed to the teeth and because they do not know what to do with these arms. . . . It is equally absurd to leave military circles to determine and recommend to governments and peoples what they should do.

These theses of Tito form the basis of the reasoning of the Yugoslav revisionists on the fundamental problems of our time — the problems of the struggle between two opposing social systems, of the struggle for peace, of the struggle of peoples against colonial oppression and exploitation, of the struggle of the working class and all workers against capitalist domination, and so forth. They are an adaptation, outlined in white, of the "basic strategy" of American imperialism. They are also a franker and more advanced presentation of the substance of all modern revisionist viewpoints on the main problems of current world evolution.

Has the aggressive, warlike nature of imperialism changed?

One of the main questions dealt with by Tito in his interview is that of war and peace. Dealing with this problem, Tito repeats his familiar theses that imperialism no longer represents a danger; that it is no longer an agency and a source of aggressive wars. According to the revisionist Tito, there is at present no reason for war because "the world has outlived the period when war was waged because of economic problems"; because "from all points of view war between states is at present absurd"; because imperialism has radically changed its nature and is no longer imperialism; it is no longer the source of aggressive wars because the imperialist countries, as he himself says, have reached a high degree of productive development, are assured of everything in sufficient quantity, and consequently have no need for conquest. (!) Furthermore, according to Tito, there is at present no danger of wars being unleashed by the imperialists because the imperialist countries are headed by "sane" and "peaceable people" who "express the aspirations of mankind," such as Kennedy and associates!

With some slight differences it is in these waters that the revisionist group of N. Khrushchev is also sailing. One now knows the dangerous opportunist illusions spread by the N. Khrushchev group that one presumably can now achieve a "world without wars, without arms, and without armies"; that Eisenhower, Kennedy, De Gaulle, and other leaders of imperialism are said to stand for peace; that the imperialists, with the means made available by disarmament, could aid the economic and cultural development of backward countries, etc. In the article, "Essential Problems in the Development of a World Socialist System," published in *Kommunist,* No. 12, August 1962, N. Khrushchev says almost openly that at present there is no longer any danger of aggressive wars on the part of imperialism against the socialist countries; that the imperialists have renounced war as a means of resolving contradictions between the two systems; that "sensible Western personages" (in other words, the leaders of imperialism) "subscribe more and more to a realistic solution." "The imperialists," N. Khrushchev continues, "have taken seriously our appeal for competition in economic development. . . . We are gradually drawing the capitalist countries into peaceful competition between the two systems." According to N. Khrushchev, the imperialists have now completely renounced military preparations for aggressive wars against the socialist countries and are "tending to mobilize their whole potential for the struggle against the world socialist system in the economic, political, and ideological fields." N. Khrushchev reaches the conclusion that "at present the problem poses itself as follows: Which system will prove to be the most vital? In other words, which system will give people, in the shortest time, greater material and spiritual benefits? It is precisely in this sphere, it would seem, that the sharp battles between socialism and capitalism will take place."

From what premise does N. Khrushchev reach the conclusion that there is allegedly no longer a danger of imperialist aggression against the socialist countries? As he says in his own article, it is based on the premise of a change in the balance of power in the international arena in favor of socialism. He argues from the fact that "the imperialists cannot fail to see that in the development of modern arms, which corresponds to the latest achievements in science and technology, the socialist camp not only is not lagging behind but is in several respects ahead"; that although the imperialists "do not renounce war against the socialist countries in the military field, war leads them to an impasse, because both sides, namely the socialist and capitalist countries, have at their disposal powerful nuclear armed forces"; that under such conditions the imperialists cannot hope in our time to "settle by war the historic rivalry between socialism and capitalism"; that the imperialists do not do this willingly, but are forced into it "by the new balance of power in the international arena which has been created as a result of the growth of the power of the socialist system."

It is more than true that the balance of power in the international arena has changed in favor of socialism; that the world socialist system has now become a colossal international force; that the Soviet Union has modern war weapons and is, in several respects, superior to the imperialist powers. This is indeed a factor which the imperialists cannot fail to reckon with: a factor which restrains them, which obliges them to reflect at length before deciding on aggressive actions against the countries of the socialist camp. But can one draw, so lightly, the conclusion reached by N. Khrushchev that imperialism has now already renounced or is renouncing its aggressive aims against the socialist countries and is seriously engaging in peaceful competition with socialism? No, not at all.

While N. Khrushchev and his followers seek to convince people that the imperialists have allegedly renounced or are renouncing their efforts for an aggressive war against the socialist countries and are seriously engaged in economic competition with socialism, representatives of imperialism themselves have openly declared and are declaring that the whole strategy of imperialism, particularly United States imperialism, is imbued with the idea of preparing for aggressive war against the Soviet Union and the other socialist countries, that they believe war in general and nuclear war in particular to be the sole means of settling international problems. They do not trouble to conceal the essential aim of their policy: the extinction of the socialist system and the establishment of the world hegemony of imperialism, with American imperialism at its head.

Facts daily prove that the imperialists are not merely talking about war against the socialist countries, but are making practical preparations for it. The unbridled arms race which has assumed colossal proportions in the imperialist countries, the encirclement of the socialist countries by a thick network of American military bases, the strengthening of the aggressive military blocs of imperialism and the feverish intensification of their activity, the rebirth and arming of revanchist militarism in West Germany and the attempts to put Japanese militarism back in the saddle in the Far East, the creation of hotbeds of war in various parts of the globe so as to pass thereby from local wars to a world war, primarily against the socialist countries, and so forth, testify eloquently to these facts.

Within the framework of this strategy of imperialism and of its preparations for war, a number of dangerous actions undertaken by American imperialism in recent times can also be explained, such as the latest explosions of American nuclear weapons in the atmosphere, the war in South Vietnam, the incitement of Chiang Kai-shek to attack the Chinese People's Republic, the dispatch of American armed forces to Southeast Asia, the continual provocations in Berlin, the barbarous bombardment of Havana and the preparations of plots for fresh aggression against socialist Cuba, the sabotaging of the disarmament negotiations in Geneva, the continuation of intrusions by American U-2 spy planes over the territory of the Soviet Union and the CPR, President Kennedy's decision to call up 150,000 United States reservists, and many others.

After all these facts concerning the aggressive activity and war preparations of imperialism, who is to give us a guarantee that the danger of imperialist aggression against our countries no longer exists? Who is to give us a guarantee that the imperialists will not reckon differently and that one fine day they will not undertake a senseless military venture against the socialist countries, as Hitler did in World War II? There is no absolute guarantee of this.

The danger of war at present is also real because of the fact that the arms race is continuing at a feverish pace, that weapons are being increasingly improved, and that in these conditions, as has been proved by specialists and by life itself, war may break out even for accidental reasons such as errors which may be made by the men in control of the weapons of war, breakdowns in the warning apparatus, and so on.

We know also that military quarters exert an ever-growing influence on the policy of the imperialist countries. In his article, N. Khrushchev himself is obliged to admit that in the imperialist countries there are "sworn enemies of socialism," "madmen," "people who have lost their common sense," who openly declare that they "would rather die under capitalism than live under Communism." And these people are not just anybody. They are high military and political figures who head the governments and military staffs of imperialism.

We cannot fail to mention here that it was only three months ago that the N. Khrushchev group itself "drew attention" to the danger of an aggressive war by imperialism against the socialist countries. In the message addressed to the Soviet people on June 1, 1962, concerning the decision to increase the price of meat, meat products, and butter, it was stated, among other things: "We do not live in outer space. As long as imperialism exists, the danger of new wars also remains. It is no secret that international reaction, with the U.S.A. at its head, is rattling the saber, feverishly pursuing the arms race, and nursing plans for a surprise attack with rockets and nuclear weapons against the USSR and the other socialist countries. And its politicians and generals speak openly about all this. What is more, the President of the U.S.A., Mr. J. Kennedy, has also spoken openly of this. He has stated: 'In certain circumstances we might take the initiative in a nuclear conflict with the Soviet Union.'"

One may legitimately ask how this statement by the N. Khrushchev group can be reconciled with what Khrushchev wrote in the magazine *Kommunist,* No. 12. Has imperialism in the last three or four months changed so radically as to renounce its aims and aggressive actions against the Soviet Union and the other socialist countries? It would be difficult to believe this. It seems that at the time the N. Khrushchev group required one interpretation, while at the present time it requires another. This is not the first time that the N. Khrushchev group juggled with the principles of Marxism-Leninism, subordinating them pragmatically to its daily objectives.

The views expressed by N. Khrushchev in his recent article in *Kommunist* are in flagrant contradiction to the Leninist teachings on imperialism and to the program documents of the international Communist movement — the Moscow Declarations of 1957 and 1960. The 1960

Declaration clearly emphasizes that "the aggressive nature of imperialism has not changed," that "as long as imperialism exists, the basis for aggressive wars also exists," that "the peoples of all countries know that the danger of a nuclear third world war is not yet past," and that only "the world victory of socialism will finally remove the social and national causes of wars of all kinds." Proceeding from these tenets and from the policy and practical activity of the imperialists, the statement sets forth the task "not to permit the underestimation of the danger of war" and emphatically states that "particularly high vigilance is now, more than ever, required of the peoples."

For what purpose did N. Khrushchev need assertions that the imperialists have allegedly renounced preparation for aggression against the socialist countries and have accepted seriously the call for peaceful economic competition with the socialist camp? It appears that he needs them to justify his opportunist policy of rapprochement and open reconciliation with imperialism, of the establishment of broad economic and political collaboration with the imperialist countries, on which we will dwell in greater detail later. At this point we would only point out that N. Khrushchev's views are very dangerous to the interests of the security of the socialist countries and of world peace.

It is well known that at the present time — as was stressed in two Moscow Declarations — as a result of the growth of the forces of peace throughout the world and especially as a result of the strengthening of the world socialist system, headed by the Soviet Union, a real possibility has been created for preventing another world war and the local wars unleashed by imperialism. Conviction concerning the possibility of preventing imperialist wars bolsters the faith of the peace-loving peoples in their strength, makes them optimistic about attaining the goal in their struggle for the defense of peace, and increasingly mobilizes them in the struggle. However, in spite of the great changes which have taken place in the balance of power, in spite of the new possibilities for preventing war which have been created, the danger of war and the possibility of its being unleashed by the imperialists have not been eliminated. As long as imperialism exists there is no absolute guarantee that there will be no war. To stress on the one hand the possibility of preventing war and on the other the danger of its being unleashed is hardly the same thing as frightening people, throwing them into panic and uncertainty. It is rather to make them conscious of the real situation existing in the world, to keep high their vigilance and preparedness so as not to be taken unawares, so as to stay the hand of the imperialist aggressors in time.

The struggle to safeguard and consolidate peace is inseparable from the struggle to unmask imperialism — in particular, American imperialism, which is the principal bastion of aggression and strife in the world. The peoples must be made to understand clearly where the threat of war comes from and who is threatening the peace; otherwise their struggle for peace will be illusory and devoid of aim. To talk of peace in the abstract without unmasking the imperialist warmongers and, even more, to create illusions as to the "good peaceful designs" of imperialism and its leaders, as the N. Khrushchev group does, to say that imperialism has today renounced or is renouncing aggression against the socialist countries, and so on — all this is very dangerous since it lowers the vigilance of the peace-loving peoples, leads to the weakening of the defensive might of the socialist countries, which is the determining factor in the safeguarding of world peace, weakens the struggle of the peoples against the imperialist warmongers, and leaves their hands free to carry out their aggressive plans more easily.

Adversaries of the anti-imperialist national liberation struggle of the peoples

The aggressive nature of imperialism, headed by American imperialism, appears not only in its hostile activity against the socialist countries but also in its aggressive actions against other countries and peoples and against world peace in general. Every day it commits aggressive acts in various parts of the world; every day it seriously threatens the peace and security of the peoples. Everywhere, in Asia, Africa, and Latin America, in the struggle against the revolutionary and progressive movement in Europe, can be seen the bloody hand of American imperialism. Life itself rejects the absurd allegations of the revisionists that the aggressive and warlike character of imperialism has changed, that the very economic basis of the unleashing of imperialist wars has now been eliminated, that imperialism has renounced economic expansion, as the renegade Tito would have us believe. . . .

Despite blows to the colonial system, the imperialists are applying every effort and using every means to preserve colonial exploitation in the newly liberated countries. They are seeking to retain former positions, primarily economic and military, and to link the new states of Asia and Africa to their aggressive policy. To this end they are using every means and every method, from colonial warfare, as in Laos and the Congo, to the corruption of national bourgeois leaders. The imperialist powers, under the guise of aid to underdeveloped countries, are endeavoring to retain their over-all power in these countries and to transform their independence into purely formal independence. Even in the countries from which the colonialist powers have been obliged to withdraw, they have remained by means of new forms of domination such as neocolonialism, military infiltration, etc. The imperialists are constantly initiating colonial wars against the peoples of Asia, Africa, and Latin America. Not a year passes without the colonialists' starting a war in some region of the world. . . .

These facts show that imperialism makes wide use of aggressive war, that colonialism has not yet expired, that to maintain its positions it stops short of nothing. But the very fact of the existence of these pacts, the very fact of the unleashing of aggressive wars by imperialism, reveal its fear of the national liberation movement, reveal that the national liberation struggle has developed very much and has been extended, that it has become an irresistible force, a major factor of our time for the destruction of imperialism, for the progress of mankind, and for the consolidation of the cause of peace.

Naturally, the revisionists are not so blind as not to see this reality. But they desire to come to the aid of imperialism by reducing the vigilance of the peoples and by splitting the ranks of the anti-imperialist national liberation struggle. If at the present time, as Tito claims, there are no longer any colonies or colonialism, if the highly developed imperialist powers allegedly no longer need conquests and expansion because they themselves produce all they need, then, according to his logic, it is no longer necessary for these oppressed people to struggle for their national liberation, to consolidate their independence, and to develop their economies independently of imperialism. Through these theses, therefore, the revisionist Tito, as a devoted servant of imperialism, tries to convince the peoples to abandon the national liberation struggle, to cease resisting the policy of neocolonialism conducted by the U.S.A. and the other imperialist powers. He recommends that these peoples "collaborate" with imperialism, accept "aid" and "credits" from it, because it nurtures no evil designs against them. Briefly, he recommends that they submit completely to imperialism. The most outstanding example of this is provided by Tito's group itself, which has so far obtained more than $5,000,000,000 from the U.S.A. and other imperialist powers.

But the Yugoslav revisionists do not limit themselves solely to the ideological and theoretical field. They are also working intensively in the practical field. Under the mask of "positive neutrality," Tito's clique has tried to draw the neutral countries onto the United States imperialist bandwagon; it has tried to stifle the anti-colonialist and anti-imperialist spirit of those countries which have only just won their freedom and independence in order to make them deviate from the road of rapprochement with the countries of the socialist camp. More than once the "Galeb" of the chief of the Yugoslav revisionists has crossed the seas and oceans to transport this "neutral" missionary of United States imperialism to various countries of Asia and Africa whenever the interests of imperialism demand this. Now that the national liberation struggle of the Latin American peoples is shaking the American continent, a new cruise of the "Galeb" to these parts is being prepared.

In the same way, the views and actions of N. Khrushchev's revisionist group and its supporters are doing great harm to the cause of the liberation of the peoples and to their anti-imperialist national liberation movement. They are imposing conditions on the struggle of the oppressed peoples and are making it dependent on the question of general and complete disarmament. They preach that "disarmament is the prime condition for the success of the independence struggle," "the most important factor in the liberation of the colonial peoples," and even that it is "the main objective of the peoples struggling for national liberation." This means *in fact* that the subjugated peoples must renounce the national liberation struggle and struggle only for general and complete disarmament, which, according to the N. Khrushchev group, will ensure the peoples liberty and national independence "through negotiations." (!) These are nothing more than beautiful dreams and harmful delusions.

There is no question that general and complete disarmament is to the advantage of all the peoples of the world, including those struggling for liberty and national independence. It is precisely for this reason that the correct proposals of the Soviet Government on disarmament have found support from all progressive mankind. But life and facts have shown, and continue to show with each passing day, that the imperialists are putting up fierce resistance to disarmament, that they have systematically rejected and continue to reject any reasonable proposals and have sabotaged and continue to sabotage all disarmament negotiations. In these conditions it is a crime to put a brake on the struggle of the oppressed peoples for their national liberation from the colonial yoke of imperialism, to condemn them to live in untold suffering and misery, while awaiting with folded arms the achievement of general and complete disarmament. As was clearly stated in the Moscow Declaration of 1960, the decisive factor in the liberation of the oppressed peoples is their resolute struggle against the imperialist-colonialists: "they win sound victory on the basis of the powerful national liberation movement." This is the commonly held view of the whole international Communist movement on this question.

Contrary to the wishes and advice of the revisionists, many peoples in Asia, Africa, and Latin America, who are fighting with rifle in hand against the imperialist occupiers, cannot throw down their arms and wait for freedom until the imperialists accept disarmament. They must arm themselves to disarm the imperialists occupying their countries.

By directing itself against imperialism, by weakening its positions, and narrowing its sphere of domination, the national liberation movement of the oppressed peoples is one of the main forces in the struggle for peace and is an effective and important factor in imposing disarmament on imperialism. Thus these peoples are, through their struggle, making a direct contribution to the maintenance and strengthening of peace. At the same time, they are supporting and upholding all movements for peace and all actions in the interest of peace and against the aggressive and warmongering plans of imperialism, which constitute a grave threat to all peoples. For its part, the peace partisan movement has the task of giving unreserved support with all its strength, to the national liberation movement of the oppressed peoples. The national liberation movement and the struggle for peace and disarmament are two fronts in the struggle against the same enemy — imperialism.

The attempts by the N. Khrushchev group to wean the peace partisan movement away from the support it ought to give to the national liberation struggle of the peoples and to subject the latter completely to the policy of disarmament, attempts which were once more clearly evident at the World Congress for Peace and Disarmament in Moscow last July, weaken both the national liberation movement and the peace movement by doing great harm both to the cause of the liberation of the peoples and to that of world peace.

At the present time the imperialist powers, with the U.S.A. at the head, are exerting great efforts to maintain by new methods and forms the colonial exploitation of the peoples of the former colonies and to consolidate their economic, political, and military positions in the newly liberated countries; they are trying to drag these countries along in their wake and to set their ruling circles against the socialist countries. To this end the imperialists are trying to establish military dictatorships, their own puppets, in these countries. They are trying to buy off various elements of the national bourgeoisie and put them at the service of their own interests. On the other hand the N. Khrushchev group and its supporters, by distorting the Leninist principle of peaceful coexistence, are also supporting by every means certain reactionary elements and bourgeois circles in the former colonial countries, such as reactionary Indian circles which in their foreign policy are ever more openly expressing tendencies to draw closer to the imperialists and adopting unfriendly attitudes toward the socialist countries, while in domestic policy they are persecuting the democratic and progressive forces of their country and leaning ever further toward reaction. The N. Khrushchev group, while seeking to weaken the defensive might of the socialist countries — as, for example, in the case of the People's Republic of Albania — has even gone so far as to sell Indian reactionary circles arms and airplanes, which are in fact used to oppress the Communists and progressives and for armed provocations against the socialist countries.

It is thus clear that, although the N. Khrushchev group tries to pose as a supporter of the national liberation movement of the peoples, in fact its viewpoints, actions, and attitudes do not help at all in strengthening the struggle against imperialism and for freedom and national independence; on the contrary they weaken it, render difficult the struggle of the progressive and anti-imperialist forces, and encourage the pro-imperialist and anti-socialist reactionary forces in the newly liberated countries.

Tito clarifies his position

Even the concrete problems of contemporary international life, whose solution rightly concerns all the peoples of the world, are being intentionally complicated by the Yugoslav revisionists, who place on an equal plane the policy of the imperialist countries and the policy of the socialist countries in order to protect the imperialist and to place the responsibility for the tension in international relations upon the socialist countries.

In his interview with the *Washington Post* correspondent, the leader of the Yugoslav revisionists exposes his positions and openly supports imperialist policy, with regard to the German problem and the problem of Berlin as well as the question of disarmament.

It is known that the N. Khrushchev group, with a view to justifying its rapprochement with the traitorous Belgrade clique, has started making a great noise to the effect that the Yugoslav viewpoint on these questions allegedly "is fully compatible with the foreign policy of the USSR"; that Yugoslavia allegedly supports the proposals of the Soviet Union, the GDR, and all the other socialist countries on the question of the peace treaty with Germany and the solution of the

West Berlin problem by transforming it into a free and demilitarized city; and that Yugoslavia supports the Soviet proposals on disarmament.

But in his recent interview Tito makes his position very clear to those who might not have understood it correctly. (!?) He says: "The question of Berlin is still the problem of the great victorious powers in World War II, the Soviet Union, the U.S.A., Great Britain, and France, who are the ones who must settle it. And because this question is in their province, I do not visualize particular possibilities of its settlement. In my opinion, this question should be left to the German people themselves to settle." This roundabout and "too principled" solution means in fact that the Berlin problem would never be settled. The view that "this question should be left to the German people themselves to settle" is in practice nonsense, demagogy, a smoke screen thrown up before the eyes of naive people, and an "argument" for further deception in the hands of those who are supporting the Tito clique. There is only one way to solve the Berlin problem: firm and immediate implementation of the proposals of the Soviet Union to sign a peace treaty with the two German states and, if this is impossible, with the GDR only, and simultaneously to transform West Berlin into a free demilitarized city. As for the solution of the German problem, this is, indeed, a problem of the German people themselves, as long as two states exist in Germany with different social and political systems. This aim would be served by the signing of a peace treaty with both German states, which is not even mentioned by Tito in his interview. Tito's obscure viewpoint is only an "amicable" retreat, an echo of the positions of the American imperialists and their allies with regard to alleged "free elections," which are being mentioned now and then by imperialist propaganda in connection with the settlement of the German question. Tito thinks that it is time to change his stand on this question, too, to aviod making the American imperialists or Adenauer angry.

On the subject of Berlin Tito goes even further. He encourages the imperialists to hold to their positions when, in reply to another question by Drew Pearson, he says: "Khrushchev has given broad interpretations to his former positions on the subject of Berlin, and the whole question has eased considerably." From this and from the whole tone of the interview it can clearly be seen that Tito is in favor of an "easing" of the Berlin question, of concessions in this direction in order to draw out its settlement. From their point of view, the foreign policy of the Yugoslav revisionists fully corresponds with the policy of the N. Khrushchev group.

Tito openly defends the positions of American imperialism on the question of disarmament too. Not only does he not say a word in condemnation of the unbridled arms race, which the imperialists are engaging in, or of their policy of sabotaging disarmament, but, on the contrary, he tries in a diabolical manner to slander the Soviet Union by accusing it of an arms race on the same level as the United States. Moreover, the only thing that preoccupies Tito is the question of United States prestige, which has gone down greatly in the eyes of the world as a consequence of its warmongering and aggressive actions. The leader of the Yugoslav revisionists, like a faithful lackey, speaking about the agreement on the ban of atomic weapons, takes the liberty of advising his master that "if the U.S.A. took the initiative in this situation, it would be of great political importance for them. . . . By such an agreement the United States would gain more politically than by pursuing nuclear tests." In other words, Tito tells the American imperialists: There is no harm in your carrying out nuclear tests, but you are not gaining *much politically!* Moreover, Tito told the American journalist that "atomic weapons tests do not give any of the parties any military superiority whatsoever" and that "they are now simply political in nature." This statement by Tito, made after the decision by the Soviet Government to resume atomic tests, forced on it by the latest series of atomic weapons tests by the United States, means that he is opposed to this just decision of the Soviet Government, which is aimed at raising the defensive capacity of the Soviet Union and the whole camp of socialism.

It is clear that the "support" which Tito seemed to give to the Soviet and other countries' proposals, either on the German and Berlin questions or on the question of disarmament, was only a bluff, a piece of demagogy, which is necessary for Tito and his revisionist friends in order to prepare the ground, to have another "argument" for penetration into the bosom of the socialist camp in order better to play his divisive role. And those who have assumed the task of "rehabilitating" Tito's clique or, to be more precise, who have entered on the road of total reconciliation with Tito by trampling upon the Moscow Declaration of 1960 have many times used and are still using the "convincing argument" that on the German question and on Berlin, as well as on the disarmament question, Tito is taking the position of the socialist countries, that "in foreign policy there is an identity of views between the Soviet Union and Yugoslavia"!

One knows that a policy of bluff is a short-lived one. This time, too, Tito used it as long as he needed it. These political tergiversations are common to all revisionists and, therefore, also to the Yugoslav revisionists, whom we have come up against before. It could not be otherwise. In fact Tito's clique has shown itself to be clever in these tergiversations, but this is not so much its merit as that of its allies, the modern revisionists, who for purposes which are now well known allow this clique of traitors to maneuver however and whenever required.

In opposition to the path of the modern revisionists, Marxism-Leninism teaches us that peace, peaceful coexistence, national independence, disarmament, and the settlement of other international problems cannot be begged from the imperialists but must be imposed on them. It is incontestable that negotiations and meetings between statesmen are useful. But the peoples cannot place all their hopes for ensuring peace on this path *alone*. Life has shown that the ruling circles of the imperialists states have gone to the negotiating table when under pressure from the peoples, not moved by good intentions to reach a concrete agreement on peace, but to deceive the peoples by pretending to be for peace in order to gain time and to prepare war behind their backs. Replying to this interviewer's question as to how America could convince Khrushchev that it is also for peace, Tito replied: "It is necessary to negotiate and negotiate not once but many times."

At a time when the imperialists have rejected for several years the proposals of the Soviet Union and other countries of the socialist camp for disarmament and continue to arm themselves to the teeth, when they sabotage all efforts to conclude a peace treaty with Germany, to settle the Berlin problem and other international problems, it is clear that the efforts of the Titoist clique, of N. Khrushchev's group, and of other revisionists to convince the peoples that one can secure peace, that one can carry out general and total disarmament, and that one can solve other important international problems with the approval, desire, and free will of the imperialists and solely through negotiations with the chiefs of imperialism or through meetings and other international forms controlled by them, are very harmful and give rise to dangerous illusions. The problem of preserving peace is the problem of the peoples themselves. It is only by throwing the masses into the struggle against imperialism, by mobilizing them for concrete actions in support of peace, that it is possible to tie the hands of the warmongering imperialists and to impose peace, disarmament, and peaceful coexistence upon them. It is only by relying on the broad struggle of the peoples and of the international working class that negotiations and various meetings in the interest of peace can yield positive results.

For anyone who attentively follows the views and practical activities of the Titoist clique and of N. Khrushchev's revisionist group and who is not deceived by their demagogical phrases it is clear that they aim at the same target: to divert the peoples and the Communist and workers parties from a resolute struggle against imperialism, to stifle their militant revolutionary spirit, and to reduce them to a state of passivity. This totally opportunist line pursued by Khrushchev and his group stems from illusions that, allegedly, imperialism has now lost its aggressive and belligerent nature and that the important problems now confronting the peoples of the world can be resolved without a resolute struggle, by "peaceful" means and through agreement with the imperialists. Moreover, it seems that the N. Khrushchev group thinks that in following this opportunist line of conciliation toward imperialism, they will make the imperialists "peaceable," "sensible," and will thus create conditions for rapprochement and multilateral economic and political collaboration with the world of capitalism, with imperialism, and particularly American imperialism, this being one of Khrushchev's main objectives. It is not difficult to understand that this totally anti-Marxist and opportunist line, which sacrifices the vital interests of the peoples for the sake of rapprochement with imperialism, in fact only serves the interests of the imperialists.

The opportunist and traitorous line of N. Khrushchev's revisionist group is being increasingly unmasked and is becoming discredited in the eyes of the Communists and the peoples. From time to time they are obliged to engage in demagogical practices and to say a few "hard words" against imperialism. But these are merely efforts to embellish a policy which is becoming threadbare.

2. *Rapprochement with imperialism — the general line of the modern revisionists*

The synthesis of all the revisionists' views, expressing the ultimate objective which modern revisionists have fixed for themselves, is rapprochement and then fusion with imperialism, or, in other words, the so-called "integration" of the world. In the recent interview granted to Drew Pearson, Tito declared openly that "our prospect is economic and political integration." In the final analysis, the entire line followed by the modern revisionists is subordinated to the implementation of this prospect.

World economic and political integration — the revisionist interpretation of Kennedy's theory of "peaceful evolution"

The idea of the "economic and political integration" of the world is not an innovation in the theories of the Yugoslav revisionists; but the fact that the renegade Tito raises this question at this precise time is by no means accidental.

It is known that the Western countries are today raising a big hullabaloo over the question of the "economic and political integration" of the capitalist world, which has found concrete expression in the form of the European Economic Community (the Common Market). Integration in the capitalist world is nothing but an attempt to solve, or at least to smooth over, the contradictions and difficulties of modern capitalism, in order to heal its wounds as best it can for the benefit of the big capitalist monopolies and to the detriment of the broad working masses; it constitutes a counterweight against the might and power of attraction of the world socialist system, which daily gives proof of its superiority over the capitalist system; it is a form of collective colonialism, tending by new means and new methods to preserve colonial domination and to bring about the submission of the underdeveloped countries; it is a tool of the "cold war" which serves to reinforce the aggressive military blocs of imperialism, as a basis for the realization of a political union, by creating respective supranational bodies; it is a weapon for the preparation of aggressive war against the Soviet Union and the other socialist countries, and for the suppression of liberation movements and revolutionary and democratic movements in various countries. Monopolist integration has been and is a component of the basic strategy of American imperialism which aims at extending European integration on an Atlantic scale and later on a world scale, under the direction of the U.S.A., in other words, at achieving world domination by American imperialism. "Once a total European union has been assured," President Kennedy declared, "we shall be ready to discuss . . . the ways and means of creating a concrete Atlantic Alliance. This Atlantic Alliance will serve as a nucleus for the eventual union of all free men, of those who are free today and of those who will win freedom one day." Therefore, this is what the imperialists, especially the American imperialists, understand by "integration."

Tito in his interview also speaks of "world integration." But he does not state explicitly what integration he has in mind, on a socialist or capitalist basis, and this is not unintentional because "the serpent never shows its feet." He only says that he is not for integration "of a discriminatory nature," that he "will not become reconciled to such integration." Despite the care taken by Tito to hide his tracks, his theory of "integration" means in fact the melting of socialism into capitalism, the swallowing-up of the world by American imperialism.

Tito says that in order to achieve integration, wars of every kind must be renounced, because "wars prevent us from integrating," making no distinction whatsoever between different kinds of war. Therefore, in order to achieve the integration of the world, it is necessary, according to him, to renounce the revolutionary struggle of the working class and all workers for the overthrow of the capitalist order and the triumph of socialism, plus the national liberation struggle of enslaved peoples against imperialist oppression and exploitation, plus the ideo-political struggle of socialism against capitalism, against the aggressive and warmongering plans and activities of imperialism. What does all this mean? It means, on the one hand, the preservation intact of the capitalist order and, on the other, the securing of every latitude for the imperialists to apply without hinderance their policy of war and aggression, the final objective of which is the overthrow of the socialist order and the restoration of capitalism in all countries where it has been overthrown. We are therefore dealing here with the swallowing-up of socialist countries by imperialism, the integration of the world on a capitalist basis.

For Marxist-Leninists and for all realistic men it is clear that, under conditions of the division of the world into two opposing systems, there can be no question of any economic, much less political, integration, because it is impossible to imagine one world in which socialism and capitalism are fused together. The world can only be one on a single social basis, either on the basis of capitalism or on that of socialism. There is not and there cannot be any intermediate way. The Yugoslav revisionists deem it possible to create a single world, integrated even today, because in their view the existence of two opposing systems, the socialist and the capitalist, is not something objective, conditioned by the laws of development of human society in the present epoch, but an artificial division into military-political blocs which, as the Program of the LCY states, "has resulted in the economic division of the world" and "hinders the process of world integration and the social progress of mankind."

But one knows that formerly the world was "one." There was one world system, that of capitalism. This "unity" has been breached as a result of the triumph of the socialist revolution in Russia and in a good many other countries and by the creation of the world socialist system. It is clear, therefore, that Tito deplores the breach of the former "unity" of the capitalist world and regards the creation of the world socialist system as something negative "which hinders the process of world integration and the social progress of mankind." Therefore, according to Tito's logic, to create a single world one must liquidate the source of its division, the existence of the world socialist system. It transpires once again that Tito thereby means the economic and political integration of the world on the basis of capitalism, therefore the merging of socialism with capitalism.

It clearly transpires from all this that Tito is giving public support to Kennedy's "basic strategy," one of whose principal objectives is "the creation of possibilities for a long constructive evolution of the Communist bloc and the inclusion of the Communist states in the community of the free world." The thesis of the Yugoslav revisionists on "world economic and political integration" in fact presupposes the peaceful integration of socialism into capitalism, the liquidation of socialism, and the re-establishment of total domination by imperialism.

Rapprochement with imperialism under the guise of peaceful coexistence

In his capacity as an agent of imperialism and as an advanced revisionist, Tito speaks more openly of the prospect of integration with capitalism, of submission to imperialism. But the views and actions of the other revisionists also lead, in fact, along this road. The views of N. Khrushchev's revisionist group on the fundamental questions of our epoch and particularly its anti-Marxist conception of peaceful coexistence testify to this.

N. Khrushchev's group, on the one hand, overestimates the forces of imperialism, whose atomic blackmail and war threats it fears, and therefore it tries by every means to have good relations with imperialism, to come closer to it and reconcile itself to it, flattering it, making concessions of principle, and going so far as to sacrifice the interests of the world revolutionary and national liberation movement. On the other hand, by overestimating our forces and by underestimating the forces of imperialism, N. Khrushchev's group spreads the illusion that, allegedly, imperialism, particularly American imperialism, is confronting a new balance of power, has changed or is changing its nature, has become peaceful, has renounced and is renouncing its aggressive and warlike designs against the socialist countries and the other peoples, and is seriously engaged in peaceful economic competition with socialism.

Inasmuch as these are two contradictory evaluations, they lead Khrushchev's group to the unique revisionist conclusion: to renounce concretely the ideological and political struggle against imperialism and the firm unmasking of its policy of war and aggression, to renounce support for the national liberation struggle and for revolution, to establish all-round economic and political collaboration between socialism and capitalism. This is, in effect, the line of rapprochement and fusion with imperialism which constitutes the core of the anti-Marxist concept of N. Khrushchev's group on peaceful coexistence.

According to N. Khrushchev's group, peaceful coexistence is "the general line of foreign policy of the socialist countries"; it is "the only correct road for solving all the current vital problems of human society." Thus, according to him, all other tasks and all other problems must be subordinated to peaceful coexistence, namely, world revolution and the national liberation struggle, while the peoples must remain with their arms folded and wait for their national and social liberation through the implementation of the policy of peaceful coexistence. In truth, this means the perpetuation of capitalist and imperialist oppression and exploitation of the peoples.

It is by no means necessary to pause here in order to submit to close analysis the anti-Marxist and revisionist conception of N. Khrushchev's group on peaceful coexistence, because this question has been discussed at length in previous articles and materials of our party published by the press. We shall merely indicate that this conception has nothing to do with Lenin's teachings and with the theses of the two Moscow Declarations on peaceful coexistence. The Moscow Declaration of 1960 stresses that "in the conditions of the division of the world into two systems, the only just and reasonable principle of international relations is the principle of the peaceful coexistence of states with different social systems." However, peaceful coexistence, the Declaration notes, "does not mean, as the revisionists say, the renunciation of the class struggle. Peaceful coexistence between states with different social systems is a form of class struggle between socialism and capitalism." It "does not mean the reconciliation of socialist ideology with bourgeois ideology. Quite the contrary, it presupposes the strengthening of the struggle of the working class, of all Communist parties, for the triumph of socialist ideas." The Declaration also stresses that "the successes of the class revolutionary struggle and of the national liberation struggle contribute to the strengthening of peaceful coexistence," because they result "in the weakening and and ever more pronounced contraction of the positions of imperialism." To struggle for peace and peaceful coexistence, the Declaration stresses, "means to give evidence of very great vigilance, to denounce persistently the policy of imperialism, to follow most attentively the intrigues and machinations of the warmongers, and to direct the holy wrath of the peoples against those who practice the policy of unleashing war. It means to go about organizing all peace-loving forces, steadfastly to intensify the active moves of the masses, to safeguard the peace, and to strengthen collaboration with all states interested in preventing new wars."

The anti-Marxist and revisionist conception of N. Khrushchev and his group regarding peaceful coexistence, such as the line of rapprochement with imperialism and of cessation of the struggle against it, is also closely bound to their opportunist preaching on the roads of transition to socialism, which divert the workers and the Communist and workers parties from a firm and effective struggle to overthrow capitalism and from the socialist revolution while they await the creation of favorable conditions for a peaceful transition to socialism as a result of the policy of peaceful coexistence. Thus, in practice, N. Khrushchev's group stresses in a one-sided manner the possibility of the peaceful road alone, neglecting the necessity simultaneously to prepare for the two possibilities, the peaceful and the non-peaceful. This idea alleges that the possibility of the peaceful path grows from day to day, and, what is worse, it presents the peaceful path as a purely parliamentary one, as simply the winning of a majority in a bourgeois parliament, and totally neglects the fundamental teaching of Marxism-Leninism on the need to smash the bourgeois state machine and to replace it by organs of the dictatorship of the proletariat.

N. Khrushchev's propagandists recently have gone so far as to present the state monopoly capitalism of capitalist countries as one of the principal factors in the overthrow of the monopolist bourgeoisie and as almost the first step toward socialism. Thus, in his closing speech at the international meeting of Marxist scholars in Moscow devoted to current problems of the capitalist world, transmitted by TASS in summarized form September 3, 1962, the director of the Institute of World Economy and International Relations of the USSR Academy of Sciences, A. Arzumanyan, said *inter alia:* "At present, in the third state of the general crisis of capitalism, nationalization cannot be regarded as an ordinary reform. It is bound up with the revolutionary struggle for the liquidation of monopolies, for the overthrow of the power of the financial oligarchy. Through the correct policy of the working class, relying on an upsurge in the struggle of the broad popular masses, it may become a radical means of abolishing the domination of the monopolist bourgeoisie. The nationalization of industry and of the banks is now becoming the slogan of the antimonopolist coalition." What is the difference between this concept and the well-known, fundamentally opportunist point of view in the Program of the LCY that "specific forms of capitalist state relations can be the first step toward socialism," that "the ever growing impact of state-capitalist tendencies in the capitalist world is the most outstanding proof that mankind is entering ever more deeply, in an uncontrollable manner and in the most varied ways, into the epoch of socialism"?

It is not necessary to dwell here in detail on arguments showing how ill-founded are these clearly opportunist views of the Yugoslav revisionists and N. Khrushchev's group. It is sufficient only to recall that not very long ago the propagandists of N. Khrushchev's group, polemicizing on the draft program of the LCY, stressed that "the development of state monopoly capitalism means the further strengthening of monopolies, the further concentration of economic and political power in their hands. It means that the state is exploited by the monopolies for their egotistical purposes and to the detriment of the workers' interests." (See the article, "On the Draft Program of the League of Communists of Yugoslavia," published in the sixth issue of *Kommunist,* 1958.) Commenting on the previously cited points of the program of the LCY, the current Secretary of the CPSU Central Committee, B. Ponomarev, wrote in the periodical *Kommunist,* No. 8, 1958, that this was "point by point what was said by Bernstein and Kautsky, that capitalist society spontaneously merges of its own accord with socialism." It therefore turns out that N. Khrushchev's group formerly criticized unnecessarily the Yugoslav revisionists, Bernstein, and Kautsky because they now propagate, in substance, the same opportunist views. (!)

We cannot fail to recall in this connection that in his time V. I. Lenin harshly criticized the bourgeois reformist notion that state monopoly capitalism is a noncapitalist order, a step toward socialism, which is necessary to the opportunist and reformist denial of the inevitability of the socialist revolution and their embellishing of capitalism. (See V. I. Lenin, *Works,* Vol. 25, pp. 414–415, Russian edition.) V. I. Lenin emphatically stressed that "steps toward greater monopolism and state control of production are inevitably followed by an increase in the exploitation of the working masses, the intensification of oppression, difficulty in resisting exploiters, and the strengthening of reaction and military despotism. Parallel with this, they result in an extraordinary increase in the profits of the big capitalists to the detriment of all other strata of the population." (Lenin's *Works,* Vol. 24, pp. 275–277, Russian edition.) The previously quoted thesis of N. Khrushchev's group is also in flagrant opposition to the Moscow Declaration of 1960, in which it is stated that "by strengthening the domination of monopolies in the nation's life, state monopoly capitalism unites the strength of the state in a single mechanism in order to save the capitalist order and to increase to the maximum the profits of the imperialist bourgeoisie, by means of the exploitation of the working class and the robbing of broad strata of the population."

By loudly propagating "the great and ever-growing possibilities" of the peaceful path, N. Khrushchev engages in wishful thinking. What do the facts of contemporary life show? They show that monopoly capital is demonstrating, in an increasingly obvious manner, its reactionary and antidemocratic essence. It does not even accommodate itself to the former bourgeois democratic freedoms; it deprives the popular masses of the opportunity to express their will and to place the true defenders of their interests in government bodies. When the bourgeoisie sees that even those mutilated rights which the constitution grants to the workers constitute a danger to its domination, it simply tramples on them, arbitrarily modifies the electoral system, proclaims elections "illegal," and unhesitatingly liquidates elected bodies, as recently happened in Argentina, for example. In fact, the monopolist bourgeoisie has installed fascist regimes in certain countries, and it shows an increasing tendency to install such regimes under new forms in a number of other countries. Are not the terrorist actions of the OAS in France, the persecution of the Communist Party and the activities of the "ultras" in the United States, the installation of military dictatorships in Latin American countries, South Korea, and elsewhere proof of this? At present the reactionary bourgeoisie relies more and more on armed forces — the army, police, and gendarmerie — to safeguard its domination and crush any revolutionary and progressive movement of the working masses. How can one underestimate or even fail to take into consideration this reality, which N. Khrushchev's group is obliged to admit in certain cases (naturally, for the sake of appearances), and stress, unilaterally only, the possibility of the peaceful path, to preach that the possibilities of this path are growing day by day in present circumstances?

Recent attempts of N. Khrushchev's group to establish broad economic collaboration with the imperialist countries and with their monopolist associations also form part of the framework of reconciliation and rapprochement with imperialism. In his article in the twelfth issue of *Kommunist,* N. Khrushchev specifies that, taking into account "the objective tendencies toward the internationalization of production which are active in the capitalist world, we establish our policy and our economic measures." But what is this policy and what are these economic measures which N. Khrushchev mentions? Among other things, he wants to engage in economic cooperation not only with particular capitalist countries but also with their economic communities, with the Common Market to be precise, and not only in trade but also in production, "to process raw materials in short supply, to increase the sources of power, jointly to utilize shipping routes," and so forth.

Naturally, the socialist countries are in favor of developing trade with the capitalist countries on the basis of mutual advantage — this is in the interest of the peoples of both parties — of lessening international tension and of improving relations between states. But the line propounded by N. Khrushchev on economic collaboration and links with the capitalist world, viewed through the prism of his general opportunist line, clearly testifies to his inclination toward an unprincipled rapprochement with imperialism. This is even clearer if we take into account the fact that, while he is so preoccupied with tightening economic links and cooperation with the capitalist world and with a rapprochement with it, N. Khrushchev's group does not hesitate to inflict colossal harm to economic cooperation between countries of the socialist camp and even to go so far as to effect a total break of all economic relations, even simple commercial exchanges. The clearest example of this is the anti-Marxist discriminatory positions of N. Khrushchev's group toward Albania, which are already well known to all. All this takes place at a time when, in the face of imperialist attempts to create a united economic, political, and military front, directed primarily against the socialist camp, the socialist countries should deem it an indispensable and urgent task to strengthen their unity on all sides and their internationalist collaboration in all fields. This is verbally granted by N. Khrushchev himself, certainly not to give it reality but to conceal his anti-Marxist and revisionist actions against the unity of the socialist camp.

The measures proposed by N. Khrushchev in his article rightly raise questions and doubts among Communists and all reasonable men. On the other hand, he points out that "the so-called economic communities of the imperialists have the same aims as the aggressive military blocs

(NATO and SEATO, etc.)," and that "the leaders of the Western powers do not conceal the links and direct interdependence between the economic organization of the Common Market and the aggressive NATO alliance." He therefore calls on Communists and the peoples to struggle against the Common Market, against other capitalist communities like it, and to unmask their antipopular and aggressive aims. On the other hand, N. Khrushchev asks for the establishment of broad cooperation between the socialist countries and the imperialist economic communities in all fields of the economy, including the field of production; he asks, as it were, for a certain international division of labor between the two systems. However, as N. Khrushchev himself recognizes, since the Common Market has the same aims as the aggressive NATO bloc and since, as is rightly stated in the theses "On Imperialist Integration in Western Europe," published in August of this year by the Institute of World Economy and International Relations of the USSR Academy of Science, "it is being converted into an economic base for this bloc in Europe"; since these things are so, to ask for the establishment of broad economic cooperation in all fields with the Common Market is, in reality, equivalent to asking for vast cooperation with the aggressive NATO military bloc itself, which is directed primarily against the Soviet Union and the other socialist countries.

Does not all this create a harmful illusion, for which N. Khrushchev is an open spokesman, that at the present time imperialism has renounced and is renouncing its aggressive aims and actions, notably against the socialist camp, that it is willing from now on to enter the road of peaceful competition with socialism and is seriously devoting itself to this task, that each day ever greater possibilities are created for multilateral collaboration between the two systems — socialism and capitalism? It is not difficult for anyone to see how close and similar these views of N. Khrushchev's group are to the anti-Marxist views of the Yugoslav revisionists on world economic and political integration, expressed clearly in Tito's recent interview.

Tito, the counselor and mediator in the rapprochement of the N. Khrushchev revisionist group with imperialism

It is now becoming ever more clear that both the imperialists and revisionists are seeking understanding, rapprochement, and an increase in mutual trust, in order to pave the way for "world economic and political integration." In the interview he granted to Drew Pearson, Tito tries with great zeal to make a contribution in this very direction — but no longer in the role of a lackey. At least in the eyes of the world he presents himself this time as a "counselor." The American journalist openly said to Tito: "You understand the Soviet Union and the United States and you have friends on both sides. Could you become a mediator?" Tito replied, as if moved: "I do not wish to become a mediator, but when I meet Premier Khrushchev I shall acquaint him with my view. This will be my personal view, and I can express it both to Premier Khrushchev and to President Kennedy, if I have the opportunity to meet him." To assure the American imperialists that he might well be successful in his mission as "counselor," the chief of the Yugoslav revisionists declares: "So far I have spoken openly to Premier Khrushchev, orally or in writing, about the way we view international problems, and I must add that I have not encountered any resistance. Premier Khrushchev knows how to weigh opinions, and I have found that this is also the case with American leaders." To let it be understood that he would not limit himself to this, Tito announced in his interview: "I have been invited to spend a holiday in the Soviet Union. . . . Probably at the end of this year or next spring I shall go there for a rest. I shall certainly enter into discussions on this occasion."

The position of "counselor" and the notion of as close a rapprochement as possible between the imperialists and the revisionists seem to possess a powerful appeal for the revisionist Tito. That is why, in order to abolish mistrust, to convince the two sides that each is struggling for peace (from the revisionist point of view, of course) Tito "advises," not without boasting: "It is necessary to negotiate and negotiate again, not once but several times. It is necessary to establish continual contacts," because in this way one will advance "toward the consolidation of peace, and in this way mistrust will be eliminated."

Tito advises his imperialist bosses not to "dramatize" things, and he tells them that he knows N. Khrushchev well, and that he is deeply convinced that it is easy to achieve understanding with him. Replying to the American journalist's question about whether he thinks that "one day in the future the U.S. and the USSR will become good friends," Tito told him with profound conviction that the time for realizing such a thing would come. "Why not realize it?" he adds. Nothing opposes this; all roads are open.

As you can see, therefore, Tito does not play badly his role of "the servant of two masters," or, raised to the rank of counselor, his mission of rapprochement and reconciliation between N. Khrushchev's revisionist group and the imperialists.

3. *The revisionists — splitters of the unity of the socialist camp and of the international Communist and workers movement*

Tito's interview clearly shows the other objective of the revisionists, that of splitting the socialist camp and the international Communist movement. We are dealing here neither with a new role nor with a new task of the revisionists. The splitting of the socialist camp and the Communist movement is one of the essential objectives of the activity of all the contemporary revisionists.

It is well known that one of the most subtle and dangerous forms of the struggle by imperialism and its agency against the world socialist system is the effort to undermine the unity of the socialist camp from within, to set the socialist countries and the Communist workers parties against each other. The star role in achieving this aim of its fundamental strategy has been assigned by imperialism — headed by the United States — to the revisionists, first and foremost to the traitorous clique of Belgrade revisionists.

The facts demonstrate that the Tito clique has not spared its efforts to carry out well its role of "Trojan horse," not only by spreading its anti-Marxist views but also by its hostile practical activity against the socialist countries and the Communist and workers parties. The role of the Yugoslav revisionists in inspiring and organizing the counterrevolutionary coup in Hungary and in organizing plots against the Albanian People's Republic is already well known, as are their subversive and undermining activities against the socialist countries. The whole world knows of their slanderous and schismatic attacks against the Soviet Union, the other socialist countries, the Marxist-Leninist parties and their leaders, and so forth.

In his recent interview as well, Tito attempts to cause division. The object of his schismatic attacks this time is the Chinese People's Republic and Soviet-Chinese friendship. Drew Pearson pointedly asked Tito: "What do you think about the divergencies between China and the Soviet Union?" And Tito pointedly dwelt at length on this question. He slanders the Chinese People's Republic and its peaceful foreign policy and indirectly accuses it of being opposed to disarmament, opposed to peace, and of almost being opposed to any agreement, and so forth. He even goes so far as to say almost openly to the American imperialists that China wants war and not peace, that the threat comes from China, so direct toward that country not only your attention but also your acts and your provocations; direct toward that country your armies, the muzzles of your guns, your rockets! All this is being done at a time when the American imperialists in cooperation with the Chiang Kai-shek clique and their allies of the aggressive SEATO bloc are hatching dangerous plots and provocations against the Chinese People's Republic and against peace in the Far East. This is yet another proof of the co-ordinated policy of the Yugoslav revisionists and the American imperialists.

Tito deliberately put forward once more the well-known thesis of the Yugoslav revisionists, which is loudly taken up by all modern revisionists, that there are some socialist states which are for war. "I think," Tito told the American journalist, "that the Soviet Union is acting in a conciliatory manner regarding the problem of the Chinese islands and Chiang Kai-shek, and is exerting influence so that things do not get worse and so that no greater conflicts occur." He goes on to add that "the same applies to the Indian-Chinese border dispute, which the Soviet Union is trying to stop." On this subject Tito also openly supports the American plan for the creation of two Chinas, which, as everyone knows, seeks to prolong forever the occupation of the Chinese territory of Taiwan and the other Chinese islands by the American imperialists and the Chiang Kai-shek clique. On this issue, too, the Belgrade revisionists do not take the side of the Chinese people and its lawful leaders but the side of the imperialist occupiers and their aggressive policy. Ever consistent in his attitude, Tito openly aligns himself on the side of the reactionary Indian circles on the subject of the Chinese-Indian border conflict, a conflict which, as everyone knows, has been instigated by American imperialism and serves its interests, serves the American policy of aggression and war to aggravate tension in the relations between two great neighboring countries and in this important part of Asia in general. Precisely the same attitude was adopted toward the Chinese-Indian border conflict by A. Mikoyan during his visit to India last July. Replying to a speech by Indian Minister of State Mr. Krishnamachari, who alleged openly that it was not India but the Chinese People's Republic that was supposedly committing aggressive actions on the Chinese-Indian border, Mikoyan stated: "My honorable host has made such a good speech that it only remains for me to go along with his words. He has found particularly clear and apt terms for his speech." (*Pravda,* 26 July 1962.)

Taking advantage of the opportunity, Tito here again tries to drive wedges into the unity and friendship between the Soviet Union and the Chinese People's Republic. But Tito's wedges as well as the activity of the modern revisionists to undermine this friendship will be in vain, as they have been thus far. The friendship between the peoples of the Soviet Union and China will strengthen and grow through the ages, for it is not the product of opportunist political combinations, but is rather a friendship of peoples, a friendship molded by the immortal ideology of Marxism-Leninism, animated by the common ideals of the building of socialism and Communism.

This is not the first nor yet the last time that the modern revisionists have aimed their attacks directly and indirectly against the Chinese People's Republic. The modern revisionists, like the American imperialists, see in the Chinese People's Republic an insurmountable menace to their plans, a great power which is struggling resolutely against imperialism and for the defense of the cause of socialism, peace, the freedom and independence of peoples. They see in the Chinese Communist Party the principal obstacle to the achievement of their plans, a resolute fighter for the defense of the purity of Marxism-Leninism and the unity of the socialist camp and the international Communist and workers movement. Time has shown and will show that all attacks, calumniations, and provocations and all plots of the imperialists and revisionists against the Chinese People's Republic will always fail shamefully. The Chinese People's Republic, guided by its glorious Communist Party headed by its Chairman Comrade Mao Tse-tung, will march victoriously forward, holding high the banner of socialism and Communism, of peace and national independence, the banner of the unity of the socialist camp and of the international Communist and workers movement.

In his interview, Tito, with the hypocrisy which is a mark of the revisionists, tries to present himself as a friend of the Soviet Union. He even goes so far as to allow himself to give an "interpretation" of the foreign policy of the Soviet Union, to speak in the name of the Soviet Union. But the entire spirit and content of Tito's interview are a proof of the opposite, of his hatred of the Soviet Union, of his old and tested anti-Soviet attitude. The Yugoslav revisionists have not been and can never be the sincere friends of the Soviet Union, as Nikita Khrushchev tries to present them. Yugoslav revisionists are and will remain the same: agents of American imperialism who are trying to raise themselves from the role of lackey to the role of counselor. They are seasoned provocateurs and conspirators against the unity of the socialist camp.

In the divisive activities against the unity of the socialist camp and of the international Communist and workers movement, the imperialists and the Yugoslav revisionists are stimulated and encouraged by the very anti-Marxist and anti-socialist attitudes and actions of N. Khrushchev's group. N. Khrushchev's group began its divisive and undermining activities a long time ago, and at the 22nd Congress of the Communist Party of the Soviet Union it went as far as launching hostile public attacks against a Marxist-Leninist party and a socialist country — the PPSh and the Albanian People's Republic. It also launched open counterrevolutionary appeals for the overthrow of the leadership of the party and state in Albania, while after the 22nd Congress it even broke off diplomatic relations with the Albanian People's Republic. By its attacks and its hostile acts against fraternal parties and fraternal socialist countries, N. Khrushchev's group has undermined and is seriously undermining the unity of the socialist camp and of the international Communist movement, and has given weapons with which to fight us to imperialist enemies.

N. Khrushchev's revisionist group has never ceased its divisive and unfriendly activity against our unity. N. Khrushchev's beautiful words about unity are nothing but bluff and demagogy, a mask which he needs to deceive, to gain time to conduct calmly his divisive activity, to undertake new measures even more dangerous to the unity of the socialist camp and the Communist movement.

Modern revisionists, as life shows, do not care at all about the unity of the socialist camp and of the international Communist movement. They could not care less about the interests of socialist countries. They try to destroy this unity, to betray the high interests of the socialist system. We have no intention of dwelling at length on the Yugoslav revisionists, who have publicly declared that they are against the existence of the socialist camp and who have organized, in cooperation with the imperialists, various plots against the socialist countries, like the chauvinist plan of Tito and of King Paul of Greece for dismembering our country, or the plots organized by the Titoist clique, together with the Greek monarchofascists and the United States imperialists, against the Albanian People's Republic. What must be noted is that N. Khrushchev's group, in the name of the rapprochement at any price with imperialism, with the bourgeois governments and personages, and under the pretext of "peaceful coexistence," does not hesitate to trample underfoot the sovereign rights of the socialist countries. One knows already about N. Khrushchev's unscrupulous bargaining with S. Venizelos to the detriment of the territorial integrity of the Albanian People's Republic. It was precisely N. Khrushchev's group which came to the defense of the traitors and enemies of the Albanian people who had played a role in organizing the plot of the Yugoslav revisionists, the Greek monarchofascists, and the American imperialists to commit aggression against Albania. When our party and our people rightly condemn the Greater Serbia inhuman chauvinistic policy of the Belgrade band of revisionists, which it practices against more than a million Albanian brothers in Kossovo, Montenegro, and Macedonia, when we unmask with facts the policy of discrimination, the crimes of genocide, the judicial repressions, the administrative deportations, and the massive annihilation of our brothers by the Belgrade clique, N. Khrushchev's group does not hesitate to accuse us of being "nationalist," thus approving the inhuman and anti-Albanian actions of the renegade Belgrade group. Such anti-internationalist attitudes of N. Khrushchev's group are not applied solely against the Albanian People's Republic and the Albanian people.

But facts show that on the question of the unity of the socialist camp and of the international Communist and workers movement, the line of the traitorous Titoist clique and that of N. Khrushchev's revisionist group are entirely at one and that they both, in fact, serve the objectives and the plans of imperialism. On this question, too, N. Khrushchev's group unscrupulously violates the Moscow Declaration of 1960, which specifies that under conditions in which imperialist reaction is uniting its forces for a struggle against Communism, it is particularly indispensable to strengthen at any price the unity of the socialist camp and of the international Communist movement, that solicitude for the continual strengthening of this unity is the supreme internationalist task of every Marxist-Leninist party.

Our Party of Labor has been and always is in favor of unity of the socialist camp and of the international Communist movement; it has fought and is fighting firmly and in a principled manner to strengthen this unity on the firm basis of Marxism-Leninism. Our party has always seen in this unity the indomitable strength of the camp and of our movement, the important factor for the construction of socialism in our country, the guarantee of the successful advance of the struggle for the triumph of the great cause of socialism and Communism, of national liberation, of democracy and peace. Starting from this principled position, our party has been and remains ever faithful to the common line of the international Communist movement, expressed in the two historic Moscow Declarations of 1957 and 1960, and has firmly applied this line. In its relations with the fraternal parties and with the fraternal socialist countries, our party has adhered and is rigorously adhering to the principles of proletarian internationalism, to the Marxist-Leninist norms which govern relations among Communist parties and socialist countries.

Inasmuch as it is a firm fighter for unity, the Albanian Party of Labor has been, is, and always will be in favor of the maintenance and strengthening of the friendship and love of our people for the glorious fraternal peoples of the Soviet Union, in favor of preserving love and respect for the great party of Lenin, because as hitherto the Albanian Party of Labor regards friendship with the Soviet peoples and unity with the Soviet Union and the Communist Party of the Soviet Union as one of the fundamental questions of principle in its revolutionary activity. Our party has never confused and never confuses the Soviet Union and its Communist Party with N. Khrushchev's revisionist group. Independently of N. Khrushchev's hostile positions toward our country and our party, independently of his efforts to bring harm to Albanian-Soviet friendship, this sacred friendship is preserved intact in the hearts of the Communists and of our entire people.

Our party has struggled and is struggling for the firm unity of the socialist camp and of the international Communist movement, based on the principles of Marxism-Leninism and proletarian internationalism, for the rigorous application of the Moscow Declarations, for unity in the struggle against imperialism and the renegades of Marxism-Leninism — the modern revisionists. The struggle for unity and the struggle against the disruptions of unity, the modern revisionists, are inseparable. Only such Marxist-Leninist unity can be a truly effective and stable unity, which the international Communist movement needs.

From an analysis of the interview granted by Tito to the American journalist Drew Pearson, from an analysis of the views and practical activities of Yugoslav revisionists, their true nature, their role as traitors and enemies in the service of American imperialism, of its fundamental strategy, is once again clearly seen. It is precisely this activity in the service of American imperialism which has unmasked the Belgrade revisionists in the eyes of the whole world. Communists, progressive men, and the peoples clearly see what Tito's clique represents and the danger which it represents for the cause of Communism, for the cause of peace, freedom, and the national independence of peoples. In the Moscow Declaration of the 81 Communist and workers parties of 1960 the Yugoslav revisionist leaders are branded as traitors to Marxism-Leninism, as lackeys of imperialism, as enemies of the national liberation movement and of peace.

But Tito's clique has friends, comrades, and allies who, through numerous schemes try to preserve its lost "prestige," try to give it back its lost "credit"; to this end also toil their imperialist patrons, headed by the United States, who try to squeeze the lemon dry; to this end work also the modern revisionists headed by N. Khrushchev's group, who seek to find in Tito and in his whole clique active comrades-in-arms and effective allies in the struggle against Marxism-Leninism and intermediaries in their machinations with imperialism. These bilateral efforts have been particularly noticeable lately.

American imperialists, on the one hand, are noisily asserting that Tito is allegedly in the process of establishing links with the East. Proposals are made in the United States Senate and Congress to cut aid to Yugoslavia, because "it is flirting." On the other hand, N. Khrushchev's group and his followers, contrary to the Moscow Declaration of November 1960, loudly proclaim that "Yugoslavia is a socialist country," that "Yugoslavia's foreign policy on the most important questions fully corresponds to that of the Soviet Union and the other socialist countries," that "the Yugoslav experience should be carefully studied"; and — as if to bring this recommendation to life — exchanges of various delegations are taking place, the Yugoslavs are even being invited — for the time being as "observers" — to meetings of the socialist countries, the way to mass meetings is being opened, etc., etc.

It is clear that the two sides are bluffing, that they are trying to foster illusions among the peoples and among the Communists, that they help provide one another with opportunities, according to their means and for their own purposes, to make use of Tito's revisionist clique in the future as well, because, in fact, nothing has changed. Regardless of the rumpus created in Congress or in the United States Senate, Tito continues to be the servant of imperialists; he continues to receive credits and "aid," and he continues to be bound hand and foot to the imperialist bandwagon. Similarly, regardless of the pompous declarations of N. Khrushchev's group on "socialist Yugoslavia," and so on and on, socialism continues to be nothing but an empty phrase in Yugoslavia, nothing but a mask which enables Tito's clique the more easily to undermine the socialist camp, to carry out diversionary acts, as his role of "Trojan horse" demands.

In short, Tito's clique remains what it has been, regardless of the illusions which the imperialists or N. Khrushchev's group is trying to create concerning it. Tito's clique continues its role of servant of two masters, that is, to serve both the imperialists in their designs against Communism, the liberation movement, and peace among peoples and N. Khrushchev's revisionist group in its struggle against Marxism-Leninism and in its goal of rapprochement with imperialism.

The N. Khrushchev group did not reply to the Tito interview, thus accepting and approving everything that Tito said about N. Khrushchev. This proves that the Tito clique and the N. Khrushchev group are following the same path. But the N. Khrushchev group could not adopt any other attitude to the Tito interview for another reason, too: It would otherwise have been obliged to take back everything it had said in defense of the Tito clique; it would have had to admit that it had been mistaken in its policy of conciliation and rapprochement with the Yugoslav revisionists. Events of recent times have now demonstrated that the rapprochement between the N. Khrushchev group and the Tito clique is becoming closer and closer. As has been announced, L. Brezhnev is shortly going to Yugoslavia, while toward the end of this year or next spring Josip Broz Tito is to go to the Soviet Union at the invitation of N. Khrushchev. These visits are not made without reason. It seems that they are being made to coordinate better their common work and activities.

It becomes clearer with each passing day what a great danger to the destinies of socialism and the struggle of the peoples against imperialism are the views and actions of the modern revisionists, particularly those of the *agentura* of imperialism, the Tito clique. To be silent, not to denounce these dangerous views and actions of the revisionists, would mean bearing a heavy responsibility to the Communist movement and all the peoples of the world who are struggling for their national liberation and socialism. The task emphatically stressed by the two Moscow Declarations of 1957 and 1960 is more urgent than ever: to wage a resolute struggle against modern revisionism, which is the essential danger to the international Communist and workers movement, and to denounce still further the Yugoslav revisionists as traitors to Marxism-Leninism and as enemies of socialism, peace, and the liberty and independence of the peoples.

DOCUMENT 32

"A Great Betrayal of Marxism-Leninism," Zëri i Popullit, *October 13, 1962 (complete text).*

Soviet President L. Brezhnev recently made an eleven-day official visit to Yugoslavia at the invitation of Tito. The Soviet and Yugoslav press announced that Brezhnev's visit was in response to the one made by Tito to the Soviet Union in 1956.

At the Moscow airport he was seen off by N. Khrushchev. Upon his arrival in Belgrade, where he was given a great welcome by Tito and his clique, Brezhnev hastened to express to "esteemed Comrade Tito" his gratitude for this friendly invitation and to convey to him, on behalf of N. S. Khrushchev, "cordial greetings and good wishes for success in his life and work, in the struggle for lasting peace and for socialism."

During the visit the two presidents made many speeches. In them Tito hastened to express his great joy at being able to show Comrade Brezhnev "the results attained in the development and construction of socialism in Yugoslavia" under the guidance of the League of Communists of Yugoslavia. He said that "the existence of certain differences must not be an obstacle along this road, inasmuch as they represent a natural phenomenon which is frequently engendered in today's world because of the fact that the concrete paths followed by the economic and social development of different countries are different, due to differing historical and other conditions." Tito dealt with the aid and support Yugoslavia has given to the national and progressive liberation movements throughout the world and to the independent countries of Asia and Africa. He loudly proclaimed in front of the President of the Supreme Soviet that "the positions of the Yugoslav Government and those of the Government of the Soviet Union either coincide or are identical on a number of fundamental international questions." Recalling the time when a certain obscurity reigned in USSR-Yugoslav relations, Tito enjoined: "There is no need for us to insult each other. We must put an end to this once and for all and become good friends. I am convinced that your visit is a great step forward in the development of relations between our two countries." In his speech at Kragujevać, Tito said: "We can tell our friends frankly that they have come to a country where socialism is being built and where there cannot be another road of development. We shall continue to advance along this path, and we possess the means with which to build our socialist regime. [Note well, he did not speak about American "aid."] In conclusion I would like to thank Comrade Brezhnev and our other friends for their visit and for the words they have spoken, which are in complete accordance with our views on socialism."

In his turn the President of the Supreme Soviet and member of the Presidium of the Central Committee of the Communist Party of the Soviet Union, Brezhnev, praised Tito's speeches and made several statements. During his first speech on September 24 and several times thereafter, he repeated that "cooperation with Yugoslavia is in the interests of all countries building socialism and Communism." (?!) After indicating that "the scope of activities in Soviet-Yugoslav relations is vast," he continued: "We greatly appreciate the efforts made by the government, and personally by the President of the YFPR, Comrade Josip Broz Tito, toward a policy of peace and cooperation among states," etc. During a speech made at a meeting in Split, Brezhnev spoke to "the Yugoslav comrades" about the liquidation of the personality cult and its odious consequences. He underlined that "the uncovering and bold unmasking of the personality cult of Stalin and its condemnation was of tremendous importance for the successful building of a Communist society." Here Brezhnev also gave his impression of the construction of socialism in Yugoslavia by saying that "we have seen how the peoples of Yugoslavia are working as a fraternal and united family in the construction of their new life." He often mentioned his "interesting and valuable conversations with President Tito and other eminent Yugoslav personalities," as well as "the interesting things he had seen," the "very interesting visit," and the "interesting trip he made across Yugoslavia."

The most important person among those accompanying the Soviet President on his trip across the country was A. Ranković, known for organizing the tortures and slaughter of thousands of Yugoslav Communists who had the courage to oppose the revisionist course of the Tito clique since 1948.

In taking "cordial" leave of Tito, Brezhnev spoke once more about "the sincere conversations" he had had with him "on many problems concerning the joint struggle for peace and the general development of Soviet-Yugoslav relations in the interests of peace and socialism." He once more "warmly thanked" his "dear friend, the President of the republic, Comrade Tito," and on behalf of N. Khrushchev begged him to pay a visit to the Soviet Union. According to TASS, Tito accepted this invitation with pleasure and said he would visit N. Khrushchev in December of this year.

Borba, speaking with frenzied joy about Brezhnev's visit, said: "The friendly relations and fruitful cooperation between the Soviet Union and Yugoslavia will no doubt become a long-term phenomenon, will become more stable and will continue to improve."

That is what was said publicly. But what attracts attention is what was not said or what was intentionally evaded, both in the speeches and the published communiqué. We do not wish to speak of the secret talks which have been in progress for a long time between the group of N. Khrushchev and Tito, of their plans to cooperate and coordinate their divisive activities. Time will reveal the secrets, as has been the case on earlier occasions. We want to speak about the questions on which silence is being maintained, or which are being approached in a distorted manner. Anyone who has followed Brezhnev's trip from the beginning and carefully read the final communiqué on the Tito-Brezhnev talks will note that the danger presented by American imperialism to peace, to the national independence of peoples, and to socialism is not stressed; that the illusion is created that there will come a time when the imperialists will, as a result of disarmament, transfer large funds to the promotion of the well-being of peoples, particularly in underdeveloped countries; that, when speaking of Cuba, the finger is not pointed at American imperialism, which is threatening that country with aggression, but mention is made only of certain aggressive circles of imperialism; that when speaking about the admission of the CPR to the United Nations, nobody recalls the necessity of driving the Chiang Kai-shek clique from the UN; that the imperialist policy of "two Chinas" is not condemned; etc.

It therefore appears that Brezhnev's visit, the visit of N. Khrushchev's personal envoy to Tito, was not a simple and ordinary trip to see "beautiful and wondrous parts of Yugoslavia," in spite of the efforts made to keep it officially within the framework of peaceful coexistence and relations between states. This visit was paid only a short time after N. Khrushchev's speech at Varna in Bulgaria, where he eulogized the Tito clique, "which is building socialism," where he characterized his relations with Tito as being "not only normal but good," and where he launched an appeal for a rapprochement and multilateral improvement of relations with Yugoslavia, describing cooperation with and aid to Yugoslavia as a factor which "not only will contribute to an improvement in mutual relations between the Soviet Union and Yugoslavia but which will also be of advantage to all countries building socialism and Communism." (?!) Brezhnev's visit, if considered in the context of the divisive activities engaged in by the Tito clique against the socialist camp, the national liberation movement, the revolutionary movements within the working class, and progressive movements in general, if considered within the context of the revisionist views and disruptive machinations of N. Khrushchev's group and within the context of the bilateral attempts made by N. Khrushchev and Tito to come together and to coordinate their anti-Marxist activities, leaves no doubt that it went beyond the limits of a courtesy visit decreed by diplomatic protocol. Brezhnev's journey, this "friendship mission," this "important visit" — to quote the Soviet press — reveals its strongly accentuated political and ideological nature and constitutes a link in the chain of N. Khrushchev's efforts to achieve a rapprochement with the Yugoslav revisionists, to coordinate with them a new revisionist course to split the socialist camp and liquidate socialism.

It is known that N. Khrushchev publicly began seeking a rapprochement with the Yugoslav renegades in 1955 when he knelt down before Tito in Belgrade, begged his pardon for the mistakes allegedly committed by the Communist and workers parties of the socialist countries against "the Yugoslav leaders," and forgave the Titoists their sins in the name of the Soviet Union. That was the first step. Having again clothed the Yugoslav revisionists in the robes of Marxist-Leninists, N. Khrushchev systematically adopted one measure after another — as has been verified and is being verified by life — to achieve an ever closer rapprochement with them.

Developments which took place after Tito's visit to the Soviet Union in 1956, particularly the counterrevolution in Hungary and the publication of the revisionist program of the LCY, created obstacles to N. Khrushchev's progress along this road. The Moscow meetings in 1957 and 1960, which justly and severely unmasked the revisionist Yugoslav clique as traitors to Marxism-Leninism, as saboteurs of the camp of socialism in the service of American imperialism, etc., worried Khrushchev considerably. Therefore, as a result of the pressure of the struggle carried out by the Communist and workers parties against revisionism — and in particular against

Yugoslav revisionism — as the main danger to the Communist movement, he sometimes had to say a word against the clique of Tito. But throughout his speeches, made opportunely or otherwise — and as verified by the numerous facts now publicly known — Khrushchev always left the door open for an agreement with the Tito clique. He always in one way or another urged others not to worsen relations, not to fight the Yugoslav revisionists, under the absurd pretext that it would "increase their importance."

And finally, at the 22d Congress, Khrushchev revealed himself as the unmasked splitter of the socialist camp and of the Communist movement. At that time the first thing he did was to remove all obstacles and restore official state and party relations with the Tito clique. This was indispensable for the continuation of his divisive activities, and the best ally in this undertaking was undoubtedly Tito, who had given evidence of treason to Marxism-Leninism. To achieve this aim, he had to trample the 1960 Moscow Declaration underfoot; and intent upon the fulfillment of his plans, he did not hesitate to do such a thing.

Thus collaboration in the economic field began. Since 1961, trade has increased 2.5 times compared with 1955. In 1962, trade will be 30 per cent greater than last year. Last July, "in cordial talks held in an atmosphere of friendship and complete mutual understanding," all questions of mutual economic cooperation were solved without any difficulties. One after the other, various agreements were signed providing for a considerable increase in trade between 1963 and 1965, in comparison with the volume of trade set for this period in the existing long-term agreement. All measures have been taken for cooperation in the fields of industry and technical-scientific collaboration, for the mutual exchange of specialists, etc.

After solving economic questions, N. Khrushchev had to settle fully ideological and political questions with the Tito clique. A close collaborator of N. Khrushchev, V. Spiridonov, chairman of the Soviet of the Union of the Supreme Soviet, has said: "If one is aiming at increasing points of contact between states on questions of foreign policy, economics, and culture, then one can also set upon the path of removing differences in the ideological field" (from the speech made by Spiridonov on July 2, 1962, during the reception in honor of the Yugoslav parliamentary delegation). Cooperation began to assume large proportions through the exchange of many delegations in all fields, including delegations in the political and ideological fields. The exchange of delegations comprised mass organizations such as those of trade unions, journalists, writers, artists, scientists, etc. The rumors which Khrushchev and his propagandists spread now and then on the agreement of his policy with that of the Tito group were only prologues to the visit of Brezhnev.

The rapprochement with the Tito clique was masked by Khrushchev with statements that "Yugoslavia is a country which is building socialism." Such a mask is too transparent to conceal the great treason which is being carried out in collaborating with the renegades of Belgrade.

Upon what basis and what logic are N. Khrushchev and his followers relying when they say that Yugoslavia is building socialism? How can a group of traitors to Marxism-Leninism be building socialism when one knows that Marxism-Leninism is the scientific ideology of the construction of socialism? How can one build socialism by giving free rein to capitalist development in the countryside, by turning the economy more and more into a capitalist economy? How can one build socialism with billions of American dollars which are strangling the entire Yugoslav economy? How can one build socialism in a country whose leaders are undermining the unity of the socialist camp? How can they be saboteurs of socialism and the builders of socialism at the same time? How can one call a country socialist whose leadership, under the pretext of a policy of nonalignment, is pursuing a line harmful to the unity of all peaceful forces and states? What changes have taken place in Yugoslavia since the 1960 Moscow meeting that enable one to arrive at views such as those of the Khrushchev group? No changes have taken place. Not only have the Yugoslav revisionists made no changes, but each day they have put themselves more deeply in the service of imperialism and have set about restoring capitalism in Yugoslavia.

The N. Khrushchev group needs the Tito clique for its traitorous and disruptive activities. Tito's experience in this field is useful in implementing Khrushchev's revisionist course. Therefore, he is intentionally closing his eyes to the present situation in Yugoslavia, which is marching toward the restoration of the capitalist system; he is forgetting everything he has said against the Yugoslav revisionists. This explains all the various ideological concessions and efforts to bring their views into agreement which were made during the course of the visit of Brezhnev in Yugoslavia.

It was not without purpose that Brezhnev, during his visit, never mentioned the words "the socialist camp" in his speeches. He was obliged not to mention them because, first of all, Tito would not accept it — for he is "against all camps" and "above camps." Second and more importantly, it is plain from Brezhnev's speeches that he is trying to find adequate ways to liquidate the socialist camp, to introduce a wolf into the sheep pen, to admit "friendly socialist Yugoslavia" into the family of socialist countries and achieve common aims which are already known by all. This is why he avoided referring to the "socialist camp" and instead spoke about the "world of socialist countries," the "socialist forces in the world," and the "society of socialist states."

To achieve his aims of rapprochement, N. Khrushchev gave Brezhnev reliable support consisting of the latter's party during his visit to Yugoslavia. This included the closest and most reliable adherents of his revisionist line — Adzhubei, Firyubin, and Andropov. Adzhubei, whose only merit as a "political figure" is that he married a daughter of Khrushchev, is known as the man who, following in the steps of his father-in-law, called the multimillionaire president of American monopolies, Kennedy, a "hero in whom the American people should take pride," and he has acted as the direct agent of Khrushchev in his transactions with Kennedy. Firyubin was ambassador in Belgrade, served as an official liaison agent between N. Khrushchev and the Tito clique, and has figured prominently in the Tito-Khrushchev rapprochement. Andropov, former ambassador to Hungary and at present an important official in the apparatus of the CPSU Central Committee, is known as a proponent of the sinister activities of Khrushchev and his group during the events of the Hungarian counterrevolution in 1956 and in the plots of Khrushchev against the PPSh and against other Communist and workers parties of the world.

The N. Khrushchev group, and Tito himself, consider that the most timely moment for a many-sided rapprochement has come, that it is now time for open collaboration in all directions and in all forms. This was clearly expressed in Tito's speech addressed to Brezhnev: "Let us have done with insults. We must not quarrel any longer. We must be good friends." In other words, Tito said: "Let us stop throwing dust in the eyes of others as if we were adversaries. Let us abandon our masks. It is time to openly shake hands and work together for our joint aims."

During his visit to Yugoslavia, Brezhnev mentioned more than once the known formula of N. Khrushchev on the "accord" of views and positions on questions of foreign policy.

In our previous articles we have closely analyzed and proved by facts that the positions of the Yugoslav revisionists have nothing in common with the foreign policy of the Soviet Union and the other socialist countries. That is why it is not necessary to deal with it at length. We will only stress that precisely when Brezhnev was touring Yugoslavia, trying to round off the positions and policy of the Yugoslav revisionists and present them as identical to Soviet policy, Popović, the representative of the Yugoslav revisionists at the present session of the U.N. General Assembly, once more attacked the policy of the Soviet Union and the other socialist countries, comparing it with the policy of aggression and war of American imperialism. The attempts of the N. Khrushchev group to equate the policies of the Yugoslav revisionists and the Soviet Union and to bring into harmony and make identical the Soviet-Yugoslav positions concerning international questions are only a bluff and a mask used by N. Khrushchev to present the renegade clique of Belgrade as socialist. In fact, these attempts have been refuted by many facts and by Tito himself in his recent interview when he said: "Our representatives do not always vote on the side opposing the United States. . . . There were cases when our representatives adopted, in accordance with our points of view, attitudes which corresponded to the positions of the American representatives."

It is no secret that Yugoslav policy in international questions follows the policy of aggression and war followed by the American imperialists, and that there can be no question of conformity with the policies of the Soviet state and the other socialist countries. The policy of the Yugoslav revisionists is fully in conformity with the views and aims of the revisionist group of N. Khrushchev.

It is of great importance for N. Khrushchev that the positions of the Tito clique on various international issues be in accord with the fundamental strategic questions uniting the N. Khrushchev group with the Tito clique. These questions are: class conciliation between socialism and capitalism, political and ideological coexistence between them, peace and coexistence at any price, negation of all revolutionary movements, and the economic and political integration of the world. As for actions and positions on given concrete questions, N. Khrushchev himself is in many instances in contradiction with the basic policy of the Soviet state and the CPSU. In support of this there are many instances showing that Khrushchev has contradicted what he said the day before. One day he praises Eisenhower, the next day he insults him; one day he declares that the question of Germany must be settled without delay — setting a time limit — then he declares without blushing that the question of time limits has no importance; one day he says that Yugoslav revisionism is a Trojan horse, the next he alleges that it is building socialism. This tactic constitutes one of the characteristic traits of modern revisionists: lack of principles. Like anti-Marxists — and this is what they are — they try to adapt themselves to shifts caused by small political events, but they forget the vital interests of the proletariat and the nature of the capitalist order.

It was in vain that the N. Khrushchev group tried to give Brezhnev's visit an anti-imperialist character and thus camouflage the real purpose of the visit — to coordinate their views and revisionist actions. *Izvestiya,* in an article entitled "In the Name of Common Objectives," which points out eagerly "the clear atmosphere of Soviet-Yugoslav relations," tried to indicate that the visit by Brezhnev allegedly was viewed "with anxiety and nervousness by the ruling circle of Adenauer" and imperialist circles in general. But the truth is different. Indeed, Brezhnev was not particularly concerned with this question, and *Izvestiya* did not insist on pressing it. On the contrary, concerned lest the imperialists get angry and turn their backs on the Tito clique, the Khrushchev group particularly stressed that "the Soviet Union, in desiring the expansion of good relations with Yugoslavia, is not trying to aggravate its relations with other countries" (*Izvestiya* of September 29). And this is not done without a purpose; it is not in N. Khrushchev's interest that the Yugoslav revisionists break with the imperialists, particularly with the American imperialists. The Tito clique represents an important bridge between Khrushchev and Kennedy. The hubbub being made these days in the U.S.A. over the U.S. Senate's decision to deprive Yugoslavia of the right of the most-favored-nation trade clause is not fortuitous. The truth is that the reactionary press could not hide its joy over this visit and enthusiastically described the demonstration of friendship of Khrushchev's group toward Tito as "the spring of Soviet-Yugoslav relations."

It is clear from the above that the N. Khrushchev group and the renegade Tito gang are in accord politically and ideologically on all fundamental questions, on their tactics and their strategy with a view to a rapprochement with the imperialists; that they agree on their strategy and tactics in their struggle against Marxism-Leninism and the unity of the socialist camp, in their joint efforts to lure into treason and to corrupt certain leaders of the Communist and workers parties of some socialist countries of Europe and some capitalist countries. They are in accord in their strategy and tactics aimed at undermining the national liberation movement by subjecting it to general and complete disarmament; they are in accord in their strategy and tactics for the economic and political integration of the world.

All this indicates that we are faced with a great betrayal of Marxism-Leninism. This betrayal is not obvious to those and only those who do not wish to see it, to those whose interest it is not to see it.

We must look things straight in the eye and call a spade a spade. Modern revisionism has become a very great danger to the great historic victories scored by the proletariat, to the revolution, and to socialism. It has become aggressive and shameless.

Modern revisionism, as an anti-Marxist trend, has not been completely unmasked — and precisely herein lies its dangerous character. It is true that Yugoslav revisionism has been greatly discredited, but today one must completely unmask the common front which the modern revisionists are about to create in their struggle against socialism, against revolutionary Marxism-Leninism.

Wherein lies the force of modern revisionism? We have to deal today not with an opportunism like that of the Second International during the 1894–1917 period, which relied solely on the alms given it by the dominant bourgeoisie from unlimited profits derived from the exploitation of colonial and dependent peoples. The great tragedy which has struck the international Communist movement today is that revisionism is represented by the group of N. Khrushchev, who is at the head of the Soviet Union and the Communist Party of the great Lenin.

By engaging in frenzied demagogy, the revisionists are profitably exploiting the great international authority acquired by the Communist Party of the Soviet Union under the leadership of Lenin and Stalin, as well as the glorious revolutionary past of some Communist parties in various countries. Modern revisionism uses Marxism-Leninism, particularly the name of Lenin, as a label to propagate its theories and anti-Marxist views, to deceive the masses. Naturally, one cannot prevent Khrushchev, Tito, and their followers from using any labels they wish in order to sell their antiquated goods; but they are dangerous when they are used by men whose mask has not been completely torn off, whose anti-Marxist faces are still hidden. V. I. Lenin continuously stressed that obvious opportunism is not so dangerous and harmful as the one which presents itself under the guise of Marxism-Leninism.

Moreover, modern revisionism also has the support of international imperialism, which is aiding it through various ways and devices, overtly or covertly. Suffice it to mention Yugoslavia, where the United States monopolies have given Tito, one of the leaders of modern revisionism, 5 billion dollars to achieve their essential objective, namely, the liquidation of the socialist system and restoration of the world hegemony of imperialism.

The source of modern revisionism was

exposed and best defined at the meetings of the representatives of the Communist and workers parties held in Moscow in 1957 and 1960. "The existence of bourgeois influence," the 1957 declaration stated, "is the internal source of revisionism, whereas capitulation before imperialist pressure is its external source."

Therefore, revisionism is not something fortuitous; it has not been suddenly brought forth, as Athena from the head of Zeus. It has arisen as a result of the ceaseless struggle which is taking place between socialism — to which the future belongs — and the imperialist bourgeoisie, which is heading for doom. It is the embodiment in this struggle of the aristocraticized and unstable section of the representatives of the working class, which capitulated as a result of powerful and continuous pressure exerted by imperialism.

As in the past, the substance of opportunism today is the idea of collaboration between the classes. The entire activity of modern revisionism rests upon this idea.

The revisionist group of N. Khrushchev never talks about the scientific definition of our epoch, as given in the 1960 Moscow Declaration, because this grates on its ears. In this Declaration our epoch was defined as an epoch of struggle between two different social systems, an epoch of the disintegration of imperialism and the liquidation of the colonial system, an epoch of the transition to socialism of other countries and the triumph of socialism and Communism on an international scale. Khrushchev and his followers, however, present our epoch as one of peaceful coexistence during which, by peaceful means and negotiations, the social and political problems dividing the world at the moment are to be settled. To them the essential content of our time is peaceful economic competition between the world social systems — socialism and capitalism. Peaceful coexistence has also been proclaimed with much hue and cry by the Khrushchev group as the general line of the foreign policy of the socialist countries, as the general road leading to the victory of socialism on a world scale. The evaluation by the Tito group of our present epoch, which they describe as the epoch of the peaceful integration of the world into socialism, makes the same point.

We have stressed the essential difference in the definition given to our epoch by the Moscow Declaration of 1960, on the one hand, and by the revisionists, on the other hand, because it is here that the diametrically opposed paths of revolutionary Marxism-Leninism and modern revisionism diverge.

Proceeding from a scientific definition of our time, Marxist-Leninists draw correct revolutionary conclusions from the radical changes which have taken place in the new balance of power in the international arena, a balance which is in favor of socialism. The waxing strength of the forces of Communism in the world and the strengthening of the influence of the socialist system are conceived by revolutionary Marxist-Leninists as factors which have created extremely favorable conditions and new opportunities for the Communist and workers parties, for the working class and all revolutionary forces in the capitalist countries, as well as for the peoples oppressed by imperialism, *for the certain triumph of socialist revolutions and national liberation movements,* for the triumph of socialism and Communism throughout the world. But victory never falls from heaven nor does anyone make you a present of it. It is gained by struggle and by the efforts of the popular masses, strongly united to a revolutionary leadership determined to defend the interests of the people and the revolution to the end. This is the lesson of history. Today more than ever before the situation demands that the Communist and workers parties remain always at the head of the efforts exerted by the masses against imperialism, that they show by deeds their ability to guide the proletariat and its allies in the struggle for the triumph of the socialist revolution and the national liberation revolution. "It is not sufficient to call oneself the vanguard unit," Lenin has said. "One must also act in a way that all other units see us marching at the head and are forced to admit it" (*Selected Works,* Vol. I, p. 174). The historical development of events never asks what name you bear, whether it be "Communist Party" or any other, what program and what slogan you proclaim. Revolution has no need of words but of actions. If you cannot master a situation through action, it will eliminate you; it will eliminate you so violently that it will smash you and nobody will give you any further consideration. There is no shortage of examples; indeed, there are living examples which show how severely the development of revolutionary events has condemned those who have lagged behind events as a result of their degeneration through following the revisionist course of Khrushchev.

American imperialism today represents the essential force of aggression and war; it is also the most vicious enemy of all humanity. The world witnesses its numerous acts of aggression and war unleashed in various countries. It witnesses the feverish preparations for new aggressive wars made by the American imperialists and their partners in aggressive blocs against the socialist countries, against the peoples who have barely emerged into freedom and independence, against the peoples who arose and continue to arise with each passing day in order to free themselves from the yoke of the colonialists and imperialists and in order to liquidate the odious regime of oppression and capitalist exploitation.

The present situation demands urgently and more than ever before the creation of a united front in the struggle against imperialism for peace, national independence, and socialism on the part of the socialist countries, the revolutionary workers movement in capitalist countries, the revolutionary movement for national liberation and democracy in all countries, and all peace-loving peoples, because imperialism is at present the chief and common enemy of mankind. It is only in this way that it is possible to ensure a durable peace and stave off a new world war, and, at the same time, to liquidate imperialist domination and achieve the triumph of socialism on an international scale.

However, the creation of a strong front against imperialism is impeded through all available means by the modern revisionists. They resort to anything, even the vilest criminal actions, to sabotage the struggle for liberation of the oppressed peoples against the imperialists, to prevent the union of all anti-imperialist forces struggling for peace, national independence, and socialism, and to prevent the ideas of revolutionary Marxism-Leninism from spreading and taking roots. In this respect the modern revisionists make great concessions of principle to the imperialist.

In the meantime, the imperialists, mainly the American imperialists, exploit as best they can the weaknesses and concessions of the modern revisionists, particularly those of Khrushchev. The policy of anti-revolutionary opportunist activity, the policy of conciliation with the imperialists which is being practiced by the revisionists, splits and weakens the socialist camp, weakens the revolutionary movement of the peoples against imperialism, and allows the imperialists to strengthen their positions in various parts of the world which have been turned into centers of aggression against the Soviet Union, the Chinese People's Republic, other socialist countries, and the liberation movements of the oppressed peoples.

In spite of the savage measures and billions of dollars used by the imperialists and supported by the revisionists in order to stifle the revolutionary and anti-imperialist movements, the revolutionary movement and the international Communist movement in general spread and grow stronger with each passing day. It could not be otherwise. Contradictions of all kinds within imperialism are continuously becoming more serious. Today more than ever the old capitalist world is pregnant with socialist and national liberation movements. A very severe class struggle is taking place in the international arena. In the greater part of the oppressed countries in Asia, Africa, and Latin America the flame of revolutionary struggle is spreading unceasingly. Even in the most advanced capitalist countries the class struggle has not ceased and will never cease, because this does not depend on the will of the revisionists or on the will of the imperialist bourgeoisie. It is caused by the objective conditions of oppression and exploitation of man by man which can disappear only with the overthrow of the capitalist order and the installation of the socialist order. A certain increase, out of the ordinary, in the production of some capitalist countries is nothing but an incidental and temporary phenomenon, because there has not been and cannot now be a permanent peaceful development of capitalism. The world capitalist system is plunged into a profound general crisis; therefore, the situation of the "peaceful development" of capitalism in certain countries of the world cannot continue indefinitely.

As was underlined by the Moscow Declaration of 1960, no efforts by imperialism can obstruct the advance of society, the liquidation of the imperialist system, and the complete triumph of socialism on a world scale. This may happen more quickly or may take a much longer time. It depends on the extent to which the proletariat and the other oppressed and exploited masses are ready and prepared to act in every respect in the revolutionary situations which at present are inevitable; on the extent to which the Communist and workers parties are able to prepare the masses in a many-sided manner for the revolution, to make them completely conscious, and to lead them to a complete victory over internal and external enemies. No party of the working class is able to accomplish this task if it is infected with the dangerous disease of revisionism, if revisionist leaders are at its head, if the solidarity of the world revolutionary movement, the unity of the international Communist movement, and the unity of the socialist camp are not safeguarded and strengthened in the struggle against revisionism. The dissemination and strengthening of revisionism within the international Communist movement not only prolongs the existence of imperialism and considerably retards the triumph of socialism in other countries, but it seriously threatens the victories attained by the workers' masses in those countries where socialism has triumphed.

The definition of revisionism at the Moscow meetings of 1957 and 1960 as the chief danger within the international Communist movement and the task set to fight and destroy revisionism to its very roots are, ideologically speaking, more topical and concrete today than ever before. The struggle against and the ideological destruction of modern revisionism have become at present a historically indispensable and urgent task.

Revisionism not only numbs the revolutionary energy of the masses but it finds in this torpor a fertile soil for development. We note this phenomenon in countries where revisionists are at the head of Communist parties. Marxism-Leninism, however, and Marxist-Leninist parties find support in and derive strength precisely from the revolutionary energy of the masses. Thus, by fighting revisionism and by unmasking its agents, the revolutionary energy of the masses is revitalized. They become conscious and learn to fight for their interests, for the revolution, for complete national independence, for democracy, socialism, and Communism.

One cannot fight imperialism successfully and attain victory over it without fighting and unmasking revisionism. V. I. Lenin used to stress continuously that "the fight against imperialism becomes an empty and false gesture unless it is tied closely to the fight against opportunism" (*Selected Works,* Vol. 1, p. 858).

In order to fight revisionism successfully, which has become a very great danger, it is necessary for Communists and the masses to understand clearly what revisionism actually is. Now and then even

N. Khrushchev's group is obliged to say something about the struggle against revisionism. Certainly for N. Khrushchev's group "the struggle against revisionism" is something abstract, without an object; it is merely an empty phrase. Formerly, when mention was made of "the struggle against revisionism" in the press or speeches of the present Soviet leaders, it was sometimes possible to interpret this as a reference to the Yugoslav revisionists. But now that we are confronted with the accomplished fact of the coordination in all fields of the policy of N. Khrushchev with that of Tito, there is no doubt that Khrushchev's group not only does not fight against any form of revisionism but has itself taken into its hands the banner of modern revisionism.

In the present circumstances of the difficult class struggle between Communism and imperialism when imperialist reaction is more and more uniting its forces against Communism, it is particularly indispensable to preserve and strengthen the unity of the socialist camp, of the Communist and workers international revolutionary movement. To every true Marxist-Leninist it is clear that this unity has been greatly damaged by the modern revisionists. One of the main goals of the revisionist group of Tito has always been to disrupt the unity of the socialist camp and the forces of international Communism. The revisionist group of Khrushchev now works against this unity through its attacks, plots, and other most odious and criminal actions against the Albanian Party of Labor, other revolutionary Marxist-Leninist parties, the socialist camp, and all world revolutionary movements.

The preservation of the unity of the socialist camp and of the international Communist movement as well as the further strengthening of this unity require firm opposition to modern revisionism, combating and unmasking it in all its forms and in all its domains in order to fix once and for all the demarcation line with revisionism. Revisionism is a sore point in the Communist movement. One must heal this wound as soon as possible in spite of the terrible pain this operation may cause.

Topical today once again, just as in the heroic period of Marx and Lenin, is the revolutionary watchword which for more than 100 years has guided the violent class battles and the victories of the proletarians and of the oppressed and exploited masses: *"Workers of all countries unite."* As always, today too this unity can be achieved only on the basis of revolutionary Marxism-Leninism, around the immortal ideas of Marx, Engels, Lenin, Stalin, and never around the revisionists and their rotten ideas.

Even though they occupy commanding positions in a party, the modern revisionists, except for a segment of privileged people which they have created as a means of support for their anti-Marxist activities, are deprived of the essential support of the mass of Communists; they are deprived of the support of the workers and revolutionary peasantry, although it has become a habit with the revisionists to refer to "the masses" every time they want to advertise their theories and anti-Communist doings as perfect. The mass of Communists and workers are becoming more and more aware of the great betrayal at their expense and at the expense of Marxism-Leninism, and of the fact that the revisionists are renegades from Communism and are beyond rehabilitation. It is precisely these masses in these historic moments who have the heavy task of saying their word and, as quickly as possible, of putting revisionism and the revisionists in their places because revolution and counterrevolution, Marxism and anti-Marxism, proletarian ideology and bourgeois ideology, whose creature revisionism is, cannot live together for long, neither within the framework of a party nor within the framework of the movement as a whole.

Moreover, those Communists who are wading in the mire of N. Khrushchev and who now have the possibility of more or less seeing the betrayal of Marxism-Leninism must, from now on, find the energy and the courage to stop and detach themselves from the revisionists. They are faced with two alternatives: either to fall into the abyss where the Khrushchev group leads or courageously and firmly to react and, uniting with the mass of the party and resolutely relying on the working masses, to deal a mortal blow to the revisionists. It is only in this way that one can help the party, the country, socialism, Communism, and peace.

This is not the first time that the Communist and workers movement has been faced with such a great betrayal, the betrayal of the modern revisionists. The history of the struggle of the international proletariat has several times confirmed that in severe moments of a general crisis of capitalism, opportunism, as the creation and agency of the bourgeoisie, has gone into action, renovated itself, and tried to stifle the parties of the working class, thus aiding the international imperialist bourgeoisie in its struggle and efforts to establish world domination and the oppression of the revolutionary movements of the masses. Now everyone knows well the betrayal of the Second International and its failure, the betrayal of Kautsky, Plekhanov, Trotsky, and their failure, the betrayal of Zinoviev, Kamenev, and Bukharin and their failure. The true Marxist-Leninists, at moments of decisive danger from opportunism, have acted firmly, have courageously risen, and have waged an uncompromising and very bitter principled struggle against the enemies of Marxism-Leninism. Lenin and his Bolshevik comrades, who themselves were in the crossfire from several directions — from the vicious Tsarist autocracy and later from the bourgeois dictatorship of Kerensky, from the international imperialist bourgeoisie and from the traitorous leaders of the Second International — were never afraid but bravely defended the principles of Marxism-Leninism and drew the line against the Mensheviks, Trotskyites, and so forth, in order to unite more closely around the ideas of Marxism-Leninism. We know very well how the Bolsheviks acted, with Lenin at the head, when they saw that there was no hope of setting the Mensheviks right and that to remain with them further in a united party was harmful and impossible. It was only by definitely eliminating the Mensheviks in 1912 that real unity was established in the Bolshevik Party, and it was only in this way that it became a revolutionary party, a vanguard of the entire international Communist movement. In 1917 in answer to those who continued to demand the union of all Russian Social Democrats, Lenin wrote: "There can be no question at all about a union with the Russian Social Democrats. We would rather remain with two people like Liebknecht — and this would mean staying with the revolutionary proletariat — than accept even for a moment the idea of a union with the party of the organization committee [Mensheviks — Ed.], with Cheixen and Ceretelin . . ." (Vol. 26, p. 62, fourth edition in Russian).*

Marxism-Leninism has always come out triumphant in the struggle against capitalism and opportunism, primarily because the Marxist-Leninists have drawn the line against the traitors to the proletariat, because the working class and all the classes exploited and oppressed by international imperialism and the domestic bourgeoisie have been on the side of the revolutionary Communists.

The process of the unmasking, isolation, and ideological destruction of modern revisionism as a very dangerous disease within the international Communist movement has begun and is progressing with great strides. This is a dialectical process which nothing can stop. It cannot be stopped by the demagogy of Khrushchev's group; it cannot be stopped for long by N. Khrushchev or his followers who abusively use the authority of the great party of Lenin. The great authority of the Soviet Union and the Communist Party of Lenin cannot be considered as the property of one or another person and even less of a group of renegades and revisionists, such

* Presumably the reference is to Chkheidze and Tseretelli, although neither these names, nor their Albanian version, nor the quotation itself appears on p. 62, Vol. 26, in the fourth Russian edition of Lenin's *Works* [W.E.G.].

as the group of N. Khrushchev. The authority of the Soviet Union and the Communist Party of Lenin is maintained and defended not through words but through deeds by those who consistently pursue the path of Lenin and his triumphant teachings. It is defended by the fraternal parties which are struggling for the purity of Marxism-Leninism; it is defended by the Albanian Party of Labor, by the Bolsheviks of the Lenin party itself who are devoted to its revolutionary path. It is preserved by Communists and revolutionaries the world over. By combating the modern revisionists, they express at the same time their love and respect for the fatherland of the October Revolution, for the party and ideas of the great Lenin, which a group of revisionists is trying to besmirch.

The creation of a revisionist common front — Khrushchev and Tito, their collaboration and joint sharpening of arms — deepens and accelerates the process of the political and ideological destruction of modern revisionism because, in their obvious and coordinated activity, the Communist parties, the international Communist movement, and the working class see more clearly each day the great danger which today threatens the unity of the socialist camp, the unity of the international Communist and workers movement, and the unity of the progressive and peace-loving forces generally. Therefore, profoundly convinced of the inexhaustible revolutionary energy of Marxism-Leninism, we can say that there is no force on earth which can stop the triumphant march of its ever victorious ideas.

DOCUMENT 33

Speech of Comrade Enver Hoxha to the representatives of the capital's intelligentsia, Zëri i Popullit, *November 4, 1962* (*excerpts*).

. . . We can now speak with pride of the more noble traits which characterize our cadres and our entire intelligentsia, traits which should be developed and further strengthened in the future. . . .

Of course, Nikita Khrushchev and his associates cannot agree with this appraisal, for it is known that he has always underestimated our people's abilities and creative capacities which, among other things, manifest themselves in the inventions and improvements made by our workers, of which we are proud. It is also known that he and his followers have more than once affirmed that allegedly it was they who created our intelligentsia. But we take no notice of that. As to inventions and improvements and proposals, the unprecedented upsurge in this direction, which occurred with particular force after the attacks against our party, and the exposure of N. Khrushchev's betrayal of Marxism-Leninism — of these we are and shall always be proud and without in the least becoming conceited or resting on our laurels. We are proud, not because we have made or are making inventions of world significance, but because our cadres, struggling under the difficult conditions of capitalist geographical encirclement and revisionist blockades, are making tremendous efforts to give the people what they need. All this is of great importance because it strengthens the Albanian People's Republic, which has heroically defied this sworn enemy of the socialist camp and the international Communist and workers movement represented by the contemporary revisionism of the group of Khrushchev, Tito, and company. With regard to the other claim that they — Khrushchev and his companions — created our cadres, this is not true. Our cadres who studied in the Soviet Union were sent not to his domain but to the great land of the October Revolution, where they were able to absorb — and of that too we are proud — the great culture of the glorious Soviet people, the immortal teachings of Lenin and Stalin, which they are very ably putting into the service of the fatherland and of the general cause of socialism. They rejected with disdain and fought like men against the hostile views of this revisionist and his followers. On the contrary, when matters reached

Khrushchev's hands, it is known that he not only refused all aid but closed the doors of the institutions of higher learning and scientific institutes to our students and our cadres as he did with all other things as well.

The boys and girls of our country should study the sciences on a large scale and in a scientifically organized manner, should study them not superficially but in great depth. The University of Tirana should become the center of this endeavor, but every other possibility in our country should also be explored. In addition, you should be well acquainted with the inventions and works of foreign scholars, and strengthen the bonds with the foreign academies and universities of the Soviet Union, etc., despite the obstacles which have been created for us.

Nikita Khrushchev, who is a revisionist and holder of antiscientific views, is seeking to represent the development of science in the Soviet Union as the fruit of the period of his tenure of power. He and his followers are trying to obscure the consistent efforts of forty-five years of Soviet science and of the scientists who worked, built the foundations, and created the conditions for scientific socialism, who worked and created while guided by Marxism-Leninism and enlightened by the Communist Party of the Soviet Union, by Lenin, by Stalin, who illumined with their genius the road they traversed.

Khrushchev prevents the friends of the Soviet Union from profiting from the great benefits of Soviet science, but he is openhanded with his revisionist friends and with the scientists of capitalist countries. Can you imagine that, in this age of the swift progress of science, of the atom, of the conquest of space, of the triumph of socialism, there is a group of persons at the head of the first socialist state who would close the doors of schools, of universities, and of science to the sons and daughters of socialist Albania, to the sons and daughters of a small nation, heroic and eager for knowledge? Such a scandalous act is being committed by the renegade anti-Marxist group of Nikita Khrushchev and his followers. Such a thing has not been witnessed even in countries ruled by the bourgeoisie!

Only chauvinists, obscurantists, megalomaniacs, those who abuse the peoples and the masses, those who are strangers to the great cause of the proletariat, could act this way and think that the little nations and the little people have no place in the bright sunlight of science, that they are destined to live in the shadows of "the great," at the feet of "the great," that knowledge and skill find suitable soil for development in the "brains and make-up of the chosen élite," of only a few great and powerful peoples and states.

. . . We rejected Tito's nonsensical idea to plant only sunflowers, on the pretext that he would supply us with wheat from the Vojvodina; likewise, we rejected Khrushchev's "advice" that we should grow only fruit trees and vineyards, since he would supply us with wheat grown on his virgin lands; he said the quantity we needed was "no more than that consumed by our mice," yet he did not give it to our people when they needed it.

. . . We must rely basically on our own means, because the opportunity to continue specialized studies in the Soviet Union or other socialist countries of Europe has been, as you know, denied to us or greatly restricted. . . . In this way, a broad base of scientific cadres, also required for the long run, will gradually be formed in our country. We shall thus have the opportunity to create the conditions for our own Academy of Sciences in the near future. We have an intelligentsia which in general is well informed from the point of view of politics and ideology. This has been demonstrated not only by their active participation in the building of socialism but also by their principled and consistent stand and active participation in the party's struggle in the ideological and political field. Let us consider, for instance, the attitude of the intellectuals on the question of our party's principled struggle against the modern revisionism of the Khrushchev-Tito group, their unswerving determination to stand by the party during the most difficult political moments. There is no intellectual who has not felt proud of the honesty and unprecedented courage with which our party has defended and is defending Marxism-Leninism, the socialist camp, and the interests of its people against the intrigues and plots of the group of Tito, Khrushchev, and their followers, in spite of the fact that we are a small nation which lives, fights, and triumphs encircled by enemies. There is no intellectual among us who has not fought with the party to confront and smash the poisoned arrows of the imperialists and of their tools, the modern revisionists.

Recently the imperialists and revisionists launched a new attack against Marxism-Leninism, which they are trying to refute and misrepresent. Of course, this is not new. How many times have the bourgeois ideologists proclaimed its "defeat"? How many times have the revisionists wanted to "correct" it? Yet, more than a century has passed since the publication of the *Communist Manifesto*. During this time, fierce battles have been fought with anti-Communists of every shade, traitors and various renegades have detached themselves from the revolutionary center, and, in spite of all this, the ideas of Marx, Engels, Lenin, and Stalin are alive and will live for ages to come. The period in which we live is one of the most heroic. The most rabid colonialist and imperialist reactionaries, the traitorous Social Democrats, and the revisionist renegades are feverishly engaged in subversive activity against Marxism-Leninism, but revolutionary Marxism-Leninism will triumph. No force in the world can stop the forward march of society.

The revisionists are at present playing a particularly important role; therefore, the struggle to unmask them and completely smash them politically and ideologically is for us a task of primary importance. The revisionists are now attacking Marxism-Leninism from every direction, on the question of revolutionary strategy and tactics as well as on that of philosophy, political economy, etc., by attacking in one way or another the theoretical and methodological basis of other sciences, particularly the social sciences.

Characteristically, the revisionists do not attack openly, but, under the pretext of "new conditions," they attack particular theses of Marxism-Leninism, opposing them with their revisionist theses.

Another characteristic of the modern revisionists is that they direct their blows essentially at points where demagogy can more easily conceal their treason as shown by their efforts — starting from the premise of the change in the balance of power in the international arena — to reject the entire theory of revolution, etc., without hesitating to touch on other fields of revolutionary theory and practice as well.

Revisionism has now become so uncontrollable and shameless in its swift march toward the precipice that it does not hesitate to attack even dialectical and historical materialism, even economic theory, even the historical sciences, even Marxist esthetics, etc. The tendency is clear: Everything is being done to pass from materialism to idealism and from dialectics to metaphysics, in order to replace the revolution with evolution, and the class struggle with peaceful economic competition, in order to reject socialist realism in literature and the arts and clear the way for decadent trends. In France last year certain philosopher members of the French Communist Party began to question a number of fundamental issues of dialectical and historical materialism. Discussing the object of Marxist philosophy, some of them — the most advanced revisionists — reached the conclusion that, since knowledge has reached the stage where concrete knowledge is being developed by particular sciences, Marxist philosophy must limit itself to the study of the theory of thought and its laws. You understand where this leads. This aims at reducing Marxist philosophy from a science which studies general laws on the evolution of nature, society, and human thought to a science which studies only the latter. From there it is not difficult to pass on to what has always been the aim of bourgeois and revisionist ideology — namely, to deny that Marxism-Leninism is able to study and scientifically explain the evolution of nature and society, to deny Marxism-Leninism itself.

Similar discussions are also taking place within the Italian Communist Party. In particular, the theses published in connection with the 10th Congress of this party, which will be held in December of this year, constitute a new code of modern revisionism; for it is almost explicitly stated that many questions of Marxism-Leninism should be revised because they are not correct. And let us not forget, comrades, that all this is being done with the blessing and under the direction of the revisionist group of N. Khrushchev. Moreover, it is he and his bankrupt "theoreticians" who lay down the directives and call the tune for all these and other attacks on Marxism-Leninism. After all, what was the object of the meeting of so-called Marxist economic theoreticians held recently in Moscow to discuss modern capitalism? What were the conclusions of these "theoreticians"? They proclaimed as a great discovery of our age that modern capitalism is not like the capitalism of yesteryear, that this or that thesis previously expounded by Marx and Lenin is not true, that life proves the contrary, or something or other, etc. The whole business consisted of a theoretical "verification" of the revisionist theses of N. Khrushchev.

That is how the matter stands. By turning the facts upside down, they are trying with all their strength to revise Marxism-Leninism. Thus, it is necessary that, under the wise guidance of our Party, you should engage still more vigorously in the struggle against these revisionist "theories," against these ugly features of our time, know the enemy, know what he is doing, and fight him without mercy. Naturally we are faced with both objective and subjective difficulties which can impede our work. The fact remains, however, that we are not now in the position of 10 or 15 years ago; we do not have the difficulties we had then. We have got used to struggling, wrestling with, and triumphing over difficulties. There are plenty of examples to prove this. On the whole, we now enjoy certain advantages in dealing with difficulties. We have a powerful material base; we have gained much experience which ensures that we will overcome subjective difficulties and that we will reduce and eliminate defects in our work. We shall also overcome our objective difficulties thanks to our efforts and the aid of our friends, primarily of our Chinese comrades. All we have to do is work conscientiously and loyally apply the correct party line. Our internal situation is stronger than ever. Labor solidarity and enthusiasm are exemplary. We look to the future with optimism, and feel certain that our intelligentsia can face any storm and overcome any obstacle. The cadre problem, as I said, must be very seriously examined also because of the international situation in which our country and the whole world now find themselves. While in the past we were able in tackling this problem to rely on aid from the Soviet Union and other socialist countries, at present we receive effective assistance only from the Chinese People's Republic, which accepts our students and renders us technical-scientific aid. For this and other generous assistance, we are profoundly grateful to our Chinese comrades. At the same time we are building socialism under conditions of capitalist and revisionist encirclement and of intensified efforts by the imperialists and their tools to unleash war. You know that with his total blockade of Cuba and other measures, the President of the United States of America, Kennedy, most seriously challenged the Soviet Union and all peace-loving peoples, pushing mankind to the brink of atomic world war. This compels us to strengthen our economy and defenses to the utmost so that we can cope with any eventuality.

As you know, things are going well in our country. Industry, agriculture, culture, the arts, and science are rapidly advancing. Plans are being fulfilled and overfulfilled.

In the future, too, we shall score victories. The guarantee for these victories — that we shall build socialism, and later on Communism, at any price, that we shall implement all our plans — is our party and people, our heroic working class and our collective farmers, our splendid cadres, our people's intelligentsia, our ever victorious Marxism-Leninism — to which we shall remain faithful forever and to our last breath — the international solidarity of Marxists and Leninists, the proletarians and the peoples of the whole world who will always be on our side.

DOCUMENT 34

"Solemn Meeting Dedicated to the 45th Anniversary of the Great October Socialist Revolution," speech by Hysni Kapo, Zëri i Popullit, *November 8, 1962 (excerpts).*

. . . On this heroic path the genius of V. I. Lenin, that glorious architect of the revolution and the building of socialism, emerges majestically as does also the great role of J. V. Stalin, that invincible fighter for the cause of Communism who, as the successor of Lenin, led the Communist Party of the Soviet Union for more than thirty consecutive years on the path set by the great October Revolution toward the shore foreseen by Lenin.

Under Stalin's leadership, the Communist Party of the Soviet Union showed itself capable of coping with its historic tasks. It never wavered in the face of difficulties and enemies. It stood without flinching, liquidated the adversaries of Leninism, and successfully achieved the Leninist plan for the building of socialism in the Soviet Union, laying sound foundations for the present magnificent achievements of the land of the Soviets.

The revisionist falsifiers can scribble new texts and distort the glorious history of the Communist Party of the Soviet Union or of the Patriotic War by wiping out the name and glorious work of Josif Stalin or by inventing various kinds of lies about him. But Stalin will remain forever in the hearts and minds of the Communists and workers of the world. The revisionists and traitors are capable of all kinds of fabrications and slanders, but the sun cannot be hidden with a sieve, and the black clouds cannot obscure his brilliance for long. The party of the Bolsheviks, the Soviet people, and the Communists and the peoples throughout the world do not believe the revisionist falsifiers and cannot be deceived by their maneuvers with the so-called "documents" and "new facts." They believe the living fact and the indisputable document that J. V. Stalin, in spite of any mistake which he might have made during his revolutionary life, courageously defended and developed further than anyone else the teachings of Lenin regarding the building of the new type of party and the leading role of the Communist Party in the period of the transition from capitalism to socialism. He defined the main thesis and practical paths for the socialist industrialization of the Soviet Union for the collectivization of agriculture, for the increase of the defensive force of the Soviet state, for the development of socialist culture, science, and technology, and, as leader of the Soviet party and Government, he ably implemented them in practice. The Communists and the peoples of the world cannot forget that J. V. Stalin always maintained and defended with dignity the name of Communist and internationalist; he always kept high the dignity, prestige, and authority of the Soviet Union and its Communist Party and the Soviet people. In the most difficult moments, he never wavered and never yielded to the blackmail, threats, and pressures of imperialism and class enemies.

The enemies of socialism, the imperialists and the various opportunists, struggled against Stalin for years, but always failed shamefully. Not once during his lifetime could they denigrate his person and discredit Leninism. What others could not do, N. Khrushchev now, after the death of Stalin, is trying to do; like all previous traitors, by attacking Stalin he is attempting to prepare the way for dethroning Leninism, for discrediting and denigrating the socialist system, for rejecting the glorious experience of the Soviet Union in the revolution and the building of socialism, for propagating opportunism and treason, for ideologically and politically rehabilitating, as experience shows, the Bukharins and all the anti-Marxist deviationists upon whose ideas the N. Khrushchev group bases its own view.

This unprincipled and anti-Marxist struggle against J. Stalin by N. Khrushchev has given great comfort to the imperialists. For this reason, speaking at a dinner of the Anglo-American Society on October 1 of this year, the British foreign minister Lord Home pointed out that "it is of great importance that the Western world should not underestimate the importance and consequences of the open denunciation of Stalin and his thoughts" and "should understand the current facts of life and follow a deft policy in dealing with them."

However, the efforts of the revisionists to discredit the name and the great work of J. V. Stalin will undoubtedly fail shamefully. Marxism-Leninism, to whose triumph J. V. Stalin devoted all his energy and his life, is invincible. It is marching victoriously in the world, terrifying the imperialists and the revisionists and ensuring new victories for the forces of peace, democracy, national independence, and socialism in the world.

. . . Imperialism and international reaction, pursuing their reactionary aims of poisoning the international atmosphere, discrediting and denigrating the Chinese People's Republic, and justifying their participation in the aggressive provocations against it, are conducting a furious propaganda campaign of lies to present People's China as a warmonger and aggressor and the reactionary Indian circles, headed by Nehru, as "angels of peace." The Marxist-Leninist parties and all the Communists and honest people of the world cannot remain indifferent and "neutral" in the face of a situation in which the imperialists are arming Indian reaction in a coordinated manner. They consider it their internationalist duty mercilessly to unmask the ugly slanders and provocations of the imperialists and reactionary Indian circles against the Chinese People's Republic, resolutely to denounce and condemn the aggression against China and to support socialist and peace-loving China with all their strength. To maintain a neutral position on this question, under present conditions, means in practice to support the aggressive and provocative actions of imperialism and reactionary circles against the Chinese People's Republic.

. . . Comrades,

In the realization of the strategic objectives of imperialism, with American imperialism at the head, the contemporary revisionists, who are actually helpmates of imperialism and its "Trojan horse" in the world Communist and revolutionary movement, are playing a special, primary role. By discharging their mission, as "watchdogs of capitalism," to keep intact the capitalist order in various places where it still remains in power and to restore capitalism where it has been overthrown, the contemporary revisionists are trying by all possible means to build up capitalism and imperialism and to denigrate the socialist system, to divert by all possible means the working masses and the peoples from their resolute struggle against imperialism, from the revolution and the national liberation struggle, and to dampen their revolutionary upsurge. To achieve this end, the revisionists reject the revolutionary core of Marxism-Leninism and its fundamental teachings, reach for those offshoots which Lenin and Stalin cut off long ago in the struggle against the traitorous leaders of the Second International, against the Trotskyites, Zinovievists, Bukharinists, and other renegades, and spread those opportunist theories which were shattered to bits by the triumph of the Great October Socialist Revolution and its glorious experience.

V. I. Lenin revealed, on the basis of a profound scientific analysis of imperialism, the deeply reactionary, oppressive, and aggressive character of imperialism, attested that imperialism is the source of wars and aggressions and that, as long as imperialism exists, the basis for aggressive wars will remain. The renegades of Marxism-Leninism and the contemporary revisionists, such as the group of N. Khrushchev and Tito's traitorous band, have rejected these important and principled teachings of Lenin as "outdated" and "worthless" in the present era. They maintain that now, as a result of the change in the balance of power in favor of socialism and because of the destructive character of war in the present era, the imperialists, and primarily the United States imperialists, have either abandoned or are abandoning their aggression against the socialist countries, that they "have now accepted and take seriously the appeal of the socialist countries for peaceful competition," and that growing "realistic trends" are appearing among the leading circles of imperialism, including the group led by President Kennedy to avoid war and to settle international problems in a peaceful manner. (!) This is what N. Khrushchev writes in the No. 12, 1962, edition of *Kommunist.* The same is said by the revisionist leadership of the Italian Communist Party in its theses drafted for the Tenth Party Congress, not to mention the traitorous Titoist revisionist clique. However, life and facts mercilessly refute these dangerous pacifist illusions which the revisionists are trying to create in order to divert the peoples from their resolute struggle against imperialism. These illusions evaporated like dew under the sun before the recent furious provocations of American imperialism against revolutionary Cuba, the Soviet Union, and general world peace. It is only declared reactionaries, capitulators, and simple-minded people who can consider Kennedy's provocative and warmongering activities as an "understandable preoccupation with the security of the United States," as "proof of his concern to preserve peace" which "merits appreciation," and other statements like these, which we read in the cables and messages sent to President Kennedy by N. Khrushchev. . . .

The "peaceful" path noisily advocated by the contemporary revisionists under the pretext of "new conditions" and "national peculiarities" means in fact to depart from the basic teachings of Marxism-Leninism on the socialist revolution and proletarian dictatorship. In this connection, the views propagated by the leadership of the Italian Communist Party, headed by P. Togliatti, are very characteristic. P. Togliatti and his comrades are strongly emphasizing that the roads to socialism will be *very different* not only in form but also *in content,* and that the proletarian dictatorship in various countries will also be different not only in form but *also in content.* They say that the basic experience of the Soviet Union and of the peoples' democracies, which they consider as an accumulation of "grave errors," "dogmatic and bureaucratic distortions," and "impermissible violations of socialist legality," is neither imperative nor useful for other countries. Togliatti has openly stated that certain theses of Marx, Engels, and Lenin, such as the thesis on the destruction of the bourgeois state apparatus and its replacement by the organs of the dictatorship of the proletariat as an absolute condition for the transition to socialism, the thesis on the leading role of the Marxist-Leninist party in the struggle for the victory of socialism, the Leninist thesis on just and unjust wars, and so forth, which according to him were once correct, must now be "reviewed" and "corrected" on the basis of the new conditions of the present time. The leaders of the Italian Communist Party preach that the transition to socialism can be made without even destroying the present bourgeois state, which can be used as the primary weapon for smashing the power of the big capitalist monopolies and liquidating them, and that the transition to socialism can be achieved by carrying out the "structured reforms" envisaged by the present bourgeois constitution of Italy, and so forth.

All these, which are nothing but a repetition in new words and terms of the opportunist, revisionist, and reformist theories of Bernstein, Kautsky, and "the Economists" and other renegades of the working class, are presented to us as "the last word in creative Marxism." They are, in fact, attempts aimed at weaning the working class away from the revolution and serving the bourgeoisie. The words of the great Lenin unmasking the treason of the leaders of the Second International fit today's revisionists very well:

> It has been proved in practice that the militants within the workers movement who participate in the opportunist trend are the best defenders of the bourgeoisie, better even than the bourgeoisie itself. If the workers were not led by such persons, the bourgeoisie would not be able to stand on its feet (*Works,* Vol. 31, p. 254).

The views spread by the revisionist leaders of the Italian Communist Party, headed by P. Togliatti, are very significant because they constitute, as it were, the intermediate link that unites into a single entity, into a unique code of modern revisionism, the views spread by Khrushchev at the 20th Congress of the Communist Party of the Soviet Union and thereafter about the so-called "peaceful" and "parliamentary" path of the transition to socialism with the openly opportunist and revisionist views of the traitorous and revisionist Tito clique. . . .

Life is illustrating with new examples that in order to safeguard and effectively strengthen the unity of the socialist camp and of the Communist and workers movement, which is seriously threatened by the divisive activities of the revisionists who are attempting to sow discord and cause contradictions among the fraternal socialist countries and the fraternal parties, thus facilitating the work of imperialism, it is indispensable to conduct a broad struggle against revisionism in all fields and by every means. There cannot be sound Marxist-Leninist unity, which is as vital as air and light to the socialist countries, the international Communist and workers movement, and the peoples in the world, as long as the border line with the revisionists is not properly defined, as long as the revisionists are not thrown out of the ranks of our movement, and as long as they are not liquidated ideologically and politically. True unity and cohesion can only be obtained on the basis of revolutionary Marxism-Leninism and by a means of a principled and uncompromising struggle against the anti-Marxist views and actions of the modern revisionists.

The modern revisionists are now coordinating their anti-Marxist views and their disruptive activity everywhere; they are creating a united revisionist front, all the way from the N. Khrushchev group to the traitorous revisionist Tito clique, in the struggle against Marxism-Leninism in order to breach the unity of the socialist camp and the international Communist movement, and to split and degrade the revolutionary movement of the peoples. Striking proof of the efforts of the revisionists to form this united front is the many steps which the modern revisionists have recently taken for ever closer rapprochement with the traitorous Belgrade clique and which were crowned by Brezhnev's visit to Yugoslavia.

Particularly because it has created a united front, contemporary revisionism represents a great danger. For this reason, today it is more necessary than ever to execute the task assigned by the Declaration of the Moscow meeting of the 81 Communist and workers parties calling for a resolute struggle to destroy completely modern revisionism, ideologically and politically. This is an essential and urgent historic imperative. The struggle against revisionism, the unmasking of its proponents, animates the revolutionary energies of the working masses, makes them alert, and teaches them how to fight to protect their interests, the revolution, and freedom and national independence. The struggle against imperialism itself cannot be successful and will remain an empty gesture unless it is linked with the struggle against revisionism.

The Albanian Party of Labor is fully convinced that Marxism-Leninism will always triumph over opportunism, because the truth, the revolutionary Communists, and the broad masses of the working people in the world are with it.

Index

Index